WELLES-TURNER MEMORIAL LIBRARY
GLASTONBURY, CT 06033

lonely planet

# Cancún, Cozumel & the Yucatán

DISCARDED BY
WELLES-TURNER
MEMORIAL LIBRARY
GLASTONBURY, CT

Cancún
& Around
p55

Isla Mujeres
p79

Riviera Maya
p103

Yucatán State &
the Maya Heartland
p151

Isla Cozumel
p89

Costa Maya
& Southern
Caribbean Coast
p133

Campeche
State
p209

Chiapas & Tabasco
p235

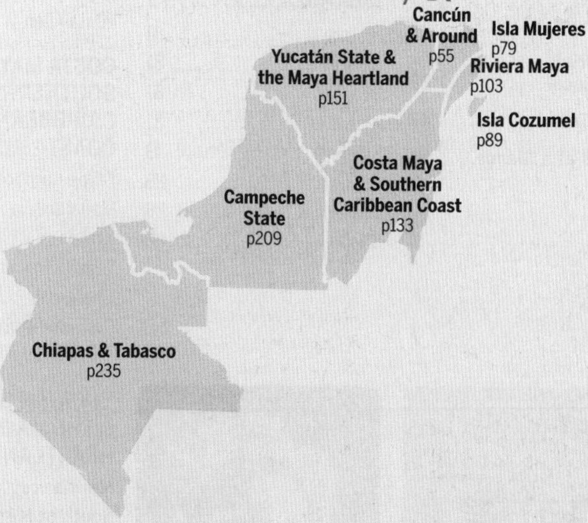

Ashley Harrell, Ray Bartlett, Stuart Butler, John Hecht, Tom Masters

# Contents

PLAYA DEL CARMEN P108

POLA DAMONTE VIA GETTY IMAGES/GETTY IMAGES ©

DÍA DE MUERTOS P21

BONNIEBC/SHUTTERSTOCK ©

# Contents

## COVID-19

We have re-checked every business in this book before publication to ensure that it is still open after the COVID-19 outbreak. However, the economic and social impacts of COVID-19 will continue to be felt long after the outbreak has been contained, and many businesses, services and events referenced in this guide may experience ongoing restrictions. Some businesses may be temporarily closed, have changed their opening hours and services, or require bookings; some unfortunately could have closed permanently. We suggest you check with venues before visiting for the latest information.

Right: El Castillo (p191),
Chichén Itzá

WELCOME TO

# Cancún, Cozumel & the Yucatán

*Maybe I've been living in gritty Mexico City too long but every time I see the peninsula's Caribbean beaches and biodiverse jungles I'm blown away by the rich color palette of blues and greens. I love the things that make this corner of Mexico so unique, from the sublime limestone swimming holes and intriguing Maya ruins to the impressive old haciendas and world-class diving sites. And even though it's been some 15 years since I first visited, I still crave the Yucatán's insanely delicious regional cuisine.*

**John Hecht, Writer**
🐦 @john_hecht
For more about our writers, see p320

# Cancún, Cozumel & the Yucatán

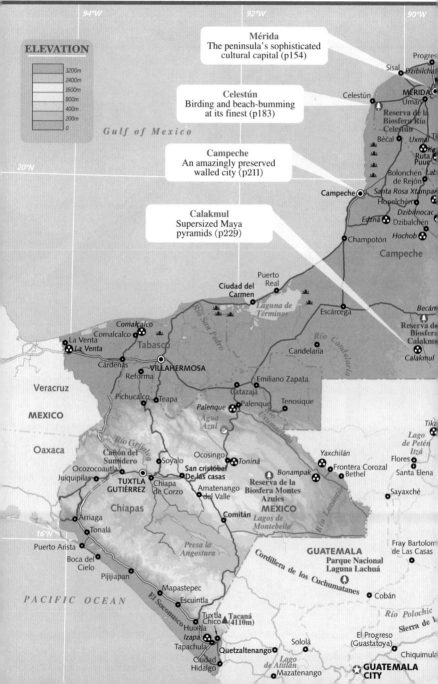

**ELEVATION**

3200m
2400m
1600m
800m
400m
200m
0

**Mérida**
The peninsula's sophisticated cultural capital (p154)

**Celestún**
Birding and beach-bumming at its finest (p183)

**Campeche**
An amazingly preserved walled city (p211)

**Calakmul**
Supersized Maya pyramids (p229)

| | |
|---|---|
| **Isla Holbox** | Whale sharks and bird-watching (p72) |
| **Isla Contoy** | A nature buff's paradise (p72) |
| **Isla Mujeres** | Low-key island living (p79) |
| **Cancún** | Resort glitz meets Caribbean blue (p57) |
| **Isla Cozumel** | Mexico's top diving destination (p89) |
| **Playa del Carmen** | Relaxing beach and party getaway (p108) |
| **Tulum** | Jaw-dropping oceanfront Maya ruins (p119) |
| **Cobá** | Bike at a Maya jungle site (p128) |
| **Chichén Itzá** | World-famous Maya wonder (p190) |
| **Laguna Bacalar** | Snorkel in an azure lake (p140) |

# Yucatán Peninsula's Top Experiences

## 1 MARVEL AT MAYA RUINS

The Yucatán Peninsula boasts some of the best-preserved and most remarkable ruins in Mexico. Here you'll experience ruins with an ocean view or bike along jungle paths leading to a towering Maya pyramid. Meanwhile, the Ruta Puuc provides a moving picture of sites both big and small, culminating with a visit to the spectacular Uxmal.

## Drive the Ruta Puuc

Feast your eyes on some of the most sophisticated ancient architecture you'll ever see as you tour Uxmal and the Ruta Puuc region. The road along the Puuc Route traverses hilly countryside dotted with seldom-visited Maya ruins. p171

Right: Ancient carvings
Left: Gran Pirámide (p173)

## Bike Among Jungle Ruins

See the tallest pyramid in Quintana Roo when you visit the sprawling jungle-set Cobá ruins, which are best explored along dirt trails on a rented bicycle. In town, pedal out to a series of cenotes to cool off in sublime swimming holes. p128

Above: Bicycling near Cobá

## Swim Below Cliffside Temples

Visit dramatically situated Maya ruins that afford jaw-dropping views of the aquamarine Caribbean coast below. A visit to Tulum brings together cultural exploration and relaxing beach time as you enjoy a gorgeous stretch of sand along the Riviera Maya. p119

Above: Tulum

## 2 UNDERWATER EXPLORING

Not only does the Yucatán have some of the best ocean diving on the planet, it also offers intriguing experiences in subterranean caverns and cenotes (limestone sinkholes). Off the turquoise Caribbean coast, you'll find a slew of breathtaking sites dotting the world's second-largest coral reef system, known as the Mesoamerican Barrier Reef.

### Dive at World-Famous Sites

It's hard to imagine a more exhilarating aquatic experience than what awaits you in the Mexican Caribbean, home to some of the planet's top dive destinations for their abundant marine life, primo drift diving and steep walls. p96

Above left: Isla Cozumel

### Plunge into Majestic Sinkholes

Submerge yourself into one of the largest underwater cave systems in the world, at the Maya-run Dos Ojos. Diving enthusiasts come from far and wide to plunge into these waters, some of which contain ancient human remains. p113

Above right: Dos Ojos

### Beat the Crowds

Serious divers head for the largest coral atoll in the northern hemisphere, a remote marine reserve off the southern Quintana Roo coast. Banco Chinchorro wows visitors with its spectacular shipwreck sites, coral walls and wildlife-rich canyons. p137

Top right: Diving at Banco Chinchorro

# 3 GETTING AWAY

Some folks love the creature comforts of the Yucatán's tourist-friendly resorts, others just want to get as far away from that as possible. When visiting these remote places, expect spotty (if any) wi-fi, minimal nightlife and hit or miss cuisine. For anyone seeking a little solitude or a quiet place to open that book you've been meaning to read, welcome to the Mexico where time stands still.

DUARTE DELL ARQLE/SHUTTERSTOCK ©

AKSENOVDEN/SHUTTERSTOCK ©

### Chilling & Diving

No streetlights, no banks, no problem. Hit Xcalak for a diving adventure and a taste of what things looked liked before the development boom in this corner of the Caribbean coast. p139

Top left: Xcalak

### Remote Ruins

Given its remote location, fewer people visit Calakmul than other Maya cities, but it's worth the trek. Meander between sites, climb a pyramid or three and take a picnic. p229

Bottom left: Calakmul

### Wildlife-Watching

The long bumpy ride from Tulum to the remote fishing village of Punta Allen is well worth the effort. Wildlife-watching is awesome here, just don't expect 24/7 electricity. p130

Above: Frigate bird

# 4 CULTURAL CITIES

CGE2010/SHUTTERSTOCK ©

GEO/GETTY IMAGES ©

GUMBAO/SHUTTERSTOCK ©

### Yucatán's Cultural Capital

History comes alive in Mérida, the so-called White City, where you can admire a cathedral that's nearly as old as the city itself and stay in mansions that have been converted into gorgeous hotels. p154

### Ahoy Mateys!

Let your swashbuckling fantasies run wild as you stand before protective fortresses once used to fend off pirate attacks, then walk the colonial streets of Campeche, full of pastel buildings and well-preserved mansions. p211

Top: Campeche

### Heavenly Highlands

Roam the cobbled streets in the small town of San Cristóbal de las Casas while visiting colorful open-air markets and atmospheric restaurants set in old mansions. p238

Bottom: Church, San Cristóbal de las Casas

Even if you don't consider yourself much of an architecture buff, the cities in this corner of Mexico will leave you thoroughly impressed with their intricately designed churches, imposing hilltop fortresses and charming, lively plazas. These places have long been regarded as the region's cultural capitals, meaning they also have an interesting offering of cool museums, art galleries and tasty regional cuisine.

# 5 INTO THE WILD

Sitting pretty between two seas in Mexico's easternmost region, the Yucatán Peninsula spoils nature lovers with its extraordinary variety of wildlife in its biosphere reserves and national parks. Whether you like watching sea turtles as they nest on beaches, swimming alongside massive whale sharks or venturing out on a boat to spot crocs and bird species, you'll always find plenty of nature activities to enjoy here.

## Primo Nature-Watching

Spy pink flamingos and crocodiles on a boat tour through Celestún's sprawling biosphere reserve. The flamingos, always the center of attention, come out in full force from November to mid-March. p183

Below right: Flamingos

LUNAMARINA/SHUTTERSTOCK ©

## Whale Sharks & Wildlife-Rich Mangroves

Swim with enormous whale sharks off the coast of low-key Isla Holbox, or paddle out on a kayak and take in the island's mangroves. p72

Above: Isla Holbox

## Birding and Turtle-Watching

Birding is a delight on uninhabited Isla Contoy, home to some 170 species, and you'll also see turtles coming ashore when nesting season begins in May. p72

Right: Frigate bird

# 6 MAKING A SPLASH

SVEN HANSCHE/SHUTTERSTOCK ©

With Caribbean beaches, majestic cenotes and stunning lagoons, there's more than one way to cool off in the Yucatán. Sure, you'll find plenty of water parks, too, but nothing beats a refreshing swim far away from the crowds and surrounded by natural beauty. Cenotes (sublime limestone swimming holes draped with dangling vines) offer a uniquely Yucatecan experience, and with an estimated 7000 of them dotting the peninsula, they're never far away.

### Swimming in Cenotes

Plunging into a cenote leaves a lasting impression, and even more so when you can find that special place such as Hacienda San Lorenzo Oxman, a quiet, old *henequen* plantation out in the sticks. p199

### Snorkeling in Paradise

Swimming and snorkeling in the shallow turquoise waters of Playa Norte might just be the best beach experience in the country. p81

Above: Playa Norte

### Freshwater Fun

Take in the rich color palette of blues and greens while frolicking along the shores of the peninsula's largest lagoon, Laguna Bacalar. p140

# Need to Know

**For more information, see Survival Guide (p285)**

## Currency

Mexican peso (M$)

## Language

Spanish, Maya

## Visas

Tourist permit required; some nationalities also need visas.

## Money

ATMs are widely available in medium-sized and large cities. Credit cards are accepted in some hotels and restaurants, most often in midrange and top-end establishments.

## Cell Phones

Many US cell-phone companies offer Mexico roaming deals. Local SIM cards can only be used on phones that have been unlocked.

## Time

Central Standard Time (GMC/UTC minus six hours) in the states of Yucatán, Campeche and Chiapas; Eastern Standard Time (GMC/UTC minus five hours) in Quintana Roo.

## When to Go

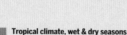

- Tropical climate, wet & dry seasons
- Tropical climate, rain year-round
- Dry climate

**Cancún**
GO May–Jun

**Mérida**
GO Nov–Feb

**Playa del Carmen**
GO Jan–Apr

**Campeche**
GO Nov–Mar

**San Cristóbal de las Casas**
GO Feb–May

### High Season
(Dec–Apr)

➡ Mostly dry, but so-called *nortes* bring northerly winds.

➡ Hotel rates increase, some more than double around Christmas and Easter.

➡ Mérida Fest is held in January; the weather is much cooler.

### Shoulder Season
(Jul & Aug)

➡ Very hot and humid throughout the peninsula. Hurricane season underway.

➡ Vacationing Mexicans flock to the beaches to beat the heat; hotel rates rise.

### Low Season
(May–Jun & Sep–Nov)

➡ Weather cools down from September to November. Hurricane and rainy seasons end in December; hurricane season begins in June.

➡ Great hotel deals. Crowds thin out at ruins and other popular attractions.

# Useful Websites

**Yucatán Today** (www.yucatan today.com) All things Yucatán.

**Yucatán Travel** (www.yucatan. travel) Yucatán state tourism site.

**Loco Gringo** (www.locogringo. com) Book homes and hotels in Riviera Maya.

**Lonely Planet** (www.lonely planet.com/mexico) Destination information and more.

# Important Numbers

Mexican toll-free numbers start with ☑800, followed by seven digits; they always require the ☑01 long-distance prefix.

| | |
|---|---|
| **Country code** | ☑52 |
| **Directory assistance** | ☑040 |
| **Emergencies** | ☑911, ☑066 |
| **International access code** | ☑00; ☑011 from USA and Canada |
| **Roadside assistance** | ☑078 |
| **Domestic/ international operator** | ☑020/090 |

# Exchange Rates

| | | |
|---|---|---|
| **Australia** | A$1 | M$15.23 |
| **Belize** | BZ$1 | M$9.74 |
| **Canada** | C$1 | M$16.26 |
| **Euro zone** | €1 | M$23.96 |
| **Guatemala** | Q1 | M$2.54 |
| **Japan** | ¥100 | M$17.95 |
| **New Zealand** | NZ$1 | M$14.15 |
| **UK** | UK£1 | M$27.78 |
| **USA** | US$1 | M$19.62 |

For current exchange rates, see www.xe.com.

# Daily Costs

**Budget:**
**Less than M$1000**

➡ Dorm bed: M$150–300

➡ Double room in budget hotel: M$400–800

➡ Street eats or economical set menu: M$20–80

➡ City bus: M$4–12

**Midrange:**
**M$1000–1500**

➡ Double room in comfortable hotel: M$600–1500

➡ Lunch or dinner in restaurant: M$80–240

➡ Short taxi trip: M$20–50

➡ Sightseeing, activities: M$100–250

**Top End:**
**More than M$1500**

➡ Double room in upscale hotel: from M$1500

➡ Dining in fine restaurant: M$250–800

➡ Car rental including liability insurance: from M$650 per day

➡ Tours: M$1000–2500

# Opening Hours

Hours may decrease during shoulder and low seasons. Some shops, restaurants and hotels may close for weeks or months during low season.

**Archaeological sites** 8am–5pm

**Banks** 9am–5pm Monday to Friday, some open 10am–2pm Saturday

**Cafes** 8am–9pm

**Cenotes** 9am–5pm

**Museums** 9am–5pm Tuesday to Sunday

# Arriving in Cancún, Cozumel & the Yucatán

**Aeropuerto Internacional de Cancún** Green Line shuttles and Super Shuttle charge US$35 per person to Ciudad Cancún or the Zona Hotelera. ADO buses (M$98) go to the downtown bus station. Regular taxis charge M$650.

**Aeropuerto Internacional de Mérida** Curbside taxis charge M$200 per carload to downtown. Buses (M$8) do not enter the airport; catch one on the main road if you don't mind walking.

**Cozumel International Airport** Shared shuttles from the airport into town cost about M$85. For hotels on the island's north and south ends, they charge M$140 to M$200.

**Ángel Albino Corzo International Airport** Minibuses run between Tuxtla Gutiérrez's airport and San Cristóbal de las Casas' bus terminal.

# Getting Around

**Shared Van** *Colectivos* (shared vans) are cheaper than buses. Most have frequent departures. They can get crammed and go rather rapidly, however.

**Bus** 1st- and 2nd-class buses go pretty much everywhere in the Yucatán.

**Car** Great option for traveling outside big cities. Expect to pay about M$750 a day for rental and gas.

**Ferry** Frequent boats depart from Playa del Carmen to Cozumel, Chiquilá to Isla Holbox and Cancún to Isla Mujeres.

For much more on **getting around**, see p299

# First Time
## Cancún, Cozumel & the Yucatán

**For more information, see Survival Guide (p285)**

## Checklist

➡ Ensure your passport is valid.

➡ Check if you need a visa.

➡ Inform your debit-/credit-card company of your travels.

➡ Get vaccinations.

➡ Book high-season hotels.

➡ Get travel insurance.

➡ Check whether you can use your cell phone.

➡ Confirm your airline's baggage restrictions.

## What to Pack

➡ Passport

➡ Credit or debit card

➡ Driver's license (if driving)

➡ Cell phone and charger

➡ Power adapter/s

➡ Sunscreen

➡ Sunhat

➡ Insect repellent

➡ Swimsuit

➡ Phrasebook

➡ Camera

➡ Pocketknife

➡ Snorkel gear

➡ Toiletries

➡ Flashlight (torch)

## Top Tips for Your Trip

➡ For beaches and scuba diving, visit the peninsula's Caribbean side. For culture, Maya ruins and nature experiences, go west. Cancún and Riviera Maya are very touristy.

➡ Avoid mosquitoes. If you get pricked by one carrying dengue or chikungunya, it's usually not life-threatening but expect to spend days in bed.

➡ Visiting Maya communities brings money into local economies and the experience leaves you with a lasting impression.

➡ Night driving can be dangerous due to livestock or potholes. Toll roads have better lighting than *libre* (free) roads.

## What to Wear

Keep in mind that the Yucatán, particularly Mérida, gets extremely hot from April through August, so bring light and loose-fitting clothes to stay cool. If you're staying on the coast or in cool inland areas, bring a light sweater or jacket for evenings. Take long-sleeve shirts and long pants/skirts for protection against mosquitoes, especially if you plan to be near mangroves or jungles; this attire is also good for formal restaurants and for visiting nonbeach towns, where you'll see fewer people wearing shorts and tank tops.

## Sleeping

Accommodations in the Yucatán range from hammocks and *cabañas* to hotels of every imaginable standard, including world-class luxury resorts.

**Guesthouses** Family-run houses (called *posadas* in Spanish) that usually provide good value and personable service.

**B&Bs** Usually more intimate and more upscale than guesthouses.

**Bungalows** Anything from cheap rustic cabins to elegant boutique setups.

**Hotels** Range from budget digs to expensive all-inclusive resorts.

**Hostels** The most affordable option and a way to meet travelers.

## Discounts & Peso-Pinching

**Discounts** Many museums and archaeological sites have discounts for kids, while some hotels and bus lines offer good savings for online reservations.

**Colectivos** Shared vans are a very affordable and efficient way to move around the peninsula.

**Hammocks** Some hotels will allow you to hang a hammock on their property for a fraction of what it would cost to get a room.

## Bargaining

Most stores have set prices. You can do some friendly haggling in some arts and crafts markets, but don't get carried away – most of the artisans are just trying to make a living. Some hotels are willing to negotiate rates with walk-ins, especially during low season.

## Tipping

**Hotels** About 5% to 10% of room costs for staff.

**Restaurants** 15% if service is not already included.

**Supermarket baggers/gas station attendants** Usually around M$5.

**Porters** M$25 per bag.

**Taxis** Drivers don't expect tips unless they provide an extra service.

**Bars** Bartenders usually don't get tips so anything is appreciated.

# Language

English is widely spoken in Cancún and the Riviera Maya. Elsewhere on the peninsula, you can get by with English in the main tourist centers, but outside of these Spanish is useful. Any effort to speak Spanish is appreciated and Yucatecans are generally very patient and helpful when they see that you're trying to speak their language. Most Maya speakers also speak Spanish. See Language (p304) for more.

 **Where can I buy handicrafts?**
**¿Dónde se puede comprar artesanías?**
don·de se pwe·de kom·prar ar·te·sa·nee·as

Star buys in Mexico are the regional handicrafts produced all over the country, mainly by the indigenous people.

 **Which *antojitos* do you have?**
**¿Qué antojitos tiene?** ke an·to·khee·tos tye·ne

'Little whimsies' (snacks) can encompass anything – have an entire meal of them, eat a few as appetisers, or get one on the street for a quick bite.

 **Not too spicy, please.**
**No muy picoso, por favor.** no mooy pee·ko·so por fa·vor

Not all food in Mexico is spicy, but beware – many dishes can be fierce indeed, so it may be a good idea to play it safe.

 **Where can I find a *cantina* nearby?**
**¿Dónde hay una cantina cerca de aquí?**
don·de ai oo·na kan·tee·na ser·ka de a·kee

Ask locals about the classical Mexican venue for endless snacks, and often dancing as well.

 **How do you say … in your language?**
**¿Cómo se dice … en su lengua?**
ko·mo se dee·se … en su len·gwa

Numerous indigenous languages are spoken around Mexico, primarily Mayan languages and Náhuatl. People will appreciate it if you try to use their local language.

# Etiquette

**Greetings** A handshake is standard when meeting people for the first time. Among friends, men usually exchange back-slapping hugs; for women it's usually a kiss on the cheek.

**Conversation** Yucatecans are generally warm and entertaining conversationalists. As a rule, they express disagreement more by nuance than by open contradiction. The Maya can be slightly more reserved in conversation.

**Getting directions** Mexicans are very cordial and eager to please, so much so that some folks will steer you in the wrong direction rather than saying they don't know where a particular place is. It can be frustrating at times, but keep in mind that it's done with good intentions.

# Month by Month

## TOP EVENTS

**Mérida Fest**, January

**Carnaval**, February

**Vernal Equinox**, March

**Día de Muertos**, November

## January

The first week of January is one of the busiest times of the year, meaning hotel rates spike. Weather-wise, it's relatively cool.

### ✺ Mérida Fest

This cultural event celebrates the founding of Mérida with art exhibits, concerts, plays and book presentations. (p160)

### ✺ Día de los Reyes Magos

Three Kings' Day (January 6) is the day Mexican children traditionally receive gifts, rather than at Christmas. Weeklong celebrations take place in Tizimín.

## February

Temperatures rise slightly and it remains fairly dry. It's still considered high season but most destinations have quietened down significantly.

### ✺ Carnaval

A big street bash preceding the 40-day penance of Lent, Carnaval usually falls in February or early March. It's festively celebrated in Mérida, Campeche, Chetumal and Isla Cozumel with parades, music, dancing and lots of partying.

### ✺ Cruzando Fronteras

A weeklong cultural festival in Mahahual featuring concerts, art exhibits and food stalls along the boardwalk. Usually held in late February or early March. (p137)

## March

The thermometer rises a few notches in more ways than one as US spring breakers flock to the peninsula for tequila-fueled revelry.

### ☉ Spring Break

Beer bong, anyone? Most US university students have a midterm break in March and many descend on Cancún – so either join the party or head for the hills.

### ☉ Vernal Equinox

On the day of the spring equinox (usually around March 20) and for about a week thereafter, thousands head to Chichén Itzá to witness the shadow formation of a serpent appear on the staircase of the El Castillo pyramid. Dzibilchaltún shines with glowing temple doors. (p190) (p185)

## April

One of the hottest and driest months of the year on the peninsula. Semana Santa brings out Mexican tourists in droves as they look to cool off at the beach.

### ☉ Semana Santa

Held throughout Holy Week (starting on Palm Sunday, in March or April), solemn processions move through the streets. On Good Friday (Viernes Santo) there are dramatic reenactments of the Passion play.

### ✺ Feria de San Cristóbal

Starting on Easter Sunday, this weeklong fair features art shows, song and dance, amusement rides, bullfights, fireworks and, of course, lots of food.

## May

A scorcher of a month, especially in Mérida where the daily high averages around 36°C. Not surprisingly, great hotel deals can be found.

### ✵ Feria del Cedral

On Isla Cozumel, the entertaining Feria del Cedral honors a group of Caste War refugees who settled on the island in 1848. The fairgrounds have rides, rodeo events and you can see the time-honored 'Dance of the Pigs' Heads.' (p97)

## June

It is still very hot and June 1 marks the beginning of hurricane season, which runs to November 30. Tourism slows down.

### ✵ Día de la Marina

On June 1 in Río Lagartos a crown of flowers dedicated to the Virgin is taken out to the water as an offering to fisherfolk who have perished at sea.

## July

Expect warm, wet and humid weather. This is a summer holiday month for Mexicans and North Americans so book hotels in advance.

### ✵ Fiesta de la Virgen de Carmen

For the last two weeks of July, the patron saint of Ciudad del Carmen, Campeche, is taken on a journey over land and across the harbor. The fiesta features artistic and cultural events and craft shows. See www.feriacarmen.gob.mx.

## August

The summer holiday season continues, as do the rains. Inland spots tend to be sticky.

### ✵ Festival Jats'a-Já

Held in Mahahual, this festival is a prayer offering of sorts to the hurricane gods. Traditional Maya dancing, art exhibits and culinary events take place. (p137)

## September

The height of the hurricane season, though it shouldn't present a problem if you keep an eye out for alerts.

### ✵ Día de la Independencia

Independence Day (September 16) marks the anniversary of the start of Mexico's War of Independence in 1810. On the evening of the 15th, the famous call to rebellion is repeated from the balcony of every town hall in the land.

## October

Slightly cooler climes and slightly less rainfall.

### ☕ Halloween

Playa del Carmen is the scene of a wild, all-night costume party that draws a sizable crowd of inebriated zombies.

## November

The rainy season has passed and temperatures start to subside. Some accommodations drop prices by as much as 50%.

### ◉ Día de Muertos

Families build altars in their homes and visit graveyards to commune with their dead on November 1, taking garlands and gifts. Many cities place giant altars in their main squares. In Pomuch they actually disinter their loved ones and display them in special boxes. (p220)

## December

Hurricane season ends. *Nortes* (northerly winds that bring showers) are prevalent along the coast from November to January. The first two weeks of December are quiet ahead of Christmas.

### ✵ Día de Nuestra Señora de Guadalupe

A week or more of celebrations leads up to the Day of Our Lady of Guadalupe (December 12), which honors the Virgin who appeared to an indigenous Mexican, Juan Diego, in 1531, and has since become Mexico's religious patron.

### ✵ Posadas

Over nine nights from December 16 to 24, candlelit parades reenact the journey of Mary and Joseph to Bethlehem. More important in small towns than cities.

# Plan Your Trip
# Itineraries

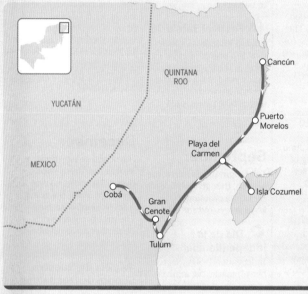

NATALIYA HORA/GETTY IMAGES ©

## 1 WEEK  Cancún & the Riviera Maya

The road from Cancún to Cobá is chock-full of surprises. Along the way you'll find fun-filled cenotes (limestone sinkholes), astonishing Maya ruins and sweet little beach towns with sugar-white sands.

Get things started with a dip in the sapphire waters along the Zona Hotelera (hotel zone) of **Cancún** or hit the secluded beaches north of downtown on Isla Blanca, then return to town for dinner, drinks and perhaps some salsa dancing.

After a day or two in Cancún, make your way south about 30km and stop in **Puerto Morelos** to duck out to the beach, browse for handmade crafts and get in some snorkeling or diving.

Next, spend a little time beach-bumming and partying in uberchic **Playa del Carmen**, a large city with a dizzying array of restaurants, bars and discos.

Playa, as it's called, is a good jumping-off point for **Isla Cozumel**, where you can enjoy some of the best diving in the world, quiet beaches on the island's windswept side and a pleasant town plaza. Frequent ferries run between Playa and Cozumel.

Puerto Morelos (p105)

Back on the mainland, you'll definitely want to make time for **Tulum**, where Maya ruins are perched atop a spectacular cliff overlooking the Mexican Caribbean. While at the site, take the stairs down to the beach and have a refreshing swim to cool off. Stay the night in Tulum's town, where the main drag is lined with happening bars and restaurants, or head 3km south to the coast and get a bungalow in Tulum's hip and happening Zona Hotelera.

With an early start, take off for the Maya ruins of **Cobá** (find the road to Cobá at Tulum's north end). Once inside this archaeological site, rent a bicycle and marvel at jungle ruins connected by ancient paths. Stop for lunch at a lakeside restaurant in Cobá, then on the way back to Tulum, drop by the **Gran Cenote** for a swim or snorkel in a large sinkhole with small fish.

This easy 170km trip stays close to Cancún and there's frequent transport to all of these destinations, or you can just rent a car.

# Maya Country

**PLAN YOUR TRIP ITINERARIES**

The architectural and artistic achievements of the Maya are prominently displayed across the peninsula. Though the ancient cities are long abandoned, the Maya people and their traditions are still very present. One can spend weeks, even months, visiting all the ruins, archaeological museums and small Maya towns.

For background, visit the shiny Museo Maya de Cancún in the heart of the Zona Hotelera in **Cancún**, where admission includes access to adjoining Maya ruins.

Hit the road the next day and spend a day or two in the colonial town of **Valladolid**, a former Maya ceremonial center with a climbable pyramid near the town square. For some respite from your Maya itinerary, drop by **Cenote X'Kekén y Samulá** on your way out of town and take a plunge into a spectacular limestone cavern pool.

Next set aside a day for **Chichén Itzá**, a Maya archaeological site that was named one of the 'new seven wonders of the world.' Get an early start to beat the tour-bus crowds.

A route then leads to **Oxkutzcab** and **Tekax**, offering glimpses of traditional Maya life. While in Oxkutzcab, check out the nearby **Grutas de Loltún**, the largest cave system on the peninsula.

The following day move on to **Santa Elena**, which makes a fine base for exploring the impressive ruins of **Uxmal**, Kabah and several other archaeological sites tucked away in the rolling Puuc hills.

After crossing the Yucatán-Campeche border, stop at **Hopelchén**, where in a nearby village, you can see the tradition of beekeeping.

Make your way to the walled city of **Campeche**, a good base for visiting **Edzná**, a formidable Maya site with a five-story temple. The peninsula's south harbors numerous fascinating but scarcely visited remnants of classic Maya civilization ensconced in the vast **Reserva de la Biosfera Calakmul**.

Extend your explorations for several days to the ruins of **Palenque** and the contemporary Maya domain of **San Cristóbal de las Casas**, both in Chiapas.

Most destinations on this route are reachable by bus or shared transport vehicles, but for some you'll need to hire a car, taxi or go with a tour operator.

Top: Edzná (p223)
Bottom: Grutas de Loltún (p176)

Cancún

Chichén Itzá

Valladolid

Uxmal

Cenote X'Kekén y Samulá

Santa Elena

Oxkutzcab

Tekax

Campeche

Grutas de Loltún

Hopelchén

Edzná

Reserva de la Biosfera Calakmul

Palenque

San Cristóbal de las Casas

MEXICO

GUATEMALA

BELIZE

# Off the Beaten Track: Cancún, Cozumel & the Yucatán

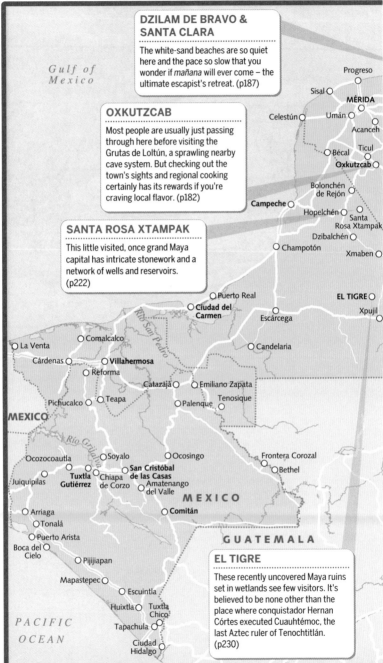

**DZILAM DE BRAVO & SANTA CLARA**

The white-sand beaches are so quiet here and the pace so slow that you wonder if *mañana* will ever come – the ultimate escapist's retreat. (p187)

**OXKUTZCAB**

Most people are usually just passing through here before visiting the Grutas de Loltún, a sprawling nearby cave system. But checking out the town's sights and regional cooking certainly has its rewards if you're craving local flavor. (p182)

**SANTA ROSA XTAMPAK**

This little visited, once grand Maya capital has intricate stonework and a network of wells and reservoirs. (p222)

**EL TIGRE**

These recently uncovered Maya ruins set in wetlands see few visitors. It's believed to be none other than the place where conquistador Hernan Córtes executed Cuauhtémoc, the last Aztec ruler of Tenochtitlán. (p230)

Gulf of Mexico

Progreso
Sisal
**MÉRIDA**
Celestún
Umán
Acanceh
Bécal
Ticul
Oxkutzcab
Bolonchén de Rejón
**Campeche**
Hopelchén
Santa Rosa Xtampak
Dzibalchén
Champotón
Xmaben
Puerto Real
**Ciudad del Carmen**
**EL TIGRE**
Xpujil
Escárcega
Comalcalco
La Venta
Candelaria
Cárdenas
**Villahermosa**
Río San Pedro
Reforma
Catazajá
Emiliano Zapata
Pichucalco
Teapa
Palenque
Tenosique
**MEXICO**
Río Grijalva
Ocozocoautla
Soyalo
Ocosingo
Frontera Corozal
**Tuxtla Gutiérrez**
Chiapa de Corzo
**San Cristóbal de las Casas**
Bethel
Juiquipilas
Amatenango del Valle
**MEXICO**
Arriaga
**Comitán**
Tonalá
Puerto Arista
**GUATEMALA**
Boca del Cielo
Pijijiapan
Mapastepec
Escuintla
Huixtla
Tuxtla Chico
*PACIFIC OCEAN*
Tapachula
Ciudad Hidalgo

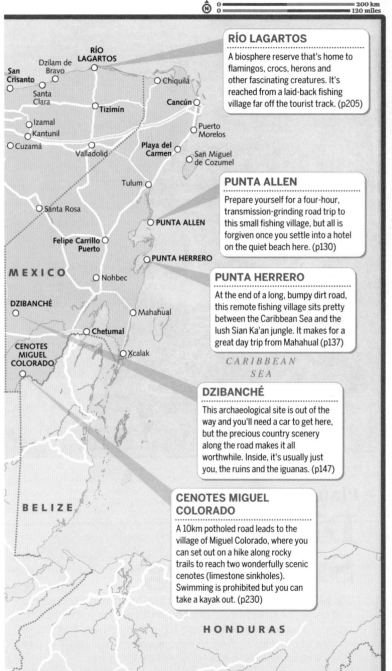

0        200 km
0        120 miles

## RÍO LAGARTOS

A biosphere reserve that's home to flamingos, crocs, herons and other fascinating creatures. It's reached from a laid-back fishing village far off the tourist track. (p205)

## PUNTA ALLEN

Prepare yourself for a four-hour, transmission-grinding road trip to this small fishing village, but all is forgiven once you settle into a hotel on the quiet beach here. (p130)

## PUNTA HERRERO

At the end of a long, bumpy dirt road, this remote fishing village sits pretty between the Caribbean Sea and the lush Sian Ka'an jungle. It makes for a great day trip from Mahahual (p137)

## DZIBANCHÉ

This archaeological site is out of the way and you'll need a car to get here, but the precious country scenery along the road makes it all worthwhile. Inside, it's usually just you, the ruins and the iguanas. (p147)

## CENOTES MIGUEL COLORADO

A 10km potholed road leads to the village of Miguel Colorado, where you can set out on a hike along rocky trails to reach two wonderfully scenic cenotes (limestone sinkholes). Swimming is prohibited but you can take a kayak out. (p230)

RÍO LAGARTOS

Dzilam de Bravo

San Crisanto

Santa Clara

Chiquilá

Cancún

Tizimín

Izamal

Kantunil

Puerto Morelos

Cuzamá

Valladolid

Playa del Carmen

San Miguel de Cozumel

Tulum

Santa Rosa

PUNTA ALLEN

Felipe Carrillo Puerto

PUNTA HERRERO

MEXICO

Nohbec

DZIBANCHÉ

Mahahual

Chetumal

CENOTES MIGUEL COLORADO

Xcalak

CARIBBEAN SEA

BELIZE

HONDURAS

Diving off Isla Cozumel (p95)

## Plan Your Trip
# Diving & Snorkeling

The Mexican Caribbean is world famous for its colorful coral reefs and translucent waters full of tropical fish so, not surprisingly, diving and snorkeling are the area's top activity draws. Add cenote (limestone sinkhole) dives to the mix and you truly have one of the most intriguing dive destinations on the planet.

J.S. LAMY/SHUTTERSTOCK ©

# Best Dives

## Isla Cozumel

Hands-down Mexico's most popular scuba-diving location, Cozumel gets high praise for its excellent visibility and wide variety of marine life. The amazing sights are sure to keep even the most experienced diver in a constant state of awe.

## Banco Chinchorro

The largest coral atoll in the northern hemisphere, Banco Chinchorro boasts a glorious underwater fantasy world of wrecked ships and vivid reefs. Best of all, rarely will you find crowded dive sites at Chinchorro.

## Isla Mujeres

With snorkeler-friendly shallow reefs, shark caves and an underwater sculpture museum, Isla Mujeres' sites appeal to both novice and advanced divers. From mid-May to mid-September you can snorkel with enormous whale sharks.

## Cenote Dos Ojos

Belonging to one of the largest underwater cave systems in the world, divers have the unforgettable experience of exploring the mysteries of the deep at this cenote.

# Diving

## Isla Cozumel

If you can visit only one dive destination in Mexico, the wonderful underwater world of Isla Cozumel (p89) is your best bet. Once a pilgrimage site of the Maya and little more than a small fishing community up until the late 1950s, today Cozumel and its astoundingly rich reefs draw divers from far and wide.

Drift diving is the norm in Cozumel – local divers say there's nothing like the sensation of gliding through the water as you're carried by the strong currents.

## WHEN TO GO

Generally you can dive year-round in the Yucatán; however, before you leave for Mexico you should take into account several considerations.

➡ From November through January the peninsula gets northerly winds and showers known as *nortes*. In Cozumel they can blow so strongly that the harbormaster closes ports – sometimes for days. While this won't affect the ferry between Cozumel and Playa del Carmen, it could alter diving plans.

➡ If you're planning to visit from June through November, you'll want to keep a watchful eye out for hurricane alerts.

➡ The best time to see whale sharks is between mid-June and late August, but be aware that the water will be crowded with tour boats at this time of year.

So what can you see? Imposing drop-off wall reefs, sea turtles, moray eels, black grouper, barracuda, rainbow parrotfish, large coral and giant Caribbean anemones.

If you're a diver heading to this area, Cozumel's Punta Sur and Palancar Gardens are well worth visiting. Snorkelers will want to check out Dzul-Há, near the town of San Miguel de Cozumel, and Colombia Shallows on the island's south side.

## Other Diving Spots

Recreational and serious divers alike will be happy to know that there are great dive sites to be enjoyed all along the eastern coast of the Yucatán Peninsula. Cancún, Isla Mujeres, Puerto Morelos, Playa del Carmen, Mahahual and Xcalak all are prime places to plan a vacation around diving and snorkeling.

The Banco Chinchorro (p137), a sprawling coral atoll off the southern Quintana Roo coast, was pounded by Hurricane Dean in 2007, but the government designated new dive sites so that the hardest-hit areas could recover, which they have. Home to more than 90 coral species, the biosphere reserve of Chinchorro gets fewer visitors than the reefs of Cozumel and Isla

Caribbean Sea reef

Mujeres, making it a very attractive option. Here you can see rays, eels, conch and giant sponges.

In and around Cancún there's an interesting snorkeling and diving attraction called the Museo Subacuático de Arte (p83), aka MUSA, an underwater sculpture museum created by British artist and diving aficionado Jason deCaires Taylor. Built to divert divers away from deteriorating coral reefs, this one-of-a-kind aquatic museum features some 500 life-size sculptures in the waters of Cancún and Isla Mujeres. The artificial reefs are submerged at a depth of 28ft, making them ideal for snorkelers and first-time divers.

## Cenote Dives

When you find yourself yawning at the green morays, eagle rays, dolphins, sea turtles, nurse sharks and multitudinous tropical fish, you're ready to dive a cenote (a deep limestone sinkhole containing water). Hook up with a reputable dive shop and prepare for (in the immortal words of Monty Python) 'something completely different.' The Maya saw cenotes as gateways to the underworld.

You won't see many fish on a typical cenote dive. Trade brilliance for darkness, blue for black, check that your regulator is working flawlessly and enter a world unlike anything you've ever dived before. Soar around stalactites and stalagmites, hover above cake frosting–like formations and glide around tunnels that will make you think you're in outer space. Some of the best cenote dives include Dos Ojos (p113) and Cenote Manatí (p128).

Keep in mind that these are fragile environments. Avoid applying sunscreen or insect repellent before entering. Use care when approaching, entering or exiting, as the rocks are often slippery. Loud noises such as yelling disturb bats and other creatures – though most people find themselves subdued by the presence in these caverns. In rare cases, tourists have been seriously injured or killed by climbing on the roots or stalactites.

Be very careful when cenote diving; it can be an extremely dangerous activity, especially in caves. A good rule of thumb is to go with local dive shops that have knowledge of the cave system. And above all, do not attempt cave diving without proper certification.

Snorkeling in Gran Cenote (p127)

## Snorkeling

Many spots on the Yucatán's Caribbean side make for some fine snorkeling. The best sites are generally reached by boat, but areas near Akumal, Isla Mujeres and Cozumel all offer decent beach-accessed spots. In Cozumel, you'll find some of the most popular snorkeling sites along the western shore.

Inland you can snorkel in some of the Yucatán's famed cenotes. Some places rent gear, but, when in doubt, take your own.

Snorkeling with whale sharks (p73) has become very popular in recent years...too popular some might say. Just about all the dive shops in Isla Mujeres and Isla Holbox offer whale-shark tours. Just make sure before signing up that the tour operator abides by responsible practices recommended by the World Wildlife Fund. Only three swimmers (including your guide) are allowed in the water at a time. Also, you are not allowed to touch these giant fish, and you must wear either a life jacket or wetsuit to ensure you do not dive below the shark.

Keep in mind that tour operators can never fully guarantee that they'll actually track down a whale shark – sometimes nature has its own plans.

## Responsible Diving & Snorkeling

Remember that coral reefs and other marine ecosystems are particularly fragile environments. Consider the following tips when diving to help preserve the ecology and beauty of the reefs.

➡ Avoid touching or standing on living marine organisms or dragging equipment across the reef. Polyps can be damaged by even the gentlest contact. If you must hold on to the reef, only touch exposed rock or dead coral.

➡ Be conscious of your fins. Even without contact, the surge from fin strokes near the reef can damage delicate organisms. Take care not to kick up clouds of sand, which can smother them.

➡ Practice and maintain proper buoyancy control and avoid over-weighting. Major damage can be done by divers descending too fast and colliding with the reef.

➡ Take great care in underwater caves. Spend as little time in them as possible as your air bubbles may be caught within the roof and thereby leave organisms high and dry. Take turns to inspect the interior of a small cave.

*Understanding* by Elier Amado Gil (Punta Nizue Gallery), Museo Subacuático de Arte (p59)

➡ Resist the temptation to collect or buy corals or shells or to loot marine archaeological sites (mainly shipwrecks).

➡ Ensure that you take home all your rubbish and any litter you may find. Plastics in particular are a serious threat to marine life.

➡ Do not feed the fish. In doing so you may be encouraging aggressive behavior or giving them food that may be harmful to their health.

➡ Minimize your disturbance of marine animals. Never ride on the backs of turtles.

## Safety

Most dive shops rent equipment. If you do rent diving equipment, make sure that it's up to standard. Before embarking on a scuba-diving or snorkeling trip, consider the following tips to ensure a safe and enjoyable experience.

➡ If scuba diving, carry a current diving-certification card from a recognized instruction agency.

➡ Regardless of skill level, you should be in good condition and know your physical limitations.

➡ If you don't have your own equipment, ask to see the dive shop's before you commit. Also, make sure you feel comfortable with your divemaster.

➡ Obtain reliable information about physical and environmental conditions at the dive site from a reputable local dive operation, and ask how locally trained divers deal with these considerations.

➡ Be aware of local laws, regulations and etiquette about marine life and the environment.

➡ Dive only at sites within your level of experience: if available, engage the services of a competent, professionally trained dive instructor or divemaster.

➡ Avoid decompression sickness by diving no less than 18 hours prior to a high-altitude flight.

➡ Know the locations of the nearest decompression chambers and emergency numbers.

➡ Find out if your dive shop has up-to-date certification from PADI (www.padi.com), NAUI (www.naui.org) or the internationally recognized Mexican organization FMAS (www.cmas.org).

➡ Always put safety above cost considerations – in the spirit of competition, some dive shops offer great deals, but as the old saying goes, sometimes you get what you pay for.

Tulum ruins (p119)

## Plan Your Trip

# Exploring Maya Ruins

When you stop and think about it, the Maya accomplished some downright remarkable feats. Not only did they pull off very sophisticated architecture, but they also made mind-blowing contributions to mathematics, astronomy and art. The cities they left behind remind us of this brilliant legacy.

# Planning Your Trip

## When to Go

The best time to visit is from November to mid-December, when the peninsula has cooler climes and is dry. If you visit during high season, from Christmas to April, along with July and August, you'll deal with large crowds unless you arrive early.

## Where to Stay

Tulum makes a great base for visiting both the Tulum archaeological site and Cobá. For the ruins of Chichén Itzá and Ek' Balam, consider staying in colonial Valladolid. In Chiapas, Palenque has many nice accommodations nearby. An overnight in Campeche is convenient for getting an early start at Edzná, and the tranquil town of Santa Elena is the perfect hub for exploring the Ruta Puuc, Kabah and Uxmal.

## What to See

So many interesting sites, so little time. Definite must-sees include Chichén Itzá, Palenque, Tulum, Uxmal and Edzná.

## What to Take

Ensure you have comfortable walking shoes, a hat, sunscreen and plenty of water.

# Amazing Maya

Classic Maya (250–900 CE), seen by many experts as the most glorious civilization of pre-Hispanic America, flourished in three areas.

**North** The low-lying Yucatán Peninsula.

**Central** The Petén forest of Guatemala, and the adjacent lowlands in Chiapas and Tabasco in Mexico (to the west) and Belize (to the east).

**South** Highland Guatemala and a small section of Honduras.

It was in the northern and central areas that the Maya blossomed most brilliantly, attaining groundbreaking heights of artistic and architectural expression.

Among the Maya's many accomplishments, they developed a complex writing system, partly pictorial, partly phonetic, with 300 to 500 symbols. They also refined a calendar used by other pre-Hispanic peoples into a tool for the exact recording and forecasting of earthly and heavenly events. Temples were aligned to enhance observation of the heavens, helping the Maya predict solar eclipses of the sun and movements of the moon and Venus.

They also believed in predestination and developed a complex astrology. To win the gods' favor they carried out elaborate rituals involving dances, feasts, sacrifices, consumption of the alcoholic drink *balché* and bloodletting.

They believed the current world to be just one of a succession of worlds, and the cyclical nature of their calendrical system enabled them to predict the future by looking at the past.

# Top Museums

All of the following museums provide interesting background information that's often missing from some of the archaeological sites.

**Gran Museo del Mundo Maya** (p158) Adding to Mérida's rich cultural tradition, this world-class museum showcases more than 1100 Maya pieces with permanent and temporary exhibits focusing on culture, art, science and Maya worldview. There's a free nightly light-and-sound show here as well.

**Museo Maya de Cancún** (p57) This museum houses an important collection of Maya artifacts. The adjoining San Miguelito archaeological site contains more than a dozen restored Maya structures and an 8m-high pyramid. The entrance fee for the museum includes access to San Miguelito.

**Museo Arqueológico de Campeche** (p215) Set in an old fortress, this museum exhibits pieces from the Maya sites of Calakmul and Edzná. Stunning jade jewelry and exquisite vases, masks and plates are thematically arranged in 10 halls; the star attractions are the jade burial masks from Calakmul.

**Museo de la Cultura Maya** (p143) Chetumal's pride and joy illustrates the Maya's calendrical system, among other intriguing exhibits. It's organized into three levels, mirroring Maya cosmology. The main floor represents this world; the upper floor the heavens; and the lower floor Xibalbá, the underworld. Go here before visiting the nearby sites of Kohunlich and Dzibanché. It's short on artifacts, but interesting nonetheless.

## Practicalities

➡ Admission to the Yucatán's archaeological sites ranges from free to M$254; children under 13 often cost a fraction of the adult entrance fee. Both Chichén Itzá and Uxmal project nightly light-and-sound shows.

➡ Opening hours at most major sites are from 8am to 5pm.

➡ Drink lots of water and bring protection against the sun. Insect repellent keeps the mosquitoes away when visiting jungle sites.

➡ Explanatory signs may be in Spanish only, or both Spanish and English. Audio translators are available at some sites.

➡ Multilingual guides offer one-hour tours (from M$600 to M$1000). Official tour-guide rates are posted at the entrances of some sites; legit guides carry government-issued badges.

➡ Avoid midday visits when the sun is beating down and tourists are out in full force.

Tulum ruins (p119)

➡ Seldom-visited sites have no food or water available; pack a lunch or stop off for a meal or supplies along the way.

### SITE HIGHLIGHTS AT A GLANCE

| SITE | PERIOD | HIGHLIGHTS |
| --- | --- | --- |
| Becán | 550 BCE-1000 CE | towered temples |
| Calakmul | approx 1-900 CE | high pyramids with views over rainforest |
| Chichén Itzá | approx 100-1400 CE | El Castillo pyramid, Mexico's biggest ball court, El Caracol observatory, Cenote Sagrado |
| Cobá | 600-1100 CE | colossal pyramids in jungle setting |
| Dzinbanché | approx 200 BCE-1200 CE | semi-wild site with palaces & pyramids |
| Edzná | 600 BCE-1500 CE | five-story pyramid palace, Temple of the Masks |
| Ek' Balam | approx 600-800 CE | huge Acrópolis & high pyramid with unusual carving |
| Kabah | 750-950 CE | Palace of the Masks with 300 Chaac masks |
| Kohunlich | 100-600 CE | Temple of the Masks |
| Ruta Puuc | 750-950 CE | three sites (Sayil, Xlapak, Labná), palaces with elaborate columns & sculpture, including Chaac masks |
| Tulum | 1200-1600 CE | temples and towers overlooking the Caribbean Sea |
| Uxmal | 600-900 CE | pyramids, palaces, riotous sculpture featuring masks of rain god Chaac |
| Xpujil | flourished 700-800 CE | three-towered ancient 'skyscraper' |

Grupo de las Mil Columnas (p193), Chichén Itzá

# Resources

The following books and organizations provide a wealth of information on Maya history and culture.

➡ *An Archaeological Guide to Central and Southern Mexico* (Joyce Kelly) Published in 2001 and still very useful, with coverage of 70 sites.

➡ *Archaeology of Ancient Mexico and Central America: An Encyclopedia* (Susan Toby Evans and David L Webster) An excellent reference book incorporating recent discoveries and scholarship.

➡ *Chronicle of the Maya Kings and Queens* (Simon Martin and Nikolai Grube) Looks at the dynasties and rulers of the most important ancient Maya kingdoms.

➡ *Incidents of Travel in Yucatán* (John Lloyd Stephens) A travelogue written by an American explorer documenting the Maya sites he visited with English artist Frederick Catherwood in the mid-19th century.

➡ Instituto Nacional de Antropología e Historia (INAH; www.inah.gob.mx) Mexico's National Institute of Anthropology and History offers virtual tours of its sites and museums, practical information for visiting the ruins, and details of the historical significance of each site, mostly in Spanish.

➡ Maya Exploration Center (www. mayaexploration.org) A Maya-specific nonprofit offering education programs, tours and study-abroad courses.

➡ Mesoweb (www.mesoweb.com) A great, diverse resource that focuses on the ancient cultures of Mexico and Central America.

# Behind the Names

**Calakmul** (adjacent mounds) Dubbed as such by US botanist Cyrus Lundell when he first came across the hidden jungle ruins in the 1930s.

**Chichén Itzá** (mouth of the well of the Itzaes) The ancient Maya city was built around a well known today as the 'sacred cenote.'

**Palenque** (palisade) The Spanish name has no relation to the city's ancient name, Lakamha, which translates as 'big water' and probably refers to the area's springs, streams and waterfalls.

Palenque (p247)

### AFTER THE APOCALYPSE

As you probably heard, some folks were predicting the end of the world on December 21, 2012, when the Maya long-count calendrical cycle came to an end, yet the date actually signaled the beginning of a new *bak' tun* (about a 400-year period).

Despite all the media hype focusing on doomsday scenarios, some good came out of all the attention: in the year leading up to that December day, federal and state governments poured some serious money into new Maya museums and into restoring existing archaeological sites. Some say the renewed interest in Maya culture was short-lived, but at the very least we can report that research and excavations do continue in the post-apocalypse era.

**Tulum** (wall) Refers to the stone walls that once protected the city. The original Maya name, Zamá, means 'dawn' or 'sunrise.'

**Uxmal** (thrice built) Alludes to how many times the city was built, though it was actually constructed five times.

## Tours

If you don't have a car, tours are especially convenient when you're pressed for time or find that a site is difficult to reach by bus. Youth hostels throughout the Yucatán often provide affordable outings and they welcome nonguests. The following are some of the better tour operators.

**Nómadas Hostel** (p160) Does day trips from Mérida to Uxmal, Chichén Itzá and Kabah. Tours include transportation and guide, but you pay the site entrance fees.

**Mundo Joven** (Map p62; ☏998-271-47-40; www.mundojoven.com; Av Uxmal 25; tours to Chichén Itzá/Tulum US$80/45; ⊙10am-7pm Mon-Fri, to 2pm Sat; 🚇R-1) A Cancún hostel and travel agency running day trips to Chichén Itzá and Tulum. Tours include guide, transport, entrance fee and a meal.

**Turitransmérida** (p159) This Mérida-based operator goes to the hard-to-reach Ruta Puuc, Dzibilchaltún, Chichén Itzá, Kabah and Uxmal; includes transportation, lunch and guide. A four-person minimum is required for Ruta Puuc.

**Community Tours Sian Ka'an** (p121) This Maya-run ecotourism outfit will take you kayaking and swimming along an ancient canal, south of Tulum.

**Ecoturismo Yucatán** (p159) One-day excursions to Chichén Itzá and Uxmal include entrance fees, transportation, guide and lunch. The owners of this tour company are passionate about both sharing and protecting the state's natural treasures.

Corn *pozole* and accompaniments

# Eat & Drink Like a Local

The Yucatán is an endless feast of traditional regional flavors, fresh fish and seafood, and an eclectic mix of international cuisine. The wonderfully unique recipes you'll encounter on the peninsula leave no doubt: folks in this corner of Mexico are passionate about food.

TONO BALAGUER/SHUTTERSTOCK ©

# The Year in Food

## Changing dates

Celebrity chefs from Mexico and abroad descend on the Yucatán for the Cancún-Riviera Maya Wine & Food Festival (https://wineandfoodfest.com/en); a good chance to sample Mexican wines and gourmet dishes.

## Summer (June–August)

Oh yeah, lobster season begins in July! Trapping season for lobster actually runs through February. In small fishing villages that usually means you're getting the fresh catch of the day. The Jats'a Já Festival in Mahahual celebrates the town's fishing tradition with food stands in August.

## Autumn (September–November)

*Pibes* (chicken *tamales*) are cooked underground for Day of the Dead in many cities throughout the peninsula, while bakeries make *pan de muerto* (colorful seasonal bread).

## Winter (December–March)

The Mérida Fest in January brings food vendors to the main plaza; in late February or early March you'll find tasty street eats during Carnaval festivities in Cozumel, Chetumal and Campeche.

# Local Specialties

Food is a tremendous source of pride on the peninsula and the origins of some of the most popular dishes can easily become a topic of hot debate. We've broken down what's on offer in each state, but you'll definitely find variations of the most popular local dishes across state lines.

## Yucatán State

**Cochito/pollo pibil** Pork (often suckling pig) or chicken marinated in citrus juices and *achiote* (a spice made from annatto seeds). When done

properly, *cochito* is slow-cooked in an underground pit.

**Sopa de lima** Soup with shredded turkey or chicken, lime and tortilla strips.

**Papadzules** Diced hard-boiled eggs wrapped in corn tortilla and topped with pumpkin seeds and tomato sauces.

**Huitlacoche** (corn fungus) A terrible name for a delicious mushroom-like delicacy, this fungus was a Maya staple and makes fantastic crepes.

**Queso relleno** A hollowed-out ball of Edam cheese stuffed with ground pork and smothered in tomato sauce and gravy.

**Panuchos** Fried tortilla filled with beans and topped with chicken, lettuce, tomato and pickled red onion.

**Frijol con puerco** A regular weekly dish in many Yucatecan homes is *frijol con puerco,* a local version of pork and beans. Pork cooked with black beans is served with rice and garnished with radish, cilantro and onion.

## Quintana Roo

**Lobster** A popular menu item in Cancún and other coastal towns. Some restaurants prepare it with chili and tamarind sauces, giving it a very distinct Mexican taste.

**Fish and shrimp tacos** Beer-battered fish and shrimp are topped with shredded cabbage and the salsas of your choice. They're fast, cheap and highly addictive.

**Ceviche** Raw fish or seafood marinated in lime juice and spices and served with *tostadas*. Ceviche and *cerveza* (beer) go down great together on a warm day.

**Fusion** With so many Americans, Italians and other transplants living in these parts, you get some interesting blends of international and Mexican cuisine.

**Fried whole fish** Fish is deep-fried to perfection in a bubbling vat of oil, leaving it crispy on the outside and succulent inside.

## Campeche

**Pibipollo** Chicken *tamales* cooked underground and usually wrapped in banana leaves.

**Chocolomo** A hearty stew made of beef, kidneys, brain, tongue, liver etc. You get the point – nothing goes to waste.

**FOOD FACTS**
..........................................

**Chocolate**
Archaeologists in the Yucatán have detected chocolate residue on plate fragments believed to be about 2500 years old, meaning the ancient Maya may have used it as a spice or cacao sauce similar to *mole*.

**Habanero Consumers**
The strongest demand for habanero chilis grown in the Yucatán comes from Japan. Japanese companies normally buy the chili in its powder form and add it to a variety of snacks.

**Pan de Cazón** Stewed shark placed between corn tortillas and bathed in a tomato sauce.

# Chiapas

**Coffee** Optimal growing conditions (high altitude, good climate, rich soil) produce some of the finest coffee in the country.

**Tamales** If you haven't tried a tamale with the aromatic *hoja santa* herb, wrapped in a banana leaf, you're missing something truly special.

**Pozol** Another drink that is a local specialty, Pozol is a thick, heavy mixture of masa (cornmeal dough) in water, it's often mixed with sugar and sometimes has chili or chocolate added. It's the equivalent of an energy drink, and you can see indigenous people everywhere carrying it around in reused plastic 1L bottles. Travelers often take a ball of the masa and make some up when there's water available.

# Food Experiences
## Meals of a Lifetime

**Nixtamal, Laguna Bacalar** (p142) Painfully slow wood-fired cooking but worth the wait.

**Nohoch Kay, Mahahual** (p138) Try the fried whole fish in wine and garlic sauce and you'll understand why this place is called the 'Big Fish.'

**El Mirador, Ticul** (p181) It's hard to imagine a better *recado blanco* (hearty turkey stew) than the one you get at this lookout restaurant.

**Ku'uk, Mérida** (p164) Alto-gourmet takes on some Yucatecan favorites in an elegant mansion.

Shot of sangrita (left) and tequila (right)

## Cheap Treats
You'll find the best cheap eats at market stalls, street stands, cafes and *cocinas económicas* (economical eateries). Keep in mind that some budget options have sketchy hygiene standards, so it can be a bit of a crapshoot (no pun intended).

**Wayan'e, Mérida** (p163) Greet the new day with the greasy goodness of a *castacan* (pork belly) sandwich or taco.

**Lonchería El Pocito, Cancun** (p65) Yucatecan comfort food at its best with a very local ambience.

**Christian's Tacos, Laguna Bacalar** (p141) These guys can hold their own against the best of Mexico's *al pastor* (spit-roasted pork) *taquerías*.

## Dare to Try
➡ Pickled pigs feet, snout and ears in Mérida's sprawling Mercado Municipal Lucas de Gálvez (p155).

➡ The four-alarm habanero-chili salsas at Marisquería El Taco Loco (p145) in Chetumal.

➡ Lionfish at Sulumar (p138) in the Costa Maya beach town of Mahahual – hold the venom please!

Guacamole and corn chips

# Food Basics

## When to Eat

**Desayuno** (breakfast) Usually consists of fresh fruit, *pan dulce* (sweet bread) or egg dishes; served between 7am and 11am in restaurants and cafes.

**Almuerzo** (light lunch) Locals usually take a light lunch when they've missed breakfast or want something to hold them over until *la comida,* the big meal of the day.

**La comida** (heavy lunch or 'main meal') From 2pm to 5pm. Many establishments offer gut-busting four-course meals. Shops can close between these hours, especially in smaller towns.

**La cena** (supper) Some people like to grab a light dinner, between 7pm and 11pm, before hitting the bars and clubs; it's also a popular time for taco stands.

## Where to Eat

**Restaurante** Restaurants offer the widest variety in terms of menu items, price ranges and hours; most are family-friendly establishments and they're usually your best shot at finding vegetarian options.

**Cocina económica/Fonda** These affordable eateries specialize in home-style cooking and they're great spots to mingle with locals.

**Taquería** Taco shops are a perfect late-night option and the food's cheap if you're looking to pinch some pesos.

**Mercado** Many markets have a cluster of food stalls preparing decent, reasonably priced local dishes.

**Cafe** Coffee shops are a good breakfast option when you have an early start.

**Puesto** Street stalls whip up everything from tacos to ceviche cocktails. Opening hours vary considerably.

## Menu Decoder

**Menú del día/Comida corrida** Affordable set menu with three or four courses.

**Menú degustación** A menu normally consisting of six to eight tasting-size courses.

**Entradas/Antojitos** Appetizers or snacks; common in the Yucatán, especially in bars.

**Plato fuerte** Main course or main dish.

**Postre** Dessert.

**Bebida** Drink.

## A Few Tips

➡ When sharing a table with Mexicans or dining in close quarters with them, it's customary to wish them '*buen provecho*' (enjoy your meal) before you leave.

➡ Waiters will not bring you the check until you ask for it. In Mexico it is considered rude to leave a check on a table while customers are still eating.

➡ The standard tip for tourists in Mexico is around 15% of the bill.

# Drink Basics

## Where to Drink

**Cantinas** All cantinas serve *cerveza* and some, but not all, have licenses to pour tequila and other spirits. Some may even have *xtabentún*, a regional anise-flavored liqueur made from fermented honey. Cantinas usually open at high noon and close around 11pm or midnight. The cantina experience varies considerably from one watering hole to the next. Some are festive, family-friendly establishments offering live music and complimentary snacks, others have a down-and-dirty vibe that's best avoided, especially if you're a woman traveling alone.

**Nightclubs** Some nightclubs in the region charge hefty covers (that means you Cancún) with open bar included with admission. So of course you're gonna try to get your money's worth – just don't say we didn't warn you about the nasty hangover. The party usually gets started around 11pm and thumps well into the wee hours of the morning.

**Mezcalerías** Essentially small bars that specialize in mezcal, a distilled alcoholic drink made from the agave plant. Though mezcal is not actually made in the Yucatán, *mezcalerías* have grown very popular in recent years, especially in larger cities such as Mérida, Tulum and Playa del Carmen. Mezcal has a higher alcohol content than tequila, so expect the unexpected after knockin' a few back.

**Juice bars** Usually found in markets, *juguerías* sell freshly squeezed juices, *liquados* (fruits blended with milk) and *aguas frescas* (water flavored with local ingredients such as chia seed and chaya greens). Water used to prepare drinks at juice bars is purified.

Fruit and vegetable seller, Valladolid (p198)

## A BOOZY LOVE STORY

According to legend, *balché* was created as an act of love between a beautiful Maya girl, Sak-Nicté (White Flower), and a brave young warrior. As the story goes, the young couple fled their tribe when a powerful *cacique* (indigenous chief) also declared his love to Sak-Nicté. After days of wandering in the Maya forest, the lovebirds found a honeycomb. Sak-Nicté and the warrior had a feast with the sweet honey, and decided to save some inside the trunk of a *balché* tree. That night brought rain and thunder, and the water blended with the honey inside the tree, creating a luscious beverage.

When the *cacique* found them, he ordered Sak-Nicté to return to her tribe. The young warrior was devastated and, in a desperate attempt to keep his lover at his side, he offered to cook a fantastic meal for the *cacique*. The *cacique* accepted and the couple served him a banquet, crowned with the sweet drink they had discovered. The *cacique* was so impressed with the *balché* that he let the two lovers go, on condition that they share with him how to prepare it.

**Cafes** There's no shortage of cafes in the Yucatán serving quality organic coffee from Chiapas, Oaxaca and Veracruz, Mexico's top coffee-producing regions. Most cafes open early and close around 10pm.

## Alcoholic Drinks

As elsewhere in Mexico, on the peninsula you will find the popular tequila and its cousin mezcal. Both spirits are distilled from the agave plant; one difference is that tequila comes from blue agave in the central state of Jalisco and is protected with Denomination of Origin status.

*Cerveza* (beer) is also widely available; the most popular mass-produced brew is Montejo. There is a growing number of breweries producing craft beers, such as Tulum, which makes a fine IPA, and Ceiba.

*Balché* is a Maya spirit that was offered to the gods during special ceremonies. It is fermented inside the hollow trunk of the *balché* tree with water and honey. In Valladolid, during indigenous weddings, the bride is sprayed with *balché* as a sign of abundance. *Balché* is not commercially available, but another Maya spirit, *xtabentún,* is easy to find in the region. *Xtabentún* is an anise-flavored liqueur that, when authentic, is made by fermenting honey.

It's worth noting that drinking home-brewed spirits may have health consequences beyond a hangover if they use wood rather than grain. Use caution.

## Nonalcoholic Drinks

The great variety of fruits, plants and herbs that grow in the Yucatán Peninsula are a perfect fit for the kinds of nonalcoholic drinks Mexicans love. *Juguerías* (small establishments selling freshly squeezed juices) are widely available. In some cases they will serve local fruits such as mangoes, *cayumito* (a purple plum-like fruit), *zapote negro* (a black fruit with a pear-like consistency) and *marañón* (cashew fruit). *Juguerías* also sell *licuados,* a Mexican version of a milkshake that normally includes banana, milk, honey and fruit.

*Aguas frescas* (fresh drinks made with fruit, herbs or flowers) are standard Mexican refreshments. Some of them resemble iced teas. In *agua de tamarindo* the tamarind pods are boiled and then mixed with sugar before being chilled; *agua de jamaica* is made with dried hibiscus leaves. Others like *horchata* are made with melon seeds and/or rice.

Two local favorites are *agua de chia* (a plant from the salvia family), which is typical during Holy Week celebrations in Chiapas, and *agua de chaya,* enjoyed throughout the peninsula, in which the leaves of the native shrub *chaya* are mixed with lime, honey and pineapple.

# Food & Drink Glossary

### MEAT & POULTRY

| | | |
|---|---|---|
| **a la parilla** | a la pa·*ree*·ya | grilled |
| **a la plancha** | a la *plan*·cha | pan-broiled |
| **albóndigas** | al·*bon*·dee·gas | meatballs |
| **aves** | *a*·ves | poultry |
| **bistec** | *bis*·tek | steak |
| **borrego** | bo·*re*·ga | sheep |
| **carne (asada)** | *kar*·ne (a·*sa*·da) | meat (grilled beef) |
| **carne de puerco** | *kar*·ne de *pwer*·ko | pork |
| **carne de res** | *kar*·ne de res | beef |
| **chicharrones** | chee·cha·*ro*·nes | deep-fried pork skin |
| **chorizo** | cho·*ree*·so | Mexican-style sausage made with chili and vinegar |
| **frijol con puerco** | fri·*khol* kon *pwer*·ko | *Yucateco*-style pork and beans, topped with a sauce made with grilled tomatoes, and decorated with garnishes; served with rice |
| **jamón** | kha·*mon* | ham |
| **lechón** | le·*chon* | suckling pig |
| **milanesa** | mee·la·*ne*·sa | breaded beef cutlet |
| **pavo** | *pa*·vo | turkey |
| **pibil** | pee·*beel* | meat wrapped in banana leaves, flavored with *achio-te*, garlic, sour orange, salt and pepper, and baked in a pit oven; the two main varieties are *cochinita pibil* (suckling pig) and *pollo pibil* (chicken) |
| **picadillo** | pee·ka·*dee*·yo | a ground beef filling that often includes fruit and nuts |
| **poc-chuc** | pok·chook | tender pork strips marinated in sour orange juice, grilled and served topped with a spicy onion relish |
| **pollo** | *po*·yo | chicken |
| **puchero** | pu·*che*·ro | a stew of pork, chicken, carrots, squash, potatoes, plantains and *chayote* (vegetable pear), spiced with radish, fresh cilantro and sour orange |
| **tocino** | to·*see*·no | bacon |
| **venado** | ve·*na*·do | venison, a popular traditional dish |

### SEAFOOD

| | | |
|---|---|---|
| **calamar** | ka·la·*mar* | squid |
| **camarones** | ka·ma·*ro*·nes | shrimp |
| **cangrejo** | kan·*gre*·kho | large crab |
| **ceviche** | se·*vee*·che | raw fish, marinated in lime juice |
| **filete** | fee·*le*·te | fillet |
| **langosta** | lan·*gos*·ta | lobster |
| **mariscos** | ma·*rees*·kos | shellfish |
| **ostiones** | os·*tyo*·nes | oysters |
| **pescado** | pes·*ka*·do | fish as food |
| **pulpo** | *pool*·po | octopus |

## EGGS

| | | |
|---|---|---|
| **(huevos) estrellados** | *(hwe*·vos) es·tre·*ya*·dos | fried (eggs) |
| **huevos motuleños** | *hwe*·vos mo·too·*le*·nyos | 'eggs in the style of Motul'; fried eggs atop a tortilla, garnished with beans, peas, chopped ham, sausage, grated cheese and a certain amount of spicy chili |
| **huevos rancheros** | *hwe*·vos ran·*che*·ros | fried eggs served on a corn tortilla, topped with a sauce of tomato, chilies and onions |
| **huevos revueltos** | *hwe*·vos re·*vwel*·tos | scrambled eggs |

## SOUP

| | | |
|---|---|---|
| **caldo** | *kal*·do | broth or soup |
| **consomé** | con·so·*may* | broth made from chicken or mutton base |
| **sopa** | *so*·pa | soup, either 'wet' or 'dry' as in rice and pasta |
| **sopa de lima** | *so*·pa de *lee*·ma | 'lime soup'; chicken broth with bits of shredded chicken, tortilla strips, lime juice and chopped lime |

## SNACKS

| | | |
|---|---|---|
| **antojitos** | an·to·*khee*·tos | 'little whims,' corn- and tortilla-based snacks, such as tacos and *gorditas* |
| **empanada** | em·pa·*na*·da | pastry turnover filled with meat, cheese or fruits |
| **enchiladas** | en·chee·*la*·das | corn tortillas dipped in chili sauce, wrapped around meat or poultry and garnished with cheese |
| **gordita** | gor·*dee*·ta | thick, fried tortilla, sliced open and stuffed with eggs, sausage etc, and topped with lettuce and cheese |
| **panuchos** | pa·*noo*·chos | Yucatán's favorite snack: a handmade tortilla stuffed with mashed black beans, fried till it puffs up, then topped with shredded turkey or chicken, onion and slices of avocado |
| **papadzules** | pa·pad·*zoo*·les | tortillas stuffed with chopped hard-boiled eggs and topped with a sauce of marrow squash (zucchini) or cucumber seeds |
| **papas fritas** | *pa*·pas *free*·tas | french fries |
| **quesadilla** | ke·sa·*dee*·ya | cheese and other items folded inside a tortilla and fried or grilled |
| **relleno negro** | re·*ye*·no *ne*·gro | turkey stuffed with chopped, spiced pork and served in a rich, dark sauce |
| **(queso) relleno** | (*ke*·so) re·*le*·no | stuffed (cheese), Dutch edam filled with minced meat and spices |
| **salbutes** | sal·*boo*·tes | same as *panuchos* but without the bean stuffing |
| **sope** | *so*·pe | thick corn-dough patty lightly grilled, served with salsa, beans, onions and cheese |
| **torta** | *tor*·ta | sandwich in a roll, often spread with beans and garnished with avocado slices |

## DESSERTS

| | | |
|---|---|---|
| **helado** | e·*la*·do | ice cream |
| **nieve** | *nye*·ve | sorbet |
| **paleta** | pa·*le*·ta | popsicle |
| **pastel** | pas·*tel* | cake |
| **postre** | *pos*·tre | dessert |

### FRUIT & VEGETABLES

| | | |
|---|---|---|
| **aceituna** | a·say·*too*·na | olive |
| **calabacita** | ka·la·ba·*see*·ta | squash |
| **cebolla** | se·*bo*·lya | onion |
| **champiñones** | sham·pee·*nyo*·nes | mushrooms |
| **coco** | *ko*·ko | coconut |
| **elote** | e·*lo*·te | corn on the cob |
| **ensalada** | en·sa·*la*·da | salad |
| **fresa** | *fre*·sa | strawberry |
| **frijoles** | fri·*kho*·les | beans |
| **guayaba** | gwa·*ya*·ba | guava |
| **jícama** | *khee*·ka·ma | turniplike tuber, often sliced and garnished with chili and lime; sweet, crunchy and refreshing |
| **jitomate** | khee·to·*ma*·te | tomato |
| **lechuga** | le·*choo*·ga | lettuce |
| **limón** | lee·*mon* | lemon |
| **maíz** | mai·*ees* | corn |
| **papas** | *pa*·pas | potatoes |
| **piña** | *pee*·nya | pineapple |
| **plátano macho** | *pla*·ta·no *ma*·cho | plantain |
| **plátano** | *pla*·ta·no | banana |
| **toronja** | to·*ron*·kha | grapefruit |
| **verduras** | ver·*doo*·ras | vegetables |

### CONDIMENTS & OTHER FOODS

| | | |
|---|---|---|
| **achiote** | a·*cho*·te | reddish paste obtained from annatto seeds |
| **arroz** | a·*roz* | rice |
| **azúcar** | a·soo·*kar* | sugar |
| **mantequilla** | man·te·*kee*·ya | butter |
| **mole** | *mo*·le | a handmade chocolate and chili sauce |
| **pan** | pan | bread |
| **sal** | sal | salt |

### DRINKS

| | | |
|---|---|---|
| **agua mineral** | *a*·gwa mee·ne·*ral* | mineral water or club soda |
| **agua purificada** | *a*·gwa poo·ree·fee·*ka*·da | bottled uncarbonated water |
| **atole** | a·*to*·le | corn-based hot drink flavored with cinnamon or fruit |
| **café (con leche/ lechero)** | ka·*fe* (kon *le*·che/le·*che*·ro) | coffee (with hot milk) |
| **café americano** | ka·*fe* a·me·ree·*ka*·no | black coffee |
| **caguama** | ka·*gwa*·ma | liter bottle of beer |
| **horchata** | hor·*cha*·ta | rice drink |
| **jamaica** | kha·*may*·ka | hibiscus flower, chief ingredient of *agua de jamaica*, a cold tangy tea |
| **jugo de naranja** | *khoo*·go de na·*ran*·kha | orange juice |
| **leche** | *le*·che | milk |
| **té negro** | te *ne*·gro | black tea |

# Plan Your Trip
# Family Travel

Snorkeling in caves, playing on the beach, running amok in the jungle...kids will find plenty of ways to keep busy in the Yucatán. And, as elsewhere in Mexico, children take center stage – with few exceptions, they're welcome at all kinds of hotels and in virtually every cafe and restaurant.

## Yucatán Peninsula for Kids

Few places offer more to see and do for youngsters than the Yucatán, from kid-friendly theme parks to kids' menus in nearly every restaurant, to the fascinating, once-in-a-lifetime opportunities to clamber around ruins, see wildlife and birds most kids only know from books, and do things that bring wide-eyed wonderment. Horseback riding, snorkeling, ATVs, zip-lines, cenote swimming, and so on all rank way up there in the 'world's best vacation' list. So don't think your child will be thumb-twiddling.

Be aware that not all online streaming services work when you cross over the border, so if your vacation bliss does depend on screen-based entertainment, make sure it's in a non-online form like an MP4 or DVD.

### Getting Around

Car seats are compulsory for children under five, but if you'll be renting you may want to bring your own seat or booster from home, as agencies often add US$5 or even more per day to the cost of the car. Buses have comfortable seats, usually with onboard movies, and most (not all!) have bathrooms.

## Best Regions for Kids

### Riviera Maya
Kids can splash themselves silly in the Riviera at family-friendly beaches and cenotes. The area also has many theme parks if interest in the beaches starts to wane.

### Cobá
Children dig the experience of bicycling through a thick jungle among the ancient ruins, while a series of nearby cenotes make for a fun afternoon swim.

### Cancún
From pirate-ship cruises and hotels with kids clubs to a wide offering of water-related activities and tours, boredom is simply not an option (especially if mom and dad are willing spenders) here.

### Isla Mujeres
With its shallow, swimmable beaches and a great little turtle farm, Isla Mujeres is a big hit with kids.

### Celestún
What kiddo doesn't like a chance to see wild flamingos and crocodiles, or build sand castles on the beach next to gentle ocean waves? Celestún is a bit of a trek but worth it for kids of all ages.

## Health & Safety

You know your kiddo best, but the bottom line is, don't worry: this is a safe, fun, interesting place for kids of all ages, and if you run into anything unexpected, such as an injury, you'll be in good hands. If an emergency does happen, don't think you need to cut the trip short and fly home just to get stitches – Mexico has decent medical clinics and care. In fact, the hardest thing about bringing your kid(s) along may be the undeniably trying, often lengthy, and boring-for-all-ages wait in the customs and immigration lines.

That said, some activities may have inherent risks. Swimming, diving and snorkeling are obvious things to be vigilant about. Most dive shops, boat operators and cenotes have kid-sized personal flotation devices. At times, you may be quite far from a good hospital, so having an emergency medical kit (even a pre-made one) is a good idea. All *farmacias* (pharmacies) have painkillers, cortisone creams, NSAIDs and so on. Less easily found are 100% DEET products or decent sunscreen, so you may want to bring these from home.

Child safety provisions in Mexico may be less strict than what you're accustomed to. Check out things such as toddler pools, cribs, guardrails and even toys, so that you're aware of any potential hazards.

Be mindful that children are more easily affected than adults by heat, disrupted sleeping patterns and strange food, and are sometimes less able to coherently express what's wrong.

## Sleeping

The peninsula has an exciting variety of different places to stay that should please most kids – anything beachside is usually a good start, and rustic *cabañas* (cabins) provide a sense of adventure (but choose one with good screens and mosquito nets).

Many hotels have a rambling layout and a good amount of open-air space – courtyards, pool areas, gardens – allowing for some light exploring by kids. The most family-oriented hotels, with expansive grounds and facilities such as shallow pools, playgrounds and kids clubs, tend to be found in the big resorts.

Family rooms are widely available, and many hotels will put an extra bed or two in a room at little or no extra cost. You can find rooms with air-conditioning nearly everywhere, and most midrange and top-end hotels have wi-fi access and child-friendly channels on the TV and/or DVD players for when your kids just need to flop down in front of something entertaining.

## Eating

In most restaurants in Mexico you will see entire families and their kids eating together, especially on weekends. Waiters are used to accommodating children and will promptly help you with high chairs (*silla para niños* or *silla periquera*); in some places they will bring crayons or some other toys to keep them entertained.

The Yucatán has plenty of eateries serving up international comfort food

### PLANNING

#### Before You Go

➡ See a doctor about vaccinations at least two months before your trip.

➡ It's a good idea to book some accommodations for at least the first couple of nights, even if you plan to be flexible once you've arrived.

➡ Make sure when reserving a room that the establishment accepts children – some are adults-only.

➡ Lonely Planet's *Travel with Children* has lots of practical advice on the subject.

#### Practicalities

➡ Diaper-change facilities can be found in some shopping centers and restaurants.

➡ Breastfeeding in public is not common in the Yucatán.

➡ Cots for hotel rooms and high chairs for restaurants are available mainly in midrange and top-end establishments.

➡ It's usually not hard to find an inexpensive babysitter – ask at your hotel.

### UNDER-18 AIR TRAVELERS

To conform with regulations to prevent international child abduction, minors (people aged under 18) traveling to Mexico without one or both of their parents may need to carry a notarized consent form signed by the absent parent or parents, giving permission for the young traveler to make the international journey. Though Mexico does not specifically require this documentation, airlines flying to Mexico may refuse to board passengers without it. In the case of divorced parents, a custody document may be required. If one or both parents are dead, or the traveler has only one legal parent, a notarized document may be required. Regardless of whether it's required, having it can spare you needless hassle if you're stopped or questioned, so it's worth considering before you depart.

should Mexican fare not sit well with your children. Along the Riviera Maya you'll find many Italian-owned establishments preparing pizzas and pastas, while in gringo-friendly Cancún, there are so many restaurants doing burgers and the like that it'll seem like you never left home. Yucatecan *antojitos* (snacks) such as *sopa de lima* (which tastes like chicken soup) and *salbutes* (lightly fried tortillas topped with shredded poultry and other fixings) are fairly neutral options for experimenting with local flavors.

The closer you are to tourist centers, the better chance you have of finding more diverse and child-friendly menus. If your kid is a finicky eater, consider packing a lunch when visiting small towns where menu options may be more limited.

The spacious open-air character of many Yucatán eateries conveniently means that children aren't compelled to sit nicely at the table all the time. Some restaurants even have play areas or small pools to keep kids busy while the grown-ups have a drink.

# Children's Highlights
## Water Worlds

**Croc-spotting** (p205) Boat tours offer unique animal-spotting opportunities in Río Lagartos.

**Swim with whale sharks** (p73) Massive whale sharks congregate around Isla Holbox from mid-May to mid-September.

**Sail on a pirate ship** (p60) A replica Spanish galleon stages nightly swashbuckler battles off the waters of Cancún. Pirate ships sail in Campeche too.

**Snorkel in the Caribbean** (p31) Many beaches on the Yucatán's Caribbean coast provide calm waters and colorful marine life for beginners.

**Theme parks** (p108) Visitors can make their way through underground rivers and caves at Riviera Maya theme parks.

**Cruise the jungle** (p254) Reach the ancient cities of Yaxchilán by an adventurous riverboat trip.

## Inland Fun

**Selvática** (p108) An award-winning zip-line circuit through the jungle near Puerto Morelos, with its own cenote for swimming.

**Cobá** (p130) This jungle-surrounded ancient Maya site near Tulum has pyramids, a zip-line, and bicycles for pedaling around the network of dirt trails.

**Aktun Chen** (p108) This park near Akumal features a 60m-long cave, a 12m-deep cenote, 10 zip-lines and a small zoo.

**Boca del Puma** (p105) Near Puerto Morelos, Boca del Puma has zip-lining, horseback riding, wall climbing and a cenote to dip into.

## Animal Encounters

**Isla Mujeres Turtle Farm** (p81) Has hundreds of sea turtles, both big and small, and there's an aquarium, too. The staff are very friendly and will take the time to explain how and why the farm protects the turtles.

**Reserva de la Biosfera Ría Celestún** (p183) Take a boat tour through the mangroves of Ría Celestún, home to flamingos and harpy eagles.

**Crococun Zoo** (p105) Visitors can interact with the animals at this zoo near Puerto Morelos. You get an up-close look at crocodiles and wild spider monkeys.

# Regions at a Glance

## Cancún & Around

Beaches
Nature
Activities

### Beach-Bumming

Cancún was built as a resort city with its scenic beaches in mind, so the one constant is the fine white sands and turquoise blue waters, especially along the northern coast of Isla Blanca, where the coast remains relatively undeveloped.

### Wildlife-Watching

Several islands near Cancún offer unforgettable encounters with nature. Off the coasts of Islas Mujeres and Holbox, you can swim with ginormous whale sharks, while the national park Isla Contoy has excellent bird-watching. Don't miss the boat back from uninhabited Contoy or you'll be sleeping with the turtles!

### Water Sports

Name your water activity, Cancún has it: snorkeling, kayaking, wakeboarding, fishing – there's even a unique underwater sculpture museum for beginner divers. If you have kids and visit the area's water parks, the biggest problem will be convincing them it's time to leave.

p55

## Isla Mujeres

Conservation
Beaches
Activities

### Wildlife Conservation

At the Isla Mujeres Turtle Farm, more than 100,000 of the little guys are released into the great big sea each year from July through November. Turtle eggs are gathered and secured in safe sands during peak nesting season, May to October.

### Calm Beaches

The waters on Isla Mujeres' north shore, known as Playa Norte, are calm, shallow, warm and remarkably blue. On the island's south side, you'll come across some sweet snorkeling sites.

### Great Outdoors

Snorkel with whale sharks, hook big game fish on a sportfishing excursion, or go diving and spot manta rays, barracuda and sea turtles. You can also rent a golf cart and visit beach clubs on the island's quieter south side.

p79

# Isla Cozumel

Activities
Scenery
Food

### Divine Diving

Isla Cozumel is a must-visit if you're into diving – in fact, some rank the island's sites among the world's best. Cozumel is known for its drift diving, year-round visibility, spectacular walls and impressive variety of colorful marine life.

### Island Escape

A road trip on a scooter or convertible VW to the island's less-visited side is a moving picture of windswept beaches and scrubby jungle scenery. There are even small Maya ruins along the way. It all makes a nice escape from the cruise-ship crowds back in town.

### Wining & Dining

Cozumel certainly has no shortage of quality restaurants serving fine local and international cuisine. The highest concentration of restaurants and bars is near the main plaza, but many hidden gems lie outside the tourist center.

**p89**

# Riviera Maya

Beaches
Nightlife
Activities

### Beach Life

The Riviera Maya sits on prime beach real estate. In Tulum, Maya ruins are dramatically perched atop a cliff tower above the beach. In tranquil Paamul, it's just you and the sea urchins, while up north in Puerto Morelos, a colorful reef awaits just 600m offshore.

### Party Central

With beachside discos featuring fire-dancer shows and cool 'inland' salsa clubs, Playa del Carmen still rules as the Riviera's top party town. But in recent years Tulum has gained ground on Playa in its bid to claim pueblo-that-never-sleeps status.

### Cenote Diving

Take a plunge into a cenote (limestone sinkhole) and explore an intriguing underwater world of caverns and caves. Cenotes also make great swimming holes for nondivers. The Maya referred to these intricate river systems as gateways to the underworld.

**p103**

# Costa Maya & Southern Caribbean Coast

Scenery
Activities
Beaches

### Shades of Blue

Dubbed the 'lake of seven colors,' the crystalline waters of Laguna Bacalar have shades of blue that you never even knew existed. The glorious colors are on full display at Cenote Azul.

### Take the Plunge

Divers won't want to miss out on the opportunity to explore Banco Chinchorro, the largest coral atoll in the northern hemisphere and a ship graveyard. There's fantastic snorkeling here as well.

### Sleepy Beach Towns

Once tiny fishing villages, Mahahual and Xcalak are seeing more tourism these days, but fortunately they're still very chill – a far cry from the megaresort madness of Cancún.

**p133**

# Yucatán State & the Maya Heartland

Archaeology
Nature
Food

## Maya Ruins

The Yucatán has so many Maya ruins that you'd need a leave of absence to visit them all. The most famous, Chichén Itzá, draws more than a million visitors a year and has been declared one of the 'new seven wonders of the world.'

## Birdies & Crocs

The Yucatán's two largest biosphere reserves, Celestún and Ría Lagartos, are always a hit with nature buffs. Tour boats take you out to observe crocodiles, flamingos and other bird species.

## Food, Glorious Food

Yucatán state is one of Mexico's most exciting culinary destinations. In state capital Mérida, you get an interesting mix of traditional Yucatecan fare such as *cochinita pibil* (slow-cooked pork) and quality international cuisine.

p151

# Campeche State

History
Nature
Archaeology

## Pirates Ahoy

Campeche's unique feature is its pretty historical center surrounded by stone walls built to fend off pirate attacks. It's a serene destination with few tourists, where a beachside boardwalk creates an atmosphere more romantic than ravaged.

## Fins & Flippers

Laguna de Terminos' collection of estuaries and mangroves provides a rich coastal habitat for many critters. Keep a lookout for migratory birds or spot playful dolphins from a boat.

## Lofty Pyramids

Deep in a jungle full of toucans and monkeys lies Calakmul, a significant, if remote, Maya site. Originally a huge city, it covered 72 sq km and supported more than 50,000 people – and it boasts one of the tallest Maya pyramids in Mexico.

p209

# Chiapas & Tabasco

Indigenous Culture
Outdoor Adventure
Nature

## Temples & Tradition

The world of the Maya lives on everywhere you turn here, from the preserved stone temples of Classic Maya civilization to the persistence of dramatic pre-Hispanic religious rituals and the intricate hand-woven textiles and clothing still worn by many.

## In Motion

Whether you're rappelling into a jungle sinkhole, bouncing over a stretch of white water in a rubber raft, or climbing a 4000m volcano, Chiapas has multiple ways to raise your adrenaline levels.

## Birds & Beasts

Nesting turtles, roaring monkeys and flashes of rainbow plumage are standard fare in the jungles and on the misty mountains and sandy beaches of this biodiverse region that's full of rare and endangered wildlife.

p235

# On the Road

## AT A GLANCE

**POPULATION**
743,600

**CAPITAL**
Chetumal

**BEST TASTING MENU**
Tempo (p66)

**BEST ECOHOTEL**
Hotel El Rey del Caribe (p61)

**BEST PALAPA BAR**
Tribu Bar (p76)

**WHEN TO GO**
**Mar** Spring-break madness lasts through mid-April, but hotel rooms are pricier.

**May** After the dust settles, visitors see a quieter side of the city, and great online deals.

**Jul & Aug** Best months to snorkel with enormous whale sharks off the Isla Contoy coast.

Zona Hotelera (p57)
FREDERICK MILLETT/SHUTTERSTOCK ©

# Cancún & Around

One look at Cancún's aquamarine Caribbean waters and it makes perfect sense why planners back in the 1970s were so eager to develop the area as Mexico's next big resort destination. The result is a tale of two cities, with the Zona Hotelera offering 19km of powdery white-sand beaches and Cancún Centro providing the local flavor.

Certainly when most people think of Cancún, a wild party town comes to mind. But rest assured you can also soak up some indigenous culture in between the fiestas, and dine on everything from Yucatecan comfort food to haute cuisine. Outdoorsy types will appreciate the nearby diving and snorkeling sites, underwater cave systems and myriad water activities.

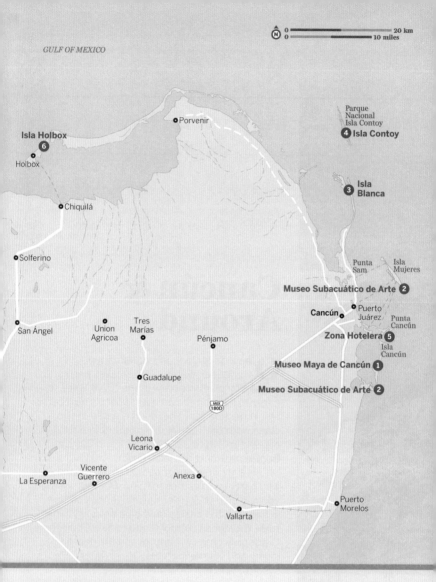

# Cancún Highlights

**1 Museo Maya de Cancún**
(p57) Wandering around a
world-class museum, home
to one of the Yucatán's most
important collections of Maya
artifacts.

**2 Museo Subacuático de
Arte** (p59) Snorkeling in the
shallow waters of a unique
underwater museum

hundreds of submerged life-
sized sculptures.

**3 Isla Blanca** (p60)
Chilling on the soft sands of a
white-sand beach flanked by
the Caribbean Sea and a calm
lagoon.

**4 Isla Contoy** (p72)
Exploring an uninhabited
island that's home to 170

bird species, including red
flamingos and frigates.

**5 Zona Hotelera** (p57)
Basking in 19km of postcard-
perfect Caribbean beaches.

**6 Isla Holbox** (p72)
Swimming with whale sharks,
kayaking through wildlife-rich
mangroves and enjoying laid-
back island living.

# CANCÚN

## History

When you look around at the towering hotels of the hotel zone and the urban sprawl
of downtown, it boggles the mind to think
that some 50 years ago there was nothing
in Cancún but sand and fishing boats. But
the course of history changed dramatically
in the early 1970s when Mexico's ambitious
planners decided to outdo Acapulco with a
brand new world-class resort that would be
located on the Yucatán Peninsula.

## ⊙ Sights

Most of Cancún's star attractions – namely
its beaches, museum, ruins and water-related activities – are in the Zona Hotelera. If
you're staying in Cancún Centro, any 'R-1,'
'R-2,' or 'Zona Hotelera' bus will drop you off
at any point along the coast.

### ★ Museo Maya de Cancún       MUSEUM
(Maya Museum; Map p58; ☑998-885-38-43;
www.facebook.com/museomayacancun;      Blvd
Kukulcán Km 16.5; adult/child under 13yr M$75/
free; ⊙9am-6pm Tue-Sun; ◻R-1) Holding one
of the Yucatán's most important collections
of Maya artifacts, this modern museum is
a welcome sight in a city known more for
its party scene than cultural attractions. On
display are some 400 pieces found at key
sites in and around the peninsula, ranging
from sculptures to ceramics and jewelry.
One of the three halls shows temporary
Maya-themed exhibits. Many of the pieces
in the collection are from Chichén Itzá.

Cancún's original anthropology museum
shut down in 2004 due to structural damage from hurricanes. The new museum features hurricane-resistant reinforced glass.
The price of admission includes access to
the adjoining San Miguelito archaeological
site.

### San Miguelito       ARCHAEOLOGICAL SITE
(Map p58; ☑998-885-38-43; www.facebook.com/
museomayacancun; Blvd Kukulcán Km 16.5; M$70;
⊙9am-5:30pm; ◻R-1) This archaeological site
contains more than a dozen restored Maya
structures inhabited between 1250 and 1550
CE, prior to the arrival of the conquistadors.
It is underwhelming if compared to some
of the nearby ruins in Tulum or Cobá, but
a nice cultural diversion if you're staying
in Cancún. A path from the Museo Maya
leads to remains of houses, a palace with 17

columns and the site's tallest structure: the
8m-high Pirámide (Pyramid), which was re-
built three times.

Access to the ruins is included in the entrance fee to the Museo Maya.

### Zona Arqueológica
### El Rey       ARCHAEOLOGICAL SITE
(Map p58; www.inah.gob.mx; Blvd Kukulcán
Km 18.5; M$55; ⊙8am-4:30pm; ◻R-1, R-2)
In the Zona Arqueológica El Rey, on the
west side of Blvd Kukulcán, there's a small
temple and several ceremonial platforms.
The site gets its name from a sculpture
excavated here of a noble, possibly a *rey*
(king), wearing an elaborate headdress. El
Rey, which flourished from 1200 to 1500
CE, and nearby San Miguelito were communities dedicated to maritime trade and
fishing.

### Yamil Lu'um       ARCHAEOLOGICAL SITE
(Map p58; off Blvd Kukulcán Km 12.5; ◻R-1)
FREE Also known as the Templo del Alácran
(Scorpion's Temple), Yamil Lu'um was used
between 1200 and 1550 CE, and sits atop
a beachside knoll in the parklike grounds
between the Park Royal and Westin Lagu-
namar hotels. The ruin makes a pleasant
venture for its lovely setting more than
anything else. Only the outward-sloping
remains of the weathered temple's walls
still stand. To reach the site, visitors must
discreetly pass through either of the hotels
flanking it.

## 🏖 Beaches

Starting from Cancún Centro in the northwest, all of Isla Cancún's beaches are on
the left-hand side of the road. (The lagoon
is on your right; don't swim in the lagoon
because of crocodiles!) The first beaches are
Playas Las Perlas, Juventud, Linda, Langos-
ta, Tortugas and Caracol. With the exception
of Playa Caracol, these are Cancún's most
swimmable beaches.

When you round Punta Cancún the water gets rougher (though it's still swimmable) and the beaches become more scenic as
white sands meet the turquoise-blue Caribbean, from Playa Gaviota Azul all the way
down south to Punta Nizuc at Km 24. Playa
Delfines, at Km 18, is about the only beach
with a public parking lot big enough to be
useful; unfortunately, its sand is coarser and
darker than the exquisite, fine sand of the
more northerly beaches.

# Cancún

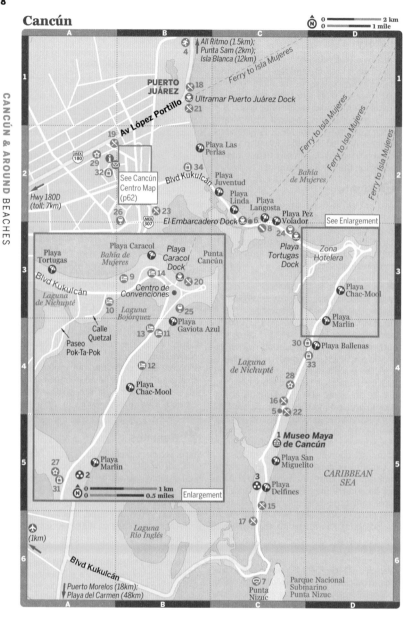

## Beach Access

Under Mexican law you have the right to walk and swim on every beach in the country except those within military compounds. In practice, it is difficult to approach many stretches of beach without walking through the lobby of a hotel, particularly in the Zona Hotelera.

However, as long as you look like a tourist (this shouldn't be hard, right?), you'll usually be permitted to cross the lobby and proceed to the beach.

# Cancún

## Beach safety

Avoid swimming along the shores of Laguna Nichupté. The lagoon is a crocodile habitat and, although attacks are rare, you're better off at the beach. In April 2015, a reportedly inebriated man ignored the many signposts warning that the lagoon was not safe for swimming and died in a crocodile attack.

Cancún's ambulance services respond to as many as a dozen near-drownings per week. The most dangerous beaches with the strongest undercurrents line the eastern shore, from Playa Chac-Mool at Km 10 to Playa Delfines at Km 18.

Though the surf is usually gentle, undertow is a possibility, and sudden storms can blacken the sky and sweep in at any time without warning. A system of colored pennants warns beachgoers of any potential danger:

**Blue** Normal, safe conditions.

**Yellow** Use caution, changeable conditions.

**Red** Unsafe conditions; use a swimming pool instead.

# 🏃 Activities

★ **Museo Subacuático de Arte**  SNORKELING
(MUSA; Map p58; www.musamexico.org; snorkeling tour US$47, 1-tank dive US$90-115) 🏊 Built to divert divers away from deteriorating coral reefs, this unique aquatic museum features hundreds of life-size sculptures in the waters of Cancún and Isla Mujeres. Only snorkeling is allowed at the 4m-deep artificial reef at Cancún's Punta Nizuc gallery, while the deeper Isla Mujeres' gallery is ideal for first-time divers. Organize outings through dive shops; Scuba Cancún is recommended.

The underwater museum is a creation of British-born sculptor Jason deCaires Taylor.

**Scuba Cancún**  DIVING
(Map p58; ☎ 998-849-52-25; www.scubacancun.com.mx; Blvd Kukulcán Km 5.2; 1-/2-tank dive US$62/77; ⊙ 7am-8pm, from 8am Sun) A family-owned and PADI-certified dive operation with many years of experience, Scuba Cancún was the city's first dive shop. It offers a variety of snorkeling and diving expeditions (including cenote and night dives). It also runs snorkeling and diving trips to the underwater sculpture museum, aka MUSA, as well as outings to see whale sharks.

## DAY-TRIPPER: FIVE GREAT EXCURSIONS FROM CANCÚN

There's a whole world beyond Cancún, and you don't have to wait to enjoy it.

And here's a quick sustainable travel tip: skip the group tour and use that extra dough to hire a local guide and buy some crafts. Staying the night in your destination will bring even more money into the local community.

**Chichén Itzá** (p190) Rent a car so you can take the old highway through Valladolid. Stop in the small Maya communities along the way for out-of-sight *panuchos* (small corn tortillas stuffed with refried beans and topped with shredded turkey or chicken).

**Isla Mujeres** (p79) Take the ferry from Puerto Juárez. Check out the southern coast in the morning, then swing up north for a swim in the stunningly beautiful turquoise waters of Playa Norte.

**Tulum** (p119) Get up early and rent a car to make your way down to Tulum, the only Maya ruin of size built right on the coast. On the way back, stop at one of the numerous cenotes clearly marked from the highway.

**Puerto Morelos** (p105) Just a half-hour ride heading south of Cancún, you'll find this quiet beach town with a small plaza, an excellent handicrafts market and surprisingly good restaurants. Playa Express buses depart frequently from in front of the bus terminal.

**Isla Blanca** See what Cancún used to look like before the development boom and do it fast because the big hotels are gradually moving in. Take the dirt road north of Punta Sam past beach club Cabañas Playa Blanca and continue north until you literally reach the end of the road, where you'll find a sublime white-sand beach flanked by a shallow lagoon and the Caribbean Sea.

**Koko Dog'z Surf Shop**      WATER SPORTS
(Map p62; ☑998-887-36-35; www.kokodogz. com; Av Náder 42; ☉noon-8pm Mon-Fri, to 4pm Sat; ☑R-1) Sells all sorts of beachwear and boards – surf, kite and wake.

**All Ritmo**      WATER PARK
(Map p58; ☑998-881-79-00; www.allritmo cancun.com; Puerto Juárez-Punta Sam Hwy Km 1.5; adult/child 5-12yr M$350/290; ☉10am-5pm Wed-Mon) Little ones can splish and splash to their hearts' content at this water park, which also has minigolf and shuffleboard. The turnoff is 2km north of the Ultramar ferry terminal. 'Punta Sam' *colectivos* on Avenida Tulum (opposite the bus terminal) will drop you at the turnoff, and it's a short walk from there.

## Tours

Most hotels and travel agencies work with companies that offer tours to surrounding attractions.

**Captain Hook**      BOATING
(Map p58; ☑998-849-44-51; www.capitanhook. com; Blvd Kukulcán Km 5, Marina Capitán Hook; adult US$89-109, child 2-12yr US$40-53; ☉tour 7-10:30pm; ☑) There's nothing like a swash-buckling adventure with sword fights and cannon battles to get kids' imaginations run-

ning wild. This 3½-hour tour aboard a Spanish galleon replica includes dinner service, and it costs a pretty doubloon if you opt for the steak and lobster option. On the other hand, kids cost only US$5 if they eat strictly from the buffet bar.

**Aquaworld**      TOURS
(Map p58; ☑998-689-10-13; www.aquaworld. com.mx; Blvd Kukulcán Km 15.3; adult/child 4-11yr US$47/24; ☉7am-8pm) Runs a hybrid submarine and glass-bottom boat out to the Museo Subacuático de Arte, an underwater museum with hundreds of submerged life-sized sculptures. This tour is a good option for kids or non-swimmers, as opposed to the snorkeling tours that go out to the site as well.

## Sleeping

The city has a variety of accommodations ranging from budget to mind- and budget-blowing. Almost all hotels offer discounts during 'low' season, but many have up to five different rate periods: Christmas and New Year are always at a premium, with high rates sometimes running from December through to US spring break in March and again in July and August (when locals have their summer vacation). Many places have great online promotions.

## 🛏 Cancún Centro

'Budget' is a relative term; prices in Cancún are higher for what you get than almost anywhere else in Mexico. There are many cheap lodging options within several blocks of the bus terminal, northwest on Avenida Uxmal. The area around Parque de las Palapas has several hostels and budget digs as well.

Midrange in Cancún is a two-tiered category; the Cancún Centro area is much cheaper than the Zona Hotelera and only a short bus ride away from the Zona's beaches.

### Mezcal Hostel                    HOSTEL $

(Map p62; 🗐 998-217-53-15; www.nomadsexpe rience.com/mezcal.php; Mero 12; dm/r US$16/70; 🔄 ✳ 🛜 🌀; 🚍R-1) Mezcal Hostel occupies a beautiful two-story house and some adjoining properties in a quiet residential area off Avenida Náder. Smoke can be thick in the common areas, but the dorms are smoke-free.

There's a pool, large bar and restaurant, lots of activities, and even a tattoo parlor. What's next, a wedding chapel?

### Los Girasoles                    HOTEL $

(Map p62; 🗐 998-887-39-90; www.losgirasoles cancun.com.mx; Piña 20; r from M$600; 🔄 ✳ @ 🛜) On a quiet downtown backstreet, this affordable hotel is one of the better budget deals you'll find in the area, despite its shortcomings (beds and wi-fi service could use upgrades). Nevertheless, the modern rooms here are clean and wi-fi works just fine in the breezy lobby.

### ★Hostel Ka'beh                    HOSTEL $

(Map p62; 🗐 998-892-79-02; www.facebook. com/hostelkabeh; Alcatraces 45; dm/r/tr incl breakfast from M$230/750/1200; 🔄 ✳ @ 🛜; 🚍R-1) A friendly central option just off the buzzing Parque de las Palapas, this small hostel has a lived-in feel that goes hand in hand with the relaxed vibe. Expect many social activities at night, most organized around food and drink. Trips depart to the beach at noon and to the Zona Hotelera after dinner.

At the time of research plans for a pool were underway, as well as expansion to give sleepers some quieter quarters away from the rebranded 'Fiesta Party House.' And what other hostel offers over 30 craft beers from its fridge?

### Náder Hotel & Suites                    HOTEL $$

(Map p62; 🗐 998-884-15-84; www.suitesnader cancun.com; Av Náder 5; d/ste incl breakfast M$1450/1950; 🔄 ✳ 🛜; 🚍R-1) The Náder caters to business travelers, but it's also a hit with families thanks to its ample rooms and suites with large common areas and kitchens. Even the 'standard' setup here gets you digs with some serious elbow room, with a work desk and chair, track lighting, and a comfy chaise to nap on.

### Cancún International Suites                    HOTEL $$

(Map p62; 🗐 998-884-17-71; www.cancuninter nationalsuites.com; Gladiolas 11, cnr Alcatraces; r/ ste M$1480/1860; 🔄 ✳ 🛜; 🚍R-1) Colonialstyle rooms and suites in this remodeled hotel are comfortable and quiet and the location is great – right off Parque de las Palapas and conveniently close to downtown's restaurant and bar zone.

### Soberanis Hotel                    HOTEL $$

(Map p62; 🗐 998-884-45-64; www.soberanis. mx; Av Cobá 5 s/n; d M$1300; 🔄 @ 🛜; 🚍R-1) Location, location, location. The Soberanis sits right on a busy intersection where you can catch buses to practically anywhere in town, including Zona Hotelera, and there's a supermarket right next door. Rooms have comfortable, clean beds with wood furnishings. No elevator means the lotsa-luggage crowd may want to look elsewhere.

### Hotel Plaza Caribe                    HOTEL $$

(Map p62; 🗐 998-884-13-77; www.hotelplaza caribe.com; Pino 19; r from M$1270; P 🔄 ✳ 🛜 🌀; 🚍R-1, R-2) Directly across from the bus terminal, this hotel offers comfortable rooms, a pool, restaurant and gardens with peacocks roaming about. Request one of the remodeled rooms, which sport newer furnishings than those in the older wing.

### Hotel Bonampak                    HOTEL $$

(Map p62; 🗐 998-884-02-80; www.hotelbonam pak.com; Av Bonampak 225; d incl breakfast M$1200; P 🔄 ✳ @ 🛜 🌀; 🚍R-1, R-2) Good value by Cancún standards, rooms at this business-style hotel have comfy mattresses, dark-wood furnishings and flat-screen TVs. Ask for one overlooking the sunny pool area.

### Hotel El Rey del Caribe                    HOTEL $$$

(Map p62; 🗐 998-884-20-28; www.elreydel caribe.com; Av Uxmal 24; r incl breakfast from US$90; 🔄 ✳ 🛜 🌀; 🚍R-1) 🌿 El Rey is a

# Cancún Centro

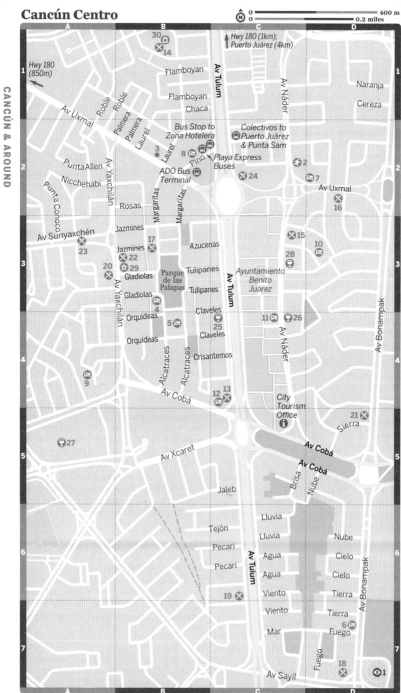

# Cancún Centro

true ecohotel – it recycles, employs solar collectors and cisterns, uses gray water on the gardens, and has some rooms with composting toilets. This beautiful spot has a swimming pool and Jacuzzi in a jungly courtyard that's home to a small family of *tlacuaches* (opossums). Each room has a fully equipped kitchenette, comfortable beds and a fridge.

Offers good online deals.

## 🛏 Zona Hotelera

With few exceptions, most hotels lining Blvd Kukulcán are of the top-end variety. Many offer all-inclusive packages, often at reasonable rates if you're willing to forgo eating elsewhere. Often the best room rates are available through hotel-and-airfare packages, so shop around.

**Mayan Monkey**　　　　　　　HOSTEL $
(Map p62; ☑998-217-53-32; www.mayanmonkey.com; Blvd Kukulkán 9.3; dm/r incl breakfast from M$200/2300; ❁❋🛜🌊; ☐R-1) This monkey-themed hostel is as clean and comfortable as they come, and it's a hell of a deal with two meals included. The rooftop pool and bar area provide sweeping city views and fun-filled nights with free activities like salsa classes.

On offer are immaculate female-only and mixed dorms, and modern private rooms adorned with hipster monkey art.

**Hostel Natura**　　　　　　　HOSTEL $$
(Map p58; ☑998-883-08-87; www.facebook.com/hostelcancunnatura; Blvd Kukulcán Km 9.5; dm US$30, r with/without bathroom US$100/75; ❁❋🛜; ☐R-1, R-2) Above a health-food restaurant of the same name, this fun, vibrant Zona Hotelera hostel offers private rooms with lagoon views and somewhat cramped dorms, offset by the airy rooftop terrace and a nice common kitchen area. The party zone is just a stumble away, and the staff are helpful and friendly.

**Grand Royal Lagoon**　　　　　HOTEL $$
(Map p58; ☑800-552-46-66, 998-883-27-49; reservar.grlagoon@hotmail.com; Quetzal 8A; r M$1500; 🅿❁❋🛜🌊; ☐R-1, R-2) Though pleasantly breezy and relatively affordable for the Zona Hotelera, rooms at the old-school Grand Royal are looking a bit worn and tired these days. Most have two double beds, while some have kings, lagoon views and balcony. The property has a small pool, and wi-fi reaches common areas only. It's 100m off Blvd Kukulcán Km 7.5.

**★ Le Blanc**　　　　　　　　RESORT $$$
(Map p58; ☑998-881-47-48, USA 800-986-5632; www.leblancsparesort.com; Blvd Kukulcán Km 10; d/ste all-inclusive from US$793/868; 🅿❁❋🛜🌊; ☐R-1, R-2) You can't miss the glaring white exterior of the aptly named Le Blanc, arguably Cancún's most sophisticated resort. This adults-only retreat comes with all the amenities you'd expect in this category:

## LIVING LARGE IN THE MEXICAN CARIBBEAN

Cancún and its surrounding areas have many establishments selling the 'resort' experience, but only some are truly worth the splurge. Non-negotiable is a prime beachfront location; after that, it's really just a question of what best suits your needs: some hotels put a premium on over-the-top comfort and elegance, others specialize in family-friendly getaways with around-the-clock activities. When booking a room, keep in mind that some resorts do not accept children and most, though not all, offer all-inclusive plans with an endless banquet of food and drink.

The 'all-inclusive' plans will likely give you an experience that's barely Mexico: you'll speak in English, eat international food (often not as good as at the nearby restaurants), and have packaged day trips and excursions. If you're looking to experience Mexico or its culture, an all-inclusive may not be the right fit for you, and you can often get excellent service and delicious food at a family-run B&B.

Here are some of the best resorts in and around Cancún.

**Le Blanc** (p63) Adults-only resort with over-the-top luxury. Butler service, anyone?

**Beachscape Kin Ha Villas & Suites** Family-friendly resort with very swimmable beach for kids.

**Petit Lafitte** (p112) Secluded and safe family vacation spot just north of Playa del Carmen.

**Grand Velas** (p112) Riviera Maya luxury resort that puts the others to shame.

---

gorgeous infinity pool, cold welcome drink on check-in, scented hand towels – the works. There's even butler service should life in Cancún become too complicated. Discounts for multiple-night stays.

Guests get free valet parking as well.

### Beachscape Kin Ha Villas & Suites
RESORT $$$

(Map p58; ☑998-891-54-00; www.beachscape.com.mx; Blvd Kukulcán Km 8.5; d/ste incl breakfast from M$5210/6060; 🅿➔❋@🛜🐕; 🚍R-1) A good family spot, Beachscape offers a babysitting service, a play area for kids and a swimmable beach with calm waters. You'll never need to leave the hotel's grounds (though we think you should), as there are bars, markets, travel agencies and more on the premises. All rooms feature a balcony and two double beds or one king-sized bed.

### Suites Costa Blanca
HOTEL $$$

(Map p58; ☑998-883-08-88; www.suitescostablanca.com; Blvd Kukulcán Km 8.5; r from M$1800; ➔❋🛜; 🚍R-1) A decent value option for the Zona Hotelera, which in itself makes this a great find, though it's tucked into a non-functional mall and it's strange wandering past closed-up stores. The hotel claims to offer 'Mediterranean-style' suites, but they're really just large (somewhat outdated) rooms with sitting areas and small balconies. Rates fluctuate significantly from month to month.

## ✖ Eating

## ✖ Cancún Centro

Eating options in Cancún Centro range from your standard taco joints to upscale seafood restaurants. You'll find many restaurants clustered around Parque de las Palapas and lining nearby Avenida Yaxchilán. Trendy new spots are popping up on or around Avenida Náder, between Avenidas Uxmal and Cobá. Mercados 23 (p69) and 28 (p68) serve up good market food, and for groceries, try Soriana (Map p62; cnr Avs Tulum & Uxmal; ⏰24hr), close to the bus station, or Chedraui Supermarket (Map p62; cnr Avs Tulum & Cobá; ⏰7am-11pm; 🅿; 🚍R-1).

### Rooster Café Sunyaxchen
CAFE $

(Map p62; ☑998-310-46-92; Av Sunyaxchen s/n, Plaza Sunyaxchen; mains M$90-180; ⏰7am-11pm; 🛜) A main go-to cafe for locals in search of a place to write, work or hang out, this trendy coffee shop has a central location in downtown Cancún, close to Market 28. Try items like Monte Cristo waffles and homemade breads from the breakfast menu, or stop by in the afternoon for desserts, salads, burgers and paninis.

### El Paisano del 23
MEXICAN $

(Map p62; Jabín 9 No 134, Mercado 23; tacos & tortas M$15-40; ⏰6am-4pm; 🚍R-1) A local favorite for more than 40 years, the *pais-*

*ano* ('fellow countryman' – it's the owner's nickname) marinates *pierna* (pork leg) in red wine and then slow cooks it. The *tortas* (sandwiches) go fast, especially on weekends.

### Los de Pescado
SEAFOOD $

(Map p62; ☑998-884-11-46; www.losdepescado .com; Av Tulum 32; tacos & tostadas M$34-35, ceviche M$104-150, burritos M$57; ⊘10am-6pm; 🕿; 🖫R-27) It's easy to order at a place where you have just a handful of choices: ceviche (seafood marinated in lemon or lime juice, garlic and seasonings), tacos, *tostadas* (fried tortilla), *caldo de camarón* (shrimp soup) and burritos. Try the fish and shrimp tacos with fixings from the salad station and you'll understand why locals dig this spot.

### Lonchería El Pocito
YUCATECAN $$

(Map p58; ☑998-252-26-54; Calle 31 Norte, btwn Calles 10 & 12; tacos M$16-17, mains M$120-130; ⊘8am-10pm Mon-Fri, to 8pm Sat) For authentic Yucatecan home-cooking, locals often recommend this fan-cooled *palapa* restaurant and it's easy to take an instant liking to the place. The changing daily menu features savory regional classics such as *queso relleno* (stuffed cheese), *papadzules* (diced egg enchiladas) and *relleno negro de pavo* (stewed turkey). Wash it down with a refreshing *agua de chaya* (Mexican tree spinach water).

### La Fonda del Zancudo
INTERNATIONAL $$

(Map p62; ☑998-884-17-41; www.facebook. com/lafondadelzancudo; Av Uxmal 23; mains M$155-295; ⊘6pm-midnight Mon-Sat; 🕿; 🖫R-1) Softly illuminated by strings of lights, lanterns and moonlight, this alluring little restaurant sits within an enchanting walled patio on downtown Cancún's central Avenida Uxmal. The main menu boasts artisanal creations made primarily with local organic ingredients, and the daily specials wall always has tempting culinary surprises and inventive cocktails to try.

### Kiosco Verde
SEAFOOD $$

(Map p58; ☑cell 998-1988402; www.facebook. com/kioscoverdemarisqueria; Av López Portillo 570, Puerto Juárez; mains M$120-273; ⊘12:30-8pm Wed-Mon; 🅿🕿; 🖫R-1) The Green Kiosk just might be the most underrated seafood restaurant in all of Cancún. It began in 1974 as a small grocery store and now it excels in well-prepared seafood dishes like grilled octopus and hogfish. The Kiosko also has a new cantina that stays open until 11pm.

### El Tigre y El Toro
ITALIAN $$

(Map p62; ☑998-898-00-41; www.facebook. com/tigreyeltoro; Av Náder 64; mains M$165-295; ⊘6pm-12:30am Mon-Sat, to 11:30pm Sun; 🕿🗷; 🖫R-1, R-2) Gourmet thin-crust pizza and homemade pastas are served in a candlelit gravel garden at El Tigre y El Toro ('Tiger' and 'Bull' are the owners' nicknames). Many locals rank this as Cancún's *numero uno* pizza joint; a seasonal lobster topping comes highly recommended.

### Picaña & Grill
STEAK $$

(Map p62; ☑998-310-52-34; www.facebook. com/picanagrillcancun; Av Yaxchilán 31; tacos M$28-33, steaks M$195-340; ⊘1pm-midnight Tue-Sun) The house specialty here is the *picaña* (top sirloin cap), which can be ordered as a tender steak or sliced off a spit for tacos. They also do loaded baked potatoes and grilled bone marrow with *carne asada* (grilled beef), but the *picaña* steak is king.

### La Playita
SEAFOOD $$

(Map p62; ☑998-898-40-15; www.laplay itabar.com; cnr Av Bonampak & Av Sayil; mains M$120-200; ⊘11am-2am, to 3am Thu-Sat; 🎮🕿) The covered terrace at this bar and restaurant affords views of the nearby bullring and towering residential buildings. Multiflavored mojitos are great accompaniments to an idyllic afternoon seafood lunch such as *camarones al coco* (coconut shrimp with mango sauce), and vegans will love the 'veganiche' ceviche option.

### Pescaditos
SEAFOOD $$

(Map p62; ☑998-884-03-05; http://pescaditos. restaurantsnapshot.com; Av Yaxchilán 69; mains M$99-250, pescaditos M$55; ⊘8am-midnight, to 1am Fri & Sat; 🕿) The namesake *pescaditos* (fried fish sticks served with a mayo-*chipotle* sauce) are the star attraction here, but the menu features plenty of other fresh fish and seafood dishes that are well worth trying.

### ★ Peter's Restaurante
INTERNATIONAL $$$

(Map p62; ☑998-251-93-10; www.facebook .com/peterscancun; Av Bonampak 71, btwn Sierra & Róbalo; dinner M$210-655; ⊘6-10pm Tue-Sat) Peter's Restaurante has a homey charm and some of the best cooking in the city. Dutch chef Peter Houben has blended European, Mexican and international cuisine, with beautifully prepared dishes like the mushroom-ravioli appetizer and fresh salmon fillet in lemon sauce with a spicy hint of *chile de arbol* (tree chili). Try the poached pear for dessert.

### Puerto Santo
SEAFOOD $$$

(Map p58; 🖉WhatsApp only 998-845-28-52; www.facebook.com/puertosantocancun; Residencial Puerta del Mar Supermanzana 84, Puerto Juárez; appetizers M$85-189, mains M$179-320; ⊙1-11pm; P🕿) In a gated residential community about 500m south of the Puerto Juárez ferry terminal, this hidden oceanfront restaurant wins over locals with dishes like chili-sautéed octopus *tostadas*, fresh ceviche and wood-fired whole fish. To get here, leave an ID with a security officer at the Puerta del Mar entrance.

### The Bears Den
INTERNATIONAL $$$

(Map p58; 🖉998-688-67-43; www.thebearsden cancun.com; 2nd fl, Av Sayil, Plaza Azuna; mains M$220-460; ⊙3-11pm Tue-Sun) In this casual open-air restaurant on the second floor of a shopping center, Québec native Christopher Vallieres prepares exquisitely refined dishes including tender pork belly with sake-and-pear purée and seared tuna with mango-jalapeño chutney and soy-ginger glaze. The dining area catches a nice lagoon breeze and service is spot-on.

### La Habichuela
FUSION $$$

(Map p62; 🖉998-884-31-58; www.lahabichuela. com; Margaritas 25; mains M$220-490, cocobichuela M$650; ⊙1pm-11pm; P🕿; ⌨R-1) This restaurant has hit-or-miss food in a lovely courtyard dining area, just off Parque de las Palapas. Known for the tasty *cocobichuela* (shrimp and lobster in curry sauce served inside a coconut with tropical fruit), but you pay premium for the elegance. Appetizers shine, but the steaks, fish, and even the Maya dishes are so-so.

A small, non-valet parking lot is convenient for those with a rental car.

## 🍴 Zona Hotelera

'Pay-per-view' takes on a whole different meaning in the Zona Hotelera. Prices sometimes reflect the location of the restaurant and what's outside the window more than the quality of food. That being said, there are a fair number of excellent seafood and gourmet restaurants along the strip too.

For budget eats in the Zona Hotelera, you can always hit the taco joints across from the nightclub zone at Km 9.5 and nearby **Surfin' Burrito** (Map p58; 🖉998-883-00-83; www.facebook.com/thesurfinburrito; Blvd Kukulcán Km 9.5; burritos M$85-145; ⊙24hr; ⌨R-1, R-2) never closes.

### Restaurante Natura
VEGETARIAN $$

(Map p58; 🖉998-883-05-85; www.restaurante natura.com; Blvd Kukulcán Km 9.5; breakfast M$69-109, lunch & dinner M$95-205; ⊙7:30am-10:30pm; 🕿🖉; ⌨R-1) This little bistro offers up a good mix of natural and vegetarian Mexican cuisine – think giant natural juices, and quesadillas with Chihuahua cheese, spinach, mushrooms and whole-wheat tortillas. There's also a vegan menu.

### El Galeón del Caribe
SEAFOOD $$

(Map p58; 🖉cell 998-2148175; www.facebook. com/elgaleondelcaribe; Blvd Kukulcán Km 19.4; pescadillas M$16, mains M$140-190; ⊙noon-7pm; ⌨R-1, R-2) Famed for its *pescadillas* (fried tortillas stuffed with fish), this low-key seafood *palapa* has an outdoor kitchen and a lagoonside setting. It's near the southern end of the Hotel Zone and easy for in-the-know tourists to access, but its out-of-the-way location and authentic Mexican seafood make it a favorite Sunday afternoon hangout for Cancún locals too.

Only the parking lot is visible from the road.

### ★ Benazuza
MEXICAN $$$

(Map p58; 🖉998-891-50-00; www.facebook. com/restaurantebenazuza; Blvd Kukulcan Km 19.5, Grand Oasis Sens Resort; per person M$1376; ⊙7-10pm Mon-Sat; ⌨R-1) Up to 30 courses of surprising molecular cuisine. The dining experience at contemporary restaurant Benazuza incorporates traditional Mexican-inspired dishes, such as tacos and chilies, that have been transformed into new shapes, flavors and textures using cutting-edge cooking technology. The price here includes molecular cocktails at the bar, all dinner courses, and desserts unlike any you've ever tried.

### ★ Tempo
BASQUE $$$

(Map p58; 🖉998-881-17-90; www.tempocan cun.com; Blvd Kukulcan Km 16.5, inside Paradisus Cancun Resort; mains M$555-875, 9-course tasting menu M$1762; ⊙6-11pm; ⌨R-1) Dazzling contemporary elegance and impeccable service characterize Tempo, but it's the nine-course tasting menu of elaborate gourmet Basque cuisine with a molecular touch that have made this restaurant one of the best in Cancun. Created by eight-Michelin-star Chef Martin Berasategui, Tempo provides an experience where each course delights and surprises the palate, from flavorful seafood recipes to lavish desserts.

## Crab House

SEAFOOD $$$

(Map p58; ☑ 998-193-03-50; www.crabhouse cancun.com; Blvd Kukulcán Km 14.7; dishes M$485-2950; ⊗noon-11:30pm; P🅿🛜; 🚻R-1, R-2) Offering a lovely view of the lagoon that complements the seafood, the long menu here includes many shrimp and fish-fillet dishes. Stone crab is the specialty, which (along with lobster) is priced by the kilo. Both are served from crystal-clear tanks. The establishment prides itself on having no holidays, not even for hurricanes.

## Fred's House

SEAFOOD $$$

(Seafood & Oyster Bar; Map p58; ☑ 998-840-64-66; www.fredshouserestaurant.com; Blvd Kukulcán Km 14.5; mains M$325-850; ⊗1pm-midnight; 🚻R-1) One of Cancún's most beautiful restaurants, Fred's House features warm contemporary style and tropical gardens by Nichupté Lagoon. At this seafood eatery, you can order oysters from the raw bar, or try their popular wood-grilled octopus and several lobster dishes.

For the perfect sunsets or a special occasion, call in advance to reserve one of the waterfront dining pavilions.

## Harry's Steakhouse & Raw Bar

STEAK $$$

(Map p58; ☑ 998-840-65-50; www.harrys.com. mx; Blvd Kukulcán Km 14.2; mains M$380-1290, steak up to M$3900; ⊗1pm-1am; 🚻R-1, R-2) Stunning, renowned Harry's serves house-aged steaks, plus superfresh fish and a famous cotton-candy treat. The architecture's impressive too, with outdoor waterfalls, plenty of decking over the lagoon and two bars – one indoors and one out. Service is impeccable.

Try the jungle-theme lounge or the new exclusive roof nightclub, and don't miss peeking at the tequila and mezcal display. Yum!

## Mocambo

SEAFOOD $$$

(Map p58; ☑ 998-883-05-88; www.mocambo cancun.mx; Blvd Kukulcán Km 9.5; mains M$265-550; ⊗noon-11pm; P🅿🛜; 🚻R-1) Definitely one of the best seafood spots in the Zona Hotelera, the *palapa*-covered Mocambo sits right on Playa Caracol and serves up excellent seafood dishes such as whole *mero* (grouper) and a savory seafood paella. A trio plays Mexican classics from 3pm to 5pm. It's past Hertz down a narrow alley that leads to the beach.

## 🍷 Drinking & Nightlife

## 🍸 Cancún Centro

Cancún Centro's clubs and bars are generally mellower than those in the rowdy Zona Hotelera. Stroll along Avenida Yaxchilán or Avenida Náder and you are sure to run into something (or somebody) you like.

Built into the **Plaza de Toros** (Bullring; Map p62; cnr Avs Bonampak & Sayil) are several bars, some with music, that draw a largely local crowd.

## ★Amarula con Acento Tropical

COCKTAIL BAR

(Map p62; ☑ cell 998-3325680; www.facebook. com/amarulaconacentotropical; Av Náder 104; ⊗9pm-3:30am Wed-Sat; 🚻R-1) Identified from the street only by a doorway and neon sign, Amarula blends dark, sultry style with the architectural details of an old Cancún house. The cocktail menu far outshines the food here: the signature drinks live up to the bar's name ('with a tropical twist'), using classic Mexican ingredients like *jamaica* (hibiscus flower), regional fruits and chili peppers.

DJs spin house, jazz and tropical sounds.

## Nomads Hostel & Bar

COCKTAIL BAR

(Map p62; ☑ 998-898-31-92; www.nomads experience.com; cnr Av Náder & Mero; ⊗7-11:30pm Tue-Sun; 🚻R-1) Showing off with an artsy vibe where geometric tiles meet concrete and brick, Nomads draws in Cancún's young 'in crowd' with creative cocktails and innovative Mexican cuisine. The indoor area allows friends to sit down to a late dinner (mains M$90 to M$170), while the back area under the stars is standing-room only. A pool table adds to the vibe.

## Marakame Café

BAR

(Map p58; ☑ 998-887-10-10; www.marakame cafe.com; Av Xpujil, Circuito Copán 19; ⊗8am-1am Mon-Fri, 9am-2am Sat, to midnight Sun; 🛜; 🚻R-27) An excellent open-air breakfast and lunch spot by day, and a popular bar with live music by night. The bartenders, or mixologists if you will, prepare martinis and mango margaritas, and they do mimosas for Saturday and Sunday brunch (adult/child M$288/128). It's a short taxi ride from downtown.

## Grand Mambocafé

CLUB

(Map p62; ☑ 998-884-45-37; www.facebook. com/grandmambocafecancunoficial; 2nd fl, Plaza Hong Kong, cnr Avs Xcaret & Tankah; cover M$60-180; ⊗9:30pm-3am Wed-Sat; 🚻R-2) The large floor at this happening club is the perfect place to practice those Latin dance steps you've been working on. Live groups play Cuban salsa and other tropical styles.

### 11:11
GAY

(Once Once; Map p62; ☑ cell 998-1352243; www. 1111gayclubcancun.com; Claveles s/n; ☺ 10pm-5am Fri-Sun; ☒ R-1) The main room in this large house stages drag shows, go-go dancers and the like, while DJs in smaller rooms spin electronica and pop tunes till the sun comes up. Look for the black and rainbow design outside.

## 🍸 Zona Hotelera

The club scene in the Zona Hotelera is young, loud and booze-oriented – the kind that often has an MC urging women to display body parts to hooting and hollering crowds. The big dance clubs charge around US$55 to US$75 admission, which includes open-bar privileges (ie drink all you want). Most don't get hopping much before midnight.

A number of clubs are clustered along the northwest-bound side of Blvd Kukulcán, all within easy stumbling distance of each other. Be careful crossing the street.

### City
CLUB

(Map p58; ☑ 998-883-33-33; www.thecitycancun.com; Blvd Kukulcán Km 9; open bar US$65; ☺ 10:30pm-4am Fri; ☒ R-1) The largest nightclub in Latin America still manages to fill up every Friday night. Frequently hosting world-famous DJs and musicians, this massive place offers wild nightlife, whether you're dancing on top of the central stage or watching it all from the stadium-style side levels. Due to the large crowds and 'party hearty' atmosphere, it can feel overwhelming at times.

### Bar del Mar
BAR

(Map p58; www.facebook.com/bardelmarcancun; Blvd Kukulcán Km 6.5, Playa Tortugas; ☺ 10am-6pm; ☒ R-1) One of Cancún's only beach bars open to the public. With just a few tables on the terrace and on the sand, Bar del Mar serves snacks, beers and cocktails on its affordable menu. Especially good here are the tuna *tostadas* and the Bloody Caesar, a Bloody Mary prepared with habanero. There's a minimum spend of M$150.

## ☆ Entertainment

### ★ H Roof Nightclub
LIVE MUSIC

(Map p58; ☑ 998-840-65-92; www.hroof.com. mx; Blvd Kukulcán Km 14.2; ☺ 11pm-6am Thu-Sat; 🚏) Part nightclub, part live music venue, exclusive H Roof has emerged as one of the Zona Hotelera's top after-hours spots. On most nights, resident or international DJs spin lounge, hip-hop and Latino sounds. Drinks are pricey but you get a fun dance party.

### Mora Mora
LIVE MUSIC

(Map p58; ☑ cell 998-3007080; www.facebook. com/mora-mora-1434309116861854; Av Palenque 10, btwn Av Chichén Itzá & Calle 6 Poniente; ☺ 5pm-1am Mon-Sat) Local musicians and artists gather at this muralled underground venue, which operates as a restaurant and gallery as well. In Mora Mora's rear garden, you're likely to catch Mexican hip-hop, punk or metal acts grinding out spirited sets. Definitely drop by here if you're looking to tap into Cancún's youth subculture.

### Cinemex
CINEMA

(Map p58; ☑ 999-242-21-26; www.cinemex.com; Blvd Kukulcán Km 12.5, La Isla Shopping Village; ☺ 1pm-midnight; ☒ R-1, R-2) Screens mostly Hollywood movies. Some are shown in English with Spanish subtitles, others are dubbed in Spanish.

### Teatro Xbalamqué
THEATER

(Map p62; ☑ 998-204-10-28; www.teatroxbalamque.com; Av Yaxchilán 31, cnr Jazmines; ☺ showtimes 8pm & 10pm Fri & Sat) Stages musicals, comedies and monologues in Spanish.

## 🛍 Shopping

Shopaholics will enjoy downtown's colorful markets and the Zona Hotelera's modern open-air malls. Locals head to either **Mercado 28** (Map p58; ☑ 998-892-43-03; www. facebook.com/mercado28cancunmexico; cnr Avs Xel-Há & Sunyaxchén; ☺ 8am-7pm) or Mercado 23 for clothes, shoes, inexpensive food stalls and so on. Of the two, Mercado 23 is less frequented by tourists. If you're looking for a place without corny T-shirts, this is the place to go.

### La Europea
DRINKS

(Map p58; www.laeuropea.com.mx; Blvd Kukulcán Km 12.5; ☺ 10am-9pm Mon-Sat, 11am-7pm Sun; ☒ R-1) A gourmet liquor store with reasonable prices, knowledgeable staff and the best booze selection in town, including top-shelf tequilas and mezcals.

### La Isla
**Shopping Village**       MALL
(Map p58; ☑998-883-50-25; www.facebook.com/laislacancun; Blvd Kukulcán Km 12.5; ⊕10am-10pm; 🚇; 🚌R-1) Unique among the island's malls, this is an indoor–outdoor place with canals, a 60m-high Ferris wheel, an aquarium, a movie theater, a boutique-stores section and enough distractions to keep even the most inveterate hater of shopping amused. Souvenir-hunters will find nice (if pricier) options here. Consider picking up a bottle of *xtabentún,* a Yucatecan anise-flavored liqueur.

### Plaza Kukulcán       MALL
(Map p58; ☑998-193-01-60; www.kukulcanplaza.mx; Blvd Kukulcán Km 13; ⊕10am-10pm; 🛜; 🚌R-1) The largest of the indoor malls is Plaza Kukulcán. Of note here are the temporary art exhibits, the many stores selling silverwork, and La Ruta de las Indias, a shop featuring wooden models of Spanish galleons and replicas of conquistadors' weaponry and body armor.

### Mercado 23       MARKET
(Map p62; www.facebook.com/mercado23cancun; Jabín 9; ⊕8am-7pm; 🚌R-1) This market is a nice reality check if you're tired of seeing the same old tourist knickknacks elsewhere.

### Puerto Cancún Marina
**Town Center**       MALL
(Map p58; ☑998-313-31-28; www.marinatowncenter.com; Blvd Kukulcán Km 1.5; ⊕11am-11pm; 🛝; 🚌R-1, R-2) A new open-air mall with more than 20 restaurants, an IMAX movie theater, international clothing stores and sweeping views of the marina and Zona Hotelera.

## 🧭 Orientation

Cancún consists of two very distinct areas: Cancún Centro (downtown) and Zona Hotelera (Isla Cancún).

The Zona Hotelera is what most people think of when they say 'Cancún': the sandy spit that encloses a scenic lagoon on one side and has the Caribbean's azure-blues on the other. Its main road, Blvd Kukulcán, is a four-lane, divided avenue that leaves Cancún Centro and heads eastward for 9km, passing condominium developments, hotels and shopping complexes, to Punta Cancún (Cancún Point) and the **Centro de Convenciones** (Convention Center; Map p58;

☑998-881-04-00; www.cancunicc.com; Blvd Kukulcán Km 9).

From Punta Cancún, the boulevard heads south for about 15km to Punta Nizuc, flanked on both sides for much of the way by huge hotels, shopping centers, dance clubs and many restaurants and bars. Here it turns westward and then rejoins the mainland, cutting through light tropical forest for several more kilometers to its southern terminus near Cancún's international airport.

Addresses in the Zona Hotelera are refreshingly simple: instead of a street name (usually Blvd Kukulcán anyway) a kilometer distance from the 'Km 0' roadside marker at the boulevard's northern terminus in Cancún Centro is given. Each kilometer is similarly marked. Most bus drivers will know the location you're heading but, if in doubt, you can just ask to be dropped off at the appropriate kilometer marker.

## 🛈 Information

### EMERGENCY
**Emergency** (☑911, ☑066)
**Fire** (☑998-884-12-02)
**Red Cross** (☑065, ☑998-884-16-16)
**Tourist Police** (☑998-885-22-77)

### MEDICAL SERVICES
**Hospital Playa Med** (☑998-140-52-58; www.hospitalplayamed.com; Av Náder 13, cnr Av Uxmal; ⊕24hr; 🚌R-1) Modern facility with 24-hour assistance.

### MONEY
There are numerous banks with ATMs throughout the Zona Hotelera and downtown on Avenida Tulum. Cancún's airport also has ATMs and money exchange.
**Banamex ATM** (Blvd Kukulcán Km 8.5, Plaza Terramar; ⊕24hr)
**Santander** (Av Tulum s/n, cnr Av Cobá; ⊕9am-4pm Mon-Fri; 🚌R-1) With several money exchange offices nearby.

### POST
There is no post office in the Zona Hotelera, but some hotels' reception desks sell stamps and will mail letters.

The **Main Post Office** (Map p58; cnr Avs Xel-Há & Sunyaxchén; ⊕8am-4pm Mon-Fri, 9am-12:30pm Sat) is downtown at the edge of Mercado 28. You can also post mail in the red postal boxes sprinkled around town, but you're best off handing them to the clerk in person. The red boxes are increasingly misused as trash bins.

## SAFE TRAVEL

The biggest danger in Cancún isn't violent crime – it's the streets themselves. Vehicles speed along narrow roads and pedestrians (often drunk) sometimes get injured. A poked eye or twisted ankle is more common than a shooting or mugging; however, if anyone *does* demand money, don't argue. Most violent incidents involve fights where tourists put themselves in danger.

That said, do not purchase drugs on the street or be seen talking to street dealers: this can be interpreted by either police or gangs as you being involved, marking you for interrogation or mugging, and you want to avoid both.

## TOURIST INFORMATION

**City Tourism Office** (Map p62; ☎ 998-887-33-79; cnr Avs Cobá & Náder; ☻ 9am-4pm Mon-Fri) A small city tourist office with supplies of printed material and knowledgeable staff.

# ⓘ Getting There & Away

## AIR

**Aeropuerto Internacional de Cancún** (Cancún International Airport; ☎ 998-848-72-00; www. asur.com.mx; Hwy 307 Km 22) is the busiest airport in southeast Mexico. It has all the services you would expect from a major international airport: ATMs, money exchange and car-rental agencies. It's served by many direct international flights and by connecting flights from Mexico City.

Low-cost Mexican carriers VivaAerobus, Interjet and Volaris have services from Mexico City.

There are flights to Cancún from Guatemala City and Flores (Guatemala), Havana (Cuba), Panama City and São Paulo (Brazil). Some Havana–Cancún flights continue to Mérida.

For a full list of the carriers with flights to Cancún, see the airport website.

Mexican carriers include the following.

**Aeroméxico** (☎ 998-884-21-54; www.aeromex ico.com; Plaza Hollywood, Local 32; ☻ 9am-6:30pm Mon-Fri, to 6pm Sat; ☐ R-1) Direct flights from Mexico City and New York. Office just west of Avenida Bonampak.

**Interjet** (☎ 998-892-02-78; www.interjet.com; Av Xcaret 35, Plaza Hollywood; ☻ 9am-7pm Mon-Fri, to 6pm Sat, 10am-3pm Sun) Flies direct to Miami and Havana.

**Magnicharters** (☎ 998-884-06-00, 800-201-14-04; www.magnicharters.com.mx; Av Náder 94, cnr Av Cobá; ☻ 9am-8pm Mon-Fri, to 2pm Sat, 10am-3pm Sun; ☐ R-1) To Mexico City.

**VivaAerobus** (☎ 818-215-01-50; www.vivaaero bus.com; Hwy 307 Km 22, Cancún International Airport) Nonstop to Mexico City.

**Volaris** (www.volaris.com; Hwy 307 Km 22, Cancún International Airport) Service to Mexico City and other parts of Mexico.

## BOAT

There are several ferry departure points for Isla Mujeres from Cancún. From the Zona Hotelera, you can depart from **El Embarcadero** (Map p58; Blvd Kukulcán Km 4), **Playa Caracol** (Map p58; Blvd Kukulcán Km 9.5; parking per day M$100) or **Playa Tortugas** (Map p58; Blvd Kukulcán Km 6.5). From Cancún Centro, there are two passenger ferry terminals in Puerto Juárez: **Ultramar** (Map p58; ☎ 998-293-90-92; www.ultramarferry.com; Juárez adult/child one-way M$160/130, Hotelera adult/child one-way US$15/10) and a less popular dock about 500m north shared by Marinsa (www. marinsaturismo.com) and Naveganto (www. navegante.mx), though at the time of research only Ultramar was running regularly. From Puerto Juárez, one-way fares cost M$140 to M$160, while leaving from the Zona Hotelera runs about M$270.

If you want to take a vehicle across you'll need to head to Punta Sam's **Marítima Isla Mujeres** (Marítima Isla Mujeres; ☎ Isla Mujeres 998-307-10-19, Punta Sam 998-201-93-76; www. maritimaislamujeres.com; Av Rueda Medina s/n, Punta Sam), 8km north of Cancún Centro (basic one-way/return auto fare M$295/590, including driver), but it's much easier to rent a golf cart or scooter on the island.

For Isla Contoy, **boats** (☎ 998-886-42-70; www.contoytours.com; Vialidad s/n, V&V Marina; adult/child 5-12yr including dock fees US$113/93; ☻ tours 9am-5:30pm Tue-Sun) depart from the V&V Marina, just north of the Punta Sam car-ferry terminal.

## BUS

Cancún's modern bus terminal (p299) is a relatively safe area, but be aware of your bags and make sure to establish the fare before getting into a taxi.

Across Pino from the bus terminal, a few doors from Avenida Tulum, is the ticket office and mini-terminal of **Playa Express** (Map p62; Pino s/n, cnr Av Tulum), which runs air-conditioned buses down the coast to Playa del Carmen every 10 minutes until early evening, stopping at major towns and points of interest. ADO covers the same ground and beyond with its 1st-class and 2nd-class lines. To reach Isla Holbox up north, take a bus to Chiquilá.

ADO sets the 1st-class standard. Mayab provides good 'intermediate class' (tending to make more stops than 1st class) to many points.

## CAR

Cars can be rented at Cancún airport, where you'll find multiple kiosks and offices in and around the terminals. **Avant** (☑ 998-883-94-34; www.avantrentacar.com; Hwy 307 Km 15.2; US$40 per day, minimum 3 days; ☺ 9am-5pm), an upstart, will pick you up at the airport and offers no-dickering: the price you've reserved for includes full insurance already, often at a fraction of the cost of the bigger rental agencies.

In the city, there are several rental offices just south of La Isla Shopping Village (p69). Be aware that Hwy 180D, the *cuota* (toll road) running much of the way between Cancún and Mérida, costs M$504. An economy-size rental car with basic liability insurance starts at about M$700 per day.

Rental offices include the following:
**Alamo** (☑ 998-886-01-01; www.alamo.com.mx; Hwy 307 Km 22, Cancún International Airport; ☺ 24hr)
**Avis** (☑ 998-883-14-36; www.avis.com.mx; Blvd Kukulcán Km 12.5, La Isla Shopping Village; ☺ 7am-10pm)
**Hertz** (☑ 999-911-80-40; www.hertz.com; Hwy 307 Km 22, Cancún International Airport; ☺ 24hr)
**National** (☑ 998-881-87-60, toll free 800 737 3722; www.nationalcar.com; Hwy 307 Km 22, Cancún International Airport; ☺ 7am-11pm)

## ⓘ Getting Around

Cancún Centro and Zona Hotelera are just a 15-minute ride away from each other. The main north–south thoroughfare, Avenida Tulum, is the easiest street to catch city buses and taxis. If you're at the beach, the 'elbow' area in the Zona Hotelera can get very congested at rush hour, so plan accordingly.

### TO/FROM THE AIRPORT

Frequent ADO buses go to Cancún Centro (M$98) between 8:15am and 11:45pm. They depart from outside the terminals. Once in town, the buses travel up Avenida Tulum to the bus terminal on the corner of Avenida Uxmal. Going to the airport from Cancún Centro, the same ADO airport buses leave regularly from the bus station. ADO also offers bus services out of the airport to Playa del Carmen, Tulum and Mérida.

Airport shuttle vans **Super Shuttle** (☑ 998-193-17-42; www.supershuttle.com; Hwy 307 Km 22, Cancún International Airport) and Yellow Transfer run to and from Cancún Centro and the Zona Hotelera for about US$10 per person for shared rides and US$60 for nonstop service.

Regular taxis run from the airport into town or to the Zona Hotelera and cost up to M$650 (up to four people). Expect to pay about M$370 for a city cab when returning to the airport.

CANCÚN & AROUND GETTING AROUND

## BUSES FROM CANCÚN

| DESTINATION | COST (M$) | TIME | FREQUENCY (PER DAY) |
| --- | --- | --- | --- |
| Bacalar | 312-467 | 5-5½hr | frequent |
| Cancún International Airport | 88 | ½hr | frequent |
| Chetumal | 487 | 5½-6hr | frequent |
| Chichén Itzá | 334 | 3-4hr | hourly |
| Chiquilá | 270 | 3-3½hr | 4 |
| Felipe Carrillo Puerto | 246 | 3½-3¾hr | frequent |
| Mahahual | 218-497 | 5½-5¾hr | 2 (6:45am & 4:45pm) |
| Mérida | 460-754 | 4-5hr | frequent |
| Mexico City (Norte) | 1588 | 27¼hr | 1 (6:30pm) |
| Mexico City (TAPO) | 1588-1770 | 25-26½hr | 5 |
| Palenque | 832-1288 | 13-13¼hr | 4 |
| Playa del Carmen | 42-88 | 1½hr | frequent ADO & Playa Express |
| Puerto Morelos | 28-37 | ½-¾hr | frequent ADO & Playa Express |
| Ticul | 296 | 8hr | frequent |
| Tizimín | 166 | 6hr | 2-5 until 6:50pm |
| Tulum | 73-181 | 2¼-2¾hr | frequent |
| Valladolid | 191-252 | 2-2¼hr | frequent |
| Villahermosa | 1036-1258 | 12¾-14¾hr | frequent |

### BUS

To reach the Zona Hotelera from Cancún Centro, catch any **bus** (Map p62; Av Tulum) with 'R-1' 'Hoteles' or 'Zona Hotelera' displayed on the windshield as it travels along Avenida Tulum toward Avenida Cobá then eastward on Avenida Cobá. South of Avenida Cobá, along Avenida Tulum, you can also catch the 'R-27' to the Zona Hotelera.

To reach Puerto Juárez and the Isla Mujeres ferries, you can either take a northbound 'Punta Sam' or 'Puerto Juárez' **colectivo** (Map p62; Av Tulum) from a bus stop across from the ADO terminal, or you can wait on Avenida Tulum for an R-1 'Puerto Juárez' bus.

### CAR

Cancún can get congested at times and driving inside the city may not be worth the stress. Park in white curb areas only unless you've been specifically told parking in yellow is OK. Red, green and anything other than white is prohibited or reserved. Most Zona Hotelera accommodations have designated parking areas where you can leave your vehicle, while in Cancún Centro you may have to leave it on the street. Use extreme caution when riding a motorcycle or scooter in the city and always wear a helmet.

### TAXI

Cancún's taxis do not have meters. Fares are set, starting as low as M$35, but you should always agree on a price before getting in; otherwise you could end up paying for a 'misunderstanding.' From Cancún Centro to Punta Cancún it's usually M$100 to M$130, to Puerto Juárez M$50 to M$70. Trips within the Zona Hotelera or downtown zones cost around M$40 to M$50. Hourly and daily rates should be about M$250 and M$2000, respectively.

# NORTH OF CANCUN

## Isla Contoy

Spectacular Isla Contoy (998-234-99-05; contoy@conanp.gob.mx) is a bird-lover's delight: an uninhabited national park and sanctuary that is an easy day trip from Cancún or Isla Mujeres. About 800m at its widest point and more than 8.5km long, it has dense foliage that provides ideal shelter for more than 170 bird species, including brown pelicans, olive cormorants, turkey birds, brown boobies and frigates, and is also a good place to see red flamingos, snowy egrets and white herons.

Whale sharks are often sighted north of Contoy between June and September. In an effort to preserve the park's pristine natural areas, only 200 visitors are allowed access each day. Bring binoculars, mosquito repellent and sunblock. Guided tours to Isla Contoy give you several hours of free time to explore the island's interpretive trails, climb a 27m-high observation tower and get in a little snorkeling.

For more information on the island, Amigos de Isla Contoy (Map p58; 998-884-74-83; www.islacontoy.org; Local E-1, 2nd fl, Plaza Bonita Mall; 9am-5pm Mon-Fri) has detailed information on the island's ecology. Tour operators based out of Cancún (p70) run trips to Contoy.

## Isla Holbox

984 / POP 1600

Isla Holbox (hol-bosh) has sandy streets, colorful Caribbean buildings, lazing, sundrunk dogs, and sand so fine its texture is nearly clay. The greenish waters are a unique color from the mixing of ocean currents, and on land there's a mixing too: of locals and tourists, the latter hoping to escape the hubbub of Cancún.

While there are no throbbing nightclubs here, and while its beaches are beautiful, it's not exactly peaceful (what with the throngs of people and constant buzzing of noisy gasoline-powered golf carts). It's also the one place in nearly all Mexico you'll find a 'tourists-go-home' attitude from (some) locals.

It's a fantastic spot for wildlife. Lying within the Yum Balam reserve, Holbox is home to more than 150 bird species, including roseate spoonbills, pelicans, herons, ibis and flamingos. In summer, whale sharks congregate nearby.

### Beaches

Most people come here for the whale sharks and to lounge on the beaches, which are generally gorgeous. At night there's even the chance of seeing bioluminescent waves. But if you get too much sun or want a change, you can also head out to observe birds and other wildlife around the island.

**Punta Coco**                                    BEACH

On the western edge of the island, about 2.5km from downtown, Punta Coco is a great sunset beach.

## SWIMMING WITH THE WHALE SHARKS

Between mid-May and mid-September, massive whale sharks congregate around Isla Holbox to feed on plankton. They are the largest fish in the world, weighing up to 15 tons and extending as long as 15m from gaping mouth to arching tail. Locals call them 'dominoes' because of their speckled skin.

The best time to track these gentle giants is in July and August, but that also happens to be the busy Mexican vacation season, when you can get up to two-dozen boats rotating around a single whale shark.

The World Wildlife Fund has been working with the local community since 2003 to develop responsible practices for visiting the whale sharks, trying to balance the economic boon of these tours with the environmental imperatives of protecting a threatened species.

If you choose to go swimming with the whale sharks, only three swimmers (including your guide) are allowed in the water at a time. You are not allowed to touch the fish, and are required to wear either a life jacket or wetsuit to ensure you do not dive below the shark.

★ **Punta Mosquito** BEACH

On the eastern side of the island, Punta Mosquito is about 2.5km east of the downtown area. It has a large sandbar and is a good place to spot flamingos. It's not named 'Mosquito' for nothing: bring repellent!

## ⚡ Activities & Tours

★ **VIP Holbox Experience** TOURS

(☑ 984-875-21-07; www.vipholbox.com; Av Damero s/n; whale-shark tours per person US$150, night kayak tours US$55; ⊙ 9am-1pm & 5-9pm) VIP Holbox Experience goes the extra mile to ensure that guests understand they are part of a delicate ecosystem – for the whale-shark tours, they offer biodegradable sunscreen, no plastic bottles and follow strict guidelines to make sure these incredible animals are properly protected. Tours include delicious ceviche (seafood marinated in lemon or lime juice, garlic and seasonings) and a stop for snorkeling.

**Explora Holbox** KAYAKING

(☑ cell 984-1387793; www.kayakholbox.com; tours per person M$700-800) English-speaking guide Carlos Brassel does beginner- to advanced-level kayak tours through the mangroves, providing excellent bird-watching opportunities.

**Los Potrillos** HORSEBACK RIDING

(☑ cell 984-1299995; www.facebook.com/lospotrillos.holbox; Av Pedro Joaquín Coldwell s/n; tours per person US$40) Bilingual guides offer horseback-riding tours along a beach that leads to a remote lagoon at Punta Coco. You'll find Los Potrillos near the beach about 500m west of Tiburón Ballena.

**Villas HM Paraíso del Mar** TOURS

(☑ 984-875-20-62; www.villashmparaisodelmar.com/en/holbox; Av Plutarco Elías s/n, Zona Hotelera; tour per person M$550) Beachfront hotel Villas HM Paraíso del Mar arranges a *tres islas* (three islands) tour, which goes to Isla Pájaros and Isla Pasión for bird-watching and to the Yalahau spring for swimming.

**El Corchal** TOURS

(☑ cell 998-1657105; pepecorcho05@gmail.com; Av Hidalgo s/n, Solferino; tour per person M$700) 🏄 Ecotourism center El Corchal, in Solferino, has an orchid garden, jungle camping sites and kayak tours.

## 🛏 Sleeping

Not surprisingly, *cabañas* (cabins) and bungalows are everywhere along the beach. Some of the most upscale places can be found east of town, out along the island's northern shore in the Zona Hotelera. Most budget and midrange accommodations are clustered within several blocks of the plaza.

**Hostel Ida y Vuelta** HOSTEL $

(☑ 984-875-23-58; www.holboxhostel.com; Av Paseo Kuka s/n; campsites/dm/cabañas/house M$180/270/900/1300, all incl breakfast; ⊛ ❄ 🔊) A great spot for young backpackers, the stilt-based camps have dorm rooms that sleep eight, or you can stay in wood- or sand-floor *cabañas* with private bathrooms. There's also a very affordable house with a kitchen – ideal for small groups. From the plaza, head two blocks north, then walk about six blocks east.

## OFF THE MAP: ALTERNATIVE TOURISM ON THE RISE

Many Maya communities are beginning to welcome tourism – it may be the only way to maintain their language and culture as mass migration to boom towns like Cancún draws away the best and brightest, and children ask to study English rather than Maya.

Maya Ka'an (www.mayakaan.travel) supports ecotourism in numerous communities throughout the state, including lagoon tours in Muyil, just south of Tulum, which could easily be visited on a day trip from Cancún. Other Maya Ka'an tours teach ancient Maya medicine and healing practices. Another good source of information for sustainable tourism is the website www.caminossagrados.org.

North of Cancún, on the road to Isla Holbox, an ecotourism center called El Corchal (p73) runs interesting tours in the seldom-visited town of Solferino. Nature enthusiasts will enjoy the center's kayaking and jungle camping trips. Even if you have no time for the tour, you should definitely make it a point to stop in Solferino and check out the town's magnificent orchid garden and its famous 700-year-old sacred ceiba tree. Soferino lies about 125km northwest of Cancún and just 15km south of Chiquila, where you can catch ferry boats to Isla Holbox.

### Hostel Tribu                                    HOSTEL $

(☑ 984-875-25-07; www.tribuhostel.com; Av Pedro Joaquín Coldwell s/n; dm/d/ste M$380/1050/1600; ❀✸✿) With so many activities available here (from salsa lessons to yoga and kayaking), it doesn't take long to settle in with the tribe. Slightly more expensive dorms come with air-con, as does the private suite, and all rooms are clean and cheerful. Tribu also has a bar that hosts weekly jam sessions. From the plaza, it's one block north and two blocks west.

Also worthy of note are the double bars (open to nonguests too) and the common areas. Oversize lockers make it easy to secure your stuff.

### Golden Paradise Town                         HOTEL $$

(☑ 984-875-24-26; www.holboxholbox.com; Gerónimo de Aguilar, btwn Lisa & Canane; US$52; ❀✸✿) Golden Paradise Town and sister property Golden Paradise Hostel (just two blocks south) offer great deals, even during the high season. Rooms in Paradise Town come with two double beds and fridges, while tidy simple digs at the Paradise Hostel (despite the name it's actually a hotel) come even cheaper and there's camping there, too. Wi-fi is spotty in both.

### Hotel Holmar                                   HOTEL $$

(☑ 984-875-21-00; www.hotelholmar.com; Calle Carito s/n; r from M$1500; ✸✿▨) Design-wise rooms at the Holmar are nothing out of this world, unless you have a thing for towel animals, but the price is fair for what you get and it's only 50m from the beach and a block east of the square. Wi-fi reaches the lobby

only. Rooms upstairs receive more natural light.

### Casa Lupita                                     HOTEL $$$

(☑ 984-875-20-17; cinelupita@sihoteles.net; Palomino s/n; r/ste M$1700/2200; ❀✸✿) A great option on the east side of the plaza, the spacious rooms catch good breezes and the suites have private balconies overlooking the action on the square. Reception area is in Oliver's Diner downstairs.

### ★ Casa Takywara                                HOTEL $$$

(☑ 984-875-22-55; www.casatakywara.com; Av Pedro Joaquín Coldwell s/n; ste/bungalow incl breakfast from M$4100/5400; ❀✸✿) Out on the quiet western end of town, this beautiful waterfront hotel stands out for its striking architecture and stylishly decorated rooms with kitchenette and sea-view balcony. It's built next to a patch of protected wetland where you'll hear the song of chirping cicadas. Rates drop considerably during the low season.

It's located 1km west of Tiburón Ballena. Wi-fi in the reception area only.

### Hotel Arena                                     HOTEL $$$

(☑ 984-875-21-69; www.hotelarenaholbox.com; Tiburón Ballena s/n; r US$109-156; ❀✸✿▨✸) A straight shoot from the ferry dock, all of the pleasant rooms here are furnished in minimalist style and some have balconies overlooking the plaza. There's not much of a lobby but who needs one when you have a rooftop bar and pool upstairs? You'll find the reception area in the hotel's craft store downstairs.

### Hotel Casa Bárbara
HOTEL **$$$**

(☑984-875-23-02; www.hotelcasabarbara.mx; Tiburón Ballena s/n; d from M$3000; ➋✳🛜🌊) A very comfortable hotel with a swimming pool surrounded by a verdant garden. Rooms are decked out with rustic furnishings and cushy beds, and most have porches overlooking the garden. It's halfway between the ferry dock and the beach.

### Hotel La Palapa
HOTEL **$$$**

(☑984-875-21-21; www.hotellapalapa.com; Morelos 231; r from US$195; ➋✳🛜) La Palapa offers cozy beachfront rooms, some with balconies overlooking the sea, and a cloistered beach area complete with an outdoor bar that serves scrumptious international food. The ocean view from the rooftop terrace is simply awesome. It's 100m east of Tiburón Ballena, along the beach.

## 🍴 Eating

Holbox has a surprising number of good restaurants for such a small island. Remember that some places close early, especially during the low season. For cheap Yucatecan eats, hit the municipal market (7pm to 3am) on Av Damero, near the airport.

### ⭐ Le Jardin
FRENCH **$**

(☑cell 984-1158197; www.facebook.com/lejardin panaderia; Lisa 30; bread M$25-35, coffee M$24-45; ⊗8:30am-12:30pm Wed-Sun; 🛜🎮) Very tasty French pastries and morning breakfast selections make this a welcome spot if you're craving something other than Mexican morning food. Coffee is delicious as well, and the airy *palapa*, surrounded by plumeria and butterflies, makes for a comfortable spot to sit and chat with fellow diners. Kids will love the large toy selection to play with as adults dine.

### Limoncito
BREAKFAST **$**

(☑984-875-23-40; Av Damero s/n; breakfast M$85-120; ⊗8am-9:30pm Fri-Wed; 🛜) This colorful little *palapa*-covered restaurant on the square slings excellent Mexican breakfasts all day long. The *motuleños* (eggs in tomato sauce served with fried plantain, ham and peas) is a local favorite, as are the enchiladas.

### Barba Negra Seafood & Tacos
TACOS **$$**

(www.facebook.com/barbanegrahbx; Av Damero, between Carito & Sierra; tacos M$30-45, seafood dishes M$85-M$155; ⊗1-10pm) With just a few tables set under a *palapa* roof, this cool and contemporary joint features tacos piled high with a flavorful mix of ingredients and drizzled salsas. Specialties include the Maya-style fish taco and the smoked chilled octopus taco, along with a few vegan options. For seafood lovers, try the palm heart aguachile or ceviches.

### Las Panchas
SEAFOOD **$$**

(☑cell 984-1208354; Esmedregal s/n; snacks M$14-39, mains M$160-280; ⊗8-11am & 1-7pm) Ask just about anyone in town where to go for Holbox seafood and they'll probably point to Las Panchas, where you can get delicious Mexican and Caribbean seafood favorites like spicy *diabla*-style octopus, refreshing ceviches, seafood soup and fish tacos, plus some excellent Yucatecan snacks. Be prepared to wait for a table, especially on weekends in high season. Cash only.

### Roots
PIZZA **$$**

(☑cell 984-2415953; www.facebook.com/pizza rootswood; Porfirio Díaz s/n, btwn Palomino & Carito; pizzas M$100-250, lobster pizza M$600; ⊗noon-11:30pm) Like most pizzerias in town, the hot item here is the seasonal lobster pizza and Roots' version ranks among the best of them. All of the wood-fired, thin-crust pies come with a zesty Morita salsa on the side. The open-air restaurant also carries a fantastic selection of Mexican-only liquor, beers and mezcal (150 different ones!).

### ⭐ El Chapulím
MEXICAN **$$$**

(☑cell 984-1376069; elchapulim@gmail.com; Tiburón Ballena s/n; mains from M$350-550; ⊗6-9pm Mon-Sat) El Chapulím has no menu and the kitchen closes when the food runs out – usually before 9pm – so come aware of the quirks involved. Food is excellent, and chef Erik comes to your table personally. This may be the only place in Holbox where you can depend on lobster to be worth the pretty price tag. Cash only.

### Mandarina
INTERNATIONAL **$$$**

(☑984-875-2129;www.holboxcasalastortugas.com/ drink-dine; Sierra s/n, Hotel Casa Las Tortugas; breakfast dishes M$75-150, dinner main courses M$180-420; ⊗7-11am, noon-5pm & 6-9:30pm) Mandarina restaurant boasts the best location for dining with an ocean view, filled with warm lighting and rustic wood furnishings right on the Holbox beach. For breakfast, try the home-baked pastries or the *huitlacoche* omelette with truffle dressing. Dinner has a blend of Mexican and international cuisine, such as duck in an orange *mole* sauce or the catch-of-the-day marinated *pastor*-style.

## LE BAZAAR BOUTIQUE

A haven for high-end beach-inspired fashion! Le Bazaar (☑ cell 984-8048597; www.facebook.com/lebazaarholbox; cnr Av Damero & Sierra; ⊗ 5-11:30pm) has an open-air atmosphere with flowy boho-chic clothing and swimsuits lining the racks, home decor on every shelf, and handmade jewelry adorning the tables. This Holbox boutique store comes with expensive price tags, but with so many products hand-created by Mexican designers, Le Bazaar is worth a look around.

**Raices**                                 SEAFOOD $$$
(Av Damero s/n; mains M$380-1300; ⊗ 11am-9pm) Despite sky-high prices, seafood here is actually hit or miss, but you can't argue with the location: any closer to the beach and waves would be washing your toes. The sign says it's a 'slow food' spot: don't plan on hurrying on to other things. If you're looking to chill, sip a beer and watch waves, it's perfect.

## 🍸 Drinking & Nightlife

Nightlife on Holbox is pretty tame for the most part, with the exception of a few late-night haunts along Tiburon Ballena, just north of the plaza.

**Hot Corner**                                   BAR
(☑ cell 984-8752293; www.facebook.com/thehot cornerholbox; Av Pedro Joaquín Coldwell s/n; ⊗ noon-2am) Truly living up to its name, this corner gastro-bar is Holbox's go-to spot for live music, dancing, spirited boozing and late-night munchies. Much to the neighbors' chagrin, the nightly fiesta often spills onto the sand street.

**Luuma**                                 COCKTAIL BAR
(☑ 984-875-2129; https://holboxcasalastortugas. com/drink-dine; cnr Av Damero & Sierra; cocktails M$140, tapas M$50-M$100; ⊗ 5pm-midnight) This stylish evening hangout sits in a garden of palm trees, hanging lanterns and candlelight on the eastern edge of Holbox town. You can indulge in an eclectic menu of tapas and cocktails that incorporates local and Mexico-sourced ingredients, such as tacos with lamb from Tizimin city or the fruity El Origen mezcal cocktail with Oaxaca agave honey.

## ☆ Entertainment

**Tribu Bar**                                 LIVE MUSIC
(☑ 984-875-25-07; www.tribuhostel.com/bar; Av Pedro Joaquín Coldwell s/n; ⊗ 7pm-2am Tue-Sun) Drop by the *palapa* bar at Hostel Tribu (p74) for live music, weekly salsa classes and Tuesday pub quizzes.

## ❶ Information

Holbox has one **bank** (Tiburón Ballena s/n, btwn Cortéz & Kuka; ⊗ 8:30am-6:30pm Mon-Sat, ATM 24hr). There's an ATM on the plaza above the police station, but it often runs out of money so bring lots of cash.

## ❶ Getting There & Around

**Ferries** (Chiquilá dock; one-way M$150; ⊗ 6am-9:30pm) run to Holbox from the port town of Chiquilá. It takes about 25 minutes to reach the island. Smaller, faster and wetter *lanchas* (motorboats) can make the crossing after dark for M$1200.

Buses to Cancún (M$200 to M$270, 3½ hours), Mérida (M$305 to M$436, five hours) and other destinations leave from the small Chiquilá ADO station a block south of the plaza. One departure to Cancún airport (M$355) leaves per day. Alternatively, you have the option of taking shared or private shuttle vans to/from Cancún airport with **Transfer Holbox** (☑ cell 984-8752104; Av Damero, cnr Carito; M$350 per person; ⊗ 9am-9pm) or Holbox Shuttle (www.holboxshuttle.com). *Colectivos* cost M$200 to Cancún Centro and M$350 to the airport.

Private air charters with **Flights Holbox** (☑ cell 984-1368852; www.flights-holbox.com; Av Pedro Joaquín Coldwell s/n, Holbox Airport) are surprisingly economical if you have a small

## BUSES FROM CHIQUILÁ

| DESTINATION | FARE (M$) | TIME (HR) | FREQUENCY (PER DAY) |
| --- | --- | --- | --- |
| Cancún | 180-244 | 3-3½ | 4 |
| Cancún airport | 324 | 3½ | 1 (1:45pm) |
| Mérida | 384 | 5 | 1 (4:45pm) |
| Playa del Carmen | 260 | 2¼-2¾ | 3 |
| Valladolid | 182 | 2½ | 1 (4:45pm) |

group. Per plane (up to five passengers), a Cancún flight costs US$545. They also run to Playa del Carmen (US$650), Cozumel (US$719), Mérida (US$1320) and other destinations.

If you're driving, your vehicle will be safe in Chiquilá parking lots for M$50 to M$100 per 24 hours. You won't be allowed to bring a tourist car to the island.

The good news is that you really won't need a car. Holbox's sand streets are narrow and deeply rutted, and golf carts have become ubiquitous, buzzing noisily up and down like giant bumblebees. You can rent them easily enough, but consider using your walking shoes instead. Golf-cart taxis cost M$30 to M$50 in town and M$100 out to Punta Coco.

Rent golf carts at **Rentadora El Brother** (⌨ 984-875-20-18; Tiburón Ballena s/n; cart per hour/day M$250/1200; ⊙ 9am-8pm).

## AT A GLANCE

**POPULATION**
19,500

**CAPITAL**
Chetumal

**BEST BAR**
La Tablita (p86)

**BEST
KID-FRIENDLY
BEACH**
Playa Secreto (p81)

**BEST LIVE MUSIC**
Poc-Na Hostel (p86)

**WHEN TO GO**
**Jul & Aug** Snorkel
with 15-ton whale
sharks in nearby
waters.

**Aug & Sep** Watch
sea turtles come
ashore for nesting
season.

**Nov** The month
before the winter
high season, when
you'll find vacancies
and low-season
discounts.

Caribbean Sea view from Isla Mujeres
© MARCO BOTTIGELLI/GETTY IMAGES ©

# Isla Mujeres

I sla Mujeres generally has a quieter and more relaxing vibe than what you'll find across the bay in Cancún, and there's just enough here to keep you entertained: scuba diving and snorkeling, visiting a turtle farm or simply swimming and lazing around on the island's gorgeous north shore.

Sure, there are quite a few ticky-tacky tourist shops, but folks still get around by golf cart and the crushed-coral beaches are undeniably lovely. As for the calm turquoise water of Isla Mujeres, well, you really just have to see it for yourself.

Come sunset, there are plenty of dining options, and the nightlife scene moves at a carefree pace.

# Isla Mujeres Highlights

**1 Playa Norte**
(p81) Relaxing on the white sands and having a swim in the shallow crystalline waters.

**2 Punta Sur**
(p81) Feeling the fresh sea breezes and marveling at the turquoise waters as you explore the island's southernmost park.

**3 Playa Garrafón**
(p81) Seeing fish, turtles, and stingrays as you snorkel the shallows off the crushed-sand beach.

**4 Sea Hawk Divers** (p83)
Diving into the deep Caribbean blue and exploring reefs or sunken ships seems almost otherworldly.

**5 Isla Mujeres Turtle Farm** (p81)
Saying 'hello' to a variety of turtles and hatchlings at the island's turtle farm.

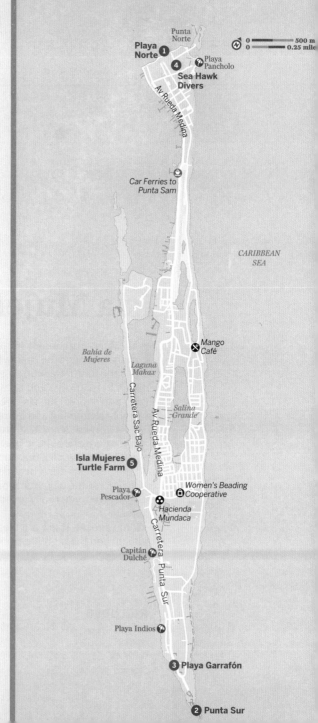

Punta Norte

Playa Norte **1**

**4**

Playa Pancholo

Sea Hawk Divers

0 — 500 m
0 — 0.25 mile

Av Rueda Medina

Car Ferries to Punta Sam

CARIBBEAN SEA

Mango Café

Bahia de Mujeres

Laguna Makax

Carretera Sac Bajo

Av Rueda Medina

Salina Grande

Isla Mujeres Turtle Farm **5**

Women's Beading Cooperative

Playa Pescador

Hacienda Mundaca

Carretera Punta Sur

Capitán Dulché

Playa Indios

**3** Playa Garrafón

**2** Punta Sur

## History

A glimpse of the sunbathers on the beach may have you thinking that the moniker 'Island of Women' comes from the bikini-clad tourists. However, the name Isla Mujeres goes at least as far back as Spanish buccaneers, who (legend has it) kept their lovers in safe seclusion here while they plundered galleons and pillaged ports on the mainland. An alternative theory suggests that in 1517, when Francisco Hernández de Córdoba sailed from Cuba and arrived here to procure slaves, the expedition discovered a stone temple containing clay figurines of Maya goddesses; it is thought that Córdoba named the island after the icons.

Today some archaeologists believe that the island was a stopover for the Maya en route to worship their goddess of fertility, Ixchel, on Isla Cozumel. The clay idols are thought to have represented the goddess. The island may also have figured in the extensive Maya salt trade, which extended for hundreds of kilometers along the coastline.

## ◉ Sights

**Punta Sur**                        VIEWPOINT, GARDENS
(ruins M$30) At the island's southernmost point you'll find a lighthouse, a sculpture garden and the worn remains of a temple dedicated to Ixchel, Maya goddess of the moon and fertility. Various hurricanes have pummeled the ruins over time and there's now little to see other than the sculpture garden, the sea and Cancún in the distance. Taxis from town cost M$105.

**Isla Mujeres Turtle Farm**                        FARM
(Isla Mujeres Tortugranja; www.facebook.com/tortugranja.mx; Carretera Sac Bajo Km 5; M$30; ◷9am-5pm; ⊞) ⚑ Although they're endangered, sea turtles are still killed throughout Latin America for their eggs and meat. In the 1980s, efforts by a local fisherman led to the founding of this *tortugranja* (turtle farm), 5km south of town, which safeguards breeding grounds and protects eggs. It's a small spot, with a number of sizes of turtles and a few species. The farm is easily reached from town by taxi (M$75 to M$100) or golf cart.

**Hacienda Mundaca**                        RUINS
(Av Rueda Medina s/n; M$20; ◷9am-4pm) A 19th-century slave trader and reputed pirate, Fermín Antonio Mundaca de Marechaja fell in love with a local woman known as La Trigueña (The Brunette). To win her, Mundaca built a two-story mansion complete with gardens and graceful archways. But while Mundaca was building the house, La Trigueña married another islander. Brokenhearted, Mundaca died, and the hacienda fell into disrepair. Even today, the grounds look neglected. The ruins are 4km south of town; they're easily reached by bike or taxi.

## 🏖 Beaches

⭐**Playa Garrafón**                        BEACH
Head to this beach for excellent snorkeling. It's 6.5km from the tourist center. A cab costs M$100.

**Playa Norte**                        BEACH
Once you reach Playa Norte, the island's main beach, you won't want to leave. Its warm, shallow waters are the color of blue raspberry syrup and the beach is crushed coral. Unlike most of the island's east coast, Playa Norte is safe for swimming and the water is only chest deep, even far from shore.

**Capitán Dulché**                        BEACH, MUSEUM
(🖂cell 998-3550012; www.facebook.com/capitandulchebeachclub; Carretera a Garrafón Km 4.5; ◷10am-7pm; ℗) To say that this beach club has a maritime museum is a bit of a stretch, but it's as close as the island comes to having some culture, plus you get to see some cool sculptures of trench-coated musicians playing on the water. Did we mention the bar has swings and looks like a boat?

**Playa Secreto**                        BEACH
(▣) The lagoon separating a large hotel complex from the rest of the island has a shallow swimming spot that's ideal for kids. Despite the depth (or lack of it), a number of pretty fish circle around the swimmers looking for handouts.

## 🏊 Activities

Within a short boat ride of the island there's a handful of lovely dives, such as **La Bandera**, **Arrecife Manchones** and **Ultrafreeze** (El Frío), where you'll see the intact hull of a 60m-long cargo ship, thought to have been deliberately sunk in 30m of water. Expect to see sea turtles, rays and barracuda, along with a wide array of hard and soft corals.

There's good shore-snorkeling near **Playa Garrafón** and at **Yunque Reef**. Watch for boat traffic when you head out snorkeling.

Snorkeling with whale sharks is another popular activity. Peak season runs from July to August, when there can be up to a dozen boats circling one whale shark. Most dive

# Isla Mujeres Town

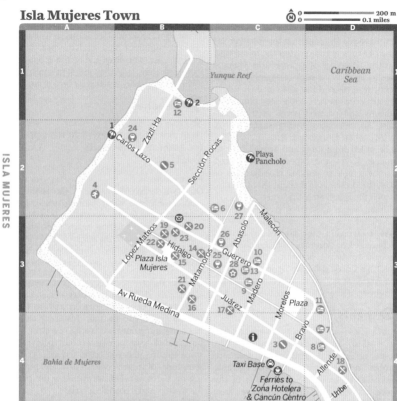

N 0 ——————— 200 m
0 ——————— 0.1 miles

# Isla Mujeres Town

shops offer whale-shark excursions; ask about their ethical practices before committing.

⭐**Hotel Garrafón de Castilla**    SNORKELING
(Carretera Punta Sur Km 6; admission M$100, snorkel-gear rental M$50; ⊘8am-5pm) Avoid the overpriced Playa Garrafón Reef Park and instead visit Hotel Garrafón de Castilla's beach club for a day of snorkeling in translucent waters. A taxi from town costs M$105.

**MUSA Isla Mujeres**    DIVING, SNORKELING
(Museo Subacuático de Arte;  ☑998-877-12-33; www.musamexico.org; Manchones reef; 1-tank dive US$70) A one-of-a-kind gallery with hundreds of life-sized sculptures submerged in the waters on the island's south side. At 8m deep, the Isla Mujeres Manchones gallery is ideal for first-time divers, though snorkelers are welcome as well. Organize outings through dive shops; Sea Hawk is recommended.

**Sea Hawk Divers**    DIVING
(☑998-877-12-33; www.seahawkislamujeres.com; Carlos Lazo s/n; 1-/2-tank dive incl equipment US$80/90, intro course US$115, whale-shark tour US$125; ⊘8am-6pm) Offers reef dives, intro courses, fishing trips and whale shark snorkeling tours. Sea Hawk also goes to the Isla Mujeres site of underwater sculpture museum MUSA, on the island's south side. Rents rooms, too, for US$85 to US$115.

**Aqua Adventures Eco Divers**    DIVING
(☑998-188-41-50, cell 998-3228109; www.diveislamujeres.com; Juárez 13; 2-tank dives incl equipment from US$120, whale-shark tour US$125; ⊘9am-7pm Mon-Sat, 10am-6pm Sun) Great option for snorkeling with whale sharks and goes to 15 sites for reef dives. Find them across from Javi's Cantina.

**Felipez Water Sports Center**    WATER SPORTS
(☑cell 998-5933403; nachankan@aol.com; Playa Norte, off Av Hidalgo; paddleboard & kayak per hr M$350, fishing per 4hr US$350; ⊘8am-6pm) Do acro-surf yoga on a paddleboard here. Also rents kayaks and does fishing expeditions.

## 🛏 Sleeping

There's a range of accommodations on Isla Mujeres, from relatively inexpensive hostels to ultra-fancy resorts. Many hotels on the island are booked solid during high season (roughly mid-December through April).

**Apartments Trinchan**    APARTMENT **$**
(☑cell 998-1666967; atrinchan@prodigy.net.mx; Carlos Lazo 46; r/apt M$800/900; ❄🖥) This is one of the best budget deals in town – and the beach is right around the corner. Opt for one of the large apartments with full kitchen, but avoid No 8, which catches noise from a nearby hostel's late-night beach parties. Unlike nearly every other hotel, you can smoke inside the rooms. (So this may be a bad choice for nonsmokers!)

**Xbulu-Ha Hotel**    HOTEL **$$**
(☑998-877-17-83; www.xbuluha.islamujeres.biz; Guerrero 4; d/ste from M$1160/1600; ⊕❄🖥) Quite a bargain, especially if you're traveling with a small group or family. Some of the standard and deluxe rooms here can accommodate three to four people, as can the larger suites, which come with kitchenette.

**Hotel Francis Arlene**    HOTEL **$$**
(☑998-877-08-61; www.francisarlene.com; Av Guerrero 7; r with fan/air-con from M$1200/1500; ⊕❄🖥) This place offers comfortable, good-sized rooms with fridge. Most have a king-sized bed or two doubles, and many have balcony and partial sea views. The lounging-frog sculptures are cute. Good low-season rates, August to September.

**Hotel Belmar**    HOTEL **$$**
(☑998-877-04-30; www.facebook.com/hotelbelmar; Hidalgo 110; d/ste from M$1511/2600; ⊕❄🖥) Run by the same family that owns the **pizza joint** (m_arquitectura_miguel@hotmail.com; Hidalgo 110; mains M$131-226; ⊘8am-11:30pm; 🖥) downstairs, Belmar offers neo-rustic rooms with tiled floors and (some) balconies. If you're looking to stumble upstairs after a night on the town, this is a perfect central location, but noise from the restaurant may bother light sleepers, so bring earplugs.

⭐**Casa Sirena**    B&B **$$$**
(☑cell  998-2425906; www.casasirenamexico.com; Hidalgo s/n; r incl breakfast from US$208; ⊕❄🖥🏊) Get the full-fledged B&B treatment in this lovingly restored historic house, where guests get excellent breakfast served in a shady courtyard along with a complimentary happy hour on a rooftop bar area featuring a plunge pool and sunny deck overlooking the ocean. The adults-only *casa* houses six elegant rooms, including one with a sea-view balcony. Two-night minimum stay required.

**Hotel Villa Kiin**    HOTEL **$$$**
(☑998-877-10-24; www.villakiin.com; Zazil-Ha 129; r with fan US$56-69, with air-con US$76-136, all

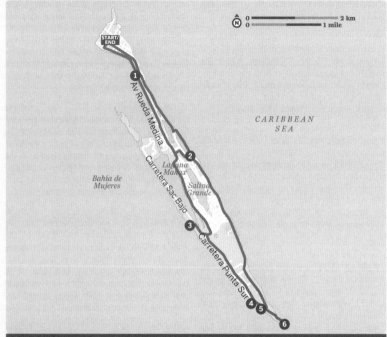

## Driving Tour
## Isla Mujeres by Golf Cart

**START** AVENIDA RUEDA MEDINA
**END** TOWN CENTER
**LENGTH** 16KM; FOUR HOURS

Puttering around the island on a rented golf cart provides hours of unforgettable entertainment, so pack your swimsuit and sunglasses and get ready to hit the open road.

After renting a cart in the town center, head south along ❶ **Avenida Rueda Medina** and make your first stop at ❷ **Mango Café** (p85) for breakfast, bottomless coffee and perhaps a jaunt around the neighborhood to soak up some local flavor.

Next, make your way back to Avenida Rueda Medina and follow the signs to the *tortugranja*, aka ❸ **Isla Mujeres Turtle Farm** (p81), where you can spend time hanging with the sea turtles before they're released into the ocean.

After some quality turtle time, drive south and make a stop at one of several beach clubs along the way. The best of the lot is at ❹ **Hotel Garrafón de Castilla** (p83), where

you should plan on snorkeling for an hour or so among colorful fish in crystalline waters. For your next stop, continue along the same road and go just past the pricey Garrafón water park to reach a ❺ **lookout** that affords a spectacular ocean view with Cancún off in the distance. It makes a fine spot to snap some pictures or simply contemplate the horizon.

Yet another photo op awaits up ahead at the oft-visited ❻ **Punta Sur** (p81), the southernmost point of the island. Punta Sur has a lighthouse and a weathered temple dedicated to the Maya goddess of fertility, Ixchel, but it's really the panoramic cliffside vistas that make it a worthwhile stop. If you're feeling a bit parched, there's an open-air restaurant where you can grab some drinks.

After Punta Sur, the coast road loops around to the island's windswept east side, where you'll motor past several undeveloped beaches. You can stop anywhere along the way for a swim, but if you do, watch out for strong currents. From this point it's a straight shoot back into the town center.

incl breakfast; ⊖❋ 🛜) With one of the safest beaches for swimming, and clean, updated rooms, Villa Kiin remains one of the island's premier hotels. Choose from a variety of accommodations ranging from fan-cooled budget digs to air-conditioned bungalows and rooms with new furniture, rocking chairs and ocean views (from some). The beachside bungalows come with hammocks. Wi-fi reaches the lobby only.

### Casa El Pío
BOUTIQUE HOTEL $$$

(www.casaelpio.com; Hidalgo 3; r from US$101; ⊖❋🛜⛱) Book rooms well in advance if you want to stay at this small – and very popular – adults-only boutique hotel. One of the five rooms has an ocean view, as does the rooftop terrace, and all rooms have interesting design details. The pool is for splashing more than swimming, wi-fi is spotty and there's a three-night minimum stay. Online reservations only.

### Hotel Rocamar
HOTEL $$$

(🖉998-877-01-01; www.rocamar-hotel.com; cnr Calle Bravo & Av Guerrero; r US$113-143, casas US$286; P⊖❋🛜⛱) Modern rooms (the glass-walled bathrooms in some do have curtains) feature private balcony with sea views. The view from the pool ain't too shabby either. *Casas* are available with a full kitchen. Prices drop considerably in low season. Wi-fi extends through the lobby area only.

## ✖ Eating

Seafood can't get fresher than it is here, so plan on eating as much as possible. The restaurants are a mixed bag and sometimes pricier than comparable mainland food. A supermarket on the plaza has a solid selection of groceries, baked goods and snacks.

For cheap eats, check the **Mercado Municipal** (Guerrero s/n, btwn López Mateos & Matamoros; mains M$50-120; ⊙7am-4pm) during the day and the food stalls on the plaza outside the Iglesia de la Inmaculada Concepción at night.

### Ruben's Restaurant
MEXICAN $

(rubenchavez_77@hotmail.com; Guerrero 18; mains M$50-145, set menu M$95; ⊙8am-9pm Mon-Sat; 🛜) There's nothing fancy about this little diner, but homemade Mexican food and great service are guaranteed. Regulars usually go for the daily set menu, which includes soup, salad and a main dish. There are also a few gringo-friendly items on the menu, for example the 'super burrito.' *Aguas* (fruit juices) are always refreshing.

### Bobo's
FISH & CHIPS $$

(www.facebook.com/bobosfishchips; Matamoros 14; mains M$95-115; ⊙3-11pm) This bar and grill fries up excellent locally caught triggerfish for its popular fish and chips, and there's malt vinegar to go along with it (a rare find in Mexico). Bobo's is also known for its burgers and convivial streetside bar.

### Mango Café
BREAKFAST $$

(www.facebook.com/mangocafeisla; Payo Obispo 101, Colonia Meterológico; mains M$105-170; ⊙7am-3pm; 🛜) See the south side of town and drop by Mango Café for some self-serve coffee and a hearty Caribbean-inspired breakfast. The hot items here are coconut French toast and eggs Benedict in a curry hollandaise sauce. It's a short bike or cab ride away, about 3km south of the ferry terminal. Cash only. No pets.

### Rooster
CAFE $$

(🖉998-274-01-52; www.facebook.com/roosterisla mujeres; Hidalgo 26; breakfasts M$105-225; ⊙7am-11pm; 🛜) The undeniable king of the breakfast providers on the island is this cute little cafe with tables out front and chilly air-con inside. The menu covers the classics and throws in a couple of inventive twists, such as eggs Benedict with lobster, and all is served with excellent coffee and attentive service.

### La Lomita
MEXICAN $$

(🖉cell 998-2903866; www.facebook.com/res taurantlalomita; Juárez Sur 25; mains M$120-205; ⊙9am-10pm) The 'Little Hill' serves good, cheap Mexican food in a small, colorful setting. Seafood and chicken dishes predominate. Try the fantastic bean and avocado soup, or the ceviche (seafood marinated in lemon or lime juice, garlic and seasonings). The walls are cutely painted and outdoors there's a little alfresco dining section with umbrellas.

### Aluxes Coffee Shop
CAFE $$

(www.aluxesisla.com; Matamoros 11; breakfast M$80-100, lunch & dinner M$95-290; ⊙8am-10pm Wed-Mon; 🛜) Aluxes serves bagels, baguettes and mighty fine banana bread, and it's one of the friendliest joints in town.

### ★ Javi's Cantina
SEAFOOD $$$

(www.javiscantina.com; Juárez 12; mains M$225-550; ⊙5-10:30pm; 🛜) More like a restaurant than a cantina, but Javi's does have happy hour and live music. The menu consists of seafood, choice beef cuts, chicken and various salad and veggie options. A house specialty is the fresh-caught parmesan-crusted fish fillet

## LOCAL EXPERIENCES

**Market eats** For affordable homestyle cooking islanders often hit the small eateries at the municipal market, and just around the corner from there, in front of the post office, a mornings-only stall slings tasty *cochinita* (slow-cooked pork) tacos and *tortas* (sandwiches).

**Hangouts** It's hard to imagine a place where you can get a better picture of local life than La Tablita, an atmospheric fan-cooled bar where the snacks and good jukebox tunes just keep coming.

**Midtown** The residential area south of downtown has some good little restaurants, a quiet church with an ocean view, a local women's beading coop and generally a much more local scene.

with tamarind sauce. Dine in the front room or sit back in the rear courtyard with a pleasant terrace. Online reservations only.

**Lola Valentina**　　　　　　FUSION $$$
(☏998-105-85-83; www.facebook.com/lolavalentina islamujeres; Hidalgo s/n; mains M$245-540; ◷8am-midnight; 🛜🖉) Overlooking the quieter north side of the restaurant strip, Lola does popular Mexican fusion with dishes like coconut shrimp, plus several vegan, gluten-free items, and the decidedly nonvegan, non-GF Latin Surf 'n' Turf. It has swings at the bar (fun!) and a tasty cocktail menu.

**Olivia**　　　　　　MEDITERRANEAN $$$
(☏998-877-17-65; www.olivia-isla-mujeres.com; Matamoros s/n; mains M$150-380; ◷5-9:45pm Mon-Sat; 🛜) This delightful Israeli-run restaurant makes everything from scratch, from Moroccan-style fish served on a bed of couscous to chicken shawarmas wrapped in freshly baked pita bread. Ask for a candlelit table out back in the garden, and save room for the house-made cherry ice cream. Usually closes September to mid-October. Reservations recommended.

**Angelo**　　　　　　ITALIAN $$$
(☏998-877-12-73; Hidalgo 14, btwn López Mateos & Matamoros; mains M$170-525; ◷4pm-midnight; 🛜) Menu standouts at this Italian-owned sidewalk steakhouse include the black grouper fillet, baked mussels and the Angus beef cuts. When he's around, owner Angelo is a great source of information.

# 🍸 Drinking & Nightlife

Isla Mujeres' highest concentration of nightlife is along pedestrian thoroughfare Hidalgo, and hot spots on or near the beach form an arc around the northern edge of town.

**★La Tablita**　　　　　　BAR
(Av Guerrero s/n; ◷noon-8pm Mon-Sat) For a little local flavor, spend a lazy afternoon over cold drinks and free snacks in this atmospheric, fan-cooled Caribbean house. The jukebox selection of Spanish-language tracks is *muy buena*.

**Poc-Na Hostel**　　　　　　BAR
(☏998-877-00-90; www.pocna.com; Matamoros 26; ◷7pm-3am; 🛜) Has a lobby bar with nightly live music and a beachfront bar with thumping music and more hippies than all the magic buses in the world. It's a scene, and an entertaining one at that. Drinks aren't expensive, but aren't magically good either.

**La Terraza**　　　　　　LIVE MUSIC
(2nd fl, Hidalgo s/n, cnr Abasolo; ◷4pm-midnight) Drinks and food are nothing special here but if the Cuban salsa band is playing it's definitely worth sticking around for some dancing.

**Buho's**　　　　　　BAR
(☏998-877-03-01; Carlos Lazo 1, Playa Norte; ◷10:30am-11pm; 🛜) The quintessential swinger experience. Literally: it has swings at the bar. You can also take morning and afternoon yoga classes here. Any closer to the beach and you'd be in the water.

**El Patio**　　　　　　BAR
(www.facebook.com/elpatioislamujeres; Hidalgo 17; ◷4:30pm-midnight; 🛜) The self-proclaimed 'house of music' has an open-air patio and rooftop terrace where you can catch mediocre rock cover bands and relatively subdued acoustic sets amid a near-100% gringo crowd. Happy hour is from 5pm to 7pm, with discount drinks and food.

# 🛍 Shopping

**Women's Beading Cooperative**　　　　JEWELRY
(☏cell 998-1619659; www.facebook.com/isla mujeresbeadingcoop; Paseo de los Peces, Colonia La Gloria; classes M$250; ◷9am-5pm Mon-Sat, to 3pm Sun) If you're headed to the island's south end, drop by this cooperative and check out the colorful handmade bead jewelry made by a group of local women and children. They also offer classes if you want to learn how to make the items yourself.

# ℹ️ Orientation

The island is 8km long and 150m to 800m wide. You'll find most restaurants and hotels in the town of Isla Mujeres, with the pedestrian corridor on Hidalgo the focal point. The ferry arrives in the town proper on the island's northern side. On the southern tip are the lighthouse and vestiges of the Maya temple. The two are linked by Avenida Rueda Medina, a loop road that follows the coast. Between them are a handful of small fishing villages, several saltwater lakes, a string of westward-facing beaches, a large lagoon and a small airstrip.

The eastern shore is washed by the open sea, and the surf there is dangerous. The most popular sand beach (Playa Norte) is at the northern tip.

# ℹ️ Information

Several banks are directly across from the ferry dock. Most exchange currency and all have ATMs.

**Hospital Comunitario Isla Mujeres** (Boquinete s/n, cnr Picuda, Colonia La Gloria; ⊘24hr) About 5km south of the town center; doctors available 24/7.

**HSBC** (🖉 998-877-00-05; Av Rueda Medina 3, btwn Bravo & Av Morelos; ⊘9am-5pm Mon-Fri)

**Hyperbaric Chamber** (🖉 cell 998-1349310, cell 998-8458147; Guerrero s/n, cnr Morelos; ⊘9am-4pm, on call 24hr) Just north of the main square. It's often closed but there's 24-hour telephone assistance.

**Post Office** (🖉 998-877-00-85; cnr Guerrero & López Mateos; ⊘8am-4pm Mon-Fri, 9am-12:30pm Sat)

**Tourist Information Office** (Av Rueda Medina 130, btwn Madero & Morelos; ⊘9am-4pm Mon-Fri) Offers a number of brochures. Some staff members speak English.

# ℹ️ Getting There & Away

There are several points of embarkation from Cancún to reach Isla Mujeres. Most people cross on Ultramar passenger ferries. The R-1 'Puerto Juárez' city bus in Cancún serves all Zona Hotelera departure points and Puerto Juárez, in Ciudad Cancún. If you arrive by car, daily parking fees in and around the terminals cost between M$100 and M$180, but can be as low as M$50 if you go further from the terminal.

Ultramar fares for ferries departing from the Zona Hotelera are in US dollars. If you're on a tight budget, it's much cheaper to leave from Puerto Juárez. Ultramar ferries (www.ultramarferry.com) depart from the following docks.

**El Embarcadero** (Blvd Kukulcán Km 4) Nine daily departures; one-way US$15.

**Playa Caracol** (Blvd Kukulcán Km 9.5) Six daily departures; one-way US$15.

**Playa Tortugas** (Blvd Kukulcán Km 6.5) Twelve daily departures; one-way US$15.

**Puerto Juárez** (4km north of Ciudad Cancún) Depart every 30 minutes; one-way M$160.

At the time of research, neither of the alternate passenger ferries Marinsa (www.marinsaturismo.com) and Naveganto (www.naveganto) were operating to or from Isla Mujeres.

Punta Sam, 8km north of Cancún Centro, is the only ferry that transports vehicles and bikes. From Punta Sam, drivers are included in prices for the following one-way fares: cars (M$295), motorcycles (M$90) and bicycles (M$20); additional passengers pay M$46. Get there an hour before if you're transporting a vehicle. See www.maritimaislamujeres.com for departure times. To reach Punta Sam, take a taxi or northbound 'Punta Sam' *colectivo* along Avenida Tulum. Car ferries for **Punta Sam** (🖉 998-293-90-92; www.ultramarferry.com; Av Rueda Medina s/n; one-way fare incl passenger M$295; ⊘6:30am-9:30pm) and **passenger ferries to Cancún** (Av Rueda Medina s/n) leave from different docks.

# ℹ️ Getting Around

Isla Mujeres has plenty of vehicle rental shops, plus a lot of touts who will set you up with rentals and extract an additional fee. It's best to deal directly with the shop supplying it, as opposed to going through a middle person.

## BICYCLE

Cycling is a great way to get around and to explore outlying areas.

**Rentadora Fiesta** (🖉 cell 998-7349862; Av Rueda Medina s/n, btwn Morelos & Bravo; bike per hour/day M$50/150, scooter/golf cart per day M$400/750; ⊘9am-5pm) Rents mountain bikes and beach cruisers.

## MOTORCYCLE & GOLF CART

Inspect all scooters carefully before renting. Costs vary, and are sometimes jacked up in high season, but generally start at about M$400 per day (9am to 5pm).

Many people find golf carts a good way to get around the island, and caravans of them can be seen tooling down the roads. The average cost is M$800 per day (9am to 5pm).

**Gomar** (🖉 998-877-16-86; cnr Av Rueda Medina & Calle Bravo; scooter/golf cart per day M$400/800; ⊘9am-9pm) Offers reasonable golf-cart and scooter rentals.

**Mega Ciro's** (🖉 cell 998-5785266; www.facebook.com/cirosgolfcartrentals; Av Guerrero 11; golf cart per day US$60; ⊘9am-5pm) Well-maintained golf carts.

## TAXI

Taxi rates are set by the municipal government and posted at the **taxi base** (🖉 998-877-18-38; Av Rueda Medina s/n; M$50-115; ⊘24hr) just south of the passenger-ferry dock.

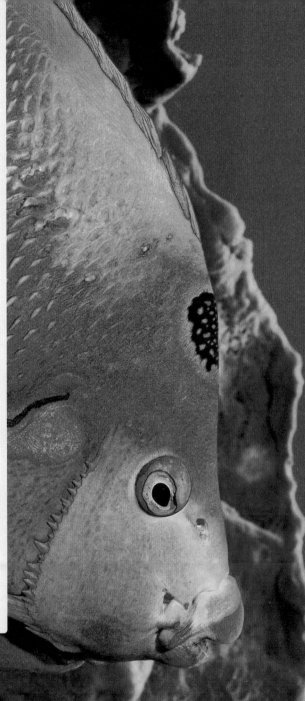

## AT A GLANCE

**POPULATION**
86,400

**CAPITAL**
Chetumal

**BEST DIVE SHOP**
Aldora Divers (p95)

**BEST ANNUAL
EVENT**
Carnaval (p97)

**BEST SHRIMP
TACOS**
Camarón Dorado
(p98)

**WHEN TO GO**
**Feb & Mar** Carnaval
brings live music,
costumes and
general revelry to the
streets.

**Apr & May** El Cedral
pays tribute to War of
the Castes refugees
with rides, rodeos
and dancing.

**Sep & Oct** The
perfect months for
diving and snor-
keling, barring a
hurricane.

Queen angelfish
STEPHEN FRINK/GETTY IMAGES ©

# Isla Cozumel

**F**ascinating for its dual personality, Cozumel offers an odd mix – quietly authentic neighborhoods existing alongside tourist-friendly playgrounds. And, of course, there are epic experiences to be had, such as diving at some of the best reefs in the world.

While diving and snorkeling are the main draws, the town square is a pleasant place to spend the afternoon, and it's highly gratifying to explore the less-visited parts of the island on a rented scooter or in a convertible car. The coastal road leads to small Maya ruins, a marine park and cliffside bars, passing captivating scenery along the unforgettable windswept shore. And while the nightlife has nothing on Playa del Carmen's or Cancún's, there's plenty to do after the sun goes down.

ISLA COZUMEL HISTORY

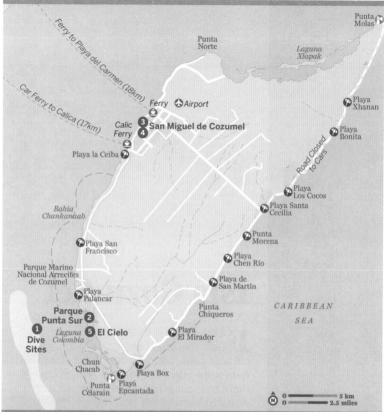

## Isla Cozumel Highlights

**1** **Dive Sites** (p95)
Plunging into the deep blue and exploring some of the world's best sites with one of the island's top dive shops.

**2** **Parque Punta Sur** (p93)
Escaping to a quiet beach park with lagoon boat tours, fine snorkeling and wildlife-watching.

**3** **Turquoise Beach Bar** (p100) Drinking in a San Miguel de Cozumel sunset over drinks and music alongside a resident pig with a hearty appetite.

**4** **Carnaval** (p97)
Celebrating and carousing in the streets of the city center during a five-day event

featuring live music, dance and colorful floats.

**5** **El Cielo** (p93)
Swimming or snorkeling at a beach with shallow waters and great opportunities for seeing undersea wildlife.

## History

Maya settlement on Cozumel dates from 300 CE. During the post-Classic period, the island flourished as a trade center and, more importantly, a ceremonial site. Every Maya woman living on the Yucatán Peninsula and beyond was expected to make at least one pilgrimage here to pay tribute to Ixchel, the goddess of fertility and the moon, at a tem-

ple erected in her honor. Archaeologists believe this temple was at San Gervasio, a little north of the island's geographical center.

At the time of the first Spanish contact with Cozumel (in 1518, by Juan de Grijalva and his men), there were at least 32 Maya building groups on the island. According to Spanish chronicler Diego de Landa, a year later Hernán Cortés sacked one of the Maya centers but left the others intact, apparently satisfied with converting the island's population to Christianity. Smallpox introduced by the Spanish wiped out half the 8000 Maya and, of the survivors, only about 200 escaped genocidal attacks by conquistadors in the late 1540s.

The island remained virtually deserted into the late 17th century, its coves providing sanctuary for several notorious pirates including Jean Lafitte and Henry Morgan. In 1848 indigenous people fleeing the War of the Castes began to resettle Cozumel. At the beginning of the 20th century the island's (by then mostly mestizo) population grew, thanks to the craze for chewing gum. Cozumel was a port of call on the chicle-export route, and locals harvested the gum base on the island. After the demise of the chicle trade – demand dropped due to the rise in production of synthetic gum – Cozumel's economy remained strong owing to the construction of a US air base here during WWII.

When the US military departed, the island fell into an economic slump, and many of its people moved away. Those who stayed fished for a living and it wasn't until the 1960s that Cozumel started to gain fame as a popular diving destination. Tourism really started to take off in the early 1980s following the construction of a commercial airport and the island's first cruise-ship dock. Today, Cozumel is one of the world's most important cruise-ship destinations.

## ◉ Sights

Cozumel's sights are spread out far enough that to do them justice you'll need to consider renting a car or scooter. With a vehicle you'll only need one day to circle around the island and visit the town of El Cedral, with time to stop at a number of beaches and cliffside bars along the way.

Access to many of Cozumel's best stretches of beach has become limited. Resorts and residential developments with gated roads create the most difficulties. Pay-for-use beach clubs occupy some other prime spots, but you can park and walk through or around them and enjoy adjacent parts of the beach without obligation. Sitting under club umbrellas or otherwise using the facilities requires you to fork out some money, either a straight fee or a *consumo mínimo* (minimum consumption of food and drink), which can add up in some places. However, charg-ing is not always strictly applied, especially when business is slow.

## ◉ San Miguel de Cozumel

It's easy to make your way on foot around the island's main town, San Miguel de Cozumel. The waterfront boulevard is Avenida Melgar; along Melgar south of the main ferry dock (*muelle fiscal*) is a narrow sand beach. The main plaza, opposite the ferry dock, has an entertaining light-and-dancing-fountains show at 8pm, accompanied by classical music.

**Sea Walls**                                    PUBLIC ART
(Map p94; www.pangeaseed.foundation/cozu mel-mexico; San Miguel de Cozumel) Local and international artists backed by the Pangea-Seed foundation created 36 large-scale public murals in 2015 to raise awareness about ocean conservation and responsible coastal development. A DIY walking tour reveals cool downtown works like a towering sea monster mural on Calle 1 Sur and Avenida 20 Sur. Ask the tourist office (p100) for a printed map of the murals.

## ◉ South of San Miguel

**El Cedral**                          ARCHAEOLOGICAL SITE
(Map p92; per person M$38; ⊘24hr) This Maya ruin, a fertility temple, is the oldest on the island. It's the size of a small house and has no ornamentation. El Cedral is thought to have been an important ceremonial site; the small church standing next to the tiny ruin today is evidence that the site still has religious significance for locals.

The town of El Cedral is 3km west of Carretera Costera Sur. The turnoff is near Km 17, across from the Alberto's Restaurant sign. Look for the white-and-red arch.

**Playa Palancar**                                  BEACH
(Map p92; ✆cell 987-1185154; www.buceopalan car.com.mx; Carretera Costera Sur Km 19.5; dives 1/2-tank incl equipment US$65/90; ⊘9am-5pm) About 17km south of San Miguel, Palancar is a great beach to visit during the week when the crowds thin out. It has a beach club renting snorkel gear (US$10) and there's a **restaurant**. Nearby, Arrecife Palancar (Palancar Reef) has some excellent diving (it's known as Palancar Gardens) and fine snorkeling (Palancar Shallows, US$35).

A dive shop here runs snorkeling and diving trips to nearby sites.

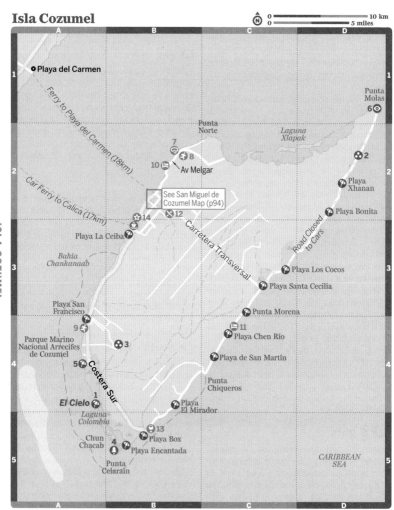

# Isla Cozumel

## Isla Cozumel

## Parque Punta Sur
NATURE RESERVE

(Map p92; ☑987-872-40-14, cell 987-8761303; www.cozumelparks.com; Carretera Costera Sur Km 27; adult/child 4-11yr US$16/10; ⊙9am-4pm Mon-Sat) For the price of admission to this park, you can visit a lighthouse, a small nautical museum and a Maya ruin. The park road leads past an observation tower from where it's possible to spot migratory birds and occasional crocodiles, and continuing further west you'll reach a beach area with a shallow reef, a restaurant and boat tours (noon, 1pm and 2pm) to Laguna Colombia. You'll need your own vehicle or a taxi (M$300 one way) to get here.

## ★El Cielo
BEACH

(Map p92) Living up to its heavenly name, El Cielo's shallow turquoise waters are ideal for snorkeling and swimming among starfish, stingrays and small fish. Located on the island's southwest side, it's only accessible by boat but all the dive shops make trips there.

## ⊙ East Coast

The eastern shoreline is the wildest part of the island and presents some beautiful seascapes and many small blowholes (there's a bunch around Km 30.5). Swimming can be dangerous on most of the east coast because of riptides and undertows; there's a swimmable saltwater pool at Playa Chen Río, just past El Pescador restaurant at Km 42.

At Punta Chiqueros (Km 37), Playa Bonita restaurant rents bodyboards and longboards.

As you travel along the coast, consider stopping at one of the several restaurant-bars with great lookout points.

### El Castillo Real
ARCHAEOLOGICAL SITE

(Map p92; road to Punta Molas; ⊙8am-5pm; 🚗4WD only) FREE Down the same intimidating road that leads to Punta Molas are the large Maya ruins known as El Castillo Real (The Royal Castle). The archaeological site, as well as the Aguada Grande ruins a few kilometers' hike away, are both quite far gone, their significance having blown off into the breeze some time ago. Still, half the fun is in getting there, right?

Other island ruins include the temple at San Gervasio, which was erected by the Maya as a tribute to Ixchel, the moon goddess of fertility. Female pilgrims came here from all over the region to pay tribute. San Gervasio sits between San Miguel and the east coast, northeast of the Carretera Transversal.

## ⊙ Punta Molas

If you'd like to explore the island's wild and undeveloped side, beyond where the east-coast highway meets the Carretera Transversal, the best bet is to arrange an off-road tour to Punta Molas (Map p92) with **Omar's Island Buggy Tours** (☑cell 987-1055892; www.omarsislandbuggytours.com; 5hr tours per person US$130). Escapists will enjoy venturing out to this remote area, where you can snorkel at secluded beaches and visit small Maya ruins and a deserted lighthouse at the northernmost point.

Only off-road vehicles can handle the difficult dirt road and a fallen sign at the entrance reads: 'Enter at your own risk. Irregular path even for 4x4 vehicles'. The truth is, it's tough to even find a place to rent a 4WD. If you do head up the road, be aware that you can't count on flagging down another motorist for help in the event of a breakdown or accident, and most car-rental agencies' insurance policies don't cover any mishaps on unpaved roads. In other words, even if you can find someone willing to rent you a vehicle for Punta Molas, you're on your own.

About 17km up the road is El Castillo Real and, a few kilometers further north, Aguada Grande. In the vicinity of Punta Molas are some fairly good beaches and a few more minor ruins.

## 🏃 Activities

Most people, understandably, visit Cozumel for its famed diving and snorkeling, but you'll find plenty of other things to do, including cycling along the island's scenic coast road, horseback riding on the beach or hitting the surf on the island's east side. You can even go spearfishing for lionfish.

**Cozumel Surfing School & Rental**
SURFING

(Map p92; ☑US 612-287-5549, cell 987-1119290; www.cozumelsurfing.com; Carretera Coastal Oriente Km 42.9, Playa Chen Río; surfboard per day US$30-40, surfing class US$110, spear-fishing US$80) Hit the surf with Nacho Gutierrez (who is rocking the Johnny Depp look in a serious way). You'll find Nacho at **El Pescador** restaurant (Km 42.9) on Playa Chen Río. He usually holds surfing classes at Punta Chiqueros, where you can rent boards at **Playa Bonita** restaurant (Km 37). Reserve ahead for surfing lessons. Nacho also runs spear-fishing outings.

# San Miguel de Cozumel

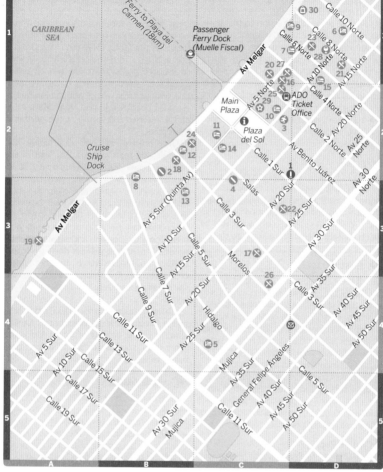

**Best Bikes Cozumel** CYCLING
(Map p94; ☑cell 987-8788602; www.bestbikes
cozumel.com; Av 10 Norte 14; per hour M$30-50, per
day M$150-250; ☺9am-6pm Apr–mid-Oct, 8am-
8pm mid-Oct–Mar) A good selection of beach
cruisers, mountain bikes and hybrids.

**Cozumel Country Club** GOLF
(Map p92; ☑987-872-95-70; www.cozumelcoun
tryclub.com.mx; off Carretera Costera Norte; rates
incl cart US$89-125, bird-watching tour US$50;
☺tee times 6:30am-3pm) 🏌 This 18-hole Nick-
laus-designed course is a challenging one,
and crocodiles inhabit all its water features,
so keep yourself at least several club lengths

from their jaws. The grounds are designated
as a certified Audubon sanctuary and you
can book early-morning bird-watching tours
led by an English-speaking biologist.

**Mr Sancho's** HORSEBACK RIDING
(Map p92; ☑987-120-22-20, cell 987-8719174; www.
mrsanchos.com; Carretera Costera Sur Km 15; 30min
US$35; ☺8am-5pm Mon-Sat) Saddle up at Mr
Sancho's for guided horseback rides along the
coast and into the surrounding jungle, where
you can trot through a mangrove-lined beach
and see wildlife. Be sure to wear clothing
appropriate for a horseback ride. Closed-toe
shoes are especially recommended.

# San Miguel de Cozumel

**ISLA COZUMEL ACTIVITIES**

## Diving

Cozumel and its surrounding reefs are among the world's most popular diving spots.

The sites have fantastic year-round visibility (commonly 30m or more) and a jaw-droppingly impressive variety of marine life that includes spotted eagle rays, moray eels, groupers, barracudas, turtles, sharks, brain coral and some huge sponges.

The island can have strong currents (sometimes around 3 knots), making drift dives the standard, especially along the many walls. Even when diving from the beach you should evaluate conditions and plan your route carefully, selecting an exit point down-current beforehand, then staying alert for shifts in currents. Always keep an eye out (and your ears open) for boat traffic as well.

There are scores of dive operators on Cozumel. All limit the size of their groups to six or eight divers, and the good ones take pains to match up divers of similar skill levels. Some offer snorkeling and deep-sea fishing trips as well as diving instruction.

Prices are usually quoted in US dollars. In general expect to pay anywhere between US$100 and US$115 for a two-tank dive (equipment included) or an introductory 'resort' course. PADI open-water certification costs US$440.

Multiple-dive packages and discounts for groups or those paying in cash can bring rates down significantly.

If you encounter a decompression emergency, head immediately to the hyperbaric chamber at Cozumel International Hospital (p100).

If diving is your primary goal, you may want to time your trip for September or October, when weather conditions are ideal. Severe weather can affect turbidity and prevent the boats from leaving, among other hassles.

**Aldora Divers** DIVING
(Map p94; ☑987-872-33-97; www.aldora.com; Calle 5 Sur 37; 1-/2-tank dive incl equipment US$92/132, 3-tank shark-cave dive US$237; ◷7am-3pm & 6-8pm) One of the best dive shops in Cozumel, Aldora will take divers to the windward side of the island when weather is bad on the western side. It also offers full-day excursions to caves with sleeping sharks; these trips include a stop at a lagoon with Maya ruins.

**Deep Blue** DIVING
(Map p94; ☑987-872-56-53; www.deepbluecozumel.com; Salas 200; 2-tank dives incl equipment US$112, snorkeling incl gear US$65; ◷7am-9pm) This PADI and National Association of Underwater Instructors (NAUI) operation has knowledgeable staff, state-of-the-art gear and fast boats that give you a chance to get

more dives out of a day. A snorkeling outing visits three sites.

### Snorkeling

The best snorkeling sites are reached by boat. Most snorkeling-only outfits in downtown go to one of three stretches of reef nearby, all accessible from the beach. If you go with a dive outfit instead, you can often get to better spots, such as Palancar Reef or the adjacent Colombia Shallows, near the island's southern end.

Your best option is to head out on a diving boat with Deep Blue (p95), which will take you to three of the finest snorkeling sites on the island.

You can save on boat fares (though you will see fewer fish) by walking into the gentle surf north of town. One good spot is beach club Buccanos (Map p92; ☎ 987-872-01-00; www.buccanos.com; Carretera San Juan Km 4.5; snorkeling incl gear US$20; ☺ 9am-4:30pm), next to Hotel Playa Azul, 4km north of the turnoff to the airport; its *palapas* offer shade, and it has a swimming area with a sheltering wharf and a small artificial reef.

It's best not to snorkel alone away from the beach area. Even when snorkeling right from the beach you need to be mindful of boat traffic, and always keep an eye on conditions and currents – plan your route, pick

## DIVING & SNORKELING SITES

With more than 60 surrounding reefs, excellent visibility and an abundance of marine life, it's no wonder the late great oceanographer Jacques Cousteau called Cozumel one of the world's top diving destinations. Among the island's many great sites you'll find everything from challenging wall dives to shallow snorkeling spots.

### Santa Rosa Wall

This is the biggest of the famous dive sites. The wall is so large that most people are able to see only a third of it on one tank. Regardless of where you're dropped, expect to find enormous overhangs and tunnels covered with corals and sponges. Stoplight parrotfish, black grouper and barracuda hang out here. The average visibility is 30m and minimum depth 10m, with an average depth closer to 25m.

### Punta Sur Reef

Unforgettable for its coral caverns, each of which is named, this reef is for very experienced divers only. Before you dive be sure to ask your divemaster to point out the Devil's Throat. This cave opens into a cathedral room with four tunnels, all of which make for some pretty hairy exploration. Only certified cave divers should consider entering the Devil's Throat. Butterfly fish, angelfish and whip corals abound at the reef.

### Colombia Shallows

Also known as Colombia Gardens, Colombia Shallows lends itself equally well to snorkeling and scuba diving. Because it's a shallow dive (maximum depth 10m, average 2m to 4m), its massive coral buttresses covered with sponges and other resplendent life forms are well illuminated. The current at Colombia Gardens is generally light to moderate. This and the shallow water allow you to spend hours here if you want; it's impossible to become bored spying all the elkhorn coral, pillar coral and anemones that live here.

### Palancar Gardens

This dive consists of a strip reef about 25m wide and very long, riddled with fissures and tunnels. The major features are enormous stovepipe sponges and vivid yellow tube sponges, and you can always find damselfish, parrotfish and angelfish around you. In the deeper parts of the reef, divers will want to keep an eye out for the lovely black corals. The Gardens can be appreciated by snorkelers in the area known as Palancar Shallows.

### Maracaibo

One of Cozumel's least visited sites, Maracaibo is the island's southernmost reef, known as a spectacular yet challenging wall dive. It's for experienced divers only – you'll be plunging to depths of 40m in waters with strong currents. Common marine life sightings in Maracaibo's deep blue waters include turtles, spotted eagle rays, nurse sharks and black tip reef sharks.

an exit strategy in advance, and stay aware of changes in currents.

As with diving (p95) the ideal time for snorkeling is September or October, when the weather and conditions are at their best.

## ⭐ Festivals & Events

### Carnaval
STREET CARNIVAL

(☺ Feb or early Mar) We know, it's not the wild Carnaval of Rio de Janeiro, but don't underestimate this nearly 150-year-old tradition. Taking place along the waterfront, the five-day celebration brings dancers festooned with feathers out into the streets, along with vibrant floats, live-music acts, food stalls and impromptu fiestas just about everywhere you turn.

### Feria del Cedral
RELIGIOUS

(El Cedral; ☺ late Apr & early May) Held in Cozumel's southern town of El Cedral, this annual celebration honors a group of War of the Castes refugees forced to flee the mainland and settle in Cozumel in 1848. The fair features rides, food stands, rodeos and traditional dance, including the time-honored Baile de las Cabezas de Cochino (Dance of the Pigs' Heads).

## 🛏 Sleeping

The official high season runs from mid-December to mid-April, but whatever the season, if business is slow, most places are open to negotiation. Almost all accommodations raise their rates during the weeks of Christmas and Easter.

San Miguel de Cozumel has many budget and midrange places, with a few big, luxury resort hotels several kilometers north and south of town.

### Casa del Solar
GUESTHOUSE $

(Map p94; 📞 987-869-30-77, cell 987-5648680; teresagonzalez230172@gmail.com; Av 5 Norte 280; d US$35-40; ❄✳🛜) Six rooms, all with comfortable beds and some with the old house's original tile floors, overlook a sunny courtyard with a large *mamey* (sapote) tree. Coffee is made each morning in a common kitchen. Like many budget guesthouses, this one has its quirks: at last visit, wi-fi was spotty and one room's electric water heater delivered harmless but eye-opening shocks.

### Beds Friends
HOSTEL $

(Map p94; 📞 987-869-18-20; www.bedsfriends hostel.com; Av 10 Norte 498; dm M$270-370, r M$770, without bathroom M$670; ❄✳🛜) This colorful spot has pretty much everything you could ask for in a hostel and then some: clean, comfortable beds in cheerful dorms and private rooms, an on-site bar and restaurant, live music, bike, scooter and snorkel gear rentals, and free weekly yoga classes. Guests hang out in a tropical gravel garden.

### Hostelito
HOSTEL $

(Map p94; 📞 987-869-81-57; www.hostelcozu mel.com; Av 10 Norte 42, btwn Av Juárez & Calle 2 Norte; dm M$200-250, d M$650-700, ste from M$750; ❄✳🛜📺) All rooms now have air-con, with your choice of mixed dorms, double rooms of varying types, and actual suites with nice beds and furnishings. Hostelito's pleasant open-air kitchen and rooftop sundeck are great spaces to hang out and exchange diving stories, or you can dip in the pool. A M$50 deposit for towels is required for the private rooms.

### Amigo's Hostel
HOSTEL $

(Map p94; 📞 987-872-38-68, cell 987-1199664; www.cozumelhostel.com; Calle 7 Sur 571, btwn Avs 25 Sur & 30 Sur; dm/d US$15/54; ❄✳🛜📺) Unlike some cramped budget digs, here you get a large garden with labeled trees, an inviting pool and a good lounge area stocked with reading material. Some guests say it's too far removed from the tourist center; others like it that way. Snorkel-gear rentals available (M$100). Air-con May to October only, from 10pm to 8am.

Recent additions include a permanent grill for guests to use, and reinforced roofing.

### Hotel Mary Carmen
HOTEL $$

(Map p94; 📞 987-872-05-81; www.hotelmary carmen.com.mx; Av 5 Sur 132; d M$900; ❄✳🛜) Clean, colorful rooms overlook a central courtyard where the owner keeps more than a dozen tortoises, so watch your step, especially at night. It's just a short walk from the ferry terminal before you reach the hotel's airy lobby, full of antique furnishings. Discounted rates are offered throughout most of the year.

### Sun Suites Cozumel
HOTEL $$

(Map p94; 📞 987-872-29-28; www.facebook.com/sunsuitesczm; Av 10 Norte 19; d incl breakfast M$1150; ❄✳🛜📺) Spacious, tile-floored rooms are spick-and-span, with large fridge, air-con, coffee maker and flat-screen TV. Guests have breakfast on a shady courtyard and there's an inviting grassy pool area at the back, with lounge chairs.

### Hotel Suites Bahía
HOTEL **$$**

(Map p94; ☑987-872-90-80, USA 877-228-6747; www.suitesbahia.com; cnr Av Melgar & Calle 3 Sur; d incl breakfast US$62-131; ⊛❀@🛜) Opt for a standard room with a street-facing balcony or a more expensive one with balcony and ocean view. You can save substantially by staying in one of the smaller, interior rooms if a view isn't vital to your sleeping equation.

### ★Hotel B Cozumel
BOUTIQUE HOTEL **$$$**

(Map p92; ☑987-872-03-00; www.hotelbcozumel.com; Carretera San Juan Km 2.5; d/ste incl breakfast US$193/287; ⊛❀🛜) This trendy hotel on the north shore may not have that sand beach you're after, but just wait till you get a look at the crystalline saltwater pool and oceanfront hot tub. Rooms are fitted with handmade furnishings, there's live jazz on Thursdays and free bikes are available. Rates quoted are for jungle-view rooms; ocean views cost extra.

### Hotel Villas Las Anclas
VILLA **$$$**

(Map p94; ☑987-872-54-76, US 305-771-8176; www.hotelvillalasanclas.com; Av 5 Sur 325; d US$131; ⊛❀) If you live having space, check out these two-story villas. A spiral staircase ascends to a snug loft bedroom, while downstairs you get a full kitchen and living room with a garden view. In the leafy patio there's a shady pool with a waterfall and a large outdoor kitchen with an integrated BBQ grill.

### Ventanas al Mar
HOTEL **$$$**

(Map p92; ☑cell 984-2672237; www.ventanasalmarcozumel.com; Carretera Costera Oriente Km 43.5; d incl breakfast from US$145; 🅿⊛❀🛜) 🏖 The only windward hotel on the island, this might be right for you if you are looking to get away from it all (*way* away from it all). The rooms have great ocean views and the constant wind will lull you to sleep – or drive you crazy if you're a light sleeper. Air-con is only on from 8pm to 6am.

### Suites Colonial Cozumel
HOTEL **$$$**

(Map p94; ☑987-872-90-80; www.suitescolonial.com.mx; Av 5 Sur, btwn Calles 1 Sur & Salas; d/ste incl breakfast US$112/133; ⊛❀🛜) Down a passageway off Avenida 5 Sur, this place has lovely 'studios' (rooms with cable TV, fridge and lots of varnished-wood touches) and nice, spacious one-bedroom suites with kitchenettes. The breakfast buffet is served at nearby sister property Casa Mexicana.

### Casa Mexicana
HOTEL **$$$**

(Map p94; ☑987-872-90-90; www.casamexicanacozumel.com; Av Melgar 457; d incl break-fast US$193-205; 🅿⊛❀@🛜) The breezy open-air lobby with swimming pool and ocean view is pretty awesome here. Rooms are standard issue for the most part, but all in all Casa Mexicana offers good value given its prime location and free breakfast buffet. The 'deluxe city view' with balcony is the best deal.

### Guido's Boutique Hotel
BOUTIQUE HOTEL **$$$**

(Map p94; ☑987-872-09-46; www.guidosboutiquehotel.com; Av Melgar 23; ste US$131-155; 🅿⊛❀🛜) Right on the main strip with an ocean view, Guido's has four chic suites with full kitchens, large common areas and private balconies, making them ideal for families or small groups. The same owners run a great Italian restaurant downstairs.

## 🍴 Eating

Cozumel pretty much has it all, from cheap market eats and taco joints to candlelit restaurants serving seafood and gourmet fare. International chains abound near the port, geared toward the cruise-ship crowd. The *comida corrida* (a set meal of several courses, usually offered at lunchtime) is always filling and is reasonably priced in most places.

### Camarón Dorado
SEAFOOD **$**

(Map p92; ☑987-872-72-87, cell 987-1181281; www.facebook.com/camaron.dorado; cnr Av Juárez & Calle 105 Sur; tortas M$29-58, tacos M$18-34; ⏰7am-1:30pm Tue-Sun; 🛜) If you're headed to the windward side of the island or just want to see a different aspect of Cozumel, drop by the Camarón Dorado for a bite, assuming you're early enough. Be warned: the *camarón empanizado* (breaded shrimp) *tortas* and tacos are highly addictive. It's 2.5km southeast of the passenger-ferry terminal.

### Taquería Los Sera's
TACOS **$**

(Map p94; Av 30 Sur, cnr Morelos; tacos M$12-40; ⏰7pm-3am Thu-Tue) The late-night, go-to spot for *al pastor* (spit-cooked pork) and *chuleta* (pork chop) tacos. Locals rave about the *al pastor* pizza; we say it's a cheesy mess.

### Burritos Gorditos
FAST FOOD **$**

(Map p94; ☑cell 987-1200037; www.facebook.com/burritosgorditos; Av 5 Norte 161; burritos M$64-128; ⏰9am-5pm Mon-Sat) This welcoming little burrito joint prepares the typical vegetarian, chicken and beef varieties, or you can experiment with Yucatán-inspired *cochinita* (slow-cooked pork). Plan on coming hungry, because the large burritos are truly *grande*.

### El Coffee Cozumel
CAFE $

(Map p94; ☑987-869-04-56; coffeecozumel@gmail.com; Calle 3 Sur 98; mains from M$60; ⊙7am-11pm; 🛜🅿) A tempting array of fresh-baked goods and organic coffee from the Mexican highlands make this place popular with locals and visitors alike. Pies are made daily, and they do a mean iced latte – perfect if you need to beat the heat.

### Mercado Municipal
MARKET $

(Map p94; Salas s/n, btwn Avs 20 & 25 Sur; snacks & mains M$25-120; ⊙8am-5pm) Visit this downtown market for your daily supply of fruit and veggies; it's also a good place for cheap eats.

### Cocina Económica
### Las Palmas
MEXICAN $

(Map p94; ☑987-872-12-95; cnr Av 25 Sur & Calle 3 Sur; mains M$100-200, comida corrida M$70-135; ⊙9.30am-6pm Mon-Sat; 🛜) This place really packs 'em in at lunchtime. And though it gets hotter than Hades, you'll love the Maya favorites such as *poc-chuc* (grilled pork) or the *pechuga rellena* (stuffed chicken breast). Mighty tasty!

### Zermatt Bakery
BAKERY $

(Map p94; Av 5 Norte s/n, cnr Calle 4 Norte; bread M$7-20; ⊙7am-2:30pm & 5-7pm Mon-Sat) Unlike many Mexican bakeries, Zermatt bakes its pastries, cakes and wholewheat bread in the early morning.

### Taquería El Sitio
TACOS $

(Map p94; Calle 2 Norte 124; tacos & tortas M$16-40; ⊙8am-2pm) For something quick, cheap and tasty, head over to El Sitio for breaded shrimp and fish tacos or a *huevo con chaya torta* (egg and tree-spinach sandwich). The folding chairs and concrete floor are nothing fancy, but the food is good.

### Jeanie's
MEXICAN $$

(Map p94; ☑987-878-46-47; www.jeaniescozumel.com; Av Melgar 790; breakfasts M$90-115, mains M$100-280; ⊙7am-10pm; 🛜) The views of the water are great from the outdoor patio here. Jeanie's serves waffles, hash browns, eggs, sandwiches and other tidbits including vegetarian fajitas. Frozen coffees beat the midday heat. Between 5pm and 7pm it does a lovely happy hour, too.

### ★ Kinta
BISTRO $$$

(Map p94; ☑987-869-05-44; www.kintarestaurante.com; Av 5 Norte 148; mains M$280-380; ⊙5-11pm; 🛜) Putting a gourmet twist on Mexican classics, this chic bistro is one of the best restaurants on the island. The Midnight Pork Ribs are a tried-and-true favorite, while the wood-fired oven turns out spectacular oven-baked fish. For dessert treat yourself to a *budín de la abuelita*, aka 'granny's pudding.' It currently has a six-course tasting menu for M$700. Yum!

### 'Ohana
PIZZA $$$

(Map p94; ☑cell 987-5641771; www.ohanacozumel.com; Av 5 Norte 341; pizzas M$250; ⊙5-11pm Mon-Sat) Known for its Chicago-style deep-dish pizza and friendly neighborhood expat bar, 'Ohana (meaning family in Hawaiian) definitely feels like home. The owner Matt (a Windy City transplant) knows a thing or two about making a proper pizza pie and he mixes his own mezcal and tequila cream liqueurs, which are fine if you like booze that tastes like dessert.

### Guido's Restaurant
ITALIAN $$$

(Map p94; ☑987-869-25-89; www.guidoscozumel.com; Av Melgar 23; mains M$250-495, pizzas M$230-280; ⊙11am-11pm Mon-Sat, from 3pm Sun; 🛜) Drawing on recipes handed down from her father, Guido, chef Yvonne Villiger has created a menu ranging from wood-fired pizzas and homemade pastas to prosciutto-wrapped scallops. To accompany the meal, order a pitcher of sangria, the house specialty. The cocktail menu is equally impressive; there is even house-made tonic syrup for your G&Ts.

### La Cocay
COCKTAIL BAR

(Map p94; ☑987-872-55-33; www.lacocay.com; Calle 8 Norte 208; mains M$160-480; ⊙5:30-11:30pm; 🛜) Operating since 1996, this restaurant's food is underwhelming and the service is slow. Opt instead to come here for a romantic, candlelit après-meal tipple, or for coffee and dessert. The full bar can fix just about any cocktail you're craving, a refreshing change from the out-of-a-can margaritas often served at other spots.

### Pepe's Grill
STEAK $$$

(Map p94; ☑987-872-02-13; www.pepescozumel.com; Av Melgar 201; mains M$220-525; ⊙10am-11pm; 🛜) This is traditionally considered Cozumel's finest restaurant and the prices reflect its reputation. The menu focuses mainly on Angus steaks, pastas, fresh fish and charbroiled lobster (available at market prices).

## 🍸 Drinking & Nightlife

San Miguel de Cozumel's nightlife is quiet and subdued. Most restaurants are open for drinks, but by 11pm things are winding

ISLA COZUMEL DRINKING & NIGHTLIFE

down – though several places around the plaza keep later hours.

**El Fish** BAR
(Map p94; Calle 8 Norte s/n, cnr Av 10 Norte; ☺noon-10pm) For the classic Cozumel *botana* bar experience (free snacks come to the table each time you order a new round), hit this fan-cooled establishment for a cold beer, tasty grub and a few laughs with the crowd of locals sat around the semi-circular bar. The kitchen closes at 7pm.

**Freedom in Paradise** BAR
(Map p92; ✆987-869-83-00, cell 987-5649164; www.bobmarleybar.com; Carretera Coastal Oriente Km 29.5; ☺10.30am-6pm) As much a viewing point as it is a great place for a chilled beer, Freedom in Paradise is a family-run endeavor that's been around for decades. The mellow *palapa* couldn't be a nicer spot to enjoy the vista. Across the street its sister location offers flavored-mezcal tastings. Long live Bob!

**Coconuts Bar & Grill** BAR
(Map p92; ✆cell 987-1077110; www.coconutscozumel.com; Carretera Coastal Oriente Km 43.3; ☺9.30am-7pm) The term 'Coconuts' is used here metaphorically, and some of the decorations are a bit tacky (the thong-wearing beach balls, for instance), but what would you expect from a cliffside bar serving tropical drinks with Jimmy Buffett tunes in the background? The view can't be beat, and on a hot day the beer can't be beat either. Cash only.

## ☆ Entertainment

**★ Turquoise Beach Bar** LIVE MUSIC
(Map p92; ✆cell 987-1155057; www.facebook.com/turquoisecozumelbeachclub; Av Melgar Km 2.8; ☺9am-8pm Mon-Sat, 10am-11pm Sun) Rock cover bands, some surprisingly good, play fun sunset shows several times a week. If you get tired of the beer routine, order a cocktail or potent mezcal. A festively plump pet pig named Taluhla roams the beach here for table scraps and she seems to be making out quite well. It's about 1km south of the car-ferry dock.

**Woody's Bar & Grill** LIVE MUSIC
(Map p94; www.cozumelradio.wixsite.com/woodys; Av Juárez s/n, btwn Avs 5 & 10; ☺9am-midnight Mon-Fri, to 1am Sat & Sun; 🛜) Though the cocktails here barely pass muster, there are some pretty decent live acts – not only covers, but some nice original stuff too. The beers are icy and this is a fun spot to people-watch, chat with new friends, or just listen.

## 🛍 Shopping

**Los Cinco Soles** ARTS & CRAFTS
(Map p94; ✆987-872-90-04; www.loscincosoles.com; Av Melgar 27; ☺8am-8pm Mon-Fri, from 9am Sat, 10am-6pm Sun) Like many shops along Avenida Melgar, this large store sells its fair share of kitsch. However, there are some keepers on the shelves if you take the time to look, such as black ceramics from Oaxaca, Talavera pottery, and colorful Day of the Dead skeleton dioramas.

## ℹ Information

### EMERGENCY
**Police, Medical, Fire** (✆911, ✆066)

### INTERNET ACCESS
Internet cafes are hard to find in Cozumel, but most hotels, restaurants and many stores offer free wi-fi. You can often ask your hotel to print out boarding passes or to help with other basic printing needs.

### MEDICAL SERVICES
**Cozumel International Hospital** (Hyperbaric Chamber; ✆987-872-14-30; www.hospitalcozumel.com; Calle 5 Sur 21B, btwn Avs Melgar & 5 Sur; ☺24hr) Has hyperbaric chamber.

### MONEY
You'll have no problem finding banks and ATMs in San Miguel. For currency exchange, try the banks near the main plaza, including:
**Banorte** (Av 5 Norte s/n, btwn Av Juárez & Calle 2 Norte; ☺8:30am-4pm Mon-Fri, 9am-2pm Sat)
**HSBC** (✆987-872-01-42; Av 5 Sur 11, cnr Calle 1 Sur; ☺9am-5pm Mon-Fri)

### POST
**Post Office** (Map p94; ✆987-872-01-06; Morelos 35, cnr Av 35 Sur; ☺9am-4pm Mon-Fri, to 1pm Sat)

### TELEPHONE
Telmex card phones are becoming rarer as most people opt for Skype or VOIP calls on their wi-fi-enabled cell phones. The payphone is still around, though its days might be numbered. Alternatively, you can buy a cheap burner phone in convenience stores; these usually come with free minutes.
**Telecomm Office** (✆987-872-00-56; Av Melgar 254, cnr Calle 7 Sur; ☺8am-7:30pm Mon-Fri) Handles faxes and money orders.

### TOURIST INFORMATION
**Tourist Information Office** (Map p94; ✆987-869-02-12; www.cozumel.travel; Av 5 Sur s/n, Plaza del Sol, 2nd fl; ☺8am-3pm Mon-Fri) Pick up maps and travel brochures here.

# ❶ Getting There & Away

## AIR

Cozumel's small **airport** (☏ 987-872-20-81; www.asur.com.mx; Blvd Aeropuerto Cozumel s/n) is some 3km northeast of the ferry terminal, and is signed along Avenida Melgar. There are direct services from the US with United, Delta and American airlines; flights from Europe are generally routed via the US or Mexico City. Cozumel is also served by Mexican airlines Interjet, Volaris and MAYAir.

**Interjet** (☏ 800-011-23-45, USA 866-285-9525; www.interjet.com; Cozumel International Airport) Direct flights to Mexico City.

**MAYAir** (☏ 987-872-36-09; www.mayair.com.mx; Cozumel International Airport) Flights to Cancún with onward service to Mérida.

**Volaris** (☏ 55-1102-8000; www.volaris.com; Cozumel International Airport) Nonstops to Guadalajara and Monterrey.

## BOAT

Passenger ferries operated by Ultramar (p117) and Winjet (p116) run frequently to Cozumel from Playa del Carmen from 7am to 11pm (one-way M$160), leaving from and arriving at the **Passenger Ferry Dock** (Map p94).

To transport a vehicle to Cozumel, go to the Calica–Punta Venado car-ferry terminal (p116) (officially known as the Terminal Marítima Punta Venado), about 8km south of Playa del Carmen. There are four daily departures (three on Sundays). See the ferries' websites for schedules. You'll need to line up at least one hour before departure, two hours before in high season. Fares cost M$500, including passengers, or more depending on the size of the vehicle.

## BUS

You can buy tickets in advance at **ADO Ticket Office** (Map p94; ☏ 987-869-25-53; Calle 2 Norte s/n, btwn Avs 5 Norte & 10 Norte; ⊙ 8am-9pm Mon-Fri, 9:30am-7pm Sat & Sun) for buses departing from Playa del Carmen on the mainland to destinations throughout the Yucatán.

# ❶ Getting Around

## TO/FROM THE AIRPORT

Frequent, shared shuttle vans run from the airport into town (M$85), to hotels on the island's north end (M$140) and to the south side (M$140 to M$200). To return to the airport in a taxi, expect to pay about M$110.

## CAR

A car is the best way to get to the island's furthest reaches, and there are plenty of places to rent one. All rental contracts should automatically include *daños a terceros* (liability insurance). Check that taxes are included in the quoted price: often they are not. Collision insurance is usually about M$380 extra, with a 10% vehicle value deductible for the cheapest vehicles.

Rates start at around M$880 all-inclusive, though you'll pay more during late December and January. There are plenty of agencies around the main plaza, but prices are about 50% lower from the dock to the fringes of the tourist zone, where you can sometimes find a jalopy or clunker for M$600 or so.

Before renting, check with your hotel to see if it has an agreement with any agencies, as you can often get discounts. Some agencies will deduct tire damage (repair or replacement) from your deposit, even if tires are old and worn. And always check your car's brakes before driving off.

If you rent, observe the law on vehicle occupancy. Usually only five people are allowed in a vehicle. If you carry more, the police will fine you. You'll need to return your vehicle with the same amount of gas it had when you signed it out or pay a premium. There's a **gas station** (cnr Avs Juárez & 30 Sur) five blocks east of the main square, and several near the town center.

**Rentadora Isis** (☏ 984-879-31-11, 987-872-33-67; www.rentadoraisis.com.mx; Av 5 Norte 181; ⊙ 8am-6:30pm) is a fairly no-nonsense, family-run place with cars ranging from great shape to total clunkers; this branch rents convertible VW Beetles, Golfs and scooters, with little seasonal variation in prices.

## SCOOTER & BICYCLE

Touring the island solo by scooter is a blast, provided you have experience with scooters and with driving in Mexico. Two people on a bike is asking for trouble, though, as the machines' suspension will be barely adequate for one. Riders are injured in crashes on a regular basis, so always wear a helmet and stay alert. Collision insurance is not usually available for scooters: you break, you pay. Be sure to carefully inspect the scooter for damage before driving off or you may get hit with a repair bill.

To rent, you must have a valid driver's license and leave a credit-card slip or put down a cash deposit. There is a helmet law, and it is enforced. Rentadora Isis is a worthwhile rental place; Best Bikes Cozumel (p94) rents good bicycles.

## TAXI

As in some other towns on the Yucatán Peninsula, the taxi syndicate on Cozumel wields a good bit of power. Fares are around M$50 (in town), M$100 (to the Zona Hotelera) and M$1500 for a five-hour day trip around the island. Fares are posted just outside the ferry terminal.

ISLA COZUMEL GETTING THERE & AWAY

## AT A GLANCE

**POPULATION**
345,200

**CAPITAL**
Chetumal

**BEST BEACH BAR**
Fusion (p114)

**BEST REMOTE
GETAWAY**
Punta Allen (p130)

**BEST TACO JOINT**
Taquería Honorio
(p124)

**WHEN TO GO**
**Oct** Playa del
Carmen throws a
Halloween bash, and
Day of the Dead is
November 1.

**Nov** Playa del
Carmen hosts the
Riviera Maya Jazz
Festival; hotels offer
good deals.

**Dec** Underground
electronic music
event Sound Tulum
runs for two weeks,
concluding in early
January.

Iguana, Tulum ruins (p119)
HOLG/GETTY IMAGES ©

# Riviera Maya

The Riviera Maya, a tourist corridor of white-sand beaches, scenic ruins and fun-filled cenotes, was made for road-tripping. Yes, it's growing fast, too fast some will say, but despite all the development, you can still find that small fishing town or head inland to catch a glimpse of the Mexico that tourism forgot.

If it's partying you want, you'll find plenty of that in boomtown Playa del Carmen. Playa still trumps fast-growing Tulum as the Riviera's wildest city, but it's got nothing on Tulum's spectacular Maya ruins perched high above the beach.

Whether traveling by car or bus, getting from one town to the next is a breeze – after all, the Riviera is basically 135km of coastline that stretches south from Puerto Morelos to Tulum.

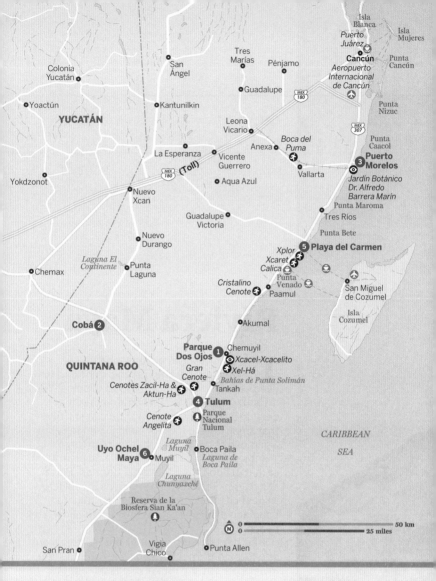

# Riviera Maya Highlights

**①** **Parque Dos Ojos** (p113) Splashing around in cenotes, or cave-diving in one of the world's largest underwater systems.

**②** **Cobá** (p128) Renting a bike to beat the hordes and then climbing the area's tallest pyramid before having a dip in nearby swimming holes.

**③** **Puerto Morelos** (p105) Diving into the waters off the coast of a quiet town that has managed to spare itself from the development boom.

**④** **Tulum** (p119) Marveling at the dramatically situated Maya ruins perched on a rugged cliff, then going for a swim down below.

**⑤** **Playa del Carmen** (p108) Hanging out at chic sidewalk restaurants and beachside bars – or, if you're feeling inspired, taking a Spanish course.

**⑥** **Uyo Ochel Maya** (p121) Touring a large lagoon system before floating down a centuries-old Maya canal.

# Puerto Morelos

🔊 998 / POP 37,500

Halfway between Cancún and Playa del Carmen, Puerto Morelos retains its quiet, small-town feel despite the encroaching building boom north and south of town. While it offers enough restaurants and bars to keep you entertained by night, it's really the shallow Caribbean waters that draw visitors here. Brilliantly contrasted stripes of bright green and dark blue separate the shore from the barrier reef – a tantalizing sight for divers and snorkelers – while inland a series of excellent cenotes beckon the adventurous. There's a nice market just south of the plaza with a good selection of crafts and handmade hammocks that are of a much higher quality than those you'll find in Cancún or Playa.

## ◎ Sights

**Crococun Zoo** ZOO

(🔊 998-850-37-19; www.crococunzoo.com; Hwy 307 Km 31; adult/child 6-12yr US$32/22; ◎9am-5pm) About 23km south of the Cancún airport, this former crocodile farm now calls itself a conservationist zoo that protects some of the area's endangered species and rescue animals. The price of admission includes a guided tour in which visitors are allowed to interact with some of the animals, such as white-tailed deer, boa constrictors, macaws, crocs and spider monkeys. Bring mosquito repellent.

**Jardín Botánico**
**Dr Alfredo Barrera Marín** GARDENS

(Jardín Botánico Yaax Che; 🔊 998-206-92-33; www.facebook.com/jbpuertomorelos; Hwy 307 Km 320; adult/child 3-10yr M$120/50; ◎8am-4pm; 🖐) One of the largest botanical gardens in Mexico, this 65-hectare reserve has about 2km of trails and sections dedicated to epiphytes (orchids and bromeliads), palms, ferns, succulents (cacti and their relatives) and plants used in traditional Maya medicine. The garden also holds a large animal population, including the only coastal troops of spider monkeys left in the region. It's 1.3km south of the Puerto Morelos turnoff. Bring mosquito repellent (June to November) and water.

**Pescadores Brewery** BREWERY

(🔊 984-175-23-19; www.pescadores.mx; Hwy 307 Km 316; tasting M$100; ◎10am-6pm; 🅿) About 5km south of Puerto Morelos you can wet your whistle at this roadside Mexican craft-beer brewery, where they run daily tours at noon and 3pm. Pescadores produces various brews, including a hoppy IPA and a popular habanero ale. After the tour, drink some suds while munching on brisket and ribs prepared at an on-site food truck.

## 🏃 Activities

The barrier reef that runs along most of the coast of Quintana Roo is only 600m offshore here, providing both divers and snorkelers with views of sea turtles, sharks, stingrays, moray eels, lobsters and loads of colorful tropical fish. Several sunken ships make great wreck diving, and the dive centers offer cenote trips as well.

**Aquanauts** DIVING

(🔊 998-206-93-65; www.aquanautsdiveadventures.com; El Cid Marina; 1-/2-tank reef dive US$85/113, 2-tank cenote dive US$210, snorkeling US$35, lionfish hunting M$140; ◎8am-4pm Mon-Sat) Runs many interesting tours, including drift diving, cenote and shipwreck dives, and lionfish fishing. Though there is an office in town, the actual dives leave from the El Cid Marina, 3km south of town.

**Wet Set** DIVING

(🔊 998-206-92-04; www.wetset.com; Av Rojo Gómez s/n, Hotel Ojo de Agua; 2-tank ocean dive US$99-124, 2-tank cenote dive US$179, snorkeling US$35-79; ◎8am-5pm) Operates trips to more than 30 dive sites, including nearby reefs, an underwater sculpture museum and Parque Dos Ojos. Also has snorkeling outings to reefs and cenotes.

**Boca del Puma** SWIMMING

(🔊 cell 998-2412855; www.bocadelpuma.com; Ruta de los Cenotes Km 16; adult/child 5-14yr US$25/15; ◎9am-5pm; 🖐) For cenote action, check out the ecopark Boca del Puma, 16km west of Puerto Morelos. Other activities available include zip-lining and ATVs.

## 🗣 Courses

**Puerto Morelos Language Center** LANGUAGE

(🔊 cell 984-8790112, cell 998-8454376; www.puertomorelosspanishcenter.com; Av Niños Héroes 46; per hr/week from US$20/100) They offer hourly and weekly classes of 10 to 20 hours, ranging from travel Spanish to business-oriented programs. The school doubles as a travel agency.

## 🛏 Sleeping

Hotels can be surprisingly full even at non-peak times, so call or book ahead if at all possible. Pickings are slim at the budget end, but midrange and top-end hotels are plentiful.

### Casitas Kinsol
GUESTHOUSE **$$**

(☑998-206-91-52; www.casitas-kinsol.com; Av Zetina Gazca 18; d with air-con/fan US$61/39; ❄✿🛜🏊) Great for people who want to see what life's like on the other side of town (yes, there are signs of life west of the highway!), Kinsol offers fan-cooled *palapa*-style huts with beautiful design details such as Talavera tile sinks and handcrafted furnishings. It's a peaceful spot where even the dogs and cats get along. It's 3km west of town.

A resident tortoise wanders around in the verdant garden. Bike rentals available.

### ★Posada El Moro
HOTEL **$$$**

(☑998-871-01-59; www.hotelelmoro.mx; Av Rojo Gómez s/n; r/ste incl breakfast from M$1900/2500; 🅿❄✿🛜🏊) A pretty property, with cheery geraniums in the halls and courtyard. Some rooms have kitchenette, most have couches that fold out into futons, and there's a small pool in a tropical garden. Prices drop substantially in low season or if you book via their website (not the booking sites). It's northwest of the plaza.

### Eden Apartments
APARTMENT **$$$**

(☑998-871-04-50; www.puertomoroloseden.com; Av Quintana Roo; apt M$1609; 🅿❄✿🛜) A great deal for families, even more so in the low season when rates drop by as much as 50%. With an emphasis on function over form, the well-managed Eden provides spotless apartments featuring a bedroom with two comfortable double beds and a separate dining room sporting a full kitchen.

### Casa Caribe
B&B **$$$**

(☑998-251-80-60; www.casacaribepuertomorelos. com; Av Rojo Goméz 768; r incl breakfast US$185; ❄✿🛜) Rooms with terra-cotta floors at this tastefully decorated B&B afford sweeping beach views from large balconies with hammocks, and all get fantastic sea breezes. Breakfast is served on a hacienda-style terrace overlooking a walled garden area.

There's a three-night minimum stay.

### Abbey del Sol
APARTMENT **$$$**

(☑998-871-01-27; www.abbeydelsol.com; Av Niñoes Héroes 806; apt from US$148, houses US$279-428; ❄✿🛜🏊) No need to hole up in a stuffy hotel room when you have this spacious option eight blocks north of the plaza. Studio and one-bedroom apartments with full kitchens overlook a well-manicured garden and pool area. Some units come with sleeper sofas to accommodate small families and groups. Other perks: free bikes and a large DVD library.

### Hacienda Morelos
HOTEL **$$$**

(☑998-871-04-48, toll-free 800-972-02-10; www. haciendamorelos.com; Av Melgar s/n; d incl breakfast from US$142; ❄✿🛜🏊) With a fantastic location right on the beach and a short walk from the plaza, the large, rather plain rooms here are a good bet. Ground-level rooms have a pool and beach at the doorstep.

### Hotel Ojo de Agua
HOTEL **$$$**

(☑998-252-60-62; www.hotelojodeagua.com; Av Rojo Gómez s/n; r garden/ocean view M$1500/1800, q M$2100; 🅿❄✿🛜🏊) Offers 36 remodeled rooms on a nice stretch of beach. You can get 'standard' rooms, but for a few hundred pesos more you get one with an ocean view. The 'habitación familiar,' which sleeps four, is good value for families. You'll find the hotel about three blocks north of the plaza.

## ✕ Eating

### Le Café d'Amancia
CAFE **$**

(☑998-206-92-42; www.facebook.com/cafe deamancia; Av Rojo Gómez s/n; mains M$55-110; ⏱7am-10pm Tue-Sun; 🛜🍴) Right on the plaza, this is a spotlessly clean place with pleasing ambience. It serves bagels, sandwiches, pies, good strong coffee, and fruit and veggie *licuados* (milkshakes).

### El Pesquero
SEAFOOD **$$**

(☑998-206-91-29; www.facebook.com/elpesquero puertomorelos; Av Melgar 4C; mains M$110-270; ⏱1-7:30pm) OK, so it's not right on the beach, but the sand floor, *palapa* roof, fan-cooled dining area and fresh fish sure make you feel like you're there. Start with a tuna *tostada*, then go with the excellent *pescado frito* (fried whole fish), which can be cooked 'natural' style or *al ajillo* (in chili-garlic sauce). If available, try the *boquinete* (hogfish).

### El Nicho
BREAKFAST **$$**

(☑cell 998-2010992; www.elnicho.com.mx; cnr Avs Tulum & Rojo Gómez; breakfast M$79-140; ⏱7:30am-2pm; 🛜🍴) Puerto Morelos' most popular breakfast spot, El Nicho serves organic egg dishes, eggs Benedict, *chilaquiles* (fried tortilla strips in salsa) with chicken and organic coffee from Chiapas. Vegetarians will find many good options here. Cash only.

### El Pirata
MEXICAN **$$**

(☑cell 55-35199040; www.facebook.com/elpirata puertomorelosrestaurant; Av Rojo Gómez 74; breakfast M$95-125, lunch & dinner M$150-365; ⏱8am-11pm Thu-Tue; 🛜) Known for its varied menu, local organic produce and casual atmosphere, this place north of the plaza does everything from tacos and classic Mexican dishes to gringo comfort food such as burgers (M$160). The grill comes on from 6pm.

**John Gray's Kitchen**  INTERNATIONAL **$$$**
(📞998-871-06-65; www.facebook.com/johngrays kitchen; Av Niños Héroes 6; breakfast M$60-100, dinner M$270-450; ⏱8am-10pm Mon-Sat Nov-Apr, from 3pm May-Oct) One block west and two blocks north of the plaza, this 'kitchen' turns out some truly fabulous food. The chef's specialty, though not listed on the regularly changing menu, is the duck in chipotle, tequila and honey sauce. It opens for breakfast too.

**★Al Chimichurri**  STEAK **$$$**
(📞998-252-46-66; www.facebook.com/alchimi churri; Av Rojo Gómez s/n; mains M$182-495; ⏱5-11pm Tue-Sun) You definitely can't go wrong with the fresh pasta and wood-fired pizza here, but this Uruguayan grill is best known for its steaks. The star cuts are a *Flintstones*-size rib eye, tender flank steak and filet mignon in homemade beef gravy. It's just south of the plaza.

## 🍷 Drinking & Nightlife

Puerto Morelos' nightlife scene is pretty calm and a new law has paved the way for beachside bar options that have nice afternoon happy hours. Only a few places stay open till the wee hours. If you need noise, you can always hop in a taxi or *colectivo* for some fun in nearby Playa del Carmen.

**Bara Bara**  BAR
(📞cell 998-1372214; Av Rojo Gómez 2; ⏱8pm-3am Tue-Sun) The party usually spills out onto the street at this popular bar just south of the plaza. Bara Bara spins the best tunes in town, prepares martinis that would have made Sinatra proud and has a foosball table!

**Posada Amor**  DANCING
(📞998-871-00-33;www.facebook.com/hotelposada amoroficial; Av Rojo Gómez s/n; ⏱11am-midnight) Posada Amor has a quiet bar where you can listen to cover bands play on Monday and Thursday night. It's located southwest of the plaza.

## 🛍 Shopping

One of the best reasons to come to Puerto Morelos is for the artisans market, one block south of the plaza. Dream catchers, pottery and textiles are popular but if you're looking for a hammock, this is the place. Unlike hammocks in the larger cities that come from Mérida, these are made right in town by a local family.

**★Artisans Market**  ARTS & CRAFTS
(Av Rojo Gómez s/n; ⏱9am-8pm) The hammocks sold here differ from what you'll find elsewhere because they're created right here in Puerto Morelos by a local family that's been making them for decades. (Ask for Mauricio or Martin!) You can also buy dream catchers, *alebrijes* (colorful wooden animal figures from San Martín Tilcajete), handbags, masks, jewelry and more.

It's refreshingly low-key and you can often see the craftspeople at work. They're happy to let you lie down in a hammock or hammock-chair. Unlike other stores or markets nearby, here the shops are owner-owned, meaning you can generally get a better deal and your money goes directly to the merchants, rather than to a big business.

**Alma Libre Books & Gifts**  BOOKS, CRAFTS
(www.almalibrebookstore.com; Av Tulum 2; ⏱10am-6pm Nov-Apr) Under new ownership, Alma Libre has a vast selection of new and used books. The store also carries art from the Yucatán, gift items and local gourmet food products. Find *Sunsets of Tulum* (set here in Yucatán) and other literature when you finish your current beach read!

## ℹ Orientation

Puerto Morelos' central plaza is 2km east of Hwy 307, nearly at the end of the main road into town (the main dock is the true end of the road). The town, all of three streets wide from east to west, stretches several blocks to the north of the plaza and about three long blocks south.

Locals refer to the neighborhood west of the highway as La Colonia, a residential area where you'll find more affordable restaurants and several decent lodging options; you can catch a *colectivo* there from the plaza.

## ℹ Information

There's an ATM on the northeast corner of the plaza.

The website www.inpuertomorelos.com is a good source of current info about the town.

## ℹ Getting There & Away

Playa Express vans and ADO buses to Puerto Morelos drop you on the highway, where you can walk the 2km into town or take a taxi (M$30) waiting at the turnoff. ADO and Playa Express have frequent departures to Cancún (M$28 to M$37) and Playa del Carmen (M$28 to M$37).

## RIVIERA THEME PARKS

Always a big hit with children, there are several theme parks between Cancún and Tulum, many with fantastic scenery – truly some of the most beautiful lagoons, cenotes and natural areas on the coast. Sure, some will find these places cheesy, but the kids couldn't care less. Some parks are pricey but their websites often offer presale online discounts.

It's worth mentioning that some parks offer an optional swim-with-dolphins activity, and though it may seem like a lovely idea, animal welfare groups suggest interaction with dolphins and other sea mammals held in captivity creates stress for these creatures.

Here are some of the most popular parks.

**Aktun Chen** (☑ cell 984-8064962, toll free 800-099-07-58; www.aktun-chen.com; Hwy 307 Km 107; full tour incl lunch adult/child 6-10yr US$128/102; ☺ 9:30am-5:30pm; ⊕ ) This small park 40km south of Playa del Carmen features a 585m-long cave, a 12m-deep cenote, 10 zip-lines and a small zoo.

**Xplor** (☑ 984-206-00-38, 998-883-31-43; www.xplor.travel; Hwy 307 Km 282; adult/child 5-11yr US$130/65; ☺ 9am-5pm & 5:30-11pm Mon-Sat; ⊕ ) This large park 6km south of Playa del Carmen operates circuits that take you zip-lining, rafting, driving amphibious jeeps, swimming in an underground river and hiking through caverns.

**Xel-Há** (☑ 984-206-00-38, 998-883-3034; www.xelha.com; Hwy 307 Km 240; adult/child 5-11yr from US$100/50; ☺ 8:30am-6pm; ⊕ ) Billing itself as a natural outdoor aquarium, it's built around an inlet 13km north of Tulum. Water-based activities include a river tour and snorkeling.

**Xcaret** (☑ 984-206-00-38; www.xcaret.com; Hwy 307 Km 282; adult/child 5-12yr from US$110/55; ☺ 8:30am-1pm; ⊕ ) One of the originals in the area, with loads of nature-based activities and stuff for grown-ups like a Mexican wine cellar and day spa. It's 6km south of Playa del Carmen. Hosts a pretty Day of the Dead festival in November.

**Selvática** (☑ 998-881-3033; www.selvatica.com.mx; Ruta de los Cenotes Km 19; adult/child 8-15yr US$199/99; ☺ tours 9am, 10:30am, noon & 1:30pm; ⊕ ) Inland from Puerto Morelos, this adventure outfit only runs prearranged tours. Come for adrenaline-pumping zip-lining, swimming in a cenote and more. Check the website for age restrictions for each tour.

You can purchase ADO tickets at a **bus station** (www.ado.com.mx; Hwy 307, cnr Morelos) next to the highway turnoff.

From **Cancún airport** (Cancún International Airport; ☑ 998-848-72-00; www.asur.com.mx; Hwy 307 Km 22), buses depart frequently to Puerto Morelos for M$127. They usually run from 7am to 8:30pm.

Cabs parked at the town plaza will take you back to the highway. Some drivers will tell you the fare is per person or overcharge in some other manner; strive for M$30 for as many people as you can stuff in. *Colectivos* to/from town to the highway cost M$8. A taxi to the airport runs M$450.

## Playa del Carmen

☑ 984 / POP 210,000

Playa del Carmen, now one of Quintana Roo's largest cities, ranks right up there with Tulum as one of the Riviera's trendiest spots. Sitting coolly on the lee side of Cozumel, the town's beaches are jammed with superfit sun worshipers. The waters aren't as clear as those of Cancún or Cozumel, and the sand isn't quite as powder-perfect as they are further north, but still Playa grows and grows.

The town is ideally located: close to Cancún's international airport, but far enough south to allow easy access to Cozumel, Tulum, Cobá and other worthy destinations. The reefs here are excellent and offer diving and snorkeling close by. Look for rays, moray eels, sea turtles and a huge variety of corals. The lavender sea fans make for very picturesque vistas.

With cruise-ship passengers visiting from Cozumel, Playa can feel crowded along the first several blocks of the tourist center.

## ◎ Sights

Playa del Carmen is primarily known for its beaches and outdoor party life, but there are a few sights worth checking out on rainy days.

**Aquarium**                    AQUARIUM
(El Acuario de Playa; ☑ 984-879-44-62, 998-287-53-13; www.elacuariodeplaya.com; 2nd fl, Calle 14

Norte 148, Plaza Calle Corazon; M$270; ⊙11am-10pm) An impressive three-story aquarium with 200 marine species and 45 exhibits. One of the few options in Playa for non-beach days. Last entry is at 9pm.

### Parque la Ceiba                                PARK
(☎984-859-23-27; www.facebook.com/parquela ceiba; 1 Av Sur, cnr Diagonal 60 Sur, Colonia Ejidal; ⊙7am-8:30pm Tue-Sat, 8am-5pm Sun; ♿🍽) **FREE** Two blocks west of the highway, this pretty park has play areas for kids, shady picnic spots and walking trails as well as activities such as movie screenings, yoga classes and the occasional concert. Every third Saturday of the month, La Ceiba hosts a crafts market with Maya artisans selling their wares.

### Quinta Avenida                               STREET
Restaurants, bars, stores and craft stalls line a 2km stretch of this busy pedestrian thoroughfare.

### Parque Fundadores                            SQUARE
(cnr 5 Av Sur & Av Juárez; ♿) **FREE** Playa del Carmen's most iconic park is bordered by the famous Quinta Avenida on one side and by a popular local beach on the other side. Here, kids can run around on the playground or try some Mexican treats at the row of fruit stands. In the afternoons, small crowds gather under the Portal Maya statue to enjoy the sunset.

### Museo Frida Kahlo Riviera Maya     MUSEUM
(☎984-980-05-95; www.museofridakahloriviera maya.org; 5 Av Norte s/n, cnr Calle 8; US$15; ⊙9am-11pm; 🅿) This 'museum' is mainly info *about* Kahlo rather than displays of her artwork. It's also small. But if you're looking for something to do on a non-beach day, you could come here and learn about one of Mexico's most famous icons.

## 🏖 Beaches

Avid beachgoers won't be disappointed here. Playa's lovely white-sand beaches are much more accessible than Cancún's: just head down to the ocean, stretch out and enjoy. Numerous restaurants front the beach in the tourist zone and many hotels in the area offer an array of water-sport activities.

If crowds aren't your thing, go north of Calle 38, where a few scrawny palms serve for shade. Here the beach extends for uncrowded kilometers, making for good camping, but you need to be extra careful with your belongings, as thefts are a possibility.

Some women go topless in Playa (though it's not common in most of Mexico, and is generally frowned upon by locals – except the young, of course). **Mamita's Beach**, north of Calle 28, is considered the best place to let loose and it's LGBTIQ+ friendly to boot.

About 3km south of the ferry terminal, past a group of all-inclusives, you'll find a refreshingly quiet stretch of beach that sees relatively few visitors.

### Punta Esmeralda                              BEACH
(via 5 Av Norte, just north of Calle 112 Norte; 🅿♿) **FREE** Emerald Point has become a favorite beach among Playa del Carmen locals, set on the northern edge of the city. Here, a shallow cenote provides a calm coastal pool where kids love to play, and the soft white sand beach is an idyllic spot to spread your beach towel for a day by the ocean.

## 🏃 Activities

In addition to great ocean diving, many outfits offer cenote dives. Prices are similar at most shops: two-tank dives (US$100), cenote dives (US$160), snorkeling (US$30), whale-shark tours (US$190) and open-water certification (US$450).

Playa used to be a fishing village, and you can still go out on small skiffs in search of kingfish, tarpon, barracuda and maybe even a sailfish. April to July is the best time.

A bike outing is a great way to discover outlying neighborhoods or visit a nearby cenote.

### ★Phocea Mexico                              DIVING
(☎984-873-12-10; www.phocea-mexico.com; Calle 10 Norte s/n; 2-tank dive incl gear US$95, cenote dives incl gear US$150; ⊙7:15am-9pm; ♿) French, English and Spanish are spoken at Phocea Mexico. The shop does dives with bull sharks (US$90) for advanced divers, usually from November to March.

### Cycling Journey                             CYCLING
(☎984-688-80-25; www.facebook.com/cycling journeyplaya; 10 Av Norte, btwn Calles 32 Norte & 34 Norte; rentals per day M$200-450; ⊙9am-8pm Mon-Sat) Bicycle shop with beach cruiser and mountain-bike rentals.

### Flora, Fauna y Cultura
### de México                              VOLUNTEERING
(☎984-871-52-89, cell 984-1880626; www.flora faunaycultura.org; Hwy 307 Km 282, Xcaret park office; ⊙9am-5pm Mon-Fri) 🌿 Contact this Xcaret-based organization to assist with conservation efforts at Playa Xcacel as turtles come ashore to lay their eggs. You can arrange a minimum one-month stay

RIVIERA MAYA PLAYA DEL CARMEN

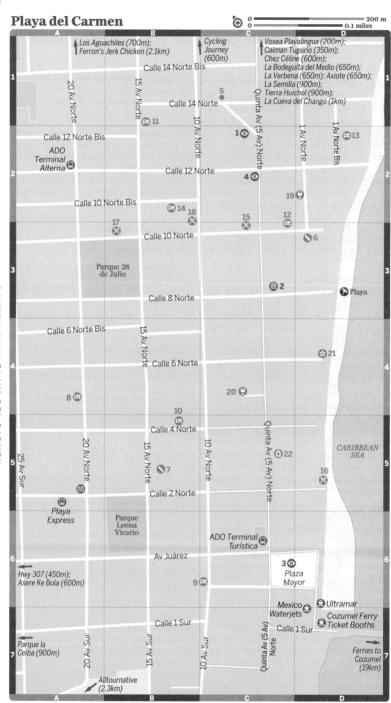

# Playa del Carmen

(M$2000) from May to October, which includes three daily meals and rustic lodging in a *palapa,* but you'll need to bring your own hammock. Volunteering for adults only.

You can also make arrangements to volunteer for one night (voluntary donation M$200) from June to August, which involves patrolling protected nesting grounds from 8pm to 5am.

**Yucatek Divers** DIVING
(☑984-803-13-63; www.yucatek-divers.com; 15 Av Norte s/n; 2-tank ocean/cavern dive incl gear US$115/160; ☺8am-5pm) Yucatek Divers has pretty good deals that include either ocean or cenote diving plus lodging at the nearby Mimi del Mar hotel. They even offer accessible diving for people with mobility needs.

**Punta Venado Bike Park** CYCLING
(☑998-206-31-45; www.pvbikepark.com; Hwy 307 Km 278; mountain biking from M$1100, horseback riding M$1200; ☺7am-4pm Tue-Sun) A sweet spot for mountain biking and horseback riding, Punta Venado lies about 11km south of Playa del Carmen and 1km further east of the highway. Bike trails of varying difficulty levels cut through a thick jungle to the coast, while a one-hour guided horseback tour makes stops at a swimmable cenote and sublime beach.

## 🐊 Courses

Playa has a couple of good language schools and you'll find plenty of people to practice Spanish with, especially if you venture out beyond the tourist center.

**International House Riviera Maya** LANGUAGE
(☑984-803-33-88; www.ihrivieramaya.com; Calle 14 Norte 141; per week US$230) Offers 20 hours of Spanish classes per week. You can stay in residence-hall rooms (US$26, no meals), even if you're not taking classes, but the best way to learn the language is to take advantage of the school's homestays (including breakfast, US$33 to US$39) with Mexican host families.

**Voxea Playalingua** LANGUAGE
(☑984-873-38-76; www.voxea-mx.com; Calle 20 Norte s/n; group/private classes per week US$230/400) Offers 20-hour-per-week Spanish classes in a group or privately, and occasionally has Mexican cooking courses.

## 🧭 Tours

**Río Secreto** ADVENTURE
(☑984-242-00-74; www.riosecreto.com; Carretera 307 Km 283.5; adult/child 4-12yr from US$79/40; ☺tours 9am-1pm) Hike and swim through a 1km-long underground cavern 5km south of Playa del Carmen. Some aspects are hyped, but there is a lot that is just plain awesome.

**Alltournative** ADVENTURE
(☑984-803-99-99; www.alltournative.com; Hwy 307 Km 287; tours per person US$139-149; ☺7am-9pm) Alltournative's packages include zip-lining, rappelling and kayaking, often combined with visits to archaeological sites, though most of these experiences are available on your own as well. But for those without transportation or who are on a tight schedule, this may be the best option. Snorkeling packages start at US$69. The office is out of the way; you're better off calling or reserving online.

RIVIERA MAYA PLAYA DEL CARMEN

## ✦ Festivals & Events

**Riviera Maya Jazz Festival**      MUSIC
(www.rivieramayajazzfestival.com; Playa del Carmen; ☻Nov) A three-day jazz fest on the beach featuring renowned international and local acts. It's usually held over the last week of November at Playa's Mamitas Beach.

## 🛏 Sleeping

Affordable budget and midrange hotels can be found within several blocks of the beach, and a number offer dorm-style lodging. High season runs from January to April, while 'super-high season' is around Christmas (when prices spike by as much as M$1000). Many rates are set in US dollars, and hotels should state the current exchange rate (*tipo de cambio*).

**Hostel 3B**      HOSTEL $
(☏984-803-29-01; www.hostel3b.com; Av 10 Sur s/n, cnr Calle 1 Sur; dm/r incl breakfast from M$180/690; ➔❄🛜≋) Known for its popular rooftop pool parties on Friday and Sunday, the electronic-music fiestas last until about 2am, something to consider if you value shut-eye. Conveniently close to the beach, bus and ferry terminals, 3B features clean, air-conditioned mixed dorms and colorful private rooms. Avoid booking rooftop rooms.

**The Yak Hostel**      HOSTEL $
(☏984-148-09-25; www.yakhostel.com; Calle 10 bis s/n; dm/r incl breakfast from M$280/800; ➔❄🛜) One of the cleanest and most comfortable hostels in town, this well-run property offers a variety of lodging options ranging from air-conditioned mixed dorms to 'deluxe' private digs with dining rooms and kitchens. Common areas include a rooftop terrace and a gravel courtyard with a fun bar scene.

**★Hotel Playa del Karma**   BOUTIQUE HOTEL $$
(☏984-803-02-72; hplayadelkarma@gmail.com; 15 Av Norte, btwn Calles 12 & 14; d M$1380; ➔❄🛜≋) The closest you're going to get to the jungle in this town; rooms here face a lush courtyard with a small – no, make that tiny – pool. All rooms have air-con and TV, sitting area and a sweet little porch with a hammock. The hotel arranges tours to nearby ruins and diving sites.

**Hotel Barrio Latino**      HOTEL $$
(☏984-873-23-84; www.hotelbarriolatino.com; Calle 4 Norte 153; r incl breakfast M$1200; ➔❄@🛜) Offers 18 clean rooms with warm,

rustic decor, good ventilation, ceiling fans or air-con, tiled floors and hammocks (in addition to beds). The place is often full and the front gate often locked. Discounted rates are available for extended stays, and the prices drop precipitously in low season. Guests get to make free international calls.

**Grand Velas**      RESORT $$$
(☏877-418-2963; www.rivieramaya.grandvelas. com; Hwy 307 Km 62; d all-inclusive from US$950; P➔❄❄🛜≋) The mother of all beach resorts, the sprawling Grand Velas boasts one of the best spas on the coast; an azure, free-form infinity pool; marble-floored rooms that put other so-called luxury accommodations to shame; loads of activities for kids and grown-ups; and the list goes on. It's 6km north of Playa del Carmen.

**Petit Lafitte**      RESORT $$$
(☏984-877-40-00; www.petitlafitte.com; Carretera Cancún–Chetumal Km 292; d/bungalow incl breakfast & dinner from US$370/515; P➔❄❄🛜≋) Occupying quiet Playa Xcalacoco, 6km north of Playa del Carmen, Petit Lafitte is an excellent and safe family vacation spot. Stay in a room or a 'bungalow' (essentially a wood cabin with tasteful rustic furnishings, some of which sleep up to five guests). Kids stay entertained with the large pool, small animal shelter, games room, paddleboards and other water activities.

**Casa de las Flores**      HOTEL $$$
(☏984-873-28-98; www.hotelcasadelasflores.com; 20 Av Norte 150; r incl breakfast from M$1600; ➔❄🛜≋) With a good mix of colonial charm and modern comfort, this sizable but intimate family-run hotel offers cheerful, colorful rooms set around a delightful plant-filled patio and pool area with hammocks.

**Kinbé Hotel**      HOTEL $$$
(☏984-873-04-41; www.kinbe.com; Calle 10 Norte s/n; r US$103-201; ➔❄🛜≋) An Italian-owned and -operated hotel, it has 29 clean, simple but elegant rooms with lovely aesthetic touches and a breezy rooftop terrace with fab views from the 3rd floor. Choose a room on the soothing 'water' side, which has an indoor pool and waterfall, or opt for the 'earth' side and surround yourself with lush vegetation.

**La Semilla**      B&B $$$
(☏984-147-32-34; www.hotellasemilla.com; Calle 38 Norte s/n; r incl breakfast from US$208; ➔❄🛜) Smallish rustic-chic rooms here are attrac-

## TOP CENOTES

Playa del Carmen makes a good base to explore the Riviera Maya's many cenotes, most of which are set in gorgeous jungles. Water activities at cenotes include swimming, snorkeling and diving in caves or caverns. Cave diving, which can be very dangerous, is for certified divers only and must be arranged through a dive shop.

**Parque Dos Ojos** (☑cell 984-1600906; www.parquedosojos.com; Hwy 307 Km 124; dives M$3000-5000, snorkeling M$400; ⊘8am-5pm) About 1km south of amusement park Xel-Há is the turnoff to the enormous Dos Ojos cave system. Operating as a sustainable tourism project by the local Maya community, Dos Ojos offers guided snorkeling tours of some amazing underwater caverns, where you float past illuminated stalactites and stalagmites in an eerie wonderland. For diving, you must go with a dive shop.

**Cenote Azul** (www.facebook.com/CenoteAzulRM; Highway 307, Km 266; adult/child 4-8yr M$100/60; ⊘8:30am-5:30pm; [P][🐕]) Conveniently located right off the main highway, Cenote Azul is one of the easiest Riviera Maya cenotes to visit. It's also one of the region's most spectacularly beautiful natural attractions. Leap off the small cliff into the clear waters at the deep end of the cenote, or spend the afternoon snorkeling among the rocks on the shallow side. Cash only. Optional life jackets and snorkel gear are available for rent. *Colectivos* run here from Playa Del Carmen.

**Cristalino Cenote** (☑cell 984-8043941; Hwy 307 Km 269; adult/child 3-12yr M$150/100, diving M$200; ⊘8am-6pm) On the west side of the highway, 23km south of Playa del Carmen, Cristalino is one of a series of wonderful cenotes. It's easily accessible, only about 70m from the entrance gate to the Barceló Maya Beach Resort, which is just off the highway. Great for diving (or just launching yourself off the rocks into the water below).

tively adorned with vintage objects purchased from flea markets and haciendas. At night guests mingle in a lush candlelit garden over complimentary wine or beer, and breakfast is served in the garden. Bikes are free for guests.

**Playa Palms**     BOUTIQUE HOTEL **$$$**
(☑984-803-39-08; www.playapalms.com; 1 Av Bis s/n; r/ste incl breakfast from US$185/224; [⊛][❄][@][🛜][🏊]) A rip-roaring deal in low season (get the best price online), Playa Palms is right on the beach. The shell-shaped rooms have balconies that look out to the ocean past the narrow, curly pool, or you can opt for the cheaper garden-view studio. Continental breakfast is delivered to your room.

## 🍴 Eating

Playa has a great range of dining choices, from cheap eats (away from the tourist center) to fancy date spots, to great regional and international food. Or hit the markets for some home-style regional cooking.

★ **Chez Céline**     BREAKFAST **$**
(☑984-803-34-80; www.chezceline.com.mx; cnr 5 Av Norte & Calle 34 Norte; breakfast M$34-118, lunch M$90-265; ⊘7:30am-11pm; [⊛][🛜][♿]) Good, healthy breakfasts (some vegan!) and a range of yummy baked goods are what keeps this French-run bakery-cafe busy. Savory croissants with smoked salmon or ham, cheese, and béchamel.

**Asere Ke Bola**     CUBAN **$**
(cnr Hwy 307 & Av Juárez; tacos & tortas M$13-25; ⊘7am-1pm) If you're pinching pesos, hit this mornings-only, Cuban-owned corner spot and try the tasty *torta de lechón,* a crunchy roast pork sandwich sprinkled with consommé and topped with pickled red onion; it's very hard to eat just one! Located in the Banorte parking lot.

**Kaxapa Factory**     SOUTH AMERICAN **$**
(☑984-803-50-23; www.kaxapa-factory.com; Calle 10 Norte s/n; mains M$75-165; ⊘8am-9pm Tue-Sun; [🛜][♿]) The specialty at this Venezuelan restaurant on the park is *arepas* (corn flatbread stuffed with your choice of shredded beef, chicken or beans and plantains). There are many vegetarian and gluten-free options here and the refreshing freshly made juices go nicely with just about everything on the menu.

**Ferron's Jerk Chicken**     JAMAICAN **$$**
(☑984-169-19-41; www.facebook.com/ferrons jerkchicken; Av 105 Norte 3, cnr Av Constituyentes; mains M$89-169; ⊘noon-6pm Tue-Sun; [🛜]) Venture out to the seldom-visited side of Playa

for some fine Jamaican jerk chicken and a cool reggae vibe. Combo meals include sweet-and-spicy grilled chicken, corn on the cob, coleslaw and a dinner roll. They also grill spicy pork ribs.

### ★La Cueva del Chango                    MEXICAN $$

(☑984-147-02-71; www.lacuevadelchango.com; Calle 38 Norte s/n, btwn Av 5 Norte & beach; breakfast M$62-138, lunch & dinner M$196-238; ☻8am-10:30pm Mon-Sat, to 2pm Sun; ☜) The 'Monkey's Cave,' known for its fresh and natural ingredients, has seating in a jungly *palapa* setting or a verdant garden out back. Service is friendly, but the kitchen can be slow. The food is delicious; try the *sopa de coco con camarones* (coconut milk with shrimp). Yum!

### Los Aguachiles                           SEAFOOD $$

(☑984-859-14-42; www.facebook.com/losagua chilesrm; Calle 34 Norte s/n; tostadas M$39-85, mains M$135-340; ☻12:30-9pm; ☜) Done up in Mexican cantina style yet with one big difference: the menu – consisting of tacos, *tostadas* and the like – was designed by a chef. The artfully prepared tuna *tostadas* found here won't be in any of the neighborhood watering holes.

### Babe's                                        FUSION $$

(☑984-879-35-69; www.babesnoodlesandbar.com; Calle 10 Norte s/n; mains M$168-228; ☻3-11:30pm Tue-Sun; ☜☑) Babe's serves some excellent Asian food, including a yummy home-style *tom kha gai* (chicken and coconut-milk soup) brimming with veggies. Vietnamese shrimp and rice noodles is another good one. Most dishes can be done vegetarian, and to mix things up a bit the Swedish owner has some tasty Korean and Indian items on the menu.

### Club Náutico Tarraya                  SEAFOOD $$

(La Tarraya; ☑984-149-42-17; www.facebook.com/tarrayaplaya; Calle 2 Norte 101; mains M$70-165; ☻noon-9pm; ☜) One of the few restaurants in Playa del Carmen that dates from the 1960s. It continues to offer good seafood at decent prices in a casual place on the beach with a nice view. Fish 'ala Tarraya' is a popular choice.

### ★Passion                                      BASQUE $$$

(☑984-877-39-00; www.passionbymb.com; 5 Av Norte, Paradisus Hotel; mains M$600-1100, tasting menu M$1950; ☻6-9:30pm Mon-Sat; ℗✲☜) With a French-Basque-inspired menu created by Michelin-starred-chef Martin Berastegui, this is unquestionably one of Playa's finest restaurants. Diners can order from the à la carte menu or opt for the exquisite seven-course tasting menu. Reserve ahead and dress appropriately for a meal served in an elegant dining room at the Paradisus Hotel.

### Axiote                                          MEXICAN $$$

(☑984-803-17-27; www.axiote.rest; Calle 34 Norte; mains M$230-268; ☻1:30-11pm) Putting a gourmet twist on tacos, tostadas and Mexican regional dishes, Axiote's diverse menu features creative treats like fish tacos with a sausage-avocado sauce and bone marrow topped with a refried bean and chili guajillo salsa. The casual *palapa* restaurant can get packed on weekends but there are some cool bars nearby if you need to kill some time.

### La Famiglia                                  ITALIAN $$$

(☑984-803-53-50; www.lafamiglia.mx; 10 Av Norte s/n, cnr Calle 10 Norte; mains M$140-550; ☻noon-11pm; ☜☑) Pay a visit to the family and enjoy superb wood-fired pizza and handmade pasta, ravioli and gnocchi. Playa is a magnet for Italian restaurants, but this definitely ranks among the best of them. Dairy-free, gluten-free and vegan options are all available.

## 🍸 Drinking & Entertainment

Playa is quite the party. You'll find everything from mellow, tranced-out lounge bars to thumping beachfront discos here. The fun generally starts on Quinta Avenida then heads down toward the beach on Calle 12.

### ★Fusion                                       LIVE MUSIC

(☑cell 984-1478420; www.facebook.com/fusion beachbarcuisine; Calle 6 Norte s/n; ☻8am-2am) This beachside bar and grill stages live music, along with a fun belly-dancing and fire-dancing show. The fire-dancing comes later in the evening (around 11:30pm). From 6pm on it's a cool spot to have a beer or cocktail and listen to rock, reggae and Latin sounds.

### Dirty Martini Lounge                        BAR

(www.facebook.com/dirtymartinilounge; 1 Av Norte 234; ☻noon-2am Sun-Thu, to 3am Fri & Sat) No foam machine, no mechanical bull and there's minimal nudity – a refreshing change for crazy Playa. The decor is something you'd find in the American West, with comfy cowhide upholstery and brown wooden panels, with a dance space and live music by locally popular bands.

## 🏃 Walking Tour
## Playa del Carmen Bar Crawl

**START** FUSION
**END** CORNER OF 1 AVENIDA NORTE AND
CALLE 12 NORTE
**LENGTH** 2.5KM; 5½ HOURS

Get things rolling at beach bar **1 Fusion** (p114) at around 10:30pm. Grab one of the candlelit tables on the sand and chat it up over drinks and live music. Stick around for at least an hour so as not to miss a cool fire-dance show on the beach.

After watching the fire dancers doing their thing, head up Calle 6 Norte, then turn right at 1 Avenida Norte and walk about 400m north to the next stop, **2 Dirty Martini Lounge** (p114). Order a round of martinis (shaken not stirred) and chill out in one of Playa's coolest bars, where you can grab the karaoke mic if you're feeling inspired by some liquid courage.

Next, after quite possibly embarrassing yourself, walk one block east and hang a right on pedestrian thoroughfare Quinta Avenida (5 Av). It's about a 1km stroll north along the Avenida to reach Calle 34 Norte, where you're

going to turn left and walk a half-block to **3 La Verbena** (p116), one of Playa's classic live music bars. At this hour, you probably won't find a table but you can bounce around to the reggae beats.

Once you've had your fill of live tunes, make your way over to **4 La Bodeguita del Medio** (p116) for some late-night salsa grooves. It's just a stumble or two away from La Verbena, 60m north along Quinta Avenida. Get into the Cuban spirit with a round of mojitos, then step onto the dance floor and show off your best salsa moves.

After lights out at the Bodeguita, make your way back toward the starting point of the bar crawl. At this juncture you can return to Dirty Martini Lounge for a nightcap, or you can hit the nearby corner of 1 Avenida Norte and Calle 12 Norte, where you'll find an after-hours street party and thumping night-clubs competing for decibel levels. Or simply call it a night.

### La Verbena
LIVE MUSIC

(🗷cell 984-128-99-91; www.facebook.com/laver benaplaya; Calle 34 Norte s/n; ⊙6pm-2am) The self-proclaimed 'Fine Music House' hosts a wide range of live music, from hip-shaking *cumbias* (music originating from Colombia) to reggae and ska beats. On warm nights, it can get downright steamy in the back room where the bands play, but you'll forget about it after swigging down some cold beers.

### La Bodeguita del Medio
DANCING

(🗷984-803-39-50; www.labodeguitadelmedio.com. mx; 5 Av Norte s/n, cnr Calle 34 Norte; ⊙6pm-1am; 🛜) The writing is literally on the walls (and on the lampshades, and pretty much every-where) at this Cuban restaurant-bar. After a few mojitos you'll be dancing the night away to live *cubana* music.

### Playa 69
GAY

(www.facebook.com/sesentaynueveplaya; off 5 Av Norte, btwn Calles 4 & 6 Norte; cover after 10pm from M$60; ⊙9pm-4am Wed-Sun) This popu-lar gay dance club proudly features foreign strippers from such far-flung places as Australia and Brazil, and it stages weekend drag-queen shows. It may also open Tues-days at key vacation times. Find it at the end of the narrow alley.

### Caiman Tugurio
BAR

(🗷984-147-16-95; www.facebook.com/caiman tugurio24; Calle 24 Norte; ⊙9pm-2am) Kind of hard to find in Playa – a bar with cool mu-sic where you can just go for a few relaxed drinks. No cover, no dance floor, just a great place to chill with friends.

## 🛍 Shopping

### Tierra Huichol
ARTS & CRAFTS

(🗷984-803-59-54; www.tierrahuichol.com; 5 Av Norte s/n, btwn Calles 38 & 40; ⊙10am-11pm) Tierra Huichol's Playa del Carmen store sells intricate yarn art and colorful beaded ani-mal figurines crafted by indigenous Huichol artists from the Pacific coast states of Jalisco and Nayarit. International delivery service available.

### Artemanos
ARTS & CRAFTS

(🗷984-803-12-72; www.facebook.com/artemanos artemexicano; 5 Av Norte; ⊙9am-11pm) A small store along the Quinta Avenida where you can pick up *alebrijes* (colorful wooden animal figures) from Oaxaca, silver jewelry and bead and yarn art crafted by indigenous Huicholes.

## ℹ Information

### EMERGENCY
**Ambulance, Fire & Police** (🗷911, 🗷066)

### MEDICAL SERVICES
**Hospiten** (🗷984-159-22-00; www.hospiten. com; Hwy 307 s/n, in front of Centro Maya; ⊙24hr) A private hospital south on Hwy 307.

**Playa International Clinic** (🗷984-803-12-15, cell 984-1088180; www.facebook.com/playa internationalclinic; 10 Av Norte s/n, cnr Calle 28; ⊙24hr) Excellent medical clinic with on-site hyberbaric chamber. The door may be locked but it is staffed 24 hours.

### MONEY
There are many ATMs and money exchange offices around town.

**Bancomer** (Av Juárez s/n, cnr 25 Av Norte; ⊙8:30am-4pm Mon-Fri, 9:30am-2pm Sat)

**Banorte** (10 Av Norte s/n, cnr Calle 8 Norte; ⊙8:30am-4pm Mon-Fri, 9am-2pm Sat)

**Scotiabank** (Av Constituyentes 39, cnr Av 10 Norte; ⊙8:30am-4pm Mon-Fri)

### POST
**Post Office** (cnr 20 Av Norte & Calle 2 Norte; ⊙8am-4pm Mon-Fri, 9am-1pm Sat)

### SAFE TRAVEL
Playa is generally safe: you are unlikely to expe-rience street crime or muggings unless you are looking for drugs or hang out with dealers/users. However, pickpockets do circulate, es-pecially in crowded dance clubs. Run-and-grab thefts while victims are swimming or sleeping, especially on the isolated beaches to the north, are not unheard of.

Note that you should not purchase drugs on the street or be seen talking to street dealers: spending time with these types can be inter-preted by either police or gangs as you being involved, marking you for interrogation or mug-ging and you want to avoid both.

## ℹ Getting There & Around

### BOAT
Passenger ferries depart frequently to Cozumel from Calle 1 Sur, where you'll find two companies with **ticket booths** (Av 1 Sur s/n, cnr Calle 1 Sur). Prices are subject to change. The **Calica-Punta Venado terminal** (Terminal Marítima Punta Venado; Hwy 307 Km 282), 8km south of Playa, operates car ferries to Cozumel.

**Winjet** (🗷984-872-15-88; www.winjet.mx; Av 1 Sur s/n; one-way adult/child 6-11yr M$170/110; ⊙8am-10pm) Online promotions can bring fares down by about 20% for all travelers.

**Transcaribe** (🗷987-872-76-71; www.trans caribe.net; Hwy 307 Km 282, Calica–Punta

Venado; one-way M$500) Daily car ferries to Cozumel. One-way fare includes passengers.

**Ultramar** (☑998-881-58-90, 998-293-90-92; www.ultramarferry.com/en; Av 1 Sur s/n; one-way adult/child 6-11yr M$220/140; ⏱7am-11pm) The most spiffy of the ferries, and claims to be the least prone to causing seasickness. Offers a 1st-class option with a lounge, more room, priority boarding and leather seats. Also operates car ferries from the Calica–Punta Venado terminal.

### BUS

Playa has two bus terminals; each sells tickets and provides information for at least some of the other's departures. You can save money by buying a 2nd-class bus ticket, but remember that it's often stop-and-go along the way.

The **ADO Terminal Alterna** (www.ado.com.mx; 20 Av Norte s/n, cnr Calle 12; ⏱24hr) is where most long-distance bus lines arrive and depart. Buses heading to destinations within the state of Quintana Roo leave from the **ADO Terminal Turística** (Terminal del Centro; www.ado.com.mx; 5 Av Norte s/n, cnr Av Juárez; ⏱24hr).

**Playa Express** (Calle 2 Norte s/n) shuttle buses are a much quicker way to get around the Riviera Maya between Playa del Carmen and Cancún. It has frequent service to Puerto Morelos (M$28, 40 minutes) and downtown Cancún (M$42, 1¼ hours).

### COLECTIVO

**Colectivos** (Calle 2 Norte s/n, cnr 20 Av; ⏱5am-11:30pm) are a great option for cheap travel southward to Tulum (M$45) and north to Cancún (M$42). They depart as soon as

they fill (about every 15 minutes) and will stop anywhere along the highway between Playa and Tulum. Luggage space is somewhat limited, but *colectivos* are great for day trips. There are also daily departures to Isla Holbox (M$250) between 8:30am and 6:30pm. Local trips around Playa cost M$15.

## Akumal

☑984 / POP 1300

Still famous for its beautiful beach and large, swimmable lagoon, Akumal (Place of the Turtles) does attract turtles, though in far fewer numbers than before due to the massive development that has encroached on nearly all of their nesting grounds. This is one of the Yucatán Peninsula's oldest resort areas and consists primarily of pricey hotels, condominiums and residential developments (occupied mostly by Americans and Canadians) on nearly 5km of wide beach bordering four consecutive bays, and it's difficult to access any of the beach (they even wall off the few places where the ocean would otherwise be visible). If you're looking to speak English and hang out with expats, Akumal won't disappoint, and the bars and food are above average.

Most sights and facilities are reached by taking the first turnoff, Playa Akumal, as you come south on the highway. It's about 500m from the highway to the entrance.

### BUSES FROM PLAYA DEL CARMEN

| DESTINATION | FARE (M$) | TIME (HR) | FREQUENCY (PER DAY) |
| --- | --- | --- | --- |
| Cancún | 79 | 1-1¼ | frequent |
| Cancún International Airport | 206 | 1 | frequent |
| Chetumal | 398 | 4½-5½ | frequent |
| Chichén Itzá | 194 | 3-4 | 3 (7:30am, 8am & 9:30am) |
| Cobá | 164 | 2 | frequent |
| Laguna Bacalar | 376 | 4-4½ | frequent |
| Mahahual | 414 | 4-4½ | 2 (8:05am & 5:55pm) |
| Mérida | 503-756 | 4¼-5¾ | frequent |
| Palenque | 986-1178 | 11½-12 | 7 |
| San Cristóbal de las Casas | 726-1216 | 20-21 | 6 |
| Tulum | 89 | 1 | frequent |
| Valladolid | 252 | 2½-3½ | frequent |

## 🏃 Activities

Increasing population is taking its toll on the reefs, but diving remains the primary attraction. For snorkeling, Laguna Yal-Kú is good value but can get crowded.

Beach access in the center costs M$100, which includes access to toilets, showers and a very swimmable beach. The hotel zone has limited free beach access.

Close to shore you'll have no problems with currents, though the surf can get rough.

### ★ Laguna Yal-Kú                    SWIMMING
(☏984-875-90-65; www.facebook.com/yalku; Yal-Kú Lagoon; adult/child 4-12yr US$14/10, snorkel gear US$12, locker US$3; ⊙9am-5pm; ♿) Located 2km north of the Playa Akumal entrance, this beautiful and rocky lagoon is, without a doubt, one of the region's highlights. It runs about 500m from its beginning to the sea and is home to large schools of brightly colored fish, and the occasional visiting turtle.

Showers, parking and bathrooms are included in the admission price, and you can rent snorkel gear. Taxis from the Playa Akumal entrance charge about M$100 to the lagoon. In an effort to protect the lagoon's fragile environment, sunblock is prohibited.

### Akumal Dive Shop                    DIVING
(☏984-875-90-32; www.akumaldiveshop.com; 1-/2-tank dive US$53/100, snorkeling US$50; ⊙8am-5pm) Dive trips and deep-sea fishing excursions are offered by Akumal Dive Shop, at the town entrance. It also does snorkeling trips to the reef and remote beaches, and it rents catamarans.

## 🛏 Sleeping

You'll find a bunch of houses for rent on www.akumalvacations.com, or you can check out one of the area's hotels, which are generally quite expensive. Across the highway lies the village of Akumal, which has very low-cost rooms that have thin walls and may possibly be shared with hourly-rate visitors.

### Que Onda                    HOTEL $$$
(☏984-875-91-01; www.facebook.com/queonda akumal; Caleta Yalkú Lote 97; d/q M$1800/2000; P✦🌐✉) Relatively affordable by Akumal standards, Que Onda has quiet, pleasant rooms overlooking a lush garden with a large pool and one of the best restaurants in town. A large two-story room sleeps four people.

### Del Sol Beachfront                    HOTEL $$$
(☏984-875-90-60; www.delsolbeachfront.com; coast road s/n; r/apt from US$129/190; P✦❄🌐✉) Del Sol looks more like Del Taco headquarters with its bright multicolored paint. The compact rooms come with beach-view patios or balconies, or you can opt for more spacious studios and two-bedroom condos. The hotel rents bikes as well (per hour US$8).

### Villa Las Brisas                    HOTEL $$$
(☏984-875-92-63, cell 984-1163985; villalasbri-sas@hotmail.com; off Hwy 307; r US$100-180, apt US$137-228; P✦❄🌐) On the beach in Aventuras Akumal, this is an attractive, modern place with two hotel-type rooms, some one- and two-bedroom condos and a studio apartment – all under two roofs. Room prices vary greatly by category and season. The friendly owners Horacio and Kersten speak five languages. The turnoff is 3km south of the turnoff for Playa Akumal.

## 🍴 Eating & Drinking

Just outside the entrance to Playa Akumal are two minimarkets that stock a reasonable selection for self-caterers. Restaurants here see many expats and foreign tourists and the prices reflect that, but the quality is fairly high.

### ★ Turtle Bay Café & Bakery                    CAFE $$
(☏984-875-91-38; www.turtlebaycafe.com; Plaza Ukana 1; mains M$105-275; ⊙7am-9pm; P🌐✐) A popular breakfast spot, this appealing cafe slings a wide variety of gringo comfort food ranging from breakfast burritos to eggs Benedict. The lunch and dinner menu include sourdough flatbread pizzas, burgers and tasty fish and seafood options, such as *pescado negro* (blackened fish). It's near the town entrance. There's also a full bar.

### La Cueva del Pescador                    SEAFOOD $$
(☏984-875-90-02; mains M$130-240; ⊙noon-9pm; P🌐) Near the town's entrance, this popular foreigners' hangout does good grilled fish dishes and shrimp tacos in a casual atmosphere with outdoor seating. Cash only.

### La Buena Vida                    BAR
(☏984-875-90-61; www.labuenavidarestaurant.com; coast road lote 35; ⊙8am-11pm; 🌐) A popular beachside restaurant-bar with sand floors, swings and a drink menu with gimmicky cocktail names such as 'The Viagra,' which offers you 'a stiff one.' The restaurant (mains M$85 to M$240) is very good here as well, with popular items such as the *Tic kin xic* fish (grilled fish in a Yucatecan sauce, M$160).

# Tulum

📞 984 / POP 32,700

Tulum's spectacular coastline – with all its confectioner-sugar sands, cobalt water and balmy breezes – makes it one of the top beaches in Mexico. Where else can you get all that *and* a dramatically situated Maya ruin? There's also excellent cave and cavern diving, fun cenotes and a variety of lodgings and restaurants to fit every budget.

Some may be put off by the fact that the town center, where the really cheap eats and sleeps are found, sits right on the highway, making the main drag feel more like a truck stop than a tropical paradise. But rest assured that if Tulum Pueblo isn't to your liking, you can always head to the coast and find that tranquil, beachside bungalow, though it's gonna cost you.

Exploring Tulum's surrounding areas pays big rewards: there's the massive Reserva de la Biosfera Sian Ka'an, secluded fishing village Punta Allen and the ruins of Cobá.

## History

Most archaeologists believe that Tulum was occupied during the late post-Classic period (1200–1521 CE) and that it was an important port town during its heyday. The Maya sailed up and down this coast, maintaining trading routes all the way down into Belize. When Juan de Grijalva sailed past in 1518, he was amazed by the sight of the walled city, its buildings painted a gleaming red, blue and yellow and a ceremonial fire flaming atop its seaside watchtower.

The ramparts that surround three sides of Tulum (the fourth side being the sea) leave little question as to its strategic function as a fortress. Several meters thick and 3m to 5m high, the walls protected the city during a period of considerable strife between Maya city-states. Not all of Tulum was situated within the walls. The vast majority of the city's residents lived outside them; the civic-ceremonial buildings and palaces likely housed Tulum's ruling class.

The city was abandoned about 75 years after the Spanish conquest. It was one of the last of the ancient cities to be abandoned; most others had been given back to nature long before the arrival of the Spanish. But Maya pilgrims continued to visit over the years, and indigenous refugees from the War of the Castes took shelter here from time to time.

'Tulum' is Maya for 'wall,' though its residents called it Zama (Dawn). The name Tulum was apparently applied by explorers during the early-20th century.

Once a small fishing town, present-day Tulum is growing fast: since 2006 the population has more than doubled and city limits continue to expand. The Zona Hotelera, once quiet and peaceful, is now full of glitz and glamour, with people there to be seen (and take selfies). Development has even run deep into the coastline of the Sian Ka'an Biosphere Reserve, as property owners sell and people put up mansions. For a trip back in time to a Tulum of 'yesterdecade,' pick up a copy of *Sunsets of Tulum*, a literary novel set in a Tulum circa 2007.

## ⊙ Sights

★ **Tulum Ruins**                          ARCHAEOLOGICAL SITE
(www.inah.gob.mx; Hwy 307 Km 230; M$75, early/late M$255, parking M$180, tours from M$700; ⊙ 6:30am-8am, 8am-5pm, 5:30-7pm; P) The ruins of Tulum preside over a rugged coastline, a strip of brilliant beach and green-and-turquoise waters that'll leave you floored. It's true the extents and structures are of a modest scale and the late-post-Classic design is

Tulum Ruins ⊛

inferior to those of earlier, more grandiose projects – but, wow! Those Maya occupants must have felt pretty smug each sunrise!

You can see (at a premium price) the sunrise yourself on a sunrise tour. Late-risers may prefer the sunset tour, though the sun sets over the jungle, not the sea. Tulum is a prime destination for large tour groups. To best enjoy the ruins without feeling like part of the herd, you should visit them early in the morning, another benefit of the sunrise tour. A train (M$55) takes you to the ticket booth from the entrance, or just hoof the 500m. You'll find cheaper parking (M$50 to M$100) just east of the main parking lot, along the old entrance road. There's a less-used southern foot entrance from the beach road.

★ SFER IK    GALLERY
(www.sferik.art; Carretera Tulum-Boca Paila Km 5; ⊙noon-6pm) FREE In this mind-bending contemporary-art gallery at Azulik resort, guests enter barefoot to interact with floors of polished concrete and *bejuco* (vine-like wood) as living organisms. Opened by the great-grandson of art collector Peggy Guggenheim, the dreamlike exhibition space of meandering expanses was conceived so viewers could experience art alongside Tulum's natural elements, all under geometrically patterned wood domes.

An adjacent 12m dome, an impressive architectural feat built according to ancient geometric principles, can be viewed here as well, but by appointment only.

## 🏃 Activities

You'll find many shops offering their services for reef dives, as well as cavern and cave dives (a big draw in Tulum's surrounding areas). Keep in mind that cave diving can be extremely dangerous and should only be attempted with proper certification. Even with certification, always dive with professionals who are familiar with the cave systems.

The spectacular Cenote Angelita (Hwy 307 Km 213; cenote dives M$300; snorkeling M$200; ⊙7am-5pm) is most notable to divers for the unique, curious, even eerie layer of hydrogen sulfide that 'fogs' the water about halfway through the descent. Look up and see the sunlight filtering down through ancient submerged tree branches that are wonderfully creepy – like outstretched witches' arms. The dive is deep and should only be done by experienced divers; make arrangements through a dive center.

### EXPLORING TULUM RUINS

Visitors are required to follow a prescribed route around the ruins. From the ticket booth, head north along nearly half the length of Tulum's enormous wall, which measures approximately 380m south to north and 170m along its sides. The tower at the corner, once thought to be a guard post, is now believed by some to have been a type of shrine. Rounding the corner, you enter the site through a breach in the north wall.

Once inside, head east toward the Casa del Cenote, named for the small sinkhole at its southern base. Next, walk south toward the bluff holding the Templo del Dios del Viento (Temple of the Wind God), which provides excellent views of El Castillo juxtaposed with the sea below.

Below the Wind God's hangout is a lovely little beach (roped off at last visit). Next, head west to Estructura 25, known for its lovely stucco frieze of the Descending God.

South of Estructura 25 lies El Palacio, notable for its X-figure ornamentation. From there, head east back toward the water and skirt the outside edge of the central temple complex (keeping it to your right). Along the back are some good sea views. Heading inland again on the south side, you can enter the complex through a corbeled archway past the restored Templo de la Estela (Templo of the Stela), where Stela 1, now in the British Museum, was found.

At the heart of the complex you can admire Tulum's tallest building, a watchtower named El Castillo (The Castle) by the Spaniards. Note the Descending God in the middle of its facade. South of the Castillo you'll find steps leading down to a (usually very crowded) beach, where you can go for a swim.

After some beach time, heading west toward the exit will take you to the two-story Templo de las Pinturas, constructed in several stages around 1400 to 1450 CE.

As you wander the grounds, you may see ring-tailed coatis and iguanas out and about.

Snorkeling and swimming from the beach are possible and fun, but be extra careful of boat traffic (a dive flag is a good idea), as the strip between the beach and reef offshore is traveled by dive boats and fishers. If there's a heavy wind onshore, strong currents can develop on the lee side of the reef. Inexperienced swimmers should stay close to shore.

**Xibalba Dive Center**                    DIVING
(☑984-8712953; www.xibalbadivecenter.com; Andromeda Oriente 7, btwn Libra Sur & Geminis Sur; 1-/2-cavern dive incl gear US$100/160) One of the best dive shops in Tulum, Xibalba is known for its safety-first approach to diving. The center specializes in cave and cavern diving, visiting sites such as Dos Ojos and the spooky Cenote Angelita. Xibalba doubles as a hotel (rooms from US$100) and offers attractive packages combining lodging, diving trips and courses.

**I Bike Tulum**                    CYCLING
(☑984-802-55-18; www.ibiketulum.com; Av Cobá Sur, btwn Sol Oriente & Gama Oriente; per day bicycle M$150-250, scooter M$670; ☉8:30am-5:30pm Mon-Sat) Rents beach cruisers with lock and helmet. Or, if you prefer, a scooter. Vehicle rentals require a hefty deposit, either cash or an important ID.

**Sian Kite Watersports**                    KITESURFING
(☑WhatsApp only 984-185-11-51; www.facebook.com/siankitetulum; Papaya Playa Project hotel, Carretera Tulum-Boca Paila Km 4.5; surfing/kiteboarding lessons per hr M$40/80; ☉9am-5pm) Offers one-hour introductory kiteboarding lessons (if you can round up other people you'll save some pesos by paying a cheaper group rate). You can also take surfing classes here. It's at Papaya Playa Project, which is 3km southeast of the Avenida Tulum–Cobá intersection and about 500m south of the coast road T-junction.

**Salsa Sunday**                    DANCING
(☑cell 984-1154726; www.lazebratulum.com; Hotel La Zebra, Carretera Tulum-Boca Paila Km 8.2; ☉6:30-11pm Sun) **FREE** Take free salsa dancing lessons at 6:30pm at beachside hotel-restaurant La Zebra, then strut your stuff with live salsa music from 8pm to 11pm. It's a festive Sunday tradition in Tulum.

## ☞ Tours

**Uyo Ochel Maya**                    TOURS
(☑WhatsApp only 983-1248001; Muyil; adult/child M$900/600, parking M$50; ☉8am-4pm) Tour

Chunyaxche and Muyil lagoons and swim in a centuries-old Maya canal. It's a lovely way to see the second-largest lagoon in Quintana Roo, and the mangroves harbor orchids, saprophytes and numerous birds. To reach the lagoon shore by car, turn down a dirt road about 250m south of the Muyil archaeological site.

**Community Tours Sian Ka'an**                    ECOTOUR
(☑984-871-22-02, cell 984-1140750; www.siankaantours.org; Osiris Sur, cnr Sol Oriente; tours per person US$85-125; ☉7am-9pm) ✐ Runs various excursions to the magnificent **Reserva de la Biosfera Sian Ka'an** (Sian Ka'an Biosphere Reserve; M$36; ☉sunrise-sunset), which include birdwatching tours, visiting Maya ruins, swimming in an ancient canal or kayaking. Community Tours is a sustainable tourism project run by locals from Maya communities.

## ☆☆ Festivals & Events

**Sound Tulum**                    MUSIC
(www.soundtulum.com; ☉late Dec & early Jan) A two-week-long music festival drawing top international names in the underground electronic music scene. .

## 🛏 Sleeping

The biggest decision, aside from budget, is whether to stay in the town center or out along the beach. Both have their advantages: most of the daytime action happens at the beach or ruins, while at night people tend to hang at restaurants and bars in town.

You'll find better deals in town, where hostels and midrange options abound.

## 🛏 Tulum Pueblo

Unless you're up for a long walk, if you stay in the town center you'll have to take a taxi, bike or *colectivo* to the beach. If you crave sand and surf, consider staying along the Zona Hotelera. Many hotels and hostels have a morning beach drop-off shuttle, but getting back you'll probably have to grab a cab or *colectivo*.

**Lum Hostal**                    HOSTEL $
(☑984-160-04-21; www.facebook.com/lumhostal; Alfa Norte, cnr Sagitario Poniente; dm/d M$500/1500; ◒🛜) This spiffy, clean, well-run hostel in the town center offers modern rooms and six-bed dorms with polished concrete floors, air-con, common kitchen and bar areas, and, best of all, free bikes to get to the beach and ruins.

# Tulum

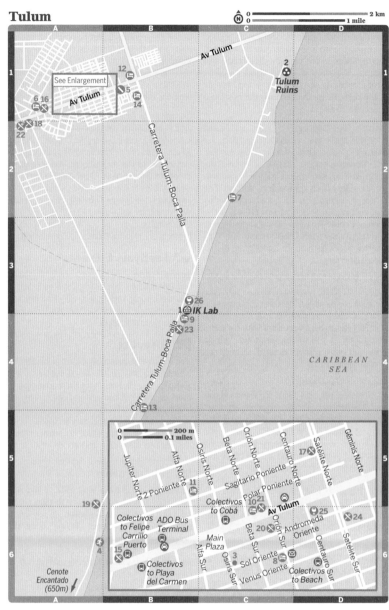

RIVIERA MAYA TULUM

**Hotel Kin-Ha**  HOTEL **$$**
(📞 984-871-23-21; www.hotelkinha.com; Orión
Sur s/n, btwn Sol Oriente & Venus Oriente; d incl
breakfast US$246-276; 🅿 ❄ ❋ 🛜) A small Ital-
ian- and Mexican-owned hotel with pleasant
rooms surrounding a small courtyard with
hammocks.

The location is ideal – the bus stop for
*colectivos* going to the beach is right around
the corner.

At last visit, Kin-Ha was still renovating
rooms and planning to install a rooftop hot
tub and bar.

# Tulum

### Casa Abanico
HOTEL $$

(☑984-160-01-25; www.facebook.com/casaaban ico.tulum; Tauro Poniente, cnr Av Kukulkán; d/q US$55/70; ☕🖭🛜) Just a few blocks from the main drag, this appealing little hotel has six welcoming rooms surrounded by pretty gardens with gravel paths. Guests have use of free bikes and an open-air common kitchen. If available, the thatch-roofed rooms upstairs have a bit more character than the ones below. The staff here are genuinely nice.

### ★ L'Hotelito
HOTEL $$$

(☑984-160-02-29; www.hotelitotulum.com; Av Tulum, btwn Beta & Orión; d incl breakfast US$100-150; ☕🖭@🛜) Brick and wood boardwalks pass through a jungle-like side patio to generous, breezy rooms at this character-packed, Italian-run hotel. The attached restaurant does good breakfasts, too. Two rooms upstairs come with wide balconies, but they also catch more street noise from the main strip down below. Towels are twisted into the shape of rabbits or swans. Check online for discounts.

### Teetotum
BOUTIQUE HOTEL $$$

(☑cell 984-1438956; www.hotelteetotum.com; Av Cobá Sur 2; r incl breakfast US$200; ☕🖭🛜🖼) There are just four stylish rooms in this hip boutique hotel. Common areas include a sundeck upstairs, a plunge pool just below and an excellent restaurant. It's a bit over-priced as it's not on the beach, but it has free bikes. It's 200m south of Avenida Tulum. Rates can drop to around US$110 at times.

## 🛏 Zona Hotelera

Gone are the days when you could bring a hammock and string it up in a hut for less than M$80. You can still find rustic, but it comes with a non-rustic price tag. Quality and price are so varied here that it's best to look around before you decide. Bedbugs, sand fleas and mosquitoes are all a possibility. Bring repellent or consider burning a mosquito coil near your door. Nights can be very cold if there's a breeze blowing.

### Cenote Encantado
CAMPGROUND $

(☑WhatsApp only 55-30282253; www.cenoteen cantado.com; Carretera Tulum–Boca Paila Km 10.5; tents per person M$500, treehouse US$120, camp-sites M$350; ☕) A rare budget option near the beach, this new-agey spot gets its name from a pretty cenote right in the campground's backyard. Guests stay in large tents with beds, rugs and nightstands, and there's a yoga and meditation room too. It's not on the beach, but you can walk there. Rates increase in December and January.

Though the area is set to get electricity, water, and (yep!) fiber-optic internet, the venerable 'Juicycle' blender-bike isn't going to the trash heap just yet. They've

RIVIERA MAYA TULUM

put some rocks in the cenote, and you can swim, kayak or snorkel here surrounded by nature, including iguanas, birds, and land crabs. It's 6.5km south of the T-junction, near the Reserva de la Biosfera Sian Ka'an entrance.

**Mango Tulum** HOTEL **$$**
(📞55-1204-0339; www.mangotulum.com; Polar Poniente, cnr Av Cobá; r from US$55; ➌❄️🛜🏊) A quiet, comfortable and relaxing mid-range stay with minimalist rooms overlooking a swimming pool and lush garden fitted with picnic benches. Ruins, cenotes and a supermarket are all nearby, and it lies just a block from the beach access road. Do not confuse it with Casa Mango, on the road to Cobá.

**★La Posada del Sol** BOUTIQUE HOTEL **$$$**
(📞cell 984-1348874; www.laposadadelsol.com; Carretera Tulum–Boca Paila Km 3.5; r incl breakfast US$300; ➌🛜) 🌱 Using recycled objects found on the property after a hurricane, Posada del Sol stands out for its natural design details and creative architecture. All 11 rooms have air-con, but the pricier ones on the beach side of the road usually catch a nice ocean breeze. The solar- and wind-powered hotel has a sweet beach and a great crafts store too.

Rooms do not have TVs. The hotel works with local turtle-nesting organizations, too. It's just before the much larger Marina del Sol hotel.

**Posada Margherita** HOTEL **$$$**
(📞WhatsApp only 984-8018493; www.posadamargherita.com; Carretera Tulum–Boca Paila Km 4.5; d US$200-300; ➌🛜) This is a beautiful spot right in the center of the Hotel Zone, with the beach just steps away. The restaurant below makes incredible food using fresh, local, organic ingredients. All rooms have good bug screening, 24-hour lights and a terrace or balcony, some with hammocks. Cash only.

**Diamante K** CABAÑAS **$$$**
(📞cell 984-8762115; www.diamantek.com; Carretera Tulum–Boca Paila Km 2.5; cabin US$250, ste US$700-800; 🅿️➌🛜) Diamante K is one of those spots that really can't be any closer to the beach. Its nine cabins have a shared bathroom and thus remain relatively affordable; all rooms are lovely, with hammocks, incredible ocean views, palm trees, and almost Tolkienesque accents and decor.

## 🍴 Eating

Tulum is ritzy and glitzy and ever-more shallow, but one good reason to come here is the food. The town has everything from cheap tourist food to high-end cuisine, all of it tasty, with lots of Italian and international options if you need a break from Yucatecan. Be aware that many of the restaurants in the Zona Hotelera cannot accept credit cards because they're off the grid. Most hotel restaurants welcome nonguests.

## 🍴 Tulum Pueblo

**★Taquería Honorio** TACOS **$**
(📞984-134-87-31; www.facebook.com/taqueriahonorio; Satélite Sur; tacos M$16-22, tortas M$35-40; ⏰6am-2pm) It began as a street stall and became such a hit that it's now a taco place with a proper roof overhead. Most folks go here for the *cochinita* (pulled pork in annatto marinade) served on handmade tortillas or *tortas* (sandwiches). Also well worth seeking out here are Yucatecan classics like *relleno negro* (shredded turkey in a chili-based dark sauce).

**Antojitos la Chiapaneca** TACOS **$**
(📞984-112-32-49; Av Tulum, cnr Acuario Norte; tacos & antojitos M$8-18, tortas M$20-28; ⏰9am-11pm Tue-Sun) A good, cheap option to get your taco fix. You'll often have to wait for a table at this popular spot, or simply belly up to the counter. In addition to *al pastor* (spit-roasted marinated pork) tacos, the Chiapaneca does tasty Yucatecan snacks, such as *panuchos* (fried tortillas with beans and toppings) and *salbutes* (similar to *panuchos* sans beans).

**La Gloria de Don Pepe** TAPAS **$$**
(📞cell 984-1524471; www.facebook.com/lagloriadedonpepe; Orión Sur, cnr Andromeda Oriente; tapas M$60-210; ⏰2-11pm Tue-Sun) With its 'A meal without wine is called breakfast' sign, this spot tickles the taste buds with delicious tapas plates and fine seafood paella. And wine – did we mention there's wine? A perfect place to come to talk to a friend for a couple of hours without being drowned out by noise. Alfresco seating is also possible.

**Barracuda** SEAFOOD **$$**
(📞984-160-03-25; www.facebook.com/barracudatulum.qr; Av Tulum, cnr Luna Norte; mains M$90-180, seafood platter M$490; ⏰9am-11pm; 🛜) A very popular seafood eatery at the south end of the center, known for its *parillada de mariscos*,

a large platter (for three people) with grilled fish, shrimp, crayfish, octopus and squid.

### El Camello Jr
SEAFOOD **$$**

(⊠984-871-20-36; www.facebook.com/restaurant eelcamellojr; Av Tulum, cnr Av Kukulkán; mains M$100-165, lobster M$380-450; ⊙10:30am-10pm Thu-Tue; ℗) Immensely popular with locals, this roadside eatery guarantees fresh fish and seafood. Regulars don't even need to look at the menu – it's all about the mixed ceviche (seafood marinated in lime juice, garlic and seasonings), seafood soup or lobster, when in season.

### Los Aguachiles
SEAFOOD **$$**

(⊠984-802-54-82; www.facebook.com/losagua chilesrm; Av Tulum, cnr Palenque; tacos & tostadas M$45-90, mains M$140-310; ⊙1-10pm; ℗⊚) If you skipped this outfit while in Playa del Carmen or Cancún, here's another chance. Fish tacos and tuna *tostadas* go down oh-so-nicely with a *michelada* (beer, lime and Clamato juice) in this airy cantina-style restaurant at the south end of town.

### La Nave
ITALIAN **$$**

(⊠984-871-25-92; www.facebook.com/lanave. tulum; Av Tulum s/n; mains M$115-250, pizzas M$90-150; ⊙8am-midnight Mon-Sat; ⊚) This open-air Italian joint is perpetually packed. There are delicious pasta dishes, such as shrimp or lobster ravioli, brick-oven pizzas, and an assortment of meat and fish dishes on offer.

### El Asadero
STEAK **$$$**

(⊠984-157-89-98; www.facebook.com/elasadero. tulummexico; Av Satélite Norte 23; mains M$160-550; ⊙4-11pm Mon-Sat; ⊚) Somewhat pricey but worth it, this spot has grilled *arrachera* (flank steak) served with sides of potato, *nopal* (cactus paddle) and sausage, which pairs nicely with the Mexican craft beers on offer. Pescatarians and vegetarians won't be disappointed with the grilled tuna and loaded potatoes.

## ✗ Zona Hotelera

### ★ Hartwood
FUSION **$$$**

(www.hartwoodtulum.com; Carretera Tulum–Boca Paila Km 7.5; mains M$365-550; ⊙5:30-10pm Wed-Sun) 🍴 Assuming you can get in (it accepts walk-ins and online reservations made one month in advance), this sweet 'n' simple nouvelle-cuisine restaurant down on the beach road will definitely impress. Ingredients are fresh and local; flavors and techniques are international. The chalkboard menu changes daily, and the solar-powered open kitchen and wood-burning oven serve to accentuate the delicious dishes.

It's about 4.5km south of the T-junction. Cash only.

### Puro Corazón
MEXICAN **$$$**

(⊠cell 984-1861152; www.facebook.com/purocora zon.tulum.1; Carretera Tulum-Boca Paila Km 5.5; mains M$160-350; ⊙8am-10pm Tue-Sun; ⊚🍴) Reasonably priced (by Zona Hotelera standards), this inviting spot serves excellent house-made cocktails that can be enjoyed immensely at sunset on the property's rear observation deck. Everything on the menu is prepared with a gourmet twist. The gravel floors, painted tables and chairs, and hookah decorations all add to the flair.

### Posada Margherita
ITALIAN **$$$**

(⊠WhatsApp only 984-8018493; www.posada margherita.com; Carretera Tulum–Boca Paila Km 4.5; mains M$345-570; ⊙7:30am-10pm) This hotel's beachside restaurant is candlelit at night, making it a beautiful, romantic place to dine. The fantastic food, including pasta, is made fresh daily and consists mostly of organic ingredients. The wines and house mezcal are excellent. It's 3km south of the T-junction. Cash only.

Parking can be a nightmare.

## ⚑ Drinking & Nightlife

### ★ Batey
BAR

(⊠cell 984-7454571; www.facebook.com/batey tulum; Centauro Sur 7, btwn Av Tulum & Andrómeda Oriente; ⊙12pm-2am Mon-Sat, 4:30pm-1am Sun) Mojitos sweetened with freshly pressed cane sugar are the main attraction at this popular Cuban bar, with fun music acts in the rear garden. Most nights the crowd spills into the street, while inside cane is pressed on top of an iconic, painted VW bug.

### Papaya Playa Project
BAR

(⊠984-871-11-60; www.facebook.com/papaya playaproject; Carretera Tulum-Boca Paila Km 4.5; ⊙10pm-3am Sat) Trendy hotel Papaya Playa Project hosts monthly full-moon parties and Saturday DJ nights with resident and guest spinsters at its beachside club. It's 500m south of the T-junction. There's usually a cover charge.

## 🛍 Shopping

Avenida Tulum is lined with shops offering many items, including hammocks, blankets and handicrafts.

# ℹ Orientation

Tulum lies 131km south of Cancún and is spread out over quite a large area. Approaching from the north on Hwy 307, the first thing you reach is Crucero Ruinas, where the old access road heads in a straight line about 800m to the ruins' ticket booth. About 400m further south on Hwy 307 (past the gas station) is the new entrance for vehicles going to the ruins; it leads to a parking lot. Another 1.5km south on the highway brings you to the Cobá junction; turning right (west) takes you to Cobá, and turning east leads about 3km to the north–south road (or T-junction) servicing the Zona Hotelera, the string of waterfront lodgings extending for more than 10km south from the ruins. This road eventually enters the Sian Ka'an Biosphere Reserve, continuing some 50km past Boca Paila to Punta Allen.

The town center, referred to as Tulum Pueblo, straddles the highway (Avenida Tulum through town) south of the Cobá junction.

A new road and development is underway for the area behind the Zona Hotelera's south side, so expect big changes to come soon.

# ℹ Information

## EMERGENCY

**Ambulance, Fire & Police** (☑ 911, ☑ 066)

## MONEY

Tulum has numerous currency exchange offices and a bank along Avenida Tulum. There's also an ATM in the ADO bus terminal.

**HSBC** (☑ 984-871-22-01; Av Tulum, btwn Alfa Sur & Osiris Sur; ⊙ 9am-5pm Mon-Fri) Bank and 24-hour ATM.

## POST

**Post Office** (☑ 984-871-21-04; Orión Sur s/n, cnr Sol Oriente; ⊙ 8am-4pm Mon-Fri, 9am-1pm Sat)

## SAFE TRAVEL

Tulum is generally safe. However, if you nod off on the beach, your valuables may disappear. Bring your own lock if you plan on staying in the cheap, no-frills beachfront *cabañas* (cabins).

Of late, perhaps due to nutrient pollution and/or climate change, sargassum seaweed has become a huge problem at times (when it arrives and for how long it stays, nobody can predict). It's not dangerous, but washes ashore in quantities so voluminous that workers are hired to rake it off the beach and haul it away by the truckload.

# ℹ Getting There & Away

The 24-hour **ADO bus terminal** (☑ 984-871-21-22; www.ado.com.mx; Av Tulum, btwn Alfa Norte & Júpiter Norte; ⊙ 24hr) is simple but adequate, with some chairs for waiting, but not much else.

*Colectivos* leave from Avenida Tulum for **Playa del Carmen** (Av Tulum s/n, cnr Júpiter Sur; M$45; ⊙ 45min). **Colectivos to Felipe Carrillo Puerto** (Av Tulum s/n, cnr Júpiter Norte; M$70; ⊙ 1hr) depart from a block south of the bus terminal. **Colectivos to Cobá** (Osiris Norte s/n, cnr Av Tulum; M$70) depart every two hours or so from 9am to 6pm.

## BUSES FROM TULUM

| DESTINATION | COST (M$) | TIME (HR) | FREQUENCY (PER DAY) |
| --- | --- | --- | --- |
| Belize City (Belize) | 831 | 6 | 1 (1:50am) |
| Cancún | 181-250 | 2-2½ | frequent |
| Cancún International Airport | 266 | 2 | 5 |
| Chetumal | 240-359 | 3¼-4 | frequent |
| Chichén Itzá | 252 | 2½-2¾ | 2 (9am & 2:45pm) |
| Chiquilá (for Isla Holbox) | 365 | 3½ | 1 (8:10am) |
| Cobá | 50 | 1 | 10:11am |
| Felipe Carrillo Puerto | 69-75 | 1¼ | 4 (consider taking a frequent *colectivo*) |
| Laguna Bacalar | 220-270 | 3 | frequent |
| Mahahual | 327 | 3-3½ | 1 (7:10pm) |
| Mérida | 264-392 | 4-4½ | frequent |
| Playa del Carmen | 44-89 | 1 | frequent |
| Valladolid | 103-148 | 1½-1¾ | frequent |

# ℹ Getting Around

**Colectivos** (cnr Venus Oriente & Centauro Sur; M$20-40; ⊗7am-midnight) to the beach run frequently from a stop from the corner of Venus Oriente and Orión Sur from 6am to 7:30pm. The shared vans turn right at the beach road T-junction and go as far south as the Sian Ka'an Biosphere Reserve entrance, before turning around.

To reach the ruins, any Playa del Carmen–bound colectivo (M$20) will drop you on the highway, where it's about a 1km walk to the site's main entrance.

Bicycles and scooters can be a good way to go back and forth between the town and beach. Many hotels and hostels have free bikes for guests. I Bike Tulum (p121) has a good selection of bike and scooter rentals.

Taxi fares are fixed, from either of the two taxi stands in Tulum Pueblo: one on the corner of Av Tulum and Jupiter Norte in front of the bus terminal, the other four blocks north on Av Tulum on the corner of Centauro Norte. They charge M$100 to the ruins and M$100 to M$150 from town to the Zona Hotelera, depending on how far south you need to go.

Tour company **iTour Mexico** (⌨ WhatsApp only 984-115-38-75; www.itourmexico.com; cnr Avs Cobá & Tulum; tour US$140) provides ground transportation to the Sian Ka'an visitors center, where you can catch a boat to Punta Allen.

# Around Tulum

There's much to be explored around Tulum. Head inland to visit cenotes, the ruins at Cobá and the grass-roots tourism project at Punta Laguna. Or cruise down the coast to Punta Allen and the wild Reserva de la Biosfera Sian Ka'an.

## ◉ Sights

**Punta Laguna**                    LAKE
(⌨985-114-86-30; www.facebook.com/puntalagu nayucatan; Hwy 109 Km 27.5; tours M$500; ⊗7am-5pm) Punta Laguna is a fair-sized lake with a small Maya community nearby, 20km northeast of Cobá on the road to Nuevo Xcan. Thus far, it's remained relatively wild. The forest around the lake supports populations of spider and howler monkeys, as well as a variety of birds, and contains small, unexcavated ruins and a cenote. A surprising jaguar population was recently discovered, though chances of seeing one are very slim. Local guides run morning and afternoon tours to spy monkeys.

**Xcacel-Xcacelito**                 BEACH
(Hwy 307 Km 112; M$81; ⊗10am-4:30pm; ℗) ✦ Between the Chemuyil and Xel-Há exits is a tiny sign on the east side of the highway marking the short dirt road that leads to the two arching bays Xcacel and Xcacelito. This is one of the loveliest and cleanest beaches along the Riviera Maya. You'll find good snorkeling here (bring your own gear) and, most notably, Quintana Roo's most important loggerhead and white sea-turtle nesting site.

**Tankah**                           BEACH
A few kilometers south of the Hwy 307 turnoff for Punta Solimán is the exit for Tankah, a picturesque stretch of beach and top-end accommodations that have the sea for a front yard and mangroves out back.

**Bahías de Punta Solimán**          BEACH
These two beautiful, protected bays are separated by a narrow point, 123km south of Cancún and 11km north of Tulum. To get here, head east (toward the sound of the ocean) on an unmarked road directly opposite Hwy 307's Oscar y Lalo's Restaurant. On the coast road's northernmost end, there's a public beach where you can eat good seafood and rent a kayak and paddle out to the reef that shelters the mouth of the bay.

## 🏃 Activities

**Gran Cenote**                      SWIMMING
(Hwy 109 s/n; adult/child under 120cm M$180/90, snorkeling gear M$80, diving M$200; ⊗8:10am-4:45pm) About 4km west of Tulum, this is a worthwhile stop on the highway out to the Cobá ruins, especially if it's a hot day. You can snorkel among small fish and see underwater formations in the caverns if you bring your own scuba gear. A cab from Tulum costs M$100 one-way (but check first to avoid surprises).

**Aktun-Ha**                         SWIMMING
(Car Wash; Hwy 109 Km 8; M$50, diving M$200, snorkel gear M$50; ⊗8am-5pm) A legend has it that taxi drivers used to wash their cabs here and to this day Aktun-Ha is still referred to as Car Wash, despite the story being somewhat embellished. It's still a good swimming spot and several dive shops teach cave and cavern diving here. It's 7.5km west of Tulum heading toward Cobá.

The cenote is part of a cool cave series with names like the Chamber of Horrors, Chamber of the Ancients and Room of Tears, to name a few.

### Zacil-Há
SWIMMING

(☑ cell 984-2037621; www.facebook.com/cenotezacilha; Hwy 109 Km 8; M$100, snorkel gear M$30, zip-line M$10; ◷ 10am-5:30pm) At this cenote you can combine swimming, snorkeling and zip-lining. It's 8km west of Avenida Tulum on the road to Cobá. There's even a bar, and if you fancy staying overnight, grab a *cabaña* for two/eight people for M$1000/1200.

### Cenote Manatí
SWIMMING

(Tankah; M$120, snorkel tour M$500, 2-person kayak per hr M$250; ◷ 8am-6pm) Named for the gentle 'sea cows' that used to frequent the beach, this is a beautiful series of seven cenotes connected by a channel that winds through the mangrove a short distance before heading back underground briefly to reach the sea. The swimming, snorkeling and kayaking are great, though prices have shot up in recent years.

# Cobá
☑ 984 / POP 1300

Cobá's ruins are a treat and exploring them is a big part of the reason for coming here: the state's tallest pyramid, a beautiful ball court and a variety of other structures make for a fun few hours. The village is quiet and cute, with a croc-filled lagoon, a series of cenotes, and a growing number of hotels and restaurants...but people mostly come for the ruins. In droves. By the busload. In fact, that's its biggest problem: arrive after 11am and you'll be one of literally hundreds of other people coming in from Cancún, Playa and Tulum. So come at 8am. You'll thank the stars you did.

From a sustainable-tourism perspective, it's great to stay the night in small communities like Cobá, but don't plan on staying up late.

## History

Cobá was settled earlier than Chichén Itzá or Tulum, and construction reached its peak between 800 and 1000 CE. Archaeologists believe that this city once covered 70 sq km and was home to some 40,000 Maya.

Cobá's architecture is a mystery; its towering pyramids and stelae resemble the architecture of Tikal, which is several hundred kilometers away, rather than the much nearer sites of Chichén Itzá and the northern Yucatán Peninsula.

Archaeologists say they now know that between 200 and 600 CE, when Cobá had control over a vast territory of the peninsula, alliances with Tikal were made through military and marriage arrangements in order to facilitate trade between the Guatemalan and Yucatecan Maya. Stelae appear to depict female rulers from Tikal holding ceremonial bars and flaunting their power by standing on captives. These Tikal royal females, when married to Cobá's royalty, may have brought architects and artisans with them.

Archaeologists are still baffled by the extensive network of *sacbeob* (ceremonial limestone avenues or paths between great Maya cities) in this region, with Cobá as the hub. The longest runs nearly 100km west from the base of Cobá's great Nohoch Mul pyramid to the Maya settlement of Yaxuna. In all, some 40 *sacbeob* passed through Cobá, parts of the huge astronomical 'time machine' that was evident in every Maya city.

The first excavation at Cobá was led by Austrian archaeologist Teobert Maler in 1891. There was little subsequent investigation until 1926, when the Carnegie Institute financed the first of two expeditions led by Sir J Eric S Thompson and Harry Pollock. After their 1930 expedition, not much happened until 1973, when the Mexican government began to finance excavation. Archaeologists now estimate that Cobá contains more than 6500 structures, of which just a few have been excavated and restored, though work is ongoing.

## ◉ Sights

### ★ Cobá Ruins
ARCHAEOLOGICAL SITE

(www.inah.gob.mx; M$75, sunset entry M$255, guides M$800-850, parking M$50; ◷ 8am-4pm & 4:30-7pm; 🅿) Cobá's ruins include the tallest pyramid in Quintana Roo (the second tallest in all of the Yucatán) and the thick jungle setting makes you feel like you're in an Indiana Jones flick. Many of the ruins are yet to be excavated; for now they are mysterious piles of root- and vine-covered rubble. Walk along ancient *sacbés*, climb up ancient mounds, and ascend Nohoch Mul for a spectacular view of the surrounding jungle.

### Grupo Cobá
ARCHAEOLOGICAL SITE

The most prominent structure in the Grupo Cobá is La Iglesia (the Church). It's an enormous pyramid; if you were allowed to climb it, you could see the surrounding lakes (which look lovely on a clear day) and the Nohoch Mul pyramid. To reach it walk just under 100m along the main path from the entrance and turn right.

# Cobá

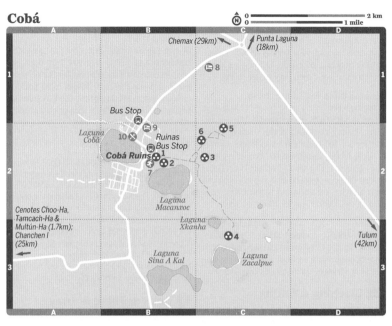

## Cobá

**Grupo Macanxoc**  ARCHAEOLOGICAL SITE

Grupo Macanxoc is notable for its numerous restored stelae, some of which are believed to depict reliefs of royal women from Tikal. Though many are worn down by the elements, a number are still in good condition and are worth a detour.

**Grupo de las Pinturas**  ARCHAEOLOGICAL SITE

The temple at Grupo de las Pinturas (Paintings Group) bears traces of glyphs and frescoes above its door and remnants of richly colored plaster inside. You approach the temple from the southeast. Leave by the trail at the northwest (opposite the temple steps) to see two stelae. The first of these is 20m along, beneath a *palapa*. Here a regal figure stands over two others, one of them kneeling with his hands bound behind him.

**Grupo Nohoch Mul**  ARCHAEOLOGICAL SITE

Nohoch Mul (Big Mound) is also known as the Great Pyramid (which sounds a lot better than Big Mound). It reaches a height of 42m, making it the second-tallest Maya structure on the Yucatán Peninsula (Calakmul's Estructura II, at 45m, is the tallest). Climbing the old steps can be scary for some. Two diving gods are carved over the doorway of the temple at the top (built in the post-Classic period, 1100–1450 CE), similar to sculptures at Tulum.

The view from up top is over many square kilometers of flat scrubby forest, with glimpses of lake.

**Juego de Pelota**  ARCHAEOLOGICAL SITE

An impressive ball court, one of several in the ruins. Don't miss the relief of a jaguar and the skull-like carving in the center of the court.

## 🏃 Activities

In addition to the ruins, the area has several cenotes south of town. If you **rent a bike** (near ruins bus stop; bikes per day M$50; ☺10am-5pm) it makes a nice ride. Otherwise, you'll need to find your own way to get there.

**Cenotes Choo-Ha, Tamcach-Ha & Multún-Ha**                    SWIMMING

(☑ cell 985-1040472; per cenote M$100; ☺8am-6pm) About 6km south of the town of Cobá, on the road to Chanchen I, you'll find a series of three locally administered cenotes: Choo-Ha, Tamcach-Ha and Multún-Ha. These cavern-like cenotes are nice spots to cool off with a swim, or a snorkel if you bring your own gear. Children under 10 enter free.

**Zip-line**                           ADVENTURE SPORTS

(zip-line M$250, lookout M$50; ☺10:30am-6:30pm) In the Cobá ruins parking lot a high tower doubles as a lookout point and zip-line allowing views of the lagoons down below.

## 🛏 Sleeping & Eating

**Hotel Maya**                              HOTEL $$

(☑ cell 984-1443006; www.facebook.com/hotel sacbecoba; Av Principal s/n; d M$800-1000; ⊜❄🛜🏊) The best deal in town. Clean, colorful and comfortable rooms (some with cable TV) await upstairs behind wooden doors designed with carvings of Maya gods, while downstairs there's an inviting blue-tiled swimming pool. It's on the main avenue and just a short walk to the ruins.

**★ Aldea Cobá**                           RESORT $$$

(☑ cell 998-1476623, cell 998-3420198; www. aldeacoba.com; Av Principal 1; M$1760-2900; 🅿⊜❄🛜) A lovingly designed jungle-set resort with cool, comfortable rooms featuring furnishings crafted by local artisans. Bungalows and the larger villas overlook an inviting pool surrounded by vegetation. On-site restaurant Pischán, which specializes in Yucatecan cuisine, welcomes nonguests and is worth visiting. It's 2.5km from the ruins, so you'll need a car or will have to hoof it into town.

**Chile Picante**                          MEXICAN $$

(☑ cell 984-1443006; www.facebook.com/restau rantechilepicante; Av Principal s/n; mains M$75-220; ☺7:30am-11pm; 🛜) Located at Hotel Maya, Chile Picante does everything from vegetarian omelettes with *chaya* (Mexican tree spinach) and fresh fruit plates to *panuchos*.

**Restaurant La Pirámide**                 MEXICAN $$

(☑984-173-74-70; Av Principal s/n; mains M$80-180, buffet M$180; ☺8am-5pm; 🛜) At the end of the town's main drag, by the lake, this restaurant is pretty touristy but does decent Yucatecan fare like *cochinita* or *pollo pibil* (*achiote*-flavored slow-cooked pork or chicken), or you can opt for the lunch buffet between noon and 3pm. The open-air setup allows for nice lagoon views.

## 🛈 Information

You may want to buy a book about Cobá before coming. On-site signage and maps are minimal and cryptic. Tours in English run about M$600 to M$650. The Nohoch Mul pyramid is the only structure the public is allowed to climb.

Be careful not to picnic beside the lake outside the entrance, as it has large crocodiles.

Cobá has an ATM in front of **Ciber Sky Planet** (☑ cell 984-1183441; Av Principal s/n; per hr M$10; ☺9am-10pm) internet cafe, but it often runs out of money so bring plenty of cash.

## 🛈 Getting There & Away

Most buses serving Cobá swing down to the ruins to drop off passengers at a small bus stop; but you can also get off in town.

Buses run eight times daily between Tulum and Cobá (M$50 to M$55, one hour) and there are about five daily departures to Playa del Carmen (M$94 to M$142, two hours). Buses also go eight times daily to Valladolid (M$52, one hour), where you'll find frequent **bus services** (☑985-856-34-48; www.ado.com.mx; cnr Calles 39 & 46; ☺24hr) to Chichén Itzá and Mérida. For Cancún (M$174, 3½ hours), a bus leaves Cobá at 3:10pm.

Day-trippers from Tulum can reach Cobá by taking colectivos (M$70) that depart every two hours or so from Calle Osiris Norte and Avenida Tulum.

The road from Cobá to Chemax is arrow-straight and in good shape. If you're driving to Valladolid or Chichén Itzá, this is the way to go.

Cobá-based taxis charge M$450 to Tulum and M$650 to Valladolid.

# Punta Allen

☑984 / POP 470

The tiny town of Javier Rojo Gómez is more commonly called by the name of the point 2km south, Punta Allen. The village, which is truly the end of the road, exudes a laid-back ambience reminiscent of the Belizean cays. There's also a healthy reef 400m from shore that offers snorkelers and divers wonderful

## RESERVA DE LA BIOSFERA SIAN KA'AN

A sprawling jungle with a pristine coastline and camping sites for intrepid travelers, Sian Ka'an is home to a small population of spider and howler monkeys, American crocodiles, Central American tapirs, four turtle species, giant land crabs, more than 330 bird species (including roseate spoonbills and some flamingos), manatees and some 400 fish species, plus a wide array of plant life.

There are no hiking trails through the heart of the reserve; it's best explored with a professional guide. If you'd like to see more of Sian Ka'an, Maya-run Community Tours Sian Ka'an (p121) runs various expeditions into the sprawling biosphere reserve.

For remote coastal camping, this is where intrepid adventuring really takes off. Bring a tent, a couple of hammocks, lots of water, mosquito nets and food supplies. Around 30km from the entrance gate is an excellent camping spot with the lagoon on one side and glorious blue ocean on the other.

sights. To get here you have to enter the incredible Sian Ka'an Biosphere Reserve, a vast tract of mangrove swamp, lagoon, beaches and jungle that supports a variety of endemic species, including the elusive jaguar.

The village is known primarily for its catch-and-release bonefishing; tarpon and snook are very popular sportfish as well. Cooperatives in town offer fishing trips, dolphin-watching outings and snorkeling expeditions.

Hurricane Gilbert nearly destroyed the town in 1988, and there was some damage and a lot of wind-scrubbed palms after Hurricane Dean in 2007. But Punta Allen is still standing.

**Cooperativa Punta Allen** TOURS
(☑ WhatsApp only 984-143-23-03; toursallen@hotmail.com; Calle Punta Nizuc s/n; per boat snorkeling & dolphin-watching M$3000, fly-fishing US$300) The Punta Allen cooperative runs various boat tours in the area, such as fly-fishing, dolphin- and turtle-watching, and snorkeling. Located north of the dock.

## 🛏 Sleeping & Eating

Sleeping options are simple and limited. A few of the higher-end places cater to fishing tours.

**★ Serenidad Shardon** GUESTHOUSE $$$
(☑ Mexico 984-146-15-87, USA 616-827-0204, WhatsApp only 984-1074155; www.shardon.com; Punta Allen Rd; cabañas M$3400, house M$11,500, camping US$25) Serenidad (serenity) couldn't be a more fitting description for this white-sand oceanfront property on the southern end of town. On offer are a large beach house that sleeps eight, a romantic honeymoon *cabaña* (cabin) for two and a larger *cabaña* with a balcony, kitchen and lovely

interior design details. There are also affordable camping options available.

**Grand Slam Fishing Lodge** HOTEL $$$
(☑ 998-800-10-47; www.grandslamfishinglodge.com; Punta Allen; r US$350; ⓟ🐕❄🖥🛎) If you have money to burn, this place at the town entrance is for you. The upscale lodge boasts 12 oceanfront rooms with Jacuzzi, large balconies and around-the-clock electricity (a true luxury in Punta Allen). Fly-fishing enthusiasts can request lodging and all-inclusive fishing packages. Rates vary based on the type of fishing, length of trip and other requirements.

**Muelle Viejo** SEAFOOD $$
(Punta Allen; mains M$95-170; ⊙12:30-9pm Tue-Sun; ⓟ) Service here can be as slow as the frigates circling overhead, but it's hard not to use this as a chance to relax and enjoy. Overlooking a dock where fishers bring in the daily catch, this colorful beach house serves fresh seafood ceviche, decent fried-fish dishes and lobster when it's in season.

**Fisherman Fishing Lodge** SEAFOOD $$
(☑ 998-277-47-68, cell 999-3220072; www.fishermanlodge.com; mains M$100-260; ⊙8am-10pm; ❄🖥) Serves breakfast meals fit for a hearty angler's appetite and a varied lunch and dinner menu featuring pizza and fresh lobster. Offers good lodging-and-fishing package deals (rooms from M$1700) and welcomes non-fisherfolk, too. Located south of the dock.

## ❶ Getting There & Away

The best way to reach Punta Allen is by driving a rental car or scooter, but prepare to drive very slowly and expect more than a few transmission-grinding bumps. The ride can take three to four hours or as little as two, depending on the condition of the road.

## AT A GLANCE

**POPULATION**
302,600

**CAPITAL**
Chetumal

**BEST SEAFOOD
RESTAURANT**
Nohoch Kay (p138)

**BEST WATERFRONT
HOTEL**
Rancho Encantado
(p141)

**BEST ECOTOURISM
CENTER**
Síijil Noh Há (p135)

### WHEN TO GO

**Feb** Catch Chetu-
mal's Caribbean-fla-
vored Carnaval in
late February or early
March.

**Mar** Attend an indie
art festival hosted
by Galeón Pirata
Espacio Cultural in
Laguna Bacalar.

**Sep–Nov** It's lob-
ster season, diving
conditions at Banco
Chinchorro are calm
and Mahahual hotels
are discounted.

Dzibanché (p147)
PHOTO SPIRIT/SHUTTERSTOCK ©

# Costa Maya & Southern Caribbean Coast

**T**he Southern Caribbean Coast, or the Costa Maya as the tourist brochures call it, is the latest region to be hit by the development boom. But if you're looking for a quiet escape on the Mexican Caribbean, it's still the best place to be.

With a coast stretching about 100km south of Sian Ka'an Biosphere Reserve down to Xcalak, you'll find many surprises along the way, including the tranquil fishing town of Mahahual.

In the interior, you'll be blown away by the mesmerizing Laguna Bacalar, while the ruins of Dzibanché and Kohunlich seem all the more mysterious without the tour vans.

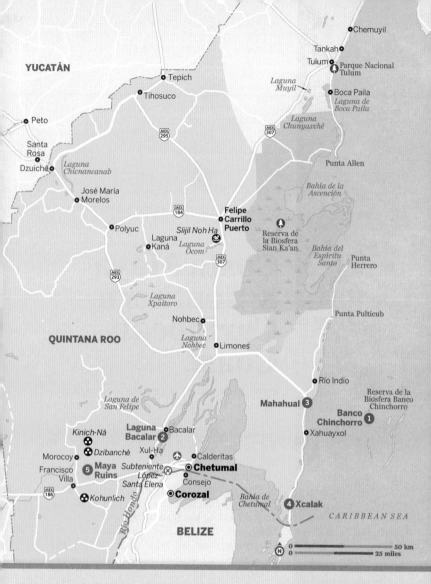

# Costa Maya & Southern Caribbean Coast Highlights

**1 Banco Chinchorro** (p137) Diving at the largest coral atoll in the northern hemisphere and visiting a fascinating ship graveyard.

**2 Laguna Bacalar** (p140) Feasting your eyes on one of the most beautiful lagoons you'll ever see and kayaking across its clear waters.

**3 Mahahual** (p136) Fishing, snorkeling, diving, bird-watching or simply chilling at a boardwalk bar or restaurant in this laid-back coastal town.

**4 Xcalak** (p139) Escaping to a remote beach village for quality R&R, diving, fly-fishing and mangrove swamps teeming with life.

**5 Maya ruins** (p147) Day-tripping from the state capital Chetumal and visiting ancient abandoned cities still overlooked by bus tours.

# Felipe Carrillo Puerto

✒ 983 / POP 26,000

Now named for a progressive governor of Yucatán, this crossroads town 95km south of Tulum was once known as Chan Santa Cruz, the rebel headquarters during the War of the Castes. Besides its historical and cultural significance, Carrillo Puerto has few points of interest other than an attractive ecotourism park about 11km south of town, and yet its lack of attention to tourist hordes may be the best reason to spend some time here. You'll experience quiet, local Maya life in an urban setting.

There's a main square with a clock tower, church and cultural center; the plaza takes center stage in late April and early May when the town celebrates its patron saint, Santa Cruz.

## History

In 1849, when the War of the Castes turned against them, the Maya of the northern Yucatán Peninsula made their way to this town seeking refuge. Regrouping, they were ready to sally forth again in 1850 when a 'miracle' occurred. A wooden cross erected at a cenote on the western edge of the town began to 'talk', telling the Maya they were the chosen people, exhorting them to continue the struggle against the government and promising victory. The talking was most likely done by a ventriloquist who used sound chambers, but the people looked upon it as the authentic voice of their aspirations.

The 'oracle' guided the Maya in battle for more than eight years, until their great victory conquering the fortress at Bacalar. For the latter part of the 19th century, the Maya in and around Chan Santa Cruz were virtually independent of governments in Mexico City and Mérida.

A military campaign by the Mexican government retook the city and the surrounding area at the beginning of the 20th century, and the talking-cross shrine was desecrated. Many of the Maya fled to small villages in the jungle and kept up the fight into the 1930s; some resisted even into the 1950s.

Carrillo Puerto today remains a center of Maya pride. The talking cross, hidden away in the jungle for many years following the Mexican takeover, has been returned to its shrine, and Maya from around the region still come to visit it, especially on May 3,

when Fiesta de Santa Cruz (Day of the Holy Cross; ☺ May 3) is celebrated.

## ◉ Sights & Activities

★ Siijil Noh Há                                    LAGOON, PARK

(✒ 983-834-05-25, cell 983-1129991; www.facebook.com/siijilnohha; off Hwy 307, Laguna Ocom turnoff; admission M$20, kayaks/bicycles per hr M$50/70, cabins M$300; ☺ 7am-7pm; ℗) ✐
About 8km south of Felipe Carrillo Puerto, off Hwy 307, you'll find a bumpy 3km dirt road leading to this sublime, solar-powered ecotourism center. Run by the local Maya community, the wooded grounds overlook a quiet lake shore. You can rent a kayak, take a dip in a freshwater spring or go biking along nature trails, and there's an on-site restaurant. If you like what you see, you can stay in a rustic cabin here.

### Xyaat Ecotourism                                    TOURS

(✒ cell 983-1067624, cell 983-1141790; www.caminossagrados.org; cnr Rojo Gómez & Borge Martín, Señor; tours per person M$1450) ✐ In the town of Señor, about 30km north of Felipe Carrillo Puerto, ecotourism center Xyaat runs two-hour tours focusing on Maya traditions and history. Visitors learn about traditional Maya medicine, henequen weaving, apiculture practices and Maya battle tactics used during the Mexican Revolution. Tours includes a meal prepared with locally produced ingredients. The proceeds go to community-based development projects.

### Museo Maya Santa Cruz
### Xbáalam Naj                                    MUSEUM

(✒ 983-834-11-25; cnr Calles 68 & 63; ☺ 9:30am-8:30pm Mon-Fri, 10am-2pm & 6-9pm Sat & Sun) FREE A small but interesting collection of Maya artifacts, clothing and cooking utensils.

### Na'atik Language Institute                                    LANGUAGE

(✒ 983-267-14-10; www.naatikmexico.org; Calle 57, btwn Calles 78 & 80; 1-week course incl homestay US$649) ✐ Study Maya or Spanish at this non-profit language school. The institute imparts 18 hours of weekly instruction and offers a homestay program that includes three meals a day with a Maya- or Spanish-speaking family. By studying here you are supporting the local community.

## 🛏 Sleeping & Eating

### Hotel Turquesa Maya                                    HOTEL $

(✒ 983-834-12-18; www.hotelturquesamaya.com; Hwy 295 No 936, cnr Calle 56; d M$635; ℗ 🐾 ❄ 🛜)

COSTA MAYA & SOUTHERN CARIBBEAN COAST FELIPE CARRILLO PUERTO

With good beds, kitchenettes and an on-site restaurant, Turquesa Maya provides the most comfortable stay in town, but it's about 15 blocks from the bus station so you may want a more centrally located hotel if you don't have wheels.

**Hotel Esquivel**                    HOTEL **$**
(☎983-834-03-44; www.hotelesquivel.blogspot. com; Calle 63 No 746, btwn Calles 66 & 68; d/ste M$570/670; P☺❄☎☀) Around the corner from the plaza and bus terminal, the Esquivel offers clean, affordable rooms but some catch noise from events held on the main square. Across the street it has quieter, family-friendly suites with kitchenettes, fridges and a swimming pool.

**Picaditas y Kekas Made**            MEXICAN **$**
(☎983-839-43-88; Calle 65, btwn Calles 64 & 66; snacks M$14-20; ☺7am-1pm & 6pm-midnight; ☀) Veracruz-style *picaditas* (tortillas with a layer of salsa, cheese and topping) are tasty and cheap at this simple eatery near the bus station. For toppings, choose between *champiñón* (mushrooms), *nopal* (cactus paddle), *rajas* (poblano chili slices), *flor de calabaza* (seasonal squash blossom) or *carne asada* (marinated grilled beef).

**Mercado Público**                   MARKET **$**
(cnr Calles 70 & 71; snacks & mains M$30-70; ☺6am-3pm) A decent spot to fuel up and do a bit of people-watching.

**El Faisán y El Venado**             MEXICAN **$$**
(☎983-834-00-43; www.facebook.com/elfaisan yelvenadocarrillo; Av Juárez 781, cnr Calle 69; mains M$120-210; ☺7am-10pm; P☎) Come here for the best eats in town. The house specialty is grilled *venado* (deer) steaks prepared *a la yucateca* (Yucatán-style). If you're here in the afternoon, get their handmade tortillas between 1pm and 3pm.

It's also a hotel, with clean, though somewhat darkish, rooms (from M$560) and a swimming pool out back.

## ❶ Information

**HSBC** (Calle 67 s/n, btwn Calle 68 & Av Juárez; ☺9am-5pm Mon-Fri) Has a 24-hour ATM.
**Post Office** (Calle 69 s/n, btwn 64 & 66; ☺9am-5pm Mon-Fri, to noon Sat)

## ❶ Getting There & Away

Buses depart from the **ADO station** (☎983-834-08-15; www.ado.com.mx; Calle 66 No 752, cnr Calle 65) on the main square.

Frequent **colectivos** (Av Juárez, cnr Calle 73) (shared vans) leave for Playa del Carmen (M$90, two hours) and Tulum (M$65, one hour) from Hwy 307 (aka Avenida Juárez), just south of Calle 73.

At Calles 66 and 63 you can catch **colectivos** (cnr Calles 63 & 66) to Chetumal (M$90, two hours).

# Mahahual

📞 983 / POP 920

Mahahual changed forever when the cruise-ship dock was completed, and it grows larger every year. Despite the (literally) boatloads of tourists, there's a lovely, relaxed, Caribbean vibe that you won't find further north, and once the passengers have returned to their ships, a quiet calm settles over the town. Mahahual is the only spot in the Costa Maya that's large enough to support a diversity of sleeping and eating options, while still being right on the beach.

New restaurants and bars are cropping up on the north side of town, a residential area known as Casitas that's home to both locals and foreigners. Or go south toward Xcalak and you'll have no problem finding

## BUSES FROM FELIPE CARRILLO PUERTO

| DESTINATION | FARE (M$) | TIME (HR) | FREQUENCY (PER DAY) |
|---|---|---|---|
| Cancún | 174-222 | 3½-4 | frequent |
| Chetumal | 99-130 | 2¼-3 | frequent |
| Laguna Bacalar | 77-114 | 1¾-2 | frequent |
| Mahahual | 166 | 1¾ | 2 (10:35am & 8:20pm) |
| Mérida | 234 | 6 | frequent |
| Playa del Carmen | 96-144 | 2½ | frequent |
| Ticul (for Uxmal) | 175 | 4 | 6 |
| Tulum | 69-104 | 1¼ | frequent |

your own private beach with sugar-white sand.

There's great diving and snorkeling in Mahahual, and just enough nightlife along the beachfront *malecón* (waterfront promenade) to keep you entertained.

## ◉ Sights & Activities

### ★ Banco Chinchorro DIVE SITE

Divers won't want to miss the reefs and underwater fantasy worlds of the Banco Chinchorro, the largest coral atoll in the northern hemisphere and known for its shipwreck sites, coral walls and canyons. Some 45km long and up to 14km wide, Chinchorro's western edge lies about 30km off the coast, and dozens of ships have fallen victim to its barely submerged ring of coral.

### ★ Amigos del Mar DIVING

(✆ cell 984-1516758; www.amigosdelmar.net; Malecón s/n, cnr Coronado; 1-/2-tank dive incl equipment US$90/150, snorkeling US$100; ⊙ 9am-6pm) One of the few dive shops in town authorized to visit the spectacular Banco Chinchorro.

### Mahahual Dive Center DIVING

(✆ 983-102-09-92; www.mahahualdive.com; Malecón Km 1, cnr Atún; 1-/2-tank dives incl equipment US$69/99, snorkeling US$25; ⊙ 9am-5pm Mon-Sat, to 4pm Sun) In a new location, right on the *malecón*, Mahahual Dive Center does scuba trips to nearby sites, snorkeling outings and day trips to the fishing village of Punta Herrero.

### Mahahual Beach BEACH

The beach right off Mahahual's beautiful *malecón* (waterfront promenade) has powdery white sand, plus water so shallow you can swim out a good 100m.

### Doctor Dive DIVING

(✆ 983-834-56-19; www.doctordive.com; cnr Malecón & Coronado; 2-tank dive US$100, snorkeling incl equipment US$25; ⊙ 8am-9pm) In addition to scuba and snorkeling excursions, the Doctor can offer training courses at many different levels, including open-water PADI certification (US$420).

## ⛩ Festivals & Events

### Cruzando Fronteras CULTURAL

(www.facebook.com/mahahualcruzandofronteras) See this cultural organization's Facebook page for upcoming events such as concerts, food festivals and art exhibits.

### Jats'a-Já Festival CULTURAL

(⊙ Aug) This festival is a prayer offering of sorts to the hurricane gods. Activities include pre-Hispanic dancing, art shows and culinary events. It's usually held during the third week of August.

## 🛏 Sleeping

The options range from cheap, backpacker spots all the way up to the way, way fancy.

### ★ Posada Pachamama HOTEL $$

(✆ 983-834-57-62; www.posadapachamama.net; Huachinango s/n, btwn Coronado & Martillo; d/q M$1500/2500; 🅿 ⊛ ❄ 🛜 🐾) Rooms at the Pachamama (which means Mother Earth in Quechua, the language of the Inca) range from small interior singles and doubles with partial ocean views to more ample digs that sleep four. The staff are very knowledgeable about local activities and the accommodations are fairly priced by Mahahual standards. The beach is a 10m stumble away.

### Travel In' GUESTHOUSE $$

(✆ cell 983-1109496; www.travel-in.com.mx; Coast road Km 6; r US$49; 🅿 ⊛ 🛜 🐾) 🚲 About 5.5km south of town, this solar-powered guesthouse is ideal for nature lovers. There are just two accommodations: a rustic, cabin-like room beside a mangrove or a more modern guesthouse with its own library. You can also camp on the beach (M$100). Even if you're not staying at Travel In', its restaurant and quiet beach are worth visiting.

### Hotel Don Kike 55 HOTEL $$

(✆ 983-834-57-11; www.hoteldonkike55.com; Carretera Cafetal-Mahahual Km 55; d M$1000; 🅿 ⊛ 🛜) About 2km from the main beach strip and 500m from Mahahual's residential area, Don Kike makes good sense for budget travelers who don't mind walking or cabbing it into town. Marketing itself as a hotel where 'size matters,' it truly does provide spacious rooms, with digs that surely won't win any design awards, but are clean, comfortable and functional.

### Hostal Jardín Mahahual HOSTEL $$

(✆ 983-834-57-22; www.mahahualjardin.com; Sardina s/n, btwn Rubia & Sierra; dm/r M$250/695; ⊛ ❄ 🛜) This is a surprisingly stylish little hostel with seven private rooms and a six-bed mixed dorm. Rooms are spotless and the dorm is the best in town by far. It's set back two blocks from the beach, near Calle Rubia.

COSTA MAYA & SOUTHERN CARIBBEAN COAST MAHAHUAL

**Palmeras de Mahahual**
Cabañas                                    CABAÑAS $$$
(⌨ cell 983-1377949; www.facebook.com/palmeras demahahual; Atún s/n, btwn Malecón & Sardina; d M$2400; 🅿 ➔ ❄ 🛜) Just four air-conditioned, wood cabin rooms are on offer at this pleasant, laid-back hotel. All have comfortable beds, mini-fridges and terraces with ocean views. At last visit, construction was going on next door but you could still catch a good eight hours of shut-eye. Prices drop considerably during low season. Rents out bikes too.

**Quinto Sole**                    BOUTIQUE HOTEL $$$
(⌨ 983-834-59-42; www.quintosole.mx; Carretera Mahahual–Xcalak Km 0.35; r/ste M$1800/2500; 🅿 ➔ ❄ 🛜) One of the fancier hotels in town, the rooms here have cushy beds and private balcony. It's on a quiet beach north of the boardwalk and 350m south of the lighthouse at the town's entrance. There's also a restaurant. Rates are for jungle views; ocean views cost more.

**Ko'ox Matan Ka'an**                    HOTEL $$$
(⌨ 983-834-56-79; www.kooxmatankaanhotel. com; Huachinango s/n, cnr Coronado; r/ste from M$3305/3965; 🅿 ❄ 🛜 ⛱ 🛜) On the south side of the soccer field, this large whitewashed hotel has a relaxed resort feel, plenty of common areas and large, clean rooms with Netflix. We only wish 'the gift from the heavens' – that's what Matan Ka'an means in Maya – included beach access, but hey, the ocean is only 100m away.

## ✕ Eating

There are about a dozen restaurants along the *malecón* (waterfront promenade), each offering an assortment of seafood, Mexican favorites and international fare. Prices are higher here than other less-touristed towns, but the selection is varied. So far there are no chain stores, either. Just local restaurants serving pretty decent food.

**★ Nohoch Kay**                    SEAFOOD $$
(Big Fish; ⌨ 983-834-59-81; miplayanohochkay@ outlook.com; cnr Malecón & Cazón; mains M$150-240; ⊙ 12:30-8:30pm; 🛜) Nohoch Kay, aka the Big Fish, definitely lives up to its name. Don't miss this beachfront Mexican-owned restaurant, where they prepare succulent whole fish in a garlic and white-wine sauce, and seafood paella for two (M$395), which includes mussels, clams, shrimp, calamari and octopus.

**Mayan Beach Garden**              INTERNATIONAL $$
(⌨ WhatsApp 983-1308658; www.mayanbeach garden.com; Camino Costera Mahahual-Punta Herrera; mains M$150-220; ⊙ 12:30-3pm & 7-9pm; 🅿) About 30km north of Mahahual, this off-grid inn and restaurant makes notably fresh seafood dishes such as mixed ceviche and fish fillet in raspberry-*chipotle* sauce. You can also book cooking classes here. After lunch, consider taking a drive up north along a coastal road toward remote fishing village Punta Herrero. It reveals spectacular scenery, but the potholed road is slow going.

**Sulumar**                              SEAFOOD $$
(⌨ 983-834-57-84; www.facebook.com/restaurante sulumar; Malecón s/n, btwn Atún & Almeja; mains M$60-210; ⊙ 9am-6:30pm; 🛜) Lobster, lionfish, octopus, you name it – this fishing cooperative cooks up the fresh catch of the day and serves it to you right on the beach at the south end of the boardwalk. Locals love this place, so be prepared to find it packed.

## ℹ Information

You'll find an ATM on Calle Coronado, between Calle Huachinango and the *malecón,* but bring plenty of cash in case the machine runs out of money.

**Entronque Casa de Cambio** (Cherna s/n, btwn Huachinango & Malecón; ⊙ 8am-8pm) The only currency-exchange office in town.

## ℹ Getting There & Around

Mahahual is 125km south of Felipe Carrillo Puerto, and 105km northeast of Laguna Bacalar.

There's no official bus terminal in Mahahual. Los Hijos del Maíz restaurant sells tickets for a twice-daily northbound bus, which departs Mahahual at 10:30am and 5:30pm for Felipe Carrillo Puerto (M$183, 1¾ hours), Tulum (M$327, three hours), Playa del Carmen (M$414, four hours) and Cancún (M$497, 5½ hours). A Xcalak-bound Caribe bus (M$52, 40 minutes) stops here as well, usually around 8:10am and 6:40pm. Hourly westbound buses to Limones (M$60, one hour), Laguna Bacalar (M$90, 1½ hours) and Chetumal (M$100 to M$244, 2½ to three hours) leave from 6:30am to 6:30pm.

Shuttle vans leave hourly from 5:20am to 8:20pm to Chetumal (M$100, 2½ hours), Laguna Bacalar (M$60, two hours) and Limones (M$60, one hour), where you can catch frequent northbound buses. The terminal is on the corner of Calles Sardina and Cherna, on the soccer field's north end.

There's a Pemex gas station in Mahahual if you need to fill your tank. The Xcalak turnoff is about 100m west of the gas station.

# Xcalak

☑ 983 / POP 375

The rickety wooden houses, beached fishing launches and lazy gliding pelicans make this tiny town plopped in the middle of nowhere a perfect escape. And by virtue of its remoteness and the Banco Chinchorro, Xcalak may yet escape the development boom.

Come here to walk along dusty streets and sip frozen drinks while frigate birds soar above translucent green lagoons. Explore a mangrove swamp by kayak, scubadive at Banco Chinchorro or do some excellent fly-fishing. Xcalak has a few nice restaurants and an easygoing mix of foreigners and locals.

The mangrove swamps stretching inland from the coastal road hide some large lagoons and form tunnels that invite kayakers to explore. They, and the drier forest, teem with wildlife; in addition to the usual herons, egrets and other waterfowl, you can see agoutis, jabirus (storks), iguanas, javelinas (peccaries), parakeets, kingfishers, crocodiles and more.

## ⚘ Activities

### XTC Dive Center                           DIVING

(☑ WhatsApp 984-2401557; www.xtcdivecenter. com; Coast Rd Km 0.3; 2-tank Chinchorro dives US$275, snorkeling trips US$50-75; ☺ dive shop 8am-6pm) XTC is the one-stop spot for all your travel needs. It offers dive and snorkel trips to the wondrous barrier reef offshore and to Banco Chinchorro. It also rents out diving equipment, provides PADI openwater certification (US$600), and operates fishing and bird-watching tours (US$75). Kayaks, free for guests, can be rented for a half/full day for US$40/60.

Additionally, XTC rents nice rooms (US$115 to US$130) and a larger apartment (US$250), and has a good restaurant-bar. It's 300m north of town.

## ⛉ Sleeping

Accommodations here are simple: even the nicer ones. Most places don't accept credit cards without prior arrangement and are best contacted through their websites, via email or WhatsApp.

### Xcalak Caribe Lodge                      LODGE $$

(☑ WhatsApp 983-1305580; www.xcalakcaribe. com; Av Guerrero s/n, Xcalak town center; d incl breakfast M$1250; ❄ ☎) Fairly affordable by Xcalak standards, this waterfront lodge has six clean, modern rooms, all with good mattresses, some with air-con and some with ocean views. Breakfast is served on a terrace upstairs. Prices vary depending on occupancy. Reservations can be made via Whatsapp messaging or email.

### Casa Paraíso                             HOTEL $$$

(☑ Canada 416-277-6774, WhatsApp 983-1587008; www.casaparaisoresort.com; Coast Rd Km 2.5; r incl breakfast US$140; ☎) Bright, cheery yellow Casa Paraíso has four guest rooms with large, hammock-equipped balconies facing the sea. Each room has a king-sized bed and a kitchen with fridge, and the bathrooms try to outdo one another with their beautiful Talavera tilework. Includes free use of kayaks, snorkel gear and bicycles.

## ✖ Eating

Food in Xcalak tends to be tourist-grade seafood or Mexican, though some of it is quite good.

### Costa de Cocos                    INTERNATIONAL $$

(☑ WhatsApp 983-1167744; www.costadecocos. com; Coast Rd Km 5.2; breakfast US$3-5, lunch & dinner US$9-26; ☺ 7am-9pm; ⓟ ☎) This fishing lodge's restaurant-bar is one of the better options in town for eating and drinking. It serves both American- and Mexican-style breakfasts and does fish tacos for the lunch and dinner crowd. The bar produces its own craft whiskey and has pale ale on tap.

### Toby's                                   SEAFOOD $$

(☑ cell 983-1075426; tobyxcalak@hotmail.com; town center; mains M$85-350; ☺ 11:30am-8pm Mon-Sat but varies) On the main drag in town, the friendly chitchat and well-prepared fish and seafood dishes make this a popular expat spot. Try the coconut shrimp or lionfish and you'll know why. Toby's also rents camping sites (M$100) across the street.

### Silvia's Restaurant                      SEAFOOD $$

(☑ cell 501-6604881; Xcalak town center; mains M$120-170; ☺ 8:30am-10pm; ⓟ) About three blocks south of the plaza and a block in from the coast, Silvia's serves mostly Yucatecan snacks, fish fillets and ceviche (seafood marinated in lemon or lime juice, garlic and seasonings). The long menu doesn't mean that everything is available...you'll likely end up having the fish. Conch shells feature large in the decor here.

## ℹ️ Getting There & Around

Buses to Chetumal (M$130) and Mahahual (M$50, where you can grab northbound buses) leave at 4:50am and 1:50pm; they stop on the coast road behind the lighthouse and pass through Mahahual before heading west. From Chetumal, buses leave at 5:40am and 4:10pm.

Cabs from Limones, on Hwy 307, cost M$1000 (including to the northern hotels).

From the Hwy 307 turnoff, drive south about 52km and then turn right at the signs pointing to Xcalak (another 60km). Keep an eye out for the diverse wildlife that frequents the forest and mangrove; a lot of it runs out onto the road. Large land crabs, snakes and tortoises are common. The cat-sized Yucatecan fox is another resident.

At last visit, the bumpy coastal road from Xcalak to Mahahual was closed, so you'll have to take the paved inland road instead: a much faster option but far less scenic.

# Laguna Bacalar

📞 983 / POP 39,000

Laguna Bacalar, the peninsula's largest lagoon, comes as a surprise in this region of scrubby jungle. More than 60km long with a bottom of sparkling white sand, this crystal-clear lake offers opportunities for camping, swimming, kayaking and simply lazing around, amid a color palette of blues, greens and shimmering whites that seems more out of Photoshop than anything real life could hold.

Some would say this area is the 'new' Tulum. Small and sleepy, yet with enough tourism to have things to do and places to eat, the lakeside town of Bacalar lies east of the highway, 115km south of Felipe Carrillo Puerto. It's noted mostly for its old Spanish fortress and popular *balnearios* (bathing places). There's not much else going on, but that's why people like it. Around the town plaza, you'll find ATMs, a money-exchange office, a small grocery store, a taxi stand and a tourist information office.

## ⭕ Sights & Activities

### ★ Los Rápidos                          KAYAKING

(📞 cell 983-1205920; www.facebook.com/losrapidosbacalar; off Hwy 307 Km 8; adult/child 2-12yr M$50/25, kayak per hr M$150; ⏱ 10am-7pm) A gorgeous spot for kayaking and bird-watching, here you can paddle up a slow-flowing,

crystalline stream brimming with large underwater stromatolites (live ancient rock-like structures formed by cyanobacteria). Some are believed to be billions of years old! Beat the crowds with a midweek morning visit and try to avoid stepping on the exceedingly rare stromatolites.

Los Rápidos is about 25km south of Bacalar's town center. Look for the signed turnoff at Km 8, off Hwy 307. A taxi from town costs about M$150.

### Balneario                             SWIMMING

(📞 983-835-55-05; Av Costera s/n, cnr Calle 14; ⏱ 9am-5pm) **FREE** This beautiful public swimming spot lies several blocks south of the fort, along Avenida Costera. Though admission is free, parking costs M$10.

### Fort                                   FORTRESS

(📞 museum cell 983-8361065; cnr Av 3 & Calle 22; adult/child 9-17yr M$100/25; ⏱ museum 9am-7pm Tue-Sun) The fortress above the lagoon was built in 1733 to protect Spanish colonists from pirate attacks and rebellions by local indigenous people. It also served as an important outpost for the Spanish in the War of the Castes. In 1859 it was seized by Maya rebels, who held the fort until Quintana Roo was conquered by Mexican troops in 1901.

### Cuco's Tours                          BOATING

(📞 cell 983-1358943, cell 983-1079980; www.cucostours.com.mx; Av Costera 479; per boat M$1800) Boat tours departing from Hotel Laguna Bacalar visit freshwater springs, a shallow white-sand beach, three cenotes (sinkholes) and a gorgeous canal. Don't forget your swimsuit.

### Cenote Azul                           SWIMMING

(Hwy 307 Km 34; adult/child under 11yr M$25/free; ⏱ 10am-6pm) Just shy of the south end of the *costera* (coastal highway) and about 3km south of Bacalar's town center is this cenote, a 90m-deep natural pool with an onsite bar and restaurant. It's 200m east of Hwy 307, so many buses can drop you nearby. Taxis to the cenote from the main square cost M$50.

## 🛏️ Sleeping

### Yak Lake House                       HOSTEL $

(📞 983-834-31-75; www.yakbacalar.com; Av Costera s/n, btwn Calles 24 & 26; dm/r M$450/2000; 🅿️🌐❄️📶) If lounging around all day in your bikini is your idea of fun, then Yak House won't disappoint. It's steps away from Laguna Bacalar and there are ample chairs, docks and decks on which to soak up the sun. Free breakfast, friendly staff, clean rooms and comfy mixed dorms make this a sweet spot to park yourself for several days.

### Pata de Perro
HOTEL $

(📞983-834-20-62; www.facebook.com/patade perrobacalar; Calle 22 No 63A, btwn Avs 3 & 5; d from M$650, ste M$950-1500; 🅿❄🛜) This hostel-turned-hotel on the square houses immaculate rooms, ranging from three-bed setups with shared bathrooms to ample suites with kitchenettes and private bathrooms. The friendly staff, central location and good on-site restaurant make this one of our favorites. The 'dog's paw' doesn't accept pets.

### Hotel Laguna Bacalar
HOTEL $$

(📞983-834-22-05; www.hotellagunabacalar.com; Av Costera 479; d with fan/air-con M$1360/1500, bungalow from M$3000; 🅿❄❄🛜🏊) This breezy, old-school place boasts a swimming pool, restaurant and fairly basic rooms with spotty wi-fi and excellent views of the lagoon, which you can explore by kayak or boat tours. It's 2km south of town and 150m east of Hwy 307, so if you're traveling by bus you can ask the driver to stop at the turnoff.

### ★Hotel Maria Maria
HOTEL $$

(📞983-834-21-16; www.facebook.com/hotelmaria maria; Av 3 No 600, cnr Calle 14; r M$950-1050, ste M$1150; 🅿❄❄🛜) Just a block away from a lovely swimming spot and a short walk from the town square, this well-run little hotel offers tastefully designed suites with lagoon views and two slightly more affordable rooms on the ground floor. Guests have use of a kitchen upstairs and the host, Maria, is very accommodating.

### Amigo's Hotelito Bacalar
HOTEL $$

(www.amigoshotelito.com; Av Costera s/n; d US$85; 🅿❄❄🛜) Right on the lake and about 500m south of the fort, this ideally located property has five spacious guest rooms with king-size beds, hammocks, satellite TV, terraces and a *palapa* (thatched-roof) common area with a lake view.

### Casa Caracol
CABAÑAS $$$

(📞cell 998-8452353, cell 998-8742207; www.casa caracol-bacalar.com; Av Costera 609; r US$136; 🅿❄🛜) If you're looking for creature comforts such as air-con and TV, this place isn't for you. If, on the other hand, you want a sublime spot to relax, Casa Caracol delivers big time. Five *cabañas'* (cabins) over-

look a lush garden and a lakeshore full of stromatolites.

Kayaks and paddle boards are available to rent. It's 3km south of town.

### Villas Bakalar
APARTMENT $$$

(📞983-834-20-49; lety@villasbakalar.com; Av 3 No 981, btwn Calles 28 & 30; d/ste incl breakfast M$2200/3200; 🅿❄❄🛜🏊) A good option for families or small groups, Villas Bakalar offers a little bit of everything: a pool area with an excellent lake view, lush gardens and large suites with full kitchens. Reserve by phone or email.

### ★Rancho Encantado
CABAÑAS $$$

(📞998-884-20-71, cell 983-1004141; www.encan tado.com; Hwy 307 Km 24; d/ste incl breakfast from M$2872/4099; 🅿❄❄🛜🏊) Laguna Bacalar is absolutely beautiful in its own right, so imagine staying at one of the most striking locations along the shore. A typical day on the *rancho* (ranch) goes something like this: wake up in comfy cabin or room; have breakfast with lagoon view; kayak or swim in calm, translucent waters; and unwind in a Jacuzzi. Wi-fi in reception only.

The ranch is 3km north of Bacalar.

## 🍴 Eating & Drinking

### El Socio
MEXICAN $

(📞cell 983-7336612; Av 7 s/n, btwn Calles 18 & 20; snacks M$12-30; ⏰7am-8pm Mon-Sat, to 2pm Sun) A local fave for more than 20 years, this simple eatery does excellent *carne asada* (grilled beef) and chicken *sopes* (tortillas with a layer of beans, cheese and salsa), as well as affordable Yucatecan snacks that usually sell out by midday, such as *panuchos* (fried tortillas with a layer of beans, chicken and other toppings).

### Christian's Tacos
TACOS $

(📞cell 983-1149094; www.facebook.com/taqueria christiansbacalar; Calle 18 s/n, btwn Avs 7 & 9; tacos M$14-30, nachos M$70-125; ⏰6pm-1am) If Christian's were in Mexico City – the *al pastor* (spit-roasted marinated pork) capital – it would compete with the best of them. The popular, yet artery-choking, *pastor* nachos are topped with slices of pork, beans and cheese. The new bar means you can wash down your food with your favorite alcoholic libations as well.

### Taquería Chepe
MEXICAN $

(Hwy 307 s/n, btwn Calles 24 and 26; tacos M$12, tortas (sandwiches) M$27; ⏰6am-12:30pm Tue-Sun) Go straight for the *taco de cochinita surtida* (slow-cooked pork), which comes prepared on a handmade tortilla and with a little extra fat for good measure. It's a few buildings north of the convenience store Oxxo on Hwy 307, past another *taquería* – don't confuse them!

**Mango y Chile**     VEGAN $$
(☑ 983-688-20-00; www.facebook.com/mangoy chile; Av 3 s/n, btwn Calles 22 & 24; mains M$100-150; ☉1-9pm Wed-Mon; P⛽✍) Bacalar's first and only all-vegan dining option, Mango y Chile has a beautiful, large deck overlooking the fort and the lagoon, and friendly service. Vegans will rejoice that there's a spot here to dine worry-free. The burgers are tasty, though the food is on the salty side.

**Los Aluxes**     MEXICAN $$
(☑ 983-834-28-17; www.losaluxesbacalar.com; Av Costera 69; mains M$120-270; ☉7am-9pm; P⛽) An open-air *palapa* restaurant serving regional and fusion dishes, this waterfront restaurant prepares interesting creations such as *pechuga sikil pak* (Yucatecan-style chicken and pasta dish). A life-sized Al Capone statue lurks in the bathroom, gun drawn. It's 1km south of town.

**Savora Bakhalal**     TAPAS $$
(☑ 983-688-20-23; www.facebook.com/bistro savorabakhalal; Calle 22 No 63, btwn Avs 3 and 5; mains M$100-240, lobster M$490; ☉8am-11pm; ⛽) With its 'smoking bench' and 'flirting bench', this al fresco spot on the plaza charms, offering tapas-style food, plus pizzas, pastas, tacos and excellent desserts. The terrace bar upstairs overlooks the plaza.

★**Nixtamal**     GRILL $$$
(☑ cell 983-1347651; www.facebook.com/nixtamal cocinaafuegoyceniza; López Mateos 525, cnr Calle 12; mains M$130-300; ☉5-11pm Wed-Mon; ⛽) The *slooow*-food experience here pushes your patience to the limit, but grill-master Rodrigo Estrada makes it well worth the wait. Exquisite dishes such as marinated rib eye and whole grilled lobster are cooked over a wood-and-charcoal grill and finished in a wood-fired oven (no gas or electrical appliances are used). The candlelit open-air restaurant stages live music on weekends.

**La Playita**     SEAFOOD $$$
(☑ 983-834-30-68; www.laplayitabacalar.com; Av Costera s/n, cnr Calle 26; mains M$160-300; ☉9am-11:45pm; ⛽) A sign outside reads, 'Eat, drink and swim' – and that about sums it up. Fish and seafood dishes are tasty, albe-

it on the smallish side, but the mezcal and fine swimming certainly make up for that. An enormous rubber tree, which provides shade in the gravel garden section, was nearly uprooted in 2007 when Hurricane Dean pummeled the coast.

This is also a lovely spot for late-night cocktails, with romantic candlelight, the quiet night and frisky toads that merrily hop around the gravel floor.

## ☆ Entertainment

**Galeón Pirata Espacio Cultural**     LIVE MUSIC
(☑ cell 983-1577558; www.facebook.com/galeon piratabacalar; Av Costera s/n, btwn Calles 30 & 32; ☉varies depending on events, to 2am Fri & Sat) This indie cultural center hosts live music, art exhibits, movie screenings and plays, while doubling as a restaurant-bar. Hours can be erratic, but when it's happening, it's a fun time. Galeón hosts an annual indie-art festival in March.

## ℹ Information

**Tourist Office** (☑ 983-834-28-86; www. bacalar.gob.mx; Av 3 s/n, btwn Calles 22 & 24; ☉8am-4pm Mon-Fri) Has useful info about local activities.

## ℹ Getting There & Away

Buses don't enter town, but taxis and some *colectivos* will drop you at the town square. Buses arrive at Bacalar's ADO station. From there it's about a 10-block walk southeast to the main square, or you can grab a local taxi for M$20.

If you're driving from the north and want to reach the town and fort, take the first Bacalar exit and continue several blocks before turning left (east) down the hill. From Chetumal, head west to catch Hwy 307 north; after 25km on the highway you'll reach the signed right turn for Cenote Azul and Avenida Costera, aka Avenida 1.

## Chetumal

☑ 983 / POP 224,000

The capital of Quintana Roo, Chetumal is a relatively quiet city going about its daily paces. The bayside esplanade hosts carnivals and events, and the modern Maya museum is impressive (though a bit short on artifacts). Excellent Maya ruins, amazing jungle and the border to neighboring Belize are all close by. Though sightings are rare (there are no tours), manatees can sometimes be seen in the rather muddy bay or nearby mangrove shores. The lagoon should not be used for swimming, as there is a risk of crocodiles, despite the locals' joke that there's only one (named Harry) and he's tame. It may be their way of getting rid of pesky tourists, so swim in your hotel pool to be safe.

## History

Before the Spanish conquest, Chetumal was a Maya port used for shipping gold, feathers, cacao and copper to the northern Yucatán Peninsula. After the conquest, it wasn't until the late-19th century when the Mexican government took full control of the city to put a stop to the arms and lumber trade carried on by descendants of the Maya who fought in the War of the Castes. The government declared May 5, 1898 as the city's 'founding' date. The town was initially dubbed Payo Obispo, and later renamed Chetumal, in 1936. In 1955, Hurricane Janet virtually obliterated it, and 2007's Hurricane Dean did a bit of damage to the town's infrastructure too.

## ◉ Sights & Activities

★ **Laguna Milagros**     LAGOON
(off Hwy 186, in Huay-Pix; 🚍 Nicolás Bravo) Paddle out on a kayak or simply have a swim in the azure waters of Laguna Milagros, about 23km west of Chetumal, in the town of Huay-Pix. Waterfront seafood restaurant El Abuelo (p145) rents kayaks (M$100 per hour) and serves tasty fresh fish.

**Museo de la Cultura Maya**     MUSEUM
(📷 983-833-38-68; www.facebook.com/museodela culturamaya; Av de los Héroes 68, cnr Av Gandhi; adult/child under 8yr M$105.61/free; ◷ 9am-7pm Tue-Sun) The Museo de la Cultura Maya is the city's claim to cultural fame – a bold showpiece that's beautifully conceived and executed, though regrettably short on artifacts. It's organized into three levels, mirroring Maya cosmology. The main floor represents this world, the upper floor the heavens and the lower floor Xibalbá, the underworld. The various exhibits cover all the Mayab (lands of the Maya). Though original pieces are in short supply, there are replicas of stelae and a burial chamber from Honduras' Copán.

**Ikadventure**     CYCLING
(📷 cell 983-1215135; www.facebook.com/ikhad venture.operadoraturistica; Blvd Bahía, cnr Emiliano Zapata; bike/in-line skates per hr M$20, kayak per hr M$150; ◷ 10am-2pm & 4pm-8pm) This outfit rents bikes and kayaks, and arranges various tours, including horseback riding and fishing. For an enjoyable bike ride, pedal north along Boulevard Bahía to Calderitas, a pleasant fishing town about 8km away.

## ⚑ Festivals & Events

**Carnaval**     RELIGIOUS
(◷ Feb/early Mar) Carnaval is particularly lively in Chetumal. Colorful nightly parades bring locals into the streets to watch floats and plumed dancers pass by.

## 🛏 Sleeping

**Hostelito**     HOSTEL, HOTEL $
(📷 983-833-34-19; www.facebook.com/hostelito chetumal; Av Othón P Blanco 187A, btwn Avs 5 de Mayo & de los Héroes; dm/d incl breakfast M$200/550; ❄ 🅿 🖥 🛜 🏊) A fine central option for budget travelers, Hostelito operates as a hotel and hostel with affordable private rooms and a 12-bed mixed dorm. Air-con is available in the dorm only when at least five people are staying in it. Guests enjoy the outdoor swimming pool, free bike loans, open-air kitchen and airy common spaces with hammocks.

★ **Hotel Urban 101**     HOTEL $$
(📷 983-834-56-27; www.hotelurban101.com; Av de los Héroes 101A, btwn Plutarco Elías Calles & Cárdenas; s/d M$890/990; ❄ 🅿 🛜) Best deal in town when it comes to comfort, convenience and friendly service. The modern rooms here stay cool thanks to their polished concrete floors, while the subtle lighting, cushy beds and coffee makers provide added value. The boardwalk, museums and bus and taxi terminals all are nearby.

**Noor Hotel**     HOTEL $$
(📷 983-835-13-00; www.hotelnoor.mx; cnr Blvd Bahía & Av Morelos; r M$1500-1800; 🅿 ❄ 🖥 🛜 🏊) Right on the bay, the Noor will appeal to those looking to get away from the bustling center. Bay-view rooms, though pricier, are your best bet, as ground-level ones tend to have poor ventilation. There's a pool, and the restaurant prepares international cuisine. The boardwalk across the way is good for afternoon strolls.

**Capital Plaza**     HOTEL $$
(📷 983-835-04-00; www.capitalplaza.mx; Av de los Héroes 171, cnr Av Gandhi; d M$1325, ste from M$1765; 🅿 ❄ 🖥 @ 🛜 🏊) One of the fanciest hotels in town; comfortable rooms overlook a courtyard with a swimming pool surrounded by tropical gardens, a restaurant

# Chetumal

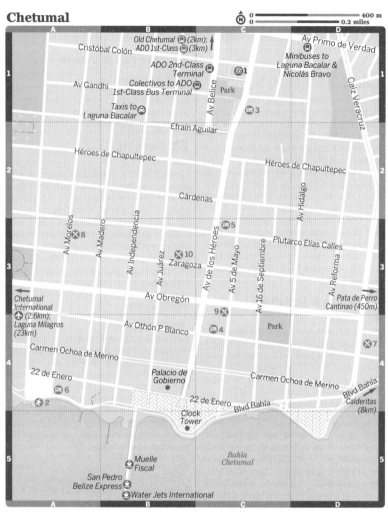

and bar. The Maya sun mirror in the lobby adds interesting flair.

## ✖ Eating & Drinking

Restaurants range from inexpensive local food to pricier seafood and international fare, but it's generally quite good, and cheaper than the more touristy northern cities and towns. There's a fun six-block strip of bars and nightclubs lining Boulevard Bahía, north of Avenida Othón Blanco, where you can dance the night away to live salsa and brass bands.

★ Lonchería La Costa                    YUCATECAN $

(📱cell 983-1800318; www.facebook.com/loncher ialacosta; Calz Veracruz 43; snacks M$22-50; ⊙6pm-midnight Mon-Sat; ✐) Yucatecan snacks such as *panuchos* (fried tortillas topped with beans, chicken and pickled onion) and *salbutes* (puffed deep-fried tortillas filled with chicken, cheese and other goodies) are delightfully prepared at this cheerful 50-year-old Caribbean house. There's no menu and most items can be prepared vegetarian-style upon request.

# Chetumal

**Taquería El Almendro**                    YUCATECAN $

(☑ 983-285-55-45; Zaragoza 213; tacos M$13-15, tortas M$24-26; ☺ 7:30am-1pm Mon-Sat, 8am-1pm Sun) Choose from more than a dozen Yucatecan-style *guisados* (home-style dishes) prepared as tacos and *tortas* (sandwiches) at this fan-cooled breakfast joint. Locals line up each morning for daily treats such as *chaya con huevo* (Mexican tree spinach with egg) and *chile xcatic relleno de queso* (chili filled with cheese), or popular weekly specials like *castacán* (pork belly).

**El Abuelo**                    SEAFOOD $$

(☑ cell 983-1171536; www.facebook.com/restaurantelabuelohuaypix; Av Laguna Milagros, Huay-Pix; mains M$140-210; ☺ 10am-7:30pm; P 🛜; 🚌 Nicolás Bravo colectivo) Overlooking the azure waters of Laguna Milagros, about 15km west of Chetumal, this open-air seafood restaurant draws deserving praise for its fried whole fish, fresh ceviche and *chicharrón de pescado* (a crispy fish appetizer). After the meal, cool off with a refreshing dip in the lagoon. Nicolás Bravo colectivos (p146) drop you at the Huay-Pix town entrance.

You can also rent kayaks here for M$150 per hour.

**Restaurante Xel-Ha**                    SEAFOOD $$

(☑ 983-285-02-87; Av Yucatán s/n, Calderitas; mains M$150-220; ☺ 11am-7pm; P) In a *palapa* (thatched-roof) restaurant right by the lagoon, Xel-Ha serves some of the best fresh fish around. Head about 8km north of Chetumal to the fishing village of Calderitas, where you'll find this classic bayside seafood restaurant. Note that they close early if there aren't any customers, so arrive well before 6pm to be sure they're open.

**Marisquería El Taco Loco**                    SEAFOOD $$

(☑ 983-129-20-90; www.tacoloco.mx; Av Morelos 87; tacos M$18-24, mains M$85-200; ☺ 8am-6pm; ❄ 🛜) A Chetumal favorite for more than three decades. Try the house specialty, *camaron empanizado* (breaded shrimp), or the fish taco *a la mantequila* (sautéed in butter), both of which are served on handmade tortillas and come with creamy garlic sauce and spicy habanero salsa on the side. The manatee mural is a fine touch.

**Sergio's Pizzas**                    PIZZA $$

(☑ 983-832-29-91; www.sergiospizzas.com.mx; Av Obregón 182, cnr Av 5 de Mayo; mains M$85-320; ☺ 7am-11pm; ❄ 🛜) Walk in here and you'll feel like you're in a Hollywood mafia movie: the service and decor are old-school, with stiff, formal waiters in starched shirts who never seem to smile. But the food's good, and it has a nice range of Mexican and Italian dishes, plus steaks and seafood.

**Pata de Perro Cantina**                    BAR

(Zaragoza 19, btwn Blvd Bahía & Isla Contoy; ☺ 8pm-1am Sun-Wed, to 3am Thu-Sat) With a more subdued vibe than some of the nearby nightclubs, this outdoor cantina stages the occasional midweek reggae act and serves ridiculously cheap large beers called *misiles* (missiles). The pleasant garden area makes a good spot to unwind over a game of dominoes or dice.

## ℹ Orientation

Chetumal is laid out on a grand plan with a grid of wide boulevards. The southern edge is bordered by the water. The main street, Avenida de los Héroes, divides the city into east and west sides, ending at the waterfront. Avenida Obregón parallels the bay and leads, heading westward, first to a *glorieta* (traffic circle), then to the airport and nearby immigration office, then to the turn for Belize.

## ℹ Information

There are numerous banks and ATMs around town, including an ATM inside the 1st-class bus terminal.

**CI Banco** (☑ 983-832-38-83; www.cibanco.com; Av Obregón 232; ☺ 8:30am-5pm Mon-Fri, 9am-2pm Sat) For ATM, bank services and money exchange.

# ℹ Getting There & Away

### AIR

Chetumal's small **airport** (☑ ext 3302 983-832-96-39; Av Revolución 660, Colonia Industrial) is roughly 2km northwest of downtown.

There are flights to Mexico City with **Interjet** (☑ 983-833-31-47; www.interjet.com; Av Revolución 660, Chetumal International Airport; ⊙ 8am-7pm Mon-Sat, from 7am Sun) and **Volaris** (☑ 55-1102-8000; www.volaris.com; Av Revolución 660, Chetumal International Airport); both have offices at the airport.

The airport is best reached by taxi (M$120).

### BOAT

Belize-bound ferries depart from the **muelle fiscal** (Dock; Blvd Bahía). Remember that in addition to the ferry fee you'll pay an exit fee of M$558 on departure, unless you can provide proof that you already paid the fee when you purchased your airline ticket, which is often the case. Immigration will need to see an itemized receipt detailing payment of the fee.

**San Pedro Belize Express** (☑ 983-832-16-48; www.belizewatertaxi.com; Av Blvd Bahía s/n, Muelle Fiscal; one-way M$950-1050; ⊙ 8:30am-4pm) Boat transportation to Belize City, Caye Caulker and San Pedro.

**Water Jets International** (☑ 983-833-32-01; www.sanpedrowatertaxi.com; Blvd Bahía s/n, Muelle Fiscal; one-way M$1100-1200; ⊙ 9am-3:30pm) Water taxis to San Pedro and Caye Caulker, in Belize.

### BUS

Long-distance buses arrive at and depart from the ADO 1st-class terminal.

**ADO 1st-Class Terminal** (☑ 983-832-51-10; www.ado.com.mx; Av Insurgentes s/n, cnr Av Palermo) Services to Cancún, Campeche, Mérida, Valladolid, Mahahual and other destinations, including points in Belize. Most 2nd-class buses also stop at the 1st-class terminal.

**ADO 2nd-Class Terminal** (www.ado.com.mx; Av Belice s/n, cnr Colón) Buses to Mahahual, Xcalak, Laguna Bacalar and Tulum.

**Minibus Terminal** (cnr Avs Primo de Verdad & Hidalgo) Minibuses serve Laguna Bacalar (M$42) from 7:30am to 1:30pm; however, you'll find more frequent departures to Bacalar at the **taxi colectivo** (Av Independencia s/n, btwn Av Gandhi & Efraín Aguilar; per person M$45) base on Avenida Independencia.

### TAXI

City cabs charge about M$25 to M$40 for short trips, but always ask the price before getting in. Taxis on Avenida Independencia charge M$45 per person for Laguna Bacalar. Night trips have an additional surcharge.

COSTA MAYA & SOUTHERN CARIBBEAN COAST CHETUMAL

## BUSES FROM CHETUMAL

Unless noted otherwise, the following buses depart from the ADO 1st-class terminal.

| DESTINATION | FARE (M$) | TIME (HR) | FREQUENCY (PER DAY) |
| --- | --- | --- | --- |
| Bacalar | 45 | ¾ | frequent |
| Belize City (Belize) | 390 | 4-4½ | 1 (4:40am) |
| Campeche | 570 | 6 | 1 (noon) |
| Cancún | 406-486 | 5½-6½ | frequent |
| Corozal (Belize) | 195 | 1 | 1 (4:40am) |
| Escárcega | 361 | 4 | 10 |
| Felipe Carrillo Puerto | 100 | 2¼-3 | frequent |
| Mahahual | 120 | 2-2½ | 1 (10:30am, 2nd-class terminal) |
| Mérida | 473 | 5½-6 | frequent |
| Orange Walk (Belize) | 300 | 2¼ | 1 (4:40am) |
| Palenque | 680-808 | 7 | 3 |
| Tulum | 323-359 | 3¼-4 | 12 |
| Valladolid | 250 | 5½ | 3 (2nd-class terminal) |
| Veracruz | 1409 | 17¾ | 1 (6:30pm) |
| Villahermosa | 767 | 8½-9 | 5 |
| Xcalak | 130 | 3-3½ | 2 (5:40am & 4:10pm, 2nd-class terminal) |
| Xpujil | 195 | 1¾ | 7 |

## BODY ARTISTS: CRANIAL DEFORMATION, PIERCING & TATTOOS

Take a second to imagine what the Maya at the height of the Classic period must have looked like. Their heads were sloped back; their ears, noses, cheeks and sometimes even genitals were pierced; and their bodies were tattooed. These were, indeed, some of the first body artists.

Cranial deformation was one of the Maya's most unusual forms of body art, and was most often performed to indicate social status. Mothers would bind the head of their infant (male or female) tightly to a board while the skull was still soft. By positioning the board either on top of or behind the head, the mother could shape the skull in many ways – either long and pointy (known as 'elongated') or long and narrow, extending back rather than up (known as 'oblique'). As the infant grew older and the bones calcified, the headboard was no longer needed: the skull would retain its modified shape for life. Apparently, compressing the skull did not affect the intelligence or capabilities of the child. Both practices became less and less common after the Spanish arrived.

**Gibson's Tours & Transfers** (☑ cell in Belize 501-6002605; www.facebook.com/gibsons storageandparking; Santa Elena-Corozal border; transportation for up to 4 people from US$100) can bring up to four people across to Corozal for US$100.

### ❶ Getting Around

Most places in Chetumal's tourist zone are within walking distance. To reach the main bus terminal from the center, catch a 'Lagunitas' **colectivo** (Gandhi s/n, btwn Avs Juárez & Belice) from the corner of Avenidas Belice and Gandhi, just around the corner from the 2nd-class bus station.

You'll find 'Calderitas' colectivos lined up across the street from the 2nd-class bus station.

## Corredor Arqueológico

The Corredor Arqueológico comprises archaeological sites that include Dzibanché, Kinich-Ná and Kohunlich, three intriguing and seldom-visited Maya ruins that can be visited on a day trip from Chetumal.

### ◉ Sights

**Dzibanché**                    ARCHAEOLOGICAL SITE
(☑983-837-24-11; off Hwy 186; M$60; ⊙8am-5pm; ℗) Though it's a chore to get to, this site is definitely worth a visit for its secluded, semi-wild nature. Dzibanché (meaning 'writing on wood') was a major city extending over more than 40 sq km and there are a number of excavated palaces and pyramids, though the site itself is not completely unearthed. On the way there you'll pass beautiful countryside.

The first restored structure you will come to is Edificio 6, the **Palacio de los Dinteles** (Palace of the Lintels), which gave the site its name. This is a perfect spot to orient yourself for the rest of the site: facing Edificio 6's steps, you are looking east. It's a pyramid topped by a temple with two vaulted galleries; the base dates from the early Classic period (300–600 CE), while the temple is from the late Classic period (600–900 CE). Climb the steps and stand directly under the original lintel on the right (south) side of the temple. Looking up you can see a Maya calendrical inscription with the date working out to 733 CE. This is some old wood.

On descending, head to your left (south) and thread between a mound on the right and a low, mostly restored, stepped structure on the left. This structure is Edificio 16, **Palacio de los Tucanes**; in the center, from the side you first approach, are the visible remains of posts that bore a mask. The path then brings you into **Plaza Gann**. Circling it counterclockwise takes you past Edificio 14 (stuck onto the north side of a larger building), decorated at the base with *tamborcillos* (little drums), in late Classic Río Bec style – look up the dirt hill to see them. The larger building to the south is Edificio 13, **Templo de los Cautivos**, so named for the carvings in its steps of captives submitting to whatever captives submitted to in those days. This seems to be the dominant (if you'll pardon the pun) theme in most Maya stelae.

On the east side of the plaza is Dzibanché's highest structure, the **Templo de los Cormoranes** (Temple of the Cormorants; Edificio 2), whose upper structure has been restored.

Exit the plaza by climbing the stone steps to the north of Edificio 2. At the top of the stairs is **Plaza del Xibalbá** (Plaza of the Underworld), though it's higher than Plaza Gann.

Opposite Palacio Norte is, of course, Palacio Sur, and from here you can see more of Edificio 2, but the most notable building is across the plaza: Edificio 1, the restored Templo del Buho (Temple of the Owl). It had an inner chamber with a stairway leading down to another chamber, in which were found the remains of a VIP and burial offerings. The nearly 360-degree views from the very top of the temple (it's a bit dicey, so be careful) are quite impressive. You can see Grupo Lamay to the west and you may spot Kinich-Ná, more than 2km to the northwest.

The ticket price for Dzibanché also includes entry to Kinich-Ná, 2km to the north.

**Kinich-Ná**                    ARCHAEOLOGICAL SITE

(off Hwy 186; ⊙8am-5pm; Ⓟ) Part of Dzibanché (p147) (ticket price includes entry to both), but well removed from the main site, Kinich-Ná consists of one building. But what a building: the megalithic Acrópolis held at least five temples on three levels and a couple of dead VIPs with offerings. The site's name derives from the frieze of the Maya sun god once found at the top of the structure. It's an easy 2km drive along a good narrow road leading north from near Dzibanché's visitors center.

**Kohunlich**                    ARCHAEOLOGICAL SITE

(☏983-837-24-11; off Hwy 186; M$75; ⊙8am-5pm; Ⓟ) This archaeological site sits on a jungle-backed grassy area. The ruins, dating from both the late pre-Classic (100–200 CE) and the early Classic (300–600 CE) periods, are famous for the great Templo de los Mascarones (Temple of the Masks), a pyramid-like structure with a central stairway flanked by huge, 3m-high stucco masks of the sun god.

## 🛈 Getting There & Away

The turnoff for Dzibanché from Hwy 186 is about 57km west of Chetumal, on the right just after the Zona Arqueológica sign. From there it's another 24km north and east along a narrow road. About 2km after the tiny town of Morocoy you'll need to turn right again. Kinich-Ná is 2km further north.

Kohunlich's turnoff is 2km west along Hwy 186 from the Dzibanché turnoff, and the site lies at the end of a 9km road. It's a straight shot from the highway.

There's no public transportation running directly to either of the sites. They're best visited by car, though Kohunlich could conceivably be reached by taking a Nicolás Bravo–bound colectivo (p146) departing from Chetumal to the turnoff in the town of Francisco Villa, then either hitchhiking or walking the 9km to the site. To return by colectivo to Chetumal or head west by bus to Xpujil or Escárcega, you'll have to flag transportation down on the highway; not all buses will stop.

Taxis can be hired in Chetumal for about M$200 per hour; to visit all three sites you'd

---

### CROSSING THE MEXICO–BELIZE BORDER

If you want to do a day trip or extended stay in Belize, or perhaps continue on to Guatemala, here are some helpful tips about crossing the Mexico–Belize border.

➡ If you enter Mexico by air, a fee called the derecho de no residente (DNR; non-resident fee) is usually included in the airfare and you will not be required to pay an 'exit fee,' as the occasional unscrupulous Mexican border official may suggest.

➡ Those entering by land and who have been in the country for more than seven days must pay M$533 at the border before leaving Mexico. If you came in on a plane, keep in mind that an itemized receipt of the airline ticket detailing payment of the DNR is the only form of proof that you did fork out the fee.

➡ If you're driving from downtown Chetumal to the Belize border, take Hwy 186 about 8km west to the 'Subteniente López' turnoff, then head about 2km south to reach the border station.

➡ The Belizean embassy says tourists entering the country for less than 24 hours are not required to show proof of a hotel reservation. However, if you plan on staying longer you'll be asked to do so (there's a terminal for booking reservations at the border station).

➡ Cabs waiting on the Belize side charge US$25 to Corozal.

➡ Visitors who have been in Belize for less than 24 hours must pay a US$15 departure fee; it's US$20 for stays longer than 24 hours.

need at least five hours or roughly M$1000. A group could pile in and split the cost.

# Corozal Town

POP 12,300

Just 9 miles south of Mexico and 29 miles north of Orange Walk Town, Corozal sits charmingly on the soapy-blue waters of Corozal Bay and has a vibe different from any other town in Belize, with its obvious Mexican influence. Most of the town's wealth comes from its position as a commercial and farming center, rather than from tourism. In fact the town's fledgling tourism sector has been hit hard by the direct boat service between San Pedro and Chetumal, which has seen many travelers bypass Corozal altogether.

But Corozal remains a fine place to be a tourist as it escapes the holiday-ville atmosphere that haunts some other places in Belize. With ocean breezes, affordable hotels, fine food and easy access to the rest of the district, Corozal is worth a stop on the way to or from Mexico – if not a detour from your Belizean itinerary further south.

## ◉ Sights

**Santa Rita** RUINS

(BZ$10; ⊙8am-6pm) Santa Rita was an ancient Maya coastal town that once occupied the same strategic trading position as present-day Corozal Town, namely the spot between two rivers – the Río Hondo (which now forms the Belize-Mexico border) and the New River (which enters Corozal Bay south of town). Much of Santa Rita remains unexcavated, but it's worth a short excursion out of town to explore the site.

## 🛏 Sleeping & Eating

**Hok'ol K'in Guest House** GUESTHOUSE $

(☑422-3329; www.corozal.net; 89 4th Ave; s/d/tr with fan BZ$77/104/109, with air-con BZ$92/120/130; ❉@🛜) With a Maya name meaning 'rising sun,' this modern, well-run, small hotel overlooking the bay may well be the best value in town. The large, impeccably clean rooms are designed to catch sea breezes. Each has two double beds, a bathroom and a balcony with hammock. Hok'ol K'in also has a cafe serving meals at reasonable prices (breakfasts are particularly good).

**★Almond Tree Resort** RESORT $$

(☑422-0006; www.almondtreeresort.com; 425 Bayshore Dr; r BZ$210-380; 🅿⊜❉🛜🏊) Tucked away on the bay south of town, Almond Tree is a gorgeous little 10-room resort and Corozal's most luxurious central offering. Most of the stylish suites have wonderful sea views, Caribbean-style furniture, Maya and Mexican artworks and modern bathrooms. Deluxe suites have full kitchenettes. The whole place is centered on lush grounds and a glorious swimming pool.

**★Serenity Sands** B&B $$

(☑669-2394; www.serenitysands.com; 50 Serenity Lane; d incl breakfast BZ$200-210, house BZ$220; 🅿❉🛜🏊) 🖉 Located about 3 miles north of Corozal Town, this B&B is off the beaten track, off the grid and out of this world. The remote beachside setting – guests have free use of the private beachfront pool – offers the perfect combination of isolation and accessibility, and the four spacious upper-story rooms are decorated with locally crafted furniture and have private balconies.

**Venky's Kabab Corner** INDIAN $

(☑402-0546; 5th St South; dishes BZ$10-15; ⊙9am-9pm) Chef Venky is the premier – and, as far as we know, only – Hindu chef in Corozal, cooking excellent Indian meals, both meat and vegetarian. The place is not much to look at on the inside – in fact there is just one table that is usually covered in assorted clutter – but the food is excellent and filling.

## ℹ Getting There & Away

In Chetumal, Mexico, buses from Corozal stop at the Nuevo Mercado (New Market), about 0.75 miles north of the town center. A taxi from the Nuevo Mercado to the intercity bus station or town center is around US$1. From Chetumal to Corozal, buses leave from the north side of the Nuevo Mercado from around 4:30am to 6pm.

## AT A GLANCE

**POPULATION**
2 million

**CAPITAL**
Mérida

**BEST BIOSPHERE RESERVE**
Celestún (p183)

**BEST CENOTES**
Valladolid (p198)

**BEST MAYA RUINS**
Uxmal (p171)

**WHEN TO GO**

**Jan** Merida hosts a month-long festival; the climate is at its coolest.

**Mar & Sep** Every equinox, Chichén Itzá visitors see the shadow serpent at El Castillo pyramid.

**Nov-Mar** Beat the heat while visiting inland cities or flamingo-watching in Celestún.

Kabah (p174)
JAVARMAN/SHUTTERSTOCK ©

# Yucatán State & the Maya Heartland

**S**itting regally on the northern tip of the peninsula, Yucatán state sees less mass tourism than its flashy and mass-market neighbor, Quintana Roo. It is the perfect spot for travelers more interested in cultural exploration than beach life. While there are a few good beaches in Celestún and Progreso, most people come to this area to explore the ancient Maya sites, like the Ruta Puuc.

Visitors also come to experience the past and present in the cloistered corners of colonial cities, to experience *henequén* haciendas (vast estates that produced agave-plant fibers, used to make rope), and to discover the energy, spirit and subtle contrasts of this diverse corner of southeastern Mexico.

# Yucatán State & the Maya Heartland Highlights

**1** **Mérida** (p154) Marveling at colonial architecture, feasting at one of the excellent restaurants, or enjoying a free concert in the cultural capital.

**2** **Chichén Itzá** (p190) Spending a full day wandering through this extraordinary Maya complex and finding out why they named this ruin one of the 'new seven wonders of the world.'

**3** **Reserva de la Biosfera Ría Lagartos** (p205) Scanning the horizon for flamingos, other birds and wildlife in the salt pans and lagoons.

**4** **Ruta Puuc** (p175) Getting goosebumps while touring archaeological (and almost magical) Maya sites on this accessible chain.

**5** **Valladolid** (p198) Spinning off the tourist track to the less-visited areas and plunging into the fabulous cenotes around the city.

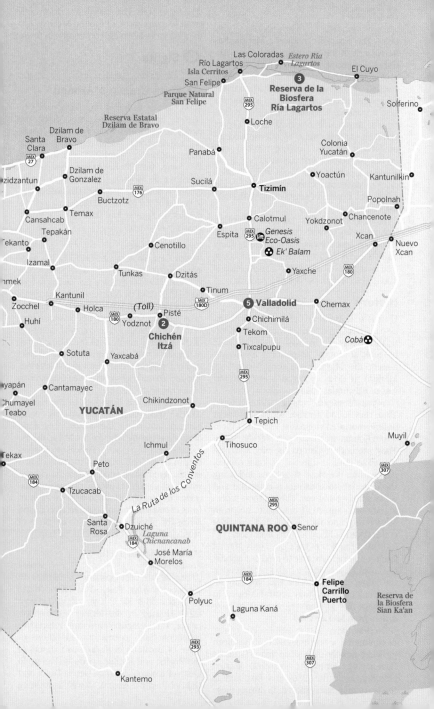

# MÉRIDA

📱 999 / POP 893,000

Since the Spanish conquest, Mérida has been the cultural capital of the entire Yucatán Peninsula. A delightful blend of provincial and cosmopolitan, it is a town steeped in colonial history, with narrow streets, broad central plazas and the region's best museums, including a fantastic collection of Maya archaeological finds. Expect excellent cuisine, some wonderful accommodations options, thriving markets and events happening just about every night. It's also a perfect place from which to kick off your adventure into the rest of Yucatán state, with dozens of sites within easy striking distance.

Long popular with European travelers looking to go beyond the hubbub of Quintana Roo's resort towns, Mérida attracts many tourists, but is too big to feel like a tourist trap. And as the capital of Yucatán state, Mérida is also the cultural crossroads of the region.

## History

Francisco de Montejo (the Younger) founded a Spanish colony at Campeche, about 160km to the southwest, in 1540. From this base he took advantage of political dissension among the Maya, conquering T'ho (now Mérida) in 1542. By decade's end Yucatán was mostly under Spanish colonial rule.

When Montejo's conquistadors entered T'ho, they found a major Maya settlement of lime-mortared stone that reminded them of the Roman architecture in Mérida, Spain. They promptly renamed the city and proceeded to build it into the regional capital, dismantling the Maya structures and using the materials to construct a cathedral and other stately buildings. Mérida took its colonial orders directly from Spain, not from Mexico City, and Yucatán has had a distinct cultural and political identity ever since.

During the War of the Castes only Mérida and Campeche were able to hold out against the rebel forces. On the brink of surrender, the ruling class in Mérida was saved by reinforcements sent from central Mexico in exchange for Mérida's agreement to take orders from Mexico City.

Mérida today is the peninsula's center of commerce, a bustling city that has been growing rapidly ever since *maquiladoras* (low-paying, for-export factories) started cropping up in the 1980s and '90s, and as the tourism industry picked up during those decades as well. The growth has drawn migrant workers from all around Mexico. and there's a large Lebanese community in town.

## ⊙ Sights

### ⊙ Plaza Grande & Around

Plaza Grande is one of the nicest plazas in Mexico, and huge laurel trees shade the park's benches and wide sidewalks. It was the religious and social center of ancient T'ho; under the Spanish it was the Plaza de Armas, the parade ground, laid out by Francisco de Montejo (the Younger). A ceremony is held daily marking the raising and lowering of the Mexican flag; there's a crafts market on Sunday and dance or live music nearly every night.

**Casa de Montejo**                              MUSEUM
(Museo Casa Montejo; 📱999-253-67-39; www.fomentoculturalbanamex.org; Calle 63 No 506, Palacio de Montejo; ⊙10am-7pm Tue-Sat, to 2pm Sun) **FREE** Casa de Montejo is on the south side of Plaza Grande and dates from 1540. It originally housed soldiers, but was soon converted into a mansion that served members of the Montejo family until the 1800s. Today it houses a bank and museum with a permanent exhibition of renovated Victorian, neo-rococo and neo-renaissance furnishings of the historic building.

Outside, take a close look at the facade, where triumphant conquistadors with halberds stand on the heads of generic barbarians (though they're not Maya, the association is inescapable). Typical of the symbolism in colonial statuary, the vanquished are rendered much smaller than the victors; works on various churches throughout the region feature big priests towering over or in front of small indigenous people. Also gazing across the plaza from the facade are busts of Montejo the Elder, his wife and his daughter.

**Museo Fernando García Ponce-Macay**            MUSEUM
(Museo de Arte Contemporáneo; 📱999-928-32-36; www.macay.org; Pasaje de la Revolución s/n, btwn Calles 58 & 60; ⊙10am-5:15pm Wed-Mon) **FREE** Housed in the former archbishop's palace, the attractive museum's impressive collection holds permanent exhibitions of three of Yucatán's most famous painters of the Realist and Ruptura periods (Fernando Castro Pacheco, Fernando García Ponce and Gabriel Ramírez Aznar), as well as rotating

exhibitions of contemporary art from Mexico and abroad.

### Catedral de San Ildefonso    CATHEDRAL

(Calle 60 s/n; ⊙6am-noon & 4:30-8pm) On the site of a former Maya temple is Mérida's hulking, severe cathedral, begun in 1561 and completed in 1598. Some of the stone from the Maya temple was used in its construction. The massive crucifix behind the altar is Cristo de la Unidad (Christ of Unity), a symbol of reconciliation between those of Spanish and Maya heritage.

To the right over the south door is a painting of Tutul Xiu, *cacique* (indigenous chief) of the town of Maní paying his respects to his ally Francisco de Montejo at T'ho. (De Montejo and Xiu jointly defeated the Cocome people; Xiu converted to Christianity, and his descendants still live in Mérida.)

In the small chapel to the left of the altar is Mérida's most famous religious artifact, a statue called Cristo de las Ampollas (Christ of the Blisters). Local legend says the statue was carved from a tree that was hit by lightning and burned for an entire night without charring. It is also said to be the only object to have survived the fiery destruction of the church in the town of Ichmul (though it was blackened and blistered from the heat). The statue was moved to the Mérida cathedral in 1645.

Other than these items, the cathedral's interior is largely plain, its rich decoration having been stripped away by angry peasants at the height of anticlerical fervor during the Mexican Revolution.

### Museo de la Ciudad    MUSEUM

(City Museum; ☑999-924-42-64; Calle 56 No 529A, btwn Calles 65 & 65A; ⊙9am-6pm Tue-Fri, to 2pm Sat & Sun) FREE The Museo de la Ciudad is housed in the old post office and offers a great reprieve from the hustle, honks and exhaust of this market neighborhood. There are exhibits tracing the city's history back to preconquest days up through the belle-epoque period, when *henequén* (sisal) brought riches to the region, and into the 20th century.

### Palacio de Gobierno    PUBLIC ART

(Calle 61 s/n; ⊙8am-7pm) FREE Built in 1892, the Palacio de Gobierno houses the state of Yucatán's executive government offices (and a tourist office). Don't miss the wonderful murals and oil paintings by local artist Fernando Castro Pacheco housed in a magnificent *sala* (hall). Completed in the late 1970s, they portray a symbolic history of the Maya and their interaction with the Spaniards and give excellent context to any trip around the region.

### Centro Cultural Olimpo    NOTABLE BUILDING

(☑999-942-00-00, ext 80130; www.merida.gob.mx/capitalcultural; cnr Calles 61 & 62; ⊙10am-8pm Tue-Sat, to 3pm Sun) Attempts to create a modern exterior for Mérida's municipal cultural center were halted by government in order to preserve the colonial character of the plaza. The modern interior serves as a venue for music and dance performances, as well as other exhibitions.

### Mercado Municipal Lucas de Gálvez    MARKET

(cnr Calles 56A & 67; ⊙6am-5pm) Mérida's main market is an ever-evolving mass of commerce, with stalls selling everything from *panuchos* (fried tortillas stuffed with beans and topped with meat and veggies) to ceviche. The chaotic surrounding streets are all part of the large market district.

---

## ◉ Calle 60

Lined with many of the city's most emblematic sights, Calle 60 cuts through the heart of the Centro, and further north it runs parallel to Paseo de Montejo, a wide main avenue known for its elegant mansions.

### Parque Santa Lucía    PARK

(cnr Calles 60 & 55) The pretty little Parque Santa Lucía has arcades on the north and west sides; this was where travelers would get on or off the stagecoaches that linked towns and villages with the provincial capital. Today it's a popular restaurant area and venue for Serenatas Yucatecas (Yucatecan Serenades), a free weekly concert on Thursday at 9pm.

### Iglesia de Jesús    CHURCH

(Iglesia de la Tercera Orden; Calle 60 s/n) The 17th-century Iglesia de Jesús was built by Jesuits in 1618. It's the sole surviving edifice from a complex of buildings that once filled the entire city block. The church was built from the stones of a destroyed Maya temple that had occupied the site. On the west wall facing Parque Hidalgo, look closely and you can see two stones still bearing Maya carvings.

### Teatro Peón Contreras    THEATER

(☑923-13-34-35; www.sinfonicadeyucatan.com.mx; cnr Calles 60 & 57; tickets from M$150; ⊙9am-9pm) The enormous Teatro Peón Contreras was built between 1900 and 1908, during Mérida's *henequén* heyday. It boasts a main staircase

# Mérida

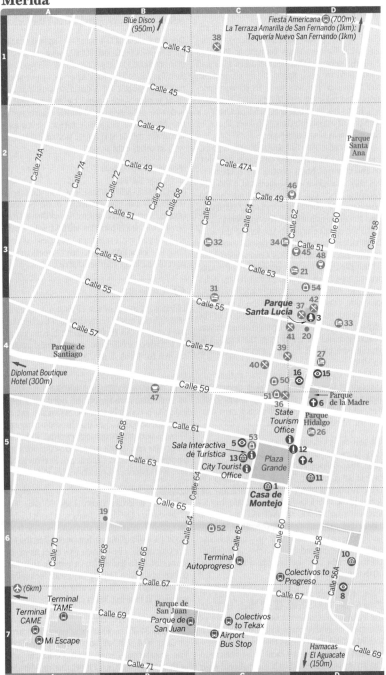

Blúe Disco (950m)

Fiesta Americana (700m);
La Terraza Amarilla de San Fernando (1km);
Taquería Nuevo San Fernando (1km)

Calle 43

38

Calle 45

Calle 47

Parque
Santa
Ana

Calle 74A

Calle 74

Calle 72

Calle 49

Calle 47A

Calle 70

Calle 68

Calle 66

Calle 64

Calle 62

Calle 60

Calle 58

46

Calle 49

Calle 51

Calle 51

34

45

48

Calle 53

32

Calle 53

21

Calle 55

54

Calle 55

31

42

37

Parque
Santa Lucía

3

33

41

20

Parque de
Santiago

Calle 57

Calle 57

39

27

Diplomat Boutique
Hotel (300m)

40

16

15

Calle 59

50

47

51

36

Parque
de la Madre

6

State
Tourism
Office

Parque
Hidalgo

Calle 68

Calle 61

26

Sala Interactiva
de Turística

5

53

Calle 63

13

City Tourist
Office

Plaza
Grande

12

4

11

1

Casa de
Montejo

Calle 70

Calle 65

19

52

Calle 64

Calle 62

Calle 60

Calle 58

Terminal
Autoprogreso

10

Colectivos to
Progreso

Calle 56A

(6km)

Calle 67

Calle 67

8

Terminal
TAME

Terminal
CAME

Calle 69

Parque de
San Juan

Colectivos
to Tekax

Mi Escape

Parque de
San Juan

Airport
Bus Stop

Hamacas
El Aguacate
(150m)

Calle 69

Calle 71

of Carrara marble, a dome with faded frescoes by Italian artists, and various paintings and murals throughout the building. The **Yucatán Symphony Orchestra** performs here Friday at 9pm and Sunday at noon (in season). See the website for more information.

**Universidad Autónoma**
**de Yucatán**     UNIVERSITY
(www.agendaculturaluady.com; Calle 60 s/n) The modern Universidad Autónoma de Yucatán was established in the 19th century by Governor Felipe Carrillo Puerto and General Manuel Cepeda Peraza. Inside you'll find the university cultural center, which stages dance, music and theater performances.

## ◉ Parque de la Mejorada

Head six blocks east of Calle 60 and you'll find this pleasant square flanked by a pretty colonial-era monastery.

**Museo de Arte Popular**
**de Yucatán**     MUSEUM
(Yucatán Museum of Popular Art; Calle 50A No 487; ⏲10am-5pm Tue-Sat, to 3pm Sun) **FREE** In a building constructed in 1906, the Museo de Arte Popular de Yucatán has a small rotating exhibition downstairs that features popular art from around Mexico. The permanent exhibition upstairs gives you an idea of how locals embroider *huipiles* (long, woven, white sleeveless tunics with intricate, colorful embroidery) and it explains traditional techniques used to make ceramics. Watch out for jaguars drinking toilet water!

**Iglesia La Mejorada**     CHURCH
(Calle 50 s/n) Across from Parque de la Mejorada stands Iglesia La Mejorada, a large 17th-century church. The building just north of it was a monastery (el Convento de La Mejorada) until the late 19th century. It now houses an academic building, but visitors are (sometimes) allowed to view the grounds.

## ◉ Paseo de Montejo

Paseo de Montejo, which runs parallel to Calles 56 and 58, was an attempt by Mérida's 19th-century city planners to create a wide boulevard similar to the Paseo de la Reforma in Mexico City or the Champs-Élysées in Paris. Though more modest than its predecessors, the Paseo de Montejo is still a beautiful green swath of relatively open space in an urban conglomeration of stone and concrete.

# Mérida

There are occasional sculpture exhibits along the paseo (promenade).

Europe's architectural and social influence can be seen along the paseo in the fine mansions built by wealthy families around the end of the 19th century. The greatest concentrations of surviving mansions are north of Calle 37, and on the first block of Avenida Colón west of Paseo de Montejo.

★ Gran Museo del
Mundo Maya                          MUSEUM
(☎999-341-04-30; www.granmuseodelmundo maya.com.mx; Calle 60 Norte 299E; adult/child under 13yr M$150/25; ☺9am-5pm Wed-Mon; 🅿) A world-class museum celebrating Maya culture, the Gran Museo houses a permanent collection of more than 1100 remarkably well-preserved artifacts, including a reclining chac-mool sculpture from Chichén Itzá and a cool underworld figure unearthed at Ek' Balam (check out his punk-rock skull belt and reptile headdress). If you're planning on visiting the area's ruins, drop by here first for some context and an up-close look at some of the fascinating pieces found at the sites.

Inaugurated in 2012, the contemporary building was designed in the form of a ceiba, a sacred tree believed by the Maya to connect the living with the underworld and the heavens above. On a wall outside, the museum offers a free light-and-sound show at night.

You'll find it about 12km north of downtown on the road to Progreso. Public transportation running along Calle 60 will leave you at the museum's entrance.

### ★ Palacio Cantón                                    MUSEUM
(Regional Anthropology Museum; ☑999-923-05-57; Paseo de Montejo 485; adult/child under 13yr M$60/free; ☺8am-5pm Tue-Sun) This massive mansion was built between 1909 and 1911, though its owner, General Francisco Cantón Rosado (1833–1917), lived here for only six years before his death. The Palacio's splendor and pretension make it a fitting symbol of the grand aspirations of Mérida's elite during the last years of the Porfiriato – the period from 1876 to 1911 when Porfirio Díaz held despotic sway over Mexico.

It hosts temporary exhibitions and the entry fee may depend on what's on.

### Quinta Montes Molina                                HOUSE
(☑999-925-59-99; www.laquintamm.com; Paseo de Montejo No 469 btwn Calles 33 and 35; M$100; ☺tours in English 9am, 11am and 3pm Mon-Fri, 9am and 11am Sat) This living history house gives you a sense of the splendor and grandeur of the 'Oro Verde' (Green Gold) *henequén* era. The only original house of its kind open to the public, it is accessed via guided tour from the in-house museum, the Casa Museo Montes Molina, by appointment only.

## 🏃 Activities

In an effort to make the city more bike-friendly, Mérida closes down stretches of Paseo de Montejo and Calle 60 to traffic on Sunday morning. For night tours, the bicycle collective Ciclo Turixes (www.facebook.com/colectivocicl_turixes) gathers at Parque Santa Ana most Wednesdays at around 8:30pm.

### Bici Mérida                                          CYCLING
(☑999-287-35-38; Paseo de Montejo s/n, btwn Calles 45 & 47; per hour M$30; ☺8am-10pm Mon-Fri, to 5pm Sat, to 3pm Sun) Rents out mountain bikes, tandems, bicycles for kids and other cool rides.

## 🍲 Courses

### Los Dos                                              COOKING
(☑999-191-26-20; www.los-dos.com; Calle 68 No 517; 1-day courses & tours from US$125) Formerly run by the late US-educated chef David Sterling, this cooking school continues to offer courses with a focus on flavors of the Yucatán under the direction of chef Mario Canul, who worked with David for many years. It offers a one-day *cocina económica*

class for US$125 per person and a Taste of Yucatán Class for US$200 per person.

### Instituto Benjamín Franklin                         LANGUAGE
(☑999-928-00-97; www.benjaminfranklin.com.mx; Calle 57 No 474A; 1hr class US$18) This nonprofit teaches intensive Spanish-language courses.

## ☞ Tours

### ★ Turitransmérida                                    TOURS
(☑999-924-11-99; http://turitransmerida.com.mx; Calle 55, btwn Calles 60 & 62; ☺8am-7pm Mon-Fri, to 1pm Sat, to 11am Sun) Turitransmérida does good day-long group tours to sites around Mérida, including Celestún (M$950 per person), Chichén Itzá (M$750), Uxmal and Kabah (M$700), and Izamal (M$700). Also does a day trip around the Ruta Puuc (M$850). You can arrange in advance for guides who speak your language. Four-person minimum.

### Transportadora Turística Carnaval                    BUS
(☑999-927-61-19; www.carnavalitocitytour.com.mx; Calle 55 btwn Calles 60 & 62; tour M$120; ☺tours 10am, 1pm, 4pm & 7pm Mon-Sat, 1pm & 3pm Sun) Run by the same folk as Turitransmérida, this outfit conducts regular two-hour guided tours of Mérida in English and Spanish on its Paseo Turístico bus departing from Parque Santa Lucía (p155).

### Historic Center Tours                                WALKING
(☑999-942-00-00; www.merida.gob.mx/turismo; Calle 62 s/n, Plaza Grande; ☺walking tours 9:30am Mon-Sat) FREE The city tourist office runs free 1½-hour guided walking tours of the historic center in both Spanish and English, departing daily from the Palacio Municipal (City Hall; Calle 62 s/n; ☺24hr) FREE.

### Nómadas Travel                                       TOURS
(☑999-924-52-23; www.nomadastravel.com; Calle 62 No 433) Nómadas arranges a variety of tours, such as day trips including transportation and guide to Reserva de la Biosfera Ría Celestún (M$1100) and outings to Chichén Itzá (M$750) and Uxmal, Yaxkopoil and a cenote (M$750). The hostel also provides informative DIY sheets with written instructions detailing costs and transportation tips for more than a dozen destinations in the region.

### Ecoturismo Yucatán                                   ECOTOUR
(☑999-920-27-72; www.ecoyuc.com.mx; Calle 3 No 235 btwn 32A & 34; day tours to Chichén Itzá US$48, Uxmal & Kabah US$51; ☺9am-6pm Mon-Fri, to 1pm Sat) The owners of reputable Ecoturismo

Yucatán are passionate about both sharing and protecting the state's natural treasures. Trips focus on archaeology, birding, natural history, biking and kayaking. The price of one-day excursions to Chichén Itzá or Uxmal and Kabah include entrance fees, transportation and lunch.

## ✻ Festivals & Events

Dates for events may vary from year to year. For more specific information, visit www.culturayucatan.com.

**Mérida Fest**                                   CULTURAL
(www.merida.gob.mx; ⊗ Jan)   This cultural event held throughout most of January celebrates the founding of the city with art exhibits, concerts, theater and book presentations at various venues.

**Carnaval**                                     RELIGIOUS
(⊗ Feb/Mar) Prior to Lent, Carnaval features colorful floats, dancers in costumes and nonstop festivities. It's celebrated with greater vigor in Mérida than anywhere else in Yucatán state.

**Festival de las Aves Toh**                       FESTIVAL
(Toh Bird Festival; www.festivalavesyucatan.com; ⊗ Feb-Nov) Toh holds various events throughout the year, culminating with a 'bird-a-thon' (bird-counting competition) in late November.

**Semana Santa**                                 RELIGIOUS
(Holy Week; ⊗ Mar/Apr) A major celebration in Mérida over Easter week. The main feature of the celebrations is the city's Passion Plays.

**Primavera Cultural**                              MUSIC
(www.culturayucatan.com; ⊗ Mar/Apr) A month-long event usually in March or April, it celebrates *trova* (troubadour-type folk music) and just about any other music genre you can imagine.

**Otoño Cultural**                                CULTURAL
(www.culturayucatan.com; ⊗ Sep & Oct) Typically held in September and October, this three-week autumn fest stages more than 100 music, dance, visual-art and theater events.

**Paseo de Ánimas**                        STREET CARNIVAL
(Festival of Souls; ⊗ around Oct 31) Hundreds of locals flaunt their skeleton-style and parade through the altar-lined streets for Day of the Dead celebrations. Musical renditions, artist performances and local food carts add to the festivities.

## 🛏 Sleeping

Budget rooms generally have fans; spending the extra money for air-con is well worth it in the hotter months. Many places market themselves as boutique hotels, but in reality are very smart B&Bs with several luxurious rooms. Unimpressive cheapie hotels are within steps of the bus stations, but you'll find better options elsewhere.

**★Nómadas Hostel**                           HOSTEL $
(📞 999-924-52-23;   www.nomadashostel.mx; Calle 62 No 433; dm from M$215, d M$640, without bathroom M$500, incl breakfast;   🅿 ❄ 🛜 🏊 )
One of Mérida's best hostels, Nómadas has mixed and women's dorms as well as private rooms with bathroom. Guests have use of a fully equipped kitchen, as well as spotless showers, toilets and hand-laundry facilities. It even has free salsa, yoga, *trova* (troubadour-type folk music) and cooking classes, and an amazing pool out back that is always buzzing with a young party-friendly crowd.

The owner, Señor Raul, was one of the first 'contemporary' hosteliers in Mexico, and he knows his stuff. See the website for various tours to nearby ruins.

**62 St Guesthouse**                        GUESTHOUSE $
(📞 999-924-30-60; Calle 62 No 448 btwn Calles 51 & 53; d M$750;   🅿 ❄ 🛜 🏊 ) Impeccably clean and about as tranquil as you can get, this old-school guesthouse offers a friendly, one-of-the-family ambience, along with nice showers, spotless bathrooms and in-room fridges. Guests have use of a kitchen and small pool out back. Charming hosts, Charlie the Cat, and a patio papaya tree add to the vibe.

**★Luz en Yucatán**                            HOTEL $$
(📞 999-924-00-35; www.luzenyucatan.com; Calle 55 No 499; r US$58-100;   🅿 ❄ 🛜 🏊 ) Luz en Yucatán has a perfect downtown location, 15 individually decorated rooms, fabulous common areas and a wonderful pool-patio area out back that combine to make it one of Mérida's very best accommodations. Knowledgeable and enthusiastic owners Tom and Donard and their helpful, English-speaking staff assist with every need and can arrange tours and activities.

A free tasting bar lets you sip tequila, triple sec or anise liqueur any time you feel like it, while a new coffee shop was being built at the time of our last visit.

★ **Hotel del Peregrino** HOTEL $$
(☎ 999-924-30-07; www.hoteldelperegrino.com; Calle 51 No 488 btwn Calles 54 & 56; r incl full breakfast from M$1200; ☯✻@☂) A former house and now guesthouse-cum-hotel, Peregrino's 13 clean, if dated, rooms comprise a mishmash of furniture and some modern creature comforts, such as Netflix. A different full breakfast is served in a patio downstairs each day of the week, and upstairs you can relax in the hotel's rooftop hot tub. Towel origami animals on the beds are a lovely touch.

The hotel has recently installed air-con units that use 60% less power, a nice boost to the environment.

**Hotel La Piazzetta** HOTEL $
(☎ 999-923-39-09; www.hotellapiazzettamerida.com; Calle 50A No 493, btwn Calles 57 & 59; d incl breakfast from M$750; ☯✻☂) Off a quiet side street overlooking Parque de la Mejorada (p157), this friendly little guesthouse-cum-hotel has lovely views of the park or the pleasant patio area. Each of the well-appointed rooms is decked out with a contemporary feel: stressed wooden tables, hanging baskets with towels and the like. Bike loans are available. An airy, pleasant on-site cafe forms the lobby.

**Casa Ana B&B** B&B $$
(☎ 999-181-66-55, 999-924-00-05; www.casaana.com; Calle 52 No 469; r incl breakfast US$50; ☯✻☂≋) Casa Ana is a casual but intimate escape and one of the best deals in town. It has a small pool and a cozy overgrown garden. The four rooms are spotless and have Mexican hammocks and mosquito screens. The Cuban owner Ana is on site, which adds a personal, friendly touch.

**Hotel Julamis** BOUTIQUE HOTEL $$
(☎ 999-924-18-18, cell 998-1885508; www.hoteljulamis.com; Calle 53 No 475B; r incl breakfast US$75-110; ✻☂) The highlight of this B&B is its breakfast, prepared by the gourmet-chef owner, Alex. The rooms are very pleasant (each features unique design details, such as colorful murals and original tiled floors), if a tad tired. But the 6pm tequila tastings and sociable happy hour make for a pleasant stay.

**Gran Hotel** HOTEL $$
(☎ 999-923-69-63; http://granhoteldemerida.com; Calle 60 No 496; s/d M$740/990, ste M$1500; ℗☯✻☂) This was indeed a grand hotel when built in 1901. Most rooms in this old-timer are pretty tired; some have slight-ly more modern features, while several still have the same old-period furnishings and faded carpets. Despite the wear, the lobby retains many elegant and delightful decorative flourishes. And the central location is a plus.

**Doralba Inn** HOTEL $$
(☎ 999-928-56-50; www.doloresalba.com; Calle 63 No 464 btwn Calles 52 & 54; s/d incl breakfast M$800/850; ℗☯✻☂≋) On a slightly gritty side of town, this well-managed hotel is surprisingly quiet inside. Rooms surround two courtyards and have two price categories; nicer ones are in the more expensive, modern wing and feature tile floors and flat-screen TVs, and face the lovely pool.

★ **Diplomat Boutique Hotel** B&B $$$
(☎ 999-117-29-72; www.thediplomatmerida.com; Calle 78 No 493A, btwn Calles 59 & 59A; r US$175-325; ☯✻☂≋) This beautiful, intimate oasis, just southwest of the historic center in a local neighborhood of Santiago, oozes style and charm. The four rooms err on minimalist, with touches of flair such as greenery and tasteful ornamentation. The hospitable Canadian hosts provide a gourmet breakfast spread served on the terrace, treats by the pool, and fabulous ideas for cuisine and exploration.

While high-season rates may be pushing the budget (and often require a minimum three-night stay), low-season rates provide better value. As if things couldn't get better, a complimentary tequila bar and welcome cocktails await.

★ **Casa Lecanda** BOUTIQUE HOTEL $$$
(☎ 999-928-01-12; www.casalecanda.com; Calle 47 No 471, btwn Calles 54 & 56; d/ste incl breakfast from US$290/393; ✻☂≋) Behind its beautiful but unassuming facade, Casa Lecanda is a cut above Mérida's other boutique options thanks to attention to detail in both the design and the guest service. A 19th-century mansion stuffed with antiques and restored to stunning effect, it only has seven rooms, each decorated with a nod to traditional styles while including plentiful amenities and luxurious bathrooms.

The courtyard surrounds a small pool, which looked like it needed a bit of a refresh on our last visit, but there's a lovely shady area for hammocks and lush gardens. Continental breakfasts are served in the colonial-style dining room and an array of tequilas and Mexican wines can be sampled at the bar.

**YUCATÁN STATE & THE MAYA HEARTLAND** MÉRIDA

**Los Arcos Bed & Breakfast**　　B&B **$$$**
(☑999-928-02-14; www.losarcosmerida.com; Calle 66 No 448B; d incl breakfast US$85-95; P❄✳🤖❄) Certainly not for minimalists – there's art on every wall and knickknacks filling every space – Los Arcos is a lovely, gay-friendly ('everyone-friendly') B&B with two guestrooms at the end of a drop-dead-gorgeous garden and pool area. Rooms have an eclectic assortment of art and antiques, plus excellent beds and bathrooms. No pets or minors.

**Hotel Casa del Balam**　　HOTEL **$$$**
(☑999-924-88-44; www.casadelbalam.com; Calle 60 No 488, btwn Calles 55 & 57; d/ste M$1800/3000; P❄✳@🤖❄) This place is centrally located, has an attractive pool and large, quiet colonial-style rooms with shiny tiles and extra-firm beds with wrought-iron bedheads. It often offers hefty discounts during quiet times, which make it solid value.

**Casa San Angel**　　BOUTIQUE HOTEL **$$$**
(☑999-928-18-00; www.hotelcasasanangel.com; Montejo 1, cnr Calle 49 & Montejo; r incl breakfast M$2725, ste M$2975; P🤖❄) Bright jungle murals and a massive vine cover the walls of the colonial patio of this welcoming spot, the home of a well-known Mexican mathematician. The 13 rooms are unpretentious and the location, at the northern end of *centro historico* and at the base of Paseo Montejo, is unbeatable. The pool is tiny but hey, it's refreshing. A restaurant is attached.

**Rosas y Xocolate**　　BOUTIQUE HOTEL **$$$**
(☑999-924-29-92; www.rosasandxocolate.com; Paseo de Montejo 480; r/ste from US$327/505; P✳🤖❄) Built from the remains of two mansions and reusing much of the original materials, this medium-sized hotel is rosy indeed, though much of its interior is painted in restrained and muted tones. It goes all out with custom-made furniture, Nespresso machines, Bose sound systems and open-air baths in each room. An air-conditioned gym, full day spa and gourmet restaurant are also onsite.

**Hotel Medio Mundo**　　HOTEL **$$$**
(☑999-924-54-72; www.hotelmediomundo.com; Calle 55 No 533; d incl breakfast US$90; ❄✳🤖❄) This former private residence exudes a casual feel: its bright colors and ample, simply furnished rooms have super-comfortable beds, Talavera-tiled sinks and windows facing on to the patio. One of the

two courtyards has a swimming pool, the other a fountain, and there's a good on-site vegan restaurant. The well-traveled, charming hosts make their guests feel at home.

## 🍴 Eating

Mérida is a culinary treat, with all kinds of cuisines for all kinds of budgets. You can dine on cheap but mind-blowingly delicious street food or try modern Mexican and international fusion at a range of world-class establishments. Don't miss Mérida en Domingo, an all-day food and crafts market in the Plaza Grande every Sunday. It's a great place to try a wide variety of regional dishes at bargain prices.

**★La Terraza Amarilla de San Fernando**　　MEXICAN **$**
(☑999-189-62-10; Av Cupules 503D; tacos & tortas M$15-24; ⊙7am-3pm) With mouthwatering cheap eats well worth detouring for, La Terraza Amarilla is a gem: you choose between four styles of mains (tacos, tortas etc) and one of seven different fillings, and in seconds your plastic plate arrives. Each menu item is the recipe of the chef-owner and his wife, who will lovingly detail each option for you given the chance.

With the different combinations you could probably eat here every night for a month without having the same item twice.

**Mercado Municipal Lucas de Gálvez**　　MARKET **$**
(cnr Calles 56A & 67; mains M$50-60; ⊙6am-5pm) Mérida's least-expensive eateries are here. Upstairs are tables and chairs and diverse menus offering main courses of beef, fish or chicken. Look for *recados* (spice pastes). Downstairs at the north end are cheap *taquerías* (taco stalls), while the south end has *coctelerías* – seafood stalls specializing in shellfish cocktails and ceviche (seafood marinated in lemon or lime juice, garlic and seasonings).

**Sukra Bar de Café**　　CAFE **$$**
(☑999-923-44-53; www.facebook.com/sukracafe; Paseo de Montejo 496, btwn Calles 43 & 45; mains M$70-135; ⊙9am-6pm Mon-Sat, to 2pm Sun; 🤖) This easygoing spot, at the beginning of Paseo de Montejo, is framed by pretty plants and features an eclectic mix of tables and chairs, more reminiscent of a great aunt's house than a cafe overlooking the poshest street in town. The excellent salads and

sandwiches are equally as down to earth. Dig in and watch the world go by.

### Wayan'e
TACOS **$**

(☎999-291-94-22; cnr Calles 59 & 46; tacos M$14-20, tortas M$22-50; ☺7am-2:30pm Mon-Sat) Popular for its *castakan* (crispy pork belly), Wayan'e (meaning 'here it is' in Maya) is one of Mérida's premier breakfast spots. Vegetarians will find options here, such as the *huevo con xkatic* (egg with chili) taco and fresh juices. But if you eat meat, it's all about the greasy goodness of the *castakan torta* (crispy pork-belly sandwich).

### Bistro Cultural
FRENCH **$$**

(Calle 66 No 377C, btwn Calles 41 & 43; mains breakfast M$60-80, lunch M$95-125; ☺8:30am-5:30pm Mon-Sat, to 4:30pm Sun; ☎) While the cuisine is French, the influence is Yucatecan, and locally grown, organic products are used where possible. The small menu varies but includes a local twist on a croque monsieur, and there is a daily special on top of the normal menu, all served in a pleasant courtyard garden.

Delectable French pastries (M$15 to M$20) are also on sale.

### Cafetería Pop
CAFE **$**

(☎999-928-61-63; www.cafeteriapop.com; Calle 57 s/n btwn Calles 60 & 62; breakfast M$20-85, lunch M$75-130; ☺7am-11pm Mon-Sat, from 8am Sun) There's a '70s feel to this little orange-and-cream cafeteria-style restaurant, which has cheap breakfast combinations and a good variety of Mexican dishes, all served ultra-efficiently. Try the chicken in dark, rich *mole* sauce. It's the type of reliable place you'll keep returning to.

---

**WORTH A TRIP**

### THE LOST HENEQUÉN HACIENDAS OF YUCATÁN

Yucatán state would have been little more than a provincial backwater if it weren't for a spiky son-of-a-bitch-of-a-plant named Agave Fourcroydes. Some call it *henequén,* others call it sisal; call it what you will, the lanced-leaved plant used to create strong maritime rope and twine was 'green gold' from the late 19th century to the end of WWII. It was during this time that the 'sisal barons' of Yucatán built their elaborate haciendas for the booming business. But the industry bottomed out post-WWII with the advent of synthetic fibers.

Not only did the demise of *henequén* force the region's haciendas to shutter operations; it had a devastating economic impact on the town of Sisal, the main seaport for *henequén* exports back in the heyday.

Most of the area's *henequén* haciendas are now in ruins, but some have been restored to past glory and make for amazing upscale retreats or simply interesting places to visit.

In recent years some haciendas have been promoted on the 'Hacienda Route'. This fascinating route allows you to appreciate some impressive old haciendas in rural Maya communities. If you're driving out of Celestún, turn south off Hwy 281 and head toward Chunchucmil, the name of both a ruined *henequén* hacienda and a nearby Maya archaeological site.

After Chunchucmil (look for the covered Maya mounds as you drive away), about every 5km you'll pass another ruined hacienda all the way to **Hacienda Granada**, shortly before the road hits old Hwy 180. Several of the buildings are hard to see from the road, so you'll need to stop frequently to really give them their due.

In some places caretakers will gladly show you around – just make sure to pay them a tip. **Hacienda Santa Rosa** (☎999-923-19-22; www.thehaciendas.com; Carretera Mérida-Campeche, Maxcanú turnoff; r incl breakfast from US$468; ☉☺❄☎☎) is the only hacienda along the route that has been converted into a hotel, and there's a gourmet restaurant there if you want to stop for lunch.

About 5km after Santa Rosa you'll reach a fork in the road. Veer right to visit Granada, where you can visit a couple of *talleres de arte popular* (artisan workshops) near the church. Drop by from Monday to Friday to watch local women create *jipijapa* (palm frond) hats and baskets as well as *henequén* crafts. Hwy 180 (the road to Mérida) is 1km east of Granada.

## LA COCHINITA QUEST

It seems like just about everyone in Mérida has an opinion on where you can get the best *cochinita pibil* (slow-cooked pork marinated in citrus juice and annatto spice). *Cochinita* is prepared in tacos, *tortas* (sandwiches) or as a main dish, and the best of the best is cooked in a pit, giving it a smoky flavor. Mérida has some very tasty options.

Out-of-towners staying in the nearby business-class hotels have been known to buy kilos of the tacos from Taquería Nuevo San Fernando (Av Cupules s/n btwn Calles 60 & 62; tortas M$25; ⊙7am-1pm; 🚍R-2) to take home with them. It's a bit of a trek to get here (near the northern end of Paseo Montejo), but the freshly made bread, roasted habanero salsa and tender *cochito* make it worth it.

### Nectar
YUCATECAN $$$

(☎999-938-08-38; www.nectarmerida.mx; Av García Lavín 32; mains M$192-605; ⊙1:30pm-midnight Tue-Sat, 2-6pm Sun) Inventive and delicious takes on traditional Yucatecan cuisine, a setting that would win design awards and superfriendly staff make for a winning combination at this north Mérida destination restaurant (take a taxi). The pork-belly tacos, *cebollas negras* (blackened onions), venison tartare and any of the fish mains are all superb and well worth the price and distance.

### Lo Que Hay
VEGAN $$

(☎999-924-54-72; www.hotelmediomundo.com; Calle 55 No 533; 3-course menu M$200; ⊙7-10pm Tue-Sat; 🖥🍴) Even nonvegans usually give an enthusiastic thumbs up to this dinner-only restaurant, where three-course themed vegan meals are served in a serene courtyard. The dishes range from Mexican and Lebanese cuisine to raw vegan. Lo Que Hay is in the Hotel Medio Mundo and it welcomes nonguests.

### ★ Ku'uk
INTERNATIONAL $$$

(☎999-944-33-77; www.kuukrestaurant.com; Av Rómulo Rozo 488, cnr Calle 27; mains M$290-550, tasting menu M$1600, with wine pairing M$2500; ⊙1:30-11pm Tue-Sat, to 5pm Sun) The stunning historic home, at the end of Paseo Montejo, sets the scene for what's to come: a high-end, gourmet meal that will end up setting a very high benchmark for Mexican cuisine. You can dine in a number of elegant, if slightly bare, rooms. The cuisine gives a nod to Yucatecan cuisine with contemporary preparation and flavor twists.

### ★ Oliva Enoteca
ITALIAN $$$

(☎999-923-30-81; www.olivamerida.com; cnr Calles 47 & 54; mains M$190-600; ⊙1-5pm & 7pm-midnight Mon-Sat; 🖥) This contemporary restaurant with black-and-white tiled floors, Edison light bulbs, designer chairs and an open kitchen is a magnet for the local smart set who descend en masse for excellent and creative Italian cuisine. Those craving something other than a margarita will love the cocktail selection, as well as the wines. Desserts are to die for.

### ★ Apoala
MEXICAN $$$

(☎999-923-19-79; www.apoala.mx; Calle 60 No 471, Parque Santa Lucía; mains M$140-480; ⊙1pm-midnight Mon-Sat, 2-10pm Sun; 🖥) With influences from Oaxaca, which like the Yucatán is known for its extraordinary regional cuisine, Apoala reinvents popular dishes such as *enmoladas* (stuffed tortillas in a rich *mole* sauce) and *tlayudas* (a large tortilla with sliced beef, black beans and Oaxaca cheese). It's in a lovely spot on Parque Santa Lucía and also boasts some of Mérida's best cocktails.

### La Chaya Maya
MEXICAN $$$

(☎999-928-47-80; www.lachayamaya.com; cnr Calles 62 & 57; mains M$100-340; ⊙7am-11pm; 🖥) This is the original branch of the popular Yucatecan restaurant, offering a near-identical menu (tasty Yucatecan specialties) but slightly different hours, and the place is a bit less fancy than the newer one (☎999-928-22-95; www.lachayamaya.com; Calle 55 No 510; mains M$100-340; ⊙7:30am-11pm; 🖥) nearby.

### La Tratto
ITALIAN $$$

(☎999-923-37-87; www.latrattomerida.com; Calle 60 s/n btwn Calles 53 & 55; mains M$185-285, set menu M$195; ⊙1pm-midnight Sun-Wed, to 1am Thu-Sat; 🖥) A bistro (one of two locations around town) that's consistently OK and best known for its gourmet pizzas and handmade pastas. You can enjoy happy hour at the bar between 6pm and 9pm. Sitting outside on the pretty Plaza Santa Lucia is a delight, especially on Thursday evenings when the local cultural concert takes place.

## Amaro
INTERNATIONAL **$$$**

(☎ 999-928-24-51; www.restauranteamaro.com; Calle 59 No 507; mains M$140-400; ⊙ 11am-1am; 🛜 🖋) An old-style spot can be romantic at night, especially when there are performing *trova* acts (after 8:30pm). It's in the courtyard of the house where Andrés Quintana Roo – poet, statesman and drafter of Mexico's Declaration of Independence – was born in 1787. The menu includes Yucatecan choices and a variety of vegetarian and continental dishes.

## 🍸 Drinking & Nightlife

You need not look far to find a friendly neighborhood bar. These range from traditional cantinas to more cutting-edge wine and cocktail bars.

### ★ Manifesto
COFFEE

(www.manifesto.mx; Calle 59 No 538, btwn Calles 66 and 68; ⊙ 8am-9pm Mon-Sat; 🛜) This place, run by a trio from Calabria, Italy, offers an ambitious 'manifesto' indeed: a revolution in coffee brought about by fusing Italian preparation methods with the very best beans Mexico has to offer. It's a compelling combination, and the sleek premises is the kind of place where you'll want to order your coffee to drink in.

They roast their beans here, too, and you can buy packets with beans originating from all over Southern Mexico.

### Mercado 60
COCKTAIL BAR

(www.mercado60.com; Calle 60, btwn Calles 51 & 53; ⊙ 6pm-late) For a fun night of booze and cheap(ish) international eats, head to this atmospheric, lively and diverse culinary market, where the margaritas will have you dancing alongside locals to live salsa music. This modern concept is a cocktail bar meets beer hall, with different businesses serving up different concoctions.

The cuisine – ranging from Mexican gourmet tacos to ramen noodles – is also served from small kiosks. Dishes, while tasty, could be better but they do the 'soaking-up' trick...

### PK2
GAY & LESBIAN

(☎ 999-154-60-12; www.facebook.com/PK2Disco BarMerida; Calle 56 btwn Calles 53 and 55; cover from M$100; ⊙ 9pm-3am Wed-Sun) One of the city's top spots for gay nightlife, the PK2 has strip shows, revues, drag queens and more, set to pumping trance- and electro-themed music. Nightly specials and the variety of acts make it one of the most popular Mérida gay venues.

### Cara Negra
BAR

(www.caranegra.mx; Calle 62 No 436; ⊙ 7pm to 1am) If you've been craving a spot to sip cocktails and look at skulls, your search is over. This dark, macabre-themed place has an excellent selection of craft beers, original cocktails, and a vibe that's not so loud or pumping that you can't chat with friends or strike up a conversation with the people nearby.

### La Negrita
DANCING

(www.facebook.com/LaNegritaMerida; Calle 62 s/n, cnr Calle 49; ⊙ noon-10pm; 🛜) This postmodern cantina (think contemporary grunge) is the current hot spot in town. If the live music doesn't inspire you to get a tropical groove on, it's just a matter of time before the mojitos and mezcals have you dancing the night away. The rear garden makes a nice spot to catch a breather and chat with locals.

Musical acts go on daily from 6pm, and the clientele often includes passengers from cruise ships docked in Progresso.

## ☆ Entertainment

Mérida organizes many folkloric and musical events in parks and historic buildings, put on by local performers of considerable skill. Admission is mostly free. The tourist publication *Yucatán Today* has a good summary of weekly events.

### Blúe Disco
KARAOKE

(☎ 999-436-04-87; www.facebook.com/Bluedisc; Av Colón No 503 btwn Calles 72 and 72A; cover from M$30; ⊙ 9pm-3:30am Wed-Sun) Strippers, drag queens and karaoke are the reasons to come to Blue, which is a bit far from the center near the Paseo de Montejo. Great shows and a casual, friendly vibe.

### Centro Cultural Olimpo
CONCERT VENUE

(☎ 999-924-00-00 ext 80130; www.merida.gob.mx/capitalcultural; cnr Calles 62 & 61) This cultural center on Plaza Grande always has something going on: films, concerts, art installations and other events, many of which are free.

## 🛍 Shopping

### Guayaberas Jack
CLOTHING

(Calle 59 No 507A; ⊙ 10am-8pm Mon-Sat) The *guayabera* (embroidered dress shirt) is the classic Mérida shirt, but in buying the wrong one you run the risk of looking like a waiter. Drop into this famous shop to avoid getting asked for the bill.

**Cielo Hamacas**  ARTS & CRAFTS
(☑999-924-04-40; www.hamacasmerida.com.mx; Calle 65 No 510, btwn Calles 62 & 64; ☺9am-7pm Mon-Fri, to 1pm Sat) Has a large catalog with all kinds of sizes, shapes and colors of locally produced hammocks, Maya hanging chairs and all accessories for creating that perfect hang-out space. It can ship purchases worldwide.

**Tejón Rojo**  GIFTS & SOUVENIRS
(www.tejonrojo.com; Calle 53 No 503; ☺noon-9pm Mon-Sat, to 6pm Sun) One of the more original places to get your Mérida souvenirs, the 'red badger' sells screen-printed graphic T-shirts and Mexican pop-culture knickknacks, including coffee mugs, jewelry, handbags, caps and – inevitably – wrestling masks.

**Librería Dante**  BOOKS
(www.libreriadante.com.mx; cnr Calles 61 & 62, Plaza Grande; ☺8am-10:30pm) Shelves a selection of archaeology and regional-history books in English and has good Yucatecan cookbooks. There are other branches throughout the city.

**Miniaturas Folk Art**  ARTS & CRAFTS
(☑999-928-65-03; Calle 59 No 507A btwn Calles 60 & 62; ☺11am-10pm Mon-Sat) Here you'll find lots of small Día de Muertos (Day of the Dead) tableaux, tinwork and figurines of every sort, from ceramics to toy soldiers. They all have two things in common: they're easy to pack and have nothing to do with Yucatán artisan traditions, originating instead from Puebla, Zacatecas or San Miguel de Allende.

**Camisería Canul**  CLOTHING
(☑999-923-56-61; www.camiseriacanul.com.mx; Calle 62 No 484; ☺9am-8pm Mon-Sat, 10am-2pm Sun) A good place for *guayaberas* (embroidered dress shirts) and *huipiles* (traditional blouses and dresses). It has been in business since 1948, offering fixed prices and custom tailoring.

**Hamacas El Aguacate**  ARTS & CRAFTS
(☑999-947-46-51; www.hamacaselaguacate.com.mx; Calle 58 No 604, cnr Calle 73; ☺9am-7pm Mon-Fri, to 5:30pm Sat) Hamacas El Aguacate stocks quality hammocks at decent prices (M$550 to M$700), and there's absolutely no hard sell. Also has mosquito nets for M$200.

## ⓘ Orientation

The Plaza Grande has been the city's heart since the time of the Maya. Though Mérida now sprawls many kilometers in all directions, many of the services and attractions for visitors are within 10 blocks of the Plaza Grande. Following the classic colonial plan, the square is ringed by several barrios (neighborhoods), each with its own park and church.

Odd-numbered streets run east–west; even-numbered streets run north–south. Addresses are usually given in this form: 'Calle 57 No 481 x 46 y 48' (between streets 46 and 48).

Lined with many of the city's most emblematic sights, Calle 60 cuts through the heart of the Centro, and further north it runs parallel to Paseo de Montejo, a wide main avenue known for its elegant mansions.

## ⓘ Information

### EMERGENCY
**Emergency** (☑066, ☑911)
**Fire** (☑999-924-92-42)
**Red Cross** (☑999-924-98-13)
**Tourist Police** (☑999-942-00-60)

---

### CRAFTS & TRADITIONAL WEAR

The Yucatán is a fine place for buying handicrafts and traditional clothes. Purchases to consider include *guayaberas*, colorfully embroidered *huipiles* and wonderfully comfortable hammocks.

Women throughout the Yucatán Peninsula traditionally wear straight, white cotton dresses called *huipiles*, with embroidered bodices. You'll come across these loose-fitting garments in many markets across the peninsula.

Men commonly wear *guayaberas* (light, elegant shirts, usually with four square pockets). They can be worn in both casual and formal settings, and the cotton and linen materials keep the body cool on warm, humid days.

You'll also find craft shops and street stalls selling wooden handicrafts of Spanish galleons and carvings of Maya deities. Campeche is the state most associated with such items, but they are made by accomplished artisans in the states of Yucatán and Quintana Roo as well.

For more on handicrafts, pick up a copy of *The Crafts of Mexico*, by Margarita de Orellana and Alberto Ruy Sánchez.

## YUCATECAN HAMMOCKS: THE ONLY WAY TO SLEEP

Yucatecan hammocks are normally woven from strong nylon or cotton string and dyed in various colors. There are also natural, undyed cotton versions. Some sellers will try to pass these off as *henequén* (agave plant fibers) or jute, telling you it's much more durable (and valuable) than cotton, and even that it repels mosquitoes. Don't be taken in: real *henequén* hammocks are very rough and not something you'd want near your skin. Silk hammocks are no longer made, but a silk-rayon blend has a similar feel.

Hammocks come in several widths, and though much is made of the quantity of pairs of end strings they possess, a better gauge of a hammock's size and quality is its weight. The heavier the better. A *sencilla* (for one person) should be about 500g and cost around M$400 to M$450. The queen, at 1100g, runs from around M$600. *De croché* (very tightly woven) hammocks can take several weeks to produce and cost double or triple the prices given here. Nylon hammocks are usually cheaper.

Mérida and its surrounding towns have some good spots for buying a hammock.

### INTERNET ACCESS

Free public wi-fi access is available on several of the main plazas and in many cafes.

### MEDIA

**Yucatán Today** (www.yucatantoday.com) is a free and very useful Spanish-English magazine devoted to tourism in Yucatán. Pick up a copy of the magazine in hotels or visit the website for great tips.

### MEDICAL SERVICES

*Yucatán Today* (www.yucatantoday.com/en/topics/healthcare-merida-yucatan) has a good list of doctors and hospitals.

**Clínica de Mérida** (☑ 999-942-18-00; www.clinicademerida.mx; Av Itzáes 242, cnr Calle 25; ☉ 24hr; ☐ R-49) Good private clinic with laboratory and 24-hour emergency service.

**Hospital O'Horán** (☑ 999-930-33-20; cnr Avs de los Itzáes & Jacinto Canek; ☉ 24hr) A centrally located public hospital for emergencies. For less urgent matters, such as prescriptions and consultations, consider going to a private clinic.

### MONEY

Banks and ATMs are scattered throughout the city. There is a cluster of both along Calle 65 between Calles 60 and 62, one block south of Plaza Grande. *Casas de cambio* (money-exchange offices) have faster service and longer opening hours than banks, but often have poorer rates.

### POST

**Post Office** (☑ 999-928-54-04; Calle 53 No 469, btwn Calles 52 & 54; ☉ 8am-7pm Mon-Fri, to 3pm Sat) Central post office.

### TOURIST INFORMATION

You'll find tourist information booths at the airport. Tourist offices downtown have basic brochures and information and maps.

**City Tourist Office** (☑ ext 80119 999-942-00-00; www.merida.gob.mx/turismo; Calle 62, Plaza Grande; ☉ 8am-8pm) Right on the main plaza, it is staffed with helpful English speakers. Here you can hook up free walking tours of the city, which depart daily at 9:30am.

**Sala Interactiva** (Calle 62, btwn Calles 61 and 63, Palacio Municipal; ☉ 9am-8pm) On the plaza, with fancy touch screens and multimedia info displays.

**State Tourism Office** (☑ 999-930-31-01; www.yucatan.travel; Calle 61 s/n, Plaza Grande; ☉ 8am-8pm) In the entrance to the Palacio de Gobierno. There's usually an English speaker on hand.

## ❶ Getting There & Away

### AIR

Mérida's Aeropuerto Internacional de Mérida (p297) is a 10km, 20-minute ride southwest of Plaza Grande off Hwy 180 (Avenida de los Itzáes). It has car-rental desks, several ATMs, currency-exchange services and an information desk for assisting you to find transportation into town.

Most international flights to Mérida make connections through Mexico City. Nonstop international services are provided by Aeroméxico and United Airlines.

**Aeroméxico** (☑ 800-021-40-00; www.aeromexico.com; Aeropuerto Internacional de Mérida) Flies direct from Miami.

**Interjet** (☑ 800-011-23-45, US 866-285-9525; www.interjet.com; Aeropuerto Internacional de Mérida) Serves Mexico City, where you can catch connecting flights to New York, Miami and Houston.

**Mayair** (☑ 800-962-92-47; www.mayair.com.mx; Aeropuerto Internacional de Mérida) Runs prop planes to Cancún that continue on to Cozumel.

**VivaAerobus** (☑ 818-215-01-50, US 888-935-9848; www.vivaaerobus.com; Aeropuerto Internacional de Mérida) Service to Mexico City and Monterrey.

**Volaris** (☑ Mexico City 55-1102-8000, US 866-988-3527; www.volaris.com; Aeropuerto Internacional de Mérida) Direct to Mexico City and Monterrey.

### BUS

Mérida is the bus transportation hub of the Yucatán Peninsula. Take care with your bags on night buses and those serving popular tourist destinations (especially 2nd-class buses): there have been reports of theft on some routes.

There are a number of bus terminals, and some lines operate from (and stop at) more than one terminal. Tickets for departure from one terminal can often be bought at another, and destinations overlap greatly among bus lines. Check out www.ado.com.mx for ticket info on some of the lines.

**Terminal CAME** (Terminal de Primera Clase; ☑ 999-924-08-30 ext 2406; Calle 70 s/n, btwn Calles 69 & 71; ⊙ 24hr; ☎) Mérida's main bus terminal has (mostly 1st-class) buses – including ADO, OCC and ADO GL – to points around the Yucatán Peninsula and faraway places such as Mexico City.

**Fiesta Americana Bus Terminal** (☑ 999-924-83-91; cnr Calle 60 & Av Colón; ☐ R-2) A small

## BUSES FROM MÉRIDA

| DESTINATION | FARE (M$) | TIME (HR) | FREQUENCY (PER DAY) & TERMINAL |
|---|---|---|---|
| Campeche | 264-341 | 2½-3 | hourly (6am-11:45pm) |
| Cancún | 476-496 | 4½-6½ | hourly; Terminal CAME, Terminal TAME |
| Celestún | 60 | 2½ | frequent; Noreste, Terminal TAME |
| Chetumal | 339-446 | 5½-6 | 3-4; Terminal TAME |
| Chichén Itzá | 99-180 | 1½-2 | frequent; Terminal CAME, Noreste, Terminal TAME |
| Escárcega | 306-430 | 4-4½ | 3 (8:30am, 2:15pm, 9pm); Terminal TAME |
| Felipe Carrillo Puerto | 234 | 6 | frequent; Terminal TAME |
| Izamal | 31 | 1½ | frequent; Noreste |
| Mayapán | 37 | 1½ | hourly; Noreste |
| Mexico City | 999-1900 | 20 | 7; Terminal CAME, Terminal TAME |
| Palenque | 662-729 | 7½-10 | 4; Terminal CAME, Terminal TAME |
| Playa del Carmen | 304-498 | 4-6 | frequent; Terminal CAME, Terminal TAME |
| Progreso | 21 | 1 | frequent; Terminal Autoprogreso |
| Río Lagartos/San Felipe | 170-250 | 3½ | 3 (5:30am, 9am, 4pm); Noreste |
| Ruta Puuc (round-trip; 30min at each site) | 99 | 8-8½ | weekly (8am Sunday); Terminal TAME |
| Ticul | 57 | 1¾ | frequent; Terminal TAME |
| Tizimín | 125-190 | 4-5 | frequent; Noreste |
| Tulum | 205-356 | 4-4½ | 5; Terminal CAME, Terminal TAME |
| Uxmal | 76 | 1½ | 5; Terminal TAME |
| Valladolid | 125-240 | 2½-3 | frequent; Terminal CAME, Terminal TAME |

1st-class terminal on the west side of the Fiesta Americana hotel complex servicing guests of the luxury hotels on Avenida Colón, north of the city center. ADO buses run between here and Cancún, Playa del Carmen, Villahermosa and Ciudad del Carmen.

**Noreste Bus Terminal** (Autobuses del Noreste y Autobuses Luz; ☑999-924-63-55; cnr Calles 50 & 67) Noreste and Luz bus lines use this terminal. Destinations served from here include many small towns in the northeast part of the peninsula, including Tizimín and Río Lagartos; Cancún and points along the way; and small towns south and west of Mérida, such as Celestún, Ticul, Ruinas de Mayapán and Oxkutzcab.

Some Oriente buses depart from Terminal TAME and stop here.

**Parque de San Juan** (Calle 69, btwn Calles 62 & 64) From all around the square and church, combis (vans and minibuses) depart for Muna (M$30), Oxkutzcab (M$55), Tekax (M$75), Ticul (M$45) and other points between about 5am and 10pm daily.

**Terminal Autoprogreso** (Progreso Bus Terminal; ☑999-928-39-65; www.autoprogreso. com; Calle 62 No 524; ◷5am-10pm) This is a separate terminal with buses leaving for the northern beach town of Progreso.

**Terminal TAME** (Terminal de Segunda Clase; ☑999-924-08-30; Calle 69, btwn Calles 68 & 70; ◷24hr) This terminal is just around the corner from Terminal CAME. ADO, Mayab, Oriente, Sur, TRT and ATS run mostly 2nd-class buses to points in the state and around the peninsula, including Ticul (M$57), Oxkutzcab (M$60), Valladolid (M$125) and Tizimín (M$115).

**Colectivo to Tekax** (Calle 62, btwn Calles 67 & 69)

**Colectivo to Progreso** (Calle 60)

### CAR

The most flexible way to tour the many archaeological sites around Mérida is to travel with a rental car. Assume you will pay M$1000 to M$2500 per day (tax and insurance included) for short-term rental of an economy-size vehicle.

Getting around Mérida's sprawling tangle of one-way streets is normally better on foot or by bus, though driving is perfectly possible in the city as well.

Several agencies have branches at the airport and on Calle 60, between Calles 55 and 57. You'll get the best deal by booking online.

**Easy Way** (☑999-930-95-00; www.easyway rentacar.com; Calle 60 No 484, btwn Calles 55 & 57; car rental incl basic insurance from US$50 per day; ◷7am-11pm)

**National** (☑999-923-24-93; www.national car.com; Calle 60 No 486F, btwn Calles 55 & 57; economy car incl basic insurance from M$2500; ◷8am-1pm & 4-8pm)

## ⓘ Getting Around

### TO/FROM THE AIRPORT

The taxi companies **Transporte Terrestre** (☑999-946-15-29; www.transporteterres tredemerida.com; per car M$250) and **ADO** (☑999-454-18-01; www.transportadoaeropuerto. mx/en; M$250) provide speedy service between the airport and downtown, charging M$200 (same price for hotel pickup). A street taxi from downtown to the airport should cost M$120. If you want to get this same price *from* the airport, you'll need to walk out to the main road and flag down a city cab.

A city bus labeled 'Aviación 79' (M$8) travels between the main road of the airport entrance. The bus does not enter the airport, but instead **stops outside** (cnr Calles 62 & 69) and connects downtown every 15 to 30 minutes until 9pm, with occasional service until 11pm. The best place to catch the same bus to the airport is at Parque San Juan, from the corner of Calles 62 and 69.

### BUS

City buses are cheap at M$8, but routes can be confusing. Some start in suburban neighborhoods, skirt downtown and terminate in another distant suburban neighborhood. **Transpublico. com** (https://merida.transpublico.com) provides detailed maps of all the routes.

To travel between Plaza Grande and the upscale neighborhoods to the north along Paseo de Montejo, catch the R-2 'Hyatt' or 'Tecnológico' lines along Calle 60. To return to downtown, catch any bus heading south on Paseo de Montejo displaying the same signs and/or 'Centro.' A bus heads to/from the airport, too.

### TAXI

More and more taxis in town are using meters these days. If you get one with no meter, be sure to agree on a price before getting in. M$30 to M$50 is fair for getting around downtown and to the bus terminals. Taxi stands can be found at most of the barrio parks (dispatch fees may cost extra).

**Radio Taxímetro del Volante** (☑999-928-30-35) For 24-hour radio taxi service.

## SOUTH OF MÉRIDA

There's a lot to do and see south of Mérida. The major draws are the old *henequén* plantations, some still used for cultivating leaves, and the well-preserved Maya ruins such as

## DAY TRIPS FROM MÉRIDA

Mérida makes a great base for day trips to all kinds of interesting destinations in the countryside, from quiet coastal towns and fun swimming holes to Maya ruins and excellent birding locations. Here are some worthwhile trips.

**Cuzamá & Homún** Amazing cenotes (limestone sinkholes) can be accessed by horse-drawn cart in Cuzamá (p177) and at Santa Barbara (p177) in Homún.

**Ruta Puuc** Ruin yourself by visiting all five sites (including megadraw Uxmal) in one day. Extend your trip by visiting Mayapán (p176) and the Grutas de Loltún (p176).

**Celestún** Head out early to catch a mangrove-birding boat tour. With a bit more time, you can visit the ruined haciendas along the way.

**Dzibilchaltún & Progreso** Visit the ruins (p185) and cenote or extend your trip for an afternoon of beach time in Progreso (p186).

---

Uxmal and the lesser-known sites along the Ruta Puuc. Beyond these tourist attractions you'll find hundreds of seldom-visited cenotes and caves, and traditional villages where life moves at an agrarian pace: women wear *huipiles* and speak Maya, and men still bike out to cut firewood or shoot a pheasant for dinner. It's a rough-and-tumble landscape, and one of the few spots on the peninsula where you'll actually find a few hills.

## Oxkintok

Archaeologists have been excited about the ruins of Oxkintok (www.inah.gob.mx; M$60; guides M$600; ⊘8am-5pm; P) for several years. Inscriptions found at the site contain some of the oldest-known dates in the Yucatán, and indicate the city was inhabited from the pre-Classic to the post-Classic period (300 BCE to 1500 CE), reaching its greatest importance between 475 CE and 860.

Three main groups of the approximately 8-sq-km site have been restored thus far, all near the site entrance. Though much of the rebuilding work looks like it was done with rubble, you can see examples of Oxkintok, Proto-Puuc and Puuc architecture. The highest structure (15m) is Ma-1, La Pirámide, in the Ah-May group, which provides good views of the area. Probably the most interesting structure is Palacio Chich (Estructura Ca-7), in the Ah-Canul group, for its original stonework and the two columns in front carved with human figures in elaborate dress. Researchers discovered a labyrinth beneath La Pirámide, though unfortunately it's closed to the public.

The ruins are reached via a west-leading fork off the road to the Grutas de Calcehtok, which is 75km southwest of Mérida off Hwy 184, a few kilometers south of the town of Calcehtok. The 4.5km dirt road to the ruins is in poor shape, so expect a slow, bumpy ride.

## Grutas de Calcehtok

The Calcehtok caves (Grutas de X'Pukil; ✆cell 999-2627292; off Hwy 184; tours M$100-300; ⊘8am-5pm; P) are said to comprise the longest dry-cave system on the Yucatán Peninsula. More than 4km have been explored so far, and two of the caves' 25 vaults exceed 100m in diameter (one has a 30m-high 'cupola'). The caves hold abundant and impressive natural formations; however, if you're claustrophobic, have a fear of dark spaces or don't like getting dirty, this definitely isn't for you.

Archaeologists have found and removed ceramic arrowheads, quartz hammers and other tools, and you can still see low fortifications built by the Maya who sheltered here during the Caste War.

All tours are guided and flashlights are provided. The opening of the main entrance is an impressive 30m in diameter and 40m deep, ringed by vegetation often buzzing with bees. It's about 1m deep in bat guano at the bottom. You can opt for a basic, intermediate or adventure tour – the latter involves belly-crawling, rope descents and possibly the 7m long by 20cm wide 'Pass of Death,' or 'El Parto' (the Birth: you figure it out). Tours last one to four hours.

Note that a 'competing' entry is (logically) also named Grutas de Calcehtok and lies on the access to to Oxkintok ruin. To get to the original entrance continue straight rather than turning right toward the ruin. Both have identical signs.

The caves are 75km southwest of Mérida off Hwy 184, a few kilometers south of the town of Calcehtok. They are best reached by car.

# Uxmal

**Uxmal** (☑ 997-976-20-64; www.inah.gob.mx/es/zonas/110-zona-arqueologica-de-uxmal; Hwy 261 Km 78; adult M$234, light & sound show M$92, parking M$30, guide M$800; ☺ site 8am-5pm, light & sound show 8pm Apr-Sep & 7pm Oct-Mar; 🚻), pronounced oosh-mahl, is an impressive set of ruins, easily ranking among the top (and unfortunately most crowded) Maya archaeological sites. It is a large site with some fascinating structures in good condition and bearing a riot of ornamentation. Adding to its appeal is Uxmal's setting near the hilly Puuc region, which lent its name to the architectural patterns in this area. *Puuc* means 'hills,' and these, rising up to about 100m, are the first relief from the flatness of the northern and western portions of the peninsula.

For an additional cost, Uxmal projects a nightly light-and-sound show.

For an entirely different experience, outside the ruins, the Choco-Story museum takes a look at the history of chocolate.

## History

Uxmal was an important city in a region that encompassed the satellite towns of Sayil, Kabah, Xlapak and Labná. Although Uxmal means 'Thrice Built' in Maya, it was actually constructed five times.

That a sizable population flourished in this dry area is yet more testimony to the engineering skills of the Maya, who built a series of reservoirs and *chultunes* (cisterns) lined with lime mortar to catch and hold water during the dry season. First settled about 600 CE, Uxmal was influenced by highland Mexico in its architecture, most likely through contact fostered by trade. This influence is reflected in the town's serpent imagery, phallic symbols and columns. The well-proportioned Puuc architecture, with its intricate, geometric mosaics sweeping across the upper parts of elongated facades, was strongly influenced by the slightly earlier Río Bec and Chenes styles.

The scarcity of water in the region meant that Chaac, the rain god or sky serpent, carried a lot of weight here. His image is ubiquitous at the site in the form of stucco masks protruding from facades and cornices. There is much speculation as to why Uxmal was abandoned in about 900 CE; a severe drought may have forced the inhabitants to relocate.

Rediscovered by archaeologists in the 19th century, Uxmal was first excavated in 1929 by Frans Blom. Although much has been restored, there is still a good deal to discover.

## ◎ Sights

**Cuadrángulo de las Monjas** ARCHAEOLOGICAL SITE
The 74-room, sprawling Nuns' Quadrangle is directly west of the Casa del Adivino. Archaeologists guess variously that it was a military academy, royal school or palace complex. The long-nosed face of Chaac appears everywhere on the facades of the four separate temples that form the quadrangle. The northern temple, the grandest of the four, was built first, followed by the southern, then the eastern and finally the western.

Several decorative elements on the exuberant facades show signs of Mexican, perhaps Totonac, influence. The feathered-serpent (Quetzalcóatl, or in Maya, Kukulcán) motif along the top of the west temple's facade is one of these. Note also the stylized depictions of the *na* (traditional Maya thatched hut) over some of the doorways in the northern and southern buildings.

Passing through the corbeled arch in the middle of the south building of the quadrangle and continuing down the slope takes you through the **Juego de Pelota** (Ball Court). From here you can turn left and head up the steep slope and stairs to the large terrace. If you have time, you could instead turn right to explore the western **Grupo del Cementerio** (which, though largely unrestored, holds some interesting square blocks carved with skulls in the center of its plaza), then head for the stairs and terrace.

**Palacio del Gobernador** ARCHAEOLOGICAL SITE
The Governor's Palace, with its magnificent facade nearly 100m long, is arguably the most impressive structure at Uxmal. The buildings have walls filled with rubble, faced with cement and then covered in a thin veneer of limestone squares; the lower part of the facade is plain, the upper part festooned with stylized Chaac faces and geometric designs, often lattice-like or fretted.

# Uxmal

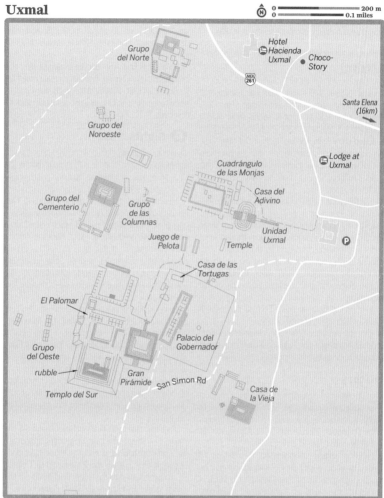

YUCATÁN STATE & THE MAYA HEARTLAND UXMAL

Other elements of Puuc style are decorated cornices, rows of half-columns (as in the Casa de las Tortugas) and round columns in doorways (as in the palace at Sayil).

Researchers recently discovered some 150 species of medicinal plants growing on the east side of the palace. Due to the high concentration of plants growing there it's believed they were cultivated by the Maya to treat stomach infections, snake bites and many other ailments.

**Casa del Adivino**        ARCHAEOLOGICAL SITE
(Pirámide del Adivino) As you approach Uxmal, the Casa del Adivino comes into view. This 35m-high temple (the name translates as 'Magician's House') was built in an unusual oval shape. What you see is a restored version of the temple's fifth incarnation, consisting of round stones held rudely together with lots of cement. Four earlier temples were completely covered in the final rebuilding by the Maya, except for the high doorway on the west side, which remains from the fourth temple.

Decorated in elaborate Chenes style (a style that originated further south), the doorway proper forms the mouth of a gigantic Chaac mask.

**Gran Pirámide** ARCHAEOLOGICAL SITE

The 30m-high, nine-tiered pyramid has been restored only on its northern side. Archaeologists theorize that the quadrangle at its summit was largely destroyed in order to construct another pyramid above it. That work, for reasons unknown, was never completed. At the top are some stucco carvings of Chaac, birds and flowers.

**Choco-Story** MUSEUM

(☑999-289-99-14; www.choco-storymexico.com; Hwy 261 Km 78, near Hotel Hacienda Uxmal; adult/child 6-12yr M$140/90; ⊙9am-7:30pm) You'll learn more than you ever wanted to know about chocolate at this interesting chain museum that follows a circuit through six exhibition spaces spread throughout the lush botanic garden, where there's also interesting text about the nutritional and medicinal values of the flora. The grounds are home to rescued jaguars and spider monkeys as well.

You cap off the visit tasting a bitter chocolate drink and then exit past, you guessed it, the gift shop. The museum is across the highway, next to Hotel Hacienda Uxmal.

**Casa de las Tortugas** ARCHAEOLOGICAL SITE

The House of the Turtles, which you'll find on top of a hillside overlooking the Juego de Pelota (Ball Court), takes its name from the turtles carved on the cornice. The Maya associated turtles with the rain god, Chaac. According to Maya myth, when the people suffered from drought, so did the turtles, and both prayed to Chaac to send rain.

The frieze of short columns, or 'rolled mats,' that runs around the temple below the turtles is characteristic of the Puuc style.

On the west side of the building a vault has collapsed, affording a good view of the corbeled arch that supported it.

**El Palomar** ARCHAEOLOGICAL SITE

West of the Gran Pirámide sits a structure whose roofcomb is latticed with a pattern reminiscent of the Moorish pigeon houses built into walls in Spain and northern Africa – hence the building's name, which means the Dovecote or Pigeon House. Honeycombed triangular 'belfries' sit on top of a building that was once part of a quadrangle.

**Casa de la Vieja** ARCHAEOLOGICAL SITE

(Old Woman's House) Off the southeast corner of the Palacio del Gobernador's platform is a small complex, now largely rubble, known as the Casa de la Vieja. In front of it is a small

*palapa* (thatch-roof shelter) that covers several large phalluses carved from stone.

## 🛏 Sleeping & Eating

There is no town at Uxmal, only several resort-style hotels aimed at tour groups, and no budget options. A good range of mid-range lodgings can be found in Santa Elena, 16km southeast, or in Ticul, 30km east, though most people press on to either Mérida or Campeche.

The only dining options in Uxmal are the hotel restaurants. For cheaper options head to Santa Elena.

**Lodge at Uxmal** LUXURY HOTEL $$$

(☑997-976-20-31, USA 877-240-5864; www.maya land.com/the-lodge-at-uxmal; Hwy 261 Km 78; r incl breakfast from US$208; 🅿❄🛜🏊) Rooms could be nicer for the price, but you can't beat the easy access to the ruins, and the pool certainly adds value. Some of the more expensive rooms have Jacuzzis. We don't suppose Stephens and Catherwood enjoyed such luxury when they passed through the area in the late 1830s. Private guides to the ruins are available for M$800.

**Hotel Hacienda Uxmal** HISTORIC HOTEL $$$

(☑800-719-54-65, US 877-240-5864; www.maya land.com/hacienda-uxmal; Hwy 261 Km 78; r incl breakfast from US$118; 🅿❄🛜🏊) This attractive Mayaland Resort is 500m from the ruins. It housed the archaeologists who explored and restored Uxmal. Wide, tiled floors, lots of wrought iron, high ceilings, great bathrooms and a beautiful swimming pool make for a pleasant stay. There are even rocking chairs to help you kick back after a hard day of exploring.

## ℹ Getting There & Away

Uxmal is 80km from Mérida. Departures (M$76, 1½ hours, four daily) on the Sur bus line leave from Mérida's Terminal TAME (p169). But going back to Mérida, passing buses may be full. If you get stuck, a taxi to nearby Santa Elena costs M$150 to M$200.

Tours offered by Nómadas Hostel (p159) in Mérida are always a good option, or rent a car and also visit other ruins in the area. Alternately, take a *colectivo* for about M$30.

# Santa Elena

☑997 / POP 3500

Originally called Nohcacab, the town today known as Santa Elena was virtually razed in

1847 in the War of the Castes. 'Ele-na' means burnt houses in Maya. The Mexican government changed the name to Santa Elena in a bold PR stunt.

If you're up for a little DIY adventure, head 4km outside town to the **Mulchic pyramid**; locals can tell you how to get there. Santa Elena also makes a great base to explore the nearby ruins of Uxmal, Kabah and those along the Ruta Puuc.

## ◉ Sights

**Santa Elena Museum**                    MUSEUM
(M$10; ⊙9am-5:30pm) The only reason you go to this tiny museum is for the view (it's perched on a hill) and to support the locals – both worth doing. Displays are modest, mainly pictures and replicas. A small section is devoted to sisal (the fiber made from *henequén*) and natural dyes. The '18th-century child mummies,' are four decomposed, desiccated bodies that were found buried beneath the adjoining cathedral, which is also well worth a look.

## 🛏 Sleeping & Eating

⭐ **Flycatcher Inn**                     B&B $$
(☑997-978-53-50; www.flycatcherinn.com; off Hwy 261; r incl breakfast US$70-117; ⊙mid-Oct–Aug; P❄🐾) Flycatcher Inn features seven squeaky-clean rooms, all with great porches, high-quality hammocks, excellent screenage and spacious bathrooms. It is surrounded by a pleasant garden, and a number of bird and animal species can be seen here, including the flycatchers that gave their name to the place. A lovely pool and high-quality breakfasts make it a great overnight stop.

**Nueva Altia**                         B&B $$
(☑cell 998-2190176; Hwy 261 Km 159; r incl breakfast M$950-1200; P❄🐾🍽) 🌿 If you're looking for some peace and quiet, this is *the* place. Geometrically designed to get nice cross breezes, the spiral-shaped bungalows were inspired by ancient Maya architecture. And, as with many locales, unearthed Maya ruins are tucked away on the pretty, wooded grounds. Each room has two double beds and its own hammock. Wi-fi is in the lobby only.

The eco-hotel runs on solar energy. The turnoff is 1km south of Santa Elena, then head 800m east down a dirt road. Prices are significantly less in low season.

**Pickled Onion**                        B&B $$
(☑997-111-79-22; www.thepickledonionyucatan.com; Hwy 261; d incl breakfast US$55-70; P❄🐾🍽) This charming spot offers modern adobe-walled huts with lovely tiled floors and bathrooms. The well-maintained rooms all come with coffeemakers and mosquito netting and keep you cool with *palapa* roofs. We love the pool and surrounding lush and landscaped gardens, and the restaurant does food to go for picnics in the nearby ruins.

**Restaurant El Chac-Mool**          MEXICAN $$
(☑997-978-51-17; www.facebook.com/chacmooluxmal; Calle 18 No 211B; mains M$80-140; ⊙9am-10pm; P🐾) Off Hwy 261 at the southern entrance to Santa Elena, Restaurant El Chac-Mool is a friendly, if basic, place but service can be slow. It serves tasty, homemade Yucatecan food that includes a hearty vegetarian plate of rice, beans and fried bananas. The smoothies are tasty.

**Pickled Onion**                     MEXICAN $$
(☑999-111-79-22; www.thepickledonionyucatan.com; Hwy 261; mains M$100-130; ⊙7:30am-8:30pm; P🐾) Situated under a large veranda, this spot provides pleasant relief from the sun. Dishes include the usual Yucatecan specialties, as well as a few options (such as gazpacho) that come as a surprise. Service is friendly and fast, and the restaurant will happily provide packed lunches for those visiting nearby archaeological sites.

# Kabah

These often-overlooked **ruins** (Hwy 261; M$60, guides M$500; ⊙8am-5pm) 23km southeast of Uxmal are right astride Hwy 261, the bulk of them on the east side of the highway. On entering the site, head right to climb the stairs of El Palacio de los Mascarones (Palace of the Masks). Standing in front of it is the Altar de los Glifos, the immediate area of which is littered with many stones carved with glyphs. The palace's facade is an amazing sight, covered in nearly 300 masks of Chaac. Most of their huge noses are broken off; the best intact beaks are at the building's south end.

These curled-up noses may have given the palace its modern Maya name, Codz Poop (Rolled Mat; it's pronounced more like 'Codes Pope' than some Elizabethan curse). This section was recently restored.

When you've had your fill of noses, head north and around to the back of the Poop to check out the two restored atlantes (an atlas – plural 'atlantes' – is a male figure used as a supporting column). These are especially interesting, as they're some of the very few 3D human figures you'll see at the main Maya sites. One is headless and the other wears a jaguar mask atop his head.

Descend the steps near the atlantes and turn left, passing the small Pirámide de los Mascarones, to reach the plaza containing El Palacio. The palace's broad facade has several doorways, two of which have a column in the center. These columned doorways and the groups of decorative columnillas (little columns) on the upper part of the facade are characteristic of the Puuc architectural style.

Steps on the north side of El Palacio's plaza put you on a path leading about 200m through the jungle to the Templo de las Columnas, which has more rows of decorative columns on the upper part of its facade. At last visit, access to the temple was closed for restoration.

West of El Palacio, across the highway, a path leads up the slope and passes to the south of a high mound of stones that was once the Gran Pirámide (Great Pyramid). The path curves to the right and comes to a large restored monumental arch. It's said that the *sacbé*, or cobbled and elevated ceremonial road, leading from here goes through the jungle all the way to Uxmal, terminating at a smaller arch; in the other direction it goes to Labná. Once, all of the Yucatán Peninsula was connected by these marvelous 'white roads' of rough limestone.

At present nothing of the *sacbé* is visible, and the rest of the area west of the highway is a maze of unmarked, overgrown paths leading off into the jungle.

The souvenir ticket office sells snacks and cold drinks. For good lodging, stay in Santa Elena, located about 8km north of Kabah.

### ⓘ Getting There & Away

Kabah is 104km from Mérida. It's easiest to reach the site by car, or from Mérida you can take a Sur bus (five daily).

Turitransmérida (p159) and Nómadas Hostel (p159) both run tours here.

# Ruta Puuc

The Ruta Puuc (Puuc Route) meanders through rolling hills dotted with seldom-visited Maya ruins sitting in dense forests. A road branches off to the east (5km south of Kabah) and winds past the ruins of Sayil, Xlapak and Labná, eventually leading to the Grutas de Loltún. The sites offer some marvelous architectural detail and a deeper acquaintance with the Puuc Maya civilization.

## ◉ Sights

★**Labná**                      ARCHAEOLOGICAL SITE
(Ruta Puuc; M$55; ⊗8am-5pm; P ) This is *the* Ruta Puuc site not to miss. Archaeologists believe that, at one point in the 9th century, some 3000 Maya lived at Labná. To support such numbers in these arid hills, water was collected in *chultunes* (cisterns); there were some 60 *chultunes* in and around the city, and several are still visible. El Palacio, the first building you encounter, is one of the longest in the Puuc region, and much of its decorative carving is in good shape.

On the west corner of the main structure's facade, straight in from the big tree near the center of the complex, is a serpent's head with a human face peering out from between its jaws, the symbol of the planet Venus. Toward the hill from this is an impressive Chaac mask, and nearby is the lower half of a human figure (possibly a ballplayer) in loincloth and leggings.

The lower level has several more well-preserved Chaac masks, and the upper level contains a large *chultún* that still holds water. The view of the site and the hills beyond from there is impressive.

Labná is best known for El Arco, a magnificent arch once part of a building that separated two quadrangular courtyards. It now appears to be a gate joining two small plazas. The corbeled structure, 3m wide and 6m high, is well preserved, and the reliefs decorating its upper facade are exuberantly Puuc in style.

Flanking the west side of the arch are carved *na* with multi-tiered roofs. Also on these walls, the remains of the building that adjoined the arch, are lattice patterns atop a serpentine design. Archaeologists believe a high roofcomb once sat over the fine arch and its flanking rooms.

Standing on the opposite side of the arch and separated from it by the *sacbé* is

## GRUTAS DE LOLTÚN

One of the largest dry-cave systems on the Yucatán Peninsula, Loltún (Loltún Caverns; adult/child under 13yr M$140/free, parking M$50; ⊙ tours 9:30am, 11am, 12:30pm, 2pm, 3pm & 4pm; 🖪), 'stone flower' in Maya, provided a treasure trove of data for archaeologists studying the Maya. Carbon dating of artifacts found here reveals that the caves were used by humans 2200 years ago. Chest-high murals of hands, faces, animals and geometric motifs were apparent as recently as 25 years ago, but so many people have touched them that scarcely a trace remains, though some handprints have been restored.

A few pots are displayed in a niche, and an impressive bas-relief, El Guerrero, guards the entrance. Other than that, you'll mostly see illuminated limestone formations.

To explore the labyrinth, you must take a scheduled guided tour, usually in Spanish but sometimes in English if the group warrants it. Please tip your guide, as this is the lion's share of their touring income. Tours last about one hour and 20 minutes, with lots of lengthy stops. Some guides' presentations are long on legends (and jokes about disappearing mothers-in-law) and short on geological and historical information. The sign says the route is 2km, but in reality it's around 1.1km. Colored lights illuminate the route.

Colectivos (shared vans) to Oxkutzcab (osh-kootz-kahb; M$60, 1½ hours, frequent) depart from Calle 67A in Mérida, beside Parque San Juan. Loltún is 7km southwest of Oxkutzcab, where you can catch colectivos (M$20) to the caves from Calle 51 (in front of the market). A taxi costs about M$120.

Renting a car is the best option for reaching the caves, though; once you're out of Mérida it's easy going on pretty good roads.

---

a pyramid known as **El Mirador**, topped by a temple. The pyramid itself is largely stone rubble. The temple, with its 5m-high roofcomb, is well positioned to be a lookout, hence its name.

Labná is 14km east of the Ruta Puuc junction with Hwy 261.

### Sayil
ARCHAEOLOGICAL SITE

(Ruta Puuc; M$55; ⊙ 8am-5pm) Sayil is best known for **El Palacio**, the huge three-tiered building that has an 85m-long facade. The distinctive columns of Puuc architecture are used often here, either as supports for the lintels, as decoration between doorways or as a frieze above them, alternating with stylized Chaac masks and 'descending gods.'

Taking the path south from the palace for about 400m and bearing left, you come to the temple named **El Mirador**, whose rooster-like roofcomb was once painted a bright red. About 100m beyond El Mirador, beneath a protective palapa, is a stela bearing the relief of a fertility god with an enormous phallus, now sadly weathered.

**Grupo Sur** is a bit further, and offers beautiful jungle-covered ruins with tree roots twisting through the walls.

The ruins of Sayil are 4.5km from the junction of the Ruta Puuc with Hwy 261.

### Xlapak
ARCHAEOLOGICAL SITE

(Ruta Puuc; ⊙ 8am-5pm) **FREE** The ornate palacio at Xlapak (shla-pak), also spelled Xlapac, is quite a bit smaller than those at nearby Kabah and Sayil, measuring only about 20m in length. It's decorated with the inevitable Chaac masks, columns and colonnettes and fretted geometric latticework of the Puuc style. The building is interesting and on a bit of a lean.

Plenty of motmots brighten up the surrounding forests. The name Xlapak means 'Old Walls' in Maya and was a general term among local people for ancient ruins.

Xlapak is about 10km east of the Ruta Puuc junction with Hwy 261.

### ❶ Getting There & Away

Public transport services the towns and villages but to do this region well it's best to have your own vehicle. If you want to do the Ruta Puuc or Uxmal only, tours operate out of Mérida.

## Ruinas de Mayapán

Though far less impressive than many Maya sites, **Mayapán** (M$45; ⊙ 8am-4:30pm) is historically significant – it was one of the last major dynasties in the region and established itself as the center of Maya civilization from 1200 to 1440. The site's main attractions are clustered in a compact core, and visitors usually have the place to themselves. It is one of few sites where you can ascend to the top of the pyramid.

The city of Mayapán was large, with a population estimated to be around 12,000; it covered 4 sq km, all surrounded by a great defensive wall. More than 3500 buildings, 20 cenotes and traces of the city wall were mapped by archaeologists working in the 1950s and in 1962. The late-post-Classic workmanship is inferior to that of the great age of Maya art.

Among the structures that have been restored is the Castillo de Kukulcán, a climbable pyramid with fresco fragments around its base and, at its rear side, friezes depicting decapitated warriors. The reddish color is still faintly visible. The Templo Redondo (Round Temple) is vaguely reminiscent of El Caracol at Chichén Itzá.

Don't confuse the ruins of Mayapán with the Maya village of the same name, which is about 40km southeast of the ruins, past the town of Teabo.

## ⓘ Getting There & Away

The Ruinas de Mayapán are just off Hwy 184, a few kilometers southwest of the town of Telchaquillo and some 50km southeast of Mérida. Although some 2nd-class buses run to Telchaquillo (M$50, 1½ hours, hourly), consider renting a car.

## Cenotes de Cuzamá

Three kilometers east of the town of Cuzamá, accessed from the small village of Chunkanan, are the **Cenotes de Cuzamá** (1-4 people M$400; ⊙8am-4pm), a series of three amazing limestone sinkholes accessed by horse-drawn railcart in an old *henequén* hacienda. The fun horse-drawn ride will jar your fillings loose while showing you attractive scenes of the surrounding, overgrown agave fields. Truly spectacular.

Iguana sightings are a sure bet here, but keen eyes can also spot vultures or caracaras, as well as other birds, lizards and the occasional rabbit or two.

One of the cenotes is featured in much of Yucatán's tourist literature, and all three are spectacular, with rope-like roots descending along with ethereal shafts of light to the crystal-clear, deep-blue water. You'll likely find yourself sharing a dip with other bathers unless you get an early start. Several cenotes have steep stairways or ladders that are often slippery, so use caution at all times.

The nearby **Cenote Santa Barbara** (☏999-138-78-43, 999-965-11-98; https://cenote-santa-barbara.negocio.site; Homún; M$150, with set lunch M$220, child 5-12yr M$75; ⊙9:30am-6pm) in Homún is upscale and a bit officious. The main cenote – where you'll spend most of your time – is a cave, with lovely stalagtites. Go early to avoid crowds, as bus tours arrive in the late morning

## ⓘ Getting There & Away

To get to Cuzamá by car, take Hwy 180 toward Cancún until you get to a turnoff for Ticopo on the right; after Akankeh (there's a small pyramid here), bear to the left to reach Cuzamá. From there, head east at the cathedral for 3km to the cenotes. Signs will lead the way. Follow the road all the way to the hacienda. Some competitors along the way will try to offer their services, telling you the hacienda no longer exists – not true; they will bring you to other spots, also with rail carts and cenotes, some of which will be quite pretty as well. To get to the official one, be sure to arrive in town (not random parking lots), where you will see the tracks actually reaching the road.

Buses leave for Cuzamá (around M$30, one hour) from the Noreste bus terminal (p169) in Mérida, or you can take colectivos (around M$30) that depart from in front of the bus terminal.

## Ticul

⟟997 / POP 28,000

Ticul, 30km east of archaeological site Uxmal, is the largest town in this ruin-rich region. It's dusty and fairly quiet, but has hotels, restaurants and transportation, so it's a good base for day trips to nearby ruins. (It's not as attractive a jumping-off point as nearby Santa Elena, though.) Ticul is also a center for fine *huipil* weaving, and ceramics made here from the local red clay are renowned throughout the Yucatán.

Ticul's main street is Calle 23, sometimes called 'Calle Principal,' starting from the highway and going past the *mercado* (market) to the main plaza, Plaza Mayor.

## ◉ Sights

**Iglesia de San Antonio de Padua**    CHURCH
(cnr Calles 25 & 26) Because of the number of Maya ruins in the vicinity, from which building blocks could be acquired, and the number of Maya in the area 'needing' conversion to Christianity, Franciscan friars built many churches in the region, including

SIMON DANNHAUER/SHUTTERSTOCK ©

1. Parque Dos Ojos (p113) 2. Gran Cenote (p127) 3. Cenote Samulá (p199) 4. Cenotes de Cuzamá (p177)

ELZBIETA SEKOWSKA/SHUTTERSTOCK ©

# Yucatán Peninsula Cenotes

One look and it's easy to see why the Maya thought cenotes (limestone sinkholes) were sacred: fathomless cerulean pools, dancing shafts of light, a darkened chamber. Even if you don't buy the spiritual aspects, they're still awe-inspiring examples of nature's beauty – and there are thousands of them dotting the peninsula.

## Dos Ojos (p113)

The cenotes at this Maya-run park on the Riviera Maya are part of one of the largest underwater cave systems on the planet. Experienced divers come from far and wide to plunge into the Pit, a 110m-deep cenote with ancient human and animal remains.

## Gran Cenote (p127)

Known for its large stalactites, stalagmites and columns, this 'grand' cenote appeals to divers, snorkelers and swimmers alike. It's 4km west of Tulum, making it a great little bike ride from town. The grounds are perfect for a picnic.

## Dzitnup (p199)

You get two lovely cenotes at one location near Valladolid, both of which are great for swimming. At X'Kekén you'll see awe-inspiring stalactites hanging from the ceiling, while Samulá is a gorgeous cavern pool with *álamo* (poplar) roots. If Dzitnup is too crowded, hit nearby Hacienda San Lorenzo Oxman, which sees fewer visitors.

## Cuzamá (p177)

A series of three cenotes reached by a horse-drawn rail cart near the town of Chunkanan, about 50km southeast of Mérida. Half the fun is getting there along tracks flanked by attractive agave fields. If you arrive early, before the crowds, you'll have a more pleasant experience in the crystal-clear blue waters.

## THE MODERN MAYA

The area between Ticul and Tihosuco is truly the Maya heartland. Indeed, the Maya in these parts continue to honor the gods of rain, wind and agriculture, just as their ancestors did before them.

Yucatán state has the fifth-highest percentage of indigenous-language speakers in Mexico, but the number of Maya speakers is rapidly declining. In 2005 about 34% of Yucatecans claimed to speak Maya; at last count, less than 30% said they spoke any type of indigenous language at all.

So where have all the Maya gone? Many have moved to big tourist cities like Cancún, while others have moved all the way up to the US. Many small Maya communities are beginning to welcome tourists in an effort to keep young folks from fleeing to the cities. It's ironic, but inviting foreigners in may prove the best way to maintain traditions.

The homes of today's rural Maya are still wood-framed huts with lean-to roofs of palm (though many now live in concrete houses; ironically, these are hot boxes and not as environmentally suited as traditional homes). The hut walls are made of bamboo poles or branches, and the spaces between the poles are often filled with mud to keep pests out. The Maya tend to prefer hammocks to beds.

Anywhere from a stone's throw to an hour's walk from a Maya hut is a *milpa* (cornfield). Corn tortillas remain a staple of the Maya diet, but the Maya also raise pigs and turkeys and produce honey, squash and other crops, which they sell at town markets. Many of the younger generation, particularly men, hitchhike out to work for a week in the larger towns such as Playa del Carmen or Cancún, returning for a day or two, or for long weekends or holidays. A *small* family will have about five children.

Many Yucatecan Maya prefer baseball to soccer. And on any given Sunday, you are likely to witness a down-home game played on the town square. It's a serious endeavor with hired hitters, uniforms and plenty of spectators.

this 16th-century one. Although looted on several occasions, it still has some original touches.

Among them are the stone statues of friars in primitive style flanking the side entrances and a Black Christ altarpiece ringed by crude medallions.

**Plaza de la Cultura** PLAZA

It's all cement and stone but nevertheless the Plaza de la Cultura is an agreeable place to take in the evening breeze, enjoy the view of the church and greet passing townspeople.

## 🛏 Sleeping

**Posada El Jardín** INN $

(☑997-972-04-01; Calle 27 No 216C btwn Calles 28 & 30; r M$600-730; 🅿️🌀❄️🛜🏊) Five rustic rooms surround a lush garden with a swimming pool and a *palapa*-covered lobby at this peaceful getaway, which feels like it's more in the jungle than in the middle of town. It's one of the coolest (we're talking temperature here) places around and has some character. The friendly hosts at this family-run inn have great tips on eating options and the nearby sights.

**Hotel Villareal** HOTEL $

(☑997-972-28-28; hotelvillareal@hotmail.com; Calle 23 s/n btwn Calles 26A & 28; d/tr M$534/615; 🅿️🌀❄️🛜) Considered one of the nicest places in town, which isn't saying much for Ticul's hotel offerings. But rooms are comfortable enough and they have balconies so that you can get some fresh air. There's a restaurant as well (mains M$80 to M$160).

**Hotel Plaza** HOTEL $

(☑997-972-04-84; www.hotelplazayucatan.com; Calle 23 No 202 btwn Calles 26 & 26A; s/d/tr M$420/550/700; 🅿️🌀❄️🛜) Spacious rooms with tiled floors and small but fun balconies make this a pretty good choice, though keep in mind that street-facing rooms may get noise. The old building adds character as does the hotel's location right off the town plaza. Sometimes offers specials including breakfast.

**Hotel San Antonio** HOTEL $

(☑997-972-18-93; hotelsan-antonioticul@hotmail.com; Calle 25A No 202 btwn Calles 26 & 26A; s/d M$275/485; 🅿️🌀❄️🛜) Some rooms have great views of the Plaza de la Cultura. The hotel lacks character, but here in Ticul that's kind of reassuring. All rooms have TV and air-con, and there's also a small parking lot.

## ✕ Eating & Drinking

### ★ El Mirador
YUCATECAN $

(☑ 997-972-13-43; off Calle 42; mains M$80-90; ☺ 11am-6pm; **P**) El Mirador means lookout in Spanish and, yes, you get an awesome view of Ticul and beyond from this large *palapa* restaurant. But it's the tasty Yucatecan comfort food that makes this place truly special. Try the *relleno blanco,* a hearty turkey stew (M$90), or go with a local favorite, *frijol con puerco* (beans and pork, M$85).

Also has excellent *jugos naturales* (juices). You'll find El Mirador's dirt-road turnoff heading south on Calle 42. A taxi from the city center costs about M$30.

### Mercado
MARKET $

(Calle 28A btwn Calles 21 & 23; snacks M$15, mains M$30-45; ☺ 8am-2pm & 5:30-9pm Mon-Sat) Ticul's lively Mercado provides all the ingredients for picnics and snacks, and offers nice photo ops, too. It also has lots of those wonderful eateries where the food is good, the portions generous and the prices low.

You can even pick up that rubber chicken you've always wanted. And if you need more than what the market offers, there's a large chain supermarket nearby.

### Bazar de Comidas
MEXICAN $

(cnr Calles 25 & 22; mains M$25-150; ☺ 8am-5pm) The friendly stalls here serve inexpensive regional food such as *poc-chuc* (grilled pork) and *queso relleno* (stuffed cheese).

### Super Willy's
SUPERMARKET $

(Calle 23 s/n btwn Calles 26 & 26A; ☺ 7am-10pm) Near the plaza, Super Willy's is a small supermarket with a big variety of groceries and household items.

### Pizzería La Gondola
PIZZA $$

(☑ 997-972-01-12; Calle 23 No 208, cnr Calle 26; pizzas M$90-140, sandwiches M$35-45; ☺ 8am-1pm & 5:30-11pm Mon-Fri, 5pm-midnight Sat & Sun) Open late, this clean place has sandwiches and pizzas with the usual toppings. 'Order by number' options make it easy for non-Spanish speakers to get exactly what they want.

## ℹ Information

You'll find banks with ATMs on Plaza Mayor.

## ℹ Getting There & Away

### BUS

Ticul's 24-hour **bus terminal** (☑ 997-972-01-62; Calle 24 s/n btwn Calles 25 & 25A) is behind the massive church. For most destinations, buses from Ticul make numerous stops along the way.

### CAR

The quickest way to Uxmal, Kabah and the Ruta Puuc sites is via Santa Elena. From central Ticul, go west to Calle 34 and turn south; it heads straight to Santa Elena.

Those headed east to Quintana Roo and the Caribbean coast can take Hwy 184 from Ticul through Oxkutzcab to Tzucacab and José María Morelos.

At Polyuc, 130km from Ticul, a road turns left (east), ending after 80km in Felipe Carrillo Puerto. The right fork of the road goes south to Laguna Bacalar. Between Oxkutzcab and Felipe Carrillo Puerto or Bacalar there are few restaurants or gas stations.

### COLECTIVO

*Colectivos* go direct to Mérida's Parque de San Juan (M$45, 1½ hours, 6am to 8:30pm) from the taxi terminal on Calle 24. There you can also catch a *colectivo* to Tekax (M$30, one hour).

Combis for Oxkutzcab (M$20, 30 minutes, 7am to 8pm Monday to Saturday, to 3pm Sunday) leave from Calle 25A, on the south side of the church.

*Colectivos* to Santa Elena (M$17, 6:50am to 8pm), which lies between the Maya sites of Uxmal and Kabah, depart from Calle 30, between Calles 25 and 25A. In Santa Elena, catch another bus northwest to Uxmal (15km) or south to Kabah (3.5km).

YUCATÁN STATE & THE MAYA HEARTLAND TICUL

## BUSES FROM TICUL

| DESTINATION | FARE (M$) | TIME (HR) | FREQUENCY (PER DAY) |
| --- | --- | --- | --- |
| Cancún | 296 | 8 | frequent |
| Chetumal | 244 | 6 | 7 |
| Mérida | 57 | 1½ | frequent |
| Oxkutzcab | 16 | ½ | frequent |
| Playa del Carmen | 284 | 7 | frequent |
| Tulum | 248 | 6 | frequent |

### TAXI

Taxis in front of the *colectivo* terminal, on the corner of Calles 24 and 25, charge around M$1200 for a full day touring the Ruta Puuc ruins. You can ask to make stops at Grutas de Loltún, Labná, Sayil, Xlapak, Kabah and Uxmal if time permits.

# Oxkutzcab

📞 997 / POP 31,000

Oxkutzcab is a rough and bustling town renowned for its daily produce market and colonial church. Markets were the principal means of trade for the ancient Maya, and the peninsula's indigenous people still travel from the countryside to central communities to exchange produce at stalls beside a main square. Oxkutzcab is such a community. A mural in the plaza across from the market depicts inquisitor Friar Diego de Landa's auto-da-fé in Maní, when he burnt thousands of idols.

The town can serve as a base for visiting sites along the Ruta Puuc. Be aware that dog fighting (though illegal in Mexico) is done here and some hotels sponsor these events. You may wish to put your tourist pesos elsewhere.

## ◉ Sights

**Iglesia de San Francisco de Asis**  CHURCH
(Calle 51 s/n) Constructed at a snail's pace from 1640 to 1693, this Franciscan convent is remarkable for its ornamental facade, at the center of which is a stone statue of St Francis, the mission patron. It's also notable for its magnificent altarpiece, one of only a few baroque altarpieces in the Yucatán to survive the revolts that have occurred since its construction.

## ⌒ Sleeping & Eating

**Hotel Ix-Chel**  HOTEL $
(📞 997-975-29-24; www.hotelix-chel.com; Calle 53 No 91A btwn Calles 44 and 46; s/d with air-con M$250/300, with air-con M$300/380; P ⊗ ❄ ⎙) The simple Ix-Chel isn't going to win any awards, but unlike several of the nearby fancier options, it doesn't sponsor dog fighting, which (though illegal) is still part of life in Oxkutzcab.

**El Príncipe Tutul-Xiu**  MEXICAN $
(📞 997-975-29-07; Calle 45 No 102 btwn Calles 50 & 52; mains M$100; ⊙ 11am-7pm; P ) Known for its *poc-chuc* (grilled pork, M$100), the massive, two-story El Principe Tutul-Xiu has

several other classic Yucatecan dishes and desserts. The menu is in indirect proportion to the number of tables, however: excluding the dessert options there are only about five options to choose from.

## ❶ Getting There & Away

Oxkutzcab is 16km southeast of Ticul on Hwy 184, which becomes a two-lane road as its passes through the town center. Buses depart frequently to Oxkutzcab from the Ticul terminal. Buses also travel to/from Mérida, departing from Terminal Tame (p169) and Noreste (p169).

# Tekax

📞 997 / POP 28,000

Tekax is a pretty little town with a central plaza and attractive church. The area is increasingly prosperous, due to a successful crop switch from corn to sugarcane and citrus.

## ◉ Sights

**San Juan Bautista**  CHURCH
Dating from around 1609, Tekax' church has been looted a couple of times, initially during the Caste War and later during the Mexican Revolution. Most noteworthy is its shape, that of a three-tiered pyramid. Since it was most likely constructed of materials taken from nearby Maya temples, it's possible that the architecture was based on a Maya structure.

## ⌒ Sleeping & Eating

**Hotel Sultán de la Sierra**  HOTEL $
(📞 997-974-21-69; hotelsultantekax@hotmail.com; Calle 50A No 211 btwn Calles 55 & 57; d/tr M$350/470; ⊗ ❄ ⎙ ≋) On the main square, the cheerfully ochre Sultán is a very simple budget option with rooms that stay fairly cool during the day, and a small swimming pool just off the lobby. Additional people cost M$50 extra.

**El Huinic de la Ermita**  YUCATECAN $$
(Calle 61 No 202B, cnr Calle 50; mains M$80-165; ⊙ 7am-3am Mon-Sun; ⎙) Arguably the best eats in town, this dark place doubles as a karaoke bar at night for wannabe crooners. It overlooks a pretty plaza and has Yucatecan classics such as *papadzules* (diced-egg enchiladas bathed in pumpkin-seed sauce), *longaniza asada* (grilled Mexican sausage) and *queso relleno* (stuffed cheese), plus steak, chicken and seafood dishes.

# WEST & NORTH OF MÉRIDA

## Celestún

📞 988 / POP 6800

West of Mérida, Celestún is a sleepy sun-scorched fishing village that moves at a turtle's pace. While it's not a historic or particularly attractive town, it does have some nice beaches, and the wonderful Reserva de la Biosfera Ría Celestún, a wildlife sanctuary abounding in waterfowl, where large colonies of flamingos are the star attraction.

It makes a good beach-and-bird day trip from Mérida, and you can even spend a night or two here if you fancy a break from Maya sights. Fishing boats dot the appealing white-sand beach that stretches north for kilometers, and afternoon breezes cool the town on most days.

### ⊙ Sights

**Hacienda Real de Salinas**    HISTORIC BUILDING

**FREE** This abandoned hacienda, a few kilometers southeast of town, once produced dyewood and salt, and served as a summer home for a Campeche family. It's 5km in from the mouth of the estuary. Out in the *ría* (estuary) you can see a cairn marking an *ojo de agua dulce* (freshwater spring) that once supplied the hacienda.

The buildings are decaying in a most scenic way; you can still see shells in the wall mixed into the building material, as well as pieces of French roof tiles that served as ballast in ships on the journey from Europe. Many intact tiles with the brickworks' name and location (Marseille) are still visible in what's left of the roofs.

The hacienda makes a good bicycle excursion from town. Coming south on Calle 4, go left at the Y junction (a dirt road that flanks Puerto Abrigo), then turn right to reach El Lastre (the Ballast), a peninsula between the estuary and its western arm. Flamingos, white pelicans and other birds are sometimes seen here. If the water is high enough, it's possible to ask your flamingo-tour captain to try stopping here on the way back from the birds. You'll find bike rentals on the town square.

### ★ Reserva de la Biosfera Ría Celestún    WILDLIFE RESERVE

The 591-sq-km Reserva de la Biosfera Ría Celestún is home to a huge variety of animals and birdlife, including a large flamingo colony. You can see flamingos (via boat tours) year-round in Celestún, but they're usually out in full force from November to mid-March.

Morning is the best time of day, though from 5pm onward the birds tend to concentrate in one area after the day's feeding, which can make for good viewing.

### 🏃 Activities

Inland from the stretches of beach north of town lies a large section of scrub stretching east to the estuary that also provides good birding opportunities.

South and east of town, toward the abandoned Hacienda Real de Salinas, is another good area for nature observation. Flamingos, white pelicans, cormorants, anhingas and many other species frequent the shores and waters of the *ría*.

The **Hotel Villas del Mar** (📞 cell 999-1544755; Calle 12 s/n; per hour M$200) does morning and afternoon horseriding tours along the coast, but it has just three horses so you should reserve ahead.

### 👉 Tours

Flamingo tours in the Reserva de la Biosfera Ría Celestún are Celestún's main draw. Normally the best months for viewing the flamingos are from around end November to mid-March.

Trips from the beach last 2½ hours and begin with a ride along the coast for several kilometers, during which you can expect to see egrets, herons, cormorants, sandpipers and many other bird species. The boat then turns into the mouth of the *ría* (estuary).

Continuing up the *ría* takes you under the highway bridge where other boat tours begin and beyond which lie the flamingos. Depending on the tide, hour, season and climate conditions, you may see hundreds or thousands of the colorful birds. Don't encourage your captain to approach them too closely; a startled flock taking wing can result in injuries and deaths (for the birds). In addition to taking you to the flamingos, the captain will wend through a 200m mangrove tunnel and visit freshwater springs welling into the saltwater of the estuary, where you can take a refreshing dip.

Tours from the bridge run 1½ hours, between 8am and 5pm daily.

Hiring a boat on the beach can be frustrating at times. Operators tend to try to collect as many people as possible, which sometimes means a lot of waiting around. Prices are often quoted based on six passengers, but if fewer people show up, the quoted price rises. You can avoid this problem by coming up with a group of six on your own. Expect to pay around M$1500 for a boat of up to six people plus the M$69 per person entry to the biosphere reserve.

With either the bridge or beach option, your captain may or may not speak English.

★ **Manglares de Dzinitún** ECOTOUR
(☎ 999-645-43-10; www.facebook.com/manglar celestun; 90min tour canoe/kayak for up to 3 people from M$1000) ✐ About 1km inland past the bridge (follow the signs to 'Paseos: canoas y kayak') you'll find an operator offering ecotours in a double kayak (where you do the work) or canoe (the guide paddles). These run through a mangrove tunnel and good birding spots, made better by the lack of engine noise and knowledgeable guides; a couple have basic English.

**Flamingo Tour** BIRDWATCHING
(Hwy 281 s/n; per boat M$1500, max 6; ◷ 8am-5pm) Motorboats (lanchas) for birdwatching tours depart from both the dock at the town's entrance, just under the bridge, plus the beach at Calle 11 (outside Restaurant Celestún). Tours from the bridge are more organized. During the trip, you'll see flamingos, Bird Island, a mangrove tunnel and a spring.

The best time to see flamingos is December through March.

## 🛏 Sleeping

Most of Celestún's hotels are on Calle 12, within a short walk of one another, though many are in poor condition. Most of the better options are along the seafront just north of town.

**Hotel Manglares** HOTEL $$
(☎ 988-916-21-04; hotelmanglares@hotmail.com; Calle 12 No 63; d/cabañas M$1100/1600; P ✦ ✳ ☎ ☀) Although the modern architecture doesn't blend perfectly with the laid-back town, this is a nice midrange choice. The 19 rooms all have sea views and private balconies. The three well-appointed cabañas face the beach and come with mini-kitchens, Jacuzzis and a small common area.

**Eco Hotel Flamingo Playa** HOTEL $$
(☎ 988-916-21-33; drivan2011@hotmail.com; Calle 12 No 67C; r from M$850; P ✦ ✳ ☎ ☀) One of

the better budget hotels in town, this rather shabby family-run hotel has direct beach access and its own pool. Weathered sinks and showers could use some maintenance, and the rooms are humid, but the place is clean. It's 800m north of Calle 11.

**Casa de Celeste Vida** GUESTHOUSE $$$
(☎ 988-916-25-36; www.hotelcelestevida.com; Calle 12 No 49E; r/apt from US$95/130; P ✦ ☎ ☀) This friendly Canadian-owned place offers two comfortably decked-out rooms with kitchenette (think toaster and coffeemaker) and an apartment that sleeps four – all with water views and the gorgeous, empty beach at your doorstep. Kayak and bike use are free for guests. The hosts are happy to arrange flamingo tours and a nighttime crocodile excursion. It's 1.5km north of the town center.

A large communal kitchen means you can cook your own meals, or you can use the barbecue. Breakfast baskets cost an extra US$10 for two people. It's open all year. Paddleboard rental is US$10 per hour.

**Castillito Kin-Nah** GUESTHOUSE $$$
(☎ 988-916-26-27, cell 999-9076419; www.cas tillito-kin-nah.com; Calle 12 No 47; r from US$85; P ✦ ✳ ☎ ☀) Known by locals as the 'little castle,' the German-run Castillito certainly feels grandiose in small-town Celestún. Behind the castle's walled gates await immaculate, if slightly dated, rooms and some pretty sweet amenities, including a nice pool and satellite TV. No breakfast is included.

## 🍴 Eating

Many restaurants close around 7pm or earlier (and are often not open on Monday evenings despite promoting the fact.) For a place smack on the sea, the seafood is hit or miss.

**Dolphin** BREAKFAST $
(Calle 14 No 104, cnr Calles 13 & 15; mains M$55-110; ◷ 8:30am-1pm Wed-Sun; P ☎) It's as casual as it comes with plastic chairs and a 'picnic' feel (sandy floor), but it's an excellent breakfast spot at Hotel Gutiérrez. Full breakfasts include coffee, juice, freshly made bread, marmalade and some mighty fine egg dishes.

**La Playita** SEAFOOD $$
(☎ 988-916-20-52; Calle 12 No 99; mains M$100-160; ◷ 10am-7pm; ☎) Of all the sandy-floored, plastic-table-and-chairs beachfront joints

---

**WORTH A TRIP**

## DIY ADVENTURES IN YUCATÁN

There are so many great adventures to be had in this region. Here are some ideas to get you started for a few days of DIY adventure.

➡ Just off the road to Mayapán, **Tekit** has a cenote worth visiting.

➡ Friar Diego de Landa burned 5000 idols, 13 altars, 27 religious and historic codices, and 197 ceremonial vases in an auto-da-fé in 1562 in the town of **Maní**. The town has a nice cathedral, and the Príncipe de Tutul-Xiu restaurant's *poc-chuc* (marinated, grilled pork) is so popular that families drive here from afar to delight in the famed dish.

➡ The rarely visited tourist route **La Ruta de los Conventos** takes you to colonial-era convents in the towns of Maní, Oxkutzcab, Teabo, Mama, Chumayel, Tekax and Yotholín.

➡ A Maya-run cenote, **Cenote de Yokdzonot** (☑ 985-121-23-28, cell 999-1499315; Calle 20 btwn 27 & 29, Yokdzonot; adult/child under 8yr M$70/40; ☺ 9am-5pm), and park in the seldom-visited town of **Yokdzonot**, west of Chichén Itzá on the old highway, makes a refreshing stop after a day at the sunbaked ruins.

➡ The weaving town of **Tixkokob**, about 20km east of Mérida on Hwy 80, is famous for its quality hammocks.

➡ **Aké**, a small town due east of Mérida, has the only continually operating *henequén* rasping machine, and even if you're not lucky enough to catch it working (only a few days a month), it's impressive to peer into the crumbling hacienda buildings and see the behemoth machine at the ready for *henequén* bales. There is also a Maya ruin here.

---

here, this one gets the thumbs-up from the locals. Fresh seafood and ceviche are its main draws, as is access to the sea and cold beers.

**La Palapa**  SEAFOOD $$
(☑ 998-916-20-63; restaurant-lapalapa@hotmail.com; Calle 12 No 105; mains M$125-235; ☺ 11:30am-6pm; 🤙) A cut above the other seaside joints, La Palapa has an expansive dining area looking down to the sea, as well as a number of tables right on the beach. The go-to dish is the coconut-coated shrimp served in a coconut shell. The perfect spot if you want to swim while waiting for your meal.

**Restaurant Los Pampanos**  SEAFOOD $$
(☑ 988-916-26-61; Calle 12 No 97C; mains M$130-170, lobster M$350; ☺ 11am-7pm) Said to be the most consistent restaurant in town. It's OK. Or you could just stick with the afternoon margaritas (M$50) overlooking the beach. Service is professional at the very least.

### ❶ Information

There are no banks in town. You'll find an ATM inside Super Willy's, located on the plaza. The best bet is to bring cash in case the ATMs run out of money (which occurs frequently).

### ❶ Getting There & Away

Calle 11 is the road into town (it comes due west from Mérida), ending at Calle 12, the road paralleling the beach.

Frequent buses head for Celestún (M$60, 2½ hours) from Mérida's Noreste bus terminal. The route terminates at Celestún's plaza, a block inland from Calle 12.

There are also *colectivos* on the plaza that will take you to downtown Mérida for around M$45.

## Dzibilchaltún

Lying about 17km due north of central Mérida, **Dzibilchaltún** (M$152, parking M$20; ☺ site 8am-5pm, museum 9am-5pm Tue-Sun, cenote 9am-3:30pm; ℙ) was the longest continuously used Maya administrative and ceremonial city, serving the Maya from around 1500 BCE until the European conquest in the 1540s. At the height of its greatness, Dzibilchaltún covered 15 sq km. Some 8400 structures were mapped by archaeologists in the 1960s; few of these have been excavated. Aside from the ruins, the site offers a lovely, swimmable cenote and a Maya museum.

In some ways it's unimpressive if you've already seen larger places, but twice a year humble Dzibilchaltún truly shines, in some ways even more than Chichén Itzá.

At sunrise on the equinoxes (approximately March 20 and September 22), the sun aligns directly with the main door of the Templo de las Siete Muñecas (Temple of the Seven Dolls), which got its name from seven grotesque dolls discovered here during excavations. As the sun rises, the temple doors glow, then 'light up' as the sun passes behind. It also casts a cool square beam on the crumbled wall behind. Many who have seen both feel the sunrise here is more spectacular than Chichén Itzá's famous snake, and is well worth getting up at the crack of dawn to witness.

Chablekal-bound *colectivos* depart frequently from Calle 58 (between Calles 57 and 59) in Mérida. They'll drop you about 300m from the site's entrance.

# Progreso

📞 969 / POP 39,000

If Mérida's heat has you dying for a quick beach fix, or if you want to see the longest pier (6.5km) in Mexico, head to Progreso (aka Puerto Progreso). The front strip *(malecón)* can get packed with diners, drinkers and oversunned tourists, as can the beach (even though it's loooong). Nevertheless, Progreso maintains a relaxed beach-town vibe. As with other Gulf beaches, the water is murky, even on calm days. Winds can hit full force in the afternoon and evenings, especially from December to March when *los nortes* (northern winds) kick up.

*Meridanos* come in droves on weekends, especially during July and August when it can be difficult to find a room with a view and, sadly, you'll see more litter on the beach. Once or twice a week the streets flood with cruise-ship tourists, but the place can feel empty on off nights, which makes a refreshing change.

## 🏃 Activities

### El Corchito
SWIMMING

(📞 999-158-51-55; Hwy 27 s/n, cnr Calle 46; adult/child under 12yr M$90/35; ⊙9am-4pm) Take a refreshing dip in one of three freshwater swimming holes surrounded by mangroves at nature reserve El Corchito. Motorboats take visitors across a canal to the reserve. El Corchito is home to iguanas, boa constrictors, small crocs, raccoons and a band of coatis. The racoons and coatis are skilled food thieves, something to consider if you bring lunch.

El Corchito sees a lot of visitors, especially on weekends, so get there early for a more peaceful swim.

'Tecnológico' buses (M$6.50) departing from a bus station at Calles 82 and 29 in Progreso will leave you a block and a half from El Corchito.

## 🛏 Sleeping & Eating

For cheaper eats, head inland away from the *malecón*, or to the market. Otherwise, expect to pay for the view...but it's a nice vibe either way.

### Maria's Nicte-Ha
HOTEL $

(📞 969-103-62-33; Calle 27 No 184 btwn Calles 86 and 88; s/d M$550/680; ⊝ ❀ 🛜 🛏) While it's not as fancy as some spots, you can't ask for better value: a rooftop terrace, a clean pool, a near-the-beach location and friendly staff make this an excellent stopover. The rooms are large and some have sliding doors that open directly on the pool area, making dipping that much easier. Hammocks on the terrace help you kick back in style.

### Hotel Yaxactún
HOTEL $$

(📞 969-103-93-26; www.hotelyrestauranteyaxactun. com; Calle 66 No 129, btwn Calles 25 & 27; r M$750; ⊝ ❀ 🛜 🛏) The brown-and-cream Yaxactún is one of the better hotels in town. Street-facing rooms get good natural light and have balconies. The hotel also has a small onsite restaurant specializing in Yucatecan food, and there's a swimming pool with a kiddie corral. It's three blocks from the beach.

There's little greenery and lots of concrete.

### Playa Linda Hotel
HOTEL $$

(📞 969-103-92-14; www.playalindayucatan.com; Calle 76 s/n btwn Calles 19 & 21; r/ste from M$750/1100; ⊝ ❀ 🛜) Rooms go fast at this hotel on the boardwalk, so book ahead. Comfy standard rooms are decked out with contemporary dark-wood furnishings, while suites come with kitchenette and beachfront balcony. Walls can be a bit thin in some rooms; avoid those near the staircase (no windows to the exterior) and upgrade to a 'studio.' The rooftop view of the pier and coastline is spectacular.

### El Naranjo
YUCATECAN $

(Calle 27 s/n, btwn Calles 78 & 80; tacos/tortas M$10/20; ⊙6am-noon) One of the best options in the market for *cochito* (slow-cooked pork) tacos and tortas – and it's squeaky clean.

**Milk Bar** CAFE $$
(Malecón s/n, btwn 72 & 74; mains M$88-155; ⏱8am-11pm; 🛜) The 'cow in a rowboat' indicates you've arrived at this laid-back Texan-run spot. Despite the name, it doesn't specialize in milk-based drinks, but is definitely the place to go for hefty sandwiches, burgers and salads. It's a popular hangout for expats who enjoy the eclectic decor and large servings. It's also a great breakfast and brunch spot.

The coffee is OK, but those obsessive about their brew shouldn't get too excited.

**Crabster** SEAFOOD $$$
(📞969-103-65-22; www.facebook.com/crab stermx; mains M$205-390; ⏱8am-8pm; 🛜) At the current posh spot on the strip, with its blond-wood chairs, pink velvet trim and designer lighting, you could be in an international hotel, not smack on the beachfront. But this spot pulls in the moneyed visitor for, you guessed it, seafood dishes. Service is a nice combo of friendly-professional.

**Flamingo's** SEAFOOD $$
(📞969-935-21-22; Calle 69 No 144, cnr Calle 72; mains M$110-210; ⏱7am-11pm; 🛜) A longtime local favorite on the boardwalk, Flamingo's fries up a tasty *pescado en mojo de ajo* (fish in garlic sauce, M$121). Tasty chips, salsas and other snacks are served while you're waiting for the main dish.

**Eladio's** SEAFOOD $$
(www.eladios.com.mx; cnr Calles 19 & 80; mains M$119-189; ⏱noon-8pm; 🅿🛜) This is a bit of an institution around town with its beachfront setting and action to boot. Some say the *botanas* (complimentary sampler plates that come to the table before the main dish arrives) are the real reason to eat here. We'll let you be the judge.

## ❶ Orientation

Progreso's even-numbered streets run north–south; odd ones, east–west. The bus terminal is five short blocks south of the waterfront *malecón* (the beach promenade along Calle 19) and the *muelle* (dock).

## ❶ Information

There are several banks with ATMs and money-exchange service along Calle 80.

Wi-fi is spotty in hotels, so you may get your best connection using cellular data.

## ❶ Getting There & Away

Progreso is 33km north of Mérida along a fast four-lane highway that's basically a continuation of the Paseo de Montejo.

To get to Progreso from Mérida, go to the Progreso bus terminal (p169) or catch a *colectivo* one block east of the terminal on Calle 60. These are not ADO buses, so if you're continuing onward beyond Mérida you'll need to have different tickets.

Traveling to Mérida, frequent buses (M$21) depart from Progreso's **bus terminal** (Calle 29 No 151, btwn Calles 80 & 82).

# East of Progreso

Heading east from Progreso, Hwy 27 parallels the coast for 70km, to Dzilam de Bravo, before turning inland. Driving along this stretch of coastline makes a lovely, if long, day drive, but it's doable from Mérida. If you are escapists, and love the solitude (especially on the secluded, breezy beaches, where time stands still), then you might want to stay.

On leaving Progreso you'll pass miles of mixed mangrove clumps and notice that on the right (south) the mud takes on a pink color. Unsurprisingly, this area is named the Laguna Rosada (Pink Lagoon).

On the seaward (north) side of the Pink Lagoon, things are less pristine, with many newly constructed timeshares, condomondos and hotels. But things are still pretty laid-back here.

From a tall wooden observation tower at the edge of the lagoon at Uaymitún, you can watch flamingos, as well as ibis, herons, spoonbills and other waterfowl.

The buildings eventually thin out beyond Uaymitún, and about 13km east of it, a road heads south from the coast some 3km across the bird-riddled lagoon to the turnoff for the Maya ruins of Xcambó (Dzemul–Xtampú road; M$70; ⏱8am-5pm). Following the road south beyond the ruins' turnoff takes you into grassy marshland with cattails and scatterings of palm trees, with ample opportunities for bird-spotting.

Back on Hwy 27 heading east, the next town you'll reach is Telchac Puerto, which has a few good eating and sleeping options. Grab a seafood meal at the casual La Picuda (📞991-917-40-07; Calle 20 s/n, Telchac Puerto; mains M$80-180; ⏱10:30am-6pm). If you decide to sleep, there are two good options: the resort-style Hotel Reef Yucatán

(☎991-917-50-00, reservations 999-941-94-94; www.reefyucatan.com; Hwy 27 Km 36.6, Zona Hotelera Telchac Puerto; s/d M$1695/2990; P ➽ ❄ �📶 ☲ ), an anomaly along these parts, or 40km further east in Dzilam de Bravo, the rustic but delightful Perla Escondida (☎cell 991-1079321; miriam_figueroa2@hotmail.com; Calle 11 Km 1, off Hwy 27, Dzilam de Bravo; r M$1000; P ➽ ❄ 📶 ☲ ). To get here, you'll pass the quaint sleepy fishing town of San Crisanto, 9km east of Telchac.

# EASTERN YUCATÁN STATE

Scrub jungle, intact colonial cities, cenotes aplenty and the Yucatán's largest coastal estuary are just a few of the attractions in the eastern portion of the state. And then there's Chichén Itzá, one of the 'new wonders of the world', as well as a smattering of less-visited (but nonetheless impressive) Maya ruins.

## Izamal

☎988 / POP 16,000

In ancient times Izamal was a center for the worship of the supreme Maya god, Itzamná, and the sun god, Kinich-Kakmó. A dozen temple pyramids were devoted to these or other gods. No doubt these bold expressions of Maya religiosity are why the Spanish colonists chose Izamal as the site for an enormous and impressive Franciscan monastery, which still stands at the heart of this town, about 70km east of Mérida.

The Izamal of today is a quiet and provincial place, nicknamed La Ciudad Amarilla (the Yellow City) for the traditional bright yellow colonial-era buildings that line its town center like a budding daisy. It's easily explored on foot, though some visitors prefer to hire a horse-drawn carriage for a tour. It's an obvious lunch stop between Mérida and Valladolid.

### ◎ Sights

It's worth taking the time to visit the talleres de arte (artisan workshops) found throughout the city. These are simple at best, but chatting with the locals, seeing where they work and buying their produce is extremely interesting. Most hotels and the Centro Cultural y Artesanal have free tourist maps with the workshop locations labeled.

★Convento de San Antonio de Padua                    MONASTERY
(Calle 31 s/n; museum M$10; ⊗5:30am-8pm, museum from 9am) When the Spaniards conquered Izamal, they destroyed the major Maya temple, the Ppapp-Hol-Chac pyramid, and in 1533 began to build from its stones one of the first monasteries in the western hemisphere. Work on Convento de San Antonio de Padua was finished in 1561. Under the monastery's arcades, look for building stones with an unmistakable mazelike design; these were clearly taken from the earlier Maya temple.

The monastery's principal church is the Santuario de la Virgen de Izamal, approached by a ramp from the main square. The ramp leads into the Atrium, a huge arcaded courtyard in which the fiesta of the Virgin of Izamal takes place each August 15.

At some point the 16th-century frescoes beside the entrance of the sanctuary were completely painted over. For years they lay concealed under a thin layer of whitewash until a maintenance worker who was cleaning the walls discovered them.

The church's original altarpiece was destroyed by a fire believed to have been started by a fallen candle. Its replacement, impressively gilded, was built in the 1940s. In the niches at the stations of the cross are some superb small figures.

In the small courtyard to the left of the church, look up and toward the Atrium to see the original sundial projecting from the roof's edge. A small museum at the back commemorates Pope John Paul II's 1993 visit to the monastery. He brought with him a silver crown for the statue of the patron saint of Yucatán, the Virgin of Izamal.

The monastery's front entrance faces west; it's flanked by Calles 31 and 33 on the north and south, respectively, and Calles 28 and 30 on the east and west.

Kinich-Kakmó                    ARCHAEOLOGICAL SITE
(Calle 27 s/n, btwn Calles 26B & 28; ⊗8am-5pm) FREE Though not worth detouring wildly for, if you're here already, three of the town's original 12 Maya pyramids have been partially restored. The largest (and the third largest in Yucatán) is the 34m-high Kinich-Kakmó, three blocks north of the monastery. Legend has it that a deity in the form of a blazing macaw would swoop down from the heavens to collect offerings left here.

**Centro Cultural y Artesanal** MUSEUM
(Calle 31 No 201; M$25; ⊙9am-8pm) 🗗 Just
across the square from the monastery, this
cultural center and museum showcases popular art from around Mexico. Explanatory
cards in English give an excellent summary.
Its excellent shop sells fair-trade-certified
crafts made by artisans from about 40 indigenous communities. Any purchase you
make is a direct source of income for rural
indigenous families.

## 🛏 Sleeping & Eating

Your best bet is Yucatecan fare. Several
*loncherías* (simple restaurants) occupy
spaces in the market on the monastery's
southwest side, but there are a few spots
that cater more to tourists.

**Hotel Tu'ul** HOTEL $
(🖉988-954-00-76; Calle 22 No 302 btwn Calles 31
& 33; d/tr M$700/800; 🅿❉🛜🌊) Hotel Tu'ul
has undergone quite the makeover, and
now offers very nice, clean rooms around a
stunning pool. For now, all 20 rooms are the
same price, so ask for the spacious ones on
the 2nd floor while you can.

**⭐Hacienda Hotel
Santo Domingo** HOTEL $$
(🖉988-967-61-36; www.izamalhotel.com; Calle 18,
btwn Calles 33B & 35; r/ste from M$1650/2375;
🅿➲🛜🌊) Set on a 13-hectare property
with lush gardens, walking trails, a pool
and *palapa* restaurant, this serene, upscale
and well-run spot (the owner is always on
site) will win over nature lovers and those
who enjoy a touch of style. All rooms are at-
tractive, some with natural stone sinks and
indoor-outdoor showers. A great reason to
stay in Izamal overnight.

**Rinconada del Convento** HOTEL $$
(🖉988-954-01-51; www.hotelizamal.com; Calle 33
No 294A; s/d/tr M$700/950/1100; ➲❉🛜🌊)

A tiered garden affords views of Izamal's
iconic monastery and Maya ruins four
blocks north of the hotel. While the hotel
(especially the pool area) is movie-set pretty, with fun staircases leading to rooms
tucked away in nooks and crannies, it's a
quirky place to spend a night in: the 'Premium' rooms face the gorgeous convent, but
are super noisy.

**Macan Ché** B&B $$
(🖉988-954-02-87; www.macanche.com; Calle 22
No 305 btwn Calles 33 & 35; r/ste incl breakfast from
M$920/1120; 🅿➲❉🛜🌊) It's about three
long (yes, long!) blocks east of the monas-
tery (take Calle 31 toward Cancún and turn
right on Calle 22) to this very Zen hotel,
which has a cluster of unpretentious, com-
fortable cottages and a small rock-bottom
pool in a woodsy setting. All of the rooms
have air-con and some have kitchenettes.

Its lovely indoor-outdoor bar-restaurant
is a good place to chill.

**Restaurante-Cafe Los Arcos** MEXICAN $
(cnr Calle 28 & 31A; mains M$90-110; ⊙5pm-
10:30pm Tue-Sun) Situated right on the plaza,
under the arches *(arcos)*, this is the go-to
place for locals who say it's the only place
open 'late' (yes, things close early around
here). It's nothing special but is the town's
best budget spot, and the perfect location to
watch the world go by. Munch on the daily
plate or grab a juice instead.

**⭐Kinich** MEXICAN $$
(🖉988-954-04-89; www.facebook.com/kinichi
zamal; Calle 27 No 299, btwn Calles 28 & 30; mains
M$150-250; ⊙11am-7pm; 🛜) Kinich showcas-
es fresh, handmade Yucatecan cuisine at
its finest. The *papadzules kinich* – rolled
tortillas stuffed with diced egg and topped
with pumpkin-seed sauce and smoky sau-
sage (M$124) – is a delightful starter that's
a house specialty. Kinich is also famous for

---

**PUEBLOS & PLACES OFF THE MAP**

There's a ton of good off-the-map adventures to be had in and around Izamal. Here are a
few of our favorites.

**Cuauhtémoc** A small community 6km south of Izamal on an extension of Calle 24, with
a 17th-century chapel.

**Kimbilá** Located 13km west of Izamal on an extension of Calle 31, this town is famous for
its embroidery.

**Iztamatul, Habuk, Chaltún Há & beyond** Some 80 pre-Hispanic structures have been
discovered within Izamal's city limits. Habuk, Itzamatul and Chaltún Há are just a few.
They are all free to the public.

its *dzic de venado,* a shredded venison dish (M$244) and its excellent empanadas.

The setting is a massive *palapa* and the servers are dressed in traditional *huipiles* (long, sleeveless tunics).

**Restaurante Zamna**  YUCATECAN **$$**
(☑988-954-02-04; www.facebook.com/restaurantezamnaizamal2015/; Calle 22 No 302 btwn Calles 31 & 33; mains M$95-145; ☺noon-8pm) Traditional, tasty and home-cooked food (you can watch your tortillas being made), prepared in a huge open-sided thatched hut, which adds to the charm. Start with a *chaya* juice and then tuck into regional specialties such as *sikil pak* (delicious pumpkin-seed dip), *papadzules* (chopped egg-filled tortillas) and *cochinita pibil* (slow-cooked pork).

It's a 10-minute walk east of the main square: take Calle 31 and then turn right on Calle 22.

## ❶ Information

Most restaurants and hotels here have a copy of the excellent free tourist map. The map is available in several languages and describes various walking tours and locations for handicraft workshops.

There is a small **tourist information** (Palacio Municipal; ☺8am-9pm Mon-Fri, to 2pm Sat & Sun) office near the convent in the **Palacio Municipal**, with friendly staff and a few brochures (and the map!).

There are several ATMs around town.

## ❶ Getting There & Around

Frequent buses run out of Izamal's **Oriente bus terminal** (☑988-954-01-07; Calle 32 s/n, cnr Calle 31A; ☺4:30am-8pm) and the nearby **Terminal de Autobuses Centro** (☑988-967-66-15; www.autobusescentro.com; Calle 33 No 302, cnr Calle 30; ☺5am-9pm).

Taxis around town charge M$25; a base is at Calles 32 and 31A.

Horse-carriage rides cost M$250 per hour.

# Chichén Itzá

☑985 / POP 5500 (PISTÉ)

The most famous and best restored of the Yucatán Maya sites, Chichén Itzá (www.chichenitza.inah.gob.mx; off Hwy 180, Pisté; adult/child under 13yr M$481/75, guided tours M$1200; ☺8am-5pm, last entry 4pm; 🅿), while tremendously overcrowded – every gawker and his or her grandmother is trying to check off the new seven wonders of the world – will still impress even the most jaded visitor. Yes, it's goosebump material. Many mysteries of the Maya astronomical calendar are made clear when one understands the design of the 'time temples' here. Other than a few minor passageways, climbing on the structures is not allowed.

The heat, humidity and crowds in Chichén Itzá can be fierce, as can competition between the craft sellers who line the paths (not to mention the irritating habit of hordes clapping to illustrate the pyramid acoustics). To avoid this, try to explore the site either early in the morning or late in the afternoon.

A nightly sound and light show gets some people fired up; others less so.

## History

Most archaeologists agree that the first major settlement at Chichén Itzá, during the late Classic period, was pure Maya. In about the 9th century CE, the city was largely abandoned for reasons unknown.

It was resettled around the late-10th century, and shortly thereafter it is believed to have been invaded by the Toltec, who had migrated from their central highlands cap-

## BUSES FROM IZAMAL

| DESTINATION | FARE (M$) | TIME (HR) | FREQUENCY (PER DAY) & TERMINAL |
| --- | --- | --- | --- |
| Cancún | 188-214 | 5 | 3 (6:10am, 2:26pm, 4:35pm), Oriente; approx every 2hr Centro |
| Mérida | 33-42 | 1½ | frequent, Centro; hourly, Oriente |
| Tizimín | 95 | 2½ | 2 (7:25am, 6:10pm), Oriente |
| Valladolid | 69 | 2 | frequent, Centro |

ital of Tula, north of Mexico City. The bellicose Toltec culture was fused with that of the Maya, incorporating the cult of Quetzalcóatl (Kukulcán, in Maya). You will see images of both Chaac, the Maya rain god, and Quetzalcóatl, the plumed serpent, throughout the city.

The substantial fusion of highland central Mexican and Puuc architectural styles makes Chichén unique among the Yucatán Peninsula's ruins. The fabulous El Castillo and the Plataforma de Venus (p192) are outstanding architectural works built during the height of Toltec cultural input.

The sanguinary Toltec contributed more than their architectural skills to the Maya: they elevated human sacrifice to a near obsession, and there are numerous carvings of the bloody ritual in Chichén demonstrating this.

After a Maya leader moved his political capital to Mayapán while keeping Chichén as his religious capital, Chichén Itzá fell into decline. Why it was subsequently abandoned in the 14th century is a mystery, but the once-great city remained the site of Maya pilgrimages for many years.

## ⊙ Sights

**Visitors Center Museum**  MUSEUM
(⊙9am-4pm) FREE The visitors center has a small museum with exhibits providing explanations in Spanish, English and French.

**El Castillo**  ARCHAEOLOGICAL SITE
Upon entering Chichén Itzá, El Castillo (aka the Pyramid of Kukulcán) rises before you in all its grandeur. The first temple here was pre-Toltec, built around 800 CE, but the present 25m-high structure, built over the old one, has the plumed serpent sculpted along the stairways and Toltec warriors represented in the doorway carvings at the top of the temple. You won't see the carvings, however, as ascending the pyramid was prohibited after a fatal accident here in 2006.

The structure is actually a massive Maya calendar formed in stone. Each of El Castillo's nine levels is divided in two by a staircase, making 18 separate terraces that commemorate the 18 20-day months of the Maya Vague Year. The four stairways have 91 steps each; add the top platform and the total is 365, the number of days in the year. On each facade of the pyramid are 52 flat panels, which are reminders of the 52 years in the Maya calendar round.

To top it off, during the spring and autumn equinoxes, light and shadow form a series of triangles on the side of the north staircase that mimic the creep of a serpent (note the carved serpent's heads flanking the bottom of the staircase).

The older pyramid inside El Castillo has a red jaguar throne with inlaid eyes and spots of jade; also lying behind the screen is a chac-mool (Maya sacrificial stone sculpture). The entrance to El Túnel, the passage up to the throne, is at the base of El Castillo's north side. You can't go in, though.

Researchers in 2015 learned that the pyramid most likely sits atop a 20m-deep cenote, which puts the structure at greater risk of collapsing.

**Gran Juego de Pelota**  ARCHAEOLOGICAL SITE
The great ball court, the largest and most impressive in Mexico, is only one of the city's eight courts, indicative of the importance the games held here. The court, to the left of the visitors center, is flanked by temples at either end and is bounded by towering parallel walls with stone rings cemented up high. Along the walls of the ball court are stone reliefs, including scenes of decapitations of players.

There is evidence that the ball game may have changed over the years. Some carvings show players with padding on their elbows and knees, and it is thought that they played a soccer-like game with a hard rubber ball, with the use of hands forbidden. Other carvings show players wielding bats; it appears that if a player hit the ball through one of the stone hoops, his team was declared the winner. It may be that during the Toltec period, the losing captain, and perhaps his teammates as well, were sacrificed.

The court exhibits some interesting acoustics: a conversation at one end can be heard 135m away at the other, and a clap produces multiple loud echoes.

**Templo del Barbado**  ARCHAEOLOGICAL SITE
The structure at the ball court's north end, called the Temple of the Bearded Man after a carving inside it, has finely sculpted pillars and reliefs of flowers, birds and trees.

**Templo de los Jaguares y Escudos**  ARCHAEOLOGICAL SITE
The Temple of the Jaguars and Shields, built atop the southeast corner of the ball court's wall, has some columns with carved

YUCATÁN STATE & THE MAYA HEARTLAND CHICHÉN ITZÁ

# Chichén Itzá

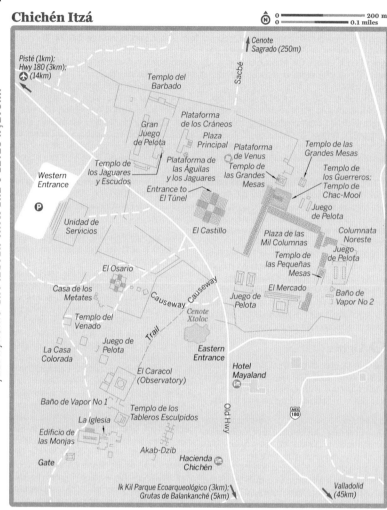

YUCATÁN STATE & THE MAYA HEARTLAND CHICHÉN ITZÁ

rattlesnakes and tablets with etched jaguars. Inside are faded mural fragments depicting a battle.

## Plataforma de los Cráneos ARCHAEOLOGICAL SITE

The Platform of Skulls (Tzompantli in Náhuatl) is between the Templo de los Jaguares y Escudos (p191) and El Castillo (p191). You can't mistake it, because the T-shaped platform is festooned with carved skulls and eagles tearing open the chests of men to eat their hearts. In ancient days this platform was used to display the heads of sacrificial victims.

## Plataforma de las Águilas y los Jaguares ARCHAEOLOGICAL SITE

Adjacent to the Platform of Skulls, the carvings on the Platform of the Eagles and Jaguars depict those animals gruesomely grabbing human hearts in their claws. It is thought that this platform was part of a temple dedicated to the military legions responsible for capturing sacrificial victims.

## Cenote Sagrado ARCHAEOLOGICAL SITE

From the Plataforma de Venus, a 250m rough stone *sacbé* (path) runs north to the huge sunken well that gave this city its name. The Sacred Cenote is some 60m in diameter and 35m deep. The walls between the summit and the water's surface are ensnared in tangled vines and other vegetation, and sadly it's hard to see much of the water, but spare a thought for the children and adults sacrificed to the gods here over the centuries.

There are ruins of a small steam bath next to the cenote.

### Grupo de las Mil Columnas
ARCHAEOLOGICAL SITE

This group east of El Castillo (p191) pyramid takes its name – which means 'Group of One Thousand Columns' – from the forest of pillars stretching south and east. The star attraction here is the Templo de los Guerreros (Temple of the Warriors), adorned with stucco and stone-carved animal deities. At the top of its steps is a classic reclining chac-mool figure, sadly not visible from behind the ropes.

Many of the columns in front of the temple are carved with figures of warriors. Archaeologists working in 1926 discovered a structure known as the Temple of the Chac-Mool lying beneath the Temple of the Warriors.

You can walk through the columns on its south side to reach the Columnata Noreste, notable for the 'big-nosed god' masks on its facade. Some have been reassembled on the ground around the statue. Just to the south are the remains of the Baño de Vapor (Steam Bath or Sweat House) with an underground oven and drains for the water. The sweat houses (there are two onsite) were regularly used for ritual purification.

### El Osario
ARCHAEOLOGICAL SITE

The Ossuary, otherwise known as the Bonehouse or the Tumba del Gran Sacerdote (High Priest's Grave), is a ruined pyramid to the southwest of El Castillo. As with most of the buildings in this southern section, the architecture is more Puuc than Toltec. It's notable for the beautiful serpent heads at the base of its staircases.

A square shaft at the top of the structure leads down into a cave that was used as a burial chamber; seven tombs with human remains were discovered inside.

### El Caracol
ARCHAEOLOGICAL SITE

Called El Caracol (the Snail) by the Spaniards for its interior spiral staircase, this observatory, to the south of the El Osario, is one of the most fascinating and important of all Chichén Itzá's buildings. Its circular design resembles some central highlands structures, although, surprisingly, not those of Toltec Tula.

In a fusion of architectural styles and religious imagery, there are Maya Chaac rain-god masks over four external doors facing the cardinal points. The windows in the observatory's dome are aligned with the appearance of certain stars at specific dates. From the dome the priests may have decreed the times for rituals, celebrations, corn-planting and harvests.

### Edificio de las Monjas
ARCHAEOLOGICAL SITE

Thought by archaeologists to have been a palace for Maya royalty, the so-called Edificio de las Monjas (Nunnery), with its myriad rooms, resembled a European convent to the conquistadors, hence their name for the building. The building's dimensions are imposing: its base is 60m long, 30m wide and 20m high.

The construction is Maya rather than Toltec, although a Toltec sacrificial stone stands in front. A smaller adjoining building to the east, known as La Iglesia (the Church), is covered almost entirely with carvings.

### Akab-Dzib
ARCHAEOLOGICAL SITE

East of the Nunnery, the Puuc-style Akab-Dzib is thought by some archaeologists to be the most ancient structure excavated here. The central chambers date from the 2nd century. The name means 'Obscure Writing' in Maya and refers to the south-side annex door, whose lintel depicts a priest with a vase etched with hieroglyphics that have yet to be successfully translated.

### Grutas de Balankanché
CAVE

(Hwy 180 Km 126; M$137; ⊗9am-4pm; P) In 1959 a guide to the Chichén Itzá ruins was exploring a cave on his day off when he came upon a narrow passageway. He followed the passageway for 300m, meandering through a series of caverns. In each, perched on mounds amid scores of glistening stalactites, were hundreds of ceremonial treasures the Maya had placed there 800 years earlier. Among the discovered objects were ritual *metates* and *manos* (grinding stones), incense burners and pots.

In the years following the discovery, the ancient ceremonial objects were removed and studied. Eventually most of them were returned to the caves, and placed exactly where they were found.

# Chichén Itzá

## A DAY TOUR

It doesn't take long to realize why the Maya site of Chichén Itzá is one of Mexico's most popular tourist draws. Approaching the grounds from the main entrance, the striking castle pyramid ❶ **El Castillo** jumps right out at you – and the wow factor never lets up.

It's easy to tackle Chichén Itzá in one day. Within a stone's throw of the castle, you'll find the Maya world's largest ❷ **ball court** alongside eerie carvings of skulls and heart-devouring eagles at the Temple of Jaguars and the Platform of Skulls. On the other (eastern) side are the highly adorned ❸ **Group of a Thousand Columns** and the ❹ **Temple of Warriors**. A short walk north of the castle leads to the gaping ❺ **Sacred Cenote**, an important pilgrimage site. On the other side of El Castillo, you'll find giant stone serpents watching over the High Priest's Grave, aka El Osario. Further south, marvel at the spiral-domed ❻ **Observatory**, the imposing Nunnery and Akab-Dzib, one of the oldest ruins.

Roaming the 47-hectare site, it's fun to consider that at its height Chichén Itzá was home to an estimated 90,000 inhabitants and spanned approximately 30 sq km. So essentially you're looking at just a small part of a once-great city.

### TOP TIPS

➡ Arrive at 8am and you'll have a good three hours or so before the tour-bus madness begins. Early birds escape the merchants, too.

➡ Remember that Chichén Itzá is the name of the site; the actual town where it's located is called Pisté.

**El Caracol**
**Observatory**
Today they'd probably just use a website, but back in the day priests would announce the latest rituals and celebrations from the dome of the circular observatory.

**Edificio de las Monjas (Nunnery)**

❻

**Akab-Dzib**

**Entrance**

**Grupo de las Mil Columnas**
**Group of a Thousand Columns**
Not unlike a hall of fame exhibit, the pillars surrounding the temple reveal carvings of gods, dignitaries and celebrated warriors.

## El Castillo
### The Castle
Even this mighty pyramid can't bear the stress of a million visitors ascending its stairs each year. No climbing allowed, but the ground-level view doesn't disappoint.

## Gran Juego de Pelota
### Great Ball Court
How is it possible to hear someone talk from one end of this long, open-air court to the other? To this day, the acoustics remain a mystery.

**Entrance**

**Parking Lot**

**Visitors Center**

**Templo de los Jaguares (Temple of Jaguars)**

**Tumba del Gran Sacerdote (High Priest's Grave)**

❶

❷

❺

**Plataforma de los Cráneos (Platform of Skulls)**

❸  ❹

## Cenote Sagrado
### Sacred Cenote
Diving expeditions have turned up hundreds of valuable artifacts dredged from the cenote (limestone sinkhole), not to mention human bones of sacrificial victims who were forced to jump into the eternal underworld.

## Templo de los Guerreros
### Temple of Warriors
The Maya associated warriors with eagles and jaguars, as depicted in the temple's friezes. The revered jaguar, in particular, was a symbol of strength and agility.

Outside the caves, you'll find a good botanical garden (displaying native flora with information on the medicinal and other uses of the trees and plants) and a tiny museum. The museum features large photographs taken during the exploration of the caves, and descriptions (in English, Spanish and French) of the Maya religion and the offerings found in the caves. Also on display is text about modern-day Maya ceremonies called Ch'a Chaac, which continue to be held in all the villages on the Yucatán Peninsula during times of drought, and consist mostly of praying and making numerous offerings of food to rain god Chaac. A recent expedition discovered additional artifacts submerged underwater as well.

Compulsory 45-minute tours (minimum six people, maximum 30) have melodramatic, not-very-informative recorded narration that is nearly impossible to make out, but if you'd like it in a particular language, English is at 11am, 1pm and 3pm; Spanish is at 9am, noon, 2pm and 4pm; and French is at 10am.

Be warned that the cave is unusually hot, and ventilation is poor in its further reaches. The lack of oxygen (especially after a few groups have already passed through) makes it difficult to draw a full breath until you're outside again.

The turnoff for the caverns is 6km east of Chichén Itzá on the highway to Valladolid. Second-class buses heading east from Pisté toward Valladolid will drop you at the Balankanché road. The entrance to the caves is 350m north of the highway.

## 🏃 Activities

**Ik Kil Parque Eco-Arqueológico** CENOTE
(Cenote Sagrado Azul; ☑ 985-851-00-02; cenote_ikkil@hotmail.com; Hwy 180 Km 122; adult/child 6-12yr M$80/40; ☺ 9am-5pm; 🐾) About 2.5km east of the western entrance of the Chichén Itzá ruins, a cenote here has been developed into a divine swimming spot. Small cascades of water plunge from the high limestone roof, which is ringed by greenery. Arrive no later than 11am to beat the tour groups.

The on-site restaurant has a good lunch buffet (M$160), and there are also spacious *cabañas* with kitchens (some sleep up to four, assuming two children; M$1250).

## 🛏 Sleeping

Most of Chichén Itzá's lodgings, restaurants and services are arranged along 1km of highway in the town of Pisté to the western (Mérida) side of the ruins. It's about 1.5km from the ruins' main (west) entrance to the nearest hotel in Pisté, and 2.5km from the ruins to Pisté's town plaza.

Don't hesitate to haggle for a bed in low season (May through June and August to early December).

**Pirámide Inn** HOTEL $
(☑ 985-851-01-15; www.piramideinn.com; Calle 15 No 30; campsite M$100, r with/without air-con M$600/400; 🅿 ❄ 🌐 🛜 ♿ 🏊) While in fairly desperate need of some TLC, this is one of the few budget options in town and is also relatively close to the ruins. Campers can pitch a tent in the large gardens, which feature an unexcavated Maya site themselves. The spacious rooms have adequate bathrooms and two double beds. Pets are welcome and vibe is super-relaxed.

**Doralba Inn Chichen Itzá** HOTEL $$
(☑ 985-858-15-55; www.doloresalba.com; Hwy 180 Km 122; r incl breakfast from M$1000; 🅿 ❄ ❄ 🛜 🏊) This is a good midrange option with substantial online discounts, and kids will dig the hotel's two pools (one has a rock bottom). The 32 semi-rustic rooms won't wow you, but they're comfy enough. Dolores Alba offers transport to Chichén Itzá at 8am, but you're on your own getting back. It's opposite the Ik Kil Parque Eco-Arqueológico, 5km from Chichén Itzá's entrance.

**Hotel Chichén Itzá** HOTEL $$
(☑ 998-887-24-95, toll free from Mexico 800-719-54-65, toll free from USA 877-240-5864; www.mayaland.com; Calle 15 No 45; r from M$1320; 🅿 ❄ ❄ 🛜 🏊) This hotel has 42 pleasant rooms with tiled floors and old-style brick-tiled ceilings. Rooms in the upper range face the pool and the landscaped grounds, and all have firm beds and good bathrooms. Parents may bring two kids under 12 years old for free. The hotel is part of the Mayaland chain, with its private entrance to the archaeological site.

**★ Hacienda Chichén** RESORT $$$
(☑ 999-920-84-07, USA 877-631-0045; www.haciendachichen.com; Zona Hotelera Km 120; d from US$198; 🅿 ❄ ❄ 🛜 🏊) About 300m from the Chichén Itzá entrance, this resort sits on the well-manicured grounds of a 16th-century hacienda with an elegant main house and towering ceiba trees. The archaeologists who excavated Chichén during the 1920s lived here in bungalows, which have been

## DREDGING CHICHÉN'S SACRED CENOTE

Around the year 1900, Edward Thompson, a Harvard professor and US consul to Yucatán, bought the hacienda that included Chichén Itzá for M$750. No doubt intrigued by local stories of female virgins being sacrificed to the Maya deities by being thrown into the site's cenote, Thompson resolved to have the cenote dredged.

He imported dredging equipment and set to work. Gold and jade jewelry from all parts of Mexico and as far away as Colombia was recovered, along with other artifacts and a variety of human bones. Many of the artifacts were shipped to Harvard's Peabody Museum, but some have since been returned to Mexico.

Subsequent diving expeditions in the 1920s and 1960s turned up hundreds of other valuable artifacts. It appears that all sorts of people – children and old people, the diseased and the injured, and the young and the vigorous – were forcibly obliged to take an eternal swim in Chichén's Cenote Sagrado. (Many guides push the sacrificial angle as tourists seem fascinated by it; other experts say this aspect is way overstressed in relationship to the real objective of the site.)

The cenote is reached by walking about 400m north from the Plataforma de Venus.

refurbished and augmented with new ones. Monthly activities on offer include Maya cooking classes and bird-watching.

One additional plus is that the spot has a private entrance to the ruins, meaning you get to skip the lines. The restaurant's prices are eye-opening (be warned), and the wi-fi is only in the public areas.

**Mayaland Hotel & Bungalows**     HOTEL **$$$**
(☑ 998-887-24-95, US 877-240-5864; www.maya land.com; Zona Hotelera Km 120; d/bungalow from M$2100/3100; P ⊜ ⊛ 🕿 🗷) Getting long in the tooth at this point, and somewhat officious rather than personal, the Mayaland is less than 100m from Chichén Itzá and has a 'private' entrance. The rooms are good, however, and the expansive public areas attractive, though there's actually very limited benefit in being so close to the site, unless you plan to visit multiple times.

As well as restaurants and all the services, it also offers cultural programs, including a popular 'Be Maya' activity where you cook Maya cuisine plus visit the resort's own replica 'observatory,' while learning about the roles of Maya people.

## ✖ Eating

**Cocina Económica Fabiola**     MEXICAN **$**
(Calle 15 s/n; mains M$45-75; ⊙ 7am-11pm) For a good, honest, cheap meal hit this humble little place at the end of the strip of simple cafes opposite the church. Since the mid-'90s it's been churning out *sopa de lima* (lime soup; M$45) and *pollo yucateco* (Yucatecan chicken; M$75). There are half a dozen similar places nearby.

**Las Mestizas**     MEXICAN **$$**
(☑ 985-851-0069; Calle 15 s/n; mains M$70-115; ⊙ 9am-10pm; ⊛ 🕿) One of the town's better restaurants, Las Mestizas serves up decent Yucatecan fare. There's indoor and outdoor seating – depending on the time of day, an outdoor table may mean you'll be getting tour-bus fumes (and lines of people) to go along with that *poc chuk* (pork marinated in orange juice and garlic and grilled; M$115).

**Restaurant Hacienda Xaybe'h d'Camara**     MEXICAN **$$**
(☑ 985-851-00-00; Calle 15A No 42; buffet lunch M$140; ⊙ 11am-5pm; P ⊛ 🗷 🍴) Set a block back from the highway opposite Hotel Chichén Itzá, this is a large place with attractive grounds. It's popular with tours and the food is a bit overpriced, but the selection of salads makes it a good option for vegetarians. Diners can use the swimming pool for free. Drinks cost extra.

## ❶ Information

Chichén Itzá's western entrance has a large parking lot and big visitors center with an ATM and restaurant serving somewhat pricey food. You'll find other ATMs in the Oxxo store on Calle 15 and at Palacio Municipal, across from the church.

## ❶ Getting There & Away

Oriente has ticket offices near the east and west sides of Pisté, and 2nd-class buses passing through town stop almost anywhere along the way.

Most 1st-class buses arrive and depart from the ruins only. These also head to Mérida and Valladolid, as well as to coastal locations in

Quintana Roo: Playa del Carmen, Tulum and Cancún. If you plan to see the ruins and then head directly to another city by 1st-class bus, to secure your seat, buy your bus ticket at the visitors center gift shop before going into the ruins.

*Colectivos* (shared vans) to Valladolid (M$35, 40 minutes) enter the car park.

## ❶ Getting Around

Buses to Pisté generally stop at the **bus station** (☑ 985-851-00-52; ⏱ 10am-6pm); you can make the hot walk to and from the ruins in 20 to 30 minutes. First-class buses stop at the ruins; for others, check with the driver.

There is a taxi stand near the west end of town; the prices are around M$50 to the ruins, M$80 to Cenote Ik Kil and M$150 to Grutas de Balankanché.

# Valladolid

☑ 985 / POP 52,000

Once known as the Sultana of the East, Yucatán's third-largest city is famed for its quiet streets and sun-splashed pastel walls. It's worth staying here for a few days or longer, as the provincial town makes a great hub for visits to Río Lagartos, Chichén Itzá, Ek' Balam and a number of nearby cenotes. The city resides at that magic point where there's plenty to do, yet it still feels small, manageable and affordable.

## History

Valladolid has seen its fair share of turmoil and revolt. The city was first founded in 1543 near the Chouac-Ha lagoon some 50km from the coast, but it was too hot and there were way too many mosquitoes for Francisco de Montejo, nephew of Montejo the Elder, and his merry band of conquerors. So they upped and moved the city to the Maya ceremonial center of Zací (sah-*see*), where they faced heavy resistance from the local Maya. Eventually the Elder's son – Montejo the Younger – took the town. The Spanish conquerors, in typical fashion, ripped down the town and laid out a new city following the classic colonial plan.

During much of the colonial era, Valladolid's physical isolation from Mérida kept it relatively autonomous from royal rule, and the Maya of the area suffered brutal exploitation, which continued after Mexican independence. Barred from entering many areas of the city, the Maya made Valladolid one of their first points of attack following the 1847 outbreak of the War of the Castes in Tepich. After a two-month siege, the city's occupiers were finally overcome. Many fled to the safety of Mérida; the rest were slaughtered.

Today Valladolid is a prosperous seat of agricultural commerce, augmented by some light industry and a growing tourist trade.

## ◉ Sights & Activities

★ Casa de los Venados                                 MUSEUM

(☑ 985-856-22-89; www.casadelosvenados.com; Calle 40 No 204, btwn Calles 41 & 43; M$100; ⏱ tours 10am or by appointment) Featuring over 3000 pieces of museum-quality Mexican folk art, this private collection is interesting in that objects are presented in an actual private house, in the context that they were originally designed for, instead of being displayed in glass cases. The tour (in English or Spanish) touches on the origins of some of the more important pieces and the story of the award-winning restored colonial mansion that houses them.

### BUSES FROM CHICHÉN ITZÁ

| DESTINATION | FARE (M$) | TIME (HR) | FREQUENCY (PER DAY) |
| --- | --- | --- | --- |
| Cancún | 172-335 | 3-4½ | hourly 8:30am-9:30pm |
| Cobá | 85 | 2 | 12:30am, 7:30am, 1pm, 5pm, 7pm |
| Mérida | 99-178 | 1¾-2¾ | hourly |
| Playa del Carmen | 174-367 | 3½-4 | 12:30am, 7:30am, 1pm, 5pm, 7pm |
| Tulum | 123-252 | 2½-3 | 12:30am, 7:30am, 8:25am, 1pm, 4:30pm, 5pm, 7pm |
| Valladolid | 34-106 | 1 | hourly |

### Templo de San Bernardino                    CHURCH

(Convento de Sisal; cnr Calles 49 & 51; M$30 Mon-Sat, Sun free; ⊙9am-7pm) The Templo de San Bernardino and the adjacent Convento de Sisal are about 700m southwest of the plaza. They were constructed between 1552 and 1560 to serve the dual functions of fortress and church. The church's charming decoration includes beautiful rose-colored walls, arches, some recently uncovered 16th-century frescoes and a small image of the Virgin on the altar. These are about the only original items remaining; the grand wooden *retablo* (altarpiece) dates from the 19th century.

### Museo de San Roque                    MUSEUM

(Calle 41 s/n btwn 38 and 40; ⊙8am-8pm Mon-Fri, from 9am Sat, 9am-6pm Sun) **FREE** Previously a 16th-century convent, San Roque has models and exhibits on the history of the city and the region. Other displays focus on various aspects of traditional Maya life.

### ★Hacienda San Lorenzo Oxman                    SWIMMING

(off Calle 54; cenote M$80, cenote & pool M$100; ⊙8am-6pm) Once a *henequén* plantation and a refuge for War of the Castes insurgents in the mid-19th century, today the hacienda's main draw is a gorgeous cenote that's usually less crowded than other sinkholes in the area, especially if you visit Monday through Thursday. If you buy the entry to both, you have a M$50 credit to use at the cafe.

### Cenote Suytun                    CENOTE

(☑cell 998-2419957; Hwy 180, Tikuch; adult/child under 11yr M$70/50; ⊙9am-5pm) If you can get in before the bus tour groups, this cenote, run by the Tikuch community, features in many brochures and guidebooks. It is the one with the stone platform (permitted to be built after some of the roof had caved in). It's a decent cenote, if a slightly more clinical experience than some of the others. It's 9km east of Valladolid off Hwy 180.

### Cenote X'Kekén y Samulá                    SWIMMING

(Cenote Dzitnup & Samulá; 1/2 cenotes M$80/125; ⊙8:30am-6:30pm) One of two cenotes at Dzitnup (also known as X'Kekén Jungle Park), X'Kekén is popular with tour groups. A massive limestone formation with stalactites hangs from its ceiling. The pool is artificially lit and easily swimmable. Here you can also take a dip in cenote Samulá, a lovely cavern pool with *álamo* roots stretching down many meters. You can also rent horses

(M$225 per 30 minutes), ATVs (M$275 per 30 minutes) or bikes (M$100 per hour).

### Cenote Zací                    SWIMMING

(☑985-856-08-18; Calle 36 s/n, btwn Calles 37 & 39; adult/child 3-11yr M$30/15; ⊙10am-5pm) One of few cenotes in Valladolid itself, Cenote Zací is a handy place to cool off. While it's a gorgeous spot, don't expect crystalline waters. You might see catfish or, overhead, a colony of bats. If you spend over M$100 at the pleasant **restaurant** under a large *palapa* (mains M$50 to M$150) here, your entry is free.

## 👣 Tours

### Xkopek Bee Tour                    ECOTOUR

(☑985-125-09-64; www.facebook.com/xkopekmx; cnr Calles 57 & 38; adult/child M$100/50; ⊙9am-5pm Tue-Sun) See bees doing their stuff on this fun and fascinating tour, taste some honey, and perhaps buy bee-related products at the shop.

### MexiGo Tours                    TOURS

(☑985-856-07-77; www.mexigotours.com; Calle 43 No 204C, btwn Calles 40 & 42; ⊙9am-1pm & 3-7pm Mon-Sat) MexiGo Tours has a good reputation for its trips that cover a range of cultural and nature activities in one day. You might be swimming in a cenote in one hour and sampling tequila the next. Not to mention visits to ruins and action further afield, such as boat tours to see flamingos at Río Lagartos. It can also arrange airport pickup in Mérida or Cancún.

Also offers bike hire per hour/day from M$25/150.

## 🛌 Sleeping

Many hotels are on or near the main plaza, Parque Francisco Cantón Rosado, with one or two excellent options slightly further out of the city center, doable if you have your own transport.

### ★Hostel Candelaria                    HOSTEL $

(☑985-856-22-67; www.hostelvalladolidyucatan.com; Calle 35 No 201F; dm/d/tr/q incl breakfast from M$200/630/860/1120; ⊕※🛜) A friendly place on a quiet little square, this hostel can get a little cramped when full, but its charming decor, good kitchen, gorgeous elongated garden complete with hammocks, female-only dorm and plenty of hangout space make it one of the best hostels in town. It also rents out bikes for M$20 per hour.

# Valladolid

**La Aurora Colonial**　　　　　　HOTEL **$**
(☎985-856-08-32; www.hotellaaurora.com; Calle 42 No 192; d/tr M$690/790; P🅿︎❄🛜🏊) Well-appointed (some slightly cramped) rooms overlook a pretty courtyard with a pool and potted plants at the colonial-style Aurora. It's good value for those on a budget. If possible, avoid the noisier street-facing rooms.

**Casa Valladolid**　　　　BOUTIQUE HOTEL **$$**
(☎985-856-55-15, 985-121-01-44; Calle 44 No 176, btwn Calles 35 & 37; r incl breakfast from M$1200;

❄🛜🏊) This spot promises big things on entry – the reception is located in a lovely colonial building with stunning floor tiles. The rooms are in a new section, set around a small pool and patio. Rooms are pleasant, if a little plain. The smaller rooms are less appealing (several don't have external windows); those with terraces and balconies are the nicest.

**Hotel Zenti'k**　　　　BOUTIQUE HOTEL **$$$**
(☎985-104-91-71; www.zentikhotel.com; Calle 30 No 192C, btwn Calles 27 & 29; cabañas incl break-

fast from M$1500; P🚗❄🛜🏊🐾) This hippyish boutique hotel some way from the town center offers a choice of 10 spacious and imaginatively designed *cabañas* within intimate surrounds. A gorgeous pool, a spa and an usual underground swimming cave are the real highlights, as is its fabulous restaurant and the fact that the owner rescues local stray animals and finds them homes.

### Casa Marlene
BOUTIQUE HOTEL $$$

(📞985-856-04-99; www.casatiamicha.com; Calle 39 No 193; r incl breakfast M$1800-2150; P🚗❄🛜🏊) A sister property of boutique hotel Casa Tía Micha (right on the same block), the Marlene house is a lovely 19th-century building with six rooms surrounding a pretty courtyard garden with an attractive little Jacuzzi.

### Casa San Roque
B&B $$$

(📞985-856-26-42; www.casasanroquevalladolid. com; Calle 41 No 193B; r M$1190-1725; P❄🛜🏊) With just seven colonial rooms on offer you'll get more privacy and personalized attention here than at some of the larger hotels on the main plaza. The full breakfast (M$100 per person) and a pool with dual fountains in the rear garden are the clinchers.

### Casa Tía Micha
BOUTIQUE HOTEL $$$

(📞985-856-04-99; www.casatiamicha.com; Calle 39 No 197; r incl breakfast from M$1450; P🚗❄🛜🏊) The corridor and rear garden are beautifully lit at night in this family-run boutique hotel just off the plaza. Some of the tastefully adorned colonial-style rooms have king-sized beds, and the upstairs suite comes with a Jacuzzi. If the Tía is booked, on the same block you'll find sister property Casa Marlene, whose pool guests here can use.

## 🍴 Eating & Drinking

### ⭐ Yerbabuena del Sisal
MEXICAN $

(📞985-856-14-06; www.yerbabuenadelsisal.com; Calle 54A No 217; mains M$80-120; ⏱8am-5pm Tue-Sun; 🛜🍴) 🍃 Wonderfully healthy dishes are served in this gorgeous open-sided space with a peaceful garden right on Parque Sisal. Tortilla chips and three delectable salsas come to the table while you look over the menu, which offers all-vegetarian and largely organic dishes, such as the delightful *tacos maculum* (with handmade corn tortillas, beans, cheese and aromatic Mexican pepper leaf).

### La Palapita de los Tamales
MEXICAN $

(📞998-106-34-72; Calle 42 s/n, cnr Calle 33; tamales from M$45; ⏱8-10pm Mon-Sat; 🍴) The menu changes daily here, but you'll always find a welcome *tamal* to snack on. Sweetcorn and pork was on the menu recently, as was excellent *pozole* (a pork-and-hominy soup). There's casual indoor or patio seating, and takeout is popular.

Great juices, breakfasts and vegan options, too.

### Bazar Municipal
MARKET $

(cnr Calles 39 & 40; breakfast M$30-50; ⏱7am-10pm) A collection of market-style eateries that are popular for their big, cheap breakfasts. At lunch and dinner some offer *comida corrida* (set meals of several courses).

### Naino
INTERNATIONAL $$

(📞985-104-90-71; www.facebook.com/zentikpro ject; Calle 30 No 192, btwn Calles 27 & 29; mains M$80-180; ⏱7am-10:30pm; P🛜) Located on the outskirts of town, on the premises of resort Zenti'k, this pleasant open-air restaurant is an option for breakfast, lunch or dinner. The food is creative with some extremely creative takes on local cooking fused with international flavors. If you're craving something a bit different then this is the spot.

### Hostería del Marqués
MEXICAN $$

(📞985-856-20-73; www.mesondelmarques.com; El Mesón del Marqués, Calle 39 No 203; mains M$120-350; ⏱7am-11pm; P❄🛜) Dine in a tranquil colonial courtyard with a bubbling fountain, or the air-con salon looking on to it. The restaurant specializes in Yucatecan fare, such as *longaniza* Valladolid (Valladolid-style sausage) and *cochinita pibil* (pulled pork), and there are also international dishes such as Angus beef cuts.

### Cafeína Bistro Bar
BAR

(📞985-858-21-26; Calle 41A s/n; mains M$90-300; ⏱noon-2am; 🛜) A little pub and bistro where you can catch a televised sporting event or chat over Mexican draft beer and well-made pizzas.

### Taberna de los Frailes
COCKTAIL BAR

(📞985-856-06-89; www.tabernadelosfrailes.com; Calle 49 s/n, cnr Calle 41A; ⏱10am-10pm; 🛜) This pretty and rather romantic spot with a verdant garden is a top spot to get a tasty cocktail at a place where you can actually have a quiet conversation. There's an excellent selection of mezcals and tequilas.

**Los Portales** CAFE
(☎ 985-856-09-99; Calle 41 No 202B; ☺ 7am-11pm)
Don't expect award-winning mixology at Los Portales, but as its name suggests, it's all about location: hard to beat the alfresco experience on the plaza if you're looking to relax, sip something and marvel at beautiful Valladolid.

## 🛍 Shopping

**La Puerta del Sol** CLOTHING
(☎ 985-856-34-20; cnr Calles 39 & 44; ☺ 8:30am-8pm Mon-Wed, Fri & Sat, to 2pm Thu & Sun) A friendly spot to find good quality *guayaberas* and other regional clothes at reasonable prices.

## ℹ Information

Various banks (most with ATMs) near the town center are generally open 9am to 5pm Monday to Friday and to 1pm Saturday.
**Grupo Médico del Centro** (☎ 985-856-51-06; www.facebook.com/grupomedicodelcentro; Calle 40 No 178B btwn Calles 33 & 35; ☺ 7:30am-12:30pm & 5:30-7:30pm) A centrally located private medical clinic.
**Main Post Office** (Calle 40 s/n btwn Calles 39 & 41; ☺ 8am-4:30pm Mon-Fri, to 1pm Sat)
**Tourist Information Office** (☎ ext 114 985-856-25-51; cnr Calles 40 & 41; ☺ 8:30am-8pm Mon-Fri, 9am-7pm Sat & Sun) With a limited budget, this place doesn't stock much printed information. Official walking guides use this as their base.

## ℹ Getting There & Away

### BUS
Valladolid's main bus terminal is the convenient **ADO bus terminal** (☎ 985-856-34-48; www.ado.com.mx; cnr Calles 39 & 46; ☺ 24hr), which has both 1st- and 2nd-class services.

Buses to Chichén Itzá/Pisté normally stop at the ruins during opening hours, though double check with the driver.

### COLECTIVO
*Colectivos* depart as soon as their seats are filled (or you can elect to pay the full fare). Most operate from 7am or 8am to about 7pm, but some leave as early as 3am or as late as 10pm.

Direct services run to **Mérida** (Calle 39, near the ADO bus terminal; M$200; ☺ 2hr) and **Cancún** (Calle 41, cnr Calle 38, 1 block east of the plaza; M$200; ☺ 2hr); confirm they're nonstop. *Colectivos* for **Pisté & Chichén Itzá** (Calle 39; M$35; ☺ 1hr) leave north of the ADO bus terminal. For **Ek' Balam** (Calle 44, btwn Calles 35 & 37; M$50) take a 'Santa Rita' *colectivo*.

## ℹ Getting Around

The old highway passes through the town center, though most signs urge motorists toward the toll road north of town. To follow the old highway eastbound, take Calle 41; westbound, take Calle 39.

Bicycles are a great way to see the town and get out to the cenotes. You can rent them at Hostel La Candelaria (p199) or MexiGo Tours (p199) for around M$20 to M$25 per hour.

It's possible to get to many of the cenotes by public transportation. *Colectivos* depart from different points around the center; ask the locals. Note that these tend to leave in the mornings only.

# Ek' Balam

The tiny village of Ek' Balam is worth a visit to see what a traditional Maya village looks like. There's not a lot here, except a handful of artisan stands (mainly selling hammocks) along the main plaza, which also serves as

## BUSES FROM VALLADOLID

| DESTINATION | FARE (M$) | TIME (HR) | FREQUENCY (PER DAY) |
| --- | --- | --- | --- |
| Cancún | 252 | 2½-3½ | frequent |
| Chichén Itzá/Pisté | 35-118 | ¾ | frequent |
| Chiquilá (for Isla Holbox) | 201 | 4 | 1 (9:50am) |
| Cobá | 51 | 1 | 6 |
| Izamal | 80 | 2½ | 1 (12:50pm) |
| Mérida | 240-250 | 2-3½ | frequent |
| Playa del Carmen | 252 | 3-4 | frequent |
| Tizimín | 31 | 1 | frequent |
| Tulum | 100-148 | 1-2 | frequent |

## CASTE WAR MUSEUM, TIHOSUCO

Tihosuco was a major military outpost for the Spanish during the late 16th century and for 300 years thereafter. During this time the town came under numerous Maya assaults, and in 1686 it was attacked, though not sacked, by pirates led by legendary Dutch buccaneer Lorencillo. During many of those attacks, the Spaniards retreated to the heavily fortified 17th-century church at the town center, which for much of its life served as a house of God, an arsenal and a stronghold. But the town and church fell to rebel hands in 1866 following a long siege, and much of the magnificent building was gutted. What remains of the once-great church is worth investigating. Services are still held inside, as in many other roofless churches in the region. Housed in an 18th-century building and with a passionate director, the small but interesting **Museo de la Guerra de Castas** (Caste War Museum; ☑ 983-208-92-03; www.facebook.com/museoguerradecastas; cnr Calles 17 & 26, Tihosuco; adult/child 6-15yr M$100/50; ◷10am-6pm Tue-Sun), does a fine job of detailing the more than four centuries of oppression suffered by the Maya on the peninsula, with its main focus on the Caste War. More recently, English explanations have been introduced. There's a small botanical garden here as well. The museum organizes cultural experiences, such as cotton weaving and traditional-medicine workshops, including tours with local food (these are for groups but you might be able to join in if you arrange in advance). Tihosuco is an easy trip on the highway, 60km south of Valladolid.

the town's soccer field, and a decent accommodations option.

## ◉ Sights

**Ek' Balam**        ARCHAEOLOGICAL SITE
(adult/child 4-12yr M$431/75, guide M$600; ◷8am-4pm) The fascinating ruined city of Ek' Balam reached its peak in the 8th century CE, before being suddenly abandoned. Vegetation still covers much of the archaeological site, but it's well organized and has a lovely, lush setting. Interesting features include a pyramid-like structure near the entrance, as well as a fine arch and a ball court. Most impressive, though, is the gargantuan **Acrópolis**, whose well-restored base is 160m long and holds a 'gallery' – actually a series of separate chambers.

Built atop the base of the Acrópolis is Ek' Balam's massive **main pyramid**, reaching a height of 32m and sporting a gaping jaguar mouth. Below the mouth are stucco skulls, while above and to the right sits an amazingly expressive figure. On the right side stand unusual winged human figures (some call them Maya angels, although a much more likely explanation is that they are shamans or medicine people).

The turnoff for the archaeological site is 17km north of Valladolid, and the ruins are another 6km east from the turnoff.

**X'Canché Cenote**       CENOTE
(☑cell 985-1009915; www.ekbalam.com.mx/cenote-xcanche; M$50; ◷8am-3:30pm) From

the Ek' Balam parking lot you can visit the X'Canché Cenote. From the entrance it's a 1.5km walk, or you can rent a bicycle (M$120) or pedicab (M$150). Also available at this ecotourist center are zip-line activities and cabin rentals (M$600 per night).

## ⌨ Sleeping & Eating

★ **Genesis Eco-Oasis**      GUESTHOUSE $$
(☑cell 985-1010277; www.genesisretreat.com; Ek' Balam pueblo; r US$45-79; ❀🐕🛜🏊) ♪ This retreat offers B&B intimacy in a quiet, laid-back ecofriendly setting. Mostly it's environmentally friendly: gray water is used for landscaping, the rooms' architecture (pitched, thatched roofs) encourages passive cooling and there's a dehydrating toilet or two. There's a swimming pool and it offers delicious veggie meals made from scratch.

The hotel closes in September and sometimes early October also. Reservations required. Wi-fi is in the lobby only.

**Dolce Vacanza**      ITALIAN $$
(☑985-124-10-80; mains M$90-120; ◷8am-8pm; 🐕) Same name, different restaurant: Dolce Vacanza (under new ownership, with a new menu to boot), now offers vegetarian food, pasta, pesto, and soups in a relaxing, bright-yellow spot.

## ❶ Getting There & Away

*Colectivos* (M$50) to Ek' Balam depart Valladolid from Calle 44, between Calles 35 and 37.

# Tizimín

986 / POP 50.000

You won't find much in Tizimín that's designed with the tourist in mind; in fact, for most folks it serves as a mere stopover point en route to the coast. If you've a couple of hours to kill before a bus, there's an interesting church and monastery that fronts Tizimín's main plaza, the Parque Principal.

Historically, however, it's important as it's believed to be one of the first villages founded by the Spanish.

If you have your own transport, 6km away is a community-run cenote with a restaurant. The cenote is in a lush, landscaped setting.

## Sights

### Templo & Exconvento de Los Santos Reyes
CHURCH
(Church of the Three Wise Kings) The Church of the Three Wise Kings and the attached convent (on opposite sides of Calle 51 on the plaza) was built in 1563 by the Franciscans. It's believed that even then, the church and convent were separated, due to the urbanization of the city at the time; these days, a road still divides the two buildings.

### Cenote Kikil
CENOTE
(986-118-31-14; www.tzn.mx; Km 4.5 Carretera Tizimín - Rio Lagartos Kikil; adult/child under 12yr M$100/20; ⊙8am-7pm) Six kilometres northwest of Tizimín, this community-run cenote comes as a lovely surprise after the grittier town. It's well run, clean, set in pretty landscaped gardens and even has an attractive restaurant (8am to 6:30pm, mains M$80 to M$200) that serves breakfast for early comers. If you've had fun, ask for a marker and add some doodle and scrawl to the walls.

## 🛏 Sleeping & Eating

### Hotel 49
HOTEL $
(986-863-21-36; contacto@hotel49.com; Calle 49 No 373 btwn Calles 46 & 48; s/d M$650/750; P❋🐾) A centrally located option with parking and rooms with air-con. Note that it does allow smoking inside, so nonsmokers may want to look elsewhere.

### Hotel San Carlos
HOTEL $
(986-863-20-94; www.hotelsancarlostizimin.com; Calle 54 No 407 btwn Calles 51 & 53; r with fan/air-con M$390/520; P❋🐾) Two blocks west of the plaza, this is one of the nicest hotels in town, though don't expect luxuries (the exterior is modern but the rooms less so). Some rooms have private balconies looking on to the shared garden area.

### Ricardo's
MEXICAN $
(Calle 48 No 371 btwn Calles 45 & 47; mains M$70-110; ⊙8:30am-6pm; 🐾) With the brightest laminated menus this side of the Yucatán, Ricardo's is known for its affordable hearty daily lunch specials.

### Cocteleria El Barco de Ana
SEAFOOD $$
(986-863-73-87, cell 986-1064496; Calle 54A No 415 btwn 57 & 59; M$70-200; ⊙11am-6pm Wed-Mon) In a tiny spot in an incongruous part of town, a few blocks from the plaza, this tiny and casual place fills up quickly, especially between 1pm and 3pm when the fish-lovin' folk head in to chomp on fresh *mariscos* and other seafood delights, all from nearby Río Lagartos.

## ℹ Getting There & Away

The **ADO bus terminal** (986-863-24-24; www.ado.com.mx; Calle 47 btwn Calles 46 & 48; ⊙3am-11pm) is east of the market. You'll find Mérida-bound *colectivos* (M$140) here, too. The **Noreste bus terminal** (Calle 46; ⊙2am-8pm) is just around the corner. Río Lagartos/San Felipe-bound *colectivos* (M$45/50, five daily) depart from the market.

### BUSES FROM TIZIMÍN

| DESTINATION | FARE (M$) | TIME (HR) | FREQUENCY (PER DAY) |
|---|---|---|---|
| Cancún | 140-185 | 3½ | frequent |
| El Cuyo | 70 | 2 | 4-5 |
| Izamal | 95 | 2½ | 3 |
| Mérida | 115-190 | 4 | 8 |
| Río Lagartos/San Felipe | 45/50 | 1¼ | 9 |
| Valladolid | 30 | 1 | frequent |

# Río Lagartos

📞 986 / POP 3000

On the windy northern shore of the peninsula, sleepy Río Lagartos (Alligator River) is a fishing village that also boasts the densest concentration of flamingos in Mexico, supposedly two or three flamingos per resident, if one believes the provided math. Lying within the Reserva de la Biosfera Ría Lagartos, this mangrove-lined estuary shelters bird species, including snowy egrets, red egrets, tiger herons and snowy white ibis, as well as the crocodiles that gave the town its name. It's a beautiful area. At the right time of year you can see numerous species of birds without even getting out of your vehicle.

## 👉 Tours

The brilliant orange-red flamingos can turn the horizon fiery when they take wing. Depending on the time of year and the forces of nature, you'll see either hundreds or thousands of them. Normally the best months for viewing them are from April through September; March and October are not so great and you might see a few only.

To see the flamingos, you'll need to rent a boat and driver. You'll see more birdlife if you head out at sunrise or around 5pm. Prices vary by boat, group size (maximum six), number of hours and destination. A two-hour trip costs around M$1200 to M$1800. Plan on packing something to eat the night before, as most restaurants open long after you'll be on the water. Ask to stop at the *arcilla* (mud bath) on the way back.

You can negotiate with one of the eager men along the boardwalk. They speak English and will connect you with a captain (who usually doesn't), but the best option is going with one of the knowledgeable English-speaking guides operating out of restaurants Ria Maya (p206) and Balneario Chiquilá.

⭐ **Río Lagartos Adventures**    BOATING
(📞986-100-83-90; www.riolagartosadventures. com; Calle 19 No 134; per boat 4hr from M$3425, 2hr flamingo tour per boat M$2000) This outfit run by local expert Diego Núñez Martinez does various water and land expeditions, including flamingo- and crocodile-watching, fly-fishing and excursions designed for photography. Diego is a licensed, fluent-English-speaking guide with formal training as a naturalist. He's well up to date on

the area's fauna and flora, which includes some 400 bird species.

He organizes the tours out of Ría Maya Restaurante (p206) and trains local guides.

**Ismael Navarro**    BOATING
(📞986-862-00-00, cell 986-8665216; riolaga@ hotmail.com; Calle 9; per boat 2hr M$1200, fly-fishing M$1200-3500) Ismael is worth seeking out for a tour of the local flora and fauna, although if he's not available he'll send one of his guides whose English is so-so. Besides the flamingo and fly-fishing outings (M$1200), Ismael can do shorebird tours along the mudflats or crocodile trips in the evenings.

You'll find him and his partner, captain 'Chino Mosca', at their HQ, Balneario Chiquilá, a casual eatery (next to a stagnant swimming hole) on the east end of Calle 9.

## 🛏 Sleeping & Eating

**Punta Ponto Hotel**    HOTEL $
(📞986-862-05-09; www.facebook.com/Hotel Puntaponto; Calle 9 No 140, cnr Calle 19; r incl breakfast M$700-750; 🅿️😊❄️🛜) It's simple and clean and one of the best deals in town. Kind host Roger is a great source of information. We love the two front rooms with balconies with the estuary views. Even if you're in a different room, the breezy, open-air common spaces seal the deal. (And there are toilet seats!)

**Hotel Villas de Pescadores**    HOTEL $
(📞986-862-00-20; www.hotelvilladepescadores. com; cnr Calles 14 & 9; d M$750; 🅿️😊❄️🛜) Near the water's edge and in a central location, this nice bright green-and-white themed hotel offers 12 very clean rooms, each with good cross-ventilation (all face the estuary), satellite TV and air-con. Upstairs rooms have balconies, and a spiral staircase leads up to a rooftop lookout tower where guests can watch the sunset.

**El Perico Marinero**    HOTEL $$
(📞986-862-00-58; www.elpericomarinero.com; Calle 9, near Calle 19; d incl breakfast M$650-950; 🅿️❄️🛜🏊) This cozy hotel offers 14 pleasant rooms, some with estuary vistas and handmade wood furnishings, and all with excellent beds. The pool isn't enormous, but is adequate for cooling off. Breakfasts are simple, but coffee is brewed, not instant.

**El Perico Marinero**    SEAFOOD $$
(📞986-862-05-55; www.elpericomarinero.com; Calle 9; mains M$150-350; ⏱7am-9:30pm) Right

## BEST FESTIVALS IN RÍO LAGARTOS

Río Lagartos knows how to party, and two festivals, La Feria de Santiago and Día de la Marina, are well worth checking out. **La Feria de Santiago** (☉ Jul 20-25), the patron-saint festival of Río Lagartos, is held in July. A bullfight (really bullplay) ring is erected in the middle of town, and every afternoon anyone who wishes is able to enter it and play matador with a young bull. The animal is not killed or even injured, just made a little angry at times.

Another big annual event in Río Lagartos is **Día de la Marina** (Day of the Marine Force; ☉ Jun 1). On this day, following a morning Mass, a crown of flowers is dedicated to the Virgin and carried from the church to a boat, where it is then taken 4km out to sea and placed in the water as an offering to all the fisherfolk who have perished at sea.

The boats are heavily decorated on this day, and tourists are welcome to ride to the site for free. Just ask if you can go, and be friendly and respectful. A tip for their kindness, following the service, is a grateful gesture (M$50 to M$100 per visitor).

on the waterfront, this simple seafood spot is a nice place to wind down after a day of flamingo-viewing. Fresh seafood and fish, some Yucatecan options, and friendly service go nicely with the last rays of sunset and the lap of the waves.

**Ría Maya Restaurante** SEAFOOD **$$**
(www.riolagartosadventures.com; Calle 19 No 134, cnr Calle 14; mains M$120-300; ☉9am-8:30pm) A popular two-story *palapa* with waterside sunset views, this is a good place to meet other travelers and form groups for boat tours. Lobster, at market price, is a delicious seasonal specialty. Hummingbird feeders (lots of them) add to the fun.

### ❶ Getting There & Away

Several Noreste buses run daily between Río Lagartos and Tizimín (M$47, 1¼ hours), Mérida (M$250, three to four hours) and San Felipe (M$20, 20 minutes). Noreste serves Valladolid and Cancún, but you'll need to transfer in Tizimín. If you are traveling to Valladolid, be sure to catch the 4pm bus from Río Lagartos; the 5pm doesn't make the connection in Tizimín.

The bus terminal is on Calle 19, between Calles 8 and 10.

## El Cuyo

☎ 986 / POP 3000

El Cuyo lies along the shore at the end of the road from Río Lagartos. This tiny fishing village has a clear white-sand beach, muddy waters and a windy coast. In recent years it's become a kiteboarding mecca for those in the know, and several outfits offer classes. The town sees a few local tourists looking for a short beach vacation, but not many foreigners visit here. Maybe this is the off-the-beaten-track spot you've been looking for.

At El Cuyo the road travels through broad expanses of grassy savanna with palms and some huge-trunked trees, passing the site of the original founding of Valladolid, in 1543. At Colonia Yucatán, 38km south of El Cuyo, you can head east to pick up the road to Chiquilá and Isla Holbox or west to Tizimín.

### 🏃 Activities

**El Cuyo Kite School** KITESURFING
(☑ cell 985-8582357; www.elcuyokiteschool.com; private/group classes from US$210/150) Fly high at one of El Cuyo's recommended kitesurf schools; El Cuyo is *the* place to catch the northern winds. Operates all year except August to October. Also has accommodations for those who get hooked and want to do the three-day course.

### 🛏 Sleeping & Eating

**Posada El Faro** HOTEL **$**
(☑986-853-40-15; s/d M$600/700; P ❄ ☀ 🛜) The five basic rooms here are comfortable enough; with beds and hammocks. It's just south of the plaza.

**Villas Chac Chi** APARTMENT **$$**
(☑ cell 998-5773380; www.facebook.com/villas chacchi; apt M$1300; P ☀ 🛜) About 1km east of the plaza along the main dirt road are six ample apartments with full kitchen and air-con, and they're just a hop, skip and a jump to the beach. The delightful owner, Johnny, is on hand to assist. Reservations required.

**La Conchita** SEAFOOD **$$**
(☑986-853-40-62; Calle 21 s/n; mains M$80-170, lobster M$340-380; ☉8am-6pm) Fish paradise under a *palapa* at this simple, no-fuss place.

Grab a beer, some ceviche and prawns and remember what life was like before technology took over. Also rents bikes for M$50 per hour.

**Miramar**                                    SEAFOOD **$$**
(mains M$100-140, lobster M$300; ⊙ 7am-6pm) Try the delicious crispy shrimp served in a coconut (M$130) at this large fan-cooled eatery on the plaza's west side.

## ℹ Getting There & Away

There are several Noreste departures to El Cuyo (around M$70, one hour) from Tizimín; going the other way, three buses head to Tizimín from the town plaza; some continue on to Valladolid (M$95). *Colectivo* vans are faster (M$70). Hitchhiking may be possible, but a rental car is by far the better way to go.

# San Felipe

🖉 986 / POP 2500

San Felipe is notable for its orderly streets, cheery Caribbean feel and painted wooden houses. With its laid-back air, this fishing village is a good alternative to staying in the 'metropolis' of Río Lagartos. About 12km west of Río Lagartos, it's seldom visited by travelers. Getting there you'll pass mangrove-dotted lagoons, and perhaps surprise a turtle or two crossing the road. Its beach lies across the mouth of the estuary, at Punta Holchit, and the mangroves there and on the western edge of town are a bird-watcher's paradise. Just looking out the windows of the town's main hotel you can see white and brown pelicans, terns, cormorants, great blue herons, magnificent frigate birds and jabirus (storks).

## ◎ Sights & Activities

*Lancheros* (boat owners) on the east end of waterfront Calle 9 charge around M$150 per boatload to take passengers across to Playa Bonita beach and M$600 to a nearby cenote. They also do fishing excursions and birding expeditions to Isla Cerritos (M$1000). Flamingo tours cost M$1800.

**Isla Cerritos**                              ISLAND
Just 5km from San Felipe, tiny Isla Cerritos was an important Maya port city back in the day. And while the entire island was covered with buildings during this era – archaeological expeditions have turned up nearly 50,000 artifacts – it's virtually deserted today, and none of the buildings have been restored. You can get there with a tour or catch a motorboat on the east side of the San Felipe boardwalk for around M$1000 per boat.

## 🛌 Sleeping & Eating

**Hotel San Felipe de Jesús**                  HOTEL **$**
(🖉 986-862-20-27; hotelsfjesus@hotmail.com; Calle 9A No 59 btwn Calles 14 & 16; d M$620-670, ste M$740; ⊙ restaurant 8-10am & 7-9pm) A friendly, clean and cleverly constructed hotel at the west edge of San Felipe's harbor, it's definitely worth a few extra pesos for a room with private balcony and water views. The restaurant (breakfast and dinner) offers good seafood at low prices. To get here, turn left at the *malecón* and proceed about 200m.

**El Popular Vaselina**                        SEAFOOD **$$**
(🖉 986-862-20-83; mains M$89-169; ⊙ 9am-6pm) Possibly the village's best for seafood; efficient service and it's right on the *malecón*.

## ℹ Getting There & Away

Noreste buses from Tizimín pass through Río Lagartos and continue to San Felipe (M$50, one hour, four to five daily). The bus ride from Río Lagartos takes 20 minutes. San Felipe–bound *colectivos* depart from the market in Tizimín (M$50, one hour). Buses bound for Mérida (M$220) leave at 5am.

## AT A GLANCE

**POPULATION**
928,400

**CAPITAL**
Campeche

**BEST NATURE
RESERVE**
Reserva de la Bios-
fera Calakmul (p229)

**BEST MUSEUM**
Museo Arqueológico
de Campeche (p215)

**BEST BOUTIQUE
HOTEL**
Hacienda Puerta
Campeche (p216)

**WHEN TO GO**
**Dec-Apr** High season
means hotels are
at peak price, but
there are also lots of
festivities.

**Jun-Aug** Tur-
tle-hatching time in
Sabancuy (the full
season lasts from
April to October).

**Nov-Mar** Dry months
are pleasant for vis-
iting Calakmul; in the
rainy season access
is limited.

Museo Arqueológico de Campeche & Fuerte de San Miguel (p215)
ABALCAZAR/SHUTTERSTOCK

# Campeche State

**T**ucked into the southwestern corner of the Yucatán Peninsula, Campeche state is home to low-key villages, vast stretches of tangled jungle, bird-dotted mangroves and lagoons, and some of the region's most imposing Maya ruins – many of which you might have all to yourself. The walled capital city of Campeche is the quiet-but-gorgeous colonial town at the center of it all, providing a great jumping-off point for your adventures into this offbeat hinterland.

Campeche is the least visited of the Yucatán's states, laced through with lonely back roads, friendly people, quiet coastlines and a provincial, lost-land charm. Here you'll find peace, surprising attractions and very genuine local experiences.

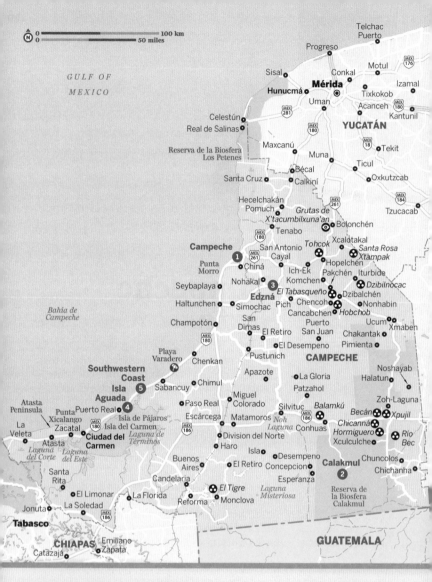

## Campeche State Highlights

**1 Campeche** (p211)
Strolling through the wedding-cake-hued streets of this pretty city, and along its stone ramparts to relive its exciting pirate history.

**2 Calakmul** (p229) Hauling yourself up massive pyramids and wandering through this incredible complex, while

the calls of howler monkeys reverberate in the surrounding jungle.

**3 Edzná** (p223) Exploring the large and impressive complexes of one of the most significant and accessible Maya ruins, and marveling at this extraordinary culture of both past and present.

**4 Isla Aguada** (p226) Spotting dolphins, seabirds and more from a local fishing boat while learning about the local ecology from the driver.

**5 Southwestern Coast** (p225) Munching on fresh seafood at a waterfront eatery or finding yourself a little patch of deserted beach.

# CAMPECHE

📞 981 / POP 250,000

Campeche is a historical fairyland, its walled city a tight enclave of restored pastel buildings, narrow cobblestone streets, fortified ramparts and well-preserved mansions. Added to Unesco's list of World Heritage sites in 1999, the state capital may lack the buzz and smarts of nearby Mérida, but wandering its near perfectly preserved colonial streets is a wonderful experience. Leave the inner walls and you'll find a genuine Mexican provincial capital complete with a frenetic market, peaceful *malecón* (boardwalk) and old fishing docks.

Besides the walls and numerous mansions built by wealthy Spanish families during Campeche's heyday in the 18th and 19th centuries, seven of the *baluartes* (bastions or bulwarks) have also survived. Two preserved colonial forts guard the city's outskirts, one of them housing the Museo Arqueológico de Campeche, an archaeological museum with many world-class pieces.

## History

Once a Maya trading village called Ah Kim Pech (Lord Sun Sheep-Tick), Campeche was first briefly approached by the Spaniards in 1517. Resistance by the Maya prevented the Spaniards from fully conquering the region for nearly a quarter-century. Colonial Campeche was founded in 1531, but later abandoned due to Maya hostility. By 1540, however, the conquistadors had gained sufficient control, under the leadership of Francisco de Montejo (the Younger), to found a permanent settlement. They named the settlement Villa de San Francisco de Campeche.

The settlement soon flourished as the major port of the Yucatán Peninsula, but this made it subject to pirate attacks. After a particularly appalling attack in 1663 (p214) left the city in ruins, the king of Spain ordered construction of Campeche's famous bastions, putting an end to the periodic carnage.

Today the city's economy is largely driven by tourism.

## ⊙ Sights & Activities

### ⊙ Plaza Principal & Around

Shaded by carob trees and ringed by tiled benches and broad footpaths radiating from a belle epoque kiosk, Campeche's appealingly modest central square started life in 1531 as a military camp. Over the years it became the focus of the town's civic, political and religious activities and remains the core of public life. *Campechanos* come here to chat, smooch, have their shoes shined or cool off with an ice cream after the heat of the day. The plaza is at its best on weekend evenings, when it's closed to traffic and concerts are staged.

**Centro Cultural Casa Número 6**
CULTURAL CENTER
(Calle 57 No 6; M$20; ⊙ 8am-9pm Mon-Fri, from 9am Sat & Sun) During the prerevolutionary era, when this mansion was occupied by an upper-class *campechano* family, Número 6 was a prestigious plaza address. Wandering the premises, you'll get an idea of how the city's high society lived back then. The front sitting room is furnished with Cuban-style pieces of the period. Inside are exhibition spaces, a tourist information desk and a gift shop.

**Catedral de Nuestra Señora de la Purísima Concepción**
CATHEDRAL
(Calle 55; ⊙ 7am-9pm) FREE Dominating Plaza Principal's east side is the two-towered cathedral. The limestone structure has stood on this spot for more than three centuries and it still fills beyond capacity most Sundays for mass. Statues of Sts Peter and Paul occupy niches in the baroque facade; the sober, single-nave interior is lined with colonial-era paintings. And at night, the gauzy lights on the illuminated church and other central landmarks create a magical atmosphere.

**Biblioteca de Campeche**
LIBRARY
(Centro Cultural del Palácio; State Library; ⊙ 9am-8pm Mon-Fri, to 1pm Sat) On the northern (seaward) side of Plaza Principal stands a replica of the old government center, now housing the modern Biblioteca de Campeche. The impressive porticoed building on the opposite side housed an earlier version of the city hall; it is now occupied by shops and restaurants.

**Mansión Carvajal**
HISTORIC BUILDING
(Calle 10, btwn Calles 51 & 53; ⊙ 8am-2:45pm Mon-Fri) FREE Once the mansion of wealthy landowner Fernando Carvajal, this beautiful building now houses state offices. Visitors are welcome to take a peek inside, however. Black-and-white tiled floors, Doric columns, elaborate archways and a dramatic marble-and-ironwork staircase are highlights. Note the historical plaque.

CAMPECHE STATE CAMPECHE

# Campeche

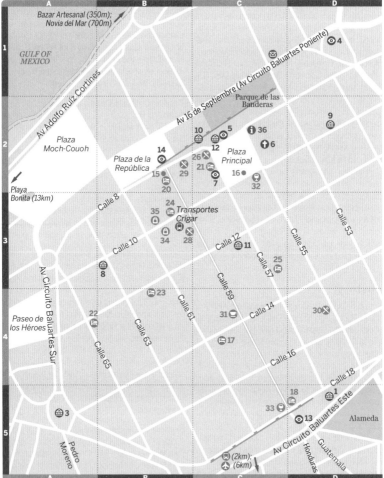

### Museo del Archivo General de Estado
MUSEUM

(981-816-09-39; Calle 12 No 159; 8am-3pm Mon-Fri) FREE At this small museum, learn how Campeche came to be. It's free and air-conditioned, and you get to check out old documents and maps, and watch a video (in Spanish or English) that recounts the history of the state.

### Museo El Palacio
MUSEUM

(981-811-03-66; http://sic.gob.mx; Calle 8 No 257, Plaza Principal; 10am-7pm Tue-Sun) This large museum at the plaza has exhibits about the city's logwood industry and salt trading; a section is designed to make you feel like you're inside a ship's hull.

### Ex-Templo de San José & Bazar Artesanal
HISTORIC BUILDING

(former San José Church; cnr Calles 10 & 63; 10am-8pm) Faced with blue-and-yellow tiles, the Ex-Templo de San José is a wonder; note the lighthouse, complete with weather vane, atop the right spire. Built in the early-18th century by Jesuits, who ran it as an institute of higher learning until they were booted out of Spanish domains in 1767.

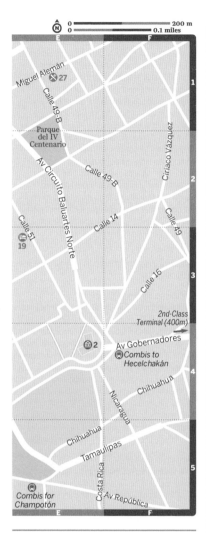

# Campeche

## ⊙ Baluartes

After a particularly blistering pirate assault in 1663, the remaining inhabitants of Campeche set about erecting protective walls around their city. Built largely by indigenous labor with limestone extracted from nearby caves, the barrier took more than 50 years to complete. Stretching more than 2.5km around the urban core and rising to a height of 8m, the hexagonal wall was linked by eight bulwarks. The seven that remain display a treasure trove of historical paraphernalia and artifacts of varying degrees of interest. You can climb atop

## RIBALD TALES: MARAUDING PIRATES OF CAMPECHE

Where there's wealth, there are pirates – this was truer in the 1500s than it is today. And Campeche, which was a thriving timber, chicle (gum) and logwood (a natural source of dye) port in the mid-16th century, was the wealthiest place around.

Pirates (or 'privateers,' as some preferred to be called) terrorized Campeche for two centuries. Time and time again the port was invaded, ships sacked, citizens robbed and buildings burned – typical pirate stuff. The buccaneers' hall of shame included the infamous John Hawkins, Francis Drake, Henry Morgan and the notorious 'Peg-Leg' himself. In their most gruesome assault, in early 1663, the various pirate hordes set aside rivalries to converge as a single flotilla upon the city, massacring Campeche's citizens.

This tragedy finally spurred the Spanish monarchy to take preventive action, but it was another five years before work on the 3.5m-thick ramparts began. By 1686 a 2.5km hexagon incorporating eight strategically placed bastions surrounded the city. A segment of the ramparts extended out to sea so that ships literally sailed into a fortress to gain access to the city. With Campeche nearly impregnable, pirates turned to other ports and ships at sea. In 1717 the brilliant naval strategist Felipe de Aranda began a campaign against the buccaneers, and eventually made this area of the Gulf safe from piracy.

the bulwarks and stroll sections of the wall for sweeping views of the port.

Two main entrances connected the walled compound with the outside world. The **Puerta del Mar** (Sea Gate; cnr Calles 8 & 59) provided access from the sea, opening on to a wharf where small craft delivered goods from ships anchored further out. (The shallow waters were later reclaimed so the gate is now several blocks from the waterfront.) The **Puerta de Tierra** (Land Gate; Calle 18; ⊙9am-6pm), on the opposite side, was opened in 1732 as the principal ingress from the suburbs.

**Museo de la Arquitectura Maya**   MUSEUM
(Calle 8; M$45; ⊙8:30am-5:30pm Tue-Sun) The Baluarte de Nuestra Señora de la Soledad, designed to protect the Puerta del Mar, contains the fascinating Museo de la Arquitectura Maya. It provides an excellent overview of the sites around Campeche state and the key architectural styles associated with them. Currently, four halls display stelae taken from various sites, accompanied by graphic representations of their carved inscriptions with brief commentaries in flawless English.

**Baluarte de Santiago**
**& Jardín Botánico**
**Xmuch Haltún**   GARDENS, HISTORIC BUILDING
(cnr Calles 8 & 49; M$15; ⊙8am-9pm Mon-Fri, from 9am Sat & Sun) Completed in 1704 – the last of the bulwarks to be built – the Baluarte de Santiago houses the Jardín Botánico Xmuch Haltún, a botanical garden with numerous endemic and some introduced plants. It's not a huge place, but provides a green and

peaceful respite when the sun gets particularly brutal.

**Baluarte de San Francisco**
**& Baluarte de San Juan**   HISTORIC BUILDING
(Calle 18; M$25; ⊙8am-9pm Mon-Wed, to 6pm Thu & Fri, from 9am Sat & Sun) **FREE** Once the primary defensive bastion for the adjacent Puerta de la Tierra, the Baluarte de San Francisco houses a pirate exhibition in both English and Spanish. You also enter here to walk along the Baluarte de San Juan, the smallest of the seven bulwarks. Here you can see the bell that was rung to alert the population in times of danger – different bells around the city had different sounds and meanings.

**Baluarte de Santa Rosa**   HISTORIC BUILDING
(cnr Calle 14 & Av Circuito Baluartes Sur; ⊙8am-8pm) **FREE** The Baluarte de Santa Rosa has a gallery that houses temporary exhibitions.

**Baluarte de San Pedro**   HISTORIC BUILDING
(cnr Avs Circuito Baluartes Este & Circuito Baluartes Norte; M$15; ⊙8am-3pm) **FREE** Directly behind Iglesia de San Juan de Dios, the Baluarte de San Pedro served a post-piracy defensive function when it repelled a punitive raid from Mérida in 1824. Carved in stone above the entry is the symbol of San Pedro: two keys to heaven and the papal tiara. Inside you'll find a few small rooms with exhibitions on pirate history.

## ⊙ Malecón

A popular path for joggers, cyclists, strolling friends and cooing sweethearts, the *malecón*, Campeche's 7km-long waterfront promenade, makes for a breezy sunrise ramble or sunset bike ride.

A series of monuments along a 2.5km stretch of the *malecón* allude to various personages and events in the city's history. Southwest of the Plaza Moch-Couoh (under construction at time of research) stands a statue of Campeche native Justo Sierra Méndez, a key player in the modernization of Mexico's educational system. Next to the plaza is a monument of the walled city's four gates. Three blocks up is a monumental sculpture of native son Pedro Sáinz de Baranda, who played a key role in defeating the Spanish at their last stronghold in Veracruz, thus ending the War of Independence.

Just beyond the Centro de Convenciones Campeche XXI, the girl gazing out to sea is the Novia del Mar. According to a poignant local legend, the *campechana* fell in love with a foreign pirate and awaits his return. About 1km further north, the Plaza Cuatro de Octubre (October 4 Plaza) commemorates the date of the city's 'founding,' depicting the fateful meeting of a Maya *cacique* (chief), the conquistador Francisco de Montejo and a priest.

At the *malecón*'s northern tip, 4.5km northeast from downtown, lies a cluster of seafood restaurants called Parador Gastrónomico de Cocteleros (p218). It's a good place for lunch, despite the overzealous waiters touting for customers.

---

## ◉ Outside the City Center

### ★ Museo Arqueológico de Campeche & Fuerte de San Miguel
MUSEUM, FORT

(Campeche Archaeological Museum; Av Escénica s/n; M$55; ⊘8:30am-5pm Tue-Sun; P) Campeche's largest colonial fort, facing the Gulf of Mexico some 4km southwest of the city center, is now home to the most important of Maya museums, the excellent Museo Arqueológico de Campeche, the city's one must-see museum. Here you can admire emblematic pieces from the sites of Calakmul and Edzná, and from Isla de Jaina, an island north of town once used as a burial site for Maya aristocracy. Much of the info is in English.

Stunning jade jewelry and exquisite vases, masks and plates are thematically arranged in different exhibit halls. The star attractions are the jade burial masks from Calakmul. Also displayed are stelae, seashell necklaces and clay figurines. You can even (using an interactive exhibit) view how you yourself might have looked as a Maya warrior.

Equipped with a dry moat and working drawbridge, the fort itself is a thing of beauty. The roof deck, ringed by 20 cannons, affords wonderful harbor views.

To get here take a bus or combi (minibus; marked 'Lerma') from the market. Ask the driver to let you off at the access road (just say 'Fuerte de San Miguel'), then hike 300m up the hill. Taxis cost around M$70.

### Playa Bonita
BEACH

(pedestrians free, cars M$10; ⊘8am-5pm; P) About 13km south of downtown, just past the port village of Lerma, Playa Bonita is the closest real beach to Campeche. Don't expect an isolated paradise though – this is a gated, developed resort with gritty sand and sandbagged swimming areas (to keep sand from washing away). Still, it's not unpleasant – plenty of *palapas* provide shade (M$50 to M$100) and there's a restaurant and *fútbol* pitch. Come on weekdays to avoid the crowds.

To get here, take one of the frequent *combis* from the market labeled '*Lerma Tecnológico*' (M$7, 20 minutes) and ask to be dropped at the beach entrance. Taxis cost around M$120.

## ☞ Tours

### Kankabi' Ok
TOUR

(📞 981-811-27-92; www.kankabiok.com.mx; Calle 59 No 3; ⊘9am-1pm & 5-9pm Mon-Sat) This reliable outfit offers a huge number of tours from four-hour guided walks around Campeche to day trips to archaeological sites such as Edzná, Chenes, Calakmul and the Ruta Puuc. Also rents out bikes (per hour M$30) and does ecotourism and beach trips. Prices vary depending on group size and itinerary, so it's best to ask. Minimum numbers may apply.

### Tranvía de la Ciudad
TOURS

(tours adult/child 11 yr & under M$100/40; ⊘hourly 9am-12pm & 5-8pm) Daily bilingual tours by *tranvía* (trolley) depart from the Plaza Principal (minimum six people, 45 minutes). They cover Campeche's historical center, traditional neighborhoods and part of the *malecón*. Occasionally another trolley, *El Guapismo*, goes to Fuerte de San Miguel leaving half an hour to visit the Museo Arqueológico de Campeche. Check schedules at the ticket kiosk in the Plaza Principal.

## ✦✦ Festivals & Events

### Carnaval
CULTURAL

(☺ Feb, date varies) Campeche pulls out all the stops for Carnaval, with two weeks of festivities leading up to Sábado de Bando (Carnaval Saturday), when everyone dresses up in outrageous costumes and parades down the *malecón*. The official conclusion is a week later, when a pirate effigy is torched and hurled into the sea.

### Feria de San Román
RELIGIOUS

(☺ Sep 14) This festival honors the beloved Cristo Negro (Black Christ) of the Iglesia de San Román. Fireworks and Ferris wheels take over the zone around the church, along with beauty contests, boxing matches and a music-and-dance competition that brings in traditional ensembles from around the peninsula.

### Día de Nuestra Señora de Guadalupe
RELIGIOUS

(☺ Dec 12) Pilgrims from throughout the peninsula travel to the Iglesia de Guadalupe, 1.5km east of the Plaza Principal, the second church of Guadalupe built after the Virgin of Guadalupe in Mexico City.

## 🛏 Sleeping

Campeche has some fine hotels but generally doesn't offer great-value accommodations, though a few hostels are notable exceptions. At Christmas and Easter prices can skyrocket.

### Hostal Viatger
HOSTEL $

(☑ 981-811-45-00; Calle 51 No 28, btwn Calles 12 & 14; dm/d/tr incl breakfast M$245/500/550; P ⊝ ❋ 🖥) This hostel enjoys a good location in the historic center (but away from the crowds) and has a friendly atmosphere. Dorms are nothing fancy, but women can enjoy their own space and there's the option of private doubles and triples, some with TVs and air-con. There's a kitchen and an outdoor social area out the back in the yard.

### Hotel Campeche
HOTEL $

(☑ 981-816-51-83; Calle 57, btwn Calles 8 & 10; s/d with fan M$285/345, with air-con M$380/450; ❋ 🖥) Not much in the way of frills here, but the plaza-side location and big rooms in this classically crumbling building make this about the best budget hotel in town. Of the 40 rooms, seven have little balconies looking out over the plaza, which are a steal at this price.

### H177 Hotel
HOTEL $

(☑ 981-816-44-63; www.h177hotel.com; Calle 14 No 177; s/d/ste M$695/790/948; P ❋ 🖥) With its slick and trendy lines, this hotel is different from anything else in traditional Campeche. It boasts 24 spacious and modern-styled rooms decked out in strong natural colors, most of which are set around a small courtyard. Bathrooms have glass-walled showers. The best rooms are on the top terrace. Call to check for discounts in low season.

### ★ Hotel López
HOTEL $$

(☑ 981-816-33-44; Calle 12 No 189; r/ste M$750/850; ⊝ ❋ 🖥 🖥) This business hotel is by far one of Campeche's best midrange options. Modern, comfortably appointed rooms open on to curvy art-deco-styled balconies around oval courtyards and pleasant greenery. There's also a lovely pool out back. Prices are considerably lower outside high season, though the standard rooms are on the small side and it's worth paying a little extra for more space.

### Hotel Misión Campeche
HOTEL $$

(☑ 981-816-45-88; www.hotelesmision.com.mx; Calle 10 No 252; r from M$1220; P ❋ 🖥) Part of a national chain of midrange hotels, this excellently located and atmospheric place enjoys a traditional courtyard and has 42 large, clean rooms spread along various arcade corridors. The downside is that the rooms can vary widely in size and brightness, so check some out first.

### Hotel Francis Drake
HOTEL $$

(☑ 981-811-56-26; www.hotelfrancisdrake.com; Calle 12 No 207; incl breakfast s/d M$935/1030, ste from M$1300; ⊝ ❋ 🖥) A somewhat baroque lobby leads to 25 cool, but now rather faded looking rooms with a sprinkling of tasteful decoration. Bathrooms and balconies are tiny, but the rooms are huge (other hotels would call them suites) with king-sized beds and separate sitting areas. Wi-fi is in the lobby only.

### ★ Hacienda Puerta Campeche
BOUTIQUE HOTEL $$$

(☑ 981-816-75-08; www.luxurycollection.com; Calle 59 No 71; r from US$240; ❋ 🖥 🖥) This beautiful Marriott-run hotel has 15 suites with high ceilings and separate lounges. Perfectly manicured gardens and grassy lawns offer peace, while the creatively designed pool cuts through the property and has nearby hammocks fit for a Maya king. There's an on-site spa, restaurant and bar in case you really don't want to leave the premises, and service is charming.

It also runs a luxury hacienda 26km outside the city, on the way to the Edzná ruins.

## Hotel Socaire

BOUTIQUE HOTEL $$$

(☑ 981-811-21-30; www.hotelsocaire.com; Calle 57 No 19, btwn Calles 12a & 14a; r/ste from M$1550/1990; ☎ 🖥) A charmingly converted colonial building leads through to a variety of spacious rooms in the rear. The walls have curios and antiques in the nooks and crannies, and the lovely pool is a perfect way to cool down in the heat of the day. It's in a great central location and is excellent value.

## Hotel Boutique
## Casa Don Gustavo

BOUTIQUE HOTEL $$$

(☑ 981-816-80-90; www.casadongustavo.com; Calle 59 No 4; r/ste from M$3300/4000; P ❄ ☎ 🖥) The 10 rooms here are decorated with antique furniture and have huge modern bathrooms, while the public areas look more like a museum than anything else. There's a small pool with hammocks and colorful tiled hallways line an outdoor courtyard. Its location on the main pedestrian street can make some rooms a little noisy, however.

## ✖ Eating

You can try some good local dishes in Campeche, especially seafood and the likes of *cochinita pibil* (roasted suckling pig). Overall the city doesn't have a particularly interesting foodie scene, but a few places offer an escape from the bland offerings of many restaurants in the historic center.

## Sotavento Café

CAFE $

(☑ 981-811-38-92; www.facebook.com/Cafeteria Sotavento; Calle 55 No 20, btwn Calles 14 & 16; coffee M$26-55, lunch mains M$69-169; ⊙ 7am-11pm; ☎) Nice, clean and quirky, with interesting art and curios around the multicolored walls, this cafe-gallery has tasty espresso drinks, plus a variety of sandwiches, burgers, pastas and veggie options. Those staying within the old city walls will find it's in a convenient central location too.

## Marganzo

MEXICAN $$$

(☑ 981-811-38-98; Calle 8 No 267; mains M$180-350; ⊙ 7am-10:45pm; ☎) Marganzo is a popular with tourists and locals alike for good reason – the food is great, the portions large and the complimentary appetizers numerous. An extensive menu offers everything from international fare to regional treats such as *cochinita pibil* and a famous seafood platter. Wandering musicians provide entertainment.

## El Bastión de Campeche

MEXICAN $$

(☑ 981-816-21-28; Calle 57 No 2; mains M$115-215; ⊙ 6:30am-11:30pm) Don't let the drab exterior fool you – this plaza-side stalwart serves up some good *campechano* dishes. Cool off with a chaya juice (M$29) before tucking in to a chicken breast stuffed with *chile xcatic* (a hot, yellow chili; M$139).

---

## THE MENNONITES OF CAMPECHE

Campeche is in the midst of a quiet arrival by an unlikely community – the Mennonites. Seeing them waiting in bus stations, hanging about the main plazas of villages or crowding a pickup, you may wonder if you've somehow stumbled on to the set of *Little House on the Prairie*. Clad in black coveralls and long-sleeved flannel shirts in the midday heat, the men tower over their Maya neighbors. The women wear dark floral-print dresses and straw hats with broad ribbons.

Tracing their origins to 16th-century Reformist Germany, the Mennonites have inhabited some northern Mexican states since the 1920s. Drawn by cheap land, they first migrated down to Hopelchén, Campeche, in 1983 and since then have established agricultural communities around Dzibalchén, Hecelchakán and Edzná. Once they've settled in, the Mennonites work relentlessly, growing corn, melons and other crops, raising cattle and producing cheese for the domestic market. They live in *campos* (self-contained communities with their own schools and churches), and speak among themselves in a form of Low German.

Mennonite men customarily fraternize and conduct business with the Mexicans and many converse fluently in colloquial Spanish (the women only speak with their own). These days, they are generally accepted by the local community and local shop owners, and businesses welcome their patronage. Locals, too, comment on the fact that they work extremely hard.

The film *Luz silenciosa (Silent Light)* by Mexican director Carlos Reygadas looks at life in Mexico's Mennonite communities. It won the coveted Jury Prize at Cannes in 2007.

### Luz de Luna
INTERNATIONAL **$$**

(☑ 981-811-06-24; Calle 59 No 6; mains M$110-190; ☺ 8am-11pm Mon-Sat) Carved, painted tables and folksy decor lend a creative atmosphere to this popular restaurant. The menu choices are reasonable – try the shrimp salad, chicken fajitas, flank steak or vegetarian burritos. There are plenty of breakfast options as well, especially omelettes. They also have a gallery next door.

### Parador Gastrónomico de Cocteleros
SEAFOOD **$$**

(Av Costera; mains M$150-400; ☺ 9am-6:30pm) This is a great place to sample the area's bountiful seafood. Over a dozen thatched-roof restaurants all serve pretty much the same thing: shrimp cocktails, fried fish and other seafood dishes. It's 4.5km from Plaza Principal at the north end of the *malecón* (taxis from center around M$40).

### La Pigua
SEAFOOD **$$$**

(☑ 981-811-33-65; www.lapigua.com.mx; Miguel Alemán 179A; mains M$200-380; ☺ 1-6pm) Campeche's most upscale restaurant can be found just outside the old city walls and is an elegant space with white linen tablecloths. Service is attentive and the specialties include *camarones al coco* (coconut shrimp), fish fillet in cilantro sauce and grilled squid with ground almonds and paprika. Reservations advised.

## 🍷 Drinking & Entertainment

Besides a few bar-restaurants along Calle 59 (often turned pedestrian-only and a fun spot to dine or bar-hop), the center sees relatively little nightlife. For a more lively experience, head 1km south of the center along the *malecón* past the Torres de Cristal, where you'll find a cluster of bars, cafes and discos.

### Chocol-Ha
CAFE

(☑ 981-811-78-93; Calle 59 No 30; drinks M$25-55, snacks M$35-80; ☺ 8am-10:30pm Mon-Sat; 🛜) For chocolate cravings, head to this cute little cafe with a patio in front and grassy yard in back. Try bittersweet hot chocolate with green tea or chili, and a chocolate frappé. Sweet treats such as cake, crepes and even tamales (yep, all chocolate!) will give you a sugary high, while nonchocolate dishes are also available.

### Salón Rincón Colonial
BAR

(☑ 981-816-83-76; Calle 59 No 60; ☺ 10am-9pm) With ceiling fans high over an airy hall and a solid wood bar amply stocked with rum, this Cuban-style drinking establishment appropriately served as a location for *Original Sin*, a 2001 movie with Antonio Banderas and Angelina Jolie that was set in Havana. The *botanas* (appetizers) are exceptionally fine and go down well with a local beer.

### La Casa Vieja de Río
BAR

(☑ 981-811-80-16; Calle 10 No 319A; cocktails M$140-260; ☺ 3:30-11:30pm) There's no better setting for an evening cocktail than La Casa Vieja's colonnaded balcony overlooking the Plaza Principal. Look for the stairs next to the McDonald's ice-cream counter.

You can eat here, too, if you are enjoying the view that much.

## 🛍 Shopping

### Casa de Artesanías Tukulná
ARTS & CRAFTS

(☑ 981-127-17-68; Calle 10 No 333; ☺ 9am-9pm) A central collection of shops selling a lovely, high-quality range of textiles, clothing, hats, hammocks, wood chairs, sweets and so on – all made in Campeche state.

### Ora et Labora
ARTS & CRAFTS

(☑ 981-127-14-10; Calle 10 No 260, btwn 59 & 61; ☺ 9am-9pm Mon-Sat, from 10am Sun) Quirky curios and nature-inspired art, crafts, minerals, gems, incense, fridge magnets, jewelry and a few dogs (the latter not for sale).

### Bazar Artesanal
ARTS & CRAFTS

(Plaza Ah Kim Pech; ☺ 10am-8pm) The state-run Folk Art Bazaar, down by the *malecón* near the Centro de Convenciones Campeche XXI, offers one-stop shopping for regional crafts. One section of the market is reserved for demonstrations of traditional craft techniques. At the time of research, it was being remodeled as a government initiative.

The artisans, however, have a new temporary location in the center's Ex-Templo de San José, so we're not sure what might happen on completion.

## ℹ️ Information

Campeche has numerous banks with ATMs.

**Central Post Office** (cnr Av 16 de Septiembre & Calle 53; ☺ 8:30am-4pm Mon-Fri, 8-11:30am Sat)

**Hospital Dr Manuel Campos** (☑ 981-811-17-09; Av Circuito Baluartes Norte, btwn Calles 14 & 16)

**Hospital General De Especialidades** (☑ 981-127-39-80; Las Flores)

**HSBC Bank** (Calle 10, btwn Calles 53 & 55; ☺ 9am-5pm Mon-Fri, to 3pm Sat) Open Saturday.

**Módulo de Información Turística del Município de Campeche** (☎ 981-811-39-89; www.campeche.travel; Puerta del Mar, Calle 8; ⊗8am-9pm Mon-Fri, from 9am Sat & Sun) Basic information on Campeche city.

**Secretaría de Turismo** (☎ 981-127-33-00; www.campeche.travel) About the only thing this place has going for it is its website with information on the state, though the site is now riddled with pop-up ads and dead links.

## ⓘ Getting There & Away

### AIR

Campeche's small-but-modern airport is 6km southeast of the center; it has car-rental offices and a tiny snack bar. Aeroméxico and Interjet provides services to Mexico City.

### BUS

Campeche's **main bus terminal** (☎ 981-811-99-10; Av Patricio Trueba 237), usually called the ADO or 1st-class terminal, is about 2.5km south of Plaza Principal via Av Central. Buses provide 1st-class and deluxe service to Mérida, Cancún, Chetumal (via Xpujil), Palenque, Veracruz and Mexico City, along with 2nd-class services to Sabancuy (M$142, two hours), Hecelchakán (M$48, one hour) and Candelaria (M$215, four hours).

The **2nd-class terminal** (Terminal Sur; ☎ 981-816-34-45; Av Gobernadores 479), often referred to as the 'old ADO' station' or 'Autobuses del Sur', is 700m east of the Mercado Principal. Second-class destinations include Hopelchén (M$71, 1½ hours), Xpujil (M$232, four hours) Uxmal (M$137, one hour) and Bécal (M$60, 1¾ hours).

**Transportes Crígar** (☎ 981-145-61-62; Calle 10 No 329; ⊗8am-10pm) is a handy spot to buy ADO (1st-class) bus tickets. Or try other travel agencies around town.

To get to the main bus terminal, catch any 'Las Flores,' 'Solidaridad' or 'Casa de Justicia' microbus by the post office. To the 2nd-class terminal, catch a 'Terminal Sur' bus from the same point.

### CAR

If you're arriving in Campeche from the south, via the *cuota* (toll road), turn left at the roundabout signed for the *universidad* and follow that road straight to the coast, then go north.

If you're heading to either Edzná, the long route to Mérida or the fast toll road going south, take Calle 61 to Av Central and follow signs for the airport and either Edzná or the *cuota*. For the non-toll route south, just head down the *malecón*. For the short route to Mérida go north on the *malecón*.

In addition to some outlets at the airport, several car-rental agencies can be found downtown, including **Avis** (☎ 981-811-07-85; www.avis.mx; Calle 10, btwn 57 & 59; per day from M$400; ⊗8am-2pm & 4-6pm). Rates start from M$400 per day depending on the season.

## ⓘ Getting Around

Taxis from the airport to the center cost M$160 (shared taxis M$70 per person); buy tickets at the taxi booth inside the terminal. Going to the airport, some street taxis (ie those not called from your hotel, which are more expensive) charge M$150; penny-pinchers can try taking the hourly bus to Chiná (a village outside Campeche; around M$15) from the market, and getting off at the airport entrance, then walking 500m to the airport doors.

Within Campeche city, taxis charge M$30 to M$60; prices are 10% more after 10pm, and 20% more from midnight to 5am.

Most local buses (around M$7) have a stop at or near the Mercado Principal.

## BUSES FROM CAMPECHE

| DESTINATION | FARE (M$) | TIME (HR) | FREQUENCY (PER DAY) |
| --- | --- | --- | --- |
| Cancún | 755 | 7 | 2 |
| Chetumal | 570 | 6½ | 1 |
| Ciudad del Carmen | 240-270 | 3 | hourly |
| Mérida | 264 | 2½ | hourly |
| Mérida (via Uxmal) | 120-180 | 4½ | 5 from 2nd-class terminal |
| Mexico City | 1200-2100 | 18 | 3 |
| Palenque | 497 | 5 | 4 |
| San Cristóbal de las Casas | 709 | 15 | 2 |
| Villahermosa | 380-609 | 6 | frequent |
| Xpujil | 240-414 | 4½ | 1 (2pm) |

Consider pedaling along the *malecón;* get bike rentals at Kankabi' Ok (p215).

Drivers should note that even-numbered streets in the *centro histórico* take priority, but go slowly until you get the hang of the cross streets.

# NORTHERN CAMPECHE

Northern Campeche offers a fascinating blend of experiences. An enticing mix of colonial and Maya elements, blended with centuries-old tradition and lush nature, it's worth spending time here. Wander through the alluring complex of Edzná (one of the region's finest sets of ruins) or marvel over the unique features of architecture at the Chenes sites. Most of these places are doable as separate day trips from Campeche.

## Pomuch

🖉 996 / POP 9000

Quiet and dusty, Pomuch may not even warrant a stop unless one of two things is true: if you're hungry, the bread shops here are so famous that people detour up to an hour to snack on the rolls, sweets and loaves. Denser, chewier and (sorry to be harsh, Mexico) fresher than the Mexican norm, the breads here hit the spot, and they travel well – grab one or two for the road.

The other reason to stop by is for its unique, somewhat macabre *Dia de los Muertos* (Day of the Dead) display. Unlike the typical Mexican *ofrendas* (altars), residents here actually disinter and clean the real bones of their ancestors and display them in special boxes. While it may seem gruesome, it's perhaps one tradition that has its origins in the ancient Maya, a culture where death, life and sacrifice were interlinked.

### ✕ Eating

**Panadería La Huachita**                BAKERY $
(☑996-432-00-14; Calle 12 No 61; snacks M$7, loaves M$70; ☺8am-9pm) One of the famous bread shops here, La Huachita has been around more than a century. Flags fly and the shelves are filled with a variety of comestibles and kitch, but the *pan* (bread) remains so popular it flies off the shelf every morning. Get it while you can.

**Panadería El Pan de Pomuch**          BAKERY $
(☑996-432-00-01; Calle 15; snacks M$7, loaves M$50; ☺8am-10pm) Tasty bite-sized morsels

in apple or cheese, loaves with a variety of fillings, and cheerful (if busy) staff.

### ❶ Getting There & Away

Pomuch is served by ATS as a stop between Mérida and Campeche. You can also get here from Hecelchakán in a quick M$8 *combi* ride.

## Hecelchakán

🖉 996 / POP 11,000

Bicycle taxis (M$7 per ride) with canvas canopies navigate the tranquil central plazas of Hecelchakán, a pleasant town 60km northeast of Campeche known for its culinary treats and a decent small museum. Hecelchakán's inhabitants, who include a Mennonite community, are primarily devoted to agriculture.

### ◉ Sights

**Iglesia de San Francisco
de Asis**                                CHURCH
Dating from the 16th century, the Iglesia de San Francisco de Asis (on the main plaza) is a former Franciscan monastery with woodbeam ceiling and striking altar; note the flaming hearts flanking a crucifix. It's often only open in the late afternoon.

**Museo Arqueológico del
Camino Real**                            MUSEUM
(Calle 18 s/n; M$40; ☺8am-5pm Tue-Sun) This tiny museum, on the north corner of the plaza, doesn't get much traffic. But it should. It contains a small but compelling collection of ceramic art excavated from Isla de Jaina, a tiny island due west of Hecelchakán that flourished as a commercial center during the 7th century. Portraying ballplayers, weavers, warriors and priests, the extraordinary figurines on display here paint a vivid portrait of ancient Maya life. There's also a collection of stelae in the courtyard.

Look for the entrance to the left of the church and at the end of the yellow building.

### 🛏 Sleeping & Eating

*Campechanos* sometimes visit Hecelchakán for its famous snacks. From 6am to 10am, outside the church, locals serve up *cochinita pibil* and *relleno negro* (turkey stuffed with pork and a chili sauce) in tacos or baguettes, plus *horchata* (a rice-based drink) and *agua de cebada* (a barley beverage).

## Hotel Margarita
HOTEL $

([telephone] 996-827-04-72; Calle 20 No 80; s/d/tr with fan M$250/300/350, with air-con M$350/400/450; [icons]) On the main drag about 200m from the plaza (look for the bright green building) is Hotel Margarita, a very basic, but clean, place with budget rooms around a patio that are good enough for a night.

## Chujuc Haa
MEXICAN $

([telephone] 996-827-07-07; Calle 20 s/n; mains M$52-93; [clock] 7am-10pm Mon-Fri, 8am-11pm Sat & Sun) It's nothing special to look at, but this popular restaurant serves regional cuisine such as *poc-chuc,* the local pork steak (M$52) that comes with rice, beans and salad. A half order is plenty. Located four doors left of the ADO/ATS bus office.

## ℹ Information

For tourist information there's the **Dirección de Turismo** (Edifício Jaina; [clock] 8am-3pm Mon-Fri), in a building across from the ADO/ATS bus office and near the plaza. Head up the stairs just left of the Telecomm office and it's the first door on your left (unmarked).

## ℹ Getting There & Away

The ADO/ATS **bus office** ([telephone] 996-827-06-32; [clock] 7:30am-10pm) is across from the post office and just south of the plaza on Calle Principal. ATS buses from Campeche's 2nd-class terminal stop here en route to Mérida every half-hour till around 10:30pm (M$41 to M$95, 1¾ to three hours). In addition, frequent **combis** (M$30, one hour) shuttle passengers between Campeche's Mercado Principal and Hecelchakán's plaza.

Bicycle taxis around town cost M$7. To Pomuch in a *combi* costs M$8.

# Bécal

[telephone] 996 / POP 6500

Bécal, about 90km north of Campeche just before you enter the state of Yucatán, is a center of the Yucatán panama-hat trade. Some inhabitants here make their living weaving *jipijapas,* as the soft, pliable hats are known locally. The finest hats are destined for export to connoisseurs in foreign cities. The tranquil town clearly identifies with its stock-in-trade, as is made obvious by the centerpiece of its plaza.

In April the Fiesta de Flor del Jipi is celebrated with dancing and bullfights.

To find out where *jipijapas* are crafted and sold in town, hail a bicycle taxi on Bécal's plaza and ask the rider for his recommendation. You'll likely be approached by a young guide (perhaps on a bicycle) – some work on donation. A half-block from the plaza, on the road into town, is Artesania Becaleña, one of several shops where you can check out some hats.

## 🛍 Shopping

### Looljipi Alfredo
FASHION & ACCESSORIES

([telephone] 996-431-43-26; Calle 30 No 231; [clock] 9am-7pm) An option for *jipi*-made crafts, including unique earrings and other non-hat fashionwear.

### Artesania Antonio Acosta
FASHION & ACCESSORIES

([telephone] 996-431-42-82; Calle 29 No 230A; hats from M$400; [clock] 9am-9pm) More than 40 years ago the Acosta family dug a *jipi* cave in their backyard and they're still making hats like their grandparents did. In 10 minutes they'll give you a fascinating tour, showing the plant

---

### DISCOVER THE ROOTS OF THE JIPIJAPA HAT

While on the surface Bécal may look like a somnolent *campechano* town, underground (literally!) people are laboring away at the traditional craft of hat making. Called *jipijapas* (or *jipis* for short), these soft, pliable hats have been woven by townsfolk from the fibers of the *huano* palm tree since the mid-19th century, when the plants were imported from Guatemala by a Catholic priest.

The stalk of the plant is cut into strands to make the fibers; the quality of the hat depends on the fineness of the cut. The work is done in humid limestone caves that provide just the right atmosphere for shaping the fibers, keeping them moist and pliable. These caves – often no bigger than a bedroom – are reached by a hole in the ground in someone's backyard. Once exposed to the relatively dry air outside, the panama hat is surprisingly resilient and resistant to crushing.

Today, Bécal's hat-making art is a dying industry due to cheap global competition. So if you want to shade your head in style while supporting a worthy cause, buy a hand-made *jipi*. Prices range from around M$350 for coarsely woven hats made in a couple of days, to nearly M$3000 for the finest hats that can take months to complete.

fibers and the cave, and ending with the variety of hats and souvenirs they have on sale. It's impressive, and the family is sweet.

# Hopelchén

📞 996 / POP 10,000

The municipal center for the Chenes region, Hopelchén (Maya for 'Place of the Five Wells') makes a pleasant base for visiting the various archaeological sites in the vicinity while also providing a glimpse of everyday life in a small Campeche town.

On a typical morning here, Maya *campesinos* (agricultural workers) and Mennonites congregate under box-shaped laurels as bicycle taxis glide past.

On the central plaza, the 16th-century Parroquia de San Antonio de Padua church features an intricate *retablo* (altarpiece), with a gallery of saints and angels amid lavishly carved pillars.

Herbalists, midwives and shamans practice traditional Maya medicine at the Consejo Local de Médicos Indígenas, five blocks east of the plaza.

Sleeping options are limited in Hopelchén; you are better off staying in Campeche and heading here for the day. Few restaurants offer anything for tourists, but for a good *caldo de pollo* (chicken soup), try the stalls beside the church, which are open from 7am to 3pm and 5pm to midnight.

## ℹ️ Getting There & Away

Hopelchén's bus terminal is at the market northeast of the church. Get tickets at the 'Sur' office in the market (4:30am to 9pm). There are buses to Campeche (M$68, 1½ hours, hourly) and Mérida (M$119, three hours, six services).

Penny-pinchers may get a good deal on the buses, as the *combis* (located on the main road a half-block toward the center from Campeche's 2nd-class bus terminal) cost more and may even take longer. They run every half-hour from Campeche (M$80, 1½ hours) to Hopelchén's plaza, stopping at villages along the way.

## Chenes Sites

Northeastern Campeche state is dotted with more than 30 sites in the distinct Chenes style, recognizable by the monster motifs around doorways in the center of long, low buildings of three sections, and temples atop pyramidal bases. Most of the year you'll have these sites to yourself. The three small sites of El Tabasqueño, Hochob and Dzibilnocac make for an interesting day trip from Campeche if you have your own vehicle, though even if you don't, you can take a tour from Campeche with Kankabi' Ok Tours (p215).

### ☉ Sights

Santa Rosa Xtampak                                    RUINS
(www.inah.gob.mx; adult/child under 13yr M$45/free; ☉ 8am-5pm) Though less excavated than Edzná, Uxmal or Calakmul, Santa Rosa Xtam-

---

### AROUND HOPELCHÉN

There are a couple of worthwhile points of interest within striking distance of Hopelchén.

Spelled Tacob on signs, Tohcok (☉ 8am-5pm) is 3.5km northwest of Hopelchén. Of the 40-odd structures found at this Maya site, the only one that has been significantly excavated displays features of the Puuc and Chenes styles. The talkative custodian, Pepe, can point out a *chultún* (Maya underground cistern), one of around 45 in the zone.

Some of the most significant caves in the peninsula, the Grutas de X'tacumbilxuna'an (M$100; ☉ 9am-5pm; 🅿️) are found 31km north of Hopelchén, shortly before you reach the town of Bolonchén de Rejón. The local Maya have long known of the existence of the Grutas de X'tacumbilxuna'an, a series of underground cenotes in this water-scarce region. In 1844 the caves were 'discovered' by the intrepid John L Stephens and Frederick Catherwood, who depicted the Maya descending an incredibly high rope-and-log staircase to replenish their water supply.

Today the cenote is dry but X'tacumbilxuna'an (*shtaa-koom-beel-shoo-nahn*) is open for exploration and admiration of the vast caverns and incredible limestone formations within. A light-and-sound extravaganza accompanies the tour, and you can hear the sounds of motmots echoing off the walls as you descend.

Buses traveling between Hopelchén and Mérida can drop you at the cave entrance before Bolonchén (around M$40, 25 minutes). In addition, *combis* depart for Bolonchén from Hopelchén's plaza, passing near the caves. Check with the driver for return times.

## TRADITIONAL HARVEST: THE SWEET HISTORY OF MAYA HONEY

The Yucatán's flowers yield a sweet, mellifluous harvest, and bees have held an exalted place throughout its honeyed history. Records show that at the time of the conquest, the Maya produced vast amounts of honey and Yucatecan villages paid tribute to the Spanish in honey, which was valued more for its curative properties than as a sweetener. Bees were important in the Maya pantheon: bee motifs appear in the surviving Maya codices, and the image of Ah Mucenkab, god of bees, is carved into the friezes of Chichén Itzá, Tulum and Sayil.

Mexico remains the world's number-four producer of honey, and the nectar of the Yucatán is especially coveted for its blend of flavors and aromas, a result of the diversity of the region's flowers. Many *campesinos* (agricultural workers) keep bees to supplement their agricultural output. However, the stingless variety known to the ancient Maya has long since been supplanted by European bees, which in turn are being pushed aside by the more aggressive African bees, notorious among handlers for their nasty sting.

**Koolel Kab** (Women Who Work With Bees; ☑ 996-102-39-27, 996-105-30-05; www.facebook.com/koolelkab.campeche; Domicilio Conocido s/n, Ich-Ek) is a Maya women's cooperative in the village of Ich-Ek, near Hopelchén, that wants to preserve the ancient heritage. The women produce honey with indigenous *melipona* bees, which take up residence in hollow trees. Using techniques much like those of their ancestors, the women place sections of tree trunk under a shelter, capping each end of the trunk with mud. An average trunk yields 12L of honey, which is marketed chiefly for its medicinal properties as throat lozenges, eye drops, soaps and skin creams. If you're in the area you can pay Koolel Kab a visit, and buy honey, soaps and farm produce from their small store.

pak is considered to be the largest and most important site in the Chenes region, and was perhaps the area's one-time capital. The long drive in means you're likely to have the ruin entirely to yourself, and (for now anyway) it's off the bus-tour circuit. The excavated area is compact and impressive, with ornate Chenes-style decorations surrounding temple doors, and around 50 *chaltuns* (wells).

**Dzibilnocac** ARCHAEOLOGICAL SITE
(⊙8am-5pm) FREE Though it only has one significant structure, Dzibilnocac possesses an eerie grandeur that merits a visit. Unlike the many hilltop sites chosen for Chenes structures, Dzibilnocac ('big painted turtle' is one translation) is on a flat plain, like a large open park. As Stephens and Catherwood observed in 1842, the many scattered hillocks in the zone, still unexcavated today, attest to the presence of a large city.

**Hochob** ARCHAEOLOGICAL SITE
(M$45; ⊙8am-5pm) About 60km south of Hopelchén, Hochob, 'the place where corn is harvested,' is among the most beautiful and terrifying of the Chenes-style sites. The **Palacio Principal** (Estructura 2, though signposted as 'Estructura 1') is on the north side of the main plaza, faced with an elaborate doorway representing Itzamná, creator of the ancient Maya, as a rattlesnake with open jaws.

**El Tabasqueño** ARCHAEOLOGICAL SITE
(⊙8am-5pm) FREE Supposedly named after a local landowner from Tabasco, El Tabasqueño boasts a **temple-palace** (Estructura 1) with a striking monster-mouth doorway, flanked by stacks of eight Chaac masks with hooked snouts. Estructura 2 is a solid **free-standing tower**, an oddity in Maya architecture.

To reach El Tabasqueño, go 30km south from Hopelchén. Just beyond the village of Pakchén, there's an easy-to-miss sign at a turnoff on the right; follow this rock-and-gravel road 2km to the site. You must walk another 500m or so to the site itself.

### ❶ Getting There & Away

If you don't have your own wheels, head off on a day trip from Campeche with Kankabi' Ok Tours (p215). There is no easy public transportation to these or other Chenes sites.

## Edzná

If you only have the time or inclination to visit one archaeological site in northern Campeche, **Edzná** (M$60, guide M$500; ⊙8am-5pm) should be your top pick. It's located about 60km southeast of Campeche.

Edzná's massive complexes, which once covered more than 17 sq km, were built by a highly stratified society that flourished from about 600 BCE to the 15th century. During that period the people of Edzná built more than 20 complexes in a melange of architectural styles, installing an ingenious network of water-collection and irrigation systems. (Though it's a long way from such Puuc Hills sites as Uxmal and Kabah, some of the architecture here has elements of the Puuc style.) Most of the visible carvings date from 550 CE to 810.

The causes leading to Edzná's decline and gradual abandonment remain a mystery; the site remained unknown until its rediscovery by *campesinos* in 1906.

Edzná means 'House of the Itzáes,' a reference to a predominant governing clan of Chontal Maya origin. Edzná's rulers recorded significant events on stone stelae. Around 30 stelae have been discovered adorning the site's principal temples; a handful are on display underneath a *palapa* just beyond the ticket office.

A path from the palapa leads about 400m through vegetation; follow the 'Gran Acropolis' sign. Soon, to your left, you'll come upon the **Plataforma de los Cuchillos** (Platform of the Knives), a residential complex highlighted by Puuc architectural features. The name is derived from an offering of silica knives that was found within.

Crossing a *sacbé* (stone-lined, grass walkway), you arrive at the main attraction, the **Plaza Principal**. Measuring 160m long and 100m wide, the Plaza Principal is surrounded by temples. On your right is the Nohochná (Big House), a massive, elongated structure topped by four long halls likely used for administrative tasks.

Across the plaza is the **Gran Acrópolis**, a raised platform holding several structures, including Edzná's major temple, the 31m-high Edificio de los Cinco Pisos (Five-Story Building). The current structure is the last of four remodels and was done primarily in the Puuc style. It rises five levels from its base

# Edzná

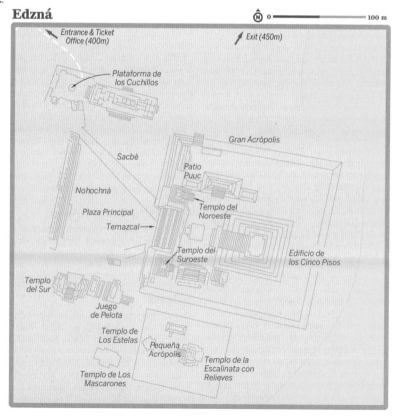

to the roofcomb and contains many vaulted rooms. Note the well-preserved glyphs along the base of the central staircase.

South of Plaza Principal is the **Templo de los Mascarones** (Temple of the Masks), with a pair of reddish stucco masks underneath a protective *palapa*. Personifying the gods of the rising and setting sun, these extraordinarily well-preserved faces display dental mutilation, crossed eyes and huge earrings, features associated with the Maya aristocracy.

The nearest place to Edzná to sleep is the luxurious **Hacienda Uayamon** (☑ 981-813-05-30; www.haciendauayamon.com; Carr Uayamon-China-Edzna Km 20; r from US$345; ⊞ ❋ ☲ ). But you can do the trip in a day from Campeche.

### ❶ Getting There & Away

**Combis** (around M$40; ⏱ 1hr) leave when full from Calle Chihuahua near Campeche's Mercado Principal. Most drop you 200m from the site entrance unless the driver is feeling generous. The last *combi* back is midafternoon (some say 2pm, others 3pm, others 5pm...you get the idea), so ask the driver to make sure. Weekdays you'll likely find a last return as late as 6pm; weekends it may be 3pm.

A taxi from Campeche with a one-hour wait at the ruins costs M$500. Kankabi' Ok (p215) in Campeche provides guided tours of Edzná (including transportation) for around M$900 per person.

## SOUTHWESTERN COAST

This sparsely developed stretch of seafront is fringed with usually deserted beaches that are ideal for watching pelicans, going on shell-searching expeditions and taking an occasional dip in the shallow aquamarine waters. Unfortunately, heading south from Campeche, the coastal highway passes behind it the entire way. It also passes through the city of Champotón, along with small fishing towns and small beaches, where you can stop for a cold beer and hang your hammock in a thatched shelter. Then you'll hit Laguna de Términos, a vast mangrove-fringed lagoon home to riots of migratory birds and a prime sea-turtle nesting spot. After all this, the shabbiness and noise and bustle of Ciudad del Carmen will seem like a culture shock.

## Champotón

☑ 982 / POP 34,000

Champotón, at the mouth of the river of the same name, has great historical significance

as the landing place of the first Spanish exploratory expedition from Cuba, led by Francisco Hernández de Córdoba, in 1517. Probably seeking a source of water along the river, the Spaniards were assailed by warriors under the command of the *cacique* Moch Couoh, forcing them to retreat. Hernández de Córdoba died shortly after his return to Cuba from wounds he received at Champotón, which from then on was known as the 'Bahía de la Mala Pelea' (Bay of the Bad Fight).

Now a pleasant enough city between Ciudad del Carmen and Campeche, Champotón sustains itself mainly on fishing, and perhaps the best reason to stop is to sample its seafood.

### ⊨ Sleeping & Eating

Several thatched-roofed *coctelerías* (seafood shacks, specializing in shellfish cocktails) are about 4.5km north of town, along the beach.

**Hotel Aaktun Kay** HOTEL **$**
(☑ 982-828-18-00; Calle 28 A No 1; s/d M$500/650; �ⓟ ❄ ❋ ☲ ) Like many places in this humid climate, this place could do with a paint touch-up on the outside, but inside the rooms are clean and modern with tan and orange decor. All have external-facing windows. Outside, the small pool has a '70s-style waterslide that will keep the kids happy.

**Posada La Regia** HOTEL **$**
(☑ 982-828-15-52; Carretera Champoton-Isla Aguada 443; s/d M$400/450; ⓟ ❄ ❋ ☲ ) Seriously underwhelming from the outside and on the main road, this humble little spot is nevertheless a very good deal. Simple, comfortable rooms with TV and air-con, and a pool area are among its charms. There's even free tea and coffee. It can help organize boat trips to a nearby mangrove.

**El Timón Restaurant & Bar** SEAFOOD **$$**
(☑ 982-828-18-63; Av Carlos Sansores Pérez 34; mains M$100-280) One of the town's smarter bar-restaurants, this large, modern spot is the place to munch on *camarones* (shrimp) on a deck jutting over the water. It also has a huge range of salads and meat dishes. Or just settle for the house specialty: *camarones al Timón* (M$220), a plateful of shrimps with bacon and Manchego cheese. It's as rich as it sounds.

### ❶ Getting There & Away

The bus terminal is on the coastal road into town, next to the market at the mouth of the river. Destinations include Campeche (M$39 to

M$110, one hour), Sabancuy (M$59 to M$110, one hour, two daily), Ciudad del Carmen (M$119 to M$222, two hours) and Xpujil (M$184 to M$308, four hours).

Combis cost M$35 to either Campeche or Ciudad del Carmen. From Campeche, frequent **combis** (M$35, 45 minutes) leave for Champotón from Av República near the Mercado Principal. If you're driving, note that two roads head south from Campeche to Champotón: a meandering coastal route (free) and a direct toll road (M$73).

## Sabancuy

**🖉 982 / POP 7500**

Sabancuy is a picturesque fishing town on the lower side of an estuary that branches off the northeastern end of Laguna de Términos. It's 2km inland, connected via land bridge to the coast highway. It's rustic, partly because nobody's yet cashed in (no mega-resorts here!) on the beauty.

It has a cute waterfront plaza, but beyond that there's not much to do; the most interesting things here are the beaches around Sabancuy that are major nesting grounds for hawksbill and green sea turtles.

An ATM is behind the church near Willy's.

### 🛏 Sleeping

For seafood with a seaside setting, small *palapas* are dotted here and there along the beach, about 500m south of the land bridge (*mototaxi* M$40).

**Hotel Aguilar**                          HOTEL **$**
(🖉 982-119-32-09; Aldama 21; r M$450; P ✳ 🗷 ) Rooms resemble monastic cells and downstairs ones are airless (if you want external facing windows, ask for upstairs rooms). It passes the test if you decide you really want to stay in a small town. There's a surprisingly nice garden and pool out the back.

**Hotel Sabancuy Plaza**              HOTEL **$**
(🖉 982-825-00-81; Calle Hidalgo s/n; r with fan/aircon M$250/400, ste M$700; P ✳ 🗢 ) A pretty basic spot that's convenient to the church. Tile-floor rooms have sheets, but no blankets (rarely needed in this climate). TVs are an extra M$50; suites are larger. The on-site restaurant is (currently) for looks only.

### ⓘ Getting There & Away

The bus terminal is right on the plaza. Bus destinations include Campeche (M$142 to M$182, two hours, 10 daily), Champotón (M$59 to M$110, one hour, 10 daily), Isla Aguada (M$32,

30 minutes, frequent departures) and Ciudad del Carmen (M$76 to M$122, 1¼ hours, hourly). Folks get around via *mototaxis* (in town M$10, to the beach M$20).

## Isla Aguada

**🖉 938 / POP 7000**

Isla Aguada is a large fishing town, although not quite an island as its name implies. It's known for its pretty, red-and-white striped lighthouse. Boat tours on the estuary are the thing to do here. The standard excursion stops at three islands, including Isla de Pájaros, where thousands of herons, gulls and magnificent frigate birds converge at sunset. You're almost guaranteed to see dolphins along the way, and most trips end with a cruise through the mangroves for more wildlife-spotting. Morning and dusk are the best times to take these trips, which last around two hours and cost M$1000 for up to five people.

The best place to stay is Freedom Shores (🖉 938-150-66-82; www.isla-aguada.com; s/d M$750/1168; P 🗢 🗷 🗢 ), a hotel set in a beautiful, palm-fringed garden. Rooms are as minimalist and unfussy as they are spacious and airy. Some face the sea, others the garden. RVs are permitted to camp (M$400), and there's an excellent restaurant with a beach-side palapa. A lovely owner can help organize tours.

### ⓘ Getting There & Away

Relatively frequent *combis* and buses connect Isla Aguada with nearby Sabancuy (M$30, 30 minutes) and Ciudad del Carmen (M$30, 40 minutes). If you're driving, the 3.2km Puente La Unidad (M$73 toll) spans the strait toward Ciudad del Carmen, 46km further west.

## Ciudad del Carmen

**🖉 938 / POP 180,000**

Campeche state's second-biggest city occupies the western end of a 40km-long, narrow island between the Gulf of Mexico and the Laguna de Términos. Ciudad del Carmen was once dependent on jumbo shrimp, dyewood and chicle (gum) for its livelihood, but in the late 1970s oil was discovered. Investment poured in and the population swelled. The 3.8km Puente Zacatal (Zacatal Bridge) was completed in 1994, linking the city (and its narrow streets) with the rest of Mexico. The privatization of Pemex, Mexico's largest oil company, had a huge effect on local employment and thousands of locals lost their

## LAGUNA DE TÉRMINOS

The largest lagoon in the Gulf of Mexico area, the Laguna de Términos comprises a network of estuaries, swamps and ponds that together form a uniquely important coastal habitat. Red, white and black mangroves fringe the lagoon, and the area is an important nesting ground for several species of marine turtle and numerous migratory birds.

As well as encompassing wildlife habitat, the Laguna de Términos is home to the state's second-largest city and Mexico's principal oil-production center. The lagoon's ecosystem remains threatened by various environmental dangers – including oil spills and over fishing – despite being designated a Flora and Fauna Protected Area in 1994.

Hemmed in by a narrow strip of land that is traversed by Hwy 180, the lagoon can be explored from various points along the way.

jobs. At the time of research, Ciudad del Carmen was feeling the brunt of this, with vacant buildings, many empty hotel rooms and a rather depressed ambience surrounding its otherwise very pretty plaza.

## Sights

**Playa Norte** BEACH
Playa Norte, on the Gulf of Mexico, is Carmen's beach area. It's rather bleak looking, with wide expanses of coarse sand, murky green water, parking areas and the occasional *palapa* restaurant. Development is coming fast, however, with shiny new hotels, restaurants and other services. To get here, take a bus from the center marked 'Playa Norte' or 'Zoológico'. *Combis* charge M$7; taxis cost M$35 to M$40.

**Museo Victoriano Nieves** MUSEUM
(938-384-24-14; cnr Calles 22 & 41; adult/child M$11.50/6; 9am-8pm Mon-Fri, 9am-4pm Sat & Sun) The city's decent history museum is in an interesting old hospital building. Inside are archaeological relics (including stelae from Xpuhil), a petroleum exhibition and information on the region's pirate history – plus a kids' pirate ship, complete with plank. Guides in Spanish only.

**Parque Zaragoza** SQUARE
(Central Plaza) Parque Zaragoza has a handsome 19th-century kiosk and is one of the city's most pleasant areas to hang out. On its north side is the 1856 **Santuario de la Virgen del Carmen**, which pays homage to the patron saint of sailors. Vestiges of Carmen's earlier prosperity remain in the *centro histórico*, where chicle barons' 19th-century mansions run along Calles 22 and 24, south of the plaza.

## Festivals & Events

Ciudad del Carmen has a renowned and colorful **Carnaval** (Sat-Tue, around Feb) celebration, with locals wearing elaborate costumes and dancing in the streets for four days. Another exciting event is the **Fiesta de la Virgen del Carmen** (Jul 16), which kicks off two weeks of festivities on July 16, when the port's patron saint is taken on a cruise around the harbor. There are also many exhibits of art, culture and local industries.

## Sleeping

Because of the current state of the oil industry (low local employment due to privatization), there is a glut of empty hotels. As such, prices are competitive. The nicest hotels tend to be the chain hotels.

**Hotel de Parque** HOTEL $
(938-382-30-46; www.facebook.com/hotelparquecarmen; Calle 33 s/n, btwn Calles 20 & 22; d incl breakfast M$700; P❉❀) A modern, waterfront property overlooking the *malecón* that is a refreshing change from some of the crumbling central hotels. Some (not all) rooms have been brought up to the 21st century so check beforehand. You can't beat the location, right in the middle of the action. There's also a restaurant.

**Hacienda Real** HOTEL $$
(938-381-17-00; www.hotelhaciendareal.com.mx; Calle 31 No 106; r from M$1298; ❂❀@❀❄) Big and brassy, the Hacienda lays it all out with king-sized beds, a top-notch restaurant, great balcony views and a surprisingly tasteful mosaic-inlaid pool. There's a bar-restaurant too.

## Eating

★ **Il Giglio** ITALIAN $$
(938-382-47-08; www.ilgiglio.com.mx; Calle 24 No 33; mains M$155-385; 2pm-11:30pm Mon-Sat, bar to 1am) In a classic, old-time, elegant building that used to be a pirate's house, this truly Italian restaurant with checkered floor tiles has a reputation for genuine cuisine,

## ATASTA PENINSULA

West of Ciudad del Carmen across the Puente Zacatal is the lush, tropical Atasta Peninsula. A scarcely visited ecological wonderland, it stretches along a thin strip between the Gulf and a network of small mangrove-fringed lagoons that feed into the Laguna de Términos. Various waterfront seafood shacks prepare crab and shrimp pulled out of the lagoon. Howler monkeys, manatees and river turtles may be spotted along the journey through the estuarine waterway.

Both 1st-class ADO and 2nd-class Sur buses use Ciudad del Carmen's modern **bus terminal** (Av Periférico s/n), a 15-minute drive east of the main plaza. A taxi-colectivo (shared taxi) from the terminal to the plaza should cost around M$35 (slightly more after 10pm). You can check schedules and buy tickets at the **ADO Ticket Office** (☑ 938-384-23-63; Calle 24; ☉ 8am-8pm Mon-Fri, 9am-2pm Sat & Sun) next to the Hotel Zacarías. Destinations include Campeche (M$217, three hours hourly), Mérida (M$415, five hours, hourly) and Villahermosa (M$190, three hours, every 45 minutes). Buses to Mexico City cost M$789.

Combis run to/from Isla Aguada (M$40, 40 minutes); the stop is three blocks northeast of the plaza at the corner of Calles 32 and 35.

including pasta dishes and seafood plates... just like an Italian *mamma* would make. The cellar has over 400 wines, too. Leave room for the specialty: mustache cake for dessert. You won't regret it.

**Café La Fuente** MEXICAN **$$**
(☑ 938-286-02-16; Calle 20 No 203; snacks M$35-80, mains M$140-160; ☉ 8am-midnight; 📶) This classic, open-fronted waterfront cafe is a busy gathering place for families and friends. It's an excellent spot to sample treats such as *pibipollo* (chicken tamales, M$40) and *arrachera encebollado* (marinated flank steak with onions and chilies, M$150). There are play structures nearby that should keep the kids happy for a while, and the view can't be beat.

**Restaurante El Marino** SEAFOOD **$$**
(☑ 938-384-15-83; Calle 20 No 2; mains M$116-209; ☉ 10am-7pm, shorter in winter) This large, open-air restaurant overlooks the water and affords terrific views of the Zacatal Bridge and local birdlife – there's even occasional faraway dolphin-spotting. Choose from seafood cocktails, fried fish, ceviche, shrimp cooked 14 ways and seafood paella (weekends only). A small beach is nearby; it's a 15-minute walk south of the plaza.

### ⓘ Information

There are banks with ATMs near the plaza.
**Municipal Tourist Office** (☑ 938-381-28-70; Calle 20 s/n, cnr Calle 31; ☉ 8am-3pm Mon-Fri) Small module inside the city hall with a few brochures.

### ⓘ Getting There & Away

**Interjet** (☑ 866-285-95-25; www.interjet.com.mx) has daily flights to/from Mexico City.

# SOUTHEASTERN CAMPECHE

The southern peninsular region from Escárcega to Xpujil, which borders modern-day Guatemala, was the earliest established, longest inhabited and most densely populated region in the Maya world. Here you'll find the most elaborate Maya archaeological sites on the Yucatán Peninsula.

Among the region's archaeological sites, the Río Bec architectural style dominates. To see all elements in one place you'll need to arrange a visit to the Río Bec ruin (p233), but more accessible ruins contain some of these distinct characteristics. It is actually a hybrid of styles fusing elements from the Chenes region to the north and Petén to the south. The most significant is the spectacular Calakmul set amid the ecologically diverse, and very lush, Reserva de la Biosfera Calakmul, however each site contains unique structures, carvings or discoveries that will fascinate ruin explorers.

## Balamkú

'Discovered' only in 1990, Balamkú (Temple of the Jaguar; M$45; ☉ 8am-5pm) boasts a remarkably ornate, stuccoed frieze that bears little resemblance to any of the known decorative elements in the Chenes or Río Bec styles. Well preserved, with traces of its original red paint, the frieze is a richly symbolic tableau that has been interpreted as showing the complementary relationship between our world and the underworld.

Along the base of the scene, stylized seated jaguars (referred to in the temple's Maya name) represent the earth's abundance.

These figures alternate with several grotesque fanged masks, upon which stand amphibian-like creatures (possibly toads or crocodiles) that in turn support some royal personages with fantastically elaborate headdresses. Readers of Spanish can find more details in the explanatory diagrams that front the frieze.

The solid stone that hid the frieze for centuries has been replaced by a protective canopy with slit windows that let in a little light. The door is kept locked, but the site custodian will usually appear to open it and give you a tour (no flash photography allowed).

Balamkú is 91km east of Escárcega and 60km west of Xpujil (2km past the Calakmul turnoff), then about 3km north of the highway along a sealed road.

# Calakmul

Possibly the largest city during Maya times, Calakmul (combined admission M$198; ⊘ 8am-5pm) was 'discovered' in 1931 by American botanist Cyrus Lundell. The site bears comparison in size and historical significance to Tikal in Guatemala, its chief rival for hegemony over the southern lowlands during the Classic Maya era. It boasts the largest and tallest known pyramid in Mexico's Yucatán, and was once home to over 50,000 people.

A central chunk of the 72-sq-km expanse has been restored, but most of the city's approximately 6000 structures lie covered in jungle. In 2004, amazingly well-preserved painted murals were discovered at the Chiik Naab acropolis of Estructura 1. They depicted something never before seen in Maya murals – the typical daily activities of ordinary Maya (as opposed to the usual political, ceremonial or religious themes). A few years before that, a significant 20m-long, 4m-high stucco frieze was uncovered at Estructura II, whose features seemed to mark a transition between Olmec and Maya architecture.

Unfortunately, the murals and frieze are not open to the public, but their reproductions can be seen at Calakmul's modern Museo de Naturaleza y Arqueología (⊘ 8am-3pm) **FREE**, at Km 20 on the 60km side road to Calakmul. This worthwhile museum also has geological, archaeological and natural-history exhibits.

Visiting Calakmul is not just a historical experience, it's also an ecological one. Lying at the heart of the vast, untrammeled Reserva de la Biosfera Calakmul (⊘ 6am-5pm), which covers close to 15% of the state's total territory, the magnificent ruins of Calakmul are surrounded by rainforest, an endless canopy of vegetation. While wandering amid the ruins, you might glimpse ocellated turkeys, parrots and toucans among the over 350 bird species that reside or fly through here. It's also possible to see or hear spider and howler monkeys, but you're much less likely to spot a jaguar – one of five kinds of wildcat in the area. There are also many other mammal, reptile and amphibian species that call this biosphere home. Animals are most active during the morning and evening.

## History

From about 250 CE to 695, Calakmul was the leading city in a vast region known as the Kingdom of the Serpent's Head. Its decline began with the power struggles and internal conflicts that followed the defeat of Calakmul's King Garra de Jaguar (Jaguar Claw) by Tikal. Calakmul flourished again in the late Classic period by forming alliances with the Río Bec powers to the north.

As at Tikal, there are indications that construction occurred over a period of more than a millennium. Beneath Edificio VII, archaeologists discovered a burial crypt with some 2000 pieces of jade, and tombs yielded spectacular jade burial masks; some of these objects are on display in Campeche city's Museo Arqueológico de Campeche & Fuerte de San Miguel (p215). The cleared area of Calakmul holds at least 120 carved stelae, the oldest dating from 435 BCE, registering key events (or so it is believed), such as the ascent to power of kings and the outcome of conflicts with rival states.

## ◉ Sights

Ideally, give yourself at least two days to visit Calakmul. This will allow you a day to get there (and possibly visit the bat cave (p230) at sunset), and another to drive the 60km to visit the extensive ruins – both driving and walking distances are long. Just this 60km side road off Hwy 186 to the ruins takes around an hour and a half.

You will be charged three separate entry fees: M$50 on Hwy 186 at the turnoff (here you are crossing community land), M$78 to the entrance to the biosphere a further 20km in and M$70 to the entrance to the site. (This combination can change frequently).

## EL TIGRE & CENOTES MIGUEL COLORADO

Off Hwy 186, heading southwest from Escárcega, is one of Campeche's most recently uncovered Maya sites, El Tigre (M$45; ⊗8am-5pm). Archaeologists are almost certain it is none other than Itzamkanac, the legendary capital of the Itzáes. This is supposedly the place where Hernan Córtes executed Cuauhtémoc, the last Aztec ruler of Tenochtitlán.

Unlike other Campeche sites, El Tigre occupies a wetlands environment crisscrossed by rivers, with two excavated pyramids amid swaying palms and diverse birdlife. From Candelaria take the road toward Monclova; a short distance beyond the village of Estado de México is the turnoff to the site.

The rather remote village of Miguel Colorado, 70km south of Champotón, has two large scenic cenotes (Cenotes Agua Azul y Los Patios; Miguel Colorado village; admission & activities with/without zip-line M$200/100; ⊗7am-5pm) (limestone sinkholes) with a spiffy new ecocenter and a private nature reserve. Full admission includes kayak rental and a couple of very high zip-lines that go over one of the cenotes. You can hike (M$80) along hilly, rocky trails to each cenote, keeping an eye out for spider and howler monkeys.

It's possible to visit a bat cave in the area and a lake called Laguna de Mokú (home to crocodiles), but you'll need a guide (M$50 extra for each).

To get to the cenotes, drive 60km south of Champotón on Hwy 261, then take a 10km side road to the village of Miguel Colorado. Turn left at the village and go 3km more.

Take all water and snacks with you. Nothing is available en route to the site once you've turned off Hwy 186.

Once there, it's about a 1km walk through the woods to the ruins from the ticket booth at the end of the road. Arrows point out three suggested walks – a long, medium and short route. The short route leads straight to the Gran Plaza; the long route directs you through the Gran Acrópolis before sending you to the main attractions.

#### Gran Plaza                ARCHAEOLOGICAL SITE

The Gran Plaza, with its ancient buildings and many stelae, is a good place to begin your Calakmul explorations. Climbing the enormous Estructura II, at the south side of the plaza, is a must. A path on the left (east) side of Estructura II leads past Estructura III, then, walking south, you come to Estructura I.

#### Estructura II                ARCHAEOLOGICAL SITE

Each of this pyramid's sides is 140m long, giving it a footprint of just under 2 hectares – making it by some estimates the largest and tallest known Maya structure. After a good climb you'll come to what appears to be the top of the building, but go around to the left to reach the real apex.

#### Estructura III                ARCHAEOLOGICAL SITE

The palatial Estructura III consists of a dozen rooms atop a raised platform. Archaeologists found a tomb inside the 5th-century structure that contained the body of a male ruler of Calakmul surrounded by offerings of jade, ceramics and shell beads. He was wearing not one but three jade-mosaic masks – one each on his face, chest and belt.

#### Estructura I                ARCHAEOLOGICAL SITE

Estructura I is Calakmul's second great pyramid (surpassed by Estructura II). American botanist Cyrus Lundell named the site Calakmul, Maya for 'two adjacent mounds,' in reference to the pair of then-unexcavated pyramids that dominated the site. The steep climb pays off with top-of-the-world views.

#### Gran Acrópolis                ARCHAEOLOGICAL SITE

The Gran Acrópolis is a labyrinthine residential zone with a ceremonial sector containing a ball court. (From the northern perimeter of this zone, you can head east and follow the path back to the entrance.)

#### Cueva de los Murciélagos                CAVE

At sundown every evening some two to three million bats swirl up from the depths of a dry cenote, forming a tornado of fur and wings that's a surreal experience. There's only a few parking spots at the end of a small dirt entry. From there it's a 15-minute hike to the lip of the cave. Look for the bat crossing signs on Hwy 186, each about 500m from the turnoff.

### 🍽 Sleeping & Eating

Bring food and drinks with you when visiting Calakmul – there are no services (and no water) at the site. Your hotel may be able to pack a lunch.

**Campamento Yaax' Che**  CAMPGROUND **$**
(Servidores Turísticos Calakmul; ☑983-101-19-21, 983-134-88-18; own/fixed tent M$100/320) This is the closest campground to the Calakmul site, and the nearest thing to a camping experience in the jungle. It's several kilometers after the turnoff from Hwy 186 on the road to Calakmul and another 700m in on a rough road. It's a relaxed, wilderness-style campground with sites for BYO tents. Or you can opt for ready-pitched tents.

**Hotel Puerta Calakmul**  HOTEL **$$$**
(☑998-892-26-24; www.puertacalakmul.com.mx; Hwy 186 Km 98; cabañas from M$3000; P ➔ 🛜 🏊) This upscale jungle lodge is 700m from the highway turnoff (from Hwy 186 for the 60km to the site). The 15 spacious bungalows are tastefully decorated with polished concrete, wood and pebbly flourishes. They're nice, though not luxurious, and all come with mosquito nets and overhead fans. The howler monkeys are residents here (light sleepers, beware).

There's a decent, screened-in restaurant where you can dine from 7am to 9:30pm (mains M$160 to M$190), plus a small pool. Wi-fi in main building only.

### ⓘ Getting There & Away

Calakmul is 60km south of Hwy 186 at the end of a dirt road (the turnoff is 56km west of Xpujil). There are no buses after the turnoff, but a taxi from Xpujil can take you for M$1500 and wait while you tour the ruins. Taxis wait at the turnoff and can bring one to four people the 60km and back for M$1200 per person, including a wait at the ruin. Shuttles can take up to 14 people for M$2400.

# Chicanná & Becán

Chicanná and Becán are two interesting sites that are easily accessible from Hwy 186, located 10km and 8km respectively west of Xpujil. They represent fascinating examples of Chenes and Río Bec styles.

### ⊙ Sights

**Chicanná**  ARCHAEOLOGICAL SITE
(M$55; ⊙8am-5pm) Aptly named 'House of the Snake's Jaws,' this Maya site is best known for one remarkably well-preserved doorway with a hideous fanged visage. Located 10km west of Xpujil and 400m south of Hwy 186, Chicanná is a mixture of Chenes and Río Bec architectural styles buried in the jungle. The city attained its peak during the late Classic period, from 550 to 700 CE, as a sort of elite suburb of Becán.

**★ Becán**  ARCHAEOLOGICAL SITE
(M$60; ⊙8am-5pm) The Maya word for 'canyon' or 'moat' is *becán,* and indeed a 2km moat snakes its way around this must-visit Maya site. Seven causeways provide access across the moat to the 12-hectare site, within which are the remains of three separate architectural complexes. A strategic crossroads between the Petenes civilization to the south and Chenes to the north, Becán displays architectural elements of both, with the resulting composite known as the Río Bec style.

### 🛏 Sleeping & Eating

**Hotel Otoch Béek**  CABIN **$**
(La Casa del Roble; ☑983-135-10-43; casadel roble.oficial@hotmail.com; Hwy 186, Becán; s/d/q M$500/600/1100; P ❄) Simple, but modern, single-room cement quarters in a variety of rainbow colors in a pretty setting, away from the madding crowd of Xpujil. There's no breakfast, but you can head into the owner's eatery, Genesis (p232), in Xpujil, for reasonably priced fare. Look for the easy-to-miss sign on the yellow wall. If you reach the soccer field you've gone too far.

**★ Río Bec Dreams**  CABIN **$$**
(☑983-126-35-26; www.riobecdreams.com; Hwy 186 Km 142, Becán; cabañas M$1300-2175; P ➔ 🛜) This Canadian-run jungle lodge, 12km west of Xpujil and 2km west of Chicanná, is a little paradise and far superior to the options in Xpujil. Though it's located just off noisy Hwy 186, it features tropical grounds and a lovely restaurant. Its seven thatched-roofed *cabañas* are simple and colorful; some comprise one room only, larger ones have a screened-in patio.

**★ Río Bec Dreams Restaurant**  INTERNATIONAL **$$**
(☑983-126-35-26; www.riobecdreams.com; Hwy 186 Km 142; mains M$120-300; ⊙7:30am-9pm; P) This wonderful open-air restaurant, set amid tropical plants, has the best homemade food in the area. The wide variety of main dishes includes roasted pork loin, Mediterranean pasta, Indian curry and chili con carne. Ingredients are high quality and fresh.

### ⓘ Getting There & Away

Your own transportation is required to get to these sites. Alternatively, a taxi from Xpujil costs around M$500 with a one-hour wait at each.

# Xpujil

☑ 983 / POP 4000

Although unremarkable, the small town of Xpujil (shpu-*heel*) has expanded recently, largely due to its proximity to the area's many ruins. As such, it's a useful base, and as there's nothing else around for miles, you're pretty much bound to spend the night here between Campeche and Quintana Roo. It has a few hotels, some unexceptional cafes, several ATMs (one at supermarket Willy's), an exchange house (Elektra Dinero on Calle Chicanná near Xnantún) and a bus terminal. Most services are along the seven-block main drag, Avenida Calakmul (aka Hwy 186) and one street heading inland. There are three gas stations in the area.

## ⊚ Sights & Activities

The ruins of **Xpuhil** (M$60; ⊗8am-5pm) are a striking example of the Río Bec style. The three towers (rather than the usual two) of Estructura I rise above a dozen vaulted rooms. The 53m central tower is the best preserved. With its banded tiers and steep stairways leading up to a temple that displays traces of a zoomorphic mask, it gives you a good idea of what the other two towers must have looked like in Xpuhil's 8th-century heyday. Go around back to see a fierce jaguar mask embedded in the wall below the temple.

The ruins are located on the western edge of Xpujil town; it's about a 1km walk from the entrance to the ruins, which are in a pretty setting. **Calakmul Adventures** (☑983-184-13-13; www.calakmuladventures.com; around M$1350) and **Ka'an Expeditions** (☑983-158-26-69, 983-871-60-00; www.kaanexpeditions.com; Av Calakmul s/n; per person US$75; ⊗noon-8pm Tue-Sun) offer trips to Calakmul.

## ⨊ Sleeping & Eating

**Hotel Maya Balam** HOTEL $
(☑983-871-62-90; Calle Xpujil s/n, btwn Avs Calakmul & Silvituc; d/tr M$540/760; P⊝❋☎) The

best of a fairly basic lot in town, this quiet place has decent, clean rooms, an outdoor restaurant and friendly service. There's not much outlook (back rooms face on to the car park), but it's fine for a night or two if exploring the area. It's a short stroll from the center of town.

**Hotel Victoria** HOTEL $
(☑983-158-72-18; Hwy 186; r M$380; P❋☎) One of a clutch of simple, nondescript hotels around the main intersection, this one has clean, adequate rooms. Its main advantage is that it's convenient for the bus from Palenque that arrives at 1am. (But it's next to the bus station and, as bus engines often remain running, it's noisy). There are public bathrooms and a restaurant on-site.

**Genesis** MEXICAN $
(Av Calakmul, cnr Balakmul; M$40-100; ⊗24hr) A very basic spot that churns out *antojitos* (little bites, or snacks) plus sandwiches, hamburgers and tacos. A good spot to buy takeout meals for Calakmul and other excursions.

**Sazón Veracruzano** MEXICAN $$
(☑983-871-62-99; Av Calakmul 92; mains M$130-170; ⊗7am-11pm Mon-Sat; ☎) Even though this casual place has a bright-orange exterior and vibrant plastic tablecloths, it's as smart as you'll get in Xpujil. It offers a big menu of Mexican dishes (with a focus on Veracruz, where the owners are from), such as *fajita la arrachera* (beef strips) and fried fish fillet, all served on an elevated roadside terrace.

## ❶ Getting There & Away

The **bus terminal** (☑983-871-65-11; ⊗24hr) is just east of the Xpujil stoplight next to Hotel Victoria. Services head to/from Campeche (M$245 to M$414, 4½ hours, six daily; via Champotón) and Chetumal (M$120 to M$198, two hours, six to eight daily). There are also *colectivos* to Chetumal (M$120 per person, 1½ hours) and Escárcega (M$130, two hours). You'll find these near the traffic circle opposite the bus terminal.

## BUSES FROM XPUJIL

Several classes of bus stop here, heading mainly east or west between Campeche and Chetumal. Currently these include AU, ATS and Sur for economy travelers, plus the premium ADO line.

| DESTINATION | FARE (M$) | DURATION (HR) | FREQUENCY (PER DAY) |
| --- | --- | --- | --- |
| Campeche | 232-380 | 4-6 | 6 |
| Cancún | 438-622 | 8 | 6 |
| Chetumal | 101-176 | 2 | 6 |
| Escárcega | 124-206 | 2 | 8 |

# Zoh-Laguna

☑ 983 / POP 1100

The pretty little community of Zoh-Laguna, 9.5km north of Hwy 186 along the Hopelchén road, offers a pleasant alternative to staying in Xpujil. It's peaceful, but has only a few simple places to stay and almost no services. It's fascinating for the quaint, pitched roofed wooden houses, the legacy of its history as a lumber town that began in the 1930s.

It is best reached with your own vehicle. Taxis from Xpujil are around M$80.

**Cabañas Mercedes**                    CABIN $

(☑ 983-839-49-91, cell 983-1351261; Calle Zapote s/n; cabañas s/d M$200/300) Fifteen basic bungalows with mosquito nets, ceiling fans and open-shower bathrooms can be found at this rustic place. Decent meals are served in the thatched-roof restaurant (mains from M$50 to M$100). Delightful host Don Antonio knows about the area's ruins.

**El Viajero**                            HOTEL $

(☑ 983-103-96-13; Calle Caobas s/n; r with/without air-con M$250/400; P ⊖ ✿ ☎) Eight modern tiled rooms across the road from the owner's simple restaurant (meals M$80). The same run the identically named Hotel El Viajero at the entrance to the village (doubles M$400). These have wi-fi and air-conditioning.

# Río Bec

A collection of small but significant structures in 74 groupings, **Río Bec** (ATV/pickup M$900/1000, guide M$700, park entry M$55; ☺8am-5pm) 🆓 covers a 100-sq-km area southeast of Xpujil, and is the only place where all five elements of Río Bec style can be seen in one building: twin towers, a roof comb, checkerboard pattern sides, false stairs, and pillars carved at the base. The remoteness and ongoing excavations give it a mystique that's lacking in more established sites.

Grupo B has some of the best-restored buildings, particularly the magnificent Estructura I (700 CE). 'Discovered' in 1907 by French archaeologist Maurice de Périgny, this palatial structure features a pair of typical tiered towers crowned by matching temples with cross motifs on their sides.

The main structure at Grupo A is a 15m-long palace with intact towers and unusual bas-relief glyphs on the lower panels.

Getting here without a guide is impossible – the very rough dirt road is accessible

CAMPECHE STATE ZOH-LAGUNA

---

**THE ROAD TO RUINS**
........................................

Maya sites around Xpujil are most conveniently reached by private vehicle. If you're on public transportation, either book a tour or hire a taxi. The taxi stop is at the Xpujil junction (with the stoplight).

Typical round-trip fares:

**Balamkú and Calakmul** M$1500 with a three- to four-hour wait.

**Becán and Chicanná** M$500 with one-hour wait at each.

**Hormiguero** M$500 with one- to 1½-hour wait.

**Río Bec** M$900 to M$1000 transport, plus M$1200 for the guide.

---

only via 4WD vehicle, ATV, or (for the fit or foolhardy!) bicycle. Since it's unsigned, with many twists and turns that can change from year to year, you'll get lost without someone who knows the way. Río Bec Dreams (p231) and Ka'an Expeditions can set up tours (reservations required).

# Hormiguero

The buildings of **Hormiguero** (☺8am-5pm) 🆓 date as far back as 50 CE; the city (whose name is Spanish for 'anthill') flourished during the late Classic period. Until recent times, the site was not easy to reach: the road, although overgrown, is largely sealed. Hormiguero has two impressive and unique buildings in a stunning, lush setting that are worth the trek. You are likely to have the site to yourself.

As you enter you'll see the 50m-long Estructura II. The facade's chief feature is a very menacing Chenes-style monster-mouth doorway, jaws open wide, set back between a pair of Classic Río Bec tiered towers. Around the back is intact Maya stonework and the remains of several columns. Follow the arrows 60m north to reach Estructura V, with a much smaller but equally ornate open-jawed temple atop a pyramidal base. Climb the right side for a closer look at the incredibly detailed stonework, especially along the corner columns that flank the doorway.

This site is reached by heading 14km south from Xpujil's stoplight, then turning right and going 8km west on a sealed road (the final 2km are on a rough, dirt road).

## AT A GLANCE

**POPULATION**
7.9 million

**CAPITALS**
Tuxtla Gutiérrez (Chiapas), Villahermosa (Tabasco)

**BEST MAYA TEMPLE**
Templo de las Inscripciones (p249)

**BEST REGIONAL CUISINE**
Restaurante LUM (p244)

**BEST COCKTAILS**
Cocoliche (p244)

**WHEN TO GO**
**Jan** Drop in on Fiesta Grande de Enero in Chiapa de Corzo.

**Jun–Nov** Nesting season for sea turtles along the Pacific coast. Heavy rains in Tabasco.

**Nov–Apr** The driest months in both states, though evenings in high-elevation San Cristóbal are chilly.

**Fresco, Bonampak (p254)**
LEON RAFAEL/SHUTTERSTOCK

# Chiapas & Tabasco

From the majestic mountain rainforests to the balmy, mangrove-flanked swamp, the breathtaking historical ruins to the still-thriving indigenous populations, these two southern states offer a glimpse into Mexico's wild heart as well as its earliest traditions.

In Chiapas, Palenque and Yaxchilán are evocative vestiges of powerful Maya kingdoms, and the presence of modern Maya is a reminder of the region's rich history. The colonial hubs of San Cristóbal de las Casas and Chiapa de Corzo give way to sandbar beaches and fertile plots of coffee and cacao in the Soconusco.

To the north, the state of Tabasco has more water than land, and harbors some Maya ruins and an expansive biosphere reserve.

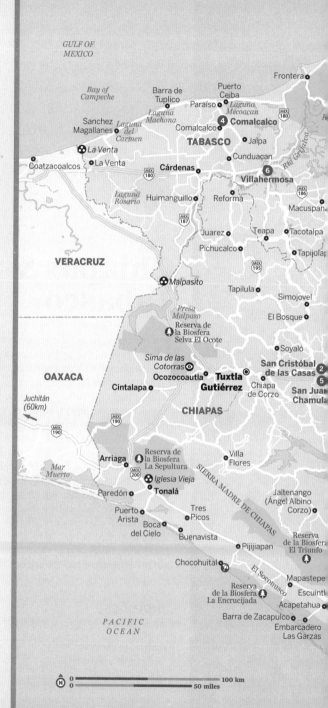

# Chiapas & Tabasco Highlights

**①** **Palenque** (p247) Scaling the jungly hills and soaring Maya temples.

**②** **San Cristóbal de las Casas** (p238) Strolling the high-altitude cobblestone streets.

**③** **Yaxchilán** (p255) Wandering amid the roar of howler monkeys at the riverside Maya ruins.

**④** **Comalcalco** (p257) Checking out a far-flung Maya site and some dreamy cacao farms.

**⑤** **San Juan Chamula** (p245) Experiencing the unique culture of the Tzotzil people.

**⑥** **Villahermosa** (p255) Dining out at some of Tabasco's top restaurants.

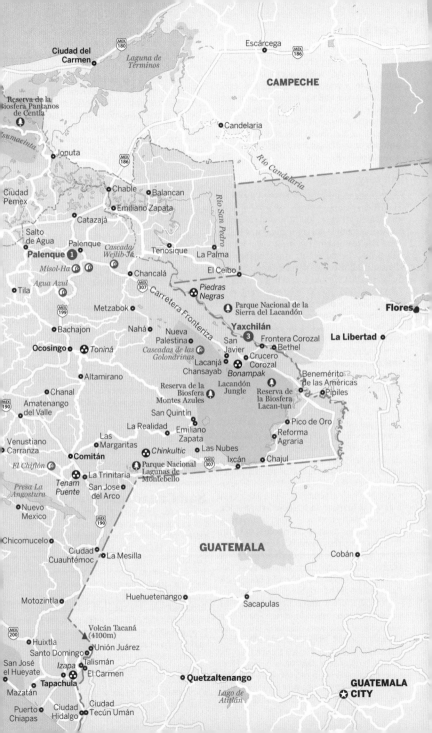

# CHIAPAS

Chilly pine-forest highlands, sultry rain-forest jungles and attractive colonial cities exist side by side within Mexico's southernmost state, a region awash with the legacy of Spanish rule and the remnants of ancient Maya civilization. Meanwhile, nature lovers willing to venture off the beaten track will swoon over the frothy cascades and exotic animals of the Lacandón Jungle and the El Triunfo reserve.

## History

The Olmec civilization, renowned for its extraordinary stone carvings, established itself in Tabasco around 1500 BCE while later, the low-lying, jungle-covered eastern Chiapas gave rise to some of the most splendid and powerful city-states of Maya civilization. During the Classic period (approximately 250–900 CE), places such as Palenque, Yaxchilán and Toniná were the centers of power, though dozens of lesser Maya powers – including Bonampak, Comalcalco and Chinkultic – prospered in eastern Chiapas and Tabasco during this time, as Maya culture reached its peak of artistic and intellectual achievement. The ancestors of many of the distinctive indigenous groups of highland Chiapas today appear to have migrated to that region from the lowlands after the Classic Maya collapse around 900 CE.

Central Chiapas was brought under Spanish control by the 1528 expedition of Diego de Mazariegos, and outlying areas were subdued in the 1530s and '40s, though Spain never gained full control of the Lacandón Jungle. New diseases arrived with the Spaniards, and an epidemic in 1544 killed about half of Chiapas' indigenous population. Chiapas was ineffectively administered from Guatemala for most of the colonial era, with little check on the colonists' excesses against its indigenous people, though some church figures, particularly Bartolomé de Las Casas (1474–1566), the first bishop of Chiapas, did fight for indigenous rights.

In 1822, a newly independent Mexico unsuccessfully attempted to annex Spain's former Central American provinces (including Chiapas), but in 1824 Chiapas opted (by a referendum) to join Mexico rather than the United Provinces of Central America. From then on, a succession of governors appointed by Mexico City, along with local landowners, maintained an almost feudal control over the state.

Periodic uprisings bore witness to bad government, but the world took little notice until January 1, 1994, when Zapatista rebels suddenly and briefly occupied San Cristóbal de las Casas and nearby towns by military force. The rebel movement, with a firm and committed support base among disenchanted indigenous people in eastern Chiapas, quickly retreated to remote jungle bases to campaign for democratic change and indigenous rights. The Zapatistas have failed to win any significant concessions at the national level, although increased government funding steered toward Chiapas did result in noticeable improvements in the state's infrastructure, the development of tourist facilities and a growing urban middle class.

In September 2017, a magnitude 8.2 earthquake struck around 87km off the coast of Chiapas. Around 98 people were killed and over 40,000 homes were damaged. The damage could have been much worse, but the earthquake occurred far underground. At time of research some reconstruction work was still taking place, mainly on the churches in and around San Cristóbal de las Casas.

Tabasco, meanwhile, continues to suffer economically as a result of the privatization of the oil industry in 2014, which saw the closure of many jobs with the formerly state-run Pemex.

The border regions, particularly around Tapachula, are busy with migrants en route to USA, including many from Sub-Saharan Africa, living in rudimentary conditions.

## San Cristóbal de las Casas

📞 967 / POP 185,000 / ELEV 2100M

Set in a gorgeous highland valley surrounded by pine forest, the colonial city of San Cristóbal (sahn cris-*toh*-bal) has been a popular travelers' destination for decades. It's a pleasure to explore San Cristóbal's cobbled streets and markets, soaking up the unique ambience and the wonderfully clear highland light. It's very much on the tourist map, and offers all the services, from good accommodations and restaurants, to tour and transport services.

Surrounded by dozens of traditional Tsotzil and Tzeltal villages, San Cristóbal is at the heart of one of the most deeply rooted indigenous areas in Mexico. A great base for local and regional exploration, it's a place where ancient customs coexist with modern luxuries.

The city shook violently during the September 2017 Chiapas earthquake; the cathedral and other buildings were damaged and, at the time of research, remained closed for renovation.

## ⊙ Sights

San Cristóbal is very walkable, with straight streets rambling up and down several gentle hills. Heading east from Plaza 31 de Marzo, Real de Guadalupe has a long pedestrian-only section with a concentration of places to eat and drink. The other principal pedestrian mall, the Andador Turístico, runs up Hidalgo and Avenida 20 de Noviembre.

★**Na Bolom**    HISTORIC BUILDING
(☑967-678-14-18; www.nabolom.org; Guerrero 33; M$60, incl tour M$70; ⊙9am-7pm) An atmospheric museum-research center, Na Bolom for many years was the home of Swiss anthropologist and photographer Gertrude Duby-Blom (Trudy Blom; 1901–93) and her Danish archaeologist husband Frans Blom (1893–1963). Na Bolom means 'Jaguar House' in the Tsotzil language (as well as being a play on its former owners' name). It's full of photographs, archaeological and anthropological relics, and books.

★**Templo & Ex-Convento de Santo Domingo de Guzmán**    CHURCH
(Av 20 de Noviembre; ⊙6:30am-1:45pm & 4-8pm Mon-Sat, 7am-9pm Sun) **FREE** Located just north of the center of town, the imposing 16th-century Templo de Santo Domingo is San Cristóbal's most beautiful church, especially when its facade catches the late-afternoon sun. This baroque frontage, with outstanding filigree stucco work, was added in the 17th century and includes the double-headed Hapsburg eagle, then the symbol of the Spanish monarchy.

**Catedral**    CATHEDRAL
(Plaza 31 de Marzo) On the north side of the plaza, the candy-colored cathedral was begun in 1528 but wasn't completed until 1815 because of several natural disasters. Sure enough, new earthquakes struck in 1816 and also 1847, causing considerable damage, but it was restored again from 1920 to 1922. The gold-leaf interior has lots of incense smoke and candlelight as well as five gilded altar-pieces featuring 18th-century paintings by Miguel Cabrera.

The cathedral was closed at time of research due to damage sustained from the 2017 earthquake.

**Museo de los Altos de Chiapas**    MUSEUM
(☑967-678-16-09; Calz Lázaro Cárdenas s/n; M$60; ⊙9am-5:45pm Tue-Sun) One of two world-class museums inside the Ex-Convento de Santo Domingo (on the western side of the Templo de Santo Domingo), this exhibits several impressive archaeological relics – including stelae from Chinkultic – as well as exhibits on the Spanish conquest and evangelization of the region. Admission is bundled with Centro de Textiles del Mundo Maya.

**Centro de Textiles del Mundo Maya**    MUSEUM
(☑967-631-30-94; www.centrotextilesmayas.org; Calz Lázaro Cárdenas; M$60; ⊙9am-2pm & 4-6pm) Upstairs inside the Ex-Convento de Santo Domingo, this excellent museum showcases over 500 examples of handwoven textiles from throughout Mexico and Central America. There's more than meets the eye here; be sure to open the drawers that showcase most of the collection! Two permanent exhibition rooms display *huipiles* (sleeveless tunics) and videos show how materials and clothes are created, with some explanations in English. Admission is bundled with the Museo de los Altos de Chiapas (note the pre-Hispanic textiles here).

**Museo del Ámbar de Chiapas**    MUSEUM
(☑967-674-58-99; www.museodelambardechiapas.org.mx; Plazuela de la Merced; M$25; ⊙10am-2pm & 4-8pm Tue-Sun) Chiapas amber – fossilized pine resin that's around 30 million years old – is known for its clarity and diverse colors. Most is mined around Simojovel, north of San Cristóbal. This small museum explains all things amber (with information sheets in English, French, German, Japanese and Italian).

**Museo del Cacao**    MUSEUM
(☑967-631-79-95; www.kakaw.org; 1ro de Marzo 16; M$30; ⊙11am-8pm Mon-Sat, to 6pm Sun) This chocolate museum runs along an open upstairs balcony of a cafe. Learn about the history of chocolate and how it was used by the Maya. Also on display are modern chocolate drinking vessels and utensils; exhibits cover the process of creating the delicious substance. Includes a small tasting. The chocolateria-cum-cafe is open later.

# San Cristóbal de las Casas

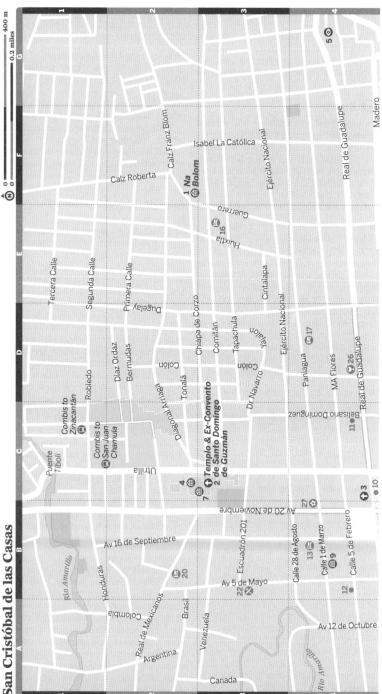

0.2 miles / 400 m

N

241

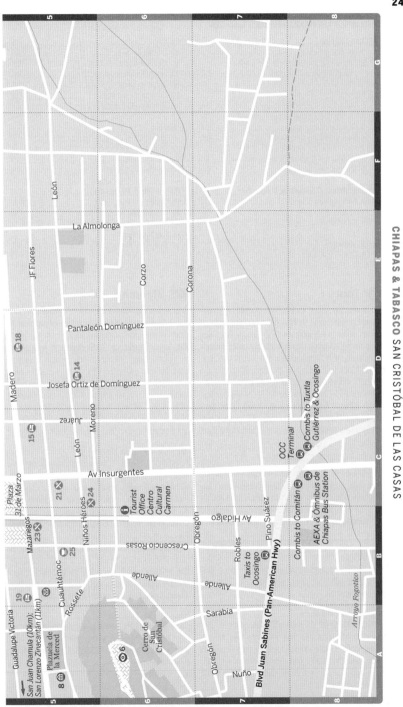

## San Cristóbal de las Casas

## 👉 Tours

Agencies in San Cristóbal (open approximately 8am to 9pm) offer a variety of tours, often with guides who speak English, French or Italian, though many offer transportation only. Typical day trips run to Chiapa de Corzo and Cañón del Sumidero (from M$350, six to seven hours), Lagos de Montebello and El Chiflón waterfalls (M$350, nine to 10 hours) and Palenque, Agua Azul and Misol-Ha (M$450, 14 hours). All prices are per person (usually with a minimum of four people).

**Raúl & Cesar Tours**               CULTURAL
(☑ 967-678-91-41; www.alexyraultours.wordpress. com; per person M$250) Enjoyable and informative minibus tours in English, French or Spanish. Raúl and/or a colleague wait at the wooden cross in front of San Cristóbal's cathedral from 8:45am to 9:30am daily, going to San Juan Chamula and Zinacantán (minimum of two people). Trips to Tenejapa, San Andrés Larraínzar or Amatenango del Valle can also be arranged for a minimum of four people.

**Jaguar Adventours**               CYCLING
(☑ 967-631-50-62; www.adventours.mx; Belisario Domínguez 8A; bicycle rental per hr/day M$50/250; ☉9am-8pm) Does bicycle tours to Chamula (M$700), plus longer expeditions. Also rents out quality mountain bikes with helmet and lock.

## 🛏 Sleeping

San Cristóbal has a wealth of budget accommodations, but also a number of appealing and atmospheric midrange hotels, often set in colonial or 19th-century mansions, along with an ever-growing number of top-end luxury choices. The high seasons here are during Semana Santa and the following week, and the months of July and August, plus the Día de Muertos and Christmas–New Year holidays. Most prices dip at least 20% (and up to 50%) outside high season.

**★ Puerta Vieja Hostel**               HOSTEL $
(☑ 967-631-43-35; www.puertaviejahostel.com; Mazariegos 23; dm incl breakfast M$180, r with/without bathroom M$450/550; ❀🐾) A spacious, modern, traveler-savvy hostel in a high-ceilinged colonial building with a large garden strung with hammocks, kitchen, temascal (pre-Hispanic steam bath) and sheltered interior courtyard. Its dorms (one for women) are a good size, and the rooftop ones have fab views. Six private rooms have one queen and a bunk bed. There's occasional karaoke in the garden.

**Rossco Backpackers**               HOSTEL $
(☑ 967-674-05-25; www.backpackershostel.com. mx; Real de Mexicanos 16; dm from M$139, d with/without bathroom M$550/400; 🅿❀@🐾) Rossco Backpackers is a friendly, sociable and well-run hostel with good dorm rooms (one for women only), a guest kitchen, a movie-watching loft and a grassy garden.

Private upstairs rooms have nice skylights. A free night's stay if you arrive by bicycle or motorcycle!

**Docecuartos** HOTEL $$
(☑ 967-678-10-53; www.docecuartos.com; Benito Juárez 1; r from M$1912; 🛜) Set around a charming courtyard, there are indeed only 12 rooms here, which adds to the intimate feel. The rooms themselves have the right balance of colonial stateliness, indigenous color and modern amenity, and the super-central location gets a thumbs up. But rooms could do with a light spruce up and disappointingly, there's no breakfast.

**Hotel Posada Jovel** HOTEL $$
(☑ 967-678-17-34; www.hoteljovel.com; Paniagua 28; r from M$1000; P ❄ 🛜) The colonial-style Jovel offers one of the better deals in town. The rooms are filled with the light, color and character of Mexico and they surround a pretty garden with fountains and tropical flowers where you can have breakfast.

**★ La Joya Hotel** BOUTIQUE HOTEL $$$
(☑ 967-631-48-32; www.lajoyahotelsancristobal. com; Madero 43A; r incl breakfast US$170-220; P ⊖ @ 🛜) This extraordinary boutique hotel is a visual feast in which every corner contains something interesting and beautiful. The five rooms have been ripped from a design magazine and have exquisite cabinetry, enormous bathrooms and antiques curated from the owners' world travels. Fireplace sitting areas and heaters grace each room, and rooftop terraces beckon with hill views.

**★ Casa del Alma** BOUTIQUE HOTEL $$$
(☑ 967-674-90-90; www.casadelalma.mx; Av 16 de Sepiembre 24; ste incl breakfast from M$3658; P ⊖ 🛜) This very central, boutique hotel has it all. The rooms, which offer a fine mix of colonial charm and modern comforts, are notable for the floor-to-ceiling artworks and creative bedheads. Each comprises the material specific to a neighborhood, such as wood or metal. Beautiful bathrooms and views over terracotta tiled roofs from the private terraces and balconies.

**Casa Santa Lucía** BOUTIQUE HOTEL $$$
(☑ 967-631-55-45; www.hotelcasasantalucia.mx; Av Josefa Ortíz de Domínguez 13; r M$1600-2000, ste M$2500-3000; P ⊖ 🛜) This discreet boutique hotel has been touched by the hand of an artist. Moroccan lamps hang from polished wood beams, geraniums add a touch

of pink, leopards and Day of the Dead skulls grin from shady corners, and ethnic textiles and antique carved furnishings fill the bedrooms. Guests enjoy the warm welcome, free laundry service and delicious breakfasts.

**Guayaba Inn** HOTEL $$$
(☑ 967-674-76-99; www.guayabainn.com; Comitán 55; r incl breakfast from M$2000; 🛜) With something of an old country farmhouse feel to it, this gorgeous, rustic and quirky place is one of the best-looking hotels in town. The artist owners' attention to detail shines through in everything from the tranquil garden spaces to the light, spacious and divinely decorated rooms. All rooms have fireplaces, big separate tubs and minibars, and there's a sauna/massage suite.

## 🍴 Eating

The region's foodie jackpot, San Cristóbal has more tantalizing food options than any other place in the state. Vegetarians are almost embarrassingly spoiled for choice. A great **food court** is in Plaza San Augustín. *¡Provecho!*

**El Caldero** MEXICAN $
(☑ 967-116-01-21; Av Insurgentes 5; soups from M$90; ⊙ 7am-10pm; 🛜) Perfect for a cold day, simple, friendly little El Caldero specializes in delicious Mexican soups – *pozole* (shredded pork in broth), *mondongo* (tripe) and *caldo* (broth). Although calling them mere 'soups' does them an injustice: these are more massive portions of thick, hearty stews than watery soups and they come with a spread of avocados, tortillas and salsas.

Vegetarian options, too.

---

**DON'T MISS**

### TWO VIEWPOINTS

Want to take in the best views in town? Well, you'll have to work for them, because at this altitude the stairs up these hills can be punishing. The **Cerro de San Cristóbal** (off Hermanos Domínguez) and **Cerro de Guadalupe** (off Real de Guadalupe) lord over the town from the west and east, respectively, and churches crown both lookouts. A church crowns the Cerro de Guadalupe. The Iglesia de Guadalupe becomes a hot spot for religious devotees around the **Día de la Virgen de Guadalupe**. These areas are not considered safe at night.

## SHOPPING FOR AMBER

Real de Guadalupe and the Andador Turístico have some upscale craft shops, but the busy daily crafts market around the Santo Domingo and La Caridad churches is also a good place to check out. In addition to textiles, another Chiapas specialty is amber, sold in numerous jewelry shops. When buying amber, beware of plastic imitations: the real thing is never cold and never heavy, and when rubbed should produce static electricity and a resiny smell.

**Te Quiero Verde**  VEGETARIAN $
(Niños Héroes 4; mains from M$80; ⊙9am-10pm; 🛜⁊) 🍴 If you've ever doubted that a vegan burger can be truly tasty, you need to head here. The soups and salads are OK too, but the burgers and homemade fries steal the show.

**★Restaurante LUM**  MEXICAN $$$
(⊋967-678-15-16; www.hotelbo.mx/restaurante-san-cristobal-de-las-casas; Hotel b¨o, Av 5 de Mayo 38; mains M$200-350; ⊙7am-11pm) This swanky indoor-outdoor restaurant in San Cristóbal's first designer hotel serves up exciting blends of Chiapas, Veracruz and Yucatán cuisine fused with tastes and ideas from around the culinary planet. Custom-made lamps, reflecting pools and walls of geometrically stacked firewood create a funky contemporary ambience. We're still in raptures of delight over the shrimp with almond sauce.

**Santo Nahual**  FUSION $$
(⊋967-678-15-47; www.santonahual.com; Hidalgo 3; mains M$130-240; ⊙9am-11pm; 🛜) This pleasant glass-roofed courtyard dining area is filled with worn timbers, smooth pebbles, glossy-leafed banana plants and even a day-glo piano. The food, is best described as modern fusion Mexican, is good, though some say it can be inconsistent.

## 🍸 Drinking & Nightlife

**Café La Selva**  CAFE
(www.cafelaselva.com; Crescencio Rosas 9; coffee M$21-35; ⊙8:30am-11pm; 🛜) One of the first coffee shops in San Cristóbal, La Selva is housed in a barn-like old building with eye-catching wall murals. There are around 10 different types of coffee on offer here and the beans for all of them are roasted on the spot, which lends a delicious aroma to the place.

**★Cocoliche**  COCKTAIL BAR
(⊋967-631-46-21; Colón 3; mains M$60-210; ⊙1pm-midnight; 🛜) By day Cocoliche is a bohemian restaurant with lots of Asian dishes, but in the evening its vintage lanterns and wall of funky posters set the scene for drinking boozy or virgin cocktails with friends. Jostle for a spot near the fireplace on chilly evenings, and check out the nightly jazz, funk and swing music.

**★Café Bar Revolución**  LIVE MUSIC
(⊋967-678-66-64; www.facebook.com/elrevomx; Calle 1 de Marzo 11; ⊙1pm-3am) There's always something fun at Revolución, with two live bands nightly and an eclectic line up of salsa, rock, blues, jazz and reggae. Dance downstairs or order a mojito or caipirinha and chat in the quieter upstairs *tapanco* (attic).

## ℹ Information

Most banks require your passport if you want to change cash, though they only change money Monday through Friday. There are also handy ATMs at the OCC bus station and on the southern side of the Plaza 31 de Marzo.

**Banamex** (Av Insurgentes, btwn Niños Héroes & Cuauhtémoc; ⊙9am-4pm Mon-Fri) Has an ATM; exchanges dollars.

**Dr Patrick Rueda Trujillo** (⊋cell 967-102-01-06) Reliable and speaks English; makes house calls.

**Hospital de la Mujer** (⊋967-678-07-70; Av Insurgentes 24; ⊙24hr) General hospital with emergency facilities.

**Main Post Office** (Allende 3; ⊙8am-5pm Mon-Fri, 10am-2pm Sat)

**Tourist Office Centro Cultural Carmen** (Av Hidalgo 15; ⊙9am-8pm) Tiny office outside the cultural center with a few fliers on local events.

## ℹ Getting There & Away

A fast toll autopista (M$60 for cars) zips to San Cristóbal from Chiapa de Corzo. Follow the highways signs that say 'cuota' (toll).

At the time of research buses were not traveling to Palenque via Ocosingo because of security concerns. Most buses were instead taking the much more circular route via Villahermosa. If you do travel to Palenque via Ocosingo it's best to travel during daylight, as highway holdups – though by no means common – do occasionally occur. When taking a bus along this route, consider stowing valuables in the checked luggage compartment.

### AIR

San Cristóbal's airport has no regular passenger flights; the main airport serving town is at Tuxtla Gutiérrez. Ten daily direct OCC minibuses (M$250) run to the Tuxtla airport from San Cristóbal's main bus terminal; book airport-bound tickets in advance, and consult www.ado.com. mx for schedules to/from 'Ángel Albino Corzo Aeropuerto.'

A number of tour agencies run shuttles to the Tuxtla airport for around M$250 to M$300 per person.

Taxis from the airport will cost at least M$650.

### BUS & COLECTIVO

The Pan-American Hwy (Hwy 190, Blvd Juan Sabines, 'El Bulevar') runs through the southern part of town, and nearly all transportation terminals are on it or nearby. From the **OCC bus terminal** (cnr Pan-American Hwy & Av Insurgentes), it's six blocks north up Insurgentes to the central square, Plaza 31 de Marzo.

The main 1st-class OCC terminal is also used by ADO and UNO 1st-class and deluxe buses, plus some 2nd-class buses. Tickets can also be purchased at **Ticketbus** (☑ 967-678-85-03; Real de Guadalupe 16; ⊙ 7am-10:30pm) in the center of town. **AEXA buses and Ómnibus de Chiapas** minibuses share a terminal across the street from the OCC terminal.

All *colectivo* vans (combis) and taxis have depots on the Pan-American Hwy a block or so from the OCC terminal. They generally run from 5am until 9pm and leave when full, including to **Comitán, Tuxtla Gutiérrez & Ocosingo**. Combis to **Zinacantán** and **San Juan Chamula** (Utrilla) leave from further north. *Colectivo* taxis to Tuxtla, Comitán and **Ocosingo** are available 24 hours; if you don't want to wait for it to fill, you must pay for the empty seats.

For Tuxtla Gutiérrez, comfortable Ómnibus de Chiapas 'sprinter' minibuses (M$60) are the best bet; they leave every 10 minutes.

### CAR & MOTORCYCLE

One of San Cristóbal's few car-rental companies, **Óptima** (☑ 967-674-54-09; optimacar1@hot mail.com; Mazariegos 39; ⊙ 9am-7pm Mon-Fri, 9am-2pm & 4-7pm Sat, 9am-1pm Sun) rents out manual-transmission cars. Rates vary wildly depending on the season and demand. Sizable discounts are given for payment in cash. Drivers must be 25 or older and have a credit card.

## ❶ Getting Around

Combis (M$7) go up Crescencio Rosas from the Pan-American Hwy to the town center. Taxis cost M$35 within town and M$40 at night.

To self-propel, Jaguar Adventours (p242) rents out good-quality mountain bikes.

**Croozy Scooters** (☑ cell 967-6832223; Belisario Domínguez 7; bicycles/scooters/motorcycles per day M$220/500/800; ⊙ 10am-7pm) rents well-maintained Italika CS 125cc scooters and 150cc motorcycles. The price includes a free tank of fuel, maps, locks and helmets; passport and M$500 deposit required.

# Around San Cristóbal de las Casas

The inhabitants of the beautiful Chiapas highlands are descended from the ancient Maya and maintain some unique customs, costumes and beliefs, and some of their villages are worth visiting. In addition to San Juan Chamula, there's San Lorenzo Zinacantán (notable for its old church) and Amatenango del Valle (famous for pottery). Those into natural wonders should head to Las Grutas de Rancho Nuevo (a long cavern).

Markets and festivals often give the most interesting insight into indigenous life, and lots of village markets are held beyond the valley bowl in which San Cristóbal nestles. Full of life and the hues of a hundred different colors, the weekly markets at the villages are today nearly always held on Sunday. Proceedings start as early as dawn, and wind down by lunchtime.

## San Juan Chamula

☑ 967 / POP 76,940 / ELEV 2200M

The Chamulans are a fiercely independent Tsotzil group, and you will feel it. Their main village, San Juan Chamula, 10km northwest

### BUSES FROM SAN CRISTÓBAL DE LAS CASAS

| DESTINATION | FARE (M$) | TIME (HR) | FREQUENCY (PER DAY) |
| --- | --- | --- | --- |
| Campeche | 408-680 | 10 | 2 OCC |
| Cancún | 1024-1422 | 18-19 | 3 OCC, 1 AEXA |
| Mérida | 564-789 | 12¾ | 2 OCC |
| Palenque | 184-332 | 5 | frequent |
| Villahermosa | 254-514 | 5½-7 | 5 OCC |

## INDIGENOUS PEOPLES OF CHIAPAS

Of the 5.2 million people of Chiapas, approximately a quarter are indigenous, with language being the key ethnic identifier. Each of the eight principal groups has its own language, beliefs and customs, a cultural variety that makes Chiapas one of the most fascinating states in Mexico.

Travelers to the area around San Cristóbal are most likely to encounter the Tzotziles and the Tzeltales. Their traditional religious life is nominally Catholic, but integrates pre-Hispanic elements. Most people live in the hills outside the villages, which are primarily market and ceremonial centers.

Tzotzil and Tzeltal clothing is among the most varied, colorful and elaborately worked in Mexico. It not only identifies wearers' villages but also continues ancient Maya traditions. Many of the seemingly abstract designs on these costumes are in fact stylized snakes, frogs, butterflies, birds, saints and other beings. Some motifs have religious-magical functions: scorpions, for example, can be a symbolic request for rain, since they are believed to attract lightning.

The Lacandones dwelled deep in the Lacandón Jungle and largely avoided contact with the outside world until the 1950s. They now number less than 700 and mostly live in three main settlements in that same region (Lacanjá Chansayab, Metzabok and Nahá), with low-key tourism being one of their major means of support. Lacandones are readily recognizable in their white tunics and long black hair cut in a fringe. Most Lacandones have now abandoned their traditional animist religion in favor of Presbyterian or evangelical forms of Christianity.

Traditionally treated as second-class citizens, indigenous groups mostly live on the least productive land in the state, with the least amount of government services or infrastructure. Many indigenous communities rely on subsistence farming and have no running water or electricity, and it was frustration over lack of political power and their historical mistreatment that fueled the Zapatista rebellion, putting a spotlight on the region's distinct inequities.

Today, long-standing indigenous ways of life are challenged both by evangelical Christianity – opposed to many traditional animist-Catholic practices and the abuse of alcohol in religious rituals – and by the Zapatista movement, which rejects traditional leadership hierarchies and is raising the rights and profile of women. Many highland indigenous people have emigrated to the Lacandón Jungle to clear new land, or to Mexican and US cities in search of work.

Despite all obstacles, indigenous identities and self-respect survive. Indigenous people may be suspicious of outsiders, and may resent interference in their religious observances or other aspects of their life, but if treated with due respect they are likely to respond in kind.

of San Cristóbal, is the center for some unique religious practices. It's an interesting place to visit, but do be aware of local sensibilities, as locals guard their privacy.

Chamulan men wear loose homespun tunics of white wool (sometimes, in cool weather, thicker black wool), but *cargo-holders* – those with important religious and ceremonial duties – wear a sleeveless black tunic and a white scarf on the head. Chamulan women wear fairly plain white or blue blouses and/or shawls and woolen skirts.

Sunday is the weekly market, when people from the hills stream into the village to shop, trade and visit the main church.

A corresponding number of tourist buses also stream in, so you might prefer to come another day (though due to local superstitions, there are fewer worshippers on Wednesdays).

## ◉ Sights

★ **Templo de San Juan** CHURCH
(M$25) Standing beside the main plaza, Chamula's main church is a ghostly white, with a vividly painted arch of green and blue. Inside the darkened sanctuary, hundreds of flickering candles, clouds of copal incense, and worshippers kneeling with their faces to the pine-needle-carpeted floor make a powerful impression. Chamulans revere San

Juan Bautista (St John the Baptist) above Christ. NOTE: It is strictly forbidden to take photos in the church. Please do not abuse the privilege of entering.

## ℹ️ Getting There & Away

From San Cristóbal, combis to San Juan Chamula (M$18) leave from spots on Calles Honduras and Utrilla frequently. It's best to come with a guide.

---

# Palenque

📞 916 / POP 43,000 / ELEV 60M

Swathed in morning jungle mists and echoing to a dawn chorus of howler monkeys and parrots, the mighty Maya temples of Palenque are deservedly one of the top destinations of Chiapas and one of the best examples of Maya architecture in all of Mexico. By contrast, modern Palenque town, a few kilometers to the east, is a sweaty, humdrum place without much appeal except as a jumping-off point for the ruins and tours to the Lacandón jungle. Many prefer to base themselves at one of the forest hideouts along the road between the town and the ruins, including the grungy travelers' hangout of El Panchán.

## History

The name Palenque (Palisade) is Spanish and has no relation to the city's ancient name, which may have been Lakamha (Big Water). Palenque was first occupied around 100 BCE, and flourished from around 630 CE to around 740. The city rose to prominence under the ruler Pakal, who reigned from 615 CE to 683. Archaeologists have determined that Pakal is represented by hieroglyphics of sun and shield, and he is also referred to as Sun Shield (Escudo Solar). He lived to the then-incredible age of 80.

Pakal's son Kan B'alam II (r 684–702), who is represented in hieroglyphics by the jaguar and the serpent (and is also called Jaguar Serpent II), continued Palenque's expansion and artistic development. During Kan B'alam II's reign, Palenque extended its zone of control to the Río Usumacinta, but was challenged by the rival Maya city of Toniná, 65km south. Kan B'alam's brother and successor, K'an Joy Chitam II (Precious Peccary), was captured by forces from Toniná in 711, and probably executed there. Palenque enjoyed a resurgence between 722 and 736, however, under Ahkal Mo' Nahb' III (Turtle Macaw Lake), who added many substantial buildings.

After 900 CE, Palenque was largely abandoned. It was not until 1837, when John L Stephens, an amateur archaeology enthusiast from New York, reached Palenque with artist Frederick Catherwood, that the site was insightfully investigated. Another century passed before Alberto Ruz Lhuillier, the tireless Mexican archaeologist, uncovered Pakal's hidden crypt in 1952. Today it continues to yield fascinating and beautiful secrets – most recently, a 1500-year-old mask depicting Pakal was uncovered in Palenque's El Palacio complex.

## 👁️ Sights

Hwy 199 meets Palenque's main street, Avenida Juárez, at the **Glorieta de la Cabeza Maya** (Maya Head Statue), a roundabout with a large statue of a Maya chieftain's head, at the west end of the town. The main ADO bus station is here, and Juárez heads 1km east from this intersection to the central square, **El Parque**.

A few hundred meters south of the Maya head, the paved road to the Palenque ruins, 7.5km away, diverges west off Hwy 199. This road passes the site museum after about 6.5km, then winds on about 1km further uphill to the **main entrance to the ruins** (Upper Entrance).

**Museo de Sitio**  MUSEUM
(Carretera Palenque–Ruinas Km 6.5; with ruins ticket free; ⊙9am-4:30pm Tue-Sun) Palenque's site museum is well worth a wander, displaying finds from the site and interpreting, in English and Spanish, Palenque's history. Highlights include a the copy of the lid of Pakal's sarcophagus (depicting his rebirth as the maize god, encircled by serpents, mythical monsters and glyphs recounting his reign) and finds from Templo XXI.

**Ancient Palenque**
The ruins of ancient **Palenque** (M$75, plus M$35 national park entry fee; ⊙8am-5pm, last entry 4:30pm) stand at the precise point where the first hills rise out of the Gulf coast plain, and the dense jungle covering these hills forms an evocative backdrop to Palenque's exquisite Maya architecture. Hundreds of ruined buildings are spread over 15 sq km, but only a fairly compact central area has been excavated. Everything you see here was built without metal tools, pack animals or the wheel.

# Palenque Ruins

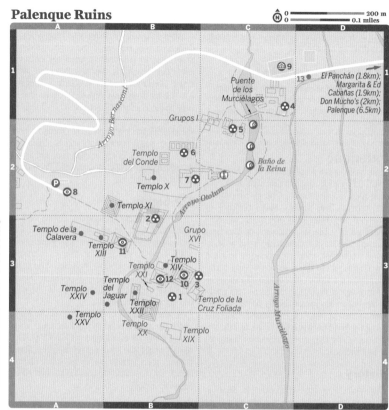

Palenque Ruins map

## Palenque Ruins

The forest around these temples is still home to howler monkeys, toucans and ocelots, and is part of Parque Nacional Palenque (a national park for which you must pay a separate admission fee at Km 4.5 on the road to the ruins).

Opening time is a good time to visit, when it's cooler and not too crowded, and morning mist may still be wrapping the temples in a picturesque haze. Refreshments, hats and souvenirs are available outside the main entrance. Vendors line many of the paths through the ruins.

Official site guides are available by the entrance and **ticket office**. Two Maya guide associations offer informative two-hour tours for up to seven people, which cost M$800 in Spanish or M$1000 in English, French, German or Italian. French, German and Italian speakers may have to wait a bit longer as there are fewer guides available.

### Exploring the Ruins

As you enter the site, a line of temples rises in front of the jungle on your right, culminating about 100m ahead at the **Templo de las Inscripciones** (Temple of the Inscriptions), the tallest and most stately of Palenque's buildings. From the top, interior stairs lead down into the tomb of Pakal (now closed to visitors indefinitely, to avoid further damage to its murals from the humidity inevitably exuded by visitors). Pakal's jewel-bedecked skeleton and jade mosaic death mask were relocated from the tomb to Mexico City, and the tomb was re-created in the Museo Nacional de Antropología. The priceless death mask was stolen in an elaborate heist in 1985 (though recovered a few years afterward), but the carved stone sarcophagus lid remains in the closed tomb – you can see a replica in the site museum.

Diagonally opposite the Templo de las Inscripciones is **El Palacio** (The Palace), a large structure divided into four main courtyards, with a maze of corridors and rooms. Built and modified piecemeal over 400 years from the 5th century on, it was probably the residence of Palenque's rulers.

Keep following the path over a bridge and up some stairs; go left at the 'Y' and you'll soon reach the **Grupo de las Cruces** (Group of the Crosses). Soon after the death of his father, Pakal's son Kan B'alam II (r 684–702) started designing the temples here. The **Templo del Sol** (Temple of the Sun), to the west, has the best-preserved roofcomb at Palenque. Nearby, steep steps climb to the **Templo de la Cruz** (Temple of the Cross), the most impressive in this group.

South of the Grupo de las Cruces is the **Acrópolis Sur**, where archaeologists have recovered some finds in recent excavations. It appears to have been constructed as an extension of the Grupo de las Cruces, but this area was closed at research time and unfortunately will probably remain closed for a few more years.

Follow the path north and back down to the river; you'll eventually reach the **Juego de Pelota** (Ball Court) and, behind it, the handsome and blissfully souvenir-free buildings of **Grupo Norte** (Northern Group). After a visit here you can follow a steep path down to mildly interesting **Grupo II**, but better yet double back to the original path and take it across the river again and down a series of steep stairs, eventually reaching the **Grupo de los Murciélagos** (Bat Group). You'll then cross a pretty bridge with a view of a small waterfall – now head up a short way to Grupo II and finally exit via the back way (this exit is open until 4pm only).

## ☞ Tours

**Palenque Guides**                                    TOURS
(1½ hr tour for up to 7 people in English/Spanish US$95/M$1300) A good guide brings the ruins to life. A bad guide can put a damp cloud over your visit. On the trail up to the ruins, you'll pass by dozens of people (including children) claiming to be guides. It's best to wait until you reach the entry gate and take an official guide. Note that prices are rather flexible!

## 🛏 Sleeping

The first choice to make is whether you want to stay in or out of Palenque town. While Palenque town hosts traffic and commerce, the surrounding area, especially between the town and the ruins, offers some magical spots where howler monkeys romp in the tree canopy and unseen animals chirp after dark. The compound of **El Panchán** (Carretera Palenque–Ruinas Km 4.5) is a traveler favorite, with mainly low-key, grungy budget *cabañas* nestled in the stream-crossed jungle and an active night scene at the one restaurant. Frequent daytime combis between town and the ruins will drop you off and pick you up anywhere along this road.

Except for the leafy La Cañada area in the west, Palenque town is not particularly attractive, but if you stay here you'll have plenty of restaurants and services nearby.

---

## 🛏 In Town

**Hotel Museo Xibalba**                          HOTEL $$
(☏916-345-04-11; www.hotelxibalba.com; Merle Green 9, La Cañada; r from M$850; 🅿❄@🛜) Located in the tranquil neighborhood of La Cañada, this midrange hotel is quirky, if okay value. It offers 35 pleasant, clean rooms, with colourful bedspreads. The common areas have rock-accented architectural details and a replica of the lid from Pakal's sarcophagus (at the time of research, a 'museum' was being constructed to house Mayan replicas).

**Hotel Maya Rue**                               HOTEL $$
(☏916-345-07-43; Aldama s/n; d/tr/f M$900/1000/1100; ❄@🛜) The nearest thing Palenque has to 'boutique' accommodations. Tree-trunk beams, dramatic lighting and

impressive black-and-white photographs hanging from the walls add a dose of style to this 13-room offering combining traditional materials and industrial chic. Some rooms have shaded private balconies, but all are spacious and come with cable TV.

**Hotel Maya Tulipanes** HOTEL **$$$**
(☎916-345-02-01; www.mayatulipanes.com.mx; Cañada 6, La Cañada; d from M$1700; ☞❄🛜🏊) Entered through a muraled foyer, this spot has plain, comfortable, air-conditioned rooms with wrought-iron double beds and minimalist decor. It's designed around a pretty garden with a small pool and a restaurant.

## 🛏 Outside Town

★**Margarita & Ed Cabañas** GUESTHOUSE **$**
(☎916-348-69-90; www.margaritaandedcabanas.blogspot.com; Carreterra Palenque-Ruinas Km 4.5, El Panchán; cabañas M$285, r with fan M$320-410, s/d with air-con M$480/570; 🅿❄) With the most spotless digs in the jungle, Margarita has welcomed travelers to her exceptionally homey place for decades. Bright, clean and cheerful rooms have good mosquito netting, and the more rustic screened *cabañas* are well kept too, with reading lights and private bathrooms. There's free drinking water, a book exchange, and a lovely newer building with super-spacious rooms.

**Cabaña Safari** CABAÑAS **$**
(☎916-345-00-26; Carretera Palenque-Ruinas Km 1; r M$1200, campsites with gear M$150; 🅿❄🛜🏊) Fourteen enjoyable, jungly *palapa*-roofed *cabañas* with air-con and private porches. Rocks, tree branches and wall murals give personality to the spacious (including some two-level) rooms. There's a plunge pool, temascal and full restaurant (open 7am to 10pm).

It's better value in low season when the price almost halves.

★**Hotel La Aldea** HOTEL **$$**
(☎916-345-16-93; www.hotellaaldea.net; Carretera Palenque-Ruinas Km 2.8; r M$1500; 🅿❄🛜🏊) The four-star Aldea has 35 large, beautiful and bright *palapa*-roofed rooms set amid lovely grounds. Each room has an outside terrace with hammock and easy chair. It's a simple, stylish place, with a peaceful hilltop restaurant and a wonderful pool area with two places for dipping! There are no TVs,

making it an ideal place to get away from it all.

**Chan-Kah Resort Village** RESORT **$$$**
(☎916-345-11-34; www.chan-kah.com.mx; Carretera Palenque-Ruinas Km 3; r/ste incl breakfast M$2450/4650; 🅿❄❄@🛜🏊) This large, quality resort on the road to the ruins is an ideal choice for families. It has arty, well-spaced wood-and-stone cottages, some of which have four beds, and all come with generous bathrooms, ceiling fans, terrace and air-con. Kids and swimmers will also love the Chan-Kah's stupendous multilayer 70m stone-lined swimming pool in lush jungle gardens.

★**Boutique Hotel Quinta Chanabnal** BOUTIQUE HOTEL **$$$**
(☎916-345-53-20; www.quintachanabnal.com; Carretera Palenque-Ruinas Km 2.2; r US$177-413; 🅿❄🛜🏊) The Maya-inspired architecture and impeccable style and service at this decadent boutique hotel will leave you swooning. Enter through heavy wood doors (carved by local artisans) into spacious stone-floor suites that contain majestically draped four-poster beds, outlandish Mexican art and cavernous bathrooms. Water features on the premises include a creek, a small lagoon and a natural rock, multitiered swimming pool.

Massages, a temascal and a fine restaurant are available. The Italian owner, Rafael, is a Maya expert and also speaks German, French, English and Spanish.

## 🍴 Eating

Palenque is definitely not the gastronomic capital of Mexico. There's a decent variety of restaurants, though some are laughably overpriced. La Cañada is the most pleasant spot for eating.

## 🍴 In Town

★**Café Jade** INTERNATIONAL **$**
(☎916-688-00-15; Prolongación Hidalgo 1; breakfast M$67-132, mains M$87-130; ◷7am-11pm; 🛜🌱) This very cool bamboo construction has indoor and outdoor seating and is one of the most popular places in town. Has fabulous staff, and serves good breakfasts, some Chiapan specialties and international traveler classics such as burgers. There is a reasonable number of vegetarian options and really good fresh juices too. Fast wi-fi to boot.

**El Huachinango Feliz**                    SEAFOOD $$
(🗹916-129-82-31; Hidalgo s/n; mains M$130-200;
⊗8am-11pm) A popular, atmospheric res-
taurant in the leafy La Cañada neighbor-
hood. It has an attractive front patio with
plastic chairs and umbrellas, and there's
also an upstairs covered terrace. Seafood is
the specialty here: order seafood soup, sea-
food cocktails, grilled fish that's beautifully
crunchy on the outside and soft on the in-
side, or shrimp served 10 different ways. The
service can be slow but the food is worth the
wait.

★**Monte Verde**                           ITALIAN $$
(mains M$120-290; ⊗2-10:30pm Sun-Tue, Thu &
Fri, to 11pm Sat) There's a real Mediterranean
vibe to this Italian restaurant tucked away
in the forest (do a bit of bird- and mon-
key-watching while waiting for your lunch!),
and though most people go for the delicious
thin-crust pizzas, the meat and pasta dishes are worthy of your time. Try the seafood
tagliatelle piled high with giant prawns and
you'll leave happy.

Frequent live music in the evenings.

**La Selva**                               MEXICAN $$
(🗹916-345-17-42; Av 7a Poniente Sur s/n; mains
M$85-220; ⊗11:30am-10:30pm) A small, neat
and slightly upscale (for Palenque anyway)
restaurant serving up well-prepared steaks,
seafood, salads and *antojitos* (snacks) un-
der an enormous *palapa* roof, with jun-
gle-themed murals at the back. Known
for its *empanadas de camarón* (shrimp
empanadas).

## ✖ Outside Town

**Don Mucho's**                       INTERNATIONAL $
(🗹916-112-83-38; Carretera Palenque-Ruinas Km
4.5, El Panchán; mains M$70-185; ⊗7am-1am Tue-
Thu, to 2am Fri, to 3am Sat, to midnight Sun & Mon)
In El Panchán, popular Don Mucho's pro-
vides great-value meals in a jungly setting,
with a candlelit ambience at night. Busy
waiters bring pasta, fish, meat, plenty of *an-
tojitos* (typical Mexican snacks), and pizzas
(cooked in a purpose-built Italian-designed
wood-fired oven).

★**Restaurante Bajlum**               MEXICAN $$$
(🗹916-107-85-18; mains M$270-370; ⊗2-10pm)
Creative and stunningly presented Maya
gastronomy fills the menu at this upmarket
but inviting restaurant. The house specials
include the delicious rabbit with 'jungle
herbs' and duck with orange. Much of the

produce is locally sourced and whatever you
order, the owner is sure to come over and
explain the story behind each dish. Impressive cocktail list.

It's a little tucked away down a side lane
on the left shortly before the ruins. Cash
only.

## ℹ Information

Both of the following banks change dollars and
euros (bring a copy of your passport).

**Banco Azteca** (Av Juárez, btwn Allende &
Aldama; ⊗9am-9pm)

**Bancomer** (Av Juárez 96; ⊗8:30am-4pm Mon-
Fri) Also has an ATM.

**Médica Palenque** (Clínica Palenque; 🗹916-
407-15-01; Velasco Suárez 33; ⊗9am-1pm &
2-6pm) Sometimes English-speaking doctors.

**Post Office** (Independencia s/n; ⊗8am-5pm
Mon-Fri, 10am-2pm Sat)

**Tourist Information Office** (cnr Av Juárez &
Calle Abasolo; ⊗9am-9pm Mon-Sat, to 1pm
Sun) The state tourism office's help center is
thin on the ground for hefty materials, though
it has regional and transportation information,
and sometimes maps. However, more accurate
information is normally available from hotel
staff.

## ℹ Getting There & Away

**AIR**

Palenque's **airport** (PQM) has twice-weekly service to Mexico City via Interjet. Otherwise, the
closest major airport is Villahermosa; ADO runs
a direct airport service (M$350) in comfortable
minibuses.

CHIAPAS & TABASCO PALENQUE

---

## ℹ SAFETY

Whichever direction you come from, it's
safer to travel to Palenque in daylight
hours as blockades (and in the past,
armed holdups) along roads leading to
Palenque are not unheard of. At the time
of research, larger buses were not trav-
elling between Ocosingo to Palenque
(taking an alternative, and much longer
but safer, route), though the tour companies were, by keeping daily check on
the status of any flare-ups. In the past,
there have also been reports of thefts
on the night bus from Mérida. When
taking buses along these routes, consider stowing valuables in the checked
luggage compartment.

## BUS

In a spacious location behind the Maya head statue, **ADO** (www.ado.com.mx) has the main bus terminal, with deluxe and 1st-class services, an ATM and left-luggage facilities; it's also used by OCC (1st class). It's a good idea to buy your outward bus ticket a day in advance. Note that due to security issues buses are not currently running direct to Ocosingo and most companies are routing buses through Villahermosa instead.

**AEXA** (www.autobusesaexa.com.mx; Av Juárez 159), with 1st-class buses, and Cardesa (2nd class) is about 300m east on Avenida Juárez.

**Línea Comitán Lagos de Montebello** (☑ 916-345-12-60; Velasco Suárez, btwn Calles 6a & 7a Poniente Norte), west of Palenque market, runs hourly vans to Benemérito de las Américas (M$150) 10 times daily, with most continuing around the Carretera Fronteriza to the Lagos de Montebello (M$330, seven hours to Tziscao) and Comitán (M$380, eight hours).

## COLECTIVOS

**Vans to Ocosingo** (M$80) wait on Calle 5a Poniente Sur and leave when full. The route is prone to security issues and vans do not always go on the most direct road. Be prepared for canceled services or very circuitous routing.

Most people do the Carretera Fronteriza (including Lacanjá Chansayab, Bonampak, Yaxchilán and Benemérito de las Américas) on a tour from Palenque or San Cristóbel. If you do decide to do it alone, it's doable, though expect to spend many hours in the crowded vans. Many combis for destinations along the Carretera Fronteriza and for Pico de Oro leave from an outdoor *colectivo* **terminal** just south of the ADO bus station.

Vans operated by **Transportes Pajchiltic** (Av 15 de Marzo) run to Metzabok (M$120, three hours) and Nahá (M$120, four hours) whenever they're full (morning is best). Transportation back again often leaves in the middle of the night.

## ℹ️ Getting Around

Taxis charge from M$55 (up to M$70 at night) to El Panchán or Maya Bell, and M$60 to the ruins. Combis (M$25) from the center ply the ruins road until dark. **Radio Taxis Santo Domingo** (☑ 916-345-01-26) has on-call service. There's a **taxi stand** on El Parque.

# Bonampak, Yaxchilán & the Carretera Fronteriza

Close to the Guatemala border, the ancient Maya cities of Bonampak and Yaxchilán might not be the largest Maya ruins, but one thing's for sure: they're certainly among the most wildly romantic. Fringed by the Lacandón Jungle, the area is characterized by bright tropical birds flitting between crumbling monuments and monkeys hooting from the trees. Bonampak, famous for its frescoes, is 152km by road from Palenque; the bigger and more important Yaxchilán, with a peerless jungle setting beside the broad and swift Río Usumacinta, is 173km by road, then about 22km by boat.

Access to Bonampak and Yaxchilán is via the Carretera Fronteriza, which also gives handy access to a number of excellent ecotourism projects, dreamy waterfalls, Lacandón villages and lesser-known archaeological ruins.

## ℹ️ Information

Drug and human trafficking are facts of life in this border region, and the Carretera Fronteriza more or less encircles the main area of Zapatista rebel activity and support. Expect a few military checkpoints along the road and from this area to Palenque and Comitán. For your own security, it's best to be off the Carretera Fronteriza before dusk. Little, if any, public transportation ever runs after dark. Aim to get to all border crossings with Guatemala early in the day.

## BUSES FROM PALENQUE

| DESTINATION | FARE (M$) | TIME (HR) | FREQUENCY (PER DAY) |
| --- | --- | --- | --- |
| Campeche | 437-470 | 5-5½ | 5 ADO |
| Cancún | 740-1458 | 12-13½ | 4 ADO |
| Mérida | 387-688 | 8 | 5 ADO |
| San Cristóbal de las Casas | 188-384 | 8-9 | 9 ADO, 4 AEXA |
| Tulum | 476-1074 | 10-11 | 4 ADO |
| Villahermosa | 95-226 | 2½ | frequent ADO & AEXA |
| Villahermosa airport | 350 | 2¼ | 4 ADO |

## EXPLORE MORE OF CHIAPAS

Here are some of our favorite DIY adventures:

➡ A respite from both the steamy lowland jungle and the chilly highlands, the bustling market town of Ocosingo sits in a gorgeous and broad temperate valley midway between San Cristóbal and Palenque. The impressive Maya ruins of Toniná are just a few kilometers away.

➡ Two spectacular water attractions – the thundering cascades of Agua Azul and the 35m jungle waterfall of Misol-Ha – are both short detours off the Ocosingo–Palenque road.

➡ The largest Lacandón Maya village, Lacanjá Chansayab, is 12km from Bonampak. Its family compounds are scattered around a wide area, many of them with creeks or even the Río Lacanjá flowing past their grassy grounds.

➡ The temperate pine and oak forest along the Guatemalan border east of Chinkultic is dotted with over 50 small lakes of varied hues, called the Lagos de Montebello. The nearby Chinkultic ruins add to the mystery.

➡ Ringed by rainforest 140km southeast of Ocosingo in the Reserva de la Biosfera Montes Azules, Laguna Miramar is one of Mexico's most remote and exquisite lakes. Rock ledges on small islands make blissful wading spots, while petroglyphs and a sea-turtle cave are reachable by canoe, which you can rent from the community tourism project in Emiliano Zapata.

➡ The luxuriant cloud forests of Reserva de la Biosfera El Triunfo, high in the remote Sierra Madre de Chiapas, are a bird-lover's paradise.

➡ The large Reserva de la Biosfera La Encrucijada protects a 1448-sq-km strip of coastal lagoons, sand bars and wetlands.

➡ Set 12km east of Tuxtla Gutiérrez on the way to San Cristóbal, Chiapa de Corzo is a small and attractive colonial town with an easygoing, provincial air. Set on the north bank of the broad Río Grijalva, it's the main starting point for trips into the Cañón del Sumidero.

➡ The dramatic sinkhole Sima de Las Cotorras punches 160m wide and 140m deep into the earth. It's about 1½ hours from Tuxtla Gutiérrez.

In the rainy months of September and October, rivers are usually too swollen for safe swimming.

Don't forget insect repellent; dengue fever has been reported here over the last couple of years.

### ℹ Getting There & Away

The Carretera Fronteriza (Hwy 307) is a good paved road running parallel to the Mexico–Guatemala border, all the way from Palenque to the Lagos de Montebello. From Palenque, Autotransporte Chamoán runs vans to Frontera Corozal (M$145, 2½ to three hours, every 40 minutes from 4am to 5pm), leaving from the outdoor *colectivo* terminal near the Maya head statue and south of the bus station. Use them for visits to Bonampak and Lacanjá Chansayab, because upon request they'll stop at the junction closest to the ruins, known as Crucero Bonampak (M$95, two hours), instead of the San Javier stop on the highway.

Línea Comitán Lagos de Montebello, west of Palenque market, runs hourly vans to Benemérito de las Américas (M$150) 10 times daily, with most continuing around the Carretera Fronteriza to the Lagos de Montebello (M$330, seven hours to Tziscao) and Comitán (M$380, eight hours).

Both companies stop at San Javier (M$90, two hours), the turnoff for Lacanjá Chansayab and Bonampak, 140km from Palenque, and at Cruce-ro Corozal (M$110, 2½ hours), the intersection for Frontera Corozal. For Cascada Welib-Já and Nueva Palestina, take any Carretera Fronteriza–bound combi from Palenque.

### Palenque to Bonampak

⭐ Cascada de las Golondrinas   WATERFALL
(Nueva Palestina; M$35, campsite M$100; ⏱ restaurant 9am-4pm; 🅿) A lovely water feature tucked 10km off the highway, where two rivers cascade dramatically from a high point of 35m and you can swim in clear blue water during the dry season. A wooden boardwalk crosses the outflow, and at dusk

## ℹ️ DAY TRIPS & ORGANIZED TOURS

Organized tours can be helpful in this region if you have limited time and aren't driving.

Day trips to Bonampak and Yaxchilán (M$1050 to M$1500) usually include two meals (breakfast and lunch) and transportation to both in an air-conditioned van – a good deal since independent transportation to both is time-consuming and tours include the Bonampak transportation fee; two-day trips (M$2000 to M$3000) include an overnight stay at Lacanjá Chansayab and jungle hiking or rafting.

In Palenque, Transportador Turística Scherrer & Barb (☑ cell 916-1032153; fermerida_69@hotmail.com; Hotel Wayak, Central Poniente 2) organizes more off-the-beaten-path trips to the region, including the Lacandón villages of Nahá and Metzabok and waterfalls in the area; San Cristóbal–based SendaSur (☑ 967-678-39-09; www.sendasur.com.mx; 5 de Febrero 29) 🍃 can help with reservations for independent travelers.

hundreds of swallows duck in to bed down in a cave beneath the falls, streaming out at dawn.

⭐ **Cascada Welib-Já**          WATERFALL

(M$30; ⏱ 8am-7pm; 🅿️) Thirty kilometers from Palenque, these 25m-high curtains of water aren't the most-dramatic water features in the area, but the turquoise river pools make excellent swimming spots and there are few people. It's in a gorgeous setting on the edge of a jungle swathe and you can hear howler monkeys as you swim. There's a fun cross-river zip-line (M$100) and a simple restaurant. From Palenque, take a combi to the well-signed highway entrance (M$25, 30 minutes); it's a 700m walk in.

The well-organized community members are keen to help with directions and activities. Life jackets are available for rent and in high season there's a life guard.

## Bonampak

It's setting in dense jungle kept Bonampak, one of the outstanding archaeological sites of Chiapas, hidden from the outside world until 1946. The site is most renowned for its vivid frescoes, which really bring the Maya world to life. Getting here is a bit of a hassle but the reward is well worthwhile. The ruins are spread over 2.4 sq km, but all the main ruins stand around the rectangular Gran Plaza.

The Bonampak site abuts the Reserva de la Biosfera Montes Azules, and is rich in wildlife. Keep your eyes peeled for monkeys and macaws.

### 👁️ Sights

The most impressive surviving monuments at the ruins (☑ 961-612-83-60; community entry

M$30, ruins M$70; ⏱ 8am-5pm) were built under Chan Muwan II, a nephew of Yaxchilán's Itzamnaaj B'alam II, who acceded to Bonampak's throne in 776 CE. The 6m-high Stele 1 in the Gran Plaza depicts Chan Muwan II holding a ceremonial staff at the height of his reign. He also features in Stele 2 and Stele 3 on the Acrópolis, which rises from the south end of the plaza.

However, it's the vivid frescoes inside the modest-looking Templo de las Pinturas (Edificio 1) that have given Bonampak its fame – and its name, which means 'Painted Walls' in Yucatecan Maya. Some archaeologists theorize that the murals depict a battle between Bonampak and the city of Sak T'zi', which is believed to be Plan de Ayutla.

Diagrams outside the temple help interpret the murals, which are the finest known from pre-Hispanic America, but which have weathered badly since their discovery. (Early visitors even chucked kerosene over the walls in an attempt to bring out the colors!)

### ℹ️ Getting There & Away

Bonampak is 12km from San Javier, the turnoff town on the Carretera Fronteriza. If you get dropped off at San Javier instead of Crucero Bonampak (8km further in), taxis from San Javier charge M$30.

Get ready to open your wallet: the community charges M$30 per person to enter the town of Lacanjá, and private vehicles are prohibited beyond the Crucero Bonampak, where van drivers charge an exorbitant M$350 to M$400 round trip per van to the ruins and back.

## Yaxchilán

Jungle-shrouded Yaxchilán (yas-chee-*lan*) has a terrific setting above a horseshoe loop in the Río Usumacinta. The control this location gave it over river commerce, and a series of successful alliances and conquests, made Yaxchilán one of the most important Classic Maya cities in the Usumacinta region. Archaeologically, Yaxchilán is famed for its ornamented facades and roofcombs, and its impressive stone lintels carved with conquest and ceremonial scenes. A flashlight is helpful for exploring parts of the site.

*Saraguatos* (howler monkeys) inhabit the tall trees here, and are an evocative highlight. You'll almost certainly hear their visceral roars, and you stand a good chance of seeing some. Spider monkeys, and occasionally red macaws, can also be spotted here at times.

### ◉ Sights

As you walk toward the **ruins** (M$70; ☉8am-5pm, last entry 4pm), a signed path to the right leads up to the **Pequeña Acrópolis**, a group of ruins on a small hilltop – you can visit this later. Staying on the main path, you soon reach the mazelike passages of **El Laberinto (Edificio 19)**, built between 742 CE and 752, during the interregnum between Itzamnaaj B'alam II and Pájaro Jaguar IV. Dozens of bats shelter under the structure's roof today. From this complicated two-level building you emerge at the northwest end of the extensive **Gran Plaza**.

Though it's difficult to imagine anyone here ever wanting to be any hotter than they already were, **Edificio 17** was apparently a sweat house. About halfway along the plaza, Stele 1, flanked by weathered sculptures of a crocodile and a jaguar, shows Pájaro Jaguar IV in a ceremony that took place in 761 CE. **Edificio 20**, from the time of Itzamnaaj B'alam III, was the last significant structure built at Yaxchilán; its lintels are now in Mexico City.

An imposing stairway climbs from Stele 1 to **Edificio 33**, the best-preserved temple at Yaxchilán, with about half of its roofcomb intact. The final step in front of the building is carved with ball-game scenes, and splendid relief carvings embellish the undersides of the lintels. Inside is a statue of Pájaro Jaguar IV, minus his head, which he lost to treasure-seeking 19th-century timber cutters.

### ❶ Getting There & Away

*Lanchas* (motorboats) take 30 to 40 minutes running downstream from Frontera Corozal, and 40 minutes to return. The boat companies are in a thatched building near the Frontera Corozal *embarcadero* (jetty), all charging about the same price for trips. The return journey with two hours at the ruins for one to four people costs M$1400, five to seven people M$1700 or eight to 10 people M$2200. *Lanchas* normally leave frequently from 7am to 3pm or so; try to hook up with other travelers or a tour group to share costs.

# TABASCO

They say that the state of Tabasco has more water than land, and looking at all the lagoons, rivers and wetlands on the map you can certainly see why, especially during the rainy season. It's always hot and sweaty here, but marginally less so when you catch a breeze along the Gulf of Mexico or venture into the southern hills. Travelers to Villahermosa and coastal Tabasco should note the region is subject to seasonal floods, though few travelers linger in Tabasco longer than it takes to see the outstanding Olmec stone sculpture in Villahermosa's Parque-Museo La Venta. Located north of Chiapas and abutting the Gulf of Mexico, Tabasco is the site of extensive onshore and offshore oil exploitation by Mexico's state oil company (Pemex), which accounts for more than half of the state's economy and nearly half of its jobs. In 2018, oil prices plummeted, gang violence soared and Tabasco became one of the nation's more troubled states.

## Villahermosa

📞 993 / POP 353,000

This sprawling, flat, hot and humid oil city, with more than a quarter of Tabasco's population, was never the 'beautiful town' its name implies. What it lacks in the looks department, though, it makes up for with its buzzy atmosphere, welcoming inhabitants and the best range of hotels and restaurants in Tabasco. The city also makes a good base for day trips to some of the state's more alluring attractions.

### ◉ Sights

★ **Parque-Museo La Venta**                    MUSEUM
(www.iec.tabasco.gob.mx/content/parque-museo-de-la-venta; Av Ruíz Cortines; M$50; ☉8am-4pm; 🅿🚻) This fascinating outdoor park and museum was created in 1958, when petroleum exploration threatened the highly important ancient Olmec settlement of La

Venta in western Tabasco. Archaeologists moved the site's most significant finds, including three colossal stone heads, to Villahermosa. There's also a zoo but the cages are shabby and depressing; this can be avoided when making your way to the sculpture trail.

★ **Museo Regional de Antropología** MUSEUM
(www.iec.tabasco.gob.mx/content/museo-antro pologia; Periférico Carlos Pellicer; M$23; ⊘9am-5pm Tue-Sun; P) Villahermosa's excellent regional anthropology museum (even the shiny modern building it's housed in is impressive) holds some stunning exhibits on Olmec, Maya, Nahua and Zoque cultures in Tabasco – including Tortuguero #6, the infamous tablet *solely* responsible for the dire 'end of world' predictions forecast for December 21, 2012, which just goes to show that you can't believe everything you read! It's in the CICOM complex, a 15-minute walk from Zona Luz and just south of the Paseo Tabasco bridge.

## 🛏 Sleeping & Eating

**One Villahermosa Centro** BUSINESS HOTEL $$
(☑ 993-131-71-00; www.onehotels.com; Carranza 101; r incl breakfast from M$1204; ❄ ☏) A large, business-style hotel, this one wins points for attentive staff and a super-central location. Rooms are what you'd expect for the price – big and comfortable but lacking much sense of place. Even so, if it's a good night's kip you want, then you won't find a better option downtown.

★ **La Cevichería Tabasco** SEAFOOD $$
(☑ 993-345-00-35; www.facebook.com/lacevicher iatabascov; Francisco José Hernández Mandujano 114; mains M$130-250; ⊘11am-6pm Tue-Fri, from 10am Sat & Sun; ❄) A stellar seafood place just over the river from downtown. With bright murals inside and out and a friendly neighborhood vibe, this busy, and slightly chaotic, place serves seafood dishes that are so arty you might prefer to just gaze in wonder at your meal rather than eat it. The tacos stuffed with marlin are especially impressive.

---

### THE LACANDÓN JUNGLE

Chiapas contains swaths of wild green landscape that have nourished its inhabitants for centuries. But this rich trove of natural resources also makes it a contentious prize in the struggle for its water, lumber and oil and gas reserves.

The Selva Lacandona (Lacandón Jungle), in eastern Chiapas, occupies just 0.25% of Mexico. Yet it contains more than 4300 plant species (about 17% of the Mexican total), 450 butterfly species (42% of the national total), at least 340 bird species (32% of the total) and 163 mammal species (30% of the Mexican total). Among these are such emblematic creatures as the jaguar, red macaw, white turtle, tapir and harpy eagle.

This great fund of natural resources and genetic diversity is the southwest end of the Selva Maya, a 42,300-sq-km corridor of tropical rainforest stretching from Chiapas across northern Guatemala into Belize and the southern Yucatán. But the Lacandón Jungle is shrinking fast, under pressure from ranchers, loggers, oil prospectors, and farmers desperate for land. From around 15,000 sq km in the 1950s, less than 5000 sq km of jungle remains today and it continues to shrink at an alarming rate. Waves of land-hungry settlers deforested the northern third of the Lacandón Jungle by about 1960. Also badly deforested are the far eastern Marqués de Comillas area (settled since the 1970s) and Las Cañadas, between Ocosingo and Montes Azules. Most of what's left is in the Reserva de la Biosfera Montes Azules and the neighboring Reserva de la Biosfera Lacan-tun.

The Mexican government deeded a large section of the land to a small number of Lacandón families in the 1970s, creating tensions with other indigenous communities whose claims were put aside. Land within the region remains incredibly contested. Lacandones and their advocates consider themselves to be an environmentally sensitive indigenous group, defending their property against invasive settlers. Other communities within the reserve, who provide some of the Zapatista rebels' strongest support, view it as an obfuscated land grab and pretext for eviction under the guise of environmental protection. Zapatista supporters also argue that the settlers are using the forests in unsustainable ways, and claim that the government seeks to exploit the forests for bio-prospecting (patenting) traditional plants.

## Coctelería Rock & Roll
SEAFOOD $$

(☑993-334-21-90; Reforma 307; mains M$160-220; ☺10am-10pm) A maelstrom of heat, swirling fans and blaring TVs. Everyone's here for the large and delicious seafood cocktails (though it also has good ceviche and seafood stew) and cheap beer. It's on a pedestrian street across from the Miraflores Hotel, and has 60 years (and three generations of owners) under its belt. A Villahermosa institution if ever there was one.

## ℹ️ Information

Most banks have ATMs and exchange dollars or euros.

**HSBC** (cnr Juárez & Lerdo de Tejada; ☺9am-5pm Mon-Fri) Bank branch on a pedestrianized street.

**Oficina de Convenciones y Visitantes de Tabasco** (OCV; ☑993-310-97-00; www. tabasco.gob.mx/turismo; Plaza Río, 1st Floor, Av Paseo Usumacinta 1504; ☺9am-3pm Mon-Fri) Statewide information.

## ℹ️ Getting There & Away

### AIR

Villahermosa's **Aeropuerto Rovirosa** (Aeropuerto Carlos Rovirosa Pérez; ☑993-356-01-57; www.asur.com.mx; Carretera Villahermosa–Macuspana Km 13) is 13km east of the center, off Hwy 186. Aeroméxico is the major airline; there are numeous daily nonstop flights between Villahermosa and Mexico City, and several other cities.

### BUS & COLECTIVO

Deluxe and 1st-class buses depart from the **ADO bus station** (☑993-312-84-22; Mina 297; 📶), which has wi-fi and 24-hour left luggage and is located 750m north of the Zona Luz.

Transportation to most destinations within Tabasco leaves from here, or other terminals within walking distance north of ADO, including the 2nd-class **Cardesa bus station** (cnr Hermanos Bastar Zozaya & Castillo) and the main 2nd-class bus station, the **Central de Autobuses de Tabasco** (CAT; ☑993-312-29-77; cnr Av Ruíz Cortines & Castillo) on the north side of Avenida Ruíz Cortines (use the pedestrian overpass).

## ℹ️ Getting Around

Comfortable ADO minibuses ferry passengers between the airport and the ADO bus terminal (M$225); they run hourly between 6am and 9pm. Taxis to the center cost around M$280. Alternatively, walk 500m past the airport parking lot for a *colectivo* (M$25) from the Dos Montes

---

### ℹ️ BUS TO PALENQUE

The Villahermosa airport has a handy counter for ADO (www.ado.com.mx), with almost hourly minibuses departing daily to Palenque (M$350, 2¼ hours) between 5:20am and 10:20pm. Check the website for schedules to/from 'Aeropuerto Villahermosa.'

---

taxi stand. These terminate in the market on Carranza, about 1km north of the Zona Luz.

A system of *colectivo* taxis (M$25) provides the backbone of the center's public transit. Private taxis charge around M$50 within the center.

# Comalcalco

☑933 / POP 40,000

The small town of Comalcalco, around 55km northwest of Villahermosa, is a scrappy, low-rise place of little visual appeal. However, just on the outskirts of town is an enjoyably under-visited Maya site that is one of the big attractions of Tabasco. The town is also known for its cacao production and small chocolate factories, some of which are open to the public. Ancient monuments and divine chocolate: what better reason to make the easy day trip from Villahermosa does a person need?

## ⊙ Sights

★**Comalcalco**
ARCHAEOLOGICAL SITE

(www.inah.gob.mx/zonas/9-zona-arqueologica -de-comalcalco; M$60; ☺8am-4pm) Surrounded by jungle and little visited by tourists, the small but impressive Maya ruins of ancient Comalcalco are the most westerly known Maya ruins. Architecturally they're unique due to many of the buildings being constructed of bricks and/or mortar made from oyster shells. Comalcalco was at its peak between 600 and 1000 CE, when it was ruled by the Chontal. It remained an important center of commerce for several more centuries, trading in a wealth of pre-Hispanic luxury goods.

**Hacienda La Luz**
PLANTATION

(☑933-337-11-22; www.haciendalaluz.mx; Bulevar Rovirosa 232; 1hr tour per person from M$100; ☺tours 9am, 11am, 1pm & 3pm) Hacienda La Luz, one of several local plantations making chocolate from home-grown cacao, offers informative guided tours (a basic tour

## EXPLORE MORE OF TABASCO

The following only scratches the surface of the adventures to be had in Tabasco.

➡ While most of the cool artifacts have been moved to the museum in Villahermosa, La Venta (☑ 923-232-04-23; M$50; ☺ 8am-5pm), 128km west of Villahermosa, is still worth a visit.

➡ Up in Tabasco's beautiful and mountainous far southwestern corner, tiny Malpasito (M$50; ☺ 7am-5pm) is the site of mysterious ancient Zoque ruins.

➡ A massive biosphere reserve, Reserva de la Biosfera Pantanos de Centla (M$36; ☺ visitor center Thu-Sun, boat trips daily) offers lakes, marshes, rivers and more.

➡ Explore riverside swimming holes and caves in southern Tabasco, using the town of Teapa, 50km south of Villahermosa, as your base.

is one hour, but longer and more detailed tours are available) round the gardens and cacao plantation (the house is still lived in). You will be shown the traditional methods of turning cacao beans into chocolate, and, yep, the bit you were waiting for, the tour concludes with a chocolate drink. For a tour in English, it's wise to reserve in advance.

### ✕ Eating

There are a number of taco stands and other cheap eats in and around the Parque Benito Juárez García, which is a little to the west of the main road through town. There is also one exceptional place close to the archaeological site.

★ Cocina Chontal                    MEXICAN $
(☑ 933-158-56-96; www.facebook.com/nelly.cor dovamorillo.5; Buenavista; mains M$150-180; ☺ noon-5pm Wed-Sun) Run by the larger-than-life, traditionally dressed Nelly Córdova, this delightful open-air restaurant is located near the archaeological site (ask to cut through the site itself). It is a basic but fun spot and specializes in rekindling half-forgotten traditional Tabasco dishes, including some from the Maya period. These include thick chocolate *moles,* turkey stew and bananas stuffed with beans and pork.

### ❶ Getting There & Away

There are frequent buses (M$100, two hours) to and from Villahermosa. They leave from the main road through town.

# Understand Cancún, Cozumel & the Yucatán

# History

Reminders of the Yucatán's storied past are just about everywhere you turn on the peninsula: from extraordinary ancient Maya ruins and old-world cities to Caste War battleground sites and crumbling *henequén* (sisal) haciendas. Even the relatively new kid on the block, the glitzy resort city of Cancún, has left an indelible mark on history as the region's cradle of mass tourism.

## The Olmec Influence

The jaguar motifs first used by the Olmecs were adopted by successive civilizations throughout Mesoamerica.

Mexico's ancestral civilization arose near the Gulf coast, in the lowlands of southern Veracruz and neighboring Tabasco. These were the Olmecs, who invented a hieroglyphic writing system and erected ceremonial centers for the practice of religious rituals. Best known for the colossal heads they carved from basalt slabs, the Olmecs developed an artistic style highlighted by jaguar motifs.

Even after their demise, aspects of Olmec culture lived on among their neighbors, paving the way for the later accomplishments of Maya art, architecture and science. Borrowing significantly from the Olmecs, the Zapotec culture arose in the highlands of Oaxaca at Monte Albán, and subsequent civilizations at Teotihuacán (near current-day Mexico City) and at El Tajín in Veracruz also show Olmec influence.

## The Maya

Legend has it the peninsula got its name when the Spanish conquistadors asked the indigenous locals what they called their land. The response was 'Yucatán' – Maya for 'We don't understand you.'

Archaeologists believe Maya-speaking people first appeared in (what is now) the highlands of Guatemala around 2500 BCE, and in the following century groups of Maya relocated to the lowlands of the Yucatán Peninsula.

Agriculture played an important role in Maya life. Watching the skies and noting the movements of the planets and stars, the Maya were able to correlate their astronomical observations with the rains and agricultural cycles. As the Maya improved their agricultural skills, their society stratified into various classes. Villages sprang up beneath the jungle canopy and temples were constructed from the abundant limestone. An easily carved substance, limestone allowed the builders to demonstrate a

| TIMELINE | 3114 BCE | 2400 BCE | 1000 BCE–250 CE |
|---|---|---|---|
| | Our current universe is created – at least according to Maya mythology. Archaeologists have even been able to pin down a specific date for the creation: August 13, 3114 BCE. | Maya-speaking farmers arrive in the Yucatán Peninsula. The Olmec culture creates a system of writing. Olmec culture later influences the Zapotec culture. | Pre-Classic period. Maya villages appear in the Yucatán, Chiapas and Guatemala. The Maya become adept farmers and astronomers. The Izapan civilization creates a calendar and writing system. |

high degree of artistic expression. The material could also be made into plaster, upon which artists painted murals to chronicle events.

Local potentates were buried beneath these elaborate temples. As each successive leader had to have a bigger temple, larger platforms were placed upon earlier ones, forming gigantic step pyramids with a thatched shelter on top. Often these temple-pyramids were decorated with huge stylized masks. More and more pyramids were built around large plazas, much in the same manner that common people built their thatched houses facing a common open space. This heralded the flourishing of the Classic Maya civilization.

Over the nearly seven centuries of the Classic Maya period (250–925 CE), the Maya made spectacular intellectual and artistic strides, a legacy that can still be admired today throughout the peninsula and beyond.

The great ceremonial centers at Copán, Tikal, Yaxchilán, Palenque and especially Kaminaljuyú (near present-day Guatemala City) flourished during the early phase of this period. Around 400 CE armies from Teotihuacán invaded the Maya highlands, imposing their rule and their culture for a time, though they were eventually absorbed into the daily life of the Maya.

After 600 CE, at the height of the late Classic period, the Maya lands were ruled not as an empire but as a collection of independent – but also interdependent – city-states. Each of these had its noble house, headed by a king who was the social, political and religious focus of the city's life. This ruler propitiated the gods by shedding his blood in ceremonies where he pierced his tongue or penis with a sharp instrument, and he led his soldiers into battle against rival cities, capturing prisoners for use in human sacrifices.

For a concise but complete account of the ancient cultures of southern Mexico and Guatemala, read *The Maya* by Michael D Coe.

## YUCATÁN'S DINOSAUR-KILLING METEORITE

Most scientists agree that a meteorite hit the Yucatán about 65 million years ago, triggering a series of events that may have caused the dinosaurs and other species to go extinct.

Using seismic monitoring equipment, geologists have found evidence for the existence of such an enormous crater (estimated to be around 200km wide) off the northern coast of the Yucatán, near the port of Chicxulub.

Scientists have theorized that the impact event kicked up enough debris to block out the sun for a decade, which either sparked a global freeze or made the air unbreathable. And now there's new research suggesting that the colossal impact also may have caused a worldwide surge in volcanic activity, which in turn blanketed the Earth's atmosphere with ashes and toxic fumes.

An international research team plans to drill 1500m below the seabed to extract geological samples from the crater. They hope the results of the investigation will once and for all reveal the mystery of why the dinosaurs disappeared from the Earth.

| 250–925 CE | 925–1530 | late 1400s | 1492 |
|---|---|---|---|
| Classic period. It's a time of high society, marked by the invasion of Teotihuacán, the rise of the Puuc, and the eventual collapse of the Classic Maya and the ascendancy of the Toltec. | Post-Classic period. The Toltecs of central Mexico establish their domain at Chichén Itzá, then the Itzáes form the League of Mayapán, which dominates politics in northern Yucatán for 200 years. | Beginning of the end of the post-Classic period. Maya decline hits full tilt, as fractious city-states replace Mayapán rule. Until the coming of the conquistadors, northern Yucatán is riddled with battles and power struggles. | Spanish arrive in the Caribbean, settling momentarily on Hispañola and Cuba, but it will be several hundred years before they truly 'conquer' the region. European diseases will eventually kill 90% of indigenous inhabitants. |

Toward the end of the Classic period, the focus of Maya civilization shifted northward to Yucatán, where new nuclei developed at what is now called Chichén Itzá, Uxmal and Calakmul, giving us the artistic styles known as Puuc, Chenes and Río Bec.

## Post-Classic Period

### The Toltecs

The collapse of Classic Maya civilization is as surprising as it was sudden. It seems as though the upper classes demanded ever more servants, acolytes and laborers, and though the Maya population was expanding rapidly, it did not produce enough farmers to feed everyone. Thus weakened, the Maya were effectively prey to the next wave of invaders from central Mexico.

In the wake of Teotihuacán's demise, the Toltec people emerged as Mexico's new boss, establishing their capital at Tula (north of present-day Mexico City). According to most historians, a Toltec faction, led by a fair-haired king named Topiltzin – the self-proclaimed heir to the title of Quetzalcóatl (Plumed Serpent) – was forced to leave its native land by hostile warrior clans. Quetzalcóatl and his followers retreated to the Gulf coast and sailed eastward to Yucatán, establishing their new base at Uucil-abnal – which would later be renamed Chichén Itzá. The culture at this Toltec-dominated center flourished after the late 10th century, when all the great buildings were constructed, but by 1200 the city was abandoned. Many Mexicans believed, however, that the Plumed Serpent king would someday return from the direction of the rising sun to reclaim his domain at Tula.

### The Itzáes

Forced by invaders to leave their traditional homeland on the Yucatán's Gulf coast, a group called the Itzáes headed southeast into northeastern Guatemala. Some continued to Belize, later making their way north along the coast and into northern Yucatán, where they settled at the abandoned Uucil-abnal around 1220 CE. The Itzá leader proclaimed himself Kukulcán (the Maya name for Quetzalcóatl), as had the city's Toltec founder, and recycled lots of other Toltec lore as well. The Itzáes strengthened the belief in the sacred nature of cenotes (limestone sinkholes that provided the Maya with their water supply), and they even named their new home Chichén Itzá (Mouth of the Well of the Itzáes).

From Chichén Itzá, the ruling Itzáes traveled westward and founded a new capital city at Mayapán, which dominated the political life of northern Yucatán for several centuries. From Mayapán, the Cocom lineage of the Itzáes ruled a fractious collection of Yucatecan city-states until the mid-15th century, when a subject people from Uxmal, the Xiú, overthrew Cocom power. Mayapán was pillaged, ruined and never repopulated. For

Mundo Maya online (http://mundo maya.travel) features articles on Maya cosmology, navigation and agriculture, among other aspects of this incredible ancient civilization.

The elite of the Classic Maya often received enemas of a sweet mead named *balché*. They also thought being cross-eyed was particularly beautiful.

| 1519–21 | 1527 | 1530–1821 | 1542 |
|---|---|---|---|
| Hernán Cortés, first landing on Isla Cozumel, begins making his way along the Gulf coast toward central Mexico, home of the Aztec empire. He captures the Aztec ruler Moctezuma II and conquers Tenochtitlán. | Francisco de Montejo and his son (the Younger) land in Cozumel and then in Xel-Há with the idea of conquering the region. Eventually they return to Mexico City in defeat. | The *encomienda* system basically enslaves the indigenous populations, and friars begin to convert the population in earnest. The Maya blend Christian teachings with their own beliefs, creating a unique belief system. | Francisco de Montejo (the Younger) avenges his father's defeat, establishing the colonial capital at Mérida upon the ruins of the Maya city of T'ho. |

the next century, until the coming of the conquistadors, northern Yucatán was alive with battles among its city-states.

## The New World Order

Led by Christopher Columbus, the Spanish arrived in the Caribbean in 1492 and proceeded to seek a westward passage to Asia. They staged exploratory expeditions to the Yucatán in 1517 and 1518, but hostile locals fiercely resisted their attempts to penetrate Mexico's Gulf coast.

Then Diego Velázquez, the Spanish governor of Cuba, asked his young personal secretary, Hernán Cortés, to lead a new expedition westward. Even though Velázquez subsequently tried to cancel the voyage, Cortés set sail on February 15, 1519, with 11 ships, 550 men and 16 horses.

Landing first at the isle of Cozumel off the Yucatán, the Spaniards were joined by Jerónimo de Aguilar, a Spanish priest who had been shipwrecked there several years earlier. With Aguilar acting as translator and guide, Cortés' force moved around the coastline to Tabasco. After defeating the inhabitants there, the expedition headed inland, winning more battles and some converts to Catholicism in the process.

Central Mexico was then dominated by the Aztec empire from its capital of Tenochtitlán (now Mexico City). The Aztecs, like many other cultures in the area, believed that Quetzalcóatl would one day return from the east, according to most historians, and – conveniently for him – Cortés' arrival coincided with their prophecies of the Plumed Serpent's return. The Aztecs allowed the small Spanish force into the capital, perhaps fearful of angering these strangers who might be gods.

By this time thousands of members of the Aztecs' subject peoples had allied with Cortés, eager to throw off the harsh rule imposed by their overlords. Many Aztecs died of smallpox introduced by the Spanish, and by the time they resolved to make war against Cortés and their subjects, they found themselves outnumbered, though they put up a tremendous fight.

Cortés then conquered central Mexico, after which he turned his attentions to the Yucatán.

## Conquest & the Colonial Period

Despite political infighting among the Yucatecan Maya, conquest by the Spaniards was not easy. The Spanish monarch commissioned Francisco de Montejo (El Adelantado, or the Pioneer) with the task, and he set out from Spain in 1527 accompanied by his son, also named Francisco de Montejo (El Mozo, or the Lad) and a band of men. Landing first at Cozumel, then at Xel-Há on the mainland, the Montejos discovered that the local people wanted nothing to do with them.

The father-and-son team then sailed around the peninsula, quelled unrest in Tabasco in 1530 and established their base near Campeche.

*Chronicle of the Maya Kings and Queens,* by Simon Martin and Nikolai Grube, tells in superbly illustrated detail the histories of 11 of the most important Maya city-states and their rulers.

Check www. sacred-texts. com for good translations of two sacred Maya books, the *Popol Vuh* and *Chilam Balam of Chumayel.*

HISTORY THE NEW WORLD ORDER

| 1562 | 1761 | 1810–41 | 1847–48 |
| --- | --- | --- | --- |
| Franciscan Friar Diego de Landa orders the destruction of 27 codices and more than 5000 idols in Maní, essentially cutting the historic record of the Maya at the root. | Maya Jacinto Canek leads an armed insurrection against the Spanish colonial government; the so-called Canek Rebellion is short-lived but inspires the Maya revolutionary movement in the 19th century. | Beginning of the War of Independence from Spain. Yucatán state joins the newly independent Mexican republic. Yucatán declares independence from Mexico in 1841. | The Caste War erupts. The Maya are whipped solidly at first, retreating to Quintana Roo. They continue to revolt for another 100 years, though an official surrender is signed in 1936. |

They pushed inland to conquer, but after four long, difficult years they were forced to return to Mexico City in defeat.

The younger Montejo took up the cause again, with his father's support, and in 1540 returned to Campeche with his cousin named…Francisco de Montejo. The two Montejos pressed inland with speed and success, allying themselves with the Xiú against the Cocomes, defeating the Cocomes and converting the Xiú to Catholicism.

The Montejos founded Mérida in 1542 and within four years subjugated almost all of Yucatán to Spanish rule. The once proud and independent Maya became peons working for Spanish masters. The Maya lands were divided into large fiefdoms of sorts, called *encomiendas*, and the Maya living on the lands were mercilessly exploited by the land owners. With the coming of Dominican friar Bartolomé de las Casas and groups of Franciscan and Augustinian friars, things improved slightly for the Maya. In many cases the clergymen were able to protect the local people from the worst abuses, but exploitation was still the general rule.

## Independence for Some

During the colonial period, Spain's New World was a highly stratified society, and nowhere was that more evident than on the peninsula, which operated under a repressive caste system. Native Spaniards were making

> Back in the 1500s traveling Maya merchants would burn incense nightly on their journeys as an offering to the god Ek-Chuah for safe passage.

### FRIAR DIEGO DE LANDA

The Maya recorded information about their history, customs and ceremonies in beautifully painted picture books made of beaten-bark paper coated with fine lime plaster. These codices, as they are known, must have numbered in the hundreds when the conquistadors and missionary friars first arrived in the Maya lands. But because the ancient rites of the Maya were seen as a threat to the adoption and retention of Catholicism, the priceless books were set aflame upon the orders of the Franciscans. Only four of the painted books survive today, but these provide much insight into ancient Maya life.

Among those Franciscans directly responsible for the burning of the Maya books was the inquisitor Friar Diego de Landa, who, in July 1562 in Maní (near present-day Ticul), ordered the destruction of 27 'hieroglyphic rolls' and 5000 idols. He also had a few Maya burned to death for good measure.

Though despised by the Maya for destroying their cultural records, it was Friar de Landa who wrote the most important existing book on Maya customs and practices. Recalled to Spain for displaying a degree of zeal that even the clerical authorities found unwarranted, he was put on trial, but was absolved. The governing body ordered him to jot down everything he knew about the Maya. The resulting book, *Relación de las Cosas de Yucatán* (An Account of the Things of Yucatán), covers virtually every aspect of Maya life in the 1560s, from Maya houses and funeral customs to the calendar and counting system.

| 1850–93 | 1876–1911 | 1901 | 1910–20 |
|---|---|---|---|
| An independent Maya republic is established with its capital at Chan Santa Cruz. The war rages on, with the Maya (getting arms from the British) winning key victories. Britain stops arming the Maya in 1893. | The Porfiriato period – the name given to the era of Porfirio Díaz' 35-year rule as president-dictator, preceding the Mexican Revolution. Under Díaz, the country is brought into the industrial age. | The Mexican army, under Porfirio Díaz, recaptures the Maya-controlled territory, executing many Maya leaders and destroying the shrine of the talking cross in Chan Santa Cruz. | Almost two million people die and the economy is shattered during the Mexican Revolution. Eventual agrarian reform gives much of the Yucatán back to local cooperatives called *ejidos*. |

the big decisions at the very top; next were the criollos, people born in the New World of Spanish stock; below them were the mestizos or *ladinos*, people of mixed Spanish and indigenous blood; and at the bottom were the pure-race indigenous people and black people. Only the native Spaniards had real power, a fact deeply resented by the criollos.

The harshness of Spanish rule resulted in frequent revolts, none of them successful for long, or at least not until the War of Independence. After Mexico proclaimed its independence from Spain in 1821, the state of Yucatán, which at that time encompassed the entire peninsula, joined the Mexican federation as a semi-autonomous entity called the Federated Republic of Yucatán.

Though independence brought new prosperity to the criollos of the Yucatán, it worsened the lot of the Maya. The end of Spanish rule meant that the Crown's few liberal safeguards, which had afforded the Maya minimal protection from extreme forms of exploitation, were abandoned. The new powers that be stole the Maya's land and forced them to work under miserable conditions.

## The Caste War

Just 20 years after Mexico's independence from Spain, Yucatán's local government voted to break away from the Mexican federation in order to establish a fully sovereign republic that would guarantee individual rights and freedom of religion. Mexican president Santa Anna sent in troops in 1843, but Yucatán's forces managed to stave them off. Economic isolation proved to be a more powerful incentive to return to the fold, however, and a treaty was signed with Mexico that same year. But Yucatán again declared independence in 1846.

For the Yucatecan Maya, independence from Mexico made little difference – they remained subordinate to a white elite. In January 1847 indigenous rebels attacked Valladolid, rampaging through the city, killing and looting. Now alerted, federal authorities caught a Maya *batab* (community leader) with a letter detailing a plot to attack the town of Tihosuco (in present-day Quintana Roo). He was shot at Valladolid. Undaunted, the plotters attacked the town of Tepich, south of Tihosuco, and killed a number of criollo families. Thus began the Caste War, which spread relentlessly across the Yucatán region and raged on in some parts until the turn of the 20th century. An estimated 40,000 men joined the insurrection.

In little more than a year after the Valladolid uprising, Maya revolutionaries had driven their oppressors from every part of the Yucatán except Mérida and Campeche. But then the rebels suddenly abandoned the attack and went home to plant the corn they would need to carry on the fight. This gave the criollos and mestizos a chance to regroup. Yucatán's governor appealed to England, Spain and the US for protection from

> When the indigenous Xiú leader was baptized, he was made to take a Christian name, so he chose what must have appeared to him to be the most popular name of the entire 16th century – and became Francisco de Montejo Xiú.

> *The Caste War of Yucatán* by Nelson Reed is a page-turning account of the modern Maya's insurrection against the criollo elite and the establishment of an independent state.

| 1940s | 1970s | 1976 | 1988 |
|---|---|---|---|
| The Yucatán's once-booming *henequén* (sisal) industry collapses due to the advent of cheaper synthetic fibers. | Mexico's oil boom: widespread extraction and exploration begins in the Gulf; environmental problems go widely unchecked. In Quintana Roo another boom is taking hold with the development of Cancún. | Yucatán state elects Francisco Luna Kan, its first governor of pure Maya descent. After his term ends in 1982, it becomes more common to see high-ranking Maya politicians in Yucatán. | Chichén Itzá, home to the Yucatán's most-visited Maya ruins, is named a Unesco World Heritage Site for its 'outstanding universal value.' |

the indigenous rebels, in exchange for annexation to any of those countries, but all three nations refused to help. Finally, in a desperate move to strengthen its military and economic position, Yucatán rejoined the Mexican federation in 1848, receiving aid from its former adversary and effectively regaining the upper hand against most of the insurgent forces.

But the Maya continued the fight in southern Quintana Roo, where they overwhelmed the Mexican garrison in Bacalar's San Felipe fortress in 1858. By about 1866 the governments in Mexico City and Mérida gave up on the area and the British in Belize recognized an independent Maya republic, which remained virtually sovereign for the latter half of the 19th century.

Of the illustrated Maya books called codices, only four survive to the present day: *Dresden Codex, Madrid Codex, Paris Codex* and *Grolier Codex.*

## Revolution, Rope & Reform

Porfirio Díaz, who definitively reclaimed current-day Quintana Roo for Mexico, ruled the country from 1876 to 1911 as a dictator, banning political opposition and free press. During this period, Díaz brought the country into the industrial age, and passed laws that created an even larger class of landless peasants and concentrated wealth in the hands of an ever-smaller elite.

In the Yucatán, fortunes were made by the owners of haciendas producing *henequén,* then a lucrative plant for making rope and other products.

Díaz was brought down by the Mexican Revolution, a major war that erupted in 1910 and plunged the country into chaos for the next 10 years. The revolution pitted Diaz' military against the forces of revolutionary leaders such as Francisco Madero, Emiliano Zapata and Pancho Villa. In the decades following the revolution, agrarian reforms redistributed much of the peninsula's agricultural land, including many of the haciendas, into the hands of peasant cooperatives called *ejidos.*

One of the forgotten victims of the Caste War is the Maya calendar: shamans were too busy with war to keep track of the days, thus losing count. Luckily, Maya priests in the Guatemalan highlands still maintain an accurate Maya calendar.

The website of the Foundation for the Advancement of Mesoamerican Studies (www.famsi.org) contains numerous resources for broadening your understanding of Maya history.

## Oil Production & Rising Tourism

In the 1970s an Organization of the Petroleum Exporting Countries (OPEC) embargo sent world oil prices soaring, around the same time that vast oil reserves were discovered in the Gulf of Mexico. Mexico became the darling of international investors, who loaned the country billions. With its newly borrowed wealth, Mexico invested heavily in infrastructure, including the installation of the Cantarell complex in the Bay of Campeche, which, by 1981, was producing over a million barrels of crude oil a day. The Cantarell field now produces about a third of that.

| 1989 | 1994 | 2000–01 | 2005 |
|---|---|---|---|
| To the delight of nature conservationists, the federal government establishes Calakmul (in Campeche) as a biosphere reserve, making it one of the largest protected areas in Mexico. | The Zapatista uprising starts in Chiapas when rebels take over San Cristóbal de las Casas. They later retreat but continue to fight to overturn the oligarchy's centuries-old hold on land, resources and power. | Vicente Fox of Partido Acción Nacional (PAN) is elected president of Mexico, ending seven decades of autocratic rule by the Partido Revolucionario Institucional (PRI). Yucatán elects PAN governor Patricio Patrón. | Hurricane Wilma, the most intense Atlantic hurricane on record, does wide-scale damage to the tourist centers of Cancún, Cozumel, Isla Mujeres and Isla Holbox, with billions of dollars in damage to Cancún alone. |

## THE TALKING CROSS

Tucked away off a quiet backstreet in the small town of Felipe Carrillo Puerto, about 95km south of Tulum, you'll find one of the most important Maya shrines at the Santuario de la Cruz Parlante. The history of the shrine is legendary, to say the least.

During the Caste War, some Maya combatants sought refuge in the jungles of what is now southern Quintana Roo. There, they were inspired to continue fighting by a religious leader believed to be working with a ventriloquist, who, in 1850 at Chan Santa Cruz (present-day Felipe Carrillo Puerto), made a sacred cross 'talk.' The talking cross convinced the Maya that their gods had made them invincible, and it guided them in a decades-long struggle to maintain independence. Even after the federal government had captured and executed the last of the rebel chiefs in 1901, local Maya kept alive a guerrilla-style resistance movement until they officially surrendered in 1936. To this day, the cross remains a tremendous source of pride for the Maya, especially on May 3 (Day of the Holy Cross), when you can see Maya communities paying their respects in religious ceremonies.

A world oil glut caused prices to plummet in 1982, leading to a serious debt crisis. As a result, the government restructured the legal framework of the *ejido* system to allow outside investment as well as privatization and sales of cooperative land.

Another drop in recent years (particularly in 2014) in international oil prices has had a significant effect on some economies, particularly around Ciudad del Carmen in Campeche, the local base for many oil operations.

During the 1970s window of prosperity, investment also poured into Quintana Roo for the development of Cancún, igniting the peninsula's tourism industry and radically transforming the economic panorama. As tourism grew, many of the region's Maya left their villages to find work in Cancún, Cozumel, Playa del Carmen and other tourist haunts. The rise of tourism is thought by many scholars to be the single greatest threat to the culture and language of the Maya.

But at the same time tourism also represents a very important source of income for many locals – and any issues that affect it have a serious impact on the economy. Hurricane Wilma, for instance, left behind billions of dollars in damage to hotels and restaurants after it ripped through Quintana Roo, plus the economy suffered a significant loss of tourist dollars when visitors stayed away from the area in the aftermath. On the flipside, in 2012, as the Maya Long Count calendar was nearing completion, the peninsula benefited from a spike in tourism as mass media hyped it as the coming of the apocalypse.

Even without the benefit of gimmicky events, the Yucatán tourism sector seems to be doing just fine, as Cancún and Mérida consistently rank among Mexico's top 10 busiest airports for national and international arrivals.

| 2006–07 | 2009 | 2015–18 | 2020-2021 |
|---|---|---|---|
| The PAN party's Felipe Calderón holds off leftist Andres Manuel López Obrador in the 2006 election. The next year, Hurricane Dean rolls over the peninsula, leveling the Quintana Roo town of Mahahual. | The misperceived dangers of swine flu and the drug war, plus the global economic crisis, trigger a 30% drop in tourist visitation. | The entire Caribbean coast is hit by an influx of Sargassum seaweed. The government spends millions in clean-up efforts to rid the white-sand beaches of the mounds of brown algae. | The Covid-19 pandemic delivers an unprecedented blow to tourism, one of the region's top industries. Construction begins on the Tren Maya, the peninsula's ambitious intercity railway. |

# Yucatecan Way of Life

Drawing from a mix of ancient Maya and Spanish colonial-era influences, many aspects of domestic and social life on the Yucatán Peninsula remain very much steeped in tradition. Whether you find yourself in a Maya village, a small fishing town or a bustling colonial city, folks in these parts will gladly share with you their passion for song, dance, art and all things uniquely Yucatecan.

## The Everyday Reality

Check out Mesoweb (www.mesoweb.com) and Maya Exploration Center (www.mayaexploration.org) for fabulous resources on the Maya, past and present.

Travelers often comment on the open, gentle and gregarious nature of the people of the Yucatán, especially the Maya. Here more than elsewhere in Mexico, it seems, you find a willingness to converse and a genuine interest in outsiders. This openness is all the more remarkable when you consider that the people of the Yucatán Peninsula have fended off domination by outsiders for so long. The situation persists today – much of the land is foreign owned and the Maya generally aren't making the big decisions when it comes to large-scale development and infrastructure.

Maya culture is facing some difficult challenges moving forward in the 21st century as more and more young Maya people gradually abandon their language and traditions (highly rooted in an agrarian way of life) and head to Cancún or Playa del Carmen to work as busboys, waiters, maids and construction workers. But survival has always been at a premium here, and the Maya (and the region's poor) are finding ways to endure, be it by working in the service and manufacturing industries in big cities or moving to the US to work.

Others are staying home and turning to community-based tourism as a means to bring in income – artisan workshops, Maya-owned tour operators and local cooperatives all have had varying degrees of success. It is always helpful whenever you purchase crafts or hire services on offer from the local community.

Despite the winds of progress and modernization, many of the age-old traditions remain. Yucatecans highly value family bonds, and are only truly themselves within the context of the family – and though they are hardworking, the people of the region still like to enjoy leisure pursuits to the fullest. They are also deeply religious; their faith is a mélange of

### SPELLING OUT OUR STYLE

While Lonely Planet tries its darndest to keep up with linguistic trends, we've decided (purposely) to skip the latest trend in Maya orthography: adding an apostrophe to indicate a glottal stop. The apostrophe was adopted by Maya linguists and historians in 1989 as a vehicle to standardize and legitimize the language. The Maya glottal stop (most often used between two vowels) closely resembles the cockney double 't,' as used in the cockney English pronunciation of bottle. Thus, if we were following the new system, Tikal would be spelled Tik'al, and Chichén Itzá would be spelled Chich'en Itza. It was a tough decision, but in the end we decided to balance the needs of travelers (signs have yet to be converted to the new orthography) with the need to accurately document language.

## THE BEEKEEPERS' STRUGGLE

Honey production, an ancient practice on the peninsula dating back to the pre-Hispanic era, is facing challenging times due to the prevalence of genetically modified crops. How? For years, agribusiness giants have been allowed to cultivate fields of genetically modified soybeans on a commercial scale. The controversial practice has spurred protests in the states of Yucatán, Quintana Roo and Campeche, where apiarists claim that transgenic herbicide-resistant crops affect honey production – and that's no small problem in a region that produces about 40% of Mexico's honey.

The problem, say researchers, is that bees in the region are collecting a genetically modified pollen that makes its way into the honey, making it more difficult to export honey from the Yucatán to foreign markets because of health concerns. Mexico is one of the world's top honey exporters.

Some locals also blame GM crops for the disappearance of entire colonies of bees in certain areas, saying the so-called Frankenstein crops are either killing off the bees or forcing them to look for pollen elsewhere.

Though farmers won a case against Monsanto's planting of GM soybeans in 2014, the plight of the bees – and the farmers who depend on them – is far from over.

pre-Hispanic beliefs and Catholicism. As elsewhere in Mexico, traditional gender roles may seem exaggerated to the outsider, though the level of machismo on the peninsula is somewhat less pronounced.

## Life in Rural Yucatán

Perhaps more than elsewhere in Mexico, ancient rhythms and customs form part of everyday life in the Yucatán. In rural areas this is apparent on the surface. Women wear colorfully embroidered, loose-fitting *huipiles* (long, woven, white sleeveless tunics, from the Maya regions, with intricate, colorful embroidery) as they slap out tortillas in the yard; families live in traditional oval thatched houses, rest in hammocks after a day's work, and consume a diet of corn, beans and chilies.

Various forms of Maya are widely spoken, and pre-Hispanic religious rituals are still observed and forms of social organization followed. In some parts of the region, Maya languages prevail over Spanish, or Spanish may not be spoken at all. More than 30 Maya dialects exist, spoken by up to three million people in southern Mexico and northern Central America. Yucatec Maya is the dialect spoken on the Yucatán Peninsula. Eight Maya languages are spoken in Chiapas; Tzeltal, Tzotzil and Chol are the most widely used, the latter believed to most closely resemble the one spoken by the Classic Maya.

Many youngsters are now choosing to leave their rural roots, heading to the *maquiladoras* (factories) of Mérida, to the megaresorts of Quintana Roo or even to the US. Rather than study Yucatec Maya, many are learning English instead. But still, there remains a broad, ubiquitous undercurrent of pride in Maya culture – a hopeful sign that the culture will endure.

In *The Modern Maya: A Culture in Transition*, Macduff Everton documents the period from 1967 to 1990 among the Yucatecan Maya with superb black-and-white photos, while reflecting on the impact of modern influences on this resilient culture.

## Popuation at a Glance

For more than a millennium the Maya of the Yucatán have intermarried with neighboring and invading peoples. Most of Mexico's population is mestizo (a mixture of indigenous and Spanish blood), but the Yucatán has an especially high proportion of pure-blooded Maya, about four times the national average. There are around 1.5 million Maya in southern Mexico, with more than 800,000 Maya speakers. Of the peninsular states, the bulk of Maya speakers (around 538,000) reside in the state of Yucatán.

**GAME OF DEATH**

Probably all pre-Hispanic Mexican cultures played some version of a Mesoamerican ritual ball game, perhaps the world's first-ever team sport. Over 500 ball courts have survived at archaeological sites around Mexico and Central America. The game varied from place to place and era to era but had certain lasting features. It seems to have been played between two teams, and its essence was to keep a rubber ball off the ground by flicking it with hips, thighs, knees or elbows. The vertical or sloping walls alongside the courts were most likely part of the playing area. The game had (at least sometimes) deep religious significance, serving as an oracle, with the result indicating which of two courses of action should be taken. Games could be followed by the sacrifice of one or more of the players – whether winners or losers, no one is sure. You can catch a weekly game in Mérida's main plaza.

Overall in Mexico, only 6% of the population (approximately 6.7 million people) speaks an indigenous language.

There are 4.5 million people living in the peninsular states. Not surprisingly, Quintana Roo (home to tourist centers Cancún and the Riviera Maya) has the highest population-growth rate at around 13%, followed by Campeche and Yucatán, at 9% and 7% respectively.

## Passion for Sports

As in most Caribbean destinations, *béisbol* (baseball) is very popular. In fact, in some towns in the states of Yucatán and Campeche you'll see more action around the baseball diamond than the soccer field.

On the semi-professional level, the quality of play is quite high, equivalent at least to AAA ball in the US. The Mexican League season runs from March through August; among its teams in the region are the Piratas de Campeche (Campeche Pirates), Delfines de Ciudad del Carmen (Ciudad del Carmen Dolphins), Olmecas de Tabasco (Tabasco Olmecs), Leones de Yucatán (Mérida Lions) and Tigres de Quintana Roo (Quintana Roo Tigers).

As elsewhere in Mexico, *fútbol* (soccer) is always present around schoolyards and playing fields on the peninsula. Fans are customarily glued to their TV sets to watch matches of the region's two professional teams: Chiapas' Jaguares and Cancún's Atlante; the latter was demoted to the second-tier league following the 2014 season. The season is divided into two big tournaments: Torneo Apertura (August to December) and Torneo Clausura (January to May). Games are played over the weekend; check newspapers for details.

Yucatecans are also passionate about *charreadas* (rodeos), which you'll usually find at ferias (fairs) around the peninsula.

Fernando Venezuela, one of the most popular Mexican baseball players of all time, pitched for the Leones de Yucatán before he was signed by the Los Angeles Dodgers. Fernandomania erupted during his surprisingly successful rookie season in 1981.

## Hybrid Religion

Among the region's indigenous populations, ancient Maya beliefs blend nearly seamlessly with contemporary Catholic traditions – the values and rituals of the two religions are often quite similar. Today's Maya identify themselves as Catholic, but they practice a Catholicism that is a fusion of shamanist-animist and Catholic ritual. The traditional religious ways are so important that often a Maya will try to recover from a malady by seeking the advice of a religious shaman rather than a medical doctor. Use of folk remedies linked with animist tradition is widespread in Maya areas.

Mestizos and criollos (Creoles; born in Latin America of Spanish parentage) are more likely to follow strict Catholic doctrine, although here, like nearly everywhere else in Latin America, Catholicism has been losing ground to fast-growing evangelical sects.

Roman Catholicism accounts for the religious orientation of around 80% of residents in Yucatán state, and 63% of those living in Quintana Roo and Campeche. In Yucatán state and Campeche, a growing segment of the population identifies itself with Pentecostalism. Congregations affiliated with churches such as the Assemblies of God, the Seventh-Day Adventists, the Church of Jesus Christ of Latter-day Saints and Jehovah's Witnesses can be found throughout the Yucatán.

# Arts & Traditional Dress

The Yucatán's cultural scene is enormously rich and varied. The influence of the Maya or Spanish cultures (or both) appears in almost every facet of Yucatecan art, from literature and dance to music and fashion.

## Literature

For some cultural and historical context, here are just some of the many Yucatán-themed books that you can read before (or during) your visit.

➡ *Chilam Balam of Chumayel* One of Yucatán's earliest-known literary works. Written in Maya after the conquest, it is a compendium of Maya history, prophecy and mythology collected by priests from the northern Yucatán town of Chumayel. It has been translated into English.

➡ *Relación de las Cosas de Yucatán* (An Account of the Things of Yucatán) Diego de Landa, the Spanish friar, could be said to have produced the first literary work from the Yucatán in Spanish, in which he relates his biased perception of the Maya's ceremonial festivals, daily life and traditions, even as he engineered their eradication.

➡ *La Hija del Judío* (The Jew's Daughter; around 1847) Aside from (unsuccessfully) seeking US intervention against the Maya during the Caste War, Justo Sierra O'Reilly is credited with writing what is possibly the first Mexican novel, a story about the ill-fated romance of a Jewish merchant's daughter in colonial Mexico.

➡ *Canek: History and Legend of a Maya Hero* (1940) Yucatecan author Ermilo Abreu Gómez synthesized the peninsula's Maya heritage in various fictional works such as this novel, which centers on an indigenous laborer's struggle against injustice.

➡ *Imagen Primera* (First Image; 1963) and *La Noche* (The Night; 1963) Novelist, playwright and art critic Juan García Ponce, who died in 2003, is perhaps the Yucatán's best-known modern literary figure. These two titles, which make good starting points for exploring his work, are collections of his short stories.

## Music

Two styles of music are traditionally associated with the Yucatán: *jarana* and *trova yucateca.*

A type of festive dance music, a *jarana* is generally performed by a large ensemble consisting of two trumpets, two clarinets, one trombone, a tenor sax, timbales and a guiro (percussion instrument made from a grooved gourd). The music pauses for the singers to deliver *bombas* – improvised verses, usually with a humorous double meaning, that are aimed at the object of their affections. A *jarana* orchestra always ends its performances with the traditional *torito,* a vivacious song that evokes the fervor of a bullfight.

A hybrid of Cuban, Spanish, Colombian and homegrown influences, *trova yucateca* is a catch-all term for romantic ballads, Cuban claves, tangos, boleros, Yucatecan folk songs and other tunes that can be strummed on a guitar by a *trovador* (troubador). The style is often played by the guitar trios who roam the squares of Mérida seeking an audience to serenade. In a *trova,* as with *jaranas,* the subject matter is usually a suitor's paean of love to an unattainable sweetheart.

*Baktun,* the first-ever Maya-language telenovela, is a portrait of a Maya migrant worker struggling to retain his cultural identity. Like any soap opera worth its salt, there's no shortage of melodrama a la Mexicana. It aired on a regional public television network in 2013.

Mel Gibson's Oscar-nominated *Apocalypto* (2006) was the first major Yucatec Maya–language film. Shot in Veracruz, it drew wide criticism for a portrayal of the Maya full of historical inaccuracies; Gibson insisted it was a fictional account.

## MIND YOUR MANNERS

Some indigenous people adopt a cool attitude toward visitors: they have come to mistrust outsiders after five centuries of rough treatment. They don't like being gawked at by tourists and can be very sensitive about cameras. Always ask for permission before taking a photo or shooting video.

A more contemporary figure of Yucatecan song is Armando Manzanero, a singer and composer from Ticul, in Yucatán state. Though Manzanero speaks to an older generation, his songs have been covered by contemporary pop stars such as Luis Miguel and Alejandro Sanz.

On the Caribbean coast, electronic music gets top billing in the party towns of Cancún, Playa del Carmen and Tulum, and you'll also find a fair share of establishments staging Cuban-style salsa acts.

Music festivals abound on the peninsula, particularly in Mérida, Playa del Carmen and Campeche. Annual fests feature traditional and contemporary performers from Mexico and abroad. The Mérida government's website (www.merida.gob.mx/cultura) is a great source of information for music festivals and live events.

*Guty Cárdenas, un Siglo del Ruiseñor,* produced by the prestigious Mexican record label Discos Corasón (www.corason.com), includes a CD and DVD covering the musical career of seminal Yucatecan composer-performer Guty Cárdenas.

### Lively Dance

The Spanish influence on Maya culture is abundantly clear in the *jarana,* a dance Yucatecans have been performing for centuries. The dance bears more than a passing resemblance to the *jota,* performed in Spain's Alto Aragón region. The movements of the dancers, with their torsos held rigid and a formal distance separating men from women, are nearly identical; however, whereas the Spanish punctuate elegant turns of their wrists with clicks of their castanets, Maya women snap their fingers.

The best place to see dancers perform to the accompaniment of *jarana* is at *vaquerías* – homegrown fiestas held in the atriums of town halls or on haciendas. The women wear their best embroidered *huipiles,* flowers in their hair and white heels; men wear a simple white cotton outfit with a red bandanna tucked into the waist. In Mérida you can catch traditional dance performances on Thursday evenings in Parque Santa Lucia.

### Traditional Attire

Women throughout the Yucatán Peninsula traditionally wear *huipiles,* the bodices of which are always embroidered. The tunic generally falls to just below the knee; on formal occasions it is worn with a lacy white underskirt that reaches the ankle. The *huipil* never has a belt, which would defeat its airy, cool design. Light and loose fitting, these garments are ideally suited for the tropics. Maya women have been wearing *huipiles* for centuries.

Similar to the *huipil* in appearance is the *gala terno,* a straight, white, square-necked dress with an embroidered overyoke and hem, worn over an underskirt with an embroidered strip near the bottom. The *gala terno* is a bit fancier than the *huipil* and is often accompanied by a hand-knitted shawl.

Men commonly wear *guayaberas* (light, elegant shirts, some made with four square pockets). They can be worn in both casual and formal settings (they're often worn at weddings), and the cotton and linen materials keep the wearer cool on warm, humid days.

# The Ancient Maya

**Not only did the ancient Maya leave behind absolutely stunning architectural monuments, but their vision of the world and beyond remains a source of mystery and intrigue to this day. In fact, all across the peninsula ancient Maya culture and knowledge live on – most certainly a testament to a wondrous past.**

## Religion & Spirituality

### The Sacred Tree of Life & Xibalbá

For the Maya, the world, the heavens and the mysterious 'unseen world' or underworld, called Xibalbá (shi-bahl-*bah*), were all one great, unified structure that operated according to laws of astrology and ancestor worship. The towering ceiba tree was considered sacred. It symbolized the Wakah-Chan (Yaxché; Tree of Life), which united the 13 heavens, the surface of the earth and the nine levels of the underworld of Xibalbá.

### Compass Cosmology

In Maya cosmology, each point of the compass had special religious significance. East was most important, as it was where the sun was reborn each day; its color was red. West was black because it represented where the sun disappeared. North was white and was the direction from which the all-important rains came, beginning in May. South was yellow because it was the sunniest point of the compass.

Everything in the Maya world was seen in relation to these cardinal points (eg the direction in which a building faced), with the Tree of Life at the center, and they were the base for the all-important astronomical and astrological observations that determined fate.

> Maya pyramids were painted in brilliant red, green, teal, yellow and white colors, and the people of the region often painted their bodies red.

### Bloodletting & Piercing

Just as the great cosmic dragon (the upper world) shed its blood, which fell to the earth as rain, so humans had to shed blood to link themselves with the underworld of Xibalbá.

As illustrated in various Maya stone carvings and painted pottery, the nobility customarily drew their own blood on special occasions, such as royal births or deaths, crop plantings, victories on the battlefield or accession to the throne. Blood represented royal lineage, and so the blood of kings granted legitimacy to these events. Often using the spine of a manta ray as a lancet, a noble would pierce his or her cheek, lower lip, tongue or genitalia and pull a piece of rope or straw through the resulting orifice to extract the sacred substance. Performed for lower-ranking members of the nobility or occasionally before dumbstruck commoners, the excruciating ritual served not only to sanctify the event but also to appease the gods, as well as to communicate with them through the hallucinogenic visions that often resulted from such self-mutilation.

> Ah Tz'ib (scribes) wrote the sacred texts of the Maya, including the Chilam Balam of Chumayel. H-menob (shamans) and Ah Tz'ib still practice their craft throughout the peninsula.

### Sacred Places

Maya ceremonies were performed in natural sacred places as well as in their artificial equivalents. Mountains, caves, lakes, cenotes (limestone sinkholes), rivers and fields were all sacred. Pyramids and temples were thought of as stylized mountains; sometimes they had secret chambers within them, like the caves in a mountain. A cave was the mouth of the creature that represented Xibalbá, and to enter it was to enter the spirit of the secret world. This is why you'll see that some Maya temples have doorways surrounded by huge masks: as you enter the door of this 'cave,' you are entering the mouth of Xibalbá.

The plazas around which the pyramids were placed symbolized the open fields or the flat land of the tropical forest. What we call stelae were to the Maya 'tree-stones'; that is, tree effigies echoing the sacredness of the Tree of Life. These tree-stones were often carved with the figures of great Maya kings, for the king was the tree of Maya society.

As these places were sacred, it made sense for succeeding Maya kings to build new and ever grander temples directly over older temples, enhancing the sacred character of a location. The temple being covered over was preserved, as it remained a sacred artifact. Certain features of these older temples, such as the large masks on the facades, were carefully padded and protected before the new construction was placed over them.

Ancestor worship and genealogy were very important to the Maya, and when they buried a king beneath a pyramid, or a commoner beneath the floor or courtyard of his or her *na* (thatched hut), the sanctity of the location was elevated.

### Similarities with Christianity

The Tree of Life had a sort of cruciform shape and when in the 16th century the Franciscan friars required the indigenous population to venerate the cross, this Christian symbolism meshed easily with established Maya beliefs.

The ceiba tree's cruciform shape was not the only correspondence the Maya found between their animist beliefs and Christianity. Both traditional Maya animism and Catholicism have rites of baptism and confession, days of fasting and other forms of abstinence, religious partaking of alcoholic beverages, burning of incense and the use of altars.

The *Popol Vuh* legends include some elements that made it easier for the Maya to understand certain aspects of Christian belief, such as

### MAYA 'BIBLE': UNRAVELING THE SECRETS OF POPOL VUH

The history, prophecies, legends and religious rites of the Maya were preserved on painted codices and through oral traditions. Nearly all these codices were destroyed during the time of the conquest (only four survive today), effectively cutting the historic record of the Maya. Luckily for Mayanologists, the *Popol Vuh*, known to many as the Maya Bible, recaptured these myths and sacred stories.

The *Popol Vuh* is said to have been written by the Quiché Maya of Guatemala, who had learned Spanish and the Latin alphabet from the Dominican friars – the text was written in Latin characters rather than hieroglyphics. The authors showed their book to Francisco Ximénez, a Dominican who lived and worked in Chichicastenango, in Guatemala, from 1701 to 1703. Friar Ximénez copied the Maya book word for word and then translated it into Spanish. Both his copy and the Spanish translation survive, but the original has been lost.

According to the *Popol Vuh*, the great god K'ucumatz created humankind first from mud. But these 'earthlings' were weak and dissolved in water, so K'ucumatz tried again using wood. The wood people had no hearts or minds and could not praise their creator, so they were destroyed, all except the monkeys who lived in the forest, who are the descendants of the wood people. The creator tried once again, this time successfully, using substances recommended by four animals – the gray fox, the coyote, the parrot and the crow. White and yellow corn were ground into meal to form the flesh, and stirred into water to make the blood.

the virgin birth. As the story goes, a virgin underworld princess named Xquic was impregnated with the seed of a calabash fruit and gave birth to a pair of Maya hero twins.

# Amazing Architecture

Maya architecture is famous for its exquisitely beautiful temples and stone sculptures. Some of the most stunning structures were built during the early and late Classic periods, many of which stand remarkably well preserved today.

## Back-Breaking Work

The achievements in Maya architecture are astounding in and of themselves – and even more so when one stops to think about how the architects and laborers went about their work.

For starters, Maya architects never seem to have used the true arch (a rounded arch with a keystone). The arch used in most Maya buildings is the corbeled arch (or, when used for an entire room rather than a doorway, corbeled vault). In this technique, large flat stones on either side of the opening are set progressively inward as they rise. The two sides nearly meet at the top, and this 'arch' is then topped by capstones. Though they served the purpose, the corbeled arches severely limited the amount of open space beneath them. In effect, Maya architects were limited to long, narrow vaulted rooms.

And consider this: boxes used to move around tons of construction materials did not have wheels. The Maya also lacked draft animals (horses, donkeys, mules or oxen). All the work had to be done by humans, on their feet, with their arms and backs.

What's more, they had no metal tools, yet could build breathtaking temple complexes and align them so precisely that windows and doors were used as celestial observatories with great accuracy.

## The Styles

Maya architecture's storied history saw a fascinating progression of styles. Styles changed not just with the times but with the particular geographic area of Mesoamerica in which the architects worked. The Classic Maya, at their cultural height from about 250–900 CE, were perhaps ancient Mexico's most artistic people. They left countless beautiful stone sculptures, of complicated design and meaning but possessing an easily appreciated touch of delicacy – a talent expressed in their unique architecture. Typical styles in the Yucatán include Esperanza, Puuc, Chenes and Río Bec.

### Early Classic (250–600 CE)

The Esperanza culture typifies this phase. In Esperanza-style temples, the king was buried in a wooden chamber beneath the main staircase of the temple; successive kings were buried in similar positions in pyramids built on top of the original.

A good example of the early Classic style is La Pirámide at the Oxkintok site (south of Mérida), where a labyrinth inside the structure leads to a burial chamber.

### Late Classic (600–900 CE)

The most important Classic sites flourished during the latter part of the period. By this time the Maya temple pyramid had a stone building on top, replacing the na of wooden poles and thatch. Numbers of pyramids were built close together, sometimes forming contiguous or even continuous structures. Near them, different structures, now called palaces,

Ixchel, the moon goddess, was the principal female deity of the Maya pantheon. Today she is linked with the Virgin Mary.

Lavishly illustrated with sections of friezes, sculpted figurines, painted pottery and other fine specimens of Maya art, *The Blood of Kings*, by Linda Schele and Mary Ellen Miller, deciphers glyphs and pictographs to explore recurring themes of Classic Maya civilization.

*The Art of Mesoamerica*, by Mary Ellen Miller, is an excellent overview of pre-Hispanic art and architecture.

were built; they sat on lower platforms and held many more rooms, perhaps a dozen or more.

> Joyce Kelly's *An Archaeological Guide to Mexico's Yucatán Peninsula* gives visitors both practical and background information on 91 sites.

In addition to pyramids and palaces, Classic sites have carved stelae and round 'altar stones' set in the plaza in front of the pyramids. Another feature of the Classic and later periods is the ball court, with the sloping playing surfaces of stone covered in stucco.

Of all the Classic sites, one of the most impressive is Uxmal, which stands out for its fascinating blend of Puuc, Chenes and Río Bec architectural styles. Equally impressive is Palenque, especially the towering Templo de las Inscripciones (Temple of the Inscriptions).

### Puuc, Chenes & Río Bec (600–800 CE)

Among the most distinctive of the late-Classic Maya architectural styles are those that flourished in the western and southern regions of the Yucatán Peninsula. These styles valued exuberant display and architectural bravado more than they did proportion and harmony – think of it as Maya baroque.

The Puuc style, named for the hills surrounding Uxmal, used facings of thin limestone 'tiles' to cover the rough stone walls of buildings. The tiles were worked into geometric designs and stylized figures of monsters and serpents. Minoan-style columns and rows of engaged columns (half-round cylinders partly embedded in a wall) were also a feature of the style; they were used to good effect on the facades of buildings at Uxmal and at the Puuc sites of Kabah, Sayil, Xlapak and Labná. Every Puuc temple features the face of Chaac, the rain god. At Kabah, the facade of the Palacio de los Mascarones (Palace of the Masks) is covered in Chaac masks.

The Chenes style, prevalent in areas of Campeche south of the Puuc region, is similar to the Puuc style, but Chenes architects seem to have enjoyed putting huge masks as well as smaller ones on their facades.

The Río Bec style, epitomized in the richly decorated temples at the archaeological sites between Escárcega and Chetumal, used lavish decoration, as in the Puuc and Chenes styles, but added huge towers to the corners of its low buildings, just for show. Adorned with stylized Chaac faces, the Palacio del Gobernador (Governor's Palace) of Uxmal is a fine example of a Río Bec building.

### Early Post-Classic (1000–1250 CE)

The collapse of Classic Maya civilization around 1000 CE created a power vacuum that was filled by the invasion of the Toltecs from central Mexico. The Toltecs brought with them their own architectural ideas, and in the process of conquest these ideas were assimilated and merged with those of the Puuc style.

The foremost example of what might be called the Toltec-Maya style is Chichén Itzá. Elements of Puuc style – the large masks and decorative

### SWEATING OUT EVIL SPIRITS IN A MAYA TEMASCAL

The temascal (sweat lodge) has always been a cornerstone of indigenous American spiritual life. The Maya, like their brothers and sisters to the north, were no different, using the temascal for both ceremonial and curative purposes.

The word temascal derives from the Aztec word *teme* (to bathe) and *calli* (house). The Maya people used these bathhouses not just to keep clean but also to heal any number of ailments. Most scholars say they were most likely used during childbirth as well. Large bath complexes have been discovered at several Maya archaeological sites. Ironically, the hygienically challenged conquistadors considered temascals dirty places and strongholds of sin. To this day, they are used by the Maya (and tourists) to bathe and keep evil spirits away.

## THE CELESTIAL PLAN

Every major work of Maya architecture had a celestial plan. Temples were aligned so as to enhance celestial observation of the sun, moon, certain stars or planets, especially Venus. The alignment might not be apparent except at certain conjunctions of the celestial bodies (eg an eclipse), but the Maya knew that each building was properly 'placed' and that this enhanced its sacred character.

Temples usually had other features that linked them to the stars. The doors and windows might frame a celestial body at an exact point in its course on a certain day of a certain year. This is the case with the Palacio del Gobernador (Governor's Palace) at Uxmal, which is aligned in such a way that, from the main doorway, Venus would have been visible exactly on top of a small mound some 3.5km away, in the year 750 CE. At Chichén Itzá, the observatory building El Caracol was aligned in order to sight Venus exactly in the year 1000 CE.

Other features might relate to the numbers of the calendar round, as at Chichén Itzá's El Castillo. This pyramid has 364 stairs to the top; with the top platform, this makes 365, the number of days in the Maya vague year. (The vague year corresponds to our 365-day solar year, with the difference that it is not adjusted every four years by adding an additional day. Therefore, the seasons do not occur at the same time each year but vary slightly from year to year. For that reason, the Maya solar year is characterized as 'vague.') On the sides of the pyramid are 52 panels, signifying the 52-year cycle of the calendar round. The terraces on each side of each stairway total 18 (nine on either side), signifying the 18 'months' of the solar vague year. The alignment of El Castillo catches the sun and makes a shadow of the sacred sky-serpent ascending or descending the side of El Castillo's staircase on the vernal and autumnal equinoxes (usually around March 20 and September 22) each year.

friezes – coexist with Toltec warrior *atlantes* (male figures used as supporting columns) and chac-mools, odd reclining statues that are purely Toltec and have nothing to do with Maya art.

Platform pyramids with broad bases and spacious top platforms, such as Chichén Itzá's Templo de los Guerreros (Temple of the Warriors), look as though they might have been imported from the ancient Toltec capital of Tula (near Mexico City) or by way of Teotihuacán (the Aztec capital also near Mexico City), with its broad-based pyramids of the sun and moon. Because Quetzalcóatl (a feathered serpent deity) was so important to the Toltecs, feathered serpents are used extensively as architectural decoration.

### Late Post-Classic (1250–1530 CE)

After the Toltecs came the Cocomes, who established their capital at Mayapán, south of Mérida, and ruled a confederation of Yucatecan states during this period. After the golden age of Palenque, even after the martial architecture of Chichén Itzá, the architecture of Mayapán is a disappointment. The pyramids and temples are small and crude compared with the glorious Classic structures. Mayapán's only architectural distinction comes from its vast defensive city wall, one of the few such walls ever discovered in a Maya city. The fact that the wall exists testifies to the weakness of the Cocom rulers and the unhappiness of their subject peoples.

Tulum, another walled city, is also a product of this time. The columns of the Puuc style are used here, and the painted decoration on the temples must have been colorful. But there's nothing here to rival Classic architecture.

Cobá has the finest architecture of this period, when the building of monumental constructions had ceased. The stately pyramids here had new little temples built atop them in the style of Tulum's two-story Templo de las Pinturas (Temple of the Paintings).

# Land & Wildlife

Sitting pretty between two seas in Mexico's easternmost corner, the Yucatán Peninsula has an insular character, in both its physical isolation from the Mexican interior and its distinct topography and wildlife.

## Land & Geology

Separated from the bulk of Mexico by the Gulf of Mexico, and from the Greater Antilles by the Caribbean Sea, the Yucatán Peninsula is a vast, low limestone shelf extending under the sea for more than 100km to the north and west. The eastern (Caribbean) side drops off much more precipitously. This underwater shelf keeps Yucatán's coastline waters warm and the marine life abundant.

The peninsula is divided into three states in a 'Y' shape, with the state of Yucatán occupying the upper portion, flanked to the west by the state of Campeche and to the east by Quintana Roo. Note that Tabasco and Chiapas are not actually part of the Yucatán Peninsula.

Unlike much of Mexico, the Yucatán remains unobstructed by mountains. It rises no more than a dozen meters above sea level in its northern section and, at its steepest, in the southern interior of Campeche state, only reaches about 300m. About 60km south of Mérida, near Ticul, the Yucatán plain gives way to the rolling hills of the Puuc ('hill' in Maya) region. South of the peninsula, in Chiapas, it's one extreme to the other – from steamy lowlands to chilly pine-covered highlands. To the east, in southern Quintana Roo, swaths of jungle meet the Caribbean coast.

More than 6000 cenotes dot the Yucatán Peninsula. And that's a moderate estimate!

### Barrier Reef

Approaching by air, you can easily make out the barrier reef that runs parallel to the Caribbean coastline at a distance of a few hundred meters to about 1.5km. Known variously as the Great Maya, Mesoamerican or Belize Barrier Reef, it's the longest of its kind in the northern hemisphere – and the second largest in the world – extending from southern Belize to Isla Mujeres off the northern coast of Quintana Roo. On the landward side of the reef, the water is usually no more than 5m to 10m deep; on the seaward side it plummets to depths of more than 2000m in the Yucatán Channel that runs between the peninsula and Cuba.

Planeta.com (www.planeta.com) brims with information and links for those wanting to delve deeper into Mexico and the Yucatán's flora, fauna and environment.

### Agriculture

Capped by a razor-thin crust of soil, the peninsula is less productive agriculturally than elsewhere in Mexico. Formed by cretaceous-era sediments, its porous limestone bedrock does not allow rivers to flow on its surface, except in short stretches near the sea where its roof has collapsed, and in the southernmost reaches of the region where the peninsula joins the rest of Mexico (and Guatemala). Some underground streams don't release their water until well offshore, while others empty into lagoons near the sea, such as the lovely Laguna Bacalar, in southern Quintana Roo.

## HURRICANE ALLEY

Hurricanes have always walloped the Yucatán, and the peninsula has certainly experienced some big ones. Blame global warming, blame regularly shifting climate patterns; whatever you decide to blame, the real loser has been the region's people, plants and animals.

For a while there, Yucatecans just couldn't catch a break. In 2005, Hurricane Wilma (a category 5 storm) pounded the Yucatán's northeast coast for more than 30 hours, causing more than 60 deaths and over US$29 billion in damage and leaving many visitors stranded in shelters. Two years later Dean struck with so much force that it leveled the beach town of Mahahual and mowed down thousands of trees along the Costa Maya, in southern Quintana Roo.

Fortunately, subsequent hurricane seasons have shown some mercy. In 2011, Hurricane Rina was bearing down on the peninsula, prompting mass evacuations of tourists staying in Cancún and along the Riviera Maya. But before making landfall, Rina was downgraded to a tropical storm, and most importantly, no deaths or major damage were reported. A similar situation occurred in 2012 when Hurricane Ernesto had many people running for cover, but it weakened before hitting land. Once again, locals and visitors skirted a potential catastrophe.

The Atlantic hurricane season runs from June 1 to November 30. Every time a storm pounds the Caribbean coast, it causes massive erosion of the white-sand beaches. Much to the chagrin of area environmentalists, the quick-fix solution is to restore the beaches by bringing in sand from other areas, such as the channel between Cancún and Isla Mujeres.

## Cenotes

A uniquely Yucatecan geological feature, cenotes (pronounced *seh-noh-tays*) – from the Maya word *d'zonot,* meaning 'water-filled cavern' – are limestone sinkholes formed by the erosive effects of rainwater drilling down through the porous limestone. Thousands of cenotes, both wet and dry, dot the peninsula landscape. Yucatecans have traditionally obtained their fresh water from these natural cisterns, while modern visitors favor their crystalline waters for swimming and snorkeling. South of the Puuc region, the inhabitants draw water from the *chenes* (limestone pools), more than 100m below ground.

# Into the Wild

The isolation of the Yucatán Peninsula and its array of ecosystems results in an extraordinary variety of plant and animal life, including a number of species that are unique to the region. Whether you like watching birds, following the progress of sea turtles as they nest on the beach, swimming next to manta rays and schools of iridescent fish, or spying wildcats through your binoculars, you'll have plenty of nature activities to do here.

## Animals

### Birds of the Yucatán

For bird-watchers, the Yucatán is indeed a banquet. Over 500 bird species – about half of those found in all of Mexico – inhabit or regularly visit the peninsula. These include dozens of regional endemics; the island of Cozumel alone boasts three unique species.

Most of the peninsula's birds are represented in the various parks and biosphere reserves, and serious birders should make for at least a few of these. Numerous coastal species can be spotted at the Reserva de la Biosfera Ría Celestún and Reserva de la Biosfera Ría Lagartos,

Birders should carry *Mexican Birds* by Roger Tory Peterson and Edward L Chalif, or *Birds of Mexico & Adjacent Areas* by Ernest Preston Edwards. The Merlin app has a comprehensive Mexican bird list as well.

on the western and eastern ends, respectively, of Yucatán state's coast. The varied panorama is due to a highly productive ecosystem where substantial freshwater sources empty into the Gulf of Mexico. A similarly diverse coastal habitat can be found at the Laguna de Términos in western Campeche. Parque Nacional Isla Contoy, off the northeastern coast of Quintana Roo, is a haven for olive cormorants, brown boobies and many other seabirds. It's home to 173 bird species.

Moving inland, the panorama shifts. The low, dry forests of the Puuc region contain two species of motmot, which nest in ruined temples. In the denser forests of the Reserva de la Biosfera Calakmul, train your binoculars on harpy eagles, ocellated turkeys and king vultures.

The Yucatán Peninsula is along the central migratory flyway, and between November and February hundreds of thousands of birds migrate here from harsher northern climes. The region's proximity to the Caribbean Sea also means it receives island species not seen elsewhere in Mexico.

In November NGO Pronatura (p296) hosts the Toh Festival (www.festivalavesyucatan.com), an annual event that attracts bird enthusiasts from far and wide. The festival culminates in a birding marathon called Xoc Ch'ich, a Maya term meaning bird count. The event is organized out of Mérida.

The Spanish-language monthly magazine *México Desconocido* (www.mexicodesconocido.com.mx) points out off-the-beaten-track destinations and wildlife-watching spots with copious color photos and maps. Check its website for details.

### Forest & Mangrove Dwellers

Around a quarter of the mammal species that exist in Mexico roam the Yucatán Peninsula. Some are the last of their breed.

There are jaguars in the forests, although, despite the Maya's traditional fascination with the New World's largest cat, poaching has all but wiped them out in southeastern Mexico. Of Mexico's estimated jaguar population of 4000, half are found on the peninsula. Your best chance of spotting one in the wild is probably in the Reserva de la Biosfera Calakmul in Campeche state. The peninsula's other native wildcat, the jaguarundi, is also at risk, as are the margay, ocelot and puma, though sightings of the latter aren't all that unusual in southern Yucatán.

The agile spider monkey also inhabits some forested areas of the region. It looks something like a smaller, long-tailed version of the gibbon (an ape native to southwest Asia). Another elusive primate, the howler monkey, frequents the forest around the ruins of Calakmul and isolated pockets elsewhere. Howlers are more often heard than seen, but you have a fair chance of seeing both them and spider monkeys at Punta Laguna.

Hiking around the forest, you may run into tapirs and piglike peccaries (javelinas), as well as armor-plated armadillos. There are several species of anteater, all with very long, flexible snouts and sharp-clawed, shovel-like front paws – the two tools needed to seek out and enjoy feeding on ants and other insects. The animal's slow gait and poor eyesight make it a common roadkill victim. Besides the *tepezcuintle* (paca) and *sereque* (agouti) – large, tailless rodents – a few species of deer can be found as well, including the smallest variety in North America.

To see recently snapped photos of jaguars, crocs, whale sharks and other Yucatán fauna in their habitat, go to the website of the environmental group Pronatura (www.pronatura-ppy.org.mx).

Crocodiles still ply the mangroves in Yucatán state and Quintana Roo. Since 1970 the government has prohibited the hunting of crocodiles and the population has recovered as a result. You can see plenty of the amphibious reptiles in biosphere reserves at Río Lagartos, Celestún and Sian Ka'an, while smaller numbers lurk up and down the Caribbean coast, including at Laguna Nichupté, which backs onto Cancún's Zona Hotelera.

## Sea Creatures

The Great Maya Barrier Reef, which parallels the length of Quintana Roo's coast, is home to a tremendous variety of colorful marine life. The coney grouper, for example, stands out for its bright-yellow suit (it varies in color from reddish brown to sun yellow). The redband parrotfish is easy to recognize by the striking red circle around its eyes and the red band that runs from the eyes to the gills. Butterflyfish are as flamboyant as their name suggests (there are six species in the area), and the yellow stingray has spots that closely resemble the rosettes of a golden jaguar.

Providing an extraordinary backdrop to these brilliant stars of the sea is a vast array of coral. It comes in two varieties: hard coral, such as the great star coral, the boulder coral and numerous types of brain coral; and soft coral, such as sea fans and sea plumes, which are particularly delicate and sway with the current. Successive generations of coral form a skin of living organisms over the limestone reef.

But there's trouble in the waters of the Mexican Caribbean – invasive lionfish, which are native to the Indo-Pacific region but were introduced to Atlantic waters in the early 1990s, are reproducing at an alarming rate and that's bad news for indigenous fish species. Protected by venomous spines and with no known predators in the Atlantic, lionfish have a fierce appetite, making them a serious threat to the balance of reef ecosystems.

In an effort to control the population explosion, fishers are being encouraged to catch lionfish for human consumption. Also, many dive shops now offer lionfish-hunting expeditions, which is capped off with a feast of lionfish ceviche at the end of the day.

The Selva Maya, which spans northern Guatemala and Belize and the southern part of the Yucatán Peninsula (including the Reserva de la Biosfera Calakmul), is the world's second-largest tropical forest after the Amazon.

## Endangered Species

Pollution, poaching, illegal traffic of rare species and the filling in of coastal areas for yet more resorts are taking an enormous toll on the Yucatán's wildlife. Deforestation is also a major threat.

Some of the species on the peninsula that are threatened with extinction or are protected include five species of cat (jaguar, puma, ocelot, margay and jaguarundi), four species of sea turtle, the manatee, the tapir and hundreds of bird species, including the harpy eagle, the red flamingo and the jabiru stork.

Efforts are being made to save these and other endangered creatures from extinction, chiefly by environmental NGOs, such as the Nature Conservancy (www.nature.org) and its local partner Pronatura (www.pronatura-ppy.org.mx). This group focuses on preservation of wildlife habitats, particularly in the biosphere reserves of Ría Celestún, Ría Lagartos and Calakmul. It's also a big promoter of ecotourism.

Camps at Ría Lagartos, Laguna de Términos, Xcacel-Xcacelito, Akumal, Sisal and Isla Holbox have been established to promote the survival of the six species of marine turtle that nest on the Yucatán's shores. Volunteers collect turtle eggs and release hatchlings into the sea, and patrols prevent poachers from snatching eggs that are laid on the beaches. In Punta Laguna environmental groups are working with local agricultural workers to establish protection zones for endangered spider monkeys, which are closely monitored by researchers. The nutrient-rich waters around Isla Holbox attract whale sharks, which are threatened by commercial fishing, and environmentalists have succeeded in getting this area categorized as a protected zone.

*Tropical Mexico – The Ecotravellers' Wildlife Guide*, by Les Beletsky, is a well-illustrated, informative guide to the land, air and sea life of southeastern Mexico.

LAND & WILDLIFE INTO THE WILD

### Plants

Vegetation varies greatly on the peninsula, with plants falling into four main categories: aquatic and subaquatic vegetation, and humid and sub-humid forest vegetation.

As you move inland from the coast, mangrove swamps are replaced first by a fairly dense forest of low deciduous trees, then by a more jungly zone with tall trees and climbing vegetation, and more than a few air plants (but without the soggy underbrush and multiple canopies you'd find further south). The taller trees of the peninsula's southern half harbor more than 100 species of orchid; for the really spectacular blooms, the avid orchid hunter will need to head into the highlands of Chiapas, where the exotic plants thrive at an elevation of about 1000m.

Dispersed among the mango and avocado trees are many annuals and perennials, such as the aptly named *flamboyán* (royal poinciana), which bursts into bloom like a red-orange umbrella, and the lavender-tinged jacaranda.

## National Parks & Reserves

There are several national parks on the peninsula, some scarcely larger than the ancient Maya cities they contain – Parque Nacional Tulum is a good example of this. Others, such as Parque Nacional Isla Contoy, a bird sanctuary in northeastern Quintana Roo, are larger and have been designated to protect wildlife.

The fact that former president Ernesto Zedillo was an avid scuba diver was likely a factor in the creation of several *parques marinos nacionales* (national marine parks) off the coast of Quintana Roo: Arrecifes de

---

### SMALL FOOTPRINTS, LARGE IMPACT: TIPS FOR STAYING GREEN

Travelers can help protect the Yucatán's environment by taking the following steps.

➡ Hire local guides. Not only does this provide local communities with a more ecologically sound way of supporting themselves, it also attaches value to nature and wildlife.

➡ Pack a water purifier and/or a refillable container to avoid unnecessary waste of plastic bottles, and use a stainless steel straw instead of a plastic one. Tourists the world over toss millions of one-time use plastic items each day!

➡ Try to observe wildlife in its natural environment and do your best not to cause disturbances; avoid dive shops that feed sharks, which can be both dangerous for humans and harmful to sharks.

➡ Don't buy souvenirs made from endangered plants and animals that have been acquired illegally. By purchasing these items you aid wildlife extinction.

➡ Don't carry away anything that you pick up at the site of an ancient city or out on a coral reef. Don't buy these items if they're offered by locals.

➡ When snorkeling or scuba diving, be careful about what you touch and where you place your feet; not only can coral cut you, but it's extremely fragile and takes years to grow even a finger's length.

➡ Keep water use down, especially in areas that have signs requesting you to do so. Most of the Yucatán Peninsula has limited water reserves, and in times of drought the situation can become grave.

➡ Before plunging into a cenote make sure you're not using sunblock, lotions, perfumes, insect repellent or any other products that pollute the water system.

Cozumel, Costa Occidental de Isla Mujeres, Punta Cancún y Nizuc and Arrecifes de Puerto Morelos.

Very large national biosphere reserves surround Río Lagartos, Celestún (both in Yucatán state) and Banco Chinchorro (Quintana Roo), spreading across thousands of hectares. The Reservas de la Biosfera Ría Lagartos and Ría Celestún are well known for their diversity of bird and animal species, including large colonies of flamingos, while Banco Chinchorro contains a massive coral atoll, many shipwrecks and a host of marine species.

Even more impressive are the two colossal Unesco-designated biosphere reserves found in the Yucatán: the Reserva de la Biosfera Calakmul and the Reserva de la Biosfera Sian Ka'an. Calakmul, covering more than 7230 sq km in Campeche, Quintana Roo and Chiapas, as well as parts of Belize and Guatemala, is home to more than 300 bird species, plus jaguars, pumas, tapirs, coatis, peccaries and many other animals. Sian Ka'an, beginning 150km south of Cancún, covers 6000 sq km, including 100 sq km of the Great Maya Barrier Reef. Its lifeforms include more than 70 species of coral, 350 species of bird (by comparison, there are 400 species of bird in all of Europe), crocodiles, pumas, jaguars and jabirus.

As of research, the largest park in Mexican history was still in the works, but the Reserva de la Biosfera Caribe Mexicano will protect the entire coastline from Cancún to Punta Allen, including the waters surrounding Isla Cozumel. The details, how it will affect the businesses and whether it can reign in some of the rampant development all remains to be seen.

## Environmental Issues

Large-scale tourism developments are affecting and sometimes erasing fragile ecosystems, especially along the 'Riviera Maya' south of Cancún. Many hectares of vital mangrove swamp have been bulldozed, and beaches where turtles once laid eggs are now occupied by resorts and condos. Ironically, tourism development is a major contributor to coastal erosion, as was made evident when 2005's Hurricane Wilma swept away the beaches (many artificial) that attract hordes of tourists annually. And with the proliferation of new hotels comes the need for freshwater sources, increasing the danger of salinization of the water table. As job-seekers converge on Quintana Roo's tourist zones, demand for building materials to construct housing for the burgeoning population is also a persistent issue.

Another key problem is the fragmentation of habitat. As patches of jungle shrink with new settlement and the construction of highways, they become isolated and species become trapped in smaller areas. Animals' movements are restricted and the gene pool cannot flow beyond the borders of each piece of fragmented habitat.

Also of concern is the need for effective waste-management systems. Some places do not have water-treatment plants, which results in untreated sewage running through underground water systems and out to sea. The so-called *aguas negras* (black waters) contain nutrients that allow for mass algal growth. Unfortunately, these oxygen-depleting algae can have an asphyxiating effect on various forms of marine life, such as coral.

Mexico's largest oil field, the Cantarell complex, is in the Bay of Campeche, 85km off the shore of Ciudad del Carmen. In 2007 there was an 11,700-barrel oil spill in the bay, adversely affecting the area's marine flora and fauna. The Cantarell field is also yielding less oil than it did

The Yucátan Wildlife website (www.yucatanwildlife.com) provides a wealth of information about the region's animal and plant species, local ecotours and Yucatán-based nature organizations.

in the past, leading the company to seek new sources in the Alacranes reef off the coast of Progreso, and at Laguna de Términos, where further habitat destruction is feared.

The good news is that the level of protection on reserves and other important natural habitats has continued on a constant basis over the years. In 2012, 380 sq km consisting of jungle area and coastline on Isla Cozumel's northern and eastern sides were given protected status, and in 2009 some 1460 sq km of waters where whale sharks congregate (off the Quintana Roo coast) was declared a protected area. And in 2004, 1497 sq km of threatened forest in the Reserva de la Biosfera Calakmul was permanently protected. In Chiapas, Parque Nacional Lagunas de Montebello was designated a Unesco biosphere reserve in 2009, adding to the conservancy potential of the area.

But Yucatán's protected zones and reserves encompass private *ejidos* (communally owned land) occupied by *campesinos* (agricultural workers) whose activities, particularly cattle raising and logging, may infringe upon the environment. Seeking a solution, some environmental organizations have begun training *ejido* inhabitants as guides for ecotourism activities, thus providing alternative livelihoods. Such programs are underway in the Reserva de la Biosfera Calakmul and on Isla Holbox, and locals say the programs have worked out well because they provide a viable source of income.

# Survival Guide

# Directory A–Z

## Accessible Travel

Lodgings on the Yucatán Peninsula generally don't cater for travelers with disabilities, though some hotels and restaurants (mostly top end) and some public buildings now provide wheelchair access. The absence of institutionalized facilities, however, is largely compensated for by Mexicans' accommodating attitudes toward others, and special arrangements are gladly improvised.

Mobility is easiest in the major tourist resorts. Bus transportation can be difficult; flying or taking a taxi is easier.

**Mobility International USA** (www.miusa.org)

**Society for Accessible Travel** (www.sath.org)

## Accommodations

Accommodations in the Yucatán range from hammocks and *cabañas* to hotels of every imaginable standard, including world-class luxury resorts. In popular destinations for high season (Christmas through Easter, plus most of July and August) it's best to book in advance.

Outside peak season, many midrange and top-end establishments in tourist destinations cut their room prices by 20% to 50%. They may also have special online offers. Some places (mostly top-end hotels) do not include a 14% to 19% tax charge in quoted prices. When in doubt, you can ask '*¿Están incluidos los impuestos?*' (Are taxes included?).

**B&Bs** Usually more intimate and more upscale than guesthouses.

**Bungalows** Anything from cheap rustic cabins to elegant boutique setups.

**Guesthouses** Family-run houses (often called posadas in Spanish) that usually provide good value and more personable service.

**Hotels** Range from budget digs to expensive all-inclusive resorts.

**Hostels** The most affordable option and a great way to meet other travelers.

### Price Categories

Room prices quoted are for high-season rates and subject to change. Rates do not reflect 'ultra' high-season prices that some midrange and top-end establishments charge from mid-December to early January, and during the two-week Easter vacation period. Budget accommodations usually keep prices the same year-round (bless their hearts!). Hotels in developed resort areas – such as Cancún and Playa del Carmen – may publish their rates in US dollars. Places that stick with the peso sometimes adjust their prices according to exchange-rate fluctuations.

#### BUDGET

The Yucatán offers an assortment of affordable sleeping options, including hostels, *cabañas* (cabins), campgrounds, guesthouses and economical hotels. Rooms in

---

### PRACTICALITIES

**Newspapers** Mérida's *El Diario de Yucatán* (www.yucatan.com.mx) is one of the country's leading newspapers. *Yucatán Today* (www.yucatantoday.com) offers good English-language info on Yucatán state.

**TV** Local TV is dominated by Televisa, which runs four national channels plus a satellite subsidiary; TV Azteca has another three.

**Smoking** Mexico has a ban on smoking in public indoor spaces, except in designated areas. Enforcement, however, is inconsistent.

**Weights & Measures** Mexico uses the metric system.

this category are assumed to have bathrooms, unless otherwise stated. Recommended accommodations in this range will be simple and no-frills but generally clean.

### MIDRANGE

Midrange accommodations are chiefly hotels, but you'll also find many appealing B&Bs, guesthouses and bungalows in this price bracket. In some areas of the Yucatán, M$800 can get you a very comfortable and atmospheric setup. Keep in mind that not all rooms are the same in many establishments (some are larger or have better views), so it's worth having a look at several options before settling in.

### TOP END

Places in this category run from classy international hotels to deluxe all-inclusive resorts and smaller boutique hotels catering to travelers with a taste for comfort and design.

## Types of Accommodations

### APARTMENTS & B&BS

In some places you can find *departamentos* (apartments) for tourists with fully equipped kitchens. Some are very comfortable and they can be good value for three or more people. The website www.locogringo.com is a good source of information. In the Yucatán, B&Bs are generally upmarket guesthouses, often aimed at foreign tourists.

### CABAÑAS

*Cabañas* are usually cabins or huts – of wood, brick, adobe or stone – with a

---

### SLEEPING PRICE RANGES

The following price ranges refer to accommodations for two people in high season, including any taxes charged.

| | |
|---|---|
| **$** | less than M$800 |
| **$$** | M$800–1600 |
| **$$$** | more than M$1600 |

palm-thatched roof. Some have dirt floors and nothing inside but a bed; others are deluxe, with electric light, mosquito net, air-con, fridge and bar. Prices vary widely depending on location and amenities provided.

### CAMPING & TRAILER PARKS

Some campgrounds are actually trailer parks set up for people with camper vans and trailers (caravans) and are open to tent campers at lower rates. They're most common along the coast. Some restaurants and guesthouses in beach spots or rural areas will let you pitch a tent on their property for about M$100 per person.

### CASAS DE HUÉSPEDES & POSADAS

*Casas de huéspedes* (guesthouses) and posadas (inns) are normally inexpensive and congenial, family-run accommodations with a relaxed atmosphere. More often than not, a *casa de huéspedes* is a home converted into guest lodgings, so it allows for plenty of interaction with the host family.

### HAMMOCKS

A hammock can be a very comfortable place to sleep in hot areas (but mosquito repellent or a net often

---

comes in handy). You can rent a hammock and a place to hang it – usually under a palm roof outside a small guesthouse or beach restaurant – for M$50 to M$100. With your own hammock, the cost comes down a bit. It's easy to buy hammocks throughout the Yucatán.

### HOSTELS

Hostels exist in nearly all the region's most popular tourist destinations. They provide dorm accommodations (for about M$200 to M$300 per person), plus communal kitchens, bathrooms and living space, and often more expensive private rooms. Standards of hygiene and security vary. Always ask if the dorms come with air-con – you might need it on a hot day.

### HOTELS

Yucatán has hotels in all price ranges, especially in developed areas. Before settling on a room, ask to see the range of options available. An additional M$200 or so in the budget and midrange categories may be the difference between a musty interior room and airy digs with a nice view. Top-end hotels offer rooms with varying degrees of luxury, depending on what you're willing to fork out.

### RESORTS

A popular option for families, particularly in Cancún and the Riviera Maya, these sprawling hotels usually offer all-inclusive packages and provide most of everything you'll need within

---

### PLAN YOUR STAY ONLINE

For more accommodations reviews by Lonely Planet authors, check out www.lonelyplanet.com. You'll find independent reviews, as well as recommendations on the best places to stay.

## Climate

### Cancún

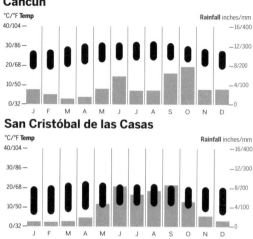

### San Cristóbal de las Casas

the confines of the property. There are also adults-only resorts, which put a premium on luxury and comfort. Some resorts still promote cheaper European plans.

## Activities

There's never a shortage of things to do on the Yucatán Peninsula, where you'll find some of the best scuba diving and snorkeling in the world, thousands of limestone swimming holes and ancient Maya ruins nearly everywhere you turn.

### Resources

**Amtave Mexican Adventure Tourism & Ecotourism Association** Has some 80 member organizations.

**Mexico Online** (www.mexonline. com) Includes listings of activities providers.

**Planeta** (www.planeta.com) Good resource on active and responsible tourism.

## Courses

Taking classes can be a great way to meet people and get an inside angle on local life and culture. Mexican universities often offer language classes. For long-term study in Mexico you'll need a student visa; contact a Mexican consulate for details. You can also arrange informal Spanish tutoring through some hostels. There are helpful links on the Lonely Planet website (www. lonelyplanet.com).

➡ You can take language courses in Mérida, Playa del Carmen and Puerto Morelos.

➡ For cooking courses you'll find good schools in culinary capital Mérida and beach town Puerto Morelos.

## Discount Cards

Reduced prices for students and seniors on Mexican buses and at museums and archaeological sites are usually only for those with Mexican residence or education credentials, but the following cards will sometimes get you a reduction (the ISIC is the most widely recognized). They are also recognized for reduced-price air tickets at student- and youth-oriented travel agencies.

**ISIC** (www.isic.org) Student card.

**ITIC** (International Teacher Identity Card) For full-time teachers.

**IYTC** (International Youth Travel Card) For those under 31 years.

## Embassies & Consulates

It's important to understand what your own embassy can and can't do to help you if you get into trouble. Generally speaking, it won't be much help in emergencies if the trouble you're in is remotely your own fault. Remember that you are bound by the laws of the country you are in. In genuine emergencies you might get some assistance, such as a list of lawyers, but only if other channels have been exhausted.

Embassy details can be found at Secretaría de Relaciones Exteriores (www.sre. gob.mx) and Embassyworld (www.embassyworld.org).

Many embassies or their consular agencies are in Mexico City (including Australia, Ireland and New Zealand); Cancún is home to several consulates, and there are some diplomatic outposts elsewhere in the region as well.

**Canadian Consulate**
**Cancún** (☏998-883-33-60; www.mexico.gc.ca; Blvd Kukulcán Km 12.5, Centro Empresarial Oficina LE7; ◷9am-1pm Mon-Fri);
**Playa del Carmen** (☏984-803-24-11; www. canadainternational.gc.ca; 3rd fl, Av 10 Sur s/n, btwn Calles 3 & 5 Sur, in Plaza Paraíso Caribe; ◷9am-1pm Mon-Fri)

**Dutch Consulate**
**Mérida** (☏999-924-31-22; http://mexico.nlambassade.org; Calle 64 No 418; ◷8:30am-5:30pm Mon-Fri)

**French Consulate**
**Mérida** (☏999-930-15-42, 999-930-15-00; merida. chfrance@gmail.com; Calle 60 No 385, btwn 41 and 43; ◷9am-5pm Mon-Fri)

**German Consulate**

**Cancún** (☏998-884-15-98; www.mexiko.diplo.de; Punta Conoco SM24; ⊙9am-3pm Mon-Fri); **Mérida** (☏999-944-32-52; merida@hk-diplo.de; Calle 51 No 329 btwn, Calles 52 & 54, Fracc Francisco de Montejo; ⊙by appt only)

**Guatemalan Consulate**

**Comitán** (☏963-110-68-16; www.minex.gob.gt; 1a Calle Sur Poniente 35, Int 3 4th fl, Comitán; ⊙9am-1pm & 2-5pm Mon-Fri); **Tapachula** (☏962-626-12-52; www.minex.gob.gt; 5a Norte 67; ⊙9am-5pm Mon-Fri)

**UK Consulate**

**Cancún** (☏Mexico City 55-1670-3200; www.gov.uk/world/mexico; Torre Europea 202, Blvd Kukulcán Km 12.5; ⊙8am-1pm Mon-Fri)

**US Consulate**

**Cancún** (☏999-316-71-68, 998-883-02-72; https://mx.usembassy.gov; Torre La Europea 301, Blvd Kukulcán Km 12.6; ⊙8:30am-1:30pm Mon-Fri); **Mérida** (☏999-942-57-00; https://mx.usembassy.gov/embassy-consulates/merida; Calle 60 No 338K; ⊙by appointment only)

**EATING PRICE RANGES**

The following price ranges refer to the cost of a main dish for lunch or dinner.

**$** less than M$100

**$$** M$100–200

**$$$** more than M$200

## Food

Yucatán is blessed with distinctive and tasty regional cuisine and the salsas run hot, due to ample use of *habanero* chiles. But it's easy to find Italian and American foods (even in smaller towns) if you need a change of pace.

## Health

Travelers to the Yucatán need to be careful chiefly about food- and water-borne diseases, though mosquito-borne infections can also be a problem, Zika and dengue being the most high profile. Most of these illnesses are not life threatening, but they can certainly impact on your trip or have other long-term consequences. Besides getting the proper vaccinations, it's important that you bring a good insect repellent and exercise care in what you eat and drink.

Be sure to keep your water intake up; it can get hot in these parts and it's easy to get dehydrated if you're not careful, whether you're lying on a beach or exploring ruins. Both are thirsty work.

Private hospitals give better care than public ones, but are more expensive.

### Before You Go
**RECOMMENDED VACCINATIONS**

Make sure all routine vaccinations are up to date and check whether all vaccines are suitable for children and pregnant women at www.cdc.gov/travel. Since most vaccines don't produce immunity until at least two weeks after they're given, visit a physician four to eight weeks before departure.

**Hepatitis A** All travelers (not recommended for pregnant women or children under two years); gamma globulin is the alternative.

**Hepatitis B** Long-term travelers in close contact with local population (requires three doses over a six-month period).

**Rabies** Recommended only for travelers who may have direct contact with stray dogs and cats, bats and wildlife.

**Typhoid** Recommended for all unvaccinated people, especially for those staying in small cities, villages and rural areas.

## Electricity

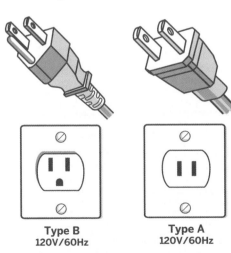

**Type B**
**120V/60Hz**

**Type A**
**120V/60Hz**

## In the Yucatán

### HEPATITIS A

➡ Hepatitis A occurs throughout Central America. It's a viral infection of the liver usually acquired by ingestion of contaminated water, food or ice, though it may also be acquired by direct contact with infected persons. Symptoms may include fever, malaise, jaundice, nausea, vomiting and abdominal pain. Most cases resolve uneventfully, though hepatitis A occasionally causes severe liver damage. There is no treatment.

➡ The vaccine for hepatitis A is extremely safe and highly effective. If you get a booster six to 12 months later, it lasts for at least 10 years. You should get it before you go to Mexico.

### DENGUE FEVER & CHIKUNGUNYA VIRUS

Dengue fever is a viral infection found throughout Central America. In Mexico, the risk is greatest along the Gulf coast, especially from July to September. Dengue is transmitted by Aedes mosquitoes, which bite preferentially during the day and are usually found close to human habitations, often indoors. They breed primarily in artificial water containers, such as cisterns and discarded tires. As a result, dengue is especially common in urban environments.

➡ Dengue causes severe flu-like symptoms, including fever, muscle aches, joint pains, headache and nausea, and it's often followed by a rash.

➡ Expect similar symptoms if infected by the mosquito-transmitted chikungunya virus.

➡ There is no vaccine and no specific treatment for dengue and chikungunya, except analgesics. Severe cases require hospitalization.

### MALARIA

Occurs in Chiapas and, in rare cases, Quintana Roo. It's transmitted by mosquito bites, usually between dusk and dawn. The main symptom is high spiking fevers, which may be accompanied by chills, sweats, headache, body aches, general weakness, vomiting or diarrhea.

➡ Taking malaria pills is strongly recommended when visiting rural areas. For Mexico, the first-choice malaria pill is chloroquine.

➡ Protecting yourself against mosquito bites is just as important as taking malaria pills, as no pills are 100% effective. If you develop a fever after returning home, see a physician, as malaria symptoms may not occur for months. It can be diagnosed by a simple blood test.

### MOSQUITO BITES

➡ To prevent bites, wear long sleeves, long pants, hats and shoes (rather than sandals). In areas with chaquistes (gnatlike sand flies that can leave welts), avoid exposing your flesh at dusk and dawn when they're out in full force.

➡ Don't sleep with the window open unless there is a functional screen. Use a good insect repellent that should be applied to exposed skin and clothing, but don't use DEET-containing compounds on children under two years.

➡ Insect repellents containing certain botanical products, including eucalyptus oil and soybean oil, are effective but last only 1½ to two hours. Where there is a high risk of malaria, use DEET-containing repellents. Products based on citronella are not effective.

➡ If sleeping outdoors or in accommodations that allow entry of mosquitoes, use a mosquito coil.

### SNAKE & SCORPION BITES

Venomous snakes in the Yucatán generally do not attack without provocation, but may bite humans who accidentally come too close. Coral snakes are somewhat retiring and tend not to bite humans unless considerably provoked.

➡ In the event of a venomous snake or scorpion bite, place the victim at rest, keep the bitten area immobilized and move them immediately to the nearest medical facility. Tourniquets are no longer recommended.

➡ To prevent scorpion stings, be sure to inspect and shake out clothing, shoes and sleeping bags before use. If stung, apply ice or cold packs.

### SUNBURN & HEAT EXHAUSTION

To protect yourself from excessive sun exposure, you should stay out of the midday sun, wear sunglasses and a wide-brimmed hat, and apply sunscreen with SPF 30 or higher, providing both UVA and UVB protection.

➡ Sunscreen should be applied to all exposed parts of the body approximately 30 minutes before sun exposure and be reapplied after swimming or vigorous activity.

➡ Do not apply sunscreen or bug repellent prior to swimming in cenotes (limestone sinkholes) – it pollutes the water.

➡ Drink plenty of fluids and avoid strenuous exercise when the temperature is high. Heat exhaustion is characterized by dizziness, weakness, headache, nausea or profuse sweating.

### TAP WATER

Tap water is generally not safe to drink.

➡ Vigorous boiling for several minutes is the most effective means of water purification.

➡ Another option is to disinfect water with iodine pills. Instructions are usually provided and should be carefully followed.

➡ Numerous water filters are on the market. Those with smaller pores (reverse osmosis filters) provide the best protection, but they are relatively large and readily plugged by debris. Those with somewhat larger pores (microstrainer filters) are ineffective against viruses, although they do remove other organisms.

**TYPHOID FEVER**

Typhoid fever is caused by ingestion of food or water contaminated by *Salmonella typhi*. Fever occurs in virtually all cases. Other symptoms may include headache, malaise, muscle aches, dizziness, loss of appetite, nausea and abdominal pain. Either diarrhea or constipation may occur.

The drug of choice for typhoid fever is usually a quinolone antibiotic, such as ciprofloxacin (Cipro) or levofloxacin (Levaquin).

**ZIKA VIRUS**

Zika has had a lot of press and is, unfortunately, present in the Yucatán, though at what density it is still unclear. What's not unclear is how to avoid it: take basic precautions to avoid mosquito bites. Use mosquito nets and repellent, wear insecticide-impregnated clothing, and avoid being outdoors without protection.

In itself, it presents as a relatively mild case of flu-like symptoms and generally goes away on its own. However, Zika has been linked to microcephaly, a birth deformation where the brain does not grow to normal size. Apparently most dangerous in the first trimester, Zika should be treated very seriously by pregnant women, women hoping to become pregnant, and their partners. At this time, research indicates that the virus can be spread by blood or unprotected sex much the same way many other STDs are. Though still not clear, the virus may also be linked to a rare nervous system disorder in men and women, Guillain–Barré syndrome.

Currently, there is no vaccine.

## Insurance

A travel-insurance policy to cover theft, loss and medical problems is a good idea. Some policies specifically exclude dangerous activities such as scuba diving and motorcycling.

Mexican medical treatment is generally inexpensive for common illnesses and minor treatment, but if you suffer some serious medical problem, you might want to find a private hospital or fly out for treatment. Travel insurance typically covers the costs but make sure the policy includes such things as ambulances and emergency flights home.

Some US health insurance policies stay in effect (at least for a limited time) if you travel abroad, but it's worth checking exactly what you'll be covered for in Mexico.

You might prefer a policy that pays medical costs directly rather than requiring you to pay on the spot and claim later. If you have to claim later, keep all documentation. There is a wide variety of policies; check the small print.

## Internet Access

Internet cafes (which charge about M$10 to M$15 per hour) still exist in the Yucatán but are going the way of the dodo; increasingly, there's free wi-fi in public plazas, and often it's available in restaurants and shops as well. Same for hotels with a computer for guests: mostly it's just wi-fi.

Many places (hotels, bars and restaurants) have wi-fi, but in some hotels the signal only reaches the lobby. We use the wi-fi icon in our reviews if the signal reaches at least some part of the premises; an internet icon refers to establishments with internet-ready computers for guests.

## Legal Matters

Mexican law presumes an accused person is guilty until proven innocent.

➡ As in most other countries, the purchase of controlled medication requires a doctor's prescription.

➡ It's against Mexican law to take firearms or ammunition into the country (even unintentionally).

➡ A law passed in 2009 decriminalized the possession of small amounts of certain drugs for personal use – including marijuana (up to 5g), cocaine (500mg), heroin (50mg) and methamphetamine (40mg). The law states that firsttime offenders do not face criminal prosecution. Selling drugs remains illegal, and people found in possession may still have to appear before a prosecutor to prove that the drugs are truly for personal use. The easiest way to stay out of trouble is to avoid drugs altogether.

## LGBTIQ+ Travelers

Mexico is more broadminded about sexuality than many might expect. LGBTIQ+ travelers rarely attract open discrimination or violence, though it's still uncommon to see open same-sex affection in the smaller rural towns. Public displays of affection, even between heterosexual couples, are uncommon in countryside Yucatán, so same-sex affection may raise an eyebrow.

## TAXES & REFUNDS

Mexico's value-added tax (IVA) is levied at 16%. By law the tax must be included in prices quoted to you and should not be added afterward. Signs in shops and notices on restaurant menus often state '*IVA incluido.*' Occasionally they state instead that IVA must be added to the quoted prices.

Some hotels in the region do not include IVA and a 3% lodging tax in their published fares, so you might be paying an additional 19% in hidden fees.

Discrimination based on sexual orientation has been illegal since 1999 and can be punished with up to three years in prison. Gay men have a more public profile than lesbians. Cancún has a small gay scene, and there are a number of gay-friendly establishments in Mérida listed at www.gaymexicomap.com.

**Gay Mexico** (www.gaymexico.com.mx) Useful online guide for gay tourism in Mexico.

**International Gay & Lesbian Travel Association** (www.iglta.org) Provides information on the major travel providers in the gay sector.

**Out Traveler** (www.outtraveler.com) Helpful general resource.

## Maps

➡ Free city and regional maps are available at tourist offices around the peninsula.

➡ Quality regional maps include the highly detailed ITMB (www.itmb.ca) 1:500,000 *Yucatán Travel Reference Map* (US$13).

➡ Guía Roji also publishes maps of each Mexican state and a national road atlas called *Por las Carreteras de Mexico* (M$220).

➡ Can-Do Maps (www.cancunmap.com) publishes various Yucatán maps that can be purchased online.

➡ A good internet source is Maps of Mexico (www.maps-of-mexico.com), with detailed maps of all states.

## Money

➡ Mexico's currency is the peso, usually denoted by the 'M$' sign. The peso is divided into 100 centavos. Coins come in five, 10, 20 and 50 centavos and one, two, five and 10 pesos; notes come in 20, 50, 100, 200, 500 and 1000 pesos.

➡ International credit cards are accepted for payment by most airlines, car-rental agencies, many midrange and upmarket hotels, and some restaurants, gas stations and shops; they can also be used to withdraw cash from ATMs. Visa is the most widely accepted card in the Yucatán.

➡ Many businesses take debit cards as well, but you'll usually wind up paying the card issuer a 3% international transaction fee. Some credit cards tack on international surcharges, too.

➡ As a backup to credit or debit cards, always carry cash, especially when visiting remote towns. US dollars, euros, British pounds and Canadian dollars are the most easily exchangeable foreign currencies. Some hotels offer discounts for cash. Many restaurants outside tourist centers accept cash only.

### ATMs

ATMs (*caja permanente* or *cajero automático*) are plentiful in the Yucatán and are the easiest source of cash, though a few tourist areas (like Río Lagartos and surrounds) still remain without. You can use major credit cards and some bank cards, such as those on the Cirrus and Plus systems, to withdraw pesos (or dollars) from ATMs. The exchange rate that banks use for ATM withdrawals is normally better than the 'tourist rate' – though that advantage is negated by transaction fees and other methods that banks have of taking your money. Use ATMs during daylight hours, and whenever possible, in secure indoor locations.

### Banks & Casas de Cambio

You can change currency in banks or at *casas de cambio* (money-exchange offices). Banks have longer lines than *casas de cambio* and usually shorter hours. *Casas de cambio* can easily be found in just about every large or medium-size town and in some smaller ones.

### International Transfers

Should you need money wired to you in Mexico, an easy and quick method is through **Western Union** (☏ toll-free USA 800-325-6000; www.westernunion.com). The service is offered by many bank branches and other businesses in the Yucatán, identified by black-and-yellow signs.

### Tipping

**Hotels** About 5% to 10% of room costs for staff.

**Restaurants** 15% if service is not already included.

**Supermarket baggers/gas-station attendants** Usually around M$5.

**Porters** M$25 per bag.

**Taxis** Drivers don't expect tips unless they provide an extra service.

**Bars** Bartenders usually don't get tips so anything is appreciated.

# Opening Hours

Hours at some places may decrease during shoulder and low seasons. Some shops, restaurants and hotels may close for several weeks – or several months – during low season.

**Archaeological sites** 8am to 5pm

**Banks** 9am to 5pm Monday to Friday; some open 10am to 2pm Saturday (hours may vary)

**Cafes** 8am to 9pm

**Cenotes** 9am to 5pm

**Museums** 9am to 5pm Tuesday to Sunday

# Photography & Video

Keep in mind the following tips when shooting.

➡ Most Mexicans don't mind having their pictures taken but it's always a good idea to ask beforehand. Some indigenous people can be especially sensitive about this.

➡ Be forewarned that a fee for use of actual video cameras (starting from around M$45) is charged at many archaeological sites.

➡ In large cities such as Cancún and Mérida, you'll find shops selling everything from waterproof disposable cameras to camcorders and memory cards for digital cameras. Some even sell film (long live analog!).

➡ If your camera breaks down, you'll be able to find a repair shop in most sizable towns.

For more information on taking travel photographs, check out Lonely Planet's *Travel Photography*.

# Post

➡ An airmail letter or postcard weighing up to 20g costs M$11.50 to send to the US or Canada, M$13.50 to Europe or South America and M$15 to the rest of the world.

➡ Delivery takes 15 to 20 days, or five to eight days if you pay for express service. (Or occasionally never; all part of the fun.)

➡ If you're sending a package internationally, be prepared to open it for inspection at the post office; take packing materials with you and don't seal it till you get there.

➡ For assured and speedy delivery, you can use one of the more expensive international courier services, such as UPS (www.ups.com/mx/es) or **FedEx** (☑toll-free 800-003-3339; www.fedex.com/mx).

# Public Holidays

Banks, post offices, government offices and many shops throughout Mexico are closed on the following national holidays.

**Año Nuevo** (New Year's Day) January 1

**Día de la Constitución** (Constitution Day) February 5

**Día del Nacimiento de Benito Juárez** (Anniversary of Benito Juárez' birth) March 21

**Día del Trabajo** (Labor Day) May 1

**Día de la Independencia** (Independence Day) September 16

**Día de la Revolución** (Revolution Day) November 20

**Día de Navidad** (Christmas Day) December 25

In addition, many offices and businesses close on the following optional holidays.

**Día de la Bandera** (National Flag Day) February 24

**Viernes Santo** (Good Friday) Two days before Easter Sunday

**Cinco de Mayo** (Commemorates Mexico's victory over French forces in Puebla) May 5

**Día de la Raza** (Columbus' 'discovery' of the New World) October 12

**Día de Muertos** (Day of the Dead) November 1 and 2

**Día de Nuestra Señora de Guadalupe** (Day of Our Lady of Guadalupe) December 12

# Safe Travel

Despite all the grim news about Mexico's drug-related violence, the Yucatán Peninsula remains relatively safe for those not engaged in illegal activities. Most of the killings you hear about happen between rival drug gangs, so tourists are rarely caught up in the disputes – especially in the Yucatán, which keeps a safe distance from the turf wars occurring elsewhere in Mexico. Cancún, Playa del Carmen and Tulum have all seen a gradual rise in drug violence, but major US cities such as New York and Chicago have higher murder rates than the entire state of Yucatán.

That said, purchasing recreational drugs or even engaging pushers in conversation can mark you as a target for interrogation or worse by police or gangs. You are best off avoiding this entirely.

## Government Travel Advice

Foreign affairs departments can supply a variety of useful data about travel to Mexico.

**Australia** (☑in Australia 02-6261-3305; www.homeaffairs.gov.au)

**Canada** (☑in Canada 800-267-8376, outside Canada 1-613-944-4000; www.dfait-maeci.gc.ca)

**UK** (☑in UK 020-7008-1500; www.gov.uk/fco)

**USA** (https://travel.state.gov/content/passports/en/alertswarnings.html)

## Theft & Robbery

Crime against tourists here is rare; however, minimizing your risks will help ensure you have a problem-free vacation. Pickpocketing and bag-snatching are relatively minor risks in the Yucatán, but it's a good idea to stay alert on buses and in crowded bus terminals and airports. Mugging is less common than purse-snatching, but more serious: resistance may be met with violence (do *not* resist). Usually these robbers will not harm you: they just want your money, fast.

➔ Don't go where there are few other people in the vicinity; this includes camping in secluded places. A simple rule: if there are families around, you're probably safe.

➔ Don't leave any valuables unattended while you swim. Run-and-grab thefts by people lurking in the woods are a common occurrence.

➔ If your hotel has a safe, leave most of your money, important documents and smaller valuables there in a sealed, signed envelope. Leave valuables in a locker when you are staying at a hostel.

➔ In the event of theft, make sure you have emailed yourself photocopies of your passport, drivers license, tourist card, and anything else that might be necessary for establishing your identity at an embassy. Having these documents on a USB key can also be useful in emergencies.

➔ Carry only a small amount of money – enough for an outing – in a pocket. If you do have to carry valuables, keep them hidden in a money belt. Keep larger bills separate from your smaller cash so that if someone sees you paying for something, they don't know that you have other money.

➔ Don't keep money, credit or debit cards, wallets or bags in open view any longer than you have to. At ticket counters, keep a hand or foot on your bag at all times.

➔ Do not leave anything valuable-looking in a parked vehicle.

➔ Be careful about accepting drinks from overly social characters in bars, especially in tourist-heavy zones; there have been cases of drugging followed by robbery and assault. Products are available – ranging from drink straws to press-on fingernails – that allow you to test for a tainted drink.

➔ Be wary of attempts at credit-card fraud. One method is when the cashier swipes your card twice (once for the transaction and once for nefarious purposes). Keep your card in sight at all times.

➔ Another swindle is when you pay for something with a M$500 bill, the clerk palms it and instantly produces a M$50 (they are both pink), asking 'Where's the rest of the money?' You scratch your head and then pay the rest, thinking you accidentally used a M$50 instead of a M$500 note. The swindler keeps the change.

➔ Purchasing illegal drugs or activities can quickly end up going sour, so avoid putting yourself in danger.

## Telephone
### Cell Phones

Using your own cell phone from home in Mexico can be extremely expensive due to high roaming fees. Roaming Zone (www.roamingzone.com) is a useful source on roaming arrangements. Alternatively, you can insert a Mexican SIM card into your phone, but your phone needs to be unlocked for international use. Some Mexican cell-phone companies will unlock it for you for a fee. The easiest option is to simply buy a new Mexican cell phone: they're inexpensive (a cheapo costs around M$500 and comes with free credit). You'll often

see cell phones on sale in convenience stores, where you can also buy more credit. Cell-phone service providers Telcel (www.telcel.com) and Movistar (www.movistar.com.mx) have the best coverage in the Yucatán region. (But ask around, in case others have entered the market.)

Like other Mexican phone numbers, every cell-phone number has an area code (usually the code of the city where the phone was bought). Here's how to make calls to and from Mexican cell phones.

➔ From local cell phone to cell phone, just dial the 10-digit number.

➔ From cell phone to landline, dial the landline's area code and number (10 digits).

➔ From landline to cell phone, dial ☎044 before the 10 digits if the cell phone's area code is the same as the area code you are dialing from, or ☎045 before the 10 digits if the cell phone has a different area code.

➔ From another country to a Mexican cell phone, dial your international access code, then the Mexican country code (☎52), then 1, then the 10-digit number.

Credit on Mexican cell phones or SIM cards burns fast, especially when making calls outside the phone's area code. Recently, however, competition has meant that there are some good short-term *paquetes* (packages) deals with unlimited calls and the like.

### Collect Calls

*Una llamada por cobrar* (a collect call) can cost the receiving party much more than if they call you, so you may prefer for the other party to call. You can make collect calls from card phones without a card. Call an operator at ☎020 for domestic calls, or ☎090 for international calls. The Mexican term for 'home country direct' is *país directo:* but don't count on Mexican international operators knowing the access codes for all countries.

Some call offices and hotels will make collect calls for you, but they usually charge for the service.

### Landlines

Mexican landlines (*telefonos fijos*) have two- or three-digit area codes.

➡ From landline to another landline in the same town, dial the local number (seven or eight digits).

➡ From landline to landline in another Mexican town, dial the long-distance prefix 01, the area code and the local number.

➡ To make an international call, dial the international prefix ☑00, the country code (☑1 for the US and Canada, ☑44 for the UK etc), and the city area code and number.

➡ To call a Mexican landline from another country, dial the international access code, followed by the Mexico country code 52, the area code and number.

### Long-Distance Discount Cards

Available at many newspaper stands, usually in denominations of M$100 and M$200, *tarjetas telefónicas de descuento* (discount phone cards) offer substantial savings on long-distance calls from landlines. Use them from most public card phones.

### Public Card Phones

These are no longer common but you'll still find a few at airports and bus stations. The most common are those of the country's biggest phone company, Telmex. To use a Telmex card phone you need a phone card known as a *tarjeta Ladatel.* These are sold at kiosks and shops everywhere in denominations of M$30, M$50 and M$100.

## VOIP

Voice Over Internet Protocol (VOIP) services such as Skype (www.skype.com) are a very economical option for travelers who have a computer and the required software. You can also use Skype at internet cafes.

## Time

The states of Campeche, Chiapas, Tabasco and Yucatán observe the Hora del Centro, which is the same as US Central Time – GMT minus six hours in winter, and GMT minus five hours during daylight saving time (*horario de verano,* summer time), which runs from the first Sunday in April to the last Sunday in October. The state of Quintana Roo observes Eastern Standard Time, GMT minus five hours in winter. Clocks go forward one hour in April and back one hour in October.

## Toilets

Public toilets are rare, so take advantage of facilities in places such as hotels, restaurants, bus terminals and museums; a fee of about M$5 may be charged. It's fairly common for toilets in budget hotels and restaurants to lack seats.

When out and about, carry some toilet paper with you because it often won't be provided. If there's a bin beside the toilet (nearly always, except in ritzy hotels), put soiled paper in it because the drains can't cope otherwise.

## Tourist Information

Just about every town of interest to tourists in the Yucatán has a state or municipal tourist office. They are generally helpful with maps, brochures and questions, and often

some staff members speak English.

You can call the Mexico City office of the national tourism ministry **Sectur** (☑55-5250-0151, 800-903-92-00, in the US 800-482-9832; www.visitmexico.com) at any time – 24/7 – for information or help in English or Spanish.

**Campeche** (www.visitmexico. com)

**Mexico Tourist Information** (www.visitmexico.com)

**Quintana Roo** (☑Cancún 998-881-90-00, Chetumal 983-835-08-60; http://qroo.gob.mx/ sedetur)

## Visas

Every tourist must have a Mexican government tourist permit, which is easily obtainable. Some nationalities also need to obtain visas.

➡ Citizens of the US, Canada, EU countries, Australia, New Zealand, Iceland, Israel, Japan, Norway and Switzerland are among the dozens of countries whose citizens do not require visas to enter Mexico as tourists.

➡ The website of the **Instituto Nacional de Migración** (☑toll-free 800-004-62-64; www.inm.gob.mx; Calle Homero 1832, Polanco, Mexico City) lists countries that must obtain a visa to travel to Mexico. If the purpose of your visit is to work (even as a volunteer), to report, to study, or to participate in humanitarian aid or human-rights observation, you may well need a visa whatever your nationality. Visa procedures can take several weeks and you may need to apply in your country of citizenship or residence.

➡ US citizens traveling by land or sea can enter Mexico and return to the USA with a passport card, but if traveling by air will need a passport. Non-US citizens passing (even in transit) through the USA on the way to or from Mexico should check well in advance on the US's complicated visa rules. Consult a US consulate, the US State Department (www.travel.state.gov) or US Customs and Border Protection (www.cbp.gov) websites.

➔ The regulations sometimes change. It's wise to confirm them with a Mexican embassy or consulate. Good sources for information on visa and similar matters are the London consulate (https://consulmex.sre. gob.mx/reinounido) and the Washington consulate (https://consulmex.sre.gob. mx/washington).

## Tourist & Permit Fee

The Mexican tourist permit (tourist card; officially the *forma migratoria multiple* or FMM) is a brief paper document that you must fill out and get stamped by Mexican immigration when you enter Mexico and keep till you leave. It's available at official border crossings, international airports, ports and often from airlines. It's also available online. Important: at land borders you won't usually be given one automatically (eg if crossing by car) – you have to ask for it; ensure you do.

A tourist permit only permits you to engage in what are considered to be tourist activities (including sports, health, artistic and cultural activities).

➔ The maximum possible stay is 180 days for most nationalities, but immigration officers will sometimes put a lower number unless you tell them specifically what you need.

➔ The fee for the tourist permit, called the *derecho de no residente* (DNR; non-resident fee), is M$533 (or US$27 equivalent), but it's free for people entering by land who stay less than seven days. If you enter

Mexico by air, however, the fee is usually included in your airfare.

➔ If you enter by land, you must pay the fee at a bank in Mexico at any time before you reenter the frontier zone on your way out of Mexico (or before you check in at an airport to fly out of Mexico). Most Mexican border posts have on-the-spot bank offices where you can pay the DNR fee. When you pay at a bank, your tourist permit will be stamped to prove that you have paid.

➔ Look after your tourist permit because it may be checked when you leave the country. You can be fined for not having it.

If you lose your tourist permit, contact your nearest Instituto Nacional de Migración (National Immigration Institute; INM) office, which will issue a duplicate for M$500 (or US$25 equivalent). All international airports have immigration offices.

## Volunteering

Volunteering is a great way of giving back to local communities. In the Yucatán there are various organizations that welcome any help they can get, from environmental and wildlife-conservation NGOs to social programs.

You can always look for opportunities at your local hostel or language school, some of which offer part-time volunteering opportunities. Most programs require a minimum commitment of at least a month, and some charge fees for room and board.

## Volunteer Directories

**Go Abroad** (www.goabroad.com)

**Go Overseas** (www.gooverseas. com)

**Idealist** (www.idealist.org)

**The Mexico Report** (www. themexicoreport.com/non-profits-in-mexico)

**Transitions Abroad** (www. transitionsabroad.com)

## Yucatán-based Programs

**Centro Ecológico Akumal** (www.ceakumal.org) Accepts volunteers for its environmental and protection programs.

**Flora, Fauna y Cultura de México** (☑984-871-52-89, cell 984-1880626; www. florafaunaycultura.org; Hwy 307 Km 282, Xcaret park office; ☺9am-5pm Mon-Fri) ◗ You can help with turtle conservation in Xcacel from June to October.

**Junax** (www.junax.org.mx) Works with indigenous communities in Chiapas; volunteers must speak Spanish.

**Pronatura** (☑999-988-44-36; www.pronatura-ppy.org.mx; Calle 32 No 269, Col Pinzón II, Mérida) Mérida-based environmental organization sometimes seeks volunteers to work on various projects in the Yucatán.

# Women Travelers

Gender equality has come a long way in Mexico, and Yucatecans are generally a very polite people. Still, women traveling alone may still be subject to some whistles, loud comments and annoying attempts to chat them up (even the impromptu marriage proposal or two).

The same precautions one would take anywhere make sense here. If something feels off, listen to your gut.

On the streets of inland cities and towns, such as in Mérida and Valladolid, you'll notice that women cover up and don't display too much leg, midriff or even their shoulders. This also makes it easier to keep valuables out of sight.

# Transportation

## GETTING THERE & AWAY

### Entering the Region

Immigration officers usually won't keep you waiting any longer than it takes to flick through your passport and enter your length of stay on your tourist permit. Anyone traveling to Mexico via the USA should be sure to check US visa and passport requirements. US citizens traveling by land or sea can enter Mexico and return to the US with a passport card, but when traveling by air will need a passport. Citizens of other countries need their passports to enter Mexico. Some nationalities also need a visa. Flights, cars and tours can be booked online at lonelyplanet.com/bookings.

## Air

Most visitors to the Yucatán arrive by air. Direct flights normally originate from an airline's hub city and connecting flights often go through Mexico City.

Mexico's flagship airline is Aeroméxico. Its safety record is comparable to major US and European airlines. Domestic low-cost carriers provide service mostly from Mexico City. MayAir runs prop planes that stop in Cozumel, Cancún and Mérida.

Low-cost carrier Interjet stopped flying in December 2020 and its longer-term future was uncertain.

### Airports & Airlines

The majority of flights into the peninsula arrive in Cancún or Mérida. The Yucatán's major airports are as follows.

**Aeropuerto Ángel Albino Corzo** (☑961-153-60-68; www.chiapasaero.com; Sarabia s/n) Aka Tuxtla Gutiérrez; serves San Cristóbal de las Casas in Chiapas.

**Aeropuerto Internacional de Cancún** (Cancún International Airport; ☑998-848-72-00; www.asur.com.mx; Hwy 307 Km 22)

**Aeropuerto Internacional de Mérida** (Mérida International Airport; ☑999-940-60-90; www.asur.com.mx; Hwy 180 Km 4.5; ☑R-79)

**Cozumel Airport** (☑987-872-20-81; www.asur.com.mx; Blvd Aeropuerto Cozumel s/n)

Other cities with airports include Campeche, Chetumal, Ciudad del Carmen, Palenque and Villahermosa.

**DOMESTIC AIRLINES FLYING TO & FROM THE YUCATÁN**

**Aeroméxico** (☑55-5133-4000; www.aeromexico.com)

**Interjet** (☑55-1102-5555, toll-free USA 866-285-9525; www.interjet.com)

**Magnicharters** (☑55-5141-1351; www.magnicharters.com.mx)

---

### CLIMATE CHANGE & TRAVEL

Every form of transport that relies on carbon-based fuel generates $CO_2$, the main cause of human-induced climate change. Modern travel is dependent on airplanes, which might use less fuel per kilometer per person than most cars but travel much greater distances. The altitude at which aircraft emit gases (including $CO_2$) and particles also contributes to their climate change impact. Many websites offer 'carbon calculators' that allow people to estimate the carbon emissions generated by their journey and, for those who wish to do so, to offset the impact of the greenhouse gases emitted with contributions to portfolios of climate-friendly initiatives throughout the world. Lonely Planet offsets the carbon footprint of all staff and author travel.

**MayAir** (☑USA 414-755-2527, toll-free 800-962-92-47; www.mayair.com.mx)

**VivaAerobus** (☑81-8215-0150, toll-free USA 888-935-9848; www.vivaaerobus.com)

**Volaris** (☑55-1102-8000, toll-free USA 855-865-2747; www.volaris.com)

## Land
### Mexico

➡ Hwy 180 runs north from Villahermosa, the state capital of Tabasco, then it heads along the coast to Campeche and makes its way inland toward Mérida, where it veers east toward Cancún. You can either take the free highway to Cancún (Hwy 180) or a toll road (Hwy 180D).

➡ In Cancún, Hwy 180 connects with Hwy 307, which runs south along the Riviera Maya and Costa Maya to Chetumal, Quintana Roo's capital. From Chetumal, Hwy 186 takes you to Hwy 199, the turnoff for Palenque and San Cristóbal de las Casas, in Chiapas.

➡ Palenque is only about two hours from Villahermosa. If you'd like to explore more of Mexico beyond the peninsula, the continuation of Hwy 180 in Villahermosa goes west to the Gulf coast state of Veracruz.

### Belize

➡ Crossing from Mexico into Belize, at the southern tip of Quintana Roo, is easy for most tourists.

➡ Each person leaving Belize for Mexico needs to pay a US$15 exit fee for visits less than 24 hours and US$20 for longer stays. All fees must be paid in cash, in Belizean or US currency – officials usually won't have change for US currency.

➡ Frequent buses run from Chetumal to the Belizean towns of Corozal (around M$50, one hour) and Orange Walk. The buses depart from the old ADO bus station and some continue on to Belize City.

➡ A boat departs from Chetumal to San Pedro; this is an easier, if more expensive route than taking a bus to Belize City and then taking a local boat.

➡ Car-rental companies do not allow you to cross the Mexico–Belize border with their vehicles.

### Guatemala

➡ The borders at La Mesilla/Ciudad Cuauhtémoc, Ciudad Tecún Umán/Ciudad Hidalgo and El Carmen/Talismán are all linked to Guatemala City, and nearby cities within Guatemala and Mexico, by plentiful buses and/or combis (minibuses).

➡ Agencies in San Cristóbal de las Casas offer daily van service to the Guatemalan cities of Quetzaltenango, Panajachel and Antigua.

➡ Additionally, several buses depart from the San Cristóbal de las Casas bus station that goes to the Ciudad Cuauhtémoc border, where you can catch Guatemalan buses on the other side in the border town of La Mesilla.

➡ **Transportes Palenque** (☑Guatemala 01-91-6345-2430; www.transportespalenque.com/home/; Calle Allende, enter Av 20 de Noviembre y Corregidora, Col Centro, Palenque Chiapas) runs vans out of Palenque to Tenosique (Tabasco), where you'll find onward connections to Guatemala.

➡ Travelers with their own vehicles can travel by road between Tenosique and Flores (Guatemala), via the border at El Ceibo.

➡ Car-rental companies do not allow you to cross the Mexico–Guatemala border with their vehicles.

## Sea

Water taxis depart from Chetumal's *muelle fiscal* (dock) on Blvd Bahía to San Pedro (Belize). Between the two companies operating water taxis, there's daily service to the island. See www.sanpedrowatertaxi.com and www.belizewatertaxi.com for more information.

Mahahual, Puerto Chiapas, Progreso and Isla Cozumel are ports of call for cruise ships. Many cruise-ship lines serve these ports.

**Carnival Cruise Lines** (☑toll-free USA 800-764-7419; www.carnival.com)

**Crystal Cruises** (☑toll-free USA 888-722-0021; www.crystalcruises.com)

**Norwegian Cruise Lines** (☑toll-free USA 866-234-7350; www.ncl.com)

---

### DEPARTURE TAX

An airport departure tax is usually included in your ticket cost, but if it isn't you must pay in cash during airport check-in. It varies from airport to airport, but costs about US$26 (price fluctuates) for international flights departing from Cancún and less for domestic flights. This tax is separate from the fee for your tourist permit, which also is usually included in airfares.

There are two taxes on domestic flights: IVA, the value-added tax (16%), and TUA, an airport tax of about US$14. In Mexico, the taxes are normally included in quoted fares and paid when you buy the ticket. But if you bought a ticket outside Mexico, you will have to pay the TUA when you check-in in Mexico.

**P&O Cruises** (☑UK 0344-338-8003; www.pocruises.com)

**Princess Cruises** (☑toll-free USA 800-774-6237; www.princess.com)

**Royal Caribbean International** (☑Mexico 55-877-3492, toll-free USA 866-562-7625; www.royalcaribbean.com)

# GETTING AROUND

## Boat

Frequent ferries depart from Playa del Carmen to Isla Cozumel, Cancún to Isla Mujeres and Chiquilá to Isla Holbox. The following prices are one-way fares.

**Isla Holbox** M$150

**Isla Cozumel** M$170 to M$220

**Isla Mujeres** M$160 from Puerto Juárez; about US$15 from Zona Hotelera

Cancún and Chiquilá have long-term parking available near the terminals. For more information about schedules, points of departure and car ferries, see www.granpuerto.com.mx and www.transcaribe.net. The Holbox ferries do not have websites.

 To reach the uninhabited island of Isla Contoy, you can hook up with tour operators with boats departing from **Cancún** (☑998-886-42-70; www.contoytours.com; Calle Vialidad s/n, V&V Marina; adult/child 5-12yr US$117/102; ☺tours 9am-5:30pm Tue-Sun) and **Isla Mujeres** (☑cell 998-1436758, cell 998-2570100; cnr Av Rueda Medina & Morelos; snorkeling from US$35, whale-shark tour US$100, Isla Contoy US$75; ☺7am-6pm).

## Bus

The Yucatán Peninsula has a good road and bus network, and comfortable, frequent, reasonably priced bus ser

vices connect all cities. Most cities and towns have one main bus terminal where all long-distance buses arrive and depart. It may be called the Terminal de Autobuses, Central de Autobuses, Central Camionera or simply La Central (not to be confused with *el centro*, the city center). If there is no single main bus terminal, different bus companies will have separate terminals scattered around town. **Grupo ADO** (☑Mexico City 55-5784-4652; www.ado.com.mx) operates many of the bus lines that you'll be using.

### Classes

#### DELUXE & EXECUTIVE

*De lujo* (deluxe) services, and the even more comfortable *ejecutivo* (executive), run mainly on the busy routes. They are swift, modern and comfortable, with reclining seats, adequate leg room, air-con, few or no stops, toilets on board (but not necessarily toilet paper), and sometimes drinks or snacks. Deluxe buses usually show movies on video screens and may offer headphones.

**ADO Platino** (www.ado.com.mx; cnr Avs Uxmal & Tulum), ADO GL and OCC provide luxury services. You can buy tickets to these services in the bus terminal before boarding.

#### 1ST CLASS

On *primera (1a) clase* (1st-class) buses, standards of comfort are adequate at the very least. The buses usually have air-con and a toilet, and they stop infrequently. They always show movies (often bad ones, unless Vin Diesel films are your idea of cinematic glory) for most of the trip.

 Bring a sweater or jacket to combat over-zealous air-conditioning. As with deluxe buses, you buy your ticket in the bus terminal before boarding. ADO sets the 1st-class standard.

#### 2ND CLASS

*Segunda (2a) clase* (2nd-class) buses serve small towns and villages, and provide cheaper, slower travel on some intercity routes. A few are almost as quick, comfortable and direct as 1st-class buses. Others are old, slow and shabby.

 Many 2nd-class services have no ticket office; you just pay your fare to the conductor. These buses tend to take slow, non-toll roads in and out of big cities and will stop anywhere to pick up passengers: if you board midroute you might make some of the trip standing. The small amount of money you save by traveling 2nd class is not usually worth the discomfort or extra journey time entailed, though traveling on these buses is a great way to meet locals and see less-traveled parts of the countryside.

 Second-class buses can also be less safe than 1st-class or deluxe buses, for reasons of maintenance, driver standards, or because of very unlikely incidents with highway bandits. In remote areas, however, you'll often find that 2nd-class buses are the only transportation available.

 The biggest 2nd-class companies are Mayab Sur, Oriente and Noreste.

 Microbuses or 'micros' are small, usually fairly new, 2nd-class buses with around 25 seats, often running short routes between nearby towns.

### Costs

First-class buses typically cost around M$1.50 to M$2 per kilometer. Deluxe buses may cost just 10% or 20% more than 1st class; *ejecutivo* services can be as much as 50% more. Second-class buses cost about 20% less than 1st class.

### Reservations

For trips of up to four or five hours on busy routes, you

can usually just go to the bus terminal, buy a ticket and head out without much delay. For longer trips, or routes with infrequent services, buy a ticket a day or more in advance. Deluxe and 1st-class bus companies have computerized ticket systems that allow you to select your seat when you buy your ticket.

Seats on deluxe and 1st-class lines such as ADO and OCC can be booked through **Mi Escape** (Map p156; ☎999-924-08-30; www.miescape.mx; Calle 70 555, btwn 69 & 71, Centro, Mérida; ☺8am-9pm Mon-Fri, 9am-5pm Sat & Sun), a reservations service with offices in Mérida, Cancún, Cozumel, Campeche and San Cristóbal de las Casas. Mi Escape adds a 10% surcharge to the cost of the ticket, so you can save a little money by simply purchasing tickets at the bus terminal.

ADO's website (www.ado.com.mx) offers online discounts.

# Car & Motorcycle

Driving in Mexico is not as easy as north of the border and rentals can get expensive for long visits, but having a vehicle gives you flexibility and freedom. To reach some of the peninsula's most remote beaches – such as faraway Punta Allen or the stretch of coast east of Progreso – having a car makes life much easier.

Drivers should ideally know some Spanish, have reserves of patience and access to extra cash for emergencies. Very big cars are unwieldy on narrow roads, particularly in the peninsula's rural areas. A sedan with a trunk provides safer storage than a hatchback. Tires (including a spare), shock absorbers and suspension should be in good condition. For security, have something

to immobilize the steering wheel.

Motorcycling around the Yucatán is not for the faint-hearted. Roads and traffic can be rough, and parts and mechanics hard to come by. Scooters are a good option for getting around on the islands of Isla Mujeres and Cozumel. Helmets are required by Mexican law.

## Bringing Your Own Car

Unless you're planning on spending a lot of time touring the Yucatán and other parts of Mexico, you're better off with a rental car. Of course, if you're bringing diving equipment or other cumbersome luggage, the long drive from the US or elsewhere may be worth your while.

You can check the full requirements for bringing a vehicle into Mexico with the American Automobile Association (www.aaa.com), a Mexican consulate or check the website of the Mexican Tourist Information (www.visitmexico.com).

## Driver's License

To drive a motor vehicle in Mexico you need a valid driver's license from your home country.

### FUEL

Gasolina (gasoline) and diesel fuel in Mexico is sold by the government-owned Pemex (Petróleos Mexicanos) and, since the deregulation of the market in recent years, other companies. All major cities and most mid-size towns in the Yucatán have gas stations. If you're heading to a remote coastal town or jungle region, you may need to fill up before leaving and wherever you can along the way.

The gasoline on sale is all sin plomo (unleaded). There are two varieties: magna, roughly equivalent to US regular unleaded, and premium, similar to US superunleaded.

At last visit, magna cost M$13.57 per liter, and premium M$14.38. Diesel fuel is widely available at M$14.20 per liter.

Before gas is added, ensure the pump is back to zero. Pump attendants at gas stations appreciate a tip of around M$5. Not all gas stations accept international credit and debit cards. A common attendant sleight-of-hand is to quickly swap your M$500 bill for a M$50 and claim you only gave them M$50...so count the money as you hand it first.

### INSURANCE

It is very foolish to drive in Mexico without Mexican liability insurance. If you are involved in an accident, you can be jailed and have your vehicle impounded while responsibility and restitution is assessed.

If you are to blame for an accident causing injury or death, you may be detained until you guarantee restitution to the victims and payment of any fines. This could take weeks or months.

Adequate Mexican insurance coverage is the only real protection – it is regarded as a guarantee that restitution will be paid. Mexican law recognizes only Mexican motor insurance (seguro), so a US or Canadian policy, even if it provides coverage, is not acceptable to Mexican officialdom. If you drive your own vehicle, you can buy Mexican motor insurance online through the well-established **Sanborn's** (☎toll-free USA 800-222-0158; www.sanbornsinsurance.com) and other companies.

Most visitors to the Yucatán rent vehicles, which come with optional insurance policies for additional insurance, but they won't rent without basic liability.

### MAPS

Signposting can be poor, especially along the Yucatán's non-toll roads, and decent maps are essential. Regional road maps such as ITMB's *Yucatán Peninsula Travel Reference Map* (US$12) are good options, or if you plan on visiting other parts of Mexico, Guatemala or Belize, Guia Roji's *Por las Carreteras de México* (M$220) will serve you well. Guia Roji maps are sold at bookstores, Sanborns department stores, some newsstands and online at www.guiaroji. com.mx.

The alternative, of course, is Google Maps, but sometimes there is no reception so don't rely solely on this. A useful offline mapping app is MapsMe, which has navigation, routes, and detailed offline map capabilities.

## RENTALS

Auto rental in the Yucatán is fairly affordable and easy to organize. You can book by internet, phone or in person, and pick up cars at city offices, airports and many of the big hotels. You'll save money by booking ahead of time over the internet. Read the small print of the rental agreement.

➡ Renters must provide a valid driver's license (your home license is OK), passport and major credit card, and are usually required to be at least 21 years old (sometimes 25, or if you're aged 21 to 24 you may have to pay a surcharge).

➡ In addition to the basic rental rate, you pay tax and insurance to the rental company, and the full insurance that rental companies encourage can almost double the base cost. You'll usually have the option of taking liability-only insurance (called *daños a terceros*) at a lower rate. Ask exactly what the insurance options cover: theft and damage insurance may only cover a percentage of costs. It's best to have plenty of liability coverage: Mexican law permits the jailing of drivers after an accident until they have met their obligations to third parties.

➡ The complimentary car-rental insurance offered with some US credit cards does not always cover Mexico. Call your card company ahead of time to check.

➡ Most rental agencies offer unlimited miles. Local firms may or may not be cheaper than the big international ones. In most places the cheapest car available costs M$600 to M$1000 a day, including unlimited miles, insurance and tax. If you rent by the week or month, the per-day cost can come down by 20% to 40%.

➡ You can cut costs by avoiding airport pickups and drop-offs, for which 10% can be added to your total check.

➡ There's usually an extra charge for drop-off in another city.

➡ Remember that you cannot take a rental car out of Mexico unless you have obtained a special permit.

**Alamo** (☏998-886-01-00; www.alamo.com.mx; Hwy 307 Km 22, Cancún airport; ☺24hr)

**Easy Way** (☏toll free 800-327-99-29; www.easywayrentacar. com)

**Hertz** (☏800-709-50-00; www. hertz.com; Hwy 307 Km 22, Cancún airport; ☺24hr)

**National** (☏998-881-87-60; www.nationalcar.com; Hwy 307 Km 22, Cancún airport; ☺8:30am-8pm Mon-Fri, 9:30am-6pm Sat & Sun)

## ROAD CONDITIONS

There are several major toll roads (mostly four-lane) in the Yucatán that connect the big cities. They are generally in much better condition and a lot quicker than the alternative free roads.

Driving during rainy season (usually May to October) can be challenging to say the least, especially along bumpy dirt roads in rural and coastal areas.

Be especially wary of Alto (Stop) signs and speed bumps (called *topes, vibradores* or *reductores de velocidad*) and holes in the road. They are often not where you'd expect, and missing one can cost you a traffic fine or cause car damage. Speed bumps are also used to slow traffic on highways that pass through built-up areas – they are not always signed and some are severe!

Driving on a dark night is best avoided – potential hazards include unlit vehicles, rocks, pedestrians and animals on the roads. Also, hijacks and robberies can occur (stay particularly alert while driving in the vicinity of the Mexico–Guatemala border).

Narrow two-lane roads, some with brush spreading onto the asphalt, are often plied by wide delivery trucks driving well over the speed limit. If you see one approaching, pull over to the side of the road (as much as you can) and let it pass rather than risking a head-on collision.

## ROAD RULES

➡ Drive on the right-hand side of the road.

➡ One-way streets are common in many towns and cities. Signs with arrows usually indicate the direction of traffic; if the arrow points both ways, it's a two-way street.

➡ Speed limits range between 80km/h and 120km/h on open highways (less when highways pass through built-up areas), and between 30km/h and 50km/h in towns and cities. Traffic laws and speed limits rarely seem to be enforced on highways.

➡ Seat belts are obligatory for all occupants of a car, and children under five years must be strapped into safety seats in the rear.

➡ Although less frequent in the Yucatán, there is the chance you will be pulled over by traffic police for an imaginary infraction. Remember that you don't have to pay a bribe, and corrupt cops would rather not work too hard to obtain one. You can also ask to see documentation about the law you have supposedly broken and always get the officer's name, badge number, vehicle number and department (federal, state or municipal). Pay any traffic fines at a police station and get a receipt, then if you wish to make a complaint head for a state tourist office.

➡ Police are sometimes stationed along highways and roads, indicated by orange safety cones and a small office. Note: by law you must slow down and put on your hazard lights on approach (they might want to see your license but more often than not, just wave you through). Note that this is different from the *Federale* checkpoints, where men in black may ask you to get out of the car to search for contraband. They usually ask where you're headed and where you came from, and if you are polite and truthful you'll be fine. It can be scary for first timers; however, they are really just looking for cartel members or shipments.

➡ Street names are often difficult to find outside city centers. Some are labeled on telephone posts or walls of corner buildings.

### Driving Tips in the Yucatán

Consider the following when behind the wheel.

➡ Fast-approaching vehicles from behind will often shine their brights or use their left-turn signal to indicate that you should change lanes and let them pass.

➡ Some streets may suddenly change direction without warning: pay close attention to the road or you may find yourself driving against the flow of traffic.

➡ Liability insurance does not include theft coverage: something to think about when parking your car overnight on the street.

➡ Insurance often does not cover damage or towing required on dirt roads.

➡ Spare tires sometimes get swiped in large cities: if you're going somewhere where you may need it, make sure it's still there before leaving.

➡ If you're pulled over at a military or police checkpoint, remain calm and courteous – they're usually just looking for vehicles transporting arms and drugs. You definitely don't want to be caught with either.

## Hitchhiking

Hitchhiking is never entirely safe in any country and even in Mexico's relatively safe Yucatán region it's best avoided. Travelers who decide to hitch should understand that they are taking a potentially serious risk. Keep in mind that kidnappings for ransom can – and still do – happen in Mexico. People who choose to hitch will be safer if they travel in pairs and let someone know where they are planning to go. A woman traveling alone certainly should not hitchhike in Mexico, and even two women together is not advisable, especially when traveling near the Mexico–Guatemala border.

However, some people do choose to hitchhike, and it's not an uncommon way of getting to some of the off-the-beaten-track archaeological sites and other places that are poorly served by

bus. If you decide to do so, keep your wits about you and don't accept a lift if you have any misgivings.

In Mexico it's customary for the hitchhiker to offer to pay for the ride, especially if it's in a work or commercial vehicle. As a general rule, offer about M$30 to M$50 per person for fairly short rides and M$100 for longer trips.

If you're driving a vehicle through rural areas, it's not uncommon for Mexican townspeople to ask for a lift. Most folks in these parts are harmless and they are only asking for a ride because there is infrequent bus service, but by no means should you feel obligated, especially if the person gives off a strange vibe.

## Local Transportation

### Bicycle

Bicycling is becoming a more common mode of transportation in some cities. Having said that, never assume that motorists will give you the right of way and be particularly careful on narrow roads. A few areas, such as Valladolid, Tulum and Chetumal, now have bicycle paths. In Mérida, a main downtown street is closed to traffic on Sundays for morning rides and on Wednesday nights a group of bicycle activists organizes mass rides. You can rent bikes in many towns for about M$30/100 per hour/day.

It's possible to purchase a bicycle in the Yucatán. Indeed, if you plan to stay on the peninsula for a few months and want to get around by bike or at least exercise on one, purchasing isn't a bad option, as there are many inexpensive models available in the big cities.

You're best off touring on bike from December through March, when the weather is cooler and it stays relatively dry.

## Bus

Generally known as *camiones* or *autobuses,* local buses are a cheap way to get around any large city, such as Cancún or Mérida.

They usually stop at fixed *paradas* (bus stops), though in some places you can hold out your hand to stop one at any street corner. Most carry change.

### Colectivos & Combis

On much of the peninsula, a variety of vehicles – often Volkswagen, Ford or Chevrolet vans – operate shared transportation services between towns or nearby neighborhoods. These vehicles usually leave whenever they are full. Fares are typically less than those of 1st-class buses. Combi is a term often used for the Volkswagen variety; *colectivo* refers to any van type. *Taxi colectivo* may mean either public or private transport, depending on the location.

## Taxi

Taxis are common in towns and cities, and surprisingly economical. City rides usually cost around M$25 to M$30 for a short trip. If a taxi has a meter, you can ask the driver if it's working (*'¿Funciona el taxímetro?'*). If there's no meter, which is usually the case, agree on a price before getting in the cab.

Many airports and some bus terminals have a system of authorized taxis: you buy a fixed-price ticket to your destination from a booth and then hand it over to the driver instead of paying cash. Fares are higher than what you'd pay on the street but these cabs offer guaranteed safety.

In tourist centers you'll often find fares posted at taxi bases. If the driver does not respect the published fare, report it to a supervisor.

Renting a taxi for a day-long, out-of-town jaunt generally costs something similar to a rental car by the time you're done with gas – M$750 to M$1000.

# Language

Although the predominant language of Mexico is Spanish, about 50 indigenous languages are spoken as a first language by more than seven million people throughout the country. There are more than 30 Maya languages still spoken today. In Chiapas the most widely spoken ones are Tzeltal, Tzotzil and Chol. Yucatec Maya is the most widely spoken indigenous language of the Yucatán.

## SPANISH

Mexican Spanish pronunciation is easy, as most sounds have equivalents in English. Note that kh is a throaty sound (like the 'ch' in the Scottish *loch*), v and b are both pronounced like a soft English 'v' (between a 'v' and a 'b'), and r is strongly rolled. Also keep in mind that in some parts of Mexico the letters *ll* and *y* are pronounced like the 'll' in 'million', but in most areas they are pronounced like the 'y' in 'yes', and this is how they are represented in our pronunciation guides. If you read our colored pronunciation guides as if they were English, you'll be understood just fine. The stressed syllables are indicated with italics.

Where both polite and informal options are given in this chapter, they are indicated by the abbreviations 'pol' and 'inf'. Masculine and feminine forms of words are included where relevant and separated with a slash, eg *perdido/a* (m/f).

### WANT MORE?

For in-depth language information and handy phrases, check out Lonely Planet's *Mexican Spanish Phrasebook*. You'll find it at **shop.lonelyplanet.com**, or you can buy Lonely Planet's iPhone phrasebooks at the Apple App Store.

## Basics

| Hello. | Hola. | o·la |
| Goodbye. | Adiós. | a·dyos |
| How are you? | ¿Qué tal? | ke tal |
| Fine, thanks. | Bien, gracias. | byen gra·syas |
| Excuse me. | Perdón. | per·don |
| Sorry. | Lo siento. | lo syen·to |
| Please. | Por favor. | por fa·vor |
| Thank you. | Gracias. | gra·syas |
| You're welcome. | De nada. | de na·da |
| Yes./No. | Sí./No. | see/no |

**My name is ...**
Me llamo ...          me ya·mo ...

**What's your name?**
¿Cómo se llama Usted?  ko·mo se ya·ma oo·ste (pol)
¿Cómo te llamas?       ko·mo te ya·mas (inf)

**Do you speak English?**
¿Habla inglés?         a·bla een·gles (pol)
¿Hablas inglés?        a·blas een·gles (inf)

**I don't understand.**
Yo no entiendo.        yo no en·tyen·do

## Accommodations

| I'd like a ... room. | Quisiera una habitación ... | kee·sye·ra oo·na a·bee·ta·syon ... |
| single | individual | een·dee·vee·dwal |
| double | doble | do·ble |

**How much is it per night/person?**
¿Cuánto cuesta por    kwan·to kwes·ta por
noche/persona?         no·che/per·so·na

**Does it include breakfast?**
¿Incluye el            een·kloo·ye el
desayuno?              de·sa·yoo·no

| air-con | aire acondicionado | ai·re a·kon·dee·syo·na·do |
| bathroom | baño | ba·nyo |
| bed | cama | ka·ma |
| campsite | terreno de cámping | te·re·no de kam·peeng |
| hotel | hotel | o·tel |
| guesthouse | pensión | pen·syon |
| window | ventana | ven·ta·na |
| youth hostel | albergue juvenil | al·ber·ge khoo·ve·neel |

## Directions

**Where's ...?**
¿Dónde está ...? — don·de es·ta ...

**What's the address?**
¿Cuál es la dirección? — kwal es la dee·rek·syon

**Could you please write it down?**
¿Puede escribirlo, por favor? — pwe·de es·kree·beer·lo por fa·vor

**Can you show me (on the map)?**
¿Me lo puede indicar (en el mapa)? — me lo pwe·de een·dee·kar (en el ma·pa)

| at the corner | en la esquina | en la es·kee·na |
| at the traffic lights | en el semáforo | en el se·ma·fo·ro |
| behind ... | detrás de ... | de·tras de ... |
| far | lejos | le·khos |
| in front of ... | enfrente de ... | en·fren·te de ... |
| left | izquierda | ees·kyer·da |
| near | cerca | ser·ka |
| next to ... | al lado de ... | al la·do de ... |
| opposite ... | frente a ... | fren·te a ... |
| right | derecha | de·re·cha |
| straight ahead | todo recto | to·do rek·to |

## Eating & Drinking

**Can I see the menu, please?**
¿Puedo ver el menú, por favor? — pwe·do ver el me·noo por fa·vor

**What would you recommend?**
¿Qué recomienda? — ke re·ko·myen·da

**I don't eat (meat).**
No como (carne). — no ko·mo (kar·ne)

**That was delicious!**
¡Estaba buenísimo! — es·ta·ba bwe·nee·see·mo

**Cheers!**
¡Salud! — sa·loo

**The bill, please.**
La cuenta, por favor. — la kwen·ta por fa·vor

**LANGUAGE** SPANISH

| I'd like a table for ... | Quisiera una mesa para ... | kee·sye·ra oo·na me·sa pa·ra ... |
| (eight) o'clock | las (ocho) | las (o·cho) |
| (two) people | (dos) personas | (dos) per·so·nas |

## Key Words

| bottle | botella | bo·te·ya |
| breakfast | desayuno | de·sa·yoo·no |
| cold | frío | free·o |
| dessert | postre | pos·tre |
| dinner | cena | se·na |
| fork | tenedor | te·ne·dor |
| glass | vaso | va·so |
| hot (warm) | caliente | kal·yen·te |
| knife | cuchillo | koo·chee·yo |
| lunch | comida | ko·mee·da |
| plate | plato | pla·to |
| restaurant | restaurante | res·tow·ran·te |
| spoon | cuchara | koo·cha·ra |

## Meat & Fish

| beef | carne de vaca | kar·ne de va·ka |
| chicken | pollo | po·yo |
| lamb | cordero | kor·de·ro |

### NUMBERS

| 1 | uno | oo·no |
| 2 | dos | dos |
| 3 | tres | tres |
| 4 | cuatro | kwa·tro |
| 5 | cinco | seen·ko |
| 6 | seis | seys |
| 7 | siete | sye·te |
| 8 | ocho | o·cho |
| 9 | nueve | nwe·ve |
| 10 | diez | dyes |
| 20 | veinte | veyn·te |
| 30 | treinta | treyn·ta |
| 40 | cuarenta | kwa·ren·ta |
| 50 | cincuenta | seen·kwen·ta |
| 60 | sesenta | se·sen·ta |
| 70 | setenta | se·ten·ta |
| 80 | ochenta | o·chen·ta |
| 90 | noventa | no·ven·ta |
| 100 | cien | syen |
| 1000 | mil | meel |

## QUESTION WORDS

| How? | ¿Cómo? | ko·mo |
|------|--------|-------|
| What? | ¿Qué? | ke |
| When? | ¿Cuándo? | kwan·do |
| Where? | ¿Dónde? | don·de |
| Who? | ¿Quién? | kyen |
| Why? | ¿Por qué? | por ke |

| lobster | langosta | lan·gos·ta |
|---------|----------|------------|
| oysters | ostras | os·tras |
| pork | cerdo | ser·do |
| shrimp | camarones | ka·ma·ro·nes |
| squid | calamar | ka·la·mar |
| veal | ternera | ter·ne·ra |

### Fruit & Vegetables

| apple | manzana | man·sa·na |
|-------|---------|-----------|
| apricot | albaricoque | al·ba·ree·ko·ke |
| banana | plátano | pla·ta·no |
| beans | frijoles | free·kho·les |
| capsicum | pimiento | pee·myen·to |
| carrot | zanahoria | sa·na·o·rya |
| cherry | cereza | se·re·sa |
| corn | maíz | ma·ees |
| cucumber | pepino | pe·pee·no |
| grape | uvas | oo·vas |
| lettuce | lechuga | le·choo·ga |
| mushroom | champiñón | cham·pee·nyon |
| nuts | nueces | nwe·ses |
| onion | cebolla | se·bo·ya |
| orange | naranja | na·ran·kha |
| peach | melocotón | me·lo·ko·ton |
| pineapple | piña | pee·nya |
| potato | patata | pa·ta·ta |
| spinach | espinacas | es·pee·na·kas |
| strawberry | fresa | fre·sa |
| tomato | tomate | to·ma·te |
| watermelon | sandía | san·dee·a |

### Other

| bread | pan | pan |
|-------|-----|-----|
| cake | pastel | pas·tel |
| cheese | queso | ke·so |
| eggs | huevos | we·vos |
| french fries | papas fritas | pa·pas free·tas |
| honey | miel | myel |
| ice cream | helado | e·la·do |

| jam | mermelada | mer·me·la·da |
|-----|-----------|--------------|
| pepper | pimienta | pee·myen·ta |
| rice | arroz | a·ros |
| salad | ensalada | en·sa·la·da |
| salt | sal | sal |
| soup | caldo/sopa | kal·do/so·pa |
| sugar | azúcar | a·soo·kar |

### Drinks

| beer | cerveza | ser·ve·sa |
|------|---------|-----------|
| coffee | café | ka·fe |
| juice | zumo | soo·mo |
| milk | leche | le·che |
| smoothie | licuado | lee·kwa·do |
| tea | té | te |
| (mineral) water | agua (mineral) | a·gwa (mee·ne·ral) |
| (red/white) wine | vino (tinto/ blanco) | vee·no (teen·to/ blan·ko) |

## Emergencies

| Help! | ¡Socorro! | so·ko·ro |
|-------|-----------|----------|
| Go away! | ¡Vete! | ve·te |

| Call ...! | ¡Llame a ...! | ya·me a ... |
|-----------|---------------|-------------|
| a doctor | un médico | oon me·dee·ko |
| the police | la policía | la po·lee·see·a |

**I'm lost.**
Estoy perdido/a.     es·toy per·dee·do/a (m/f)

**Where are the toilets?**
¿Dónde están los     don·de es·tan los
baños?     ba·nyos

**I'm ill.**
Estoy enfermo/a.     es·toy en·fer·mo/a (m/f)

**I'm allergic to (antibiotics).**
Soy alérgico/a a     soy a·ler·khee·ko/a a
(los antibióticos).     (los an·tee·byo·tee·kos) (m/f)

## Shopping & Services

**I'd like to buy ...**
Quisiera comprar ...     kee·sye·ra kom·prar ...

**I'm just looking.**
Sólo estoy mirando.     so·lo es·toy mee·ran·do

**Can I look at it?**
¿Puedo verlo?     pwe·do ver·lo

**How much is it?**
¿Cuánto cuesta?     kwan·to kwes·ta

**That's too expensive.**
Es muy caro.     es mooy ka·ro

**There's a mistake in the bill.**
*Hay un error en la cuenta.*    ai oon e·*ror* en la *kwen*·ta

| ATM | cajero automático | ka·*khe*·ro ow·to·ma·tee·ko |
| **market** | *mercado* | mer·*ka*·do |
| **post office** | *correos* | ko·*re*·os |
| **tourist office** | *oficina de turismo* | o·fee·*see*·na de too·*rees*·mo |

## Time & Dates

**What time is it?** *¿Qué hora es?* ke *o*·ra es
**It's (10) o'clock.** *Son (las diez).* son (las dyes)
**It's half past (one).** *Es (la una) y media.* es (la *oo*·na) ee *me*·dya

| morning | mañana | ma·*nya*·na |
| **afternoon** | *tarde* | *tar*·de |
| **evening** | *noche* | *no*·che |
| **yesterday** | *ayer* | a·*yer* |
| **today** | *hoy* | oy |
| **tomorrow** | *mañana* | ma·*nya*·na |

| Monday | lunes | *loo*·nes |
| **Tuesday** | *martes* | *mar*·tes |
| **Wednesday** | *miércoles* | *myer*·ko·les |
| **Thursday** | *jueves* | *khwe*·ves |
| **Friday** | *viernes* | *vyer*·nes |
| **Saturday** | *sábado* | *sa*·ba·do |
| **Sunday** | *domingo* | do·*meen*·go |

## Transportation

| boat | barco | *bar*·ko |
| **bus** | *autobús* | ow·to·*boos* |
| **plane** | *avión* | a·*vyon* |
| **train** | *tren* | tren |

| A ... ticket, please. | Un billete de ..., por favor. | oon bee·*ye*·te de ... por fa·*vor* |
|   **1st-class** | *primera clase* | pree·*me*·ra *kla*·se |
|   **2nd-class** | *segunda clase* | se·*goon*·da *kla*·se |
|   **one-way** | *ida* | *ee*·da |
|   **return** | *ida y vuelta* | *ee*·da ee *vwel*·ta |

**What time does it arrive/leave?**
*¿A qué hora llega/sale?* a ke *o*·ra *ye*·ga/*sa*·le

**Does it stop at ...?** *¿Para en ...?* *pa*·ra en ...

**What stop is this?**
*¿Cuál es esta parada?* kwal es *es*·ta pa·*ra*·da

**Please tell me when we get to ...**
*¿Puede avisarme cuando lleguemos a ...?* *pwe*·de a·vee·*sar*·me *kwan*·do ye·*ge*·mos a ...

**I want to get off here.**
*Quiero bajarme aquí.* *kye*·ro ba·*khar*·me a·*kee*

| airport | aeropuerto | a·e·ro·*pwer*·to |
| **bus stop** | *parada de autobuses* | pa·*ra*·da de ow·to·*boo*·ses |
| **ticket office** | *taquilla* | ta·*kee*·ya |
| **timetable** | *horario* | o·*ra*·ryo |
| **train station** | *estación de trenes* | es·ta·*syon* de *tre*·nes |

| I'd like to hire a ... | Quisiera alquilar ... | kee·*sye*·ra al·kee·*lar* ... |
|   **bicycle** | *una bicicleta* | *oo*·na bee·see·*kle*·ta |
|   **car** | *un coche* | oon *ko*·che |
|   **motorcycle** | *una moto* | *oo*·na *mo*·to |

| helmet | casco | *kas*·ko |
| **petrol/gas** | *gasolina* | ga·so·*lee*·na |
| **service station** | *gasolinera* | ga·so·lee·*ne*·ra |

**Is this the road to ...?**
*¿Se va a ... por esta carretera?* se va a ... por *es*·ta ka·re·*te*·ra

**(How long) Can I park here?**
*¿(Cuánto tiempo) Puedo aparcar aquí?* (*kwan*·to *tyem*·po) *pwe*·do a·par·*kar* a·*kee*

**I've run out of petrol.**
*Me he quedado sin gasolina.* me e ke·*da*·do seen ga·so·*lee*·na

**I have a flat tyre.**
*Tengo un pinchazo.* *ten*·go oon peen·*cha*·so

| SIGNS | |
| --- | --- |
| **Abierto** | Open |
| **Cerrado** | Closed |
| **Entrada** | Entrance |
| **Hombres/Varones** | Men |
| **Mujeres/Damas** | Women |
| **Prohibido** | Prohibited |
| **Salida** | Exit |
| **Servicios/Baños** | Toilets |

# YUCATEC MAYA

Yucatec Maya, spoken primarily in the Yucatán, Campeche and Quintana Roo, and in the northern and western parts of Belize, belongs to the Amerindian languages, spoken by Native American people across North America. This means that Yucatec Maya (commonly called 'Yucatec' by scholars and 'Maya' by local speakers) is related to many indigenous languages spoken in the southeastern United States, as well as far-off California and Oregon (eg Costanoan, Klamath and Tsimshian). Yucatec is just one of about 30 languages in the Maya family (together with Quiché, Mam, Kekchi and Cakchiquel), but it probably has the largest number of speakers, estimated at more than half a million people.

You can hear Yucatec spoken in the markets and occasionally by hotel staff in cities throughout the peninsula. To hear Yucatec spoken by monolingual Maya speakers, you must travel to some of the peninsula's more remote villages. Maya speakers will not assume that you know any of their language. If you attempt to say something in Maya, however, people will usually respond quite favorably.

## Pronunciation

The principles of Maya pronunciation are similar to those found in Spanish. Just follow the colored pronunciation guides included next to the Maya phrases in this section and read them as if they were English.

Maya consonants followed by an apostrophe (b', ch', k', p', t') are similar to regular consonants, but they should be pronounced more forcefully and 'explosively'. On the other hand, an apostrophe following a vowel indicates a glottal stop (similar to the sound between the two syllables in 'uh-oh').

Maya is a tonal language, which means that some words have different meanings when pronounced with a high tone or a low tone. For example, *aak* said with a high tone means 'turtle', but when said with a low tone it means 'grass' or 'vine'.

In many Maya place names the word stress falls on the last syllable. In written language, Spanish rules for indicating word stress with accent marks are often followed for these words. This practice varies, however; in this book we have tried to include accent marks whenever possible. Note also that the stressed syllable is always indicated with italics in our pronunciation guides.

Note also that words borrowed from Spanish, even if they are common ones, tend to be stressed differently in Yucatec Maya, eg *amigo* (Spanish for 'friend') is pronounced 'a·*mee*·go' in Spanish and '*a*·mee·go' in Yucatec.

## Basics

Note that Maya speakers often reiterate what is said to them, instead of saying 'yes'; eg 'Are you going to the store?' – 'I'm going'.

| | | |
|---|---|---|
| **Hello.** | *Hola.* | o·la |
| **Good day.** | *Buenos dias.* | bwe·nos dee·as |
| **How are you?** | *Bix a beel?* | beesh a bail |
| **How are you?** (less formal) | *Bix yanikech?* | beesh yaw·nee·kech |
| **OK./Well.** | *Maalob.* | ma·lobe |
| **Bye./See you tomorrow.** | *Hasta saamal.* | as·ta sa·mal |
| **Goodbye.** | *Pa'atik kin bin.* | pa'a·teek keen been |
| **Thank you.** | *Dios Bo'otik.* | dyos boe'o·teek |
| **Yes.** | *Haa./He'ele.* | haa/he'e·le |
| **No.** | *Ma'.* | ma' |
| **expensive** | *ko'o* | ko'·o |
| **pretty** | *ki'ichpam* | kee'·eech·pam |

**What's your name?**
*Bix a k'aaba?* — beesh a k'aa·ba

**My name is ...**
*In kaabae' ...* — een ka·ba·e' ...

**I don't speak Maya.**
*Ma tin na'atik mayat'aani.* — ma' teen na'·a·teek ma·ya·taa·nee

**Do you speak Spanish?**
*Teche', ka t'aanik wa castellano t'aan?* — te·che' ka t'a·neek wa ka·stay·ya·no t'an

**I want to drink water.**
*Tak in wukik ha'.* — tak een woo·keek ha'

**I'm hungry.**
*Wiihen.* — wee·hen

**It's (very) tasty.**
*(Hach) Ki'.* — (hach) kee'

**How much is that/this one?**
*Baux lelo'/lela'?* — ba·hoosh le·lo'/le·la'

| **Where is the ...?** | *Tu'ux yaan le ...?* | too'·oosh yan le ... |
|---|---|---|
| **bathroom** | *baño* | ba'·nyo |
| **doctor** | *médico* | me·dee·ko |
| **hotel** | *hotel* | o·tel |
| **road to ...** | *u be ti' ...* | u be tee ... |

| **1** | *un peel* | oom pail |
|---|---|---|
| **2** | *ka peel* | ka pail |
| **3** | *ox peel* | osh pail |

When counting animate objects, such as people, replace *peel* with *tuul* (pronounced 'tool'). Beyond three, use Spanish numbers.

# GLOSSARY

Words specific to food, restaurants and eating are listed on p44.

**Ah Tz'ib** – Maya scribes. They penned the *Chilam Balam* and still practice their craft today.

**alux** (s), **aluxes** (pl) – Maya 'leprechauns,' benevolent 'little people'

**Ángeles Verdes** – 'Green Angels;' bilingual mechanics in green trucks who patrol major highways, offering breakdown assistance

**baluartes** – bastions, bulwarks or ramparts

**barrio** – district, neighborhood

**cacique** – indigenous chief; also used to describe a provincial warlord or strongman

**cafetería** – literally 'coffee-shop,' it refers to any informal restaurant with waiter service; it is not usually a self-service restaurant

**cajero automático** – Automated Teller Machine (ATM)

**camión** (s), **camiones** (pl) – truck; bus

**camioneta** – pickup

**campechanos** – citizens of Campeche

**campesinos** – countryfolk, farm workers

**casa de cambio** – currency-exchange office

**casetas de teléfono** – call offices where an on-the-spot operator connects the call for you, often shortened to *casetas*

**Caste War** – bloody 19th-century Maya uprising in the Yucatán

**cenote** – a deep limestone sinkhole containing water

**cerveza** – beer

**Chaac** – Maya god of rain

**chac-mool** – Maya sacrificial stone sculpture

**chenes** – name for cenotes in the Chenes region

**chultún** (s), **chultunes** (pl) – Maya cistern found at Puuc archaeological sites south of Mérida

**coctelería** – seafood shack specializing in shellfish cocktails as well as *ceviche*

**cocina** – cookshop (literally 'kitchen'), a small, basic restaurant usually run by one woman, often located in or near a municipal market; also seen as *cocina económica* (economical kitchen) or *cocina familiar* (family kitchen); see also *lonchería*

**colectivo** – literally, 'shared,' a car, van (VW combi, Ford or Chevrolet) or minibus that picks up and drops off passengers along its set route; also known as *taxi colectivo*

**combi** – a catch-all term used for taxi, van and minibus services regardless of vehicle type

**comida corrida** – set meal, meal of the day

**costera** – waterfront avenue

**criollo** – a person of pure Spanish descent born in Spanish America

**cuota** – toll road

**daños a terceros** – third-party car insurance

**de lujo** – deluxe class of bus service

**DNI** – Derecho para No Inmigrante; nonimmigrant fee charged to all foreign tourists and business travelers visiting Mexico

**ejido** – communal landholding, though laws now allow sale of *ejido* land to outside individuals

**encomienda** – a grant made to a conquistador, consisting of labor by or tribute from a group of indigenous people; the conquistador was supposed to protect and convert them, but usually treated them as little more than slaves

**feria** – fair or carnival, typically occurring during a religious holiday

**gringo/a** – male/female US or Canadian visitor to Latin America (sometimes applied to any visitor of European heritage); can be used derogatorily but more often is a mere statement of fact

**gruta** – cave, grotto

**guayabera** – man's thin fabric shirt with pockets and appliquéd designs on the front, over the shoulders and down the back; often worn in place of a jacket and tie

**hacienda** – estate; Hacienda (capitalized) is the Treasury Department

**henequén** – agave fiber used to make rope, grown particularly around Mérida

**h-menob** – Maya shaman still practicing their trade in the Yucatán today

**huipil** (s), **huipiles** (pl) – indigenous women's sleeveless white tunic, usually intricately and colorfully embroidered

**iglesia** – church

**INAH** – Instituto Nacional de Arqueología e Historia; the body in charge of most ancient sites and some museums

**INM** – Instituto Nacional de Migración (National Immigration Institute)

**Itzamná** – lord of the heavens; a popular figure on the wooden panels of contemporary architecture

**IVA** – *impuesto al valor agregado* or 'ee-bah,' a 15% value-added tax added to many items in Mexico

**Ixchel** – Maya goddess of the moon and fertility

**jarana** – a folkloric dance that has been performed by Yucatecans for centuries

**jipijapa** – an alternative name for panama hats (which are made from *jipijapa* palm fronds)

**Kukulcán** – Maya name for the Aztec-Toltec plumed serpent Quetzalcóatl

**lagunas** – small lakes, lagoons

**lonchería** – from English 'lunch'; a simple restaurant that may in fact serve meals all day (not just lunch); often seen near municipal markets. See also *cocina*.

**lotería** – Mexico's version of bingo

**malecón** – waterfront boulevard

**mariachi** – small ensemble of Mexican street musicians; strolling mariachi bands often perform in restaurants

**méridanos** – citizens of Mérida

**mestizo** – also known as *ladino*, a person of mixed indigenous and European blood; the word now more commonly means 'Mexican'

**metate** – flattish stone on which corn is ground with a cylindrical stone roller

**mezcal** – a distilled alcoholic drink made from the agave plant

**na** – thatched Maya hut

**nortes** – relatively cold storms bringing wind and rain from the north

**Nte** – abbreviation for *norte* (north), used in street names

**Ote** – abbreviation for *oriente* (east), used in street names

**palapa** – thatched, palm-leaf-roofed shelter usually with open sides

**Popol Vuh** – painted Maya book containing sacred legends and stories; equivalent to the Bible

**porfiriato** – the name given to the era of Porfirio Diaz's 35-year rule as president-dictator (1876–1911), preceding the Mexican Revolution

**PRI** – Partido Revolucionario Institucional (Institutional Revolutionary Party); the controlling force in Mexican politics for much of the 20th century

**primera (1a) clase** – 1st class of bus service

**Pte** – abbreviation for *poniente* (west), used in street names

**Quetzalcóatl** – plumed serpent god of the Aztecs and Toltecs

**retablo** – altarpiece (usually an ornate gilded, carved wooden decoration in a church)

**ría** – estuary

**roofcomb** – a decorative stone-work lattice atop a Maya pyramid or temple

**sacbé** (s), **sacbeob** (pl) – ceremonial limestone avenue or path between great Maya cities

**segunda (2a) clase** – 2nd class of bus service

**Semana Santa** – Holy Week, the week from Palm Sunday to Easter Sunday; Mexico's major holiday period

**sur** – south; often seen in street names

**temazcal** – bathhouse, sweat lodge

**templo** – in Mexico, a church; anything from a wayside chapel to a cathedral

**tequila** – clear, distilled liquor produced, like pulque and *mezcal,* from the maguey cactus

**topes** – speed bumps, sometimes indicated by a highway sign depicting a row of little bumps

**torito** – a vivacious song that evokes the fervor of a bullfight

**tranvía** – tram or motorized trolley

**vaquería** – a traditional Yucatecan party where couples dance in unison to a series of songs; the parties are often held in town halls or on haciendas

**Xibalbá** – in Maya religious belief, the secret world or underworld

**xtabentún** – a traditional Maya spirit in the Yucatán; an anise-flavored liqueur made by fermenting honey

**yucateco** – someone or something of the Yucatán Peninsula

# Behind the Scenes

## SEND US YOUR FEEDBACK

We love to hear from travelers – your comments keep us on our toes and help make our books better. Our well-traveled team reads every word on what you loved or loathed about this book. Although we cannot reply individually to your submissions, we always guarantee that your feedback goes straight to the appropriate authors, in time for the next edition. Each person who sends us information is thanked in the next edition – the most useful submissions are rewarded with a selection of digital PDF chapters.

Visit **lonelyplanet.com/contact** to submit your updates and suggestions or to ask for help. Our award-winning website also features inspirational travel stories, news and discussions.

Note: We may edit, reproduce and incorporate your comments in Lonely Planet products such as guidebooks, websites and digital products, so let us know if you don't want your comments reproduced or your name acknowledged. For a copy of our privacy policy visit lonelyplanet.com/privacy.

## WRITER THANKS

### Ashley Harrell

I'd like to thank a few wonderful people (and one enthusiastic dog) for accompanying me through various parts of Mexico. Stacey Auch and Erin Morris, let us be friends and road-trip warriors forever. Amy Guthrie, Carlos Andrade, Savannah and Nico, you are fabulous hosts and people. Adam Williams and Isabella Cota, we'll always have Patrick Miller. Matt Levin, you're a joy to eat tacos with. And Dad, you're a gentleman and a champion. Love you.

### Ray Bartlett

Thanks first and always to my family and friends, for letting me go on these adventures and still remembering me when I get back, or for joining me whenever possible. Huge thanks to Sarah Stocking for the editorial wisdom and advice, to my co-author John, and the rest of the LP staff. To all people I met or who helped me along the way, especially Naomi, Vivian, Odile, Ale, Eziquiel, Fabiola, Selena, Yuli, Alex, and so many others. Thanks so much. Can't wait to be back again soon.

### John Hecht

Very special thanks to Jesus Navarrete, Ursula Reischl, Chicken Willy, destination editor Sarah Stocking, co-author Ray Bartlett and to all the *quintanarooenses* for their generous support and the good times. As always, my heartfelt gratitude to Lau for taking care of the kitties and everything else.

### Tom Masters

Many thanks to various friends for advice and suggestions about researching Yucatán and Campeche States, especially to Anna Knutson Geller, Álvaro Rodríguez Martín and Alonso Dominguez. Thanks also to the tourist information offices in Mérida, Campeche and Valladolid for their comprehensive help, and for the various guides at dozens of Maya sites across the region, but especially to Abdel Adonay Padilla Ceme at Kukulkan Rising Tours for that dawn alone at Chichén Itzá.

## ACKNOWLEDGEMENTS

Climate map data adapted from Peel MC, Finlayson BL & McMahon TA (2007) 'Updated World Map of the Köppen-Geiger Climate Classification', *Hydrology and Earth System Sciences*, 11, 1633–44.

Chichén Itzá illustration pp194–5 by Michael Weldon

Cover photograph: Palenque, Chiapas, Fer Gregory/Shutterstock ©

# THIS BOOK

This 9th edition of Lonely Planet's *Cancún, Cozumel & the Yucatán* guidebook was curated by Ashley Harrell and researched and written by Ray Bartlett, Stuart Butler, John Hecht and Tom Masters. The previous edition was researched and written by Ashley, Ray, Stuart and John.

This guidebook was produced by the following:

**Destination Editor**
Sarah Stocking

**Senior Product Editors**
Daniel Bolger, Grace Dobell, Vicky Smith

**Cartographers** Mark Griffiths, Corey Hutchison

**Product Editors** Hannah Cartmel, Sasha Drew, Ross Taylor

**Book Designers** Ania Bartoszek, Brooke Giacomin, Jessica Rose

**Assisting Editors** Judith Bamber, Samantha Cook, Barbara Delissen, Andrea Dobbin, Alison Morris, Lauren O'Connell

**Assisting Cartographer** Mick Garrett

**Cover Researcher**
Gwen Cotter

**Thanks to** Ann-Kathrin, Karen Henderson, Sandie Kestell, Genna Patterson, Kirsten Rawlings, Gabrielle Stefanos, Angela Tinson, Santiago A Vidal

# Index

**INDEX N-V**

# Map Legend

## Sights

- Beach
- Bird Sanctuary
- Buddhist
- Castle/Palace
- Christian
- Confucian
- Hindu
- Islamic
- Jain
- Jewish
- Monument
- Museum/Gallery/Historic Building
- Ruin
- Shinto
- Sikh
- Taoist
- Winery/Vineyard
- Zoo/Wildlife Sanctuary
- Other Sight

## Activities, Courses & Tours

- Bodysurfing
- Diving
- Canoeing/Kayaking
- Course/Tour
- Sento Hot Baths/Onsen
- Skiing
- Snorkeling
- Surfing
- Swimming/Pool
- Walking
- Windsurfing
- Other Activity

## Sleeping

- Sleeping
- Camping
- Hut/Shelter

## Eating

- Eating

## Drinking & Nightlife

- Drinking & Nightlife
- Cafe

## Entertainment

- Entertainment

## Shopping

- Shopping

## Information

- Bank
- Embassy/Consulate
- Hospital/Medical
- Internet
- Police
- Post Office
- Telephone
- Toilet
- Tourist Information
- Other Information

## Geographic

- Beach
- Gate
- Hut/Shelter
- Lighthouse
- Lookout
- Mountain/Volcano
- Oasis
- Park
- Pass
- Picnic Area
- Waterfall

## Population

- Capital (National)
- Capital (State/Province)
- City/Large Town
- Town/Village

## Transport

- Airport
- Border crossing
- Bus
- Cable car/Funicular
- Cycling
- Ferry
- Metro station
- Monorail
- Parking
- Petrol station
- Subway/Subte station
- Taxi
- Train station/Railway
- Tram
- Underground station
- Other Transport

## Routes

- Tollway
- Freeway
- Primary
- Secondary
- Tertiary
- Lane
- Unsealed road
- Road under construction
- Plaza/Mall
- Steps
- Tunnel
- Pedestrian overpass
- Walking Tour
- Walking Tour detour
- Path/Walking Trail

## Boundaries

- International
- State/Province
- Disputed
- Regional/Suburb
- Marine Park
- Cliff
- Wall

## Hydrography

- River, Creek
- Intermittent River
- Canal
- Water
- Dry/Salt/Intermittent Lake
- Reef

## Areas

- Airport/Runway
- Beach/Desert
- Cemetery (Christian)
- Cemetery (Other)
- Glacier
- Mudflat
- Park/Forest
- Sight (Building)
- Sportsground
- Swamp/Mangrove

*Note: Not all symbols displayed above appear on the maps in this book*